SAGA OF THE SIERRAS

A NEW FRONTIER
SAGA OF THE SIERRAS

Four Bestselling Novels Complete in One Volume

The Man from Shadow Ridge
Riders of the Silver Rim
Gold Rush Prodigal
Sequoia Scout

BROCK & BODIE THOENE

Inspirational Press
New York

First Inspirational Press edition published in 1998.

Inspirational Press
A division of BBS Publishing Corporation
386 Park Avenue South
New York, NY 10016

Inspirational Press is a registered trademark of BBS Publishing Corporation.

Published by arrangement with Bethany House Publishers.

Library of Congress Catalog Card Number: 98-72388

ISBN: 0-88486-224-0

Printed in the United States of America

CONTENTS

THE
MAN FROM
SHADOW
RIDGE

This book is dedicated
to the men of the Thoene clan—
Papa Gil, brother Jess,
sons Jacob and Luke,
who share with us a love of the West, past and present,
and to Talon Zachary,
whose timely appearance, like that of this book
foretells great things to come.

1

HARNESS LEATHER GROANED as the weary horses leaned into the last steep climb before Granite Station. The wagon was heavily loaded with flour, beans, salt and seed. Two sleeping boys and a bolt of calico cloth completed the freight.

Tom Dawson looked like a man more at ease on the back of a green-broke Indian pony than holding the lines of a team of farm horses. His rugged, sun-browned face was creviced from the weather like the landscape. His dark brown eyes matched the color of the hair that straggled across his forehead from beneath a black broad-brimmed hat. His features had the lean, angular look of a man by no means settled into an easy life, but the small wrinkles at the corners of his eyes betrayed the fact that he smiled on occasion, too.

It was late, past dark already. Tom had expected to reach his stop for the night hours before. The Army quartermaster sergeant who was to have met Tom early that morning had not arrived until midafternoon. The sergeant had sent Tom off with the warning that the stagecoach from Keyesville had been robbed. All five passengers and the driver had been brutally murdered.

Now Tom wished he had camped on the flat along the banks of Poso Creek with other travelers who had stopped for the night. His wagonload of goods might be just as tempting as gold to outlaws hiding out in the lower reaches of the Sierras. Tom's Colt Navy revolver and his Sharps carbine lay within easy reach beside him on the wagon seat.

The lights of Granite Station finally appeared atop the rise. Their friendly glow could not come too soon to suit Tom; he urged the horses to quicken their pace the last mile up the hill.

Granite boulders lined the road. The full moon cast sharp shadows from the rocky outcroppings, every one suggesting a cavernous skull. The steep ascent forced travelers to slow down; it was a natural place for an ambush. Tom knew that blood had been spilled here before.

The treeless slopes around Granite Station marked the dividing line between the oak-covered foothills of the Sierras and the grassy plains of the valley below. What thin grass grew among the boulder hissed in a fitful east wind—the dry breeze of Indian Summer that promised no rain to relieve the parched earth, but foretold winter's approach just the same. Over the rustle, Tom could just make out the tinny sound of a banjo and an occasional raucous laugh.

A rustling sound closer at hand startled Tom out of his reverie. Turning suddenly, he saw his older nephew, Jed, blinking up at him from a tangled pile of calico.

"Hold on, boy, don't wrestle that cloth. Your ma will skin us both," Tom scolded.

"I'm sorry, Tom. I thought I was home to bed an' got to reachin' for a blanket," the sleepy voice replied.

"Just lay still a mite longer; we're almost to Granite." From the long sigh that replied, Tom knew that Jed had already rejoined his brother in slumber.

Good boys, both of them, eager to go with Tom on this three-day trip—and not complainers either. But the long delay and the dusty trip up from town had worn them out.

At last the team crested the hill overlooking the little stage stop nestled below. The horses drew the wagon up and stopped across the dusty roadway from the small clapboard building that served as restaurant, saloon, and hotel of dubious accommodations. Tom planned only to grain the horses and buy a meal for himself and the boys. They would sleep on their cargo under the stars and start on at first light.

Tom could hear voices and the artlessly strummed banjo from the saloon, but no one appeared from the barn to assist Tom with the harness. He decided to let the boys sleep until he had obtained their supper, so he chocked the wheels of the wagon with two rocks that lay near for the purpose and unhitched the team. He turned them into the common corral, noting the presence of the station-keeper's chestnut gelding and three other saddle horses unknown to him. Stowing the harness on a rack in the barn, Tom strode across the road.

The stage stop appeared to lean over him as he approached. Tom reflected that even in daylight it seemed to be bracing itself away from the downhill slope on which it perched.

The music stopped abruply with a cry of "More whiskey!" just as Tom pushed open the door.

Three men sat playing cards at a table at the far end of the room. The station keeper propped his banjo against the stone fireplace and scurried behind the mahogany bar to oblige the demand for liquor.

"Howdy, Tom." The station keeper, a slightly built, balding man in his early sixties, addressed him by name. "You jest up from town?"

"Yup, Charlie. Running late and almost too tired to be hungry."

The enticing aroma of a pot of beans simmering on a cast iron hook in the fireplace made Tom's stomach rumble, giving a lie to his words.

"Reckon I will have some beans. And the boys will be waking up, now that their cradle's quit rocking."

"Heh! Cradle quit rockin'; that's a good one!" Charlie's wheezy laugh was interrupted by a growl from one of the card players.

"Whar's the whiskey? You old coot, ya gonna jabber all night?"

Tom's attention swung around to the three men at the table. The one who had just spoken was a stout, florid-faced man who mopped his forehead with a stained bandanna.

The two who flanked the speaker exchanged a furtive glance across the table; it went unnoticed by the red-faced man. One of these was lean and drawn-looking. His clothes, a faded, nondescript shade of gray, matched his hair. Even his face had an ashen cast. He watched the others with intense, dark eyes, saying nothing.

The remaining member of the group was the only one Tom knew. It was Byrd Guidett. A rough, loud bully of a man, Byrd was built like a miner—as thick through his chest as he was wide, with an enormous neck and massive shoulders. He wore his curly red hair long, and his reddish beard was untrimmed.

Byrd Guidett still claimed to be living by prospecting for gold in the high reaches on the Kern, but it was said that he more likely worked the left side of law rather than the left side of a sluice box. A mining partner of Guidett's had disappeared in a mysterious accident, and since then respectable folks had tried to walk the long way around Byrd.

"Drink up, ol' cuss," Byrd said. "Maybe yer luck will change." This was addressed to the stout man who had poured two fingers of rotgut into his glass and the other two on the table.

Charlie scampered back to the fire and, taking three none-too-clean tin plates off a sideboard, dished up three helpings of beans. He added a handful of corn-dodgers to each plate and passed the lot to Tom.

"What do I owe you?" asked Tom.

"Did ya bring my coffee?" asked Charlie. At Tom's nod, he added, "Well, if ya don't charge for freightin' my arbuckle, I reckon a few beans and 'pone is free."

"Well, much obliged, and welcome to boot." Tom started out, then stopped short at a movement in the corner behind the card players. He had been wrong about there being only four occupants of the dimly lit room, for crouched on the floor near the sweaty-browed gambler was a small Negro boy. At Tom's sudden stare, Charlie's gaze also moved to the boy, and then catching Tom's eye he shook his head slowly as a warning to say nothing.

"I'll come out directly to see to yer team," Charlie said.

With a slight narrowing of his eyes and a quick nod, Tom left with supper for him and the boys.

The boys roused themselves and eagerly lit into the beans. Because they were still nine parts tired, the boys' usual banter was absent, and they ate in silence. Presently, the saloon door opened and Charlie came across to join them. The flickering pale light that came out through the wavy glass panes gave only enough illumination for Charlie to see the questioning look on Tom's face.

"I'm glad you said nothin', Tom. That's two powerful mean men in there. Byrd you know of, and that fat Missouri fella's been yellin' at me since he an' the boy came."

When Tom made no reply, he went on. "Byrd an' that gray-lookin' fella rode in about sundown. The Missourian was already pretty likkered up, an' they got this game goin' right away like they was anxious to get started."

"How do you know the one's from Missouri?" asked Tom.

"Well, he tol' me he come from there with his *chattel*. I ain't seen no cows and then he says he means the little colored bas—" At Tom's sharp look he left the word unfinished.

"A black man? Can we see 'im?"

"No, boys, it isn't our affair. And anyway it's just a child."

Charlie resumed. "So them three been playin', with the pike drinkin' and losin' and Byrd winnin', and the slim fella jest watchin'."

"Obliged for the beans and the word," said Tom. "Guess we'll turn in now." The boys started a groan of protest, but fell silent at a look from their uncle. He handed the plates over to the station keeper. "I'll put out some grain for my team if it's all right."

"Help yerself, Tom, and g'night to y'all." Charlie moved back across the road, dropping a tin plate in the process. He appeared to inspect it briefly by the window's glow; then wiping it on the seat of his denim pants, he seemed to find it satisfactory and went in.

The shot and the crashing noise came just before dawn. Tom's mind instantly sprang awake. Grabbing the Colt Navy he ordered, "Jed! Nathan! Get in the barn and stay there!"

Crouched beside the wagon, he waited till the boys had sprung over the side and run into the barn's opening. For a moment he thought an extra shadow ran after them, but the moon had set and he shook his head to clear his vision. His attention was turned to the saloon as the door burst open and Byrd thrust himself out.

"Whar's 'at nigger? He's mine now. Whar'd he go?" Byrd moved forward as if to cross the street and enter the barn. "I'll bet he run in here!"

The click of Tom's .36 caliber as he cocked it was loud enough to be heard in the moment Byrd paused for breath. He froze in his tracks, as did the gray man who had appeared in the doorway behind him.

Slowly Byrd turned to face Tom. "What's this all about?" Tom asked quietly, but with an unmistakable edge to his voice.

"I won that nigger fair an' square, and that hunk of lard called me a cheat an' made to draw on me!"

"So you shot him," said Tom.

"It was a fair fight, wasn't it, Yance?" This last was addressed over his shoulder to the man in the doorway.

"Yup, I seen it all."

"So move outta my way," ordered Byrd with a new burst of bravado. "He's mine an' I aim to fetch him!"

"California's free territory," replied Tom softly, "so you can't *own* him. Anyway," he added, "I was right here and I didn't see him go into the barn."

"I mean to look—" Byrd began, then stopped as Tom raised the pistol to point directly at Byrd's chest.

"Nope," Tom said. "He's probably scared and still running over these hills. Besides, if you were to find him, he'd have to be held for the inquest."

Yancey started, then said, "Byrd, we don't need no inquest."

"Shut up!" Byrd snorted. Facing Tom, he added, "Yer prob'ly right about the kid. He lit a shuck out the door and he's maybe halfway back to Missouri by now." Raising his hands, open-palms toward Tom, he began to back slowly toward the saloon. "We've wasted enough time here already. If a deputy wants a statement, he can look us up. *Charlie* will say what happened, won't ya, *Charlie?*"

The old station keeper cleared his throat nervously from inside the doorway. Taking this noise to mean *yes,* Byrd added, "Bring our winnin's, Yance. I'll get the horses."

Tom watched in silence without uncocking the revolver as Byrd retrieved two bridles from the corral posts and caught his and Yancey's horses.

Charlie came out, and at a nod from Tom, entered the barn to return with two saddles and blankets. Moments later, Byrd and Yancey were mounted. As they settled into their high-cantled saddles, Byrd rode slowly over to Tom.

"I won't forget ya, Tom Dawson," he said; then he and Yancey spun their horses and loped up the road to the northeast.

2

TOM STOOD WATCHING the two ride out of sight. He thought it wise not to let down his guard too quickly, so he called out, "Charlie, do you still have that shotgun back of the bar?"

"Why sure I do, Tom!"

"You'd best bring it out here."

It was only after Charlie had returned with an ancient but serviceable double-barreled shotgun that Tom allowed his attention to turn from the knoll over which Byrd and Yancey had ridden.

"You'd better keep watch till full light," Tom directed the station keeper.

" 'Deed I will! This here load o' buck is good for polecats and other varmints—even birds!"

Tom entered the dark stable softly and called to the boys.

"Jed, Nathan. Come on out now, boys; it's all over." A rustling of hay greeted his ears; then two tousled and straw-covered heads appeared from under the hay mow.

"We heard it, Tom."

"But we was real still."

"I know, boys. You did real well."

"Can *he* come out now, too?" asked Jed, the older boy.

"What? He who?"

"You know, the little black'un!"

So there really had been a third boy-sized shape that darted into the barn! In protecting his own nephews, Tom had aided the child in staying out of Byrd's clutches as well.

"Come out and show yourself, boy. No one will harm you now."

A further rustling and a third hay-strewn head poked up. Only the outline of a round dark shape could be seen. Tom stepped to a post and took down the lantern; then reaching into his pocket, he extracted a Lucifer match and proceeded to light the lamp.

"Come on out, boy. Let's have a look at you."

At this further reassurance, the child stood up and brushed himself off, then took a place beside Nathan. The boys were almost identical in size. Both wore overalls, but the black child wore no shirt, and his clothing was ragged, here and there inexpertly mended. Both boys were barefoot. Tom stooped to nine-year-old height and asked gently, "Do you have a name, child?"

"Yassuh, massah. I be Montgomery James," he said with a shy grin.

"Well, Montgomery, you need not call me massah—nor anyone else. California is a free state."

The boy's eyes grew wide and round with wonder. He had run to escape the shooting that had killed his former owner. He had not thought of running from slavery to freedom.

"Please, suh, where does I go den?"

"Well, now, child, where are you from? Do you have family or kin?"

The boy looked troubled. His grin faltered, and he replied, "I reckon not, suh. Mistuh James, he the one what was shot, taken me off'n de farm when I was real small. I disremember any folks—"

"How do you come to be in California?"

"Mistuh James, he be a Missouri man. After order eleben come, he in trouble wid de sol'jers, an' we come away real sudden-like."

"All right, Montgomery, that will do for now. Let's get you three some breakfast. It will soon be light enough to travel and I'm anxious to be home."

While the boys hastily washed their hands and faces in the horse trough, Charlie set down the shotgun long enough to bring out more cornbread cakes and a clay jug of buttermilk. By this time the first rays of dawn had risen over the eastern hillside above the little stage stop.

The boys ate while Tom and Charlie held a conference over the Missourian's body.

"I'll help you bury him, Charlie."

"Obliged to ya, Tom. I'll fetch the shovels."

Tom leaned over the dead gambler and absently poked through his pockets. A handful of silver coins, a handkerchief, and a single cuff link engraved "J.D." Tom straightened up as Charlie entered the room carrying two shovels.

"Hadn't we best bury him outside, Charlie?" suggested Tom dryly.

"Laws yes! Killin's fluster me so," Charlie stammered. "Here, hold these." He threw the shovels to Tom. In the moment's confusion, Tom put the handkerchief and coins on the bar, but slipped the cuff link into his pocket. Leaning the shovels against a wall, Tom grasped the feet and Charlie the arms of the corpse as they half carried, half dragged it outside.

Wrapped in an old canvas slicker, the body soon lay beside four other earthen mounds on the slope a short distance below the stage stop.

"You don't worry about planting them too deep, do you?" remarked Tom.

"Naw, some kin may want to claim 'em, and then I'd jest have to dig 'em up again."

The two men walked back up the hill to where Jed and Nathan had harnessed the team and hitched them to Tom's wagon. The boys had already rejoined the freight in the wagon bed, but Montgomery James stood uncertainly alongside the rear chestnut's flank.

"What'll ya do with the black child, Tom?" inquired Charlie.

"Me?" asked Tom, startled. "I thought you'd keep him here with you."

"Naw, Tom, naw. I've got to send word to the sheriff about the killin' by the afternoon coach. I can't watch him, less'n he run off. He's a witness, ya know, and contraband to boot."

"Charlie, he has no place to run *to*. Besides, I thought I left all that contraband talk behind when I left . . ." Here Tom's voice trailed off as if he had gotten dangerously close to a topic better left alone.

"Please, Uncle," begged Jed, "let's take him home with us. Ma will look after him, and he won't run away from us, will you, Mont?"

"Now, boys, I don't want to impose on your mother without asking."

Charlie interrupted this objection by saying, "Why sure. What's one more young'un, more or less? He won't eat much, and I can tell the sheriff whar to find him."

Tom gazed down at the tight black curls and fearful eyes upturned to search his face, and sighed, "All right, child. Climb aboard."

"Oh no, suh. I nevuh rides *wid* no white folks—I jes' walks alongside."

"Well, Montgomery, if you are to be staying with us for a time, you'd best get in. We don't make our *guests* walk, whatever color they may be."

Urged on by the boys already seated in the wagon, Montgomery climbed over the tailgate and sat down on a flour sack. An unexpected smile broke over his face as though he had just seen a glimpse of heaven.

Tom climbed up, and with a nod to the gnarled station keeper to unblock the wheels, Dawson slipped the brake lever and clucked to the team.

"Be seein' ya, Tom—best be right wary now," the old man urged.

Without a reply except a pull on the brim of his hat to acknowledge the advice, Tom started the wagon out of Granite Station and up the hill toward home.

The journey was a familiar one to the team, and they needed little direction or encouragement from Tom. They stepped out smartly, confident that their home pasture lay at the end of one more day's pull. The ease of travel allowed Tom to review the night's events. He did this with a part of his mind while at the same time remaining vigilant. He thought it unlikely that Byrd would seek vengeance openly on an obviously prepared foe, but the possibility of an ambush remained. Byrd's personality ran to open force if he clearly had the upper hand, but to treachery if he didn't.

Tom mused that the Missourian's destiny to die by gunfire seemed fore-ordained. If it were true that he had recently left his native state, then he could have only just escaped the same fate as at the station. The Missouri-Kansas border was on fire. Pro-slavery and abolitionist factions raided each other's settlements with bloody results.

In fact, the bloodiest of all these clashes had just occurred in August in the sleepy little Kansas town of Lawrence. Quantrill's Confederates had swept into Lawrence, overpowered its inhabitants, and slaughtered three hundred men and boys while putting much of the town to the torch.

The reports of such sickening atrocities carried out against innocent civilians had accelerated since the outbreak of the Civil War, but the tur-moil had existed since the early 1850s. Pro-slavery elements from Missouri had sought to force their views on the newly organized Kansas territory. Abolitionist leaders like John Brown had responded with "an eye for an eye." And so it had gone.

The eastern half of the nation was embroiled in war, to be sure, but Kansas and Missouri seemed to be engaged in a blood feud, a duel to the death liable to end only with the destruction of *all* the participants.

Tom pivoted around to look at the boys in the wagon bed. Montgomery seemed to have overcome his shyness, and all three boys were talking animatedly and, glory be, comparing skin colors! He was pleased that Jed and Nathan showed no distaste for the black child, but rather a frank and open curiosity. Just now, Montgomery was elaborating on his departure from Missouri.

"An' de gen'rl, he says dat de country is lousy wid rebs. So he give out wid order 'leben. Ever'body got two days to move! Ever'body in a tizzy, throwin' things out de windas into dere wagons an' such. But Mistuh James, he catch wind dat de sol'jers comin' to arrest him. So we dasn't wait, but lit out!"

Tom resumed his thoughts. Just such turmoil had caused him to leave Missouri himself two years before. In 1861, he had been a member of the Marion Rangers, a Missouri regiment. The regiment's pro-Southern loy-alty asserted itself, and the Rangers decided to join the Confederacy. Tom had no stomach to fight on behalf of slavery, but to reenlist in a Union outfit would force him into battle against former friends and neighbors. Maybe he had been wrong not to stand up for his belief in the Union, but he had been grateful when word had come from his brother Jesse.

Tom had mixed feelings about joining Jesse; after all, other issues were involved. . . . But at last he had decided to go.

For two years, things had been peaceful in California, and the war only a distant tragic noise. Others from the Ranger group had made the same choice to come west. He had even had a letter from a former comrade-in-arms, Sam Clemens, late of Missouri, now living in Virginia City, Nevada territory.

Tom sighed. Despite what the quartermaster sergeant had said, he hoped the raid on the gold shipment was only robbery and murder and the connection to the rebel cause just a ruse. He didn't want to think that this peaceful countryside would experience the horror of Civil War, even though he knew that there were Southern sympathizers among the hill folk.

The wagon was rounding an oak-covered hillside on the last level stretch before the climb up Pruitt's Hill when Tom saw a flash ahead and just to the right of the wagon road. A gun barrel?

Tom slowed the team and cautioned the boys to be ready to jump behind a nearby clump of rocks if need be. He checked the loads in the Sharps and the Colt, then watched carefully the spot where he had seen the flash. There it was again, nearer the road this time. It appeared to be on the fork in the trail that led eastward to Poso Flat and the gold fields beyond.

The ears of the chestnuts were pricked forward, standing at attention.

In the next moment, horses and driver relaxed as the approaching sounds indicated that their maker had no sinister purpose. Muleback, with sunlight flashing from his spectacles, and singing "Old Hundred," Parson Swift rode into view.

"Hello, Tom," he called.

"Hello, Parson," Tom returned as he waited for the man of God to approach.

"Well, hello to you also, boys, and—saints alive, who's this?"

Briefly Tom explained Montgomery James's presence and the events of the shooting.

Parson Swift nodded gravely. "That explains why Byrd passed me by without a word a while back. He and a man I didn't know were riding down into Poso Flat just as I was starting up the grade. I'm heading down into the valley for a spell. I'll stop by Granite and say a few words over the man."

"I'm sure his family, if he had any, would be grateful," said Tom. Then he added, "And I'm glad Byrd's heading off east away from our track. I didn't want to see these youngsters involved in a gun battle."

"Amen, and you remember, young Tom Dawson, those that live by the sword will die that way." The lanky parson started his mule toward the valley, and the four in the wagon made their way home in the drowsy afternoon.

When the fork in the road leading to the town of Greenville appeared, Tom urged the team past it and on toward home. Shortly thereafter, they came to the ford of the Poso known as Laver's Crossing.

Shadow Ridge, which now loomed directly ahead, was aptly named. It's chaparral and oak-covered sides never appeared distinct to the eye, but were always hazy, as though enveloped in a thin blue smoke. Local Indian lore had it that the mountain was sacred; some said haunted. It was called a "ghost mountain" because it was a perfect mirror image of the Sierra Nevada peak some ten miles due east.

While the eastern range reached up to cedars and pines, it was crisply outlined against the sky. Shadow Ridge, though real enough, had a mirage-like quality. The Tuolomne elders maintained that Shadow Ridge was home to "shadow animals" and other spirits, counterparts of the real deer and grizzly bears that made their homes in the Sierras. All the tales made good storytelling material for gusty nights around a crackling fire. The trails of the Tuolomnes and Yokuts skirted the base of the peak without venturing into its precincts, but their fear had not bothered Tom's brother Jesse at all.

Jesse had brought his wife and two young sons to the property he homesteaded on the eastern slope of Shadow Ridge. His land ran from a lower oak-covered ridge down to the fertile plain watered by Poso Creek. Quail and gooseberries flourished in abundance on the hillside, while the bottom land furnished feed for cattle and good soil for planting.

Jesse's Missouri upbringing made him feel more at home as a farmer than a rancher, and his expertise soon paid off. With the army's presence at Fort Tejon and the San Joaquin Valley too swampy and malarial for farming, he rightly judged that in his corner of this mountain valley, potatoes would grow well—and travel well, too.

He had made enough money to pay for sawn cedar to build a fine home for his family, and his success with the army contract had prompted him to invite his brother to join him.

The team turned into the lane leading to the barn. Jed and Nathan jumped off before it had completely stopped, and ran to where their mother was tending her pumpkin vines in the little kitchen garden.

"Ma, can Montgomery stay with us?"

"He doesn't have any kin, but now he's free!"

"We don't have to send him away, do we?"

"Now, boys, what's all this about?" Emily asked, waiting for the flow of words to slow and a coherent explanation to emerge.

Tom lifted Montgomery down from the wagon bed. The black child trailed behind as Tom left the team standing patiently and walked over to his sister-in-law.

" 'Lo, Emily," Tom began. He felt shy in approaching, not because he doubted her kind heart, but because he was always cautious to be extra polite to his brother's wife. Tom and Jesse had been rivals for Emily's attention in Missouri. Jesse had pressed his suit and won because he had been able to present his plan for a home, a farm, and a life, while Tom had still been devil-may-care—attractive as a dashing beau but not serious enough for a prospective husband. Tom believed that Emily cherished him still, but their affection was of the purest and deepest kind now.

She stood in her garden, dressed in dark blue calico, with her fine honey-blond hair escaping the bonnet she wore to protect her face. The afternoon sun lit up her pert nose and creamy skin. Tom began again.

"Montgomery here"—he turned to beckon the child to come and stand beside him—"is an orphan. He was brought to California by a Mr. James, who got himself killed by Byrd Guidett last night. Byrd was going to take him away, but Montgomery, well, Mont doesn't need to *belong* to anyone now. Anyway, can he stay on the place for a time?" he concluded lamely.

"Of course he can, and he's welcome! Byrd Guidett is nothing but a cut-throat and a thief. Come here, Montgomery." Her beauty and easy manner won the child's heart in an instant, and he crossed to stand beside Nathan.

"Will you look at that? You two boys are the same size. Montgomery, I'll bet we can find some of Nathan's clothes that will fit you, and I'm sure he'd enjoy your assistance with his chores."

"Yessum. I'se a hard worker an' don' eat much," responded Montgomery.

"You shall eat your fill, for we've plenty and to spare. After"—she addressed herself firmly to all three youngsters—"you've washed up. I declare, you've brought home another forty acres on your faces."

"C'mon, Mont, I'll race you to the pump!" shouted Nathan as all three raced off around the corner of the house.

"Mind, now, wash those arms and necks, too," she called after them.

"Yes, Ma," and "yessum" blended together, floating back over their retreating forms.

She turned to regard Tom with an upraised eyebrow. "Was there trouble for you, Tom?" she inquired.

"Not to speak of. Byrd and his partner backed down pretty easy. I thought there might be mischief on the road, but Parson Swift said he saw them headed down Poso Flat way. Anyway, Byrd wasn't anxious to wait around for an inquest into the shooting."

"Is Jesse around?" he continued.

"No, but I expect him back most any time. He finished the work on the barn roof and went off to hunt some quail. You should wash up, too; supper's almost ready."

"I'll just unload the wagon and see to the team, and then I'll be along." They parted toward barn and house—the slim, wiry, dark man and the slender, fair woman.

Jesse appeared in the barn just as Tom was hanging up the harness. The family resemblance could be seen in their faces, but Jesse was broader and just a shade taller. His serious face showed lines of concern.

"Byrd Guidett again?"

"Yes, and a killing this time." Tom related the story to his brother, then went on.

"What's more, the stage was robbed south of Wheeler Ridge early yesterday. Everybody was gunned down."

"Did they try to make a fight of it?"

"No, and that's the worst. They were lined up beside the road and shot down in cold blood. The army thinks it's the work of reb agents who would be recognized hereabouts."

"Could that be Byrd's doing too?" asked Jesse.

"He's capable of it. Charlie said Byrd and his partner seemed anxious to settle in to a card game, like they'd nothing better to do and no hurry to be elsewhere."

Jesse added, "They could have stashed the gold somewhere, and then wanted to throw off suspicion by being purposefully seen a good distance from the killing."

"If that's so, Byrd's greed and temper may have messed up his plan. If he had the drop on that James fellow, he should have left off without another killing."

"Maybe we should share our thoughts with the sheriff."

"I was thinking that very thing. If we ride over to Greenville tomorrow, maybe Deputy Pettibone will be around to listen."

3

THE DAWSON BROTHERS had done well in their sale of the potato crop to the Union soldiers of Fort Tejon. A neat stack of twenty double-eagle gold pieces glistened on the table between them.

"When you're done admiring the profits," Emily joked, "I'll deposit those in the bank if you don't mind."

The Dawson "bank" consisted of a loose stone in the fireplace and a quart canning jar half full of assorted coins and a few gold nuggets that served as small reminders that Jesse had once dreamed of striking it rich in the gold fields. They had long since found contentment in the wealth of healthy sons, a good crop, plenty to eat and an occasional bolt of calico. It was *enough*. Jesse had come to believe that a man who wasn't satisfied with enough would never have enough to be satisfied.

Tom had dreamed of a different kind of gold mine, a different way to strike it rich. Now, as Emily scooped the meager stack of gold coins into the jar, Tom's eyes glistened with amusement.

"Wait a minute,"he said, raising a hand laconically. "That's not all."

"Not all?" Jesse leaned forward. "That's more than I expected."

Tom nodded. "For the potatoes yes." He reached into the deep pocket of his jacket and pulled out a leather bag that seemed to bulge at the seams. He hefted it twice for the effect of its weight. Emily blinked in astonishment and then looked from Tom to Jesse, then back to Tom again.

"The horses?" Jesse croaked.

Tom grinned broadly and nodded, tossing the bag onto the table with a heavy thud. "In advance."

"But they're not even broke yet!" Emily exclaimed.

"It doesn't matter." Tom took the jar from her and placed it beside the leather lump on the table. "It seems Mr. Lincoln's army is desperate for our horses."

"But they're only a scruffy bunch of mustangs," Jesse protested.

"Doesn't matter to the army anymore. I told you, for every man that falls in that cursed war, ten horses go down. Some to rifle fire, some to artillery, some to the stew pot of hungry men. North and South, the armies are all afoot now."

Emily furrowed her brow. "And they should stay afoot, too, if it makes it harder for them to kill one another."

In reply, Tom upended the sack, letting a heap of gold coins clatter to the table top among the cups and saucers. "That is not the opinion of the Union army, Emily."

She gasped at the sight. "If Mr. Lincoln would pay that in advance for wild, hook-nosed creatures that his officers have never seen, then he is a fool, indeed!"

"The South would pay that much for them as well," Tom shrugged. "Maybe more."

Jesse picked up a double-eagle and held it to the light. "Then Jefferson Davis is a fool, too."

"I won't argue with that," Tom nodded. He scooped up a handful of coins. "Two thousand dollars here." He paused for effect. "And this is only half of it. "Another two thousand when we deliver forty green-broke horses to the Union army at Fort Tejon."

Jesse gave a low whistle. "A hundred a head?"

Tom produced a neatly folded paper, emblazoned with the official seal of the Union army. "I wasn't expecting more than twenty apiece."

Emily leaned over her husband's shoulder and scanned the document. "They want the horses in a month!" she exclaimed. "But you haven't even started to break them!"

There had been nearly fifty horses corralled in five makeshift corrals since mid-July. Two journeys into the Mojave desert had yielded the half-starved mustangs for Jesse and Tom. Emily had shook her head in disapproval at the sight of the bunch and had proclaimed that no one in his right mind would mount an animal so homely, let alone spend good dollars to buy one. she had resented the feed that had disappeared down their ungrateful gullets, but after a month of good Dawson hay, she admitted that they looked a bit healthier.

"Only a month, you say?" Jesse clutched her hand and winked. "Why, I've tamed wilder things in half a day."

She blushed and turned toward the stack of dishes on the kitchen counter. "Not *forty* mustangs!"

"You'll just have to get a bigger jar for the bank, Emily," Jesse chided. "And have little faith."

"Just don't go get yourselves all busted up. You're not eighteen anymore, you know."

Tom leaned back in his chair with the casual air of a man who had won a great victory. "We're not going to break 'em," he teased. "We'll put Jed and Nathan and Montgomery to the chore."

Emily narrowed her eyes and threatened him with a swat from her dishcloth if he talked any more nonsense. "Food for the stomachs of Union soldiers," she muttered. "And now food for Southern cannons! I thought we were supposed to be far away from this war."

Dinner that night was a sumptuous affair, planned as a celebration for the successful sale of the potato crop to the army.

Emily had prepared a turkey, shot by Jed and proudly carried back to the farm by him from a manzanita thicket. She had stuffed it with corn-bread and sunflower-seed dressing, lightly spiced with fragrant sage. For the cornbread that accompanied the turkey there were gooseberry preserves and honey from their own hive of bees. A bowl of boiled potatoes brought good-natured groans from the table; but with a topping of fresh butter, salt, and a dash of red pepper, they disappeared as quickly as the rest.

Montgomery had to be coaxed to join them at the table, but once in place, he began to eat with as much enthusiasm as the others.

The conversation was of the most pleasant variety. They talked of how the money would be spent—so much for staples, so much for a new three-row cultivator, some for household furnishings and "frippery," as Jesse joked with Emily.

"That quartermaster sergeant said that next year they could take as many more loads as we could send," said Tom.

"That so? Well, it sounds like we'll need that cultivator real soon. We can open up that lower quarter section a year sooner than I expected," thought Jesse aloud.

"The sergeant told me they were getting another complement of troops to patrol the desert country clear to the Colorado."

Jed spoke up. "Yes, and he said they'd be riding camels, just like the wise men did—you know, for crossing the sand."

Nathan broke in, "With one big hump and a long snaky neck. The sergeant said they can spit tobacco juice fifty yards right in a fella's eye!"

"Now, boys," Jesse admonished, "you mustn't believe all you hear. That man was just funning with you."

"Yes, sir, Pa," replied Jed, while Nathan still looked stubbornly committed to the truth of his tale.

"But he said we'd see 'em."

"That will be enough, Nathan," Emily reproved. "Mustn't argue with your father." Then hastening to make sure no one felt too chastised, she asked, "Who's ready for pie?"

Vigorous nods of assent went around the table, and Emily retreated to the kitchen and returned moments later with a fresh baked apple pie, its flaky crust laced with sugar and cinnamon. "Now, just wait till I give you some more coffee, and then I'll dish it up."

As she completed a circuit of the table and prepared to serve the pie, Tom interrupted by getting to his feet. Raising his coffee cup he began, "Gentlemen, I give you the lady of the feast. A toast to Emily."

All the males rose, even Montgomery, who after a moment's uncertainty, grabbed his glass of milk, as did Jed and Nathan. "To Emily," said Jesse and Tom.

"To Ma," echoed Jed and Nathan.

"To Missy," added Montgomery.

Emily blushed and smiled, obviously pleased at the tribute.

As they seated themselves again and Emily began passing the pie around, Jesse observed, "Yes, sir, Tom, right here's what a man works for. A fine family and the means to feed and shelter them. A fine wife who makes a man look forward to coming home to supper. You know, Tom, you need to get married. There's nothing like it in the whole world."

After the meal the men sat smoking their pipes while Emily knitted. They had drawn their chairs up to the fireplace more for sociability than for warmth. The oak log glowed pleasantly. The three boys could be heard talking and occasionally laughing in the kitchen. Presently they finished washing the dinner dishes and came to stand in a row beside the scrubbed oak dining table.

Tom leaned forward to knock the dottle out of his pipe into the stone fireplace and stood up. "Mont, I expect you can bunk with me. Emily, that was as fine a meal and as enjoyable an evening as could be found anywhere. Good night Jesse, Jed, Nathan."

"G'night, Missy; I nevuh et bettah," added Montgomery.

"You are most welcome, both of you. Montgomery, we are pleased to have you stay with us. You must remember in your prayers tonight to thank God for your deliverance. And you, boys," addressing Jed and Nathan,"be sure to tell Him thank you for sending you a companion."

A chorus of yes'ums responded; then Jed and Nathan went up to the loft they shared, while Tom and Montgomery exited to the barn. Tom's room was actually the tack room of the barn, but it served him well, and a second cot was quickly set up for Montgomery. Soon all were fast asleep.

4

DEPUTY PETTIBONE WAS a rather small man with an enormous mustache. His graying hair was thinning on top—an observation that could not be made of his upper lip. Wiry as a bottle brush and still golden in color, the mustache seemed to precede Pettibone into rooms as if it had a presence all its own.

He was proud of that mustache and proud of his hometown of Greenville as well. From Tommy Fitzgerald's fur trading post in 1845, Greenville had grown to a population of over five thousand in less than twenty years. It boasted not one but two churches, a school, four hotels and assorted smithies, livery stables, and saloons.

For all the commerce, though, there was only one general store. Occupying the most prominent site at the juncture of the road to Laver's Crossing and the stage route to the valley, Mullins' store represented civilization and its attendant comforts to the citizens of Greenville.

Replete with food items, cookstoves, yard goods, farm implements, the latest in weapons, and ammunition, Mullins supplied the needs of the community. Through him one could order seed from Iowa, a machine from Chicago to plant it, or a mahogany casket with real silver handles from far off New York for a person to be planted in.

Robert Mullins' boast was that he could arrange to have anything one could imagine delivered in only six short months.

Mullins the man was as expansive as the horizons his store boasted. Standing three inches shy of six feet, he nevertheless tipped the scales at three hundred pounds. The apparent absence of a neck seemed not to bother him at all; indeed, the compensation of having three chins seemed more than adequate. His hands, which were like lumps of bread dough, were never idle. He constantly fidgeted with his merchandise, especially the candy jars arrayed on a shelf behind his counter, or with his watch chain that stretched across his front like the trace-chain of a four-up team.

Deputy Pettibone, like others in these mountains, saw in Mullins a man of the world, knowledgeable and prosperous. As such his advice was often sought and his presence on school board and church council accepted as his natural due.

"And when I got the news, I came up from Tailholt pronto. Do you think we should get up a posse and get after Byrd?"

"Well now, Sheriff, you know that if Byrd has faded back into those hills, he'll be next to impossible to dig out. What's more, like it or not, it appears that the stranger made the first move. Even if you could locate Mr. Guidett and compel him to come in, he'd just get acquitted."

"But shouldn't we at least dig up that feller and hold an inquest?"

"Sheriff, you do as you think best, but unless you intend to bring in the perpetrator, and I think we agree that's unreasonable, what's the point? The man is undeniably dead; he had no connections in this country, and apparently he deserved what he got—even your station-keeper Charlie admitted that, and he's the only witness."

"Well, not exactly. There was a small black child who saw it."

Mullins turned from the peppermint candy jar, which his sausage-like fingers had been exploring, and leaned across a case displaying bottles of Robin's Mild Cascara pills and Chicago Pharmaceutical's Diastalin tablets.

"A black child, you say? Did that dim-witted hostler know anything about the dead man other than that he came from Missouri?"

"Naw. He showed me a pitiful handful of stuff. 'Course Byrd had all his money. One strange thing: he had no letters, nor any papers telling who he was."

"You don't say? Well, perhaps he was a fugitive himself. Tell me, where is the child now?"

"Tom Dawson stopped there for the night. Byrd was for taking the black child away with him after the shooting, but Tom faced him down and then took the boy home."

"Did anyone think to see if the child had stolen anything?"

"No. No, least I don't think they checked. But here's Tom now; we can ask him."

Tom and Jesse entered Mullins' store and approached Deputy Pettibone.

"Hello, Jesse. Say, I was just fillin' Mr. Mullins in on what happened at Granite Station. "We—" Here he drew himself up to his full height and continued. "We think it's mighty peculiar that fella didn't have no name, nor any papers."

"The child he had along said the man's name was James—likely enough for a Missourian—and the boy had heard that name used for as long as he could remember."

"But was there no indication of the man's business?" This came from an attentive Mullins.

"No," Tom continued, "but there are many folk leaving that county who might not wish to bring any record of their past along."

"Quite, quite. And for a man who couldn't drink or gamble successfully, it's a wonder his lack of skill with guns wasn't discovered sooner also."

Deputy Pettibone felt the need to reassert his interrogation, so he asked, "Tom, are you certain that the child carried nothing away with him?"

Tom laughed. "No, Mike, that child barely had rags to cover himself. Fact is, he still thought he was a slave, and—say, there was one thing!" Tom slapped his pockets. "Yep, it's still here. When we went to bury that stranger, I must've slipped this in my pocket." Tom extracted the silver cuff link and laid it on the counter.

Before Deputy Pettibone could respond, Mullins' agitated fingers had grasped the jewelry and brought it close to his face. Just as quickly he laid it down again and commented, "It's nothing. Cheap workmanship. He probably lost the mate to it somewhere."

Jesse spoke up. "Didn't you say his name was James? Looks to me like this J is in the wrong spot. Who do you suppose J.D. could be, anyhow?"

"Ah, the man was a gambler, gentlemen. Most likely he won *some* of the time. Perhaps this J.D., whoever he was, was even unlucky enough to lose his cuff link to the unfortunate Mr. James."

Pettibone scratched his head doubtfully and made as if to reach for the cuff link, but Mullins opened a drawer below the counter top and dropped it in.

"I'm sure it's nothing, but if I have time perhaps I can examine it further for a jeweler's mark—something to tell us of its origin."

Pettibone's mouth began to work, then shut with a snap, as did the drawer when Mullins threw his girth against it.

"Mike, Jesse and I want to talk to you about Byrd anyhow. Can we visit with you a bit?"

"Shore, Tom, come on to my place."

"No need to move, gentlemen," Mullins interjected. "Just pull up a couple of chairs here. Sheriff Pettibone was here seeking my advice about Guidett, so I'm sure he wouldn't mind if I listened to your opinions. Would you, Sheriff?"

Tom and Jesse looked at each other, but Deputy Pettibone had apparently made up his mind, and he started arranging three chairs and an empty crate of Weaver's soap flakes around the fireless potbelly cast iron stove.

Jesse began. "Mike, you know that stage hold up?"

"Yes, terrible thing. So coldblooded and all. The army's out lookin' into that right now, but I hear tell whoever did it covered their tracks right smart."

"Tom and I figure that Byrd and his partner could have done it, stashed the gold and then, by hard riding, made Granite in time to throw off the scent."

"Especially if they circled around to the northwest and came in over Shadow Ridge," Tom added.

"Gentlemen, gentlemen!" Mullins interrupted. "Byrd Guidett had neither the brains nor the ambition to challenge the army for a gold shipment. He's a poor desperado at best."

Pettibone addressed Tom. "Now, Tom, I came up from Tailholt by the only trail anywhere near Shadow Ridge, and comin' that way, they couldn't have made Granite by afternoon if they rode like the wind."

"I wasn't thinking of the Tailholt trace, Mike. Jesse has heard talk of some older Indian trails—back in old Spanish days and even before. Why, even the old Yokut Chief Split Reed says that the mountain is haunted by the spirits of the Ancient Ones. Could be Byrd has found a lost trail across the south slope."

Robert Mullins' bulk obscured the ladder-back chair he occupied, but his words were anything but obscure. "Sheriff Pettibone, you know as well as I do that the south face of Shadow Ridge is a mass of deadfalls and brambles. Undoubtedly, the Indians regard it as haunted because any of their number who ventured there came to grief with a cliff or a rattlesnake. No, gentlemen, this is idle speculation. I certainly would not support endangering the lives of a posse of fine citizens for such a preposterous notion."

Tom's eyes flashed, but his brother laid a restraining hand on his arm and they both looked to the deputy for comment.

Pettibone's mustache worked vigorously as if chewing on what had been said. Finally he spoke, "Naw, boys, I'm glad you mentioned your idea but it won't wash. Like Mr. Mullins here says, there ain't no way around the south slope of old Shadow. Shucks, even pickin' his way along, Byrd would probably break his neck, let alone ridin' fast. Byrd's overdue for hangin', but this slaughter ain't his doin'."

Tom shook off Jesse's hand and stood up. "So that's it, huh? 'Thank you, Mr. Dawson, but *this* time Byrd didn't kill anybody worth bothering about?' Listen to me, Pettibone, if you ever want to be *sheriff*, as Mullins here keeps calling you, you'd better start thinking for yourself."

With that Tom and Jesse walked out, leaving a puzzled Deputy Pettibone and a complacent Mullins.

The store owner remarked, "The mark of a conscientious public servant is that he avoids irresponsible behavior. Bravo, Sheriff Pettibone, bravo."

The mustache puffed out proudly.

The dusty streets of Greenville were mostly deserted. The afternoon was hot and still. Tom's buckskin and Jesse's sorrel stood idly at the rail outside Mullins', their heads dropped and their eyes half closed. Even their tails were still, as though the oppressive heat had caused all the flies to seek shade.

"I guess that's that," Jesse commented. "You satisfied?"

"You know I'm not, but what else is there to do? What should we do with Mont?"

"He can stay, far as I'm concerned, but let's give him the choice. I'm sure Parson Swift could find a home for him, but he seems good-natured, and the boys are taken with him. Maybe he'll want to stay on."

"Before we head back, I want to get Matt to tighten that loose shoe—and maybe I can see what he thinks about old trails around Shadow Ridge."

"Good idea. If Tommy's at home, I can do the same with him. He knows most everything about this country as well as the Indians—better'n most."

Matt Green's blacksmith shop stood beneath a huge water oak just down the hill from Mullins' store. Green had taken the liberty of naming the town for himself, even though Tommy Fitzgerald had been the area's first white resident. Tommy had an Indian's outlook on land; he had never considered it something to be owned.

Matt was a wiry 60-year-old, as crusty and taciturn when sober as he was loudly abrasive when not. His face was framed by a gray beard that, together with his bushy eyebrows and craggy face, made him resemble Abraham Lincoln—until he opened his mouth. Matt seemed to have teeth only where they would meet the other jaw unopposed.

It was just as well that the likeness to Lincoln was not complete, because Matt was drunkenly outspoken in favor of the South. Not that he favored slavery, but he believed the southern states should be allowed to depart in peace.

Tom's friendly "Howdy" produced no more than a grunt of response from Matt. The blacksmith was pulling on the wooden handle of a bellows suspended from the ceiling.

With each pull the glowing coals of his forge cast a shower of sparks upward. Matt's grizzled face was streaked with grime, as though scorched by the upward flight of the escaping cinders. The bar of iron barely visible amid the flames was already cherry red. With a last heave on the bellows handle, Matt grasped a pair of tongs with his left hand and pulled the iron from the fire, laying it across his anvil. A few deft strokes of his short-handled hammer bent it into a rough U-shape; then back into the fire it went. This process of alternately heating and hammering continued until with a convulsive last stroke, Matt thrust the now-recognizable mule shoe into the tempering bucket, producing an explosive blast of steam.

"Now, what can I do for ya, Dawson?" Matt's manner was gruff, but no more than usual for him.

"Buck's fixing to throw a shoe. I thought maybe you'd tighten it for me."

"Le's see, he was jest shod two weeks ago. Musta caught it on somethin'."

The two men walked out to where the buckskin stood, and Tom watched as Matt examined the right front hoof.

"Yup, I can clench it up some. Lemme finish this batch of mule shoes so's I can let the forge go out. It's too blasted hot for this work today."

"That's fine," Tom agreed. "Mind if I watch? I need to visit with you about something, anyway."

The blacksmith's eyes narrowed with suspicion. "What about?"

Tom began slowly. "Jesse and I have been talking about Shadow Ridge. In all the time I've been here, I never heard tell of any trail around the south slope."

" 'Cause there ain't none!" Even from one as crusty as Matt Green, the vehemence with which this was uttered was surprising.

"Why, surely there must be an old Indian trail or two—

Matt's reply interrupted Tom's thoughts. "It's naught but a death trap—pits and slide rock! Don't you be messin' thereabouts, see!"

"You don't believe it's haunted, do you?"

"Mebbe I do and mebbe I don't, but there can't nobody get round thataway, and that's all there's to it!"

Matt lapsed into a stony silence as he returned to work the bellows, leaving Tom to hope that his brother was having better success with the old mountain man, Tommy Fitzgerald.

"Light and set, boy, light and set." Tommy's reception of Jesse was as warm and genuine as he was old. It was said that even Tommy didn't know what his age was.

He had crossed the plains with Walker's expedition, surviving attacks by Shoshone and later Paiute war parties, and living through a near drowning. When he reached the high pass through the Sierras near a place now called Greenhorn, he stood amazed with the first group of Anglo explorers to see the great central valley of California.

Tommy had hunted Tule elk in the swamplands of the valley, but he always returned to this mountain home, located on, as he said, "the first level spot I set my foot on west of the mountains."

When the Mexican Alcaldes held sway over the southern California ranchos, when the Russian bear's presence was still felt in the North, and San Francisco was just a miserable Hudson's Bay outpost called "Yerba Buena," Tommy already had a thriving fur trading business.

Because of ample water and abundant acorns, the Yokuts had made their fall and spring home in these mountains. They were a nomadic people, moving their camp to the valley floor in winter and to the high mountains in summer. Tommy located his home at their crossroads, built an adobe cabin, and began to trade.

The Yokuts were not an aggressive people, and because game and fowl were so readily available, the tribe never lacked food. Nor did they feel any need of horses since they didn't depend on buffalo as their brothers of the Great Plains did. There had never been much cause for fighting, so they accepted Tommy's presence gratefully, as he gave them access to iron tools. They especially prized the white man's knives, having used only obsidian blades before.

The area, with its narrow, fast-flowing streams, was not suited for beaver, but the Yokuts traded in fox furs—both gray and red—and deer and elk hides.

Tommy had watched their numbers dwindle, mostly because of white man's diseases like cholera, until after forty years, very few remained. None came to trade with Tommy anymore, and now he sat outside the crude one-room adobe with his long white hair and beard, lost in his thoughts and occasionally taunted by Greenville school children.

At Tommy's invitation, Jesse dismounted and joined the old man in the shade of a gigantic water oak.

"How stands the Union, boy?"

This was Tommy's standard greeting and called for no particular acknowledgement, but today Jesse replied to the question.

"I guess it's on shaky ground these days, Tommy. From what I hear tell, it's taken some hard knocks lately."

"Ya don't say? But, boy, we can lick the Mex. For all their trumpets, they can't match our long rifles, not by a long shot."

Jesse shook his head sadly. "No, Tommy, that Mexican war's been done these twenty years already. I mean this war between the states over slavery and all."

"Oh, I remember somethin' o' that now. I reckon I was back a ways there."

"That's all right, Tommy. I want you to remember back even further than that for me—back to old Injun days and before."

"What d'ya mean, boy?"

"Tommy, I know you know these hills like the back of your hand. Why, I bet you know every trail and blaze in them."

" 'Deed I do, boy, 'deed I do! Why, I come through here afore Fremont was a pup! I know'd Adams and Carson—all them folks. Why, I recollect one time Kit and me was—"

"Whoa up, Tommy," Jesse interrupted, for he saw that he had to jump in quickly before Tommy Fitzgerald had gotten completely wrapped up in his tale. "I want to hear you tell about these parts, especially the old trails around the south side of Shadow Ridge."

"Old Shadow? Why, boy, that mountain's haunted for sure. Plenty of good men lost their way, and ain't none of 'em come back—white nor Injun—neither."

"Think, Tommy, think. Weren't you ever on the south face?"

"Only oncet, boy, an' that were enough!"

Jesse leaned forward. "Tell me about that time."

Tommy closed his eyes for a moment as if collecting his thoughts; then with one hand gathering his beard and the other holding his forehead, he began.

"My pard, Matthews, him that's buried in Oak Grove next to the cedar stump, died up on ol' Shadow. One day he says to me, 'Tommy, I've shot a grizzly and let him get away. First light I'm goin' to track him round Shadow Ridge.'

"I says to him, 'Give it up, Frank; ya won't never find him.' And Matthews, he says, 'I cain't leave him go. If he lives he'll be rogue for sure.'

"So I said I'd go with him, and next morning we set out.

"Well, sir, we pushed round that south slope with the deer shrub and chaparral gettin' thicker an' thicker. We found a gob o' blood and we could foller that humpback real easy where he crashed through.

"When the track give up sudden-like, Matthews, he said to me, 'Be right canny now, Tommy; he's close.'

"An' jest as he said them words, all at once there riz up the biggest silver-tip I ever seed—right under his feet 'most like. Matthews tried to draw a bead, but that bear clubbed him jest as he shot. I believe Frank was dead afore he ever hit the ground.

"Well, sir, the bear never stopped to bother Matthews—jest come straight for me. I throw'd down on him and shot him in the eye—no further than from me to where you're sittin' now—but he never slowed down nor turned.

"I know'd I was a goner, but I drew my toothpick and run up the hill with that bear 'most on me.

"Do you know, I come on a path! Real faint—no more'n a trace, but goin' round the slope. I'm thinkin' maybe I'll distance this twice-shot bear when all at oncet I run plumb into a stone wall!

"I turned an' faced that there bear with jest my knife and him agrowlin' an' snarlin' real fierce an' lookin' horrible with his one eye blowed all over his head. I was abackin' toward a clump of manzanita close by when it happened."

"What, Tommy? What happened?"

"I crashed into that manzanita, and next thing I was fallin'; and then crash, my head hit an' I didn't know no more.

"Well, sir, I come to with a cracked skull an' a busted elbow an' some busted-up ribs, but I was livin'. It was dark, so I laid real still to see if that grizzly was still nosin' about. I laid there clear to daybreak, hurtin' bad an' real scared.

"Come dawn I got the biggest scare yet, 'cause right over my head, leanin' down at me, was the grizz'! But he was stone dead! Yes, sir, he died right on the edge of that cave, an' me knocked out jest fifteen feet below him!"

"A *cave*, Tommy? You're sure it wasn't just a pit you'd fallen into?"

"Naw, boy, naw. When I came to myself I seed a stream of water an' a black hole arunnin' way back in the mountain. Some Indian signs, too, boy—paintin's on the rocks, real old an' all. I clumb up a rubble pile an' bless me if I didn't have to climb over that bear agettin' out!

"It took me 'most two days to get down out o' there, what with bein' busted up. I drug poor ol' Frank down to where we'd tied the horses, an' then I couldn't load him! I finally had to leave him an' ride for help. The Injuns brought him out an' buried him, an' they tended me through a ragin' fever.

"Well, sir, those Injuns said it was a good thing I'd drug Frank as far as I did 'cause they wouldn't have set foot on the mountain proper. I said to myself, 'That's good enough for me. I ain't goin' back! An' I ain't never been back neither!"

"Didn't you ever tell this story to anyone else?"

"No, boy, I didn't. There wasn't nobody but the Injuns to tell it to at first; then later on I was afeared someone would get killed if they went lookin' for the cave, so I jest kept close till lately."

"Lately? You mean, just now?"

"Someone else asked me about a trail round ol' Shadow about a year ago. Said they'd heard Injuns talkin' about such. Well, I told 'em my story but cautioned 'em not to try an' find it—jest like I'm atellin' you now!"

"But who was it, Tommy? Who else asked about the trail?"

The old mountain man scratched his head for a moment and his eyes seemed momentarily glazed.

"What was that, boy? What did ya ask me?"

"I said, who else asked about Shadow Ridge?"

"I'm powerful sorry, boy, I can't remember. But say, did I ever tell ya about the grizzly I killed up on the Truckee? Say, that there was a bear! Why, boy, that bear was a' trackin' me!"

"Thank you, Tommy, but I'll have to hear that story another time," replied Jesse, standing up to go.

"Anytime, boy, anytime." The old man's head dropped, and he fell silent—but whether in sleep or deep thought, Jesse couldn't tell.

Riding back home, Jesse and Tom compared notes.

"I got nothin' from Matt at all—practically bit my head off for asking." Jesse recounted Fitzgerald's story, bringing an exclamation from Tom.

"A trail *and* a cave—why, Jesse, that means that not only is there a way around, but maybe even a place to keep fresh mounts!"

"Ease up, Tom. Remember, Tommy's an old man and liable to get mixed up. I was excited, too, till I noticed that he likes to tell bear stories an awful lot and I remembered that he couldn't recall what year it is!"

"But at least we should go check it out, shouldn't we?"

"Well, I suppose so, but we needn't rush off tomorrow. We've got plenty to do around the place with those horses, and it's for certain that we'll get no one to go with us—not on the strength of old Tommy's recollections. Pettibone's mind is altogether made up for him by Mullins, so we'll be on our own.

"Anyway, they're probably right. How could a trail exist and no one even know about it? And even if there were such a path and Byrd could have used it, that doesn't prove that he did."

"There you go," snorted Tom, "just like you always did. You find out that something's possible but maybe a little chancey, and you start backin' up. How'd you ever get up your nerve to move out here, anyway?"

"I knew I had to be able to offer Em something mighty special to win her away from you, old son—it was worth the risk. Now just let be till we get all our projects caught up; then I'll go with you if you still think it's so all-fired important."

5

THE CABIN SHOWED no signs of having been lived in for years. Its squared timber had once been mortared, but the chinking had been allowed to fall into such disrepair that more spaces than mortar appeared.

The windows were gaping holes only partially covered by ragged flaps of cowhide, and the wood-plank door hung crookedly from a torn leather hinge. Set in a side canyon through which flowed a seasonal tributary of

Cedar Creek, the site was the graveyard of some long-gone miner's hopes for wealth.

Mullins stopped to lean against a gnarled buckeye that stood just at the edge of the cabin's clearing. Panting for breath after his hike up the canyon from where he had left his rig hidden just off the main road to Greenville, he peered through the clumps of elderberry bushes and mopped his face.

Inwardly he swore and muttered to himself at the apparent emptiness of the scene; then he heaved his bulk forward a few more steps. He stopped short at a movement in the doorway and peered through squinted, pig-like eyes as Byrd Guidett strolled out.

"I know'd it was you. I heerd ya wheezin' and crashin' through the brush a mile off."

"Shut up, you fool, and get back inside!" snarled Mullins. "Where's Yancey?"

"Here." A voice at Mullins' elbow made him jump and caused even more sweat to pour down his florid face. Yancey stepped out from behind a brush-obscured boulder, replacing a gleaming knife into his boot top as he did so.

The three moved into the cabin. Yancey and Byrd stood on either side of the crumbling stone fireplace. On the oak beam mantel lay Byrd's rifle. The room was otherwise bare except for a rough bench on which Mullins seated himself.

"We done it!" boasted Byrd. "The strong box is hid and no one left to mark us for the law! We come over slick as ya please and made as though we hadn't a care except to play some cards. 'Course, we had a little set-to at Granite, but we came off none the worse for it."

Mullins exploded. "You cussed fool! None the worse? Do you know who it was you killed? That Missourian was Colonel James. He'd been working undercover since the secession. He was here to deliver my commission from President Davis personally and to take charge of raising the Army of the Pacific!"

"What? That ol' drunk a colonel?"

Yancey spoke up, his gray face more animated than one would have thought possible. "He didn't give no recognition sign. How was we supposed to know?"

Mullins turned on him, his jowls quivering with rage. "Did you expect him to announce himself to any cutthroat brigand he came across? He was on his way to meet with me. The gold you stole was to be used to purchase arms and train our fighting force to lead California out of the Union! *He* had the names of our contacts for making the purchases!"

"But, boss," said Byrd, "we got the gold. Cain't we jest buy the guns ourselves?"

"Do you think we can go to any arms dealer in San Francisco and say, 'Please, sir, we'd like to buy three hundred rifles'?" We'd be in Fort Alcatraz before you could cry 'Pinkerton' and hanged shortly after!"

A somewhat subdued Byrd lapsed into silence, and after a moment Yancey asked, "What's to be done?"

"The talk is that James had no papers on him—in fact, nothing but the cuff link, which I very fortunately got into my possession before anyone asked too many questions. That must mean that he had hidden the papers somewhere until after he made contact with me. Perhaps he felt that he was being followed or might be searched."

"But, boss, there's ten miles of boulders around Granite station! How'll we ever find 'em?"

Mullins calmed down a little and looked thoughtful. "Maybe that nigger boy can show us where they stopped before Granite. Or maybe Colonel James even gave the papers to the boy to carry."

"I know'd I should've catched that nigger! See, Yancey, I told ya we shoulda had him!"

Yancey replied dryly, "I seem to recall you not wantin' to press the issue with Tom Dawson and Mr. Colt's child."

Byrd glared at Yancey, but Mullins silenced any reply by saying, "Enough of this! Colonel James's death was an unfortunate accident, which luckily for you, Byrd Guidett, is reported to be not entirely your fault."

"Not entirely my fault! Why, he—"

"Shut up, I tell you! Now listen; it's clear what must be done. We must eliminate any curiosity about Shadow Ridge. There must be no snooping anywhere near the quartz ledge. Secondly, we must have that child!"

Tom and Jesse had chosen a half dozen of the stoutest old oak trees around the place to tie the broncos to. Saddled and cinched, the first six horses in the string were tied high and tight to the strongest limb of a tree. Cotton rope hobbled their legs and another rope wound around the rib cage and up through the forelegs, then through the halter to create a harness that would squeeze hard whenever the animal fought to pull away from the tree where it had been tied.

A critter what won't stand polite at a hitchin' rail is gonna come over backwards an' kill hisself an' maybe somebody else! That had been the first rule Tom and Jesse had learned from their Missouri horse-trader father. In the years since, the brothers had seen enough spoiled horses fighting a hitching rail to know the fact for themselves.

Even though there were a hundred ways to break a mustang, the brothers started by letting each animal teach itself a few manners. Some fought the rope and the tree branch more than others, jumping back and straining until they almost sat down on their hind legs, then lunging forward to relieve the pressure of the taut rope around their girth. Other horses learned to stand still after only one or two halfhearted battles. One thing was certain: they all learned sooner or later that it was easier to stand politely, regardless of the commotion around them, than to fight the rope.

It was the job of Jed, Nathan, and Montgomery—Mont as he soon came to be called—to wave flour sacks and holler like Indians within the view of the tied horses, but safely out of range of flying hoofs and the thrashing of bodies of a thousand pounds of unhappy horseflesh. *Sacking the horse* was the term Tom gave this process. After a while, the horses stopped quivering and totally ignored the bellowing of the small ranch hands.

Seven of the more stubborn animals fought for days. One powerful young bay stood sweating beneath the saddle for nearly a week, receiving from the hand of his tormentors food and a bucket of water twice a day until, at last, the brawny animal nickered happily at the sight of the man who had trussed him up like a prisoner. Tom chose this horse for his own. He had spirit and a will, and once Tom had tamed the spirit and turned the will into desire to please, the big bay had the promise of being a fine mount.

Except for his strength and size, the animal was anything but handsome. His large head had a curve like a Roman nose. The lower lip protruded slightly and moved incessantly as though he were trying to speak. His legs were black and blended into four iron-hard black hoofs. The black hoofs were an attribute that pleased Tom. An animal with white stockings meant soft, white feet, which were less likely to hold up in the harsh mountain terrain.

"This fella will go from here to the Atlantic and never need to be shod," Tom commented as he picked up the foot and examined it. "Let them have their pretty horses. I'll take good legs any day."

Emily overheard Tom's proud mumbling as she walked by with a basket of laundry in her arms. "Well, he is anything *but* pretty," she laughed. "It is lucky for us that the Union Cavalry is buying these creatures by the head. They certainly have the biggest heads of any horses I have ever seen!"

"I'm keeping this fella." Tom hefted a heavy sack of feed onto the saddle of the still-tied animal. "Jugheaded though he is."

Emily nodded. "Then name him Duncan!" she said, not missing a beat. "As a personal favor to me." She smiled brightly.

"Duncan?" Tom scratched his head. "Why Duncan?"

She continued back to the house with her basket, still giggling at her secret joke. *"Duncan!"* she called over her shoulder.

Tom shrugged and patted the thick neck of the bay. "I christen thee Duncan," he said. "Whoever he was, he must have been ugly as a mongrel dog!"

As if in agreement, the newly named Duncan nickered.

Jed, Nathan, and Mont were ready for school the morning the first twenty of the army's horses were gathered for delivery to Fort Tejon.

Tom mounted his big bay horse and then hefted Mont up for a proud ride around the barn. Duncan had learned quickly and pliantly when Tom had begun to ride him in the round pen. Now, while the rest of the rough string of mustangs were still reining reluctantly, Duncan moved easily to the leg pressure of his rider.

Emily had packed more than enough for the four-day journey. She kissed Jesse goodbye and then stepped back as he swung the pack over the saddle and mounted.

"Be careful, won't you?" She looked worried for a moment, then added, "He will give His angels charge over thee, to keep thee in all they ways!"

Jesse sounded a gruff *amen* in response, then leaned down to kiss her farewell once again. Tom looked away at their embrace. It was obvious that Jesse did not want to leave Emily for even a short journey.

Tom issued a spate of orders to the boys. Feeding and milking and other chores would have to continue even with the men gone. A chorus of eager assurance came from Jed and Nathan and Mont, who now seemed to fit into the family as easily as the others.

Tom was surprised when Emily reached up and briefly took his hand in her own. "Look after my Jesse, now," she whispered.

Tom cleared his throat and pushed his hat back on his head. "He's always been the one looking after me; you know that." Something in her eyes made him uncomfortable. He looked away, staring between the ears of the big bay horse. "When are you going to tell me why I'm calling this horse Duncan, anyway?" he asked. "Here I am taking him to a fort full of Union soldiers; Lord knows this horse is ugly enough to draw fire. Someone is gonna ask me, Emily, why I've named this jughead *Duncan!*"

"Tell us, Emily!" Jesse urged jokingly. "Just think, if we were ambushed by Indians you'd have to live with the fact that we never knew."

Her eyes flashed anger. "No such talk now, Jesse Dawson!" she scolded. "But if you must know, I've named him for an old black preacher who had a lower lip just like that! And whenever he was asked to pray, he'd tug his lip and say, 'De Lawd *done can* do it, suh! Ah knows de Lawd *done can!*'"

There was a terribly awkward moment when Mont looked startled at her rendition of the black preacher's dialect. He blinked and then looked at the horse and said loudly, "Well, I'd say de Lawd *done can* do 'bout anything He want to! He done he'ped get dem hosses broke, and now He *done can* bring Mistuh Jesse an' Mistuh Tom home safe-like!"

There was a burst of laughter all around, and then Mont patted the muscled shoulder of the horse. "Duncan!" he said with finality, and with a whistle, Jesse and Tom began to move the herd down the lane.

"Hee-yah!" shouted Jesse.

"Whoop! Whoop!" urged Tom as the last of the string of twenty green-broke mustangs were turned into the stock pens at Fort Tejon.

The steps of the adobe buildings were lined with spectators, civilians and off-duty soldiers alike. The drive from the range in Linn's Valley had taken four days, but now it was successfully concluded. The cavalry captain who gestured for the gate to be closed behind the last horse nodded with satisfaction at the sight.

"They look fine, gentlemen, just fine," he called to Tom and Jesse, who sat their horses flanking the gate. "Who would have thought that you could take wild and scrawny horseflesh and turn it into such sleek appearance in such a short span of time?"

"Well, Captain," commented Jesse, "all we did was catch this bunch at a watering hole up Mojave way inside a box canyon. We drifted out the ones we didn't want, and then we kept the others fenced away from water for a few days, only givin' them to eat and drink by our own hand. After about a week they got mostly docile."

Here Tom took up the tale. "Well, sir, next we got a rope on that lead mare over yonder." He pointed out a tall bay horse with a white blaze on her face that ran up into one blue eye. "When we started for home, she led real easy, and the rest of the herd just followed along."

Jesse resumed describing the route back to the ranch by explaining how they had gone over Walker Pass, forded the Kern River, and then followed the Bull road across the Sierra to home.

"After crossing the river, these horses were in feed like they'd never seen out in the desert. They didn't have any more reason to run away, and with this mare leading the way, the rest came on pretty easy."

"As for sleek," Tom pointed out, "all they needed was a few weeks of good feed. When we were culling the herd, we took care to pick only the sound ones that showed their ancestry back to the granddaddy horses brought to this country by the Spanish folk. Blood will tell, given time and opportunity, and this bunch has shaped up real well."

"Of course, gentlemen, how well they shape up as cavalry mounts remains to be seen," pointed out the captain. "Well fed they may be and able to be driven, but green broke to the colonel's satisfaction is another matter."

"I thought you might be interested in that, Captain," remarked Tom. "So I'd like you to look at Duncan here."

"I can already tell that you didn't select this animal for his beauty, Mr. Dawson. Perhaps you should tell me why I'm to pay attention to him."

"You see, Captain, Duncan here came out of that same herd at the same time as the rest. Now, he's had a little extra work put on him by me special, but nothing your boys couldn't do with their mounts. Watch this."

Tom spun Duncan around on his hind legs and galloped off toward the large oak tree under which explorer Peter Lebec had been killed by a grizzly. Duncan flashed around it, turning so close as to enable Tom to reach upward in passing and grasp a handful of leaves from a low branch. Halfway back across the parade ground, Tom jerked the horse to a sudden stop, and Duncan almost skidded as he sat back on his haunches.

Tom next worked the horse in a tight series of circles and figure eights, then trotted him back over to the watching crowd. Drawing rein before the grinning captain, Tom slid from Duncan's back to stand beside the bay as if to say, *See, nothing to it at all.*

"Excellent! Just excellent. And you say the rest of the string can come as far in as little time?"

"There's no doubt about it, Captain. After all, this one is not only jugheaded to look at; he's the most pigheaded and stubborn one of the bunch."

"And you say you can have the remaining twenty here in short order?"

"Absolutely," promised Jesse. "And there's more where these came from too."

"Well, then, get them to us just as quickly as possible and perhaps we'll be doing business in a regular way. Why don't we go into my office and see about your payment?"

"Suits us," said Jesse with a smile. "Then we'll be startin' back to get to work on the next batch."

As they walked up the steps, a portly quartermaster sergeant called out to Tom, "Hey, Dawson, this here crop's livelier than potatoes, huh?" To the roar of laughter which erupted, Tom waved good-naturedly and replied, "Yes, and you'd best be careful, Sergeant. Fork one of these spuds wrong, and you'll be the one gettin' peeled!"

The young lieutenant leading the detail of four troopers was preparing to leave at the same time as the Dawson brothers, so they all rode together as far as the crossing of Cottonwood Creek.

"We'll be turning west there toward the ranch of Colonel Thomas Baker," he remarked, raising his eyebrows significantly.

When neither brother reacted to this announcement, he continued, "Baker is being arrested for interfering with recruiting efforts for the Union army. He has been very open about his pro-rebel sentiments, but has recently gone too far."

"Isn't Baker some kind of government man himself?" inquired Tom.

"Yes, he's a state senator, and he's been using his political opportunities to ridicule the Union army and describe in detail the defeats we have experienced at rebel hands. He's even gone so far as to say that the war is no concern of Californians, and that boys from here ought not go off to fight in it. He stops just short of treason by pretending to favor a peaceful settlement to the conflict, but we believe that he privately favors pulling California out of the Union.

"Anyway," he concluded, "he's to be arrested on the recruiting charge, and that should interrupt his little schemes for a while."

6

BYRD CROUCHED BEHIND a cottonwood tree that grew up from the creek bed. He was peering through its leaves toward the mouth of the canyon out of which the stage would have to emerge. Dust devils chased each other across the intervening plain. Byrd scrutinized each one to see if it would resolve itself into the coach and four that he was expecting, but for over an hour each round wind had been a false alarm.

He was annoyed that the coach was late. The dust from the dry creek bed caught at his throat and irritated his eyes. For a time he amused himself by plucking cottonwood leaves and dropping them one by one at his feet, but he soon grew tired of this and drew a stained bandanna from around his neck and mopped his forehead.

He turned the bandanna over briefly in his hands, considering whether to tie it around his face. He glanced again toward the stage road, squinted upward at the sun, and threw the bandanna down on the ground in disgust.

Nervous at this delay, he decided to check his Walker Colt to make sure it was loaded properly. He reached for the four-pound pistol he wore tied down and drew its nine-inch length carefully from the holster and regarded it with squinted eyes.

Someone had once remarked that the only thing Byrd cared about in all the world besides himself was the six-shooter. Byrd would never have thought to express that observation in just that way, but it was nevertheless true, and with good reason. He earned his livelihood by his ability with the Walker's faithful performance, and it had saved his life on more than one occasion. Of course, it had not been able to save the Texas Ranger from whom Byrd had obtained it.

The weapon was loaded and capped as it had been the two earlier times Byrd had checked, and he swore at himself for this apparent nervousness. He was, he decided, tired of waiting. Being tired made him grouchy, like a petulant child in need of a nap.

He had just returned the Colt to its holster when he heard Yancey's signal—a low, whistled quail call that sounded like "chicago, chicago." Byrd's head snapped up, the revolver again in his hand.

Yancey would nag him later for not spotting the coach first. This thought only served to increase his irritation. Sure enough, out from the canyon a moving black shape had appeared, throwing up a trail of dust behind.

On through the sagebrush it came, presently drawing near enough for the form of the coach to be seen. A little closer, and the team of mules drawing it could be made out; shortly after, Byrd could see the driver and a shotgun messenger perched on the box.

Any nervousness Byrd might have felt vanished. Now he was all business. He stooped over and retrieved the bandanna, but his eyes never left the approaching stage. With his left hand he drew the cloth around his neck and swore again at the awkwardness of trying to knot it one-handed. He replaced the .44 momentarily, just long enough to tie the kerchief and pull its folds up over his nose. His bushy red beard pushed the mask out from his face.

He looked down the draw to where Yancey squatted, similarly masked and armed. Byrd had a moment to sneer again at Yancey's choice of weapons. It was a .36 caliber Allen, a "pepperbox"—good for a hideout weapon, but not a man's gun, in Byrd's opinion.

His attention returned to the stage, now less than four hundred yards away. Their plan was simple. Since the seldom-wet creek bed had no bridge, the stage drivers were in the habit of pitching violently down one bank and back up the other without even slackening speed. Just below the rim of the bank nearest the stage, Byrd and Yancey had laid the trunk of a cottonwood. This unexpected obstacle should cause the lead mules to balk, and in the confusion Byrd and Yancey would have the opportunity to get the drop on the driver and guard.

Byrd could see the pair of men clearly now. The driver was leaning forward, skillfully working the lines, getting the utmost speed out of the surging team. The guard was leaning back, bracing himself against the expected swoop into the gully. Sunlight glinted dully on the barrels of the shotgun he carried.

As expected, the coach didn't even slow as it passed the crest of the creek bank. Over it came, the team dipping below the rim so rapidly that the wagon appeared to be propelled straight across the wash for a space before dropping to follow the contour. Right in front of the leaders was the tree, its branches right in their startled faces.

The driver didn't even have time to react and had no chance to halt the suddenly pitching team; for as the leaders attempted to swerve, the sudden loss of rhythm caught the wheelers off guard, slewing the coach violently to the left, then turning it over on its side with a rending crash. The driver flew off the box after the team, and the guard pitched over the tree trunk in the direction of the tumbling coach, which finally came to rest on its side, surrounded by a great cloud of dust.

As the dust began to clear low moans could be heard coming from the coach's interior. One wheel made a mournful creaking sound as it continued to revolve lazily on its now vertical axle.

Byrd straightened up and pushed his hat up off his forehead in astonishment. He glanced to where Yancey also was taking in the scene of wreckage with an amazed look on his face. They had expected to stop the stage's headlong rush, but nothing like this.

Anticipating no resistance from the destruction that presented itself, both men put away their weapons, Yancey thrusting the pepperbox into his waistband.

They converged on the coach from opposite sides. Byrd wore a whimsical grin as if he wished he could always conduct a robbery in such a spectacular manner.

Yancey, normally silent, was moved to what was for him garrulous speech. "Did ya see that, Byrd? I'll be a suck-aig mule if that weren't the most horrific crash. Them fellers didn't have no chance atall."

Byrd studied the scene with a proprietary air, noting with satisfaction that the guard's neck was bent at an impossible angle; he was dead. Then Byrd spoke. "Where'd that driver get off to? Last I seen, he was sailin' after them mules. Well, no matter, he musta fetched up in the next county in so many little pieces, they'll have to pick 'em up with a dustpan and a broom."

That the occupants of the coach still lived was evidenced by their occasional groaning. Even though there appeared to be little chance of fight left in anyone who had experienced the crash, Yancey pulled his pistol again before stepping up on the useless thoroughbrace and peering down into the interior.

"Thar's only one in here, and he looks busted up bad," called Yancey.

"Leave 'em then, and let's get to business."

The two undid the boot and found the expected strong box. It had not broken open in the crash, but the hinges were bent, and Byrd soon was able to pry the hasp and lock off the case.

Inside was a shelf of official-looking documents, which Byrd thrust into his shirt unread. As a matter of fact, he couldn't have read them, anyway. Beneath the papers was the gold—about ten thousand dollars' worth.

Byrd hefted the box to his shoulder and turned to slog through the sand to where they had tethered the horses. Yancey trudged alongside.

An arresting pair of clicks brought them to a sudden halt. Beside the body of the guard stood the driver. His bloodless face was drawn with pain, and his left arm dangled limp at his side.

But Byrd's attention was centered on the man's right side, where he cradled the guard's shotgun under the crook of his arm and had just thumbed back the hammers.

In a halting voice he ordered, "Throw down that box and your weapons." Byrd and Yancey complied, each fingering their pistols gently in the face of the double-barreled threat.

"Now raise your hands and keep 'em up." With a glance at each other, Byrd and Yancey did so, while moving slightly apart. The driver's strength was failing; he had difficulty keeping the shotgun's muzzle elevated.

"Listen, mister, yer stove up bad, and so's yer passenger. Now ya'd best let us ride outta here, an' we'll send back some help."

"Shut up, you two, I need to think," mumbled the driver.

"But yer man here, he needs help now—cain't ya hear 'im?

As if on cue a frightened moan came from the coach. In the instant that the driver's attention wavered, Yancey's hand flashed downward toward his shirt collar and upward again with the knife that had hung between his shoulders.

The shotgun discharged both barrels into the ground with a roar, but the blade that now quivered in the man's stomach occupied all his attention.

Byrd scooped up his .44, but it wasn't needed. A moment of startled disbelief crossed the driver's face, and he swayed forward once, then pitched face-first into the sand.

Byrd and Yancey rode off, laughing at how easy it had been.

Seven men rode downward out of the narrow pass guarded by Fort Tejon, through a rocky sagebrush-covered ravine, and out onto the gentler slope that led to the floor of the San Joaquin Valley.

The dusty haze of Indian summer obscured their view up the valley, but even so it was a magnificent sight. Stretching some three hundred miles from where they rode to the San Francisco Bay and beyond, the great central valley was crisscrossed with waterways, swamps and marshes. Here and there herds of Tule elk roamed.

As they rode, Tom caught more than one of the troopers casting admiring looks at Duncan. Homely he might be, but they could tell at a glance that he had heart. These hardened men knew the value of a reliable horse. Patrolling the reaches of the Great Desert as they did, there had to exist implicit trust between man and beast. In the previous year's campaign against the Mojave Indians, the lieutenant himself had been saved from an agonizing death by his mount's ability to locate water when the tank they were depending on had turned out unexpectedly empty.

So when Duncan snorted and pricked his ears forward, not only Tom but Jesse and the whole party took note. They were just approaching the intersection of their northward-bound track and the road that led westward from the mines. The breeze was blowing toward them, and suddenly all their animals gave evidence of uneasiness.

The lieutenant called a halt and stood in his stirrups, craning his neck and peering forward. "I see something in the bend of the creek yonder," he stated. "Jones, you and Brown go forward and reconnoiter."

"Aye, sir," the troopers responded, and galloped forward. A few moments later one of them returned at high speed.

"All right, Trooper Brown, report."

An ashen-faced Brown burst out, "They're all dead, sir! I mean, it's the stage, sir, and it's been wrecked!"

"An accident, Trooper?"

"Yes, sir . . . I mean, no sir—that is, we thought it was, sir, with the coach all busted up. The guard, sir, he's got a busted neck. And the passenger, he's dead too."

"Well, what makes you think it isn't an accident?"

"It's the driver, sir, he—"

"Speak up, Brown, what is it?"

"The driver, sir, he's got six inches of knife stuck in him!"

An investigation of the area revealed in short order how the holdup had been accomplished. They could see where the outlaws had waited to surprise the stage and how successful they had been. From the position of the driver's body and the discharged shotgun lying beside it, it was even possible to reconstruct how he had met his fate.

"How could this happen?" began Jesse. "After that other holdup with everyone murdered, why wasn't this stage escorted?"

"Great scott, man!" returned the lieutenant testily. "Don't you know how short-handed we're running here? This patrol is half its normal strength, and on top of that, has twice its usual assignment to patrol!"

"Look, Lieutenant," Jesse replied, "we know you've got your problems, but this can't be allowed to continue. Pretty soon no one will feel safe traveling through the valley. Already folks are starting to talk about the need to form a California militia to mount our own patrols. People are saying that if the army can't or won't protect us, then we'll have to do it ourselves."

"May I warn you, Mr. Dawson, that kind of talk is precisely what the so-called *Colonel* Baker is being arrested for!"

"Listen," broke in Tom, "we're not talking politics here; we're talking the safety of our families. Whether this is some rebel plot or plain old highway robbery makes precious little difference to folks who lose their lives or their loved ones!"

The lieutenant looked subdued for a moment before he spoke. "Of course you're right, and the ones who did this and the other holdup must be brought to justice as quickly as possible. We still believe that this is all linked up with the plot to introduce rebel elements into the control of California gold. There may even be a bigger conspiracy afoot than you or I can imagine."

"I know," added Jesse, "that there are those in the mountains who have no use for the government in Washington; they just want to be left alone. But that doesn't necessarily make them favor the Southern cause, nor get them involved in robbery and murder!"

"I'm aware of that, Mr. Dawson, but you can certainly see we need help if this situation is to be remedied. Suppose we were to make an appearance in Greenville and other communities, pledging our increased attention to the problem, while at the same time requesting the cooperation of all the citizens in locating those who have done this?"

Jesse turned to Tom. "What do you think, Tom? Would that help matters any?"

"I don't know, Jesse. It's certain that once the news of this holdup gets out, there's going to be a real uproar. I'm not trying to tell the army its business, but it seems to me that if they'd admit we've got a problem and work together with us to solve the situation, it would be the right approach."

Tom continued to address the officer. "Don't expect any of the mountain folk to come up with information about rebel sympathizers among their friends and neighbors. They won't tolerate thieves and murderers, but they believe a man's politics are his own business—at least as far as his thoughts are concerned."

"Very well, gentlemen, I'll communicate your views to my commanding officer. I feel certain he'll agree that some immediate action will be required. Meanwhile, if you see the local deputy—what's his name, the one with the enormous mustache?"

"Pettibone?"

"That's the one. Would you inform him about what's happened and ask him to communicate it to the sheriff and others? We'll try to pass along any helpful information just as soon as we can."

The scene of the wrecked stagecoach and murdered men was still vivid in the minds of Tom and Jesse as they rode the final mile into Greenville. Neither had spoken for hours. Anger at the first sight of such a violent crime had finally dissipated into helpless frustration. Whoever had done this thing was long gone—vanished without leaving so much as a single track on the stony paths that led from the scene. Tom and Jesse would inform Deputy Pettibone that once again the gold destined for the Union coffers had been stolen. But there was little that could be done, and hardly an ounce of sentiment would be spared for the stolen Yankee gold. Wasn't there a war on, after all? Didn't people get hurt in wars, even here in California?

Tom had seen this sort of thing a hundred times in Missouri. Senseless killing. Murder in the name of a cause. Somehow people here needed to understand that there was something else at issue. Something more cruel than war. What was it? He had tried to figure it out before. How could he put a name to the cold chill that had coursed through him at the grisly sight he had seen?

As if reading his thoughts, Jesse turned to him. "Whoever did that enjoyed killing. There was an evil love of death."

Tom did not need to reply. Yes. That was it. That was what he had seen on the Kansas-Missouri border. He had even glimpsed that evil in his own soul. Now, as if to escape the landslide of emotions and memories which engulfed him, he spurred Duncan into a gentle lope up the last hill before reaching town.

At the top of the rise, a new sound greeted him. A cloud of dust rose up from the schoolyard. Boys shouted and little girls shrieked as two dozen children pressed in for a better view of a miniature battle.

"Get 'im!"

"Whallop that nigger, Sam!"

"Hit 'im . . . in the face!"

"Kill them Yankee lovers!"

Tom rose up slightly in his stirrups and tapped Duncan, who raced toward the schoolyard.

So it had come here as well. Even among the children, who mimicked their parents. . . .

7

"**R**AW PIECES OF beef steak. Just the thing for black eyes." Jesse handed out the evening's uncooked supper to each of the three boys. "Just hold it there over your shiner. I reckon it will still make a good meal after you're done using it." Jesse winked at Emily in an effort to lighten her mood. She had not smiled since her first look at the dusty, battered boys.

Mont bit his lip and peered up at Jesse through swollen eyes. He had taken the worst beating, and now Jesse wondered how the child could see. "Um, Mistuh Jesse . . ." He looked at the meat in his hand and held it timidly as though he was afraid to put it to his bruised eye.

"Yes. What is it, Mont?" Jesse knelt and put his hands on the boy's shoulders. He was keenly aware what young Mont must be feeling. After all, hadn't the fight been over the color of his skin? That and the sale of horses to the Yankees?

"Well, suh . . ." He continued to gaze at the meat. "Should ah be puttin' dis here meat on my eyes, too?"

"Of course, Mont!" Emily chimed in, wanting to reassure Mont that he was as much a part of the family as Jed and Nathan. "It's only a bit of beefsteak, and there's plenty more where that came from. You must not worry about that!"

"Yessum. Ah mean . . . no, ma'am." He still looked uneasy. "What ah means is . . . if'n dis is gonna take away my black eyes . . . is it . . . I mean, it ain't gonna make white round my eyes . . ." His small voice trailed off. "Is it? It'd be plumb awful if I was to go back to school all spotted like!"

Suppressing a laugh, Jesse reassured him that the beefsteak would simply take away the welts. Emily guided Mont's hand up to his swollen face and then sat him down firmly at the kitchen table next to Jed and Nathan.

With a solemn shake of her head, she led Jesse to the door and stepped out onto the porch.

"What next?" She wrung her hands distractedly.

Jesse lifted her chin gently and looked into her eyes. "How about a kiss hello?" he asked, pulling her close and brushing her lips with his.

"Oh, Jesse!" She leaned heavily against her husband. "I'm so worried. We had so hoped to be spared from this terrible war. But even *here* . . . people are so—" She did not finish. Jesse was stroking her hair as if she were a child to be comforted.

"It was only a kid's schoolyard fight. Nothing to fret over."

"No." She began to weep softly. "It's more than that. Not just Mont. Children can be so cruel! But . . . Jess, Mrs. Burton had harsh words for me at church, and—"

"Mrs. Burton? At church, no less. Emily you can't—"

"Listen to me, Jesse!" Emily stepped back and held the face of her husband in her hands. "I'm *frightened!* People don't take kindly to you and Tom breaking horses for the army. When I got home from church yesterday, someone had opened a gate! Five horses were turned loose! Five of the best. I thought it was just a malicious prank at first, but then I got to thinking about what Mrs. Burton said about how *many* folks are angry about those horses! I could scarcely sleep last night for thinking about it. And now, today, the boys get into it. And not only that, you come back with word that there's been another robbery—men killed and Union gold stolen . . ." She looked fiercely away at the setting sun. "I thought we would be free from this sort of thing here in California. The Promised Land. Free from war and killing and prejudice."

Jesse sighed and leaned against the porch railing as he followed her gaze to Shadow Ridge. "It wouldn't matter where we lived, Emily," he said softly as weariness crept into his voice. "You know that. Folks are always finding some reason to make trouble, to stir things up. You know it's not just the war between Yankees and rebels that has people riled up." He put his arm around her. "It's a different war. The war is inside men's hearts. Fierce and mean. And I don't suppose it's any different anywhere. No better or worse. Folks just love to hate."

The sky darkened and the trill of crickets filled the cool evening air. Neither Emily nor Jesse spoke for a long time. At last, when the corralled horses nickered for their supper, Emily said quietly, "The boys and I managed to round up three of those jugheaded horses of yours. Two are still out there wandering around Shadow Ridge, I suppose."

"Be careful how you speak of those jugheads. They are money in the bank—pure gold beneath those scruffy hides. Tom and I will go find those two."

"Jesse!" She began to protest, but he had already gone to find Tom.

Colonel Mason was trying his best to keep his temper under control. He knew if he responded emotionally to what he was hearing, he would lose the attention of the meeting. It wasn't easy, though, given what Matt Green had been saying.

"Yer bunch of blue-bellied scoundrels couldn't track a black bear on a snow-covered hillside! You ain't up here to try and catch no robbers; ye're jest makin' up stories so's to get folks to rat on their neighbors!"

"Now that's not all true, Mr. Green; we have reason—"

"I'll give you reason! I'll give you reason! You can't catch no holdup men no more'n all the Yankee gen'rls that was ever spawned can catch the likes of Jubal Early or Robert E. Lee! You ain't showed nothin' to me, 'cept that now you got an excuse to go off achasin' poor folks what don't want to fight no Yankee war!"

There were muttered growls of approval at these sentiments.

"If I may be allowed to respond—"

"Here's my ree-spond!" Matt made as if to spit, but caught himself just in time. "Sorry, Parson, I disremembered where we was."

"Thank you for recollecting that this is a church, Mr. Green. Now perhaps we should allow the colonel to continue."

Matt subsided, muttering to himself.

"Thank you, Parson Swift. Here is the situation from the army's point of view. Gold belonging to the United States government has been stolen. That makes the affair our concern. Civilians have been killed in those same attacks. That makes it a case for the civilian authorities as well. Now, whether or not you believe that the robberies are politically motivated, the fact remains that such attacks cannot be allowed to continue.

"As much as it pains me to admit it, thus far Mr. Green is correct. All our efforts to date have not apprehended the culprits, which is what brings us to the point of today's meeting.

"Contrary to what Mr. Green thinks, we are not here to pursue draft-dodgers or deserters, or to inquire into anyone's personal beliefs." Here Colonel Mason paused briefly to look Matt Green squarely in the eye before continuing. "It is necessary for us to pursue whatever information we possess, and that information is that these robberies are linked to a conspiracy to promote the rebel cause.

"Now, we are prepared to see that every stage has an armed escort and to mount regular patrols of the highways in order to prevent further oc-currences. What we want from you good people is a report of any suspi-cious activities, any strangers in town, or known outlaws whose movements seem questionable."

Matt Green burst out with another interruption. "There, ya see what

I'm atellin' ya? Who's an outlaw far's the army is concerned? What's suspicious?"

He seemed disposed to continue his tirade, but at the front corner of the room Robert Mullins rose to his feet, graciously smiling. "With all due respect, Mr. Green, I think that the colonel has made it very clear that it is up to us as good citizens to determine what is reported and what is not. It will be on each of our consciences to come forward with information that might prove helpful. After all, we want the army to participate in defending the citizenry from this wanton depredation until such time as our own capable sheriff, Mr. Pettibone here, can lay the perpetrators by the heels."

Mullins paused and looked around the room for effect. "What about this as a workable compromise? So long as the army demonstrates that they can, in fact, improve the protection of the public highways, we should have no objection to cooperation. Further, let a committee of responsible citizens be formed to whom reports can be made of suspicious actions. This committee can then pass judgment on the merits of each report before deciding whether to bring the information to the army's attention. This should satisfy Mr. Green's concern about harassment of private citizens, while at the same time filtering information so that the army's valuable time is not wasted in wild-goose chases.

"What do you say, Sheriff Pettibone? Is this a workable solution?"

Pettibone stood up next to Mullins, but given their difference in size, he appeared to be more dwarfed than ever when standing next to the storekeeper. He tugged on one end of his mustache reflectively and then commented, "It seems to me that that's a real workable answer, provided a' course that the right men be on that committee. What say you serve as the chairman, Mr. Mullins?"

Tom looked at his brother and raised his eyebrows as a low chorus of " 'At's right, Mullins'll keep 'em straight" and "Good idear" came from around the packed sanctuary.

Seeming flustered, Mullins clasped his hands in front of him and bobbed his massive head up and down as his jowls quivered. "Why, I don't know what to say. I never considered . . . But if you think I should serve, why naturally . . ."

Matt Green, who was not altogether taken with Mullins, spoke up again. "I say put the parson on that committee. He's a man of sense, an' he don't talk so much!"

Parson Swift stood to acknowledge the nomination. "Thank you, Matt. I believe you all know that I can be trusted to keep your private thoughts private, but I do agree that something needs to be done to bring the murderers to justice."

"Who else?" someone said. "We need one more."

"Don't nobody suggest Matt!" another voice added.

Finally the parson spoke up again. "I'd like to recommend Jesse Dawson. He is a member of this community with a fine reputation. He has seen first hand the awful results of the crimes we're discussing, and he has a business relationship with the army which should make him acceptable to them. What do you say, Colonel?"

"A fine choice, Parson Swift, and a good solution all around. May I take it that the matter is settled then?"

There were nods of agreement mixed with some grunts of disapproval from around the room. Deputy Pettibone frowned, chagrined that no one had thought to recommend *him*. Noting his look, Mullins pointed out, "And naturally, Sheriff Pettibone's official capacity means that he will automatically be a part of the committee's discussions as we share information." Pettibone looked pleased.

The only other markedly unsatisfied individual was still sitting next to his brother as the men began to file out of the church. Tom leaned over and whispered to Jesse, "I can tell that this committee isn't your cup of tea. Why didn't you decline the *honor?*"

"I'm not sure I can explain why I let it stand. The parson's a good, level-headed man, but with Mullins being on the church board and all, I was thinking he might be able to throw his weight around." He grinned maliciously. "But maybe the parson and I can balance him some."

"You don't really think that committee will do any good, do you?"

"Maybe not, but the parson's right about one thing: I won't be forgetting the sight of that driver any time soon. Survived the wreck of the coach, and then stuck like a pig and left to bleed to death!"

Byrd motioned for Yancey to hurry. Yancey was far more adept and quiet at slipping through brush than Byrd and so had no difficulty keeping up. In fact, he reasoned, he could have followed Byrd from two hundred yards away.

The two were slipping up on the Dawson home in obedience to Mullins' instructions to kidnap Mont. Guidett agreed wholeheartedly with the plan since he saw it as a chance to recover what he believed was his rightful property.

Yancey had some misgivings. He expressed to Robert Mullins his doubts that any information Mont had would be valuable to them, and that kidnapping a child would arouse the countryside into a protracted search.

Mullins had snorted his derision. "For an orphan nigger boy? Nobody'll give him so much as a thought, much less try to search for him.

"And," the storekeeper went on, "if you do this correctly, everyone will believe the boy is a runaway and not kidnapped at all."

So Byrd and Yancey were now creeping down the Poso Creek draw, having left their horses about half a mile from the Dawson place. They had selected this night by watching for several evenings in a row from a hilltop overlooking the farm until what they were hoping for had occurred. Tom and Jesse Dawson had left together at the end of the workday to ride into Greenville, leaving Emily and the three boys home alone.

It was all well and good for Mullins to say that they could make it look as if Mont had run away, but if they were discovered, they wanted to avoid a gun battle or any possibility of pursuit.

The gathering gloom cast pools of shadows under the scrub oaks. Twice, coveys of quail flew out of the dust with a clatter of wings as they sought to escape the night prowlers by nesting in the tree branches. Overhead the bats darted in and out of the open spaces between the oaks.

At each disturbance, Byrd and Yancey stopped short and listened. No sound came from the direction of the farm except for the nicker of a horse accepting his supper.

Even Byrd began to walk more cautiously. He made an effort to avoid the piles of brittle buckeye leaves that the breeze had gathered into heaps.

They had circled behind the Dawson place so as to approach it from the uphill side. From the rising land to the west they could look down on the barn, which was completely dark, and on the house, where only a gleam of light was visible.

Byrd motioned for Yancey to squat down beside him as they prepared to observe for a while.

Almost immediately they were rewarded as they saw the door open and Mont walk out alone. He went across the dusty yard to the tack-room door of the barn and went in. A moment later, a light peeked through the cracks in the door to show that Mont had lit a lantern or a candle.

Byrd turned to Yancey and whispered, "Looks pretty easy, don't it? Yancey, you circle the long way around to the far side of the barn while I creep up on the corral-side closest to us." He added a few more instructions and then Yancey disappeared from view.

Byrd thought he saw movement behind the corral, but he wasn't sure. Minutes passed. Then he saw Yancey moving stealthily toward the far corner of the barn. "So far, so good," Byrd said under his breath.

The plan was simple. Yancey would approach the tack-room door and tap on it lightly as though he were Emily coming for a good-night word. As Mont opened the door, Byrd would grab him. Yancey was placed to block any bolt the boy might make away from Byrd's grasp. While Byrd held the child, Yancey would make a quick grab for Mont's meager possessions to complete the illusion that he had run off. Then they would ride back to the hideout.

Byrd began his stalk. First to the tree trunk nearest the corral, then to the corral's corner. From post to post he moved, a hulking shape of sinister intent.

At the corner of the barn he stopped. The next move was the most exposed since the front of the barn had no cover and was in full view of the house. Byrd noted with satisfaction that the barn door was ajar, giving him a halfway point to reach.

As he left his last concealment and made for the barn door, Byrd felt a rising excitement. It was all going so well. He'd have the boy *and* he'd show Mullins what he was capable of.

In the midst of his self-exaltation, he heard the front door of the house open. Someone was coming out. Instinctively his hand dropped to the butt of his gun, but he forced himself to jump into the crack of the barn opening and pull the door shut behind him.

He pressed himself into the shadows in the hinged corner of the crack and waited with bated breath.

It was Emily, and she was coming straight for the barn! Byrd examined her thoughtfully. As she reached the tack-room door and opened it, the light from within fell on her. Byrd could see her shape clearly. He liked what he saw.

Byrd licked his lips. *What a woman,* he thought. *Wouldn't I like—*His gaze lingered on her. *She's too good for the old clod-kicker she's married to; she'd prob'bly appreciate a real man like me.*

Byrd's lust began to overcome his caution. *Who's to know?* he thought. *Thar she is, not ten feet away.*

He had actually begun to move toward the door when he remembered Mullins' last command: "No one must know that anyone has the slightest interest in the child. If you cannot get away cleanly, wait for another occasion."

Byrd paused, his eyes narrowed, nearly deciding to disregard Mullins' orders. Then he heard Emily speaking.

"That's right, Mont. I've given the boys permission to stay up until their father and uncle return. They'd like you to join them and play some checkers. Would you like to?"

"Oh, yessum, Miss Emily."

"Well, come on, then."

Byrd shrank back against the wall. *Blast it! We'll have to wait for another time,* he decided. *Then I'll grab the nigger, get that cussed Mullins off of my back, and have the woman, too.*

A moment more, and the door of the house opened and shut again as Emily and Mont went in.

Byrd whistled softly to Yancey and together they retraced their steps to where they had tied their horses.

When they reported their failed attempt to Mullins, he swore softly, but seemed relieved that there had been no disturbance. Byrd naturally didn't divulge any of his thoughts, but privately made his own plans for "another time."

8

TOM AND JESSE planned to look into Tommy Fitzgerald's tale of an old track around Shadow Ridge and the possibility of a cave there, but the farm delayed their exploration.

Mont worked eagerly alongside Nathan and Jed, helping with the haying and the digging of an additional root cellar to lay up potatoes, pumpkins and squash.

The boys were inseparable companions. They went exploring along the sandy banks of the level stretches of Poso Creek. Sent out to gather quail eggs and to search for late gooseberries, they would return just as often with a new variety of lizard or an unusually colorful feather.

Finally, the day came when Jesse and Tom felt free to go exploring. The boys asked to accompany them, but permission was denied.

"Boys, it's as rough a country as you'll ever see, even if it isn't haunted. Besides being steep and treacherous, it's a natural place for rattlesnakes and mountain lions." Jesse addressed himself firmly to his elder son. "Jed, I expect you to see that the littler ones don't act foolish or come to grief by being where they ought not be."

"Yes, Pa."

"Besides," added his uncle, who was tightening the girth of his saddle as he spoke, "there probably isn't a grain of truth to the story anyway—more'n likely this will be a wasted trip."

"Boys, look after your ma while we're gone. Don't run off without fetching the water for the house and seeing that the woodbox is filled. We won't be gone over two days at most."

Tom went into his room in the barn and returned with his rifle. He thrust it into the leather scabbard hanging from his saddle, then went back for a powder flask and bedroll.

Jesse stepped away from his packed horse to where Emily stood in the doorway of their home.

"We'll be back soon, Emily. We'll just take a quick look around to see if what Tommy said was fact."

"I'll be praying for a safe and quick return for both of you," promised Emily, clasping Jesse's hands and looking up into his eyes.

"You aren't afraid, are you?" Jesse asked quietly.

"Not afraid exactly, no. It's more an uneasiness. If Byrd Guidett used a hidden trail like you think, then he murdered five people in cold blood."

"Emily, Tom and I aren't looking for a gun battle, and we'll go real watchful. I thought maybe you were believing the spook stories," he teased.

"Oh, hush and get on out of here! The sooner you two get this notion out of your systems, the sooner I get my new chicken coop built and the winter's wood split."

A quick embrace and a parting kiss, and Jesse swept into his saddle, even as Tom mounted Duncan.

"So long, Emily. See you, boys." With a last look and a wave they were gone, up the slope toward Shadow Ridge, angling around its southeastern rim.

They rode easily at first, walking their horses up a hillside covered with scrub oak. Soon the gooseberry and manzanita patches grew larger and closer together.

Tom watched the ground for signs of a trail or even the marks that another rider had recently passed that way. He saw nothing to indicate the presence of anyone. The ground was thickly carpeted with decaying oak leaves, and he noted the clear impressions of deer tracks, and once where a bear had crushed the undergrowth.

Tom looked ahead to where his brother rode, and thought, not for the first time, what a fortunate man Jesse was. Tom admired him for what he had built, had carved out for himself. Emily had chosen well; Jesse was a fine provider and father for their family.

Only lately had Tom discovered in himself a desire to build. Always before his thoughts had run toward roving, seeing sights not seen before. Now he felt that the time had come to put down some roots.

Jesse turned in his saddle. "Don't you think we're wasting our time?"

Tom pulled his horse to a halt and pushed his hat back. "It sure appears so. Nobody's been on this stretch of hill in a hundred years, seems like."

Then squinting upward he added, "What do you say we split up and circle that granite face yonder? I'll try to work around the top and you push through that low spot."

"Even if we strike a path up there, that still won't explain how anyone could make their way down this slope without leaving so much as a trace.

And to get down off this slope to the Poso Creek trail, they'd have to come through here someplace."

"You're probably right, Jesse, but since we're too late to head back tonight, let's camp up in the saddle anyhow and head back tomorrow."

Jesse examined the height of the sun above Shadow Ridge's rim and nodded his agreement. The two rode together for about a quarter of a mile; then Jesse turned his mount to pick his way down the slope, while Tom urged his horse up and around a sheer rock face.

Almost immediately, both men had trouble going forward. Jesse's travel was strewn with boulders—some big as wagon boxes—that had fallen from the granite wall. Bushy thickets had grown about the rock falls, causing him to backtrack often and look for a way around. Several times he found himself moving into what appeared to be an open space, only to find his line abruptly blocked and impenetrable.

Worse yet, the ground underfoot became treacherous, the soft earth giving place to shale rock, with only a thin layer of soil covering it. Jesse's mount began to pick its way along.

Jesse didn't urge it to any great speed, preferring to trust its sense of safe footing. This was a mountain-bred horse, no stranger to hillside trails. It had been called upon before to chase deer over rocky ledges and had gone down into and out of deep mountain canyons.

The horse plainly didn't like what it saw and felt on this stretch of Shadow Ridge. Gingerly stepping around a gooseberry patch that seemed to grow out of solid rock, the mount paused after each step to test its footing.

Meanwhile, Tom was having his own share of difficulty. On the first two places he approached, the upper slope yielded dead ends against sheer granite outcroppings, and each time he had to turn farther back the way they had come in order to proceed.

"At this rate I'll be home before we ever see the top of this ridge," Tom addressed his horse. Duncan pricked his ears to listen, then seemed almost to nod in agreement.

Rounding a house-sized boulder, Tom was surprised to find a fairly open route up the face of the cliff.

Gaining the top of the granite escarpment in about half an hour, he halted on top of a sheer drop to view the countryside. Behind him the manzanita closed in, completely covering the saddle between the two nearest peaks. It was apparent that no route over Shadow Ridge could be found from this approach.

On three sides of him the land fell away, dropping several hundred feet to the slope up which he and Jesse had ridden, and then less sharply down to Poso Creek.

Tom could not see Jesse's ranch from this vantage point, but he could identify the hill behind which it lay and the bend of the Poso that contained Laver's crossing.

"Good lookout," he noted aloud, "or a place to signal from."

Far below stretched chaparral and rockslides as far as the eye could see. Tom mentally reviewed the possible travel and concluded again that no trails were visible, nor did any routes present themselves. Indeed, only one rock-filled canyon cut through the mountainside, and it provided no opportunity for travelers.

Tom observed that the canyon did intersect a bend in the path of Poso Creek but at a point where the main trail lay a few hundred yards away from the stream behind a little oak-covered knoll.

"You know, Duncan, if a body could get down from here to that canyon's mouth, he'd cut off miles of trail and come out where he could choose his moment to set out on the road to Granite."

A further study of the canyon, however, indicated the impossibility of that thought since the gorge was both deep and narrow, except near its juncture with Poso.

"Now's when we could use Tommy's cave," Tom remarked. "Some way down past these slides and, say—"

Tom stood in his stirrups for a better view. A trick of light caused by the westering sun allowed something to appear to his eye that had not been there before. Right at the bottom of the gorge, only one bend of river from the Poso Creek intersection, was a large black shadow. A cave? A moment more and the hillside reverted to its previous appearance of gooseberry thickets and fallen buckeye branches.

Tom rubbed his eyes thoughtfully, but the shadow did not reappear, or rather, the lengthening shadows of the ridge swallowed up the canyon's mouth in gloom, eliminating the momentary contrast.

At that instant Tom heard a shot, followed by a shout. As if the mountain itself were falling, a roaring crash rose up, gaining momentum like peal after peal of thunder.

The horse snorted and pranced sideways as though suddenly fearful that the rock ledge underfoot would give way. Tom stepped from the saddle, shucking the rifle from its scabbard.

"Jesse! Jesse!" he called, even though he knew his voice would not carry over the echoing rumble that coursed down the mountainside and rebounded off the canyon walls.

Tom could see by a rising cloud of dust thrown up against the evening sky just where the rock slide had occurred. After two or three minutes that felt like hours to Tom, the crashing reverberations stilled, replaced by a soft sighing sound as if the mountain were settling itself. An occasional thumping crunch was heard as dislodged boulders bounded down the slope to find new resting places against the oaks far below. In another moment, all was silent.

"Jesse, Jesse, where are you?" Tom called again. But there was no answer, nor any further sound from that direction.

Catching up the reins, Tom jumped back into his saddle and began plunging down the slope he had lately ridden up. As though sensing his rider's urgency, Duncan plunged faster downward, leaping over boulders in his way and skidding across shale-covered slide rock.

When Tom regained the point at which he and Jesse had parted, he realized that picking his way around rocks and thickets would lengthen his travel, so he abandoned Duncan and followed Jesse's trail by foot.

Hurrying furiously, he scrambled over rockfalls in his path. A new rubble field lay at the bottom of the cliff, covering chaparral and manzanita thickets that had previously blocked forward progress at the cliff's base.

Rounding a corner of the granite outcropping, Tom tore through the thicket that remained, heedless of the barbed branches grabbing at his hands and arms, even piercing the leather chaps he wore.

Finally one more wrench free and Tom was in the open. He stopped abruptly. There, at the cliff's base, lay his brother. Beside his outstretched hand lay his Colt revolver.

Tom rushed to his brother's side. Jesse was on his back, his face turned to the side. His clothes were not torn, not even disheveled. His hat was nowhere to be seen, but the hair across his forehead looked unmussed.

Tom knelt beside his brother. "Jesse, are you hurt?"

There was no reply, and as Tom gently turned his brother's face toward him, he saw the reason: the right side of Jesse's skull was crushed; he was dead.

Tom found Jesse's horse tangled in a thicket so that it could go neither forward nor back. From its location and that of Jesse's body, Tom surmised that the horse had bolted uphill, thus avoiding being buried by the slide, but unable to prevent the first falling rock from striking and killing Jesse.

The lengthening western shadows were countered from the east by a rising wind, but the sickly breeze did nothing to hold back the blackness.

Soon only the peaks of the Sierras held patches of sunlight on their heights. One by one even these tall candles were snuffed out.

Tom sat in the gathering gloom, cradling his brother's head in his lap. Tom's shoulders slumped and his neck bowed as if he were overcome with incredible weariness.

Twice he started up with a sensation of startled joy in the mistaken belief that his brother lived. Each time it was only a trick of his tear-blurred eyes that suggested movement—a ruse of the blood pounding in his ears that counterfeited breath.

A man cannot live long in the West without knowing death and its forms—sometimes peaceful, but more often sudden and frequently violent. Tom accepted the reality of his brother's death much the same way as the night fell—a few moments of lingering hope, and then black certainty.

He gave no thought to building a fire, having no energy to gather wood. He could hear the horses stamping nervously around, so he got up and unsaddled them, leaving them to graze. Then he returned to his lonely vigil.

The stars began to appear overhead, at first a handful, then hundreds, and later uncountable numbers as the Milky Way brightened into view. It was a moonless night, and the hazy starshine made all but the nearest bushes and rocks indistinguishable from the black hillside. Without the brightness of the moon, the stars appeared with more clarity and distinctness, distant as they were, than anything as near as the earth.

Tom's thoughts went back to his earliest memories of his brother. Mostly he and Jesse had fought. Jesse, the cautious, the thoughtful, the never-in-trouble one, and Tom, whom everyone thought first to blame when any mischief was discovered. And yet, there was always a deep-rooted affection between them, a sort of mutual admiration for the qualities the other possessed.

A night bird called from the brush, seemingly close by. The horses had settled down to cropping what dry grass they could find, and Tom knew that their natural caution on the steep slope would keep them from wandering far.

Tom was not by nature a fearful person, nor did the wild countryside at night hold any terror for him. Even the nearness of death made no impression of fear on him, and yet the night had an edge to it. An uneasiness penetrated his dulled senses as if part of his mind was keeping watch and sensing something amiss.

He tried to lay the blame for his jumpiness on his grief and his apprehension at the sorrow he would carry back down the mountain to Emily and the boys, but he was not entirely successful. His mind tried to reconstruct what had happened. He reviewed what he had seen of the rock face—the treacherous ground, the sudden crashing sound, the accidental discharge of Jesse's gun and his shout.

Something about the gunshot bothered Tom—something he couldn't quite put his finger on. Every time he tried to recapture the moment that perplexed him, his thoughts jumped to the tragic conclusion, and the ache he felt inside interfered with his reason.

He felt a rising anger, directed first at himself. Why were they up on this godforsaken mountain, anyway? There wasn't any trail and never had been. What was he trying to prove, and why, God, why had he dragged his brother along? Jesse, who lay dead on these stones, had never been adventurous, never courted danger. He should never have been overtaken by disaster. Why should he be dead while Tom still lived?

What would Emily do now? How could she raise the boys and keep the farm? The work was too much for one man, but they couldn't afford to pay a hired hand, so Jesse had sent for Tom.

What's more, Tom knew he couldn't stand to stay around. Emily would hate him, would hate the sight of him as a constant reminder that Tom had caused her loss. She and his nephews would sell the place and go to live with her family back in Missouri.

And Tom? He'd been wrong to think of settling down. He'd never be one to build anything or to own anything more valuable than his horse. He'd go back to drifting through the mining camps, or maybe he'd join one of the cattle ranches on the coast.

9

IT WAS ALTOGETHER too fitting that the sky was a leaden gray with the first storm of the rainy season. The trees that stood guard over Oak Grove Cemetery still wore their leaves, but without sunlight to reflect from their surfaces, they appeared drab and subdued. Grayish-green moss hung in formless folds from their branches as if nature itself had put on a crepe of mourning.

The little group gathered around the mound of earth and the raw wound of a grave over which the pine coffin rested. The people in their black coats and black shawls stood silent and still, like an awkward group of statues.

All around were the graves of earlier settlers and their families. Some had reached this place of rest in ripe old age, and some in the bloom of youth. Their granite markers and lovingly tended plots mingled with rude patches of earth with dimly lettered wooden signs. These latter graves held mute testimony to strangers who had chanced to die or be killed in the hills; their epitaph was the sober phrase: "Known only to God."

Tom stood, hat in hand, beside Emily and opposite Parson Swift. The brothers braced their mother on either side, while Mont hung back. He felt grief, but was unsure how to express it, or even whether its expression would be welcome. Behind him stood a little knot of townspeople.

The parson reminded his listeners, "We have this treasure in earthen vessels, that . . . the power may be of God and not of us. We know," he said, "that if our earthly house were dissolved, we have . . . a house not made with hands, eternal in the heavens."

He went on to explain that because Jesse was a Christian, the parting that had taken place and the sorrow they felt, however strong and painful, was only temporary. He urged them to look around at the withered grass and remember that the same God who returned the green of spring each year would reunite them in new and glorious bodies that never felt pain or suffered death.

He prayed simply but with a firm voice for the Lord to help them through their grief, and asked that all present would be reminded of the fleeting nature of life and the need to "walk uprightly before their Maker."

When he concluded with a final "amen" and a chorus of murmured "amens" replied, Parson Swift moved around the grave to take both of Emily's hands in his. Looking at her with his kind blue eyes he said, "Emily, Jesse was a fine man. God has called him to some great purpose we don't see just yet, but I know your faith will bear you up—one day at a time." She nodded, unable to speak.

At a gesture from him, his wife came up from the group of mourners to take Emily's elbow and turn her from the casket toward those waiting to offer condolences.

Tom drew apart, standing alone now at the head of his brother's grave. A seething mass of emotions boiled inside him. Grief mingled with his sense of guilt was compounded by his swelling bitterness.

Parson Swift turned aside to speak with him, but before he opened his mouth, Tom burst out with, "Don't hand me any of your pious sayings, Parson! This needn't have happened. I don't care what you say about great purposes; Jesse's family needed him here!"

"Tom, don't you think God understands what you're feeling right now? Haven't we all felt at times like shaking our fist in God's face and demanding an explanation? But what other statement can He make than what He gave to Job, 'Where were you when I laid the foundations of the earth?'"

"That may be so, Parson, but if God caused this to happen, then I don't want any part of your God!"

"Tom, I won't pretend to have an answer that will satisfy you—but I know that God does, and I'll pray that He'll let you find it."

Among the group that gathered around Emily were many of the women of the community. Miss Peavy, the schoolmarm, expressed her sympathy, then drew Jed and Nathan to her and knelt to their height.

"Boys, you must be very strong and brave for your mother. Jed, you must be manly and look after your younger brother."

"And Mont, too?" added Nathan.

Miss Peavy looked perplexed for a moment, then turned to find a wide-eyed Mont James watching her fearfully.

"Well, I don't know. Now perhaps Mont will need to . . . Your mother may not be able to . . . what I mean is—"

"Noooo!" shouted Nathan. "Mont's *got* to stay with us, doesn't he, Ma?"

Emily looked around from where she was being embraced by Mary Davis, the livery stable owner's wife.

"Of course, Mont will stay on with us. Why should he leave now?"

"But, Emily, you'll have your hands full with your two boys and taking care of your place."

"Yes, and land sakes, Emily," added Victoria Burton, wife of the hotel's proprietor, "how will it look, you raising this black child as your own—I mean, well, he *is* black."

Emily looked confused. "But what difference can that make?"

"You're just not thinking clearly, Emily," said Mrs. Davis. "This child is part of that dreadful business about Byrd Guidett. Why, Jesse would be alive today if he hadn't gone off after that foolishness about Shadow Ridge."

"No, Ma, no!" insisted Jed and Nathan. "Mont didn't do anything wrong. Don't make him go away."

Tom could stand no more and burst into their discussion. Over his shoulder he called savagely to the parson, "Is this part of your fine God's plan too, blaming Jesse's death on this small boy?"

"No, it's certainly not," the parson said sternly. "Ladies, it is very unchristian and uncalled for at a time like this—"

"You have to talk like that, Reverend, but we all know what bad luck these niggers are. Just look at this war going on now! Why didn't we just leave them in their place?"

Tom was preparing for another outburst when a soft, oily sort of voice interrupted.

"I think that our emotions are all a little raw right now, don't you, Parson?" Robert Mullins' carefully modulated tones dripped over his listeners. "I'm sure that Mrs. Davis is just expressing the frustration we all feel at the *eastern* war. Why, all of us have lost relatives in Mr. Lincoln's conflict, and this present tragic occurrence, accompanied by this Negro child, seems to bring us into that maelstrom somehow. Mrs. Davis certainly meant nothing personal. She was merely trying to suggest that the child's presence would be an unpleasant reminder. Perhaps it would be best if he stayed elsewhere for a time. With me perhaps. I could use some assistance around my store."

"Thank you, but no," replied Emily simply. "Mont will continue to stay with us for now. I'm sure he realizes that we don't hold him in any way responsible for what has happened."

She gathered up all three boys, and the group moved off toward the waiting buggies. She could not move quickly enough to escape the sound of the clods of earth falling on Jesse's coffin. Each man stepped up to the graveside to take a turn wielding one of the shovels. After a moment of silently turning the dirt, a nearby hand would reach out to take the shovel from its user before passing it on to another. As Mullins reached out to take the shovel from Tom's hand, the man murmured, "Terrible, terrible."

The service was over. The ladies of the church had prepared a meal for the family and friends to share back at the Dawson home. Each of the families represented separated at the gate of the cemetery to go to their respective homes, there to bundle up the savory meats and fragrant pies to offer as consolation to the bereaved.

Robert Mullins, the senior elder present, was in charge of locking the gate of the Oak Grove Cemetery. The last to leave, he paid his respects again to the family, shook hands all around with the other church members, and even had a moment's word with Pastor Swift about taking up a collection to provide a fine headstone for their recently departed brother, Jesse Dawson.

Nodding solemnly to each family as the buggies departed, Mullins looked the picture of respectability and Christian concern. He watched them disappear from sight around a curve of the road; then he raised his voice above its previous obsequious level and called, "All right, you two; you can come out now."

From behind a clump of brush on the knoll overlooking the burial ground stepped Byrd and Yancey. They walked down to meet Mullins where he stood beside the grave.

"Well, well. Once again a job half done. In case you didn't notice, there are *two* Dawson brothers, and one of them is still alive!"

As though he had been expecting this criticism, Byrd kept silent and let Yancey put forth their practiced defense.

"Now, boss, it's like this. When they split up on the hill up yonder, we know'd we could take one with the rockslide, see, and make it look an accident. As it is, ain't nobody thinks anything about ol' Shadow 'cept maybe it's haunted for true, and anyway it's powerful bad medicine. If we'd hauled off and shot that other one, somebody woulda gone to find 'em. Only then it weren't possible to make it be no accident—"

"You pitiful fools! Couldn't you have disposed of them in the tunnel where nobody would've been the wiser? Why should anyone have found the bodies at all?"

Byrd and Yancey looked guiltily at each other. Mullins had spotted the flaw in their excuse immediately.

Byrd figured that Yancey had not been as persuasive as he had indicated he could be, so Byrd himself decided to try.

"See, it was gettin' on to dark, and we wasn't gonna take no chance at lettin' Tom Dawson get away. But we figured it'd be worse to give away where we was for an uncertain finish than to send him down thinkin' it was an accident. We can finish with 'im later."

Mullins rubbed his face thoughtfully. "Why, Byrd, Yancey, you astonish me! I'd never have given you credit for coming to such careful restraint. This may work out for the best after all. There's clearly now no reason for anyone to explore Shadow Ridge any further."

Byrd looked pleased with himself. Completely ignoring the shake of Yancey's head, which was intended to mean *leave well enough alone,* he resumed explaining.

"Yes, sir, we know'd Tom Dawson would be comin' right wary, after that shot and all, and we—"

"What!" Mullins produced an almost piglike squeal. "What shot? I thought you said it entirely appeared to be an accident!"

"Now, jest calm yourself. The daid 'un only got off one round. We figger Tom'll put it down to a misfire when his brother's horse throw'd 'im. 'Course, it woulda been different if he'd nicked Yancey and we'd had trouble gettin' outta there our ownselves, but as it was—"

Mullins's voice and manner were icy. "You mean to say that Jesse Dawson saw you on the ledge about to push over the rocks and had time to get off a shot at you? You idiots! What if Tom figures out that it was no accidental discharge? What if the brother lived long enough to say something to him? You've already said it was near dark. How can you know for certain? Now we've got to eliminate Tom Dawson, and the sooner the better, before he has a chance to do any more thinking or to share his suspicions with anyone else."

"Cain't we jest dry-gulch 'im? Pettibone's no great shakes as a tracker. We could hole up on the ledge for a piece after."

"And have people start to question how it happens that two brothers both die so close together? We're trying to eliminate curiosity, not create more of it. Besides, have you forgotten about the black child? I can't afford to have you two in hiding for now—not after I've spent time leading

Pettibone to think that the shooting of Colonel James was entirely self-defense."

Mullins paused, breathing heavily. "No, I've got a better idea. Let's go about this completely open. Everyone knows there's bad blood between you and Dawson over the nigger boy. What about if we set up another "self-defense" situation? Why, I'll bet I could even get awarded temporary legal custody of the child after such an unfortunate incident. Yes, broad daylight, that's the way of it." Mullins rubbed his hands together gleefully as though contemplating stacks of gold coins in his office safe.

Byrd's eyes narrowed and he ground out a question. "Ya want me to kill Dawson in front of witnesses and stand trial for it? You must be nuts. I ain't aimin' to get my neck stretched for nobody."

"There won't be a trial, you fool. Now listen; here's how we'll work it."

10

THE HOUSE WAS quiet now. *Too quiet,* Tom thought as he wiped his muddy boots and knocked timidly on the frame of the screen door. Behind him on the porch dry leaves scudded forlornly over the planks, then swirled away across the empty yard where only two weeks before, Jesse had wrestled playfully with the boys as Tom and Emily had howled with laughter. Tom stared hard at the place where they had tumbled down, and the memory almost made him smile again. But the vision was only a memory. The laughter and the moment would never come again, and that thought made Tom's smile die even as it reached his lips.

Mercifully, the boys had school to keep them occupied. Reading and writing, the mysterious world of ciphers, and childhood games could ease their pain a bit. But Tom and Emily had no such escape. The absence of the children only seemed to emphasize the terrible silence that had come to the ranch since the death of Jesse. That first dull ache of shock and disbelief was now honed into a sharp blade of grief that managed to pierce their hearts every time they turned around.

A thousand times a day Tom found a thought on his lips, but Jesse was not there to answer. Talk about the crops, the stock, the weather, and the war in the East was now suddenly frozen into a silent monologue. *What would Jesse think? What would Jesse do?* Those two questions had helped Tom reason his way through a maze of confused emotions over the last days. Jesse would want him to stay here as long as Emily needed help. He would expect Tom to see her and the boys safely back to Missouri.

Tom raised his fist and knocked again. He would tell Emily that. He would let her know he planned to do his duty by her and the children. For the sake of Jesse, he would see to it that they arrived in St. Louis safe and sound beneath her parents' roof. Emily's father was a wealthy man. He would see to it that his young, widowed daughter was well cared for. Emily was never meant to live a hard life in the West. She would fit in again easily with St. Louis society. Yes, he thought, she would fit. North and South, the country was filled with widows now as husbands clad in blue or gray shared common graves in places like Gettysburg. Wasn't that why Jesse had remained in the West long after the gold fields had begun to play out? Hadn't he remained here in California just so that he would not be forced to fight against friends and neighbors in this terrible war, so that Emily would never have to wear black or sleep alone in an empty bed, or call his name in the dark?

They had come west to escape the mindless destruction, and now, somehow, death had followed them even here. How pointless it all seemed! How unjust and harsh that the hand of God had swept across the face of the mountain, and—

The door opened. Emily's face was pale with grief but seemed to radiate an inner peace. "Why, Tom! What are you doing standing out here on the porch with your hat in your hand?" She smiled and held the door open for him.

He could not bring himself to look at her. Her black mourning dress had become the uniform that united the nation's women. It did not matter which cause their husbands, sons, or brothers had died for. Tom had never expected to see that uniform on Emily, however, nor could he have imagined that she would still be so beautiful even with the gingham and calico put away.

"I thought maybe we might need to talk a bit," he said haltingly.

"Yes. I was just going through—" Her eyes moved toward a neatly folded stack of Jesse's clothes on the dining-room table. "You and Jesse are . . . were . . . close to the same size, and I was wondering . . . Jesse would like you to . . ." She did not finish. Her voice trailed off as tears clouded her eyes.

Tom remained in the center of the room, toying nervously with his hat. He could not think of wearing his brother's clothes any more than of being able to fill his brother's boots. He cleared his throat. "No. No thank you, Emily. I . . . it might be hard for the boys to see me in their father's gear." He did not add that it would also be difficult for Emily. She seemed relieved by his reply.

"You're right. Silly of me. Then perhaps you could take them to Pastor Swift when you go to town? He'll see that they are put to good use."

Tom nodded in curt agreement, wondering how he could best broach the subject of selling the ranch and returning to the East. He glanced toward the desk where Jesse kept his journals and had spent hours long into the night deep in his accounts. "Jesse would want me to stay . . . I think . . . to help you." He cleared his throat again and scratched his head. "That is, if you would like me to, until—"

"Of course, Tom," she said softly, interrupting his words.

"We'll need to sell the place and then get you and the boys back home."

She drew in her breath sharply and glared at Tom as though he had slapped her across the face. *"Sell?* Back . . . you mean Missouri? Thomas Dawson! You can't mean that you think I would take my sons back to Missouri!"

Tom was instantly sorry that he had spoken. He had not meant to upset her, but he was in it up to his neck now. "Back . . . *home,* Emily. Your folks. Your family."

She raised her chin defiantly. *"This* is my home! This is where Jesse is buried, and one day I will be buried beside him!"

Tom ran his fingers through his hair. He should not have opened his mouth. He should have let her bring it up. She always was a strong-minded woman. "You can't stay here."

"You honestly believe that Jesse would want me to take our sons back to Missouri? Of all men, Thomas, I can't believe that you have forgotten that there is a war on! I have lost two cousins who fought for Georgia, and another who died fighting for Lincoln! Not only is the country divided, Tom, my own family is torn in two by this conflict. Missouri is a border state! Jesse had only just said to me how relieved he was that we are so far away from all that! How glad he was that the hand of God had brought us here to Shadow Ridge to raise our boys in safety and peace!"

Tears began to flow now as the words *safety* and *peace* echoed hollowly in the empty house. She looked toward the pile of overalls and shirts sewn from flour sacks. Jesse had refused to exchange his mended denim for the uniform of a soldier. While others had turned in their plowshares for the weapons of destruction, Jesse had neither condemned nor joined them. When Tom had turned his back on the fighting and appeared at the ranch with tales of childhood friends firing from the opposite sides of a river-bank, Jesse had taken him in without a word of condemnation.

"When this war ends, Emily," he answered quietly, "I'll see to it you get back to St. Louis."

"Don't be such a fool, Thomas Dawson!" She whirled around to face him. "It doesn't matter who wins this war as far as you are concerned! If you go back to Missouri, you'll be hanged! And now you're telling me you're going back there!"

"Just to make sure . . ."

"To make sure there's still a price on your head? To make sure that both of the Dawson brothers die young?" Her fists were clenched as she hurled the absurdity of his thought back at him. "You don't have to go back to Missouri if you want to die young! Go back on that mountain! Back on that cursed mountain!" She began to sob now as she sank onto the settee. Blond hair fell in wisps around her face as she cried into her hands. "Do you really think this helps? Go away!" she cried. "Just get out, Tom. Let me be a while!"

Stricken, Tom stared at her in horror. What a fool he was! It was too soon to bring any of this up! Too soon! He backed toward the door. "I'm sorry, Emily," he said as he slipped out onto the porch.

The dry leaves swirled around his legs and followed him back to his cot in the barn.

Each member of the Dawson family chose a different way of dealing with grief. After Tom's unfortunate attempt to discuss relocating to Missouri, he took to finding reasons to go into town.

Jed alternately comforted and was comforted by his mother. He carried himself with a manly dignity and did his chores without being told. But when his mother brought him his father's pocket watch and said that it was right for him to have it now, he had to fight back tears and bite his lip. Emily found him later, sitting on the corral fence staring up at Shadow Ridge, the watch clutched in his fist.

Emily threw herself into housework. Given the excuse that many of their friends and neighbors would be dropping by to call, she found that the house could never be clean enough to suit her. She swept and scrubbed the wood-plank floors until they shone, and then was still able to locate imaginary crumbs to pick up. Alone at night in the empty bed, she couldn't sleep, so she took to rising at four o'clock in the morning, starting in again on chores that she had completed at midnight the night before.

Nathan, on the other hand, seemed to feel the weight of Jesse's absence the hardest—sobbing one minute, then becoming bitterly angry the next. Once when Tom returned from town, he happened to walk in and catch Nathan unawares. Nathan glanced up at his uncle, and the resemblance to his father was so great that the boy started up; then, realizing the deception, he ran crying from the room. Tom turned around and, without a word to anyone, rode back to town.

Nathan soon stopped playing with Mont. He did not intentionally ignore his friend, but he was unable to believe that his life would ever be the same again. With Jesse gone, there was no room for play.

So no one noticed how Mont was reacting to Jesse's death. He appeared at mealtimes, but they were such silent and unhappy affairs that he retreated immediately afterward to his quarters in the tack room.

Daylight had begun to fade, and Emily was busying herself in the kitchen preparing a meal of cornbread and fried chicken. Tom had not yet returned from town, but supper was nearing completion, so Emily sent Jed out to the springhouse for a jug of buttermilk, and dispatched Nathan to fetch Mont.

"Mont. Hey, Mont! Ma says come to eat," called Nathan.

There was no reply.

"Mont, don'tcha hear me? It's time to eat." Nathan pushed open the tack-room door, a long creak of the hinges announcing his entrance. He expected to see Mont perched on the edge of his cot or seated in the middle of the floor repairing a piece of harness, but Mont was nowhere to be seen.

Maybe he's gone into the barn, Nathan thought, so he walked around the corner into the barn, calling for Mont all the while. A quick inspection of the stalls still gave no evidence of the black child's whereabouts.

Raising his voice to a shout, Nathan called out, "Mont James, come down from that hayloft! I don't want to play, and Ma's waitin' supper!" When there was no answer, he marched over to the ladder that led upward to the fragrant hay storage, the scene of many pleasant hours in happier days. Still no Mont.

Nathan was not worried, but he was perplexed and growing angry. It was not like Mont to be absent at mealtimes. But then, Nathan couldn't remember having seen Mont at all since noon.

On the way back to the house, Nathan made a short loop past the corrals, the water pump, and the garden patch. No Mont.

"I'll bet he slipped around and went into the house when I was lookin' out here for him," reasoned Nathan.

"Ma," he called upon entering the house, "is Mont in here with you?"

Emily looked up from where she was filling a platter with pieces of chicken. "Why no, Nate," she replied. "Didn't you find him?"

"No, Ma, an' he's not in the barn, nor any place around."

"Perhaps he went with Jed down to the springhouse." No sooner were the words out of her mouth than Jed returned, carrying the jug of buttermilk, and without Mont.

"He wasn't with me," added Jed, having overheard their words. "And where's Uncle Tom?"

"Mercy me!" exclaimed Emily. "That must be the answer. He must have gone with Tom into town. They'll both be returning most any time now.

"You know, boys," she continued, "we must not forget about Mont no matter how bad we feel. We all have each other to lean on, but poor Mont has no family except us, and we must not shut him out.

"We all feel terrible just now," she went on, "and I know that I haven't given you the attention I should have." She waved aside their protests. "But I looked around at the house tonight, and I think it's clean enough, don't you?" This brought small grins to the faces of the boys. "Let's make a pledge to start seeing, really seeing, each other again—and that includes Mont." She might have added *and your uncle,* but she didn't.

They were interrupted by the sound of Tom's horse outside but were so confident that Mont was with Tom that no one stepped out. A couple of moments elapsed while he unsaddled and turned Duncan into the corral. When he entered the house, he was alone.

"What's for sup—What are you all staring at? Is anything wrong?"

They all began to talk at once. "Isn't Mont with you?" "We can't find him." "Didn't he go with. . . ?"

When the din subsided, Tom looked to Emily for an explanation. "Tom, it seems that Mont is gone. I sent Nathan to bring him into supper, and he's nowhere around. The last time anyone saw him was at dinner today, and we thought perhaps he'd ridden over with you."

"Why no, Emily, I haven't seen him since this morning. You may remember, I left before noon. The last I saw of him, he was sittin' on his cot all by himself."

"Oh, Tom, that's just what the boys and I have been talking about! I'm afraid we've been neglecting each other—and Mont in particular. You don't suppose he's run away, do you?"

"Now, Emily, don't get all riled up. I'm sure he's around here someplace and hasn't come to any harm. The boys and I will go look for him right now. Okay, boys?"

The boys nodded vigorously, and soon all three had lit lanterns and gathered behind the house.

"Listen carefully Jed, Nathan. I want you two to go together. Head north to where Sandy Creek joins up with the Poso; and if you haven't found Mont by then, each of you get on either side of the creek and come down to Laver's Crossing. Don't get farther away than you can see each other's lanterns clearly. Don't go past the crossing; just turn and go back to the house. I'll meet you back there."

"Which way will you go, Uncle?" asked Jed.

"I'll head up Shadow Ridge way."

Tom needn't have worried that the brothers would become widely separated. In fact, they traveled so closely together that one lantern would have been adequate.

The night was full of sounds—the familiar rustle of the long-tailed mice scurrying through the fallen leaves, the whisper-soft swoop of an owl's wings. Later on the mournful cries of the coyotes echoed from the summit of Carver Peak. The boys had no difficulty finding the juncture of the Sandy and Poso creeks, nor did they have any difficulty staying together. But they were not successful in finding Mont.

The lengthening search and the deepening night combined to stretch their imaginations. "Do ya s'pose he got snake bit?" wondered Nathan.

"Maybe," nodded Jed gravely, "or took off by Injuns more likely."

"Could be a mountain lion got 'im, or a great big ol' bear."

The same threat seemed to occur to them simultaneously. "You don't think . . . Byrd Guidett . . ."

Tom's search was all uphill. He moved in an arc, zigzagging back and forth across the slope and gaining a few yards of elevation with each swing. He tried not to think about his last trip down this hillside with the body of his brother, or how much he was coming to believe in the mountain's evil reputation. Of course, the more he tried to avoid these thoughts, the stronger they kept returning.

God, he thought, *aren't YOU supposed to be running things around here? First Jesse, and now this poor boy? Can't you make a better job of things than this? Here I am trying to get things settled at this ranch so I can take off and not be such a constant reminder to Emily of her sorrow, yet things seem to get more unsettled all the time!*

He was so lost in these thoughts that he almost missed exploring the little hollow formed by granite boulders and the fallen buckeye trunk.

Tom could never say later what it was that caught his eye. Surely no movement or flash of light—just the small dark clump that turned out to be Mont against the larger darkness. Tom jumped up on the buckeye log and raced into the rocky depression, calling out Mont's name. He began to fear the worst, saw himself carrying another corpse down to Emily—this time a slight little form. "God," he begged, "not again." And at that moment a very sleepy and bewildered Mont sat up and rubbed his eyes.

"Where is I? Mistuh Tom, is I gonna get beat?"

"Oh no, Mont. I'm so glad you're all right. You *are* all right, aren't you?"

"Yassuh, I'se fine."

"How come you're way up here on this mountain?"

"Well, suh, you and Miss Emily done been so kind to me an' all, an' now you is all so sad. Ain't no time to be alookin' after a no'count like me. Anyways, I heerd dem friends of Missy's say dat it weren't right for me to be livin' wid her no more, an' dat I'se de reason Mistuh Jesse got hisself killed. Anyways, I figgered she'd be better off if'n I went off . . . Maybe alookin' at me makes her sad mos' likely."

"Mont, nothing could be further from the truth. We all like having you around and don't want you ever to go away. Why, Nathan and Jed are out in the dark right now trying to find you."

"Is dat for true? Y'all wants me to stay?"

"I promise you, it's the truth. But say, weren't you awful scared up here by yourself tonight?"

"Oh naw, suh! I wasn't 'lone nohow."

"What do you mean, not alone?"

"You know, Mistuh Tom, Massa Jesus, He be right here beside me, so I'se got no cause to be scared."

There was a thoughtful pause; then Tom said slowly, "Mont, I want you to be my partner from now on. It seems that there are some things we can teach each other. For now, let's go home. We don't want to worry Miss Emily anymore, and I expect she's been keeping our supper warm for us."

11

THE BELLA UNION Hotel was not a fancy establishment, but neither was it a cheap saloon. A two-story affair that boasted decent food and clean beds for weary stagecoach travelers, it also attracted the business of some of the local families. Miners and cowboys, whose interests were more enticed by cheap liquor in less clean surroundings, would usually gather at the Diamondback or down at the Richbar.

So it was with some surprise that Scot McKenna noted the arrival of Byrd Guidett and Yancey into his place of business. They had been seen around town for the past few days and seemed to be minding their own business. An inquiry to Deputy Pettibone had brought the response that there was nothing Byrd could be charged with; if he caused no trouble, he was as free a citizen as the next man.

Byrd and Yancey went into the bar on the left side of the downstairs hallway, opposite the restaurant that opened on the right. McKenna watched from his place behind the counter, but made no move to interfere or question their presence. He produced whiskey and glasses without com-ment.

A moment later Tom Dawson walked into Bella Union, closely followed by Mont James. Tom and Mont had ridden over together to deliver Jesse's clothes to Parson Swift, and Tom intended to stop in for a drink before heading back. In deference to Emily's request, he sent Mont into the dining room for a lemonade rather than having the boy accompany him into the saloon.

Tom noted Byrd and Yancey seated at a table near the back of the bar, but he chose to ignore them. Instead, he stepped up and ordered his beer.

McKenna, like the name of his operation, was avowedly pro-Union. He and Tom fell to discussing the recent war news. Since the battle of Chickamauga, in which the casualties totaled almost forty thousand, the war had come to a virtual standstill. There had even been time to plan memorial services for those who had fought and died at Gettysburg. The dedication of the cemetery adjacent to the sleepy little Pennsylvania town was to have been scheduled for mid-October, but a conflict had arisen for the planned featured orator, Edward Everett, so the ceremony was postponed until November.

Neither man paid any attention when Yancey got up from the table and went out the back door.

A minute later Byrd rose to his feet and walked to the front window. "Hey, Dawson," he called, " 'pears to me yer horse is loose. Didn't anybody learn ya to tie a knot?"

Tom looked over. Sure enough, Duncan was trotting off down the street as if he had been shooed away from the rail. Tom knew the horse had been securely tied. Grimacing at McKenna, he went to retrieve Duncan, stopping by the dining room long enough to tell Mont to remain there till Tom returned. He figured that the horse would make his way down the street as far as the first livery stable, where he would stop in expectation of a handful of grain.

Byrd had remained at the window, and when he saw Tom going down the street to retrieve his horse, Byrd turned and entered the dining room.

"Hey, Nigger," he called to Mont, "come here a minute."

Mont looked scared, and said nothing.

"Are ya deaf, Nigger? I said come here, an' this is a white man talkin'."

Mont still hadn't found his speech, but he could find his feet. He jumped up and ran for the back door of the Bella Union, then skidded to a stop as Yancey appeared in the doorway. Turning around, Mont tried to duck Byrd, who had followed close behind him. But Guidett grabbed the boy by the collar, picking him completely off the floor, then carried him into the saloon.

"Here, now," began McKenna, "what's this aboot? What'er ye aimin' to do with the boy?"

"Jest mind yer own business. This nigger was s'posed to belong to me, and I aim to get some work outta him.

"Here now, Nigger, suppose ya get on down there and shine my boots." With this he gave Mont a hard thrust to the floor. "What, no shine rag? I 'spect this'll do." He jerked Mont's shirt upward, ripping it apart and spattering the buttons, then threw the cloth at the boy.

"What? Nothin' to shine 'em with?"

Mont made as if to lick the cloth and apply it to Guidett's boot. Byrd kicked him in the stomach and chest, propelling him across the floor so fast he skidded into a brass spittoon, where he lay breathing in short, pained gasps. "How could ya even *think* such a thing, boy? Nigger spit on a white man's boot? You'd best think again, coon. Now, a white man's spit'd be proper for a white man's boots. Go on, reach on down in thar and get a big slug, then crawl over here and get to shinin'."

McKenna started to protest, but Byrd whirled around. "Jest keep yer mouth shut and yer hands on the bar. I'm collectin' on some winnin's, and I aim to get paid in full."

"Paid in full sounds like a lot to expect from a small boy, Byrd Guidett. Perhaps your account would get settled more to your satisfaction with me." Tom Dawson had returned and stood in the door of the saloon. He had taken in the scene at a glance, and his hand hovered near the Colt that hung at his side.

"Are ya fixin' to draw against me, Tom Dawson? Takin' the part of a nigger against a white man—why, some folks'd be callin' you a nigger lover."

"Call me anything you like, Guidett, but touch that boy one more time and they'll be calling you dead."

Yancey moved crablike around the side wall till he was even with Byrd on the other side of the room and also facing Tom.

Byrd made as if to step forward and kick Mont again. His expectation was that this would goad Tom into drawing, and Byrd believed himself to be the better gunman. He also knew that McKenna could truthfully report Tom's threat; and in this community of largely pro-Southern sentiment, a verdict of self-defense would easily be obtained.

What he did not expect was that a very determined small black boy would see the kick coming. Grabbing the spittoon, Mont hurled it and the contents into Byrd's face.

"What the—?" Byrd clawed at the slimy goo that clung to his face and beard. He dared not lash out now, or attempt to draw, for he could only dimly see through the tobacco juice that burned his eyes.

Tom had indeed drawn his gun, but he swung it to cover Yancey, who put both his hands up slowly and backed against the wall.

"Mr. McKenna, will you be so kind as to remove Mr. Guidett's weapon? Thank you. Now, if you'll please hold it on his friend over there. I wouldn't want anything to interfere with Mr. Guidett's receiving a full accounting of what he is owed."

So saying, he released the hammer of his own gun and, calling Mont to him, gave it to the boy to hold.

A wild look of delight spread over Byrd's face as he guessed Tom's intention. "I'll break you in two!" he screamed and lunged at Tom.

Tom sidestepped the jump easily, and Byrd plowed past him like a runaway locomotive, crashing into a table. Whirling around, Byrd made as if to jump at Tom again; but this time as Tom moved to one side, Byrd also pivoted and grabbed Tom's arm.

Pinning Tom's arms to his sides, Guidett lifted his adversary off the floor bodily in a massive bear hug. This was Byrd's favorite move. With it he had crushed men's ribs and made them cry for mercy before he allowed them to crumple to the floor. But he had not reckoned with the wiry strength of Tom's arms and shoulders as he flexed his muscles and pushed Byrd's embrace away.

In the slack thus obtained, Tom leaned his body backward in Byrd's grasp, and then bent it forward suddenly, ducking his head. He drove the top of his forehead directly into Guidett's nose. With a scream of infuriated pain, Byrd dropped his hold and grabbed his face with his hands. His nose was gushing blood.

Tom followed up his advantage by driving his right fist into Byrd's midsection. This blow made Byrd back up a step, but as Tom closed in, Byrd raised his two clasped hands over his head and brought them down with a hard thrust, striking Tom over the left ear so hard he staggered back.

Byrd gave a wild cry, his face a fearful mask of gore and tobacco juice, and brought both his fists together on either side of Tom's head. Tom stumbled, his head spinning. Seeing his advantage, Byrd closed in, intending to apply his crushing hug again.

Tom knew he couldn't escape that clutch as easily this time, so he moved to step in toward Byrd at the moment when the cutthroat's arms were outstretched to encircle. Not expecting anyone to deliberately come within his reach, Byrd was unprepared to ward off the blow from Tom's left. It worked even better than Tom anticipated, for as Byrd raised his head to apply his press, Tom's fist caught him in the throat.

Byrd backed up, gasping. He couldn't breathe through his nose, and now his throat felt paralyzed and his eyes were swelling shut. He had to work fast. Again he threw himself at Tom, and this time Tom was unable to avoid the rush. Byrd's force hurled him back savagely against the counter of the bar, making him cry out at the stabbing pain from a breaking rib.

He tried to slip under Byrd's grasp, but Guidett followed him down to the floor, then jumped up for a leap that would land both his knees and all his weight on Tom's chest.

In that split second, sensing Byrd's gathering force preparing to spring, Tom reached out wildly with his arms and encountered the spittoon lying where it had rolled after being thrown by Mont. Tom's fingers closed over the rim, and in the next instant he drove it with all his remaining strength against the side of Byrd's head. The impact snapped Byrd's head against the bar, sending a shower of blood through the air.

The force of this strike was not great, but it was enough. Guidett had had difficulty breathing since the blow to his throat, and now he collapsed on top of Tom.

For a moment, neither moved. Mont was crouched on the floor, biting his lip to keep from whimpering. Yancey slouched against the far wall, casting wishful glances toward the exit—a thought which McKenna discouraged with a negligent wave of the gun. Finally, Byrd Guidett stirred, and a muffled voice underneath croaked, "Get this stinking mess off me— I'm about to be crushed!"

"Remove Guidett," directed McKenna to Yancey, "and mind that ye drag him face up, so ye get no more blood on me floor!" Yancey instantly obeyed, pulling the ugly heap away. By the time he had dragged Byrd to the front porch, he began to revive. Yancey helped the man to his feet and two staggered outside, where he doused Byrd's swollen face in the nearest horse trough.

McKenna insisted on helping Tom personally. He made him sit in a chair while the barman rubbed a towel soaked in whiskey over cuts on Tom's ears, forehead and knuckles, while muttering to himself, "This is better than that nasty carbolic, and smells nicer, too."

Tom tried to rise, but a stabbing pain in his back made him gasp and sit back down. McKenna helped Tom remove his shirt, then bent him forward gently. "Ay, he's broke one o' yer short ribs, lad. 'Tis a good thing ye're as strong as an ox, or he would have crushed yer whole ribcage like an eggshell. As it is, ye'll be mighty tender for a spell, but ye'll soon be right as rain. Here, boy"—this was addressed to Mont—"run upstairs to me room, 'tis the one jist at the top, and bring a sheet off me bed."

Mont looked first to Tom for permission, and at his nod, ran upstairs. He wasn't sure what drew him to the window, but stepping past McKenna's rumpled bed, Mont looked down into the street. What he saw there puzzled him, for he noticed a most unlikely conference. Mont saw

Byrd get up from the horse trough and shake his head like a dog shakes water from its body. Then he turned as if to reenter the Bella Union, violently throwing off Yancey's restraining hand. Next Mont saw the two seemingly being addressed by someone on the boardwalk in front of the hotel. It looked as if Byrd started to argue, placed a boot up on the step, then stopped. A moment later, Byrd and Yancey turned to walk down the dusty street leading out of town, with Byrd turning back twice and Yancey urging him along. But the one who had apparently ordered them out of town stayed out of Mont's view.

Mont returned with the sheet. McKenna tore a strip from it and, directing Tom to hold it under his arm, proceeded to wrap him around and around until, in Tom's words, he was "trussed up like a turkey."

"Do you have to make this so tight?" Tom complained. "I was having enough trouble breathing as it was."

"Ay, lad, 'tis for yer own good. We can't have that bone wanderin' around in ye. Give this but a week or so to knit, and ye can unwind it. Then ye'll be ready to fight again . . . And what a fight it was! I know of no man who's stood up to Byrd Guidett and lived." He picked up the spittoon, now completely concave where it had connected with Byrd's skull, and shook his head ruefully. "A perfectly good spittoon ruined, and him still alive after, more's the pity."

"Yes, well, I only wanted him to leave Mont alone. I'm glad I didn't have to kill him to teach him that."

"Ye may regret it later. Byrd's head is hard in more ways than one, and he'll not like bein' bested in a fight. Ye'd best watch yer back trail, and keep yer wits aboot ye."

12

BYRD WAITED UNTIL he judged that the last of the late arrivals had come. The hillside from which he watched not only overlooked the church but also gave him a view in both directions through town.

It was a frosty morning; his breath, as well as that of the bay horse on which he sat, was visible in ragged, steamy puffs. A fitful, lusterless sun was trying unsuccessfully to break through the overcast. It contributed no warmth to the day, only the promise that it would stay just above freezing.

The horses in the churchyard stood huddled together in little clumps for warmth, even normally fractious ones subdued in spirit. A row of horses still hitched to buggies and wagons stood in a row, tethered to a cable string between two iron bolts in adjacent oaks.

I'll show those crackers how it is, Byrd thought, feeling his battered nose.

Occasionally he could hear the pump organ straining to produce a hymn, but with the doors and windows tightly shut against the cold, the sound was muffled. Byrd could not be sure that all the occupants of the church building were unarmed, bundled up as they were in heavy coats, but he considered it unlikely that any carried firearms.

"Too bad for them if'n they do," he muttered sarcastically.

He couldn't see Yancey from where he waited, but he knew Yancey was watching him. "I'm blasted if'n I'm gonna freeze my tail out here any longer," he mumbled to his horse. "Let's get this show on the road." He stood in his stirrups and waved his arm three times over his head.

Yancey broke from the cover of the creek bed next to the church property, and covered the small slope to the building in a stiff lope. Both men knew that Yancey's approach could not be seen from any of the church windows. Yancey waited to the side of the church's front doors and at the bottom of the steps, where he could duck around the corner and out of sight if anyone unexpectedly appeared.

Now! Byrd thought, adjusting his mask and drawing his Colt. He urged the horse down the hillside until at the bottom it was in direct line with the church door. "Eyowhh!" he yelled, and drove his spurs into the bay's sides. The startled horse leaped forward, bolting across the road, while Byrd fired three shots. His first went into the air, but his second and third bullets went through the upper panes of two of the tall church windows.

He was at the steps, where Yancey had already flung open the doors and ducked back to the side. Byrd's excited horse never even hesitated but jumped up to the entrance in one bound, then past the doors and into the building itself. Byrd had to duck to keep from getting knocked off by the doorframe, but he came up shooting; everyone else in the building ducked, too, crying with fear as they dived for cover.

His next shot took out another window; then in a flash of devilish inspiration, he took deliberate aim at the smokestack of the potbelly stove standing in the center of the twenty-by-thirty room. With a crash and a clang, the pipe parted at the joint nearest the ceiling, showering soot on everything. The pipe folded up on itself as if exhausted from having stood so long, then collapsed into the center aisle. Grayish-brown smoke poured from the stove into the little room, only the high ceiling prevented the scene from being instantly obscured.

Byrd next turned his attention toward the pump organ at the left front of the room where a slight grayhaired lady had been playing. He shot the last bullet in the revolver directly through the side of the instrument, which erupted in a clatter of keys and stops, then gave the groan of a dying cow. The organist leaped backwards off the organ bench. There she cowered—a rumpled heap of skirts and wounded dignity.

Byrd transferred the empty weapon to his holster and drew another from his belt. Circling the prancing horse in the space between the door and the ruined stovepipe, he noted with satisfaction that all the women were huddled down between the pews, covering the heads of small children, and that not a few of the men had ducked under cover as well.

In this first moment of shocked silence, Parson Swift, who had been seated on the small platform behind the pulpit, rose to his feet. "What's the meaning of this outrage?" he demanded.

"Shut up and sit down, you old Bible-thumper! I'm here to deliver a message, an' it won't hurt my feelin's none to shoot you first!" So saying, he cocked the pistol and deliberately leveled it at the preacher's chest. "An' that goes for any of the rest of you what feels like interruptin' me!" His voice croaked awkwardly.

"This here message is to any folk what feels like lickin' them Yankee soldier boys' boots. Don't do it! They may think they got a lock on this state, but they got another think comin'! We aim to make them Yankees think that their hides'd be a whole lot safer outta these hills for good, an' that goes for any other nigger lovers in these here parts! An' don't count on no blue-bellies to protect ya; they cain't even protect their ownselves!"

Looking right into the muzzle of the gun, the parson said calmly, "Are you quite through?"

Byrd's pistol remained pointed at the parson for an instant longer; then whirling his horse around, he galloped out the door and down the steps, firing three more times as he did so.

The waters of the little cove were so deep that the dark blue color of the Pacific Ocean did not lighten at all as it swept up against the rocky headland. The small peninsula was covered with cypress trees, which further sheltered the south-facing bay from storms.

On shore a smoky fire was burning, producing a thick, greasy plume that reached up into the afternoon sky. Beached in the cove was half a carcass of a gray whale, the other half having already been drawn up the short slope to the try pots. The teams of mules that pulled the fifty-foot-long strips of blubber balked when first introduced to the smells and sights of the whaling station; but they soon discovered that the footing was more sure and the loads easier to move than the cinnabar ore they had lately been hauling on steep mountain paths.

Robert Mullins didn't believe he could ever get used to the sights and smells. The oily film that covered everything in the area disgusted him, and the view of the partially stripped whale with its ribs exposed and its blood coagulating in little pools on the shore was obscene.

And this rube of a captain is not cooperating, either, thought Mullins.

"Captain Alexander," Mullins tried again, "I really need your assistance. You have been recommended to me as a trustworthy individual whose sympathies are all correct. Surely you can see that the transportation of arms from San Francisco could be accomplished much more easily and safely from this point on the coast to the central mountains than overland past the many forts of the valley."

"I'm certain that what you say is correct, Mr. Miller," replied the captain, unaware of Mullins' real name. "But why come to me at all? I merely operate this whaling station for Mr. George Hearst, who owns this ranch. I'm not an arms merchant nor a shipper of arms. I came to this coast to get away from the cussed war and ply my trade in peace. As you can see," he said with a sweep of his hand, "I only make war on whales."

Mullins replied calmly enough, although inside he fumed like the try pots, "I've shown you the cuff links and explained how I came to have both of them. I've also shown you that I can pay. What more do you need?"

Alexander pulled his hat down over his forehead until its brim almost touched his hawklike nose, and he gazed sternly down at Mullins. "I've heard your story, all right, and I concede that your tale about one of your hirelings having mistakenly killed Mr. James in a drunken brawl is too wild for any pea-brained Yankee to have concocted.

"Nevertheless," he continued, "Mr. James should have had in his possession certain information that would confirm your status and sustain your worthiness to be privy to the name of my associate in San Francisco."

"I've already explained that we know how to locate the papers. It's merely a matter of doing so in a way that will avoid unnecessary interest on the part of federal agents."

"I applaud your caution, Mr. Miller, but its very fact should help you to understand my position. You say that you want to arm some miners who will seize the gold production for the Confederacy and then throw the Unionists out of the valley. Even if such a program were of interest to me, you must understand that there are larger wheels turning in the world than your little machinery. Plans are at work to deny the northern oppressors the use of any ports on the Pacific coast. Do you catch my drift?"

"Indeed I do, Captain, indeed. But can we not begin now to work toward that glorious day, and the inclusion of California in its rightful place under the Stars and Bars?"

"Not without your papers, Mr. Miller. You must have those papers!"

The two boys darted eagerly from tree to tree in their play, swooping and turning like a pair of swallows in flight. The morning was perfect for play; clear and crisp after the first snow of the year had left only an inch or two of pure white powder on the ground. The snow would not remain past noon; indeed, it had already slipped from the tree branches, but right now was a perfect time to practice tracking skills, mingled with a rousing game of hide-and-seek.

Nathan and Mont might have missed having Jed around if they'd stopped to think about it. But for the time being they were having too much fun to regret that the older boy, who was usually their leader, was home with the measles.

"He must rest quietly, boys, and he can't do that with you whooping around the place, so off you go. Besides, if you catch the measles, you'll have to be quiet soon enough yourselves, so get out and get to playing," Emily instructed.

They hadn't needed much urging.

"Look here, Mont, this is a rabbit's track. An' over here, slippin' up alongside Mr. Rabbit, is an ol' fox."

"I hope's Mr. Rabbit done made it home safe," commented Mont.

"Me too. An' lookit, see where this deer went by. Lessee, he stood right here nibblin' on this bush. Then somethin' musta spooked him; look at the jump he made. Clean over here, and then off he run!"

They moved from discovery to discovery throughout the morning as if the world were newly created for their enjoyment. At the juncture of Sandy Creek, they turned to follow its course mountainward into newer and less familiar territory. Presently they came to a gooseberry thicket, where a few little runways already imprinted in the snow gave evidence of the passage of a flock of quail. From the center of the thicket a soft clucking, churring sound could be heard.

"My pa always says, said, he . . ." choked Nathan, and his voice trailed off.

"Go on," urged his friend gently. "What he done said?"

Nathan drew himself up proudly. "My pa said that on cold mornin's or right after a snow, the quail family always stays close to home. See, they get right in the middle of their patch of berry thorns; they keep each other warm, and they stay good and safe that way."

"Your pa was sure enough a smart man, an' a kind one," observed Mont, "an' he made me feel right ta home wid you'uns. Jes' like the li'l quail mus' feel in de middle of his fambly."

Nathan nodded sadly. "I miss him somethin' fierce, Mont. Sometimes I forget that he's gone, and I think of somethin' I want to run and show him, and then I remember and. . . . Anyways, I like rememberin' things he taught me. When I tell 'em to you, it makes me feel better somehow, almost like he was here himself.

"Say," Nathan brightened, "I'm gettin' hungry. How 'bout you? Ma packed us some lunch, but I reckon that we could have part of it now and save the rest for later."

"Sounds mighty fine to me. What we got?"

Nathan rummaged through the burlap potato sack he had been carrying slung over his shoulder. "Let's see, here's some cold chicken and a piece of cheese each and an' some crackers. An' here"—he paused for effect—"here's provisions for us mighty trackers. Brown sugar and butter sandwiches!"

The two boys sat back-to-back on a boulder at the head of the gooseberry patch, where they could see part way down the valley that was their home. The fresh-baked bread was thickly sliced and spread with home-churned butter. The brown sugar filling made a crunching sound in the still morning air, and the delicious sweet taste complemented their camaraderie.

When they finished eating, Nathan suggested they get their game of hide-and-seek underway. "Now, we need some boundaries."

"What's a boun'dree?" inquired Mont.

"You know, markers to show how far you can go to hide so's the game is fair. Like, let's make this rock the farthest up this hill you can go, and the creek down yonder is the bottom. On the east side we'll say"—he paused to study the terrain with a judicious eye—"that there big cedar tree, and on the west that pile of rocks yonder."

"Whar's safe?"

Nathan carefully inspected again. "It needs to be somewhere's right in the middle. I know. You see that bunch of ol' buckeye trees all twisted around together? Right in the middle of that."

"Who's gonna be 'it' first?" asked Mont as they walked down the hill toward the clump of buckeyes.

"Let's peg for it. First one as can stick this Barlow knife in that buckeye trunk gets to choose."

Nathan produced his pocketknife, and the two took turns trying to make it stick in the twisted wood. On his third try, Nathan succeeded. "All right, you hide first an' I'll seek. We'll leave that knife there to mark home. I'll count to fifty, an' then I'll come lookin' for you."

"Make it a hunnert," begged Mont. "I wants to hide real good!"

"All right, a hundred it is," replied Nathan. So saying, he turned his face to the tree trunk and began counting loudly: "ONE, TWO, THREE . . ."

"Count slower!" Mont yelled back over his shoulder as he circled once around the clearing, hoping to confuse his pursuer before striking out to the west as quietly as the scrunching snow permitted. Once he stopped to throw a rock back into the middle of a brush pile; then he turned to run on, chuckling quietly to himself at the trick he was playing on his friend.

Mont knew exactly where he was headed, for the westernmost "boundary" of rocks had attracted his attention while they were eating. Directly in front of the heap of boulders an oak tree had fallen across a buckeye, and the two trees had crashed to the ground together. The gnarled buckeye, being all twists and turns, would not lie flat, but made a little archway over which the branches of the oak spread a partial cover.

As he approached his chosen hiding place, he slowed, even though behind him he heard "eighty-five, eighty-six . . ."

Mont selected his path carefully now, leaping from a rock to a pile of brush and from the brush to a clump of gooseberries and from there to the oak's trunk, and then down behind it into the space left vacant by the buckeye's fall.

Mont stood for a moment, noting with satisfaction that he could see no footprint nor any other sign of his passing in the last hundred or so feet of his path. *'Spec that'll pause 'im some,* he thought, as he settled down to wait.

Nathan was just finishing his count. "Ninety-nine, one hundred! Ready or not, here I come!" So saying, he took off directly east, toward the sound made when Mont had thrown the rock. Since Mont had circled around that way before taking off west, Nathan was supported in his choice by the sight of Mont's footprints in the snow.

I'm hot on his trail already, thought Nathan. He jumped up on a chunk of granite to survey the scene for possible hiding places. South and east he noticed a clump of brush that looked promising, and set off in that direction. He remembered to watch over his shoulder in case he was wrong and Mont broke from cover to run for "home."

Nathan skidded to a stop in front of the brush pile. Carefully he circled it, looking for Mont's tracks before his own had obscured the trail. All around the suspected hiding place the ground was clear and covered with a blanket of unmarked snow. Nathan stopped to scratch his head in thought. *He can't have come this way unless he flew.* He spotted a nearby scrubby oak with a fork about eight feet off the ground, and decided to try it as a new observation post.

Mont poked his head ever so carefully up from behind the buckeye and heard Nathan moving off to the east. He had just about decided to risk a dash toward the embedded knife when he saw Nathan climb up the oak, and from his perch in the cleft of the tree, begin a slow scan of the countryside. Quickly, Mont ducked back down.

Nathan had noticed the jumble of buckeye and oak, but from his angle, there didn't appear to be any space that offered a hiding place. Instead, he decided that a growth of manzanita over near the cedar that marked the eastern edge of their game looked promising. He jumped clear of the tree into a little pile of snow at its base and ran off to investigate the new possibility.

Mont remained hidden. He couldn't tell if Nathan had left his lookout or not, but he didn't want to offer any movement as a target. He amused himself by making a little pile of stones behind the log, all the while listening carefully for the sounds that would indicate his friend was approaching. Presently, he heard them. There was the sound of boots crunching on snow and a sharp crack of a branch breaking underfoot. Mont huddled down into the hillside, trying to breathe even quieter and willing his pursuer to go away. Mont strained his ears, but no longer could hear Nathan's footsteps. Had he succeeded in fooling his friend?

Mont eased his cramped legs just a little and thought about raising up once more to survey the hill. At that moment, a sound from behind him made him freeze. Then right over his head a booming voice exclaimed, "Wal', what's this here? If it ain't a runaway nigger, catched at last!" A brawny hand grasped Mont's coat collar and lifted him bodily out of concealment, then turned him around in midair, bringing him face-to-face with the sneering face of Byrd Guidett!

Mont kicked and struggled and tried to scream, but a huge hand clamped over his mouth, and all his efforts only got him a clout over the ear with another heavy fist.

Nathan had explored all the area around the eastern boundary. He thought about climbing another tree, but none close by had branches near enough to the ground for this to be done easily. Remembering what he had seen of the fallen trees, he put his hands together in a quick gesture of anticipation. "Sure enough, he's fooled me! Why I bet he's fixin' to make a dash for home right now."

With this thought, Nathan began running as fast as he could back across the area of their play. When he reached the tree with his pocketknife stuck in it, he was pleased that Mont hadn't gotten there ahead of him, so he continued on toward the west.

Nathan rounded the end of the oak's stump at full speed and almost collided with Byrd, who was threatening Mont with another blow if he didn't stay still. Seeing Nathan he exclaimed, "What's this? Another one?"

"Let him go!" Nathan shouted at Byrd. "You let my friend go!"

"You jest come on over here to me, boy. I'm jest havin' a little talk with this nig . . . I mean, yer friend here. Whyn't ya join us?"

Mont twisted free for an instant and called out, "Run, Nathan, run!"

Nathan took one more look and decided that getting away to get help was the best he could do. He turned to make a run for his house, but hadn't gone more than three steps when Yancey stepped out in his path with his boot knife in his hand. "You'd best do as the man says, and walk on over thar nice and easy like. It ain't real comfortable tryin' to run with this here knife astickin' betwixt yer shoulders, so ya'd best walk nice and slow."

"My uncle is coming to get us. He should be here any time now. You'd better let us go right now."

Nathan's attempted bluff was good, but it had the wrong effect. Yancey looked at Byrd and raised his eyebrows. "Could be the boy's tellin' the truth. Stead of tyin' him up, what say I jest cut his throat and be done with it?"

Mont stiffened in horror in Byrd's grasp, and Nathan stood rooted to the spot, too frightened to run, when Byrd replied, "Naw. That'd raise the whole countryside after us. If we ain't got time to tie 'im to a tree, we'll jest have to take 'im along. There ain't nothin' here to show they was around anyways, so no one will know what's happened to 'em nohow."

Yancey's lips parted in a sinister grin. "We got 'em, Byrd. We finally got 'em."

13

LIKE A DEER carcass across the saddle bow, Nathan hung head downward over the horse's withers. They were moving at a fast trot— deliberately, not in headlong flight. The bouncing motion with the saddle horn in his stomach made it hard for Nathan to breathe. Even if he hadn't been scared to death of Yancey's knife, he wouldn't have been able to yell for help. Nathan tried to concentrate on getting air into his tortured lungs and after that to pay attention to the direction of their travel. He could tell that they were skirting the edge of Carver peak and moving along parallel to, but some distance from, the side of the trail that led to the mining town of Tailholt.

Nathan tried to think what would happen to them. He believed that his uncle would come in search of them if they weren't home by nightfall. But they hadn't left any word about which direction their play would take them. Nor had they been able to leave any sign showing where they had been. Even if Tom located the trail of the two horses, how was he to know that it had anything to do with the disappearance of the two boys? Nathan began to pray silently, *Dear God, help us!*

Mont, meanwhile, was unconscious. He had attempted to struggle in Byrd's grasp, then tried to persuade the outlaws to release Nathan. But all he got for his efforts was a gruff "shut up!" from Byrd and a clout alongside his ear that had knocked him senseless. Byrd's grip kept the boy from falling headfirst to the ground.

The two outlaws drew up at the head of the canyon that sloped down around the northern flank of Shadow Ridge toward Tailholt. "Shall I kill 'em and dump 'em here?" asked Yancey, indicating the trembling Nathan.

"Naw, this is too close to our real track, an' anyways, Mullins may know of some use for the brat. Jest you be sure of this—" Byrd addressed Nathan by sidling his horse up close and yanking Nathan's head up by the hair. "If'n ya cause us any mite of trouble, ye're nothin' but crowbait. Is that right clear to ya, boy?" Nathan gave the tiniest of nods at Byrd's scowling face, and then his head was flung back down to bounce off the horse's shoulder.

Yancey motioned to the trail. "What say we split up here, jest in case Dawson do get after us?"

Byrd felt his nose and head for a moment, then remarked, "Maybe I been lookin' at this thing all wrong. I got a real hankerin' to meet up with Tom Dawson again. Maybe I oughta go on back an' make it easy for him to find me!"

For a moment Yancey looked genuinely worried that Byrd's temper and his desire for revenge would result in their getting caught. He thought for an instant, then remarked carefully, "You could sure 'nuff do that, Byrd, but we better not wait on gettin' that darkie to tell us where them papers is hid. You already know what an uproar Mullins is in. Jest hold on for a bit. You'll get yer chance soon."

Guidett looked as if he wanted to argue, but apparently saw the wisdom of Yancey's advice. He indicated with a jerk of his head that Yancey should take the right side of the canyon, while he and the still unconscious Mont rode down the left.

Now Nathan was more confused than ever. *What papers?* he wondered miserably. And they were plotting to kill his uncle. An instant before, he had wanted nothing more in the whole world than for Tom to come riding up. Now he desperately wanted his uncle to stay away! And who was Mullins? The only Mullins he knew was the fat, self-important storekeeper. Surely *he* couldn't be mixed up in this—why, he was one of the church leaders! Of course, he reminded himself, his father had never cared for the man; said he "gave himself airs."

These thoughts ran through Nathan's mind as the jolting ride resumed.

The trail they followed became narrower and steeper until the ground over which Nathan hung suspended had dropped away two hundred feet below! Now Nathan tried to hold his breath on purpose for fear that even inhaling might overbalance him and send him plummeting into the depths of White River Canyon. He tried closing his eyes, but immediately felt dizzy and sick to his stomach and in danger of losing his precarious perch.

Yancey noticed his stiffened little body and remarked dryly, "Don't go to pukin' on me, boy, or I'll figger that this here canyon is a powerful good spot to drop ya inta!"

When the gorge finally bottomed out and widened as it neared the town of Tailholt, Yancey directed his horse down the remaining six feet of bank that separated the cliff face from the river bottom. The river was dry at this time of year, but would soon enough be an outlet for the rains to find their way downward into the San Joaquin Valley.

Yancey's gelding moved silently through the soft sand toward the farther bank. There a dense thicket of cottonwoods obscured the view of the river from riders on the Tailholt road. The bay stopped of his own accord as if they had done this maneuver before. Yancey cocked his head first one direction and then the other as he listened for travelers before crossing the road.

Nathan felt a surge of hope. They must be close to the town where there was a little hotel and a few businesses. Tailholt was a rough mining camp, but there were some good people there who would surely help him to escape from this killer. If only he could give some sign, let someone know! But there wasn't anyone around to hear if he yelled; and trussed up as he was, he couldn't hope to make a run for it.

A bellowing voice floating up toward their place of concealment froze Yancey's intended movement to urge his mount up the bank. Someone was coming up the road! As quickly as Nathan's spirits soared they were brought to earth again by the cold sharp pain of Yancey's knife pressing in behind his ear. In a threatening voice made all the more sinister by its hoarse whisper, Nathan heard Yancey murmur, "Not a peep, d'ya hear? I'd as soon stick ya as look at ya."

The bellowing voice grew louder, and then a creaking sound was heard, and an intermittent popping noise—a bullwhacker and his team of oxen.

"Curse your hides you ill-gotten sons of perdition. *Crack!* Can't ya move any faster? *Crack!* I'll sell ya for hides and tallow right where ya stand! *Crack!*"

This fountain of curses and whip-cracking noise sounded as if it would pass by and go on up the hill, but all at once it stopped directly in front of Yancey and Nathan.

The drover could be heard exclaiming, "Well, how are ya, ya old horse thief?" This was apparently directed to someone whose approach down the road had been masked by the bullwhacker's carrying on.

Whoever the second party was, he was considerably more soft-spoken than the drover, and so only half the conversation could be heard. "Ya don't say? Up Havilah way? I thought that was all played out years ago."

There was a pause, then, "Not me, hoss, not me. Why, these four-legged devils are sure enough like stone, but at least they move when I tickle 'em! *Crack!* Show me the hard rock mine that'll do that, and I'll join ya."

The unseen and unheard second party to this conversation must have been riding a horse, for it chose this moment to nicker, and quite unexpectedly, Yancey's gelding answered it!

Yancey immediately leaned forward over its neck to silence it with a restraining hand, and the point of his knife pressed deeper into Nathan's flesh. The boy gasped, but remained still as a tiny trickle of blood began running down the side of his face and dripping off his nose. Both Yancey and Nathan held their breath—the one in fear of discovery, and the other in fear of death.

A moment more and both released quiet sighs, for from the road they heard, "Jim Dobber is dead? Ol' 'Mud' Dobber hisself? Why, I'da thought he was indestructible. Measles, ya say?"

At last the bullwhacker announced, "Well, ol' cuss, we'd best be movin'. I want to top the grade afore sundown. Go along, ya useless lumps! *Crack!* Rattle your hocks afore I cut out your brand marks an' sell ya for strays! *Crack!* Be seein' ya, ol' cuss!"

A short while later Yancey crept up to the edge of the cut and noted that the road was clear in both directions. Occasionally a shouted curse and the pop of the drover's whip could still be heard echoing down the canyon, but it was getting fainter and farther away.

"Ya done real good, boy. You was right smart to set so quiet. That loud-mouthed teamster may figger he can tickle his ox real clever with that fool whip, but jest you mind how good I can tickle with this little play-pretty of mine." So saying he drew the flat of his knife across Nathan's neck once more for good measure, and then they rode on across the road.

Mont was just beginning to come around. His head hurt, and his bound wrists and ankles ached. Unlike Nathan, Mont had no idea where he was or where Byrd was taking him. He was smart enough to realize that any sudden movement or sound might get him clobbered again, so he remained still, pretending unconsciousness. Byrd had naturally chosen the easier side of the canyon for himself to travel, so Mont had awakened to the view of a gently sloping hillside below him, not the rocky gorge that Nathan was being forced to watch.

Mont was not aware of it, but their travel was following the road from Greenville to Tailholt, about two hundred yards off to one side. It seemed to him that they had been traveling forever; in fact, the afternoon was drawing to a chilly close when Byrd Guidett muttered "Whoa" to his big bay horse, and they stopped in the shadows of the ridge's northwestern fringes.

Below them was the gold-mining community of Tailholt. Its thousand or so inhabitants were already indoors, away from the wind that had an increasing bite to it. In some of the windows the glow of lanterns was beginning to appear. Mont looked wistfully toward the warm, snug little homes.

"Awake finally, eh?" grunted Byrd. "You ain't the only one wishin' to get inside by a fire and hunker down with some decent food." Then, as if even this brief observation had betrayed too much gentleness, he shoved Mont roughly off the horse onto the hard ground with a thud. "Wal', we ain't goin' to no nice warm cabin, see? An' if'n ya don't tell us what we want to know and that right quick, I might jest tie you up to a rock and see how soon some bear comes to make a meal off'n ya, if'n ya don't freeze to death first!"

Both man and boy were chilled and stiff by the time Yancey and Nathan rejoined them. Byrd was even grumpier than usual. "Whar ya been? You musta stopped for supper, and me afreezin' my rear off out here!"

Yancey for once was in no mood to be cowed by Byrd's menacing talk. "Get down off yer high horse, Byrd Guidett. You know'd we had to take the long pull around Tailholt, besides pickin' our way down that canyon. An' then I had to wait near an hour to cross the road. Some bullwhacker freightin' up to Keyesville met up with some'un comin' down, and they went to palaverin' right in front of me! An' what am I s'posed to do, ride on acrost sayin', 'Pardon me, boys, whilst I get to my hideout, an' pay no mind to this trussed-up brat here'?"

Even Byrd was taken aback by Yancey's tone. "They didn't see ya, then?"

" 'Course not! Now, are we gonna stay here shootin' off our mouths, or are we gonna get on up the trail?"

When they had ridden up into the hills some mile and a half, they came to a wide expanse of shale rock with no dirt covering. Carefully, they began picking their way across the dangerous surface until at last they rode off onto broken ground about a half mile from where they had last made a track. Yancey passed his reins to Byrd and slipped off his horse, leaving Nathan to balance across the gelding with even greater difficulty. As Byrd rode and led Yancey's mount, Yancey moved along behind, smoothing out the sign of their passing with a handful of brush. He did this for perhaps another four hundred yards until satisfied that even if someone were able to trace them as far as the shale, their path after that would be impossible to pick up.

Byrd paused long enough for Yancey to mount up again; then both men urged their horses upward at a good pace. Nathan thought with a shudder that they were now climbing up Shadow Ridge itself. Somewhere up on these lonely heights his father had died. He also knew that somewhere to the east awaited his home and his mother; but this cold, inhospitable and sinister mountain lay in between!

The way the cave appeared was startling. Even Byrd and Yancey, who had seen it many times, were amazed at the suddenness with which the opening seemed to be right underfoot, where there had previously been solid granite mountainside.

The western rim had grown increasingly steep and barren for the last hour of the ride, with no features to attract anyone's attention. No entrance of any kind was visible—no boulder-strewn lip, no telltale shadow. What existed was a slightly flattened area—no more than a bench on the slope, and so near the tip that it seemed too small to contain anything worth investigating. Just inside this flattened space was the mouth of hell, so it seemed. A gaping black hole, at first a vertical shaft, resolved itself into a sloping entryway down into the earth.

The level bench near the mountain's peak coincided with an outcropping of limestone. This slight declivity caught the runoff and snowmelt, which gradually melted away the limestone, leaving a near-perpendicular crater. Some time later an earthquake had collapsed a portion of the edge, and that occurrence, combined with still later landslides, had provided access to the depths.

Byrd's horse sniffed the air over the opening as if to say, "This looks familiar, but I'm still not sure I like it." Then he stepped downward into the granite rubble that formed the ramp.

Once down the short slanting heap of debris, the cave's entrance disappeared almost immediately under a granite roof. Just inside this roof the cavern made a sharp turn to the right so that even though the crater was exposed to sunlight, very little reached the interior of the cave past the first few feet.

Byrd reached out toward the wall and grasped a lantern that sat on a rocky ledge just level with a man on horseback. Fishing around in his shirt pocket for an instant, Byrd removed a match, which he struck on the rough wall and applied to the wick.

The warm yellow glow revealed a level floor of trampled gravel, and a crude barricade of branches that blocked the entrance from the first bend of the tunnel. There, just across the rude fence were two more horses, who whinnied a greeting to the two ridden by the outlaws. Interested in spite of his aching muscles and his fear, Nathan raised up for a look. The horses may not have been signalling to their equine counterparts, after all, but reacting to the presence of Mont and Nathan. Nathan recognized both animals as having been stolen from their ranch!

Byrd and Yancey stepped from their mounts, and Yancey pulled aside two rails of the barricade. They led their horses in among the other two, with the boys still hanging over the saddles. Once through the opening Yancey replaced the fence, and then Byrd yanked both children to the ground. With a pocketknife he slit the rope that tied their ankles, but left their hands bound. "Get up," he growled roughly, gesturing for the two to precede him deeper into the cave.

Yancey lit another lantern and began to unsaddle the horses as Byrd led Mont and Nathan over another fence at the rear of the cavern. The glow from his lamp pushed back the darkness just far enough for them to see that the room they were leaving was as large as a small barn and obviously well suited for that purpose. Along one side of the passage was a channel in the rock that was filled with water like a cistern. The pool of rainwater that had formed this cave was still present, but its location was now below the surface. As the tunnel narrowed and angled downward, the pool's overflow continued downward into the mountain, as it had for ages past, and formed the tunnel through which they walked.

Mont's feet had evidently been bound more tightly than Nathan's, for he was having difficulty walking. His stumble to the fence had been managed clumsily, and now, just on the other side of it, he fell.

"My feet!" he exclaimed. "They's all needles!"

"Get up and move, ya little varmint! Do ya think I'm gonna carry ya?" With that he grabbed Mont by the collar and jerked him to his feet. "Now walk!"

"Come on," encouraged Nathan, "lean against me. I'll help you." So saying, Mont stumbled next to Nathan, and then the two lurched down the passageway.

The cave had become both narrower and lower after exiting the room for the horses; now it opened out again into a space of room-sized proportions. Byrd lifted his lantern as they entered; they had evidently arrived at the gang's living quarters. A crudely constructed fire pit stood along one wall, the surface completely blackened with soot. Black streaks ran upward until they disappeared into the shadows of the craggy ceiling, where a crevice leading to the surface provided natural ventilation.

A pile of supplies, cans of beans, and a flour barrel were jumbled together in one corner, while a heap of empty cans and other rubbish made up a garbage dump in another. Along two walls were bed frames with wooden sides and cross-laced webbing made of leather. These meager belongings and a small table with two crude chairs standing in the center of the open place comprised the entire furnishings of the room.

On the wall opposite the way they had entered were two dark holes that showed as exits. Into one ran the underground stream that had passed through this cavern along one wall and which could be heard gurgling into the passage beyond. The other opening was somewhat uphill from the rest of the cave—another stream of water had at one time flowed into this room, but it had since dried up.

Byrd gestured for the boys to sit down in the chairs, and he proceeded to light a fire in the fire pit, igniting some kindling that had been set there before. As this caught, he added small oak branches, and soon the air became noticeably warmer. He then scooped up a coffeepot full of water from the stream and set it on a flat rock next to the blaze.

Yancey came in from tending the horses just as Byrd dumped a double-handful of ground coffee into the boiling water. He tossed a can of beans to Yancey, and both men deftly opened the tops with their knives and then used the knife blades to eat with. Byrd poured himself a cup of coffee and then poured one for Yancey. All this fixing and eating and pouring had been done without a single word being spoken and without any acknowledgment of the boys.

Nathan endured the smell of the beans and the aroma of the coffee as long as he could, then remarked timidly, "Please, may we have some food too?"

Byrd flung his now empty can onto the rubbish pile and towered menacingly over the boys. "You two are a hull mess o' trouble. Why, we got blasted little here as it is, an' not to be wasted on the likes of *you.*" He raised his arm as if to strike Nathan for asking, but Yancey interrupted.

"Hold on, Byrd. 'Member, they gotta be able to talk here directly, so we'd best feed 'em some."

Byrd looked as if he begrudged them so much as one mouthful, but he opened one more can of beans and unceremoniously dumped the contents on the table. After cutting their hands free he remarked, "There it is. Now go ta eatin' an' don't waste one bean."

The boys scooped up the tiny supper and licked their fingers.

"Next I suppose you'll be wantin' milk to drink or some o' my coffee." As the two small friends looked up hopefully, Byrd concluded, "Well, ain't that jest too bad? Get on over an' lap up some water like the two scrawny curs you are."

Leaving one lighted lantern on the table, Byrd took the other in his meaty hand and growled at the boys to follow him. He led them over to the dry side passage. It was a space no bigger than a pantry, a shaft reaching upward and into the dark, out of reach of the lamplight. Thrusting them inside, he gave them a warning.

"Don't try to run off, see? Ya cain't get up the shaft, an' if'n I catch ya tryin', I'll give Yancey"—here he jerked his thumb over his shoulder—"a chance to go to carvin' on ya with his toad-sticker. Ya know, they say the Comanch can peel a man's hide like skinnin' a spud. Wal', Yance there will make ya *wish* them Injuns had you instead!" He left, taking the lantern with him and leaving the boys in total darkness and abject misery.

14

IT WAS LATE afternoon before Emily noticed that the boys had been gone longer than she expected. She had been busy all day, alternating farm chores with household cleaning and stops to visit Jed in his sickroom. He was comfortable enough, but his fever came and went, and Emily spent much of the day sponging his forehead with cool water and bringing him cups of tea with sugar when the chills were on him. Near sundown, he slept, and Emily sank into the rocking chair near the fire, exhausted.

"Where can Nathan and Mont be?" she mused. "It's getting cold outside, and I can't imagine that the lunch I packed would keep them from coming home for supper." The thought of supper reminded her that she had a pot of soup simmering in the kitchen, and so with a resigned sigh she rose and went to check on it.

Through the kitchen window she heard the sound of hoofbeats and looked out to see Tom ride into the yard on Duncan. His hat was pushed back on his head in a jaunty manner, and he was grinning as he pulled saddle and bridle from the horse and gave it a good-natured swat to turn it into the corral. He disappeared for a moment as he walked to the front door of the house and then, as she expected, she heard his knock and a shout, "Emily, it's me, Tom."

She called out, "Come on in, Tom," then returned to the front room to meet him.

"Emily," he began without preamble, "guess what? They paid me the whole amount in gold. And that cavalry officer they brought along to inspect the horses said"—he drew himself up in military fashion and puffed out his chest to support an imaginary load of medals—" 'Son, these are the finest mounts I've seen this side of the Mississippi. We'll take as many more as you can deliver—and just as soon as you can have them ready.'

'Yes, sir, Colonel,' I said, 'we'll sure have them for you.' Where are the boys? I want to tell them how good we did."

"The salt and pepper twins aren't back from playing yet. I shooed them out of the house because Jed has come down with the measles. He's been in bed all day and been running a fever, but he's asleep now and doing all right, I think."

"Measles, eh? Say, that can be pretty serious. Have you ever had them?"

"Yes, when I was just a little girl. Have you ever had measles?"

"Same with me, I guess. I must have had them about Jed's or maybe Nathan's age. I felt pretty rotten for a week or so and broke out with a terrific set of spots, but then I got over it pretty quick. How about the other two? Any sign of them catching it?"

"No, not so far, although three children over at the school have had it, so I'm almost positive these three have had an equal chance. Really, the reason I sent them off today was so I could get some work done while it stayed quiet for Jed to rest. Then, too, if they are going to be cooped up with measles, I thought it would be better for them to run off a little excitement first."

"Do we need to get a doctor?"

"I did talk to Doc Welles and he said Jed just needed rest and good food. He said kids seem to do all right as long as they keep warm and still and don't get pneumonia. He did say that it was a lot tougher on adults. But enough about measles; tell me more about your great horse trading!"

Tom paused as if gathering his thoughts before going on. Then he began in a halting voice and a more serious tone, "Emily, on the ride to Ford Tejon and back . . . well, on the trip, I had a chance to do some thinkin'."

"Yes, Tom—thinking about what?"

"Well, you know I feel responsible for you and the boys and all. I mean, not that I mind or anything, but, you know, I want to see you taken care of. Do you understand what I'm saying?"

"No, Tom, I'm not sure that I do."

Flustered, Tom began to speak, stopped, then finally tried again. "You see, since we made out so well with the horses, and since it looks like we got a steady market, with the money being good and all, I was just thinkin' . . ."

"What, Tom? What are you trying to say?"

Tom drew a deep breath and plunged ahead. "It's this way. What with this sale and the prospects of more to come, there's plenty of gold put by for you and the boys to go back to Missouri now. I mean, you could go back and buy you a place of your own. Pay cash for it, too. I should have

known you wouldn't want to be moving back in with your folks and imposing on them. Well, now you don't have to. You can get you a nice house,
and I can send back more money right along as I get more strings broke,
and . . . why, Emily, whatever is the matter?"

Tom had stopped speaking when he finally noticed that Emily's expression had changed and she appeared ready to burst.

"Ooh, you, you *dunderhead!* Didn't I tell you before that this is my
home now? I wouldn't want to go back to Missouri if I could go as the
Queen of Sheba. Get a place of my own, indeed! I *have* a place of my own,
Tom Dawson, and it's here, right here! And to think I thought you . . .
you were—ooh!"

"What, Emily, you thought what?"

"Just never mind, Tom. There's some soup on the stove. Help yourself
while I go check on Jed. Then you might go out and holler for the boys if
you've still a mind to be *helpful.* It's getting dark and past suppertime."

Tom went out to the kitchen, shaking his head and muttering as he
went. Who could understand women? Everything he'd said was perfectly
reasonable, even carefully thought out, and look how she reacted! And
what else could she have possibly thought he meant to discuss? Unless,
unless . . .

Tom shook his head again. No, it wasn't possible. It couldn't be, could
it? He decided that he needed a little fresh air to clear his head more than
he needed a bowl of soup right then, so he went out through the kitchen
door.

It was getting late. The sun was already below the top of the mountain,
and the wind had a nip to it. Even though the night was clear and the
daytime sun had all but melted the snow, winter was definitely stirring. It
might even freeze. He began to call out, "Hey, Nathan! You, Mont! Suppertime!"

When there was no response, he started walking slowly northward
toward the creek bottom where he knew the boys liked to play. When he
reached the place, they weren't there. He called to them again, but still got
no answer. Tom began to walk along the creek in the direction he thought
their games might have taken them; then he thought better of it and decided to go back for his coat and a lantern.

Emily was just coming out from checking on Jed. "Did you find them?"
she asked. "I heard you calling."

"No," he replied. "And it's getting dark and cold outside. I think I'll
grab a light from the barn and walk up the creek a ways." At Emily's
worried frown he added, "Don't get upset. They probably just were having
such a fine time that they wandered farther away than they intended. But

Nathan knows this valley real well. He can find his way back. I'll just go help them along a little."

Out in the tack room Tom put on a heavy fleece-lined coat and lit a lantern. He thought briefly about saddling a horse and riding out, but figured that tracking two small boys at night was better on foot.

Tom was pleased to find that when he returned to the creek bed with lamp in hand, he could immediately pick up their tracks in the sand. He followed them along the stream's course, lost them briefly where they had turned aside to look at something, then picked them up again a hundred yards farther on where they had rejoined the creek's path.

When Tom arrived at the juncture of Poso Creek and Sandy Creek, Tom again missed the trail where the boys had left the sand to strike out across the hillside, so he circled back until he found it. From the point at which they exited, he thought he could guess where they might have been headed. It was a large rock that stood part way up the hillside—a good "lookout post" for the upper end of the valley. Just the place two boys who were out exploring would want to visit. Tom himself had used it before to survey the countryside when he went deer hunting.

When he reached the spot, he could tell that Nathan and Mont had been there, but they were not there now; worse yet, they seemed to have milled around there a lot, without giving a clear indication of which direction they had taken next.

Tom was heading back downhill when he came upon the other sets of tracks. The boot prints of two men appeared both coming and going on the hillside, and the outward bound set was pressed deeper into the earth as if the men had been carrying something. Tom's heart began to race. How could he be sure? He couldn't bring this kind of news to Emily without proof. After all, he didn't even know for certain that Nathan and Mont had been near the men. He decided to recross the area one more time to see if he could locate anything definite, any clue to the boys' presence.

"Didn't you find them?" Emily asked when Tom returned to the house. At his negative response, she cried, "But where can they be? You don't think that someone could have. . . . ?" She stopped as a grieved look came over Tom's face. "Oh no, Tom, not Byrd Guidett! But you can't *know!* I mean, maybe you just haven't looked in the right place yet."

She stopped again and followed Tom's glance downward to his right palm outstretched in front of her; then she sank onto a bench, and with her face in her hands, began to sob.

In Tom's hand, glistening in the firelight, lay Nathan's Barlow knife, taken from the tree trunk that marked the spot where a day of fun had turned into a night of terror.

"Oh, Tom, what does it mean? Where are the boys? What could have happened to them?" gasped Emily. "Could they be lost, or was it . . . was it . . . a wild animal? But no, they'd get up a tree, wouldn't they? Oh, Tom, where can they be?"

"Take it easy, Emily. Here, sit down," instructed Tom, grasping her arms and moving her toward the rocking chair.

"Sit down? We've got to go out looking for them. Where's my other lantern and my shawl? Tom, you've got to ride to town for help! Why are you just standing there?"

Tom sighed heavily. "Now, Emily, you've got to get hold of yourself. I've got something to tell you, and it won't be easy."

"No, Tom, NO! You can't mean—"

"Emily, calm down! I don't think they're dead. In fact, I don't think they're even hurt. Do you recall that Byrd Guidett wanted to take Mont with him as some winnings in that poker game when he killed the man?"

"Why yes, of course. And you stopped him, and . . . oh, Tom, you don't think Byrd took him and Nathan!"

"Yes, I do think that's what happened, Emily. There were tracks of two men near where I found the knife, and some sign of a scuffle with the boys. I followed their trail to where they had tied their horses; then I came back here to tell you. Now, Emily, there wasn't any blood, nor any sign that the boys had been harmed. Byrd and that partner of his could have ki—hurt the boys right where they caught 'em if they'd intended to."

"But why take them away, Tom? What do they want?"

"I don't know the answer to that, Emily. Byrd may still be tryin' to get hold of Mont, but there must be more to it than that. Even the fight he and I had at the Bella Union didn't seem strictly due to Mont. It's more as if Byrd wants to get at me for something, or he thinks the boys know something . . . I don't know what . . ." His voice trailed off as he realized that he couldn't come up with anything helpful or encouraging to say.

"But he must know he'll be tracked, trailed where ever he goes, and brought to jail!"

"Yes, I'm sure he does. And that means two things."

"What, Tom, what?"

"He's not gonna leave a trail that's easy to follow, and whatever he thinks he can accomplish by taking the boys must be real important to him! Now, I'm riding to town to get help. You stay put and take care of Jed. I'll be back just as soon as I can."

The first person Tom called on when he arrived in Greenville was the Parson Swift. Even though awakened from a sound sleep, the parson came quickly to the door and admitted Tom to the parlor. As the minister listened attentively to Tom's story, Swift stoked up the fire in a small chrome and cast iron stove, his mind racing.

"Everything you say makes sense to me, Tom," he concluded. "I think we need to rouse the town and get started right away. The longer we wait, the farther ahead they'll be, and the more chance for them to cover their tracks. Let's go over to the church."

So saying, he wrapped his robe tighter around him and retrieved a worn pair of carpet slippers from his bedroom. "I explained things to Mrs. Swift," he said as they went out the door. "She'll be brewing some hot coffee for us."

Over the entryway of the little church was a narrow steeple containing one high-pitched bell. Parson Swift grasped the bell rope firmly, and with strong sweeps of his wiry arms, he began pealing the alarm. Its clanging sounded unnaturally loud in the clear, crisp night air. Soon the interrupted silence was further broken by the sounds of dogs barking and horses neighing. A few moments later lights began appearing in windows, and exclamations and slamming doors echoed off the hills around the town.

Deputy Pettibone, to his credit, was the first to arrive, his nightshirt hanging down over his trousers. In one hand he was carrying his boots, and slung over his other arm was his gun belt. "Where's the fire, Parson? Is the church burning, or what?"

"It's not a fire, Deputy, it's—" Before the Parson could complete his answer, the Volunteer Fire Company arrived, pulling their pump cart by hand. The water wagon arrived next, pulled by a team of snorting draft horses that looked far more alert than their driver, who sawed at the reins while alternately blinking, yawning and cursing.

"Come into the church, men, come in," called the parson, realizing that explanations would be futile until everyone was assembled and quiet. Confusion ruled as newcomers inquired, "What's this about, then? Ain't there a fire. No, it ain't, it's the livery stable. Naw, it's no fire atall; Jeff Davis has been captured!"

Pettibone stood up and raised his hands for silence. Gradually it grew quiet in the room, and the deputy addressed Parson Swift in a somewhat squeaky voice. "Just what's this here alarm about, Parson? Is there a fire or ain't there?

"Just quiet down, men, quiet down," instructed the preacher as the babble threatened to erupt again. "Yes, there is an emergency, and no, it's not a fire. Tom Dawson here will explain."

Quickly Tom outlined the situation—how long the boys had been gone, what he had found and where, the tracks he had followed, and what he thought it all meant. "So you can see we need to get after them right away. There's no telling what they'll do to those boys. Guidett's already shown how he treats folks in this town."

Mutters of agreement and a general movement out the door was halted by a measured voice raising carefully chosen phrases at the rear of the room. "May I suggest that we not be hasty, gentlemen? The night, while cold, is not desperately so, and the great likelihood is that the two children have merely wandered too far from home and have curled up somewhere for the night." Robert Mullins paused, then continued. "Most probably they've found some warm spot to get into, one of our neighbor's barns or haylofts, and are now peacefully sleeping—even as we all should be."

"Didn't you hear what I said, Mullins? I found my nephew's knife and the boot tracks of two men, even some sign of a struggle!" Tom Dawson burst out angrily. The parson laid a restraining hand on his arm.

"Now, Mr. Dawson. Didn't you say that you discovered this 'evidence' after dark? How can you be certain what it means?"

"You gob of lard! I'm tellin' you my nephew and Mont James are in the clutches of that bloodthirsty killer *right now* and you want stand here jawing about proof?"

"Naturally, Mr. Dawson, your emotions are running rather high just now, and I think we all understand that, don't we, men? But let's not be hasty."

"Now jest hold on a minute there, Mullins," began stocky Bill Gardell. "If it was my kid, I'd be out lookin' right now, an' I'd want my neighbors to be helpin'."

"Just so, just so, Mr. Gardell. I wasn't suggesting that we not help. But if some sort of abduction has taken place as Mr. Dawson believes, don't we stand a much better chance of tracking them by daylight? In fact, if all of us went up there now, wouldn't we obscure the marks and actually make it more difficult to proceed? Let's seek expert counsel on this. Sheriff Pettibone, what do you think?"

"Well, I . . . I don't rightly know. I mean, those is little kids an' all. Still, tracking by night is hard enough, an' if we was to trample the ground, well then, where would we be?" Pettibone stopped as if not sure what point he'd just made. On that his audience was in complete agreement, but Robert Mullins covered the awkward silence just as if Pettibone had offered a masterful summation.

"Exactly right, Sheriff. And friends, may we remember one thing? The Dawson boy, assuredly one of our *own*, is accompanied by the young Negro child, no stranger to being a runaway, I assure you. Isn't it likely that under his influence, even a fine child like young Nathan could be led astray?"

Tom could contain himself no longer. "You mean because he's black, we needn't worry if he has disappeared or been stolen? He's no concern of ours? And some of that *taint* has rubbed off on Nathan, too? Is this what all of you believe? Mullins, you no good, lousy—"

"Now, Tom, no harsh words that you'd regret later," soothed the deputy. "I'm sure Mr. Mullins meant nothin' mean about either child. He was just tryin' to keep us calm. Tell you what, we'll all go out in the mornin', at first light. Now, what do you say to that?"

"I say I'm sorry I wasted my time comin' all the way over here to get help from my *neighbors*. Now get out of my way. Move over, I say, or I'll knock you down!" Tom shoved two men aside as he went up the aisle of the church and out the door.

"We'll join you at first light, Tom, you can count on us," called Pettibone after him. Several men looked ashamed, but no one except the parson moved to follow Tom out of the building.

Parson Swift laid a hand on Tom's shoulder just as he was about to mount Duncan. Tom whirled around, his right arm raised as if to strike.

"Oh, it's you, Parson," said Tom, dropping his fist. "Sorry, I—"

"You needn't explain, Tom. I'm as disgusted as you with the whole lot, especially Mullins and that spineless Pettibone." This was an astonishing comment since the soft-spoken preacher had never been heard to say a harsh word about anyone. "I'm not a woodsman nor any kind of a tracker, but if you'll have me, I'd like to go with you."

Tom stared at the parson for a moment, then grasped his hand warmly. "Thank you, Reverend. If I don't burn this whole town to the ground, starting with Mullins' store, they'll have only you to thank. No, I'll go alone tonight. Come morning, some of these *neighbors* really might feel up to comin' to help, and they'll need someone to get 'em organized. Will you do that for me?"

"Of course I will, Tom, and I'll send my wife over to stay with Emily. I expect she's taking this pretty hard."

"You know she is. In fact, would you ask your wife to not say anything about this meeting to Emily? I'll just let her think there's folks who care in this town till maybe some of them wake up and find out they do!"

15

AT FIRST LIGHT Tom stood again by the tree where he'd found the knife. He had little trouble picking up the tracks, though he frequently walked and led Duncan for fear of missing a turn. He reasoned that the two outlaws were carrying one child apiece, and that sooner or later they would hole up. He had to believe, had to hope that he was doing the right thing. He had no other alternative.

As Tom searched, he thought often of Emily—so brave but so grief-stricken. Would she be so insistent on making this land her home if she had seen the lack of concern among those she counted as friends? Could a return to war-torn Missouri have been any worse than this?

What was wrong with those people, anyway? Could they really abandon two children because they were afraid to get involved? Could the color of a child's skin mean that his fate was of no concern at all?

And what was Mullins' role in all this? As a merchant and a church leader, one would think that he'd be strong against any lawlessness and have a heart full of compassion. "Mullins' heart must be as cold as the coins in his cash drawer," Tom muttered. Now, what was it about Mullins' cash drawer that stuck in Tom's mind? For some reason the image of Mullins standing over his counter stuck with Tom, but he couldn't for the life of him figure out why.

During the night another light snow had fallen on Shadow Ridge and the trail petered out completely. Try as he might, Tom could find no place where the two tracks had exited the snow field. Looking up the slope, with the morning sun behind him brightening the looming peak of the mountain, Tom could see no objective that any riders would have been trying to reach. There was no hideout, not even rocks big enough to conceal a horse. *They came up here purposely to lead me off,* thought Tom. *Then they backtracked their own trail, or rode down off this saddle somewhere and went toward Tailholt.* He was quite sure they would have avoided the main road only while it was light. Then when darkness had fallen, they could have returned to the highway. But how in the world could he figure out which direction or how far they had gone?

Turning his horse around, he wearily made his way back toward home. As he reached the place where he had begun to track, he came upon Parson Swift waiting for him. The parson looked expectantly at Tom, but said nothing. Tom shook his head sadly, and the two rode back to the Dawson place, where Emily and the parson's wife had kept an all-night vigil.

Mont and Nathan crouched together in their stony prison. They linked arms tightly not only out of fear but out of relief at finally, if only briefly, escaping the threatening knife point and punishing fists.

As their eyes adjusted to the light seeping from the larger cavern into their grotto, Mont could make out Nathan's tear-stained face. Nathan made no sound as he cried, but he couldn't hold back the tears any longer.

Mont listened for a moment to the noisy sounds of self-congratulations that issued from the other room, then decided he would risk a whisper. "Is you all right, Nathan?"

The hoarse, choked reply was unable to cover the lie even as Nathan spoke them. "I guess so. I'm okay."

"Is you hurt anywheres?"

Nathan's hand went up to the place behind his ear where Yancey's blade had been an inch from taking his life. "He cut me, Mont! He told me if I made a sound, I was dead! When we stopped by the road for that wagon to pass, he stuck his knife in my neck, and the blood ran down over my nose. I wanted to call out for help or jump down and run away, but I couldn't, I couldn't, you see!"   Nathan sounded close to sobs, so Mont made little hushing sounds and said, "Shh now, Nathan, we's still alive, and we's got each other."

"But I want to go home! I want my ma. What are they gonna do with us?"

"I don' rightly know what dey're fixin' to do wid us, but you know what my ol' mammie tol' me?"

"Your mama, Mont? I didn't think you remembered her."

"I dasn't talk 'bout her much, 'cause it makes me real sad, but I 'member she tol' me 'bout Massa Jesus allus takin' care of me. She say, 'Mont, Massa Jesus, He see ever' sparrow where dey go. He see 'em when dey in de nest an' He see 'em when de cat be afixin' to get 'em. I 'spects He can take care of a little blackbird like you.' "

"But what about the sparrow that the cat *does* get—what about that?"

"Den it goes up to heb'en an' fly free all de day long, I reckon. But you an' me, we'll tell Massa Jesus dat we ain't ready jes' yet. I has only jes' found out dat I is free right here. I means, dey may have catched us now, but I doesn't belong to nobody! Now we needs to pray an' den go to sleep."

For a minute when he first woke up, Nathan didn't know where he was. When he realized the predicament, he felt a moment's panic when he couldn't find Mont. In trying to find some comfort on the hard floor of the cave, they had managed to squirm past each other and were on opposite sides from where they had fallen asleep.

It was impossible to tell how long they had slept. Light was still coming in from the larger tunnel, and since no outside light reached to this depth, Nathan couldn't tell if he'd slept ten minutes or ten hours. He felt rested, though, and hungry again, so he guessed that it must be morning.

There were no sounds coming from the other room. Nathan lay very still and listened, but all he could hear was the sound of gurgling water as it made its way through the cavern beyond and plunged downward into the mountain.

Could they have been left alone? Was it possible that the outlaws had gone away? Nathan glanced over at Mont, decided against waking him, and crept slowly and cautiously over to the chamber entrance.

Quietly he lifted himself up from his huddled position and peeked around the corner. The fire in the pit was out, burned to a small pile of ashes. The two outlaws were still present, both of them asleep on the rough cots.

Nathan backed up into the smaller space. He bent down and shook his friend gently to wake him, while keeping his other hand ready to clasp over Mont's mouth to stifle any sound.

Mont awoke with a start, but didn't make any noise. His eyes opened wide, and he understood instantly when Nathan placed a finger across his lips and then gestured for Mont to follow him.

One step at a time, eyes darting back and forth from bed to bed, the two boys tiptoed out into the room. Their advance was painfully slow. It was all Nathan could do to not make a run for it. They stole past the rough table, across the open space near the upward passage, then stopped abruptly.

"You'uns wouldn't be thinkin' of runnin' away, now would ya?" a raspy voice behind them drawled.

Both boys whirled around. Yancey was sitting up on his bed eyeing them with amusement. Nathan shuddered as he noticed that Yancey already had his knife out in his hand.

"No, sir, we just needed to get a drink of water, an' we didn't want to wake you," offered Nathan.

" 'Peers to me you went the long way round to get to the crick over thar, but go on now, help yerselves." Then as the boys actually did go to the tiny stream to get a drink, Yancey added in a lower, sinister tone, "I'm right glad you wasn't asneakin' off, 'cause I mighta had to stop ya. That coulda been real unpleasant for somebody." With these words he flipped his knife, faster than they could see his wrist move, hurling the blade into the table leg.

The sudden *thok* awakened Byrd, who sat up with a start. Yancey continued speaking to the boys. "Now Byrd thar, he don't hardly wake for nothin', but me, I sleep like a rattlesnake. Do ya know how rattlesnakes sleep, boys?" When the children made no reply except to shudder, he went on. "They sleeps with one eye open, and when they strikes, they hits hard! Some'un 'most always dies."

Byrd sat rubbing his face and shaking his shaggy head. "Was they tryin' to sneak off?" he growled.

"Naw," replied Yancey. "They wouldn't even think of such a thing."

After the robbers had made coffee and fried some thick slices of bacon, they tossed a couple of biscuits to the boys. They were hard as rock, but nothing else was offered, and neither child had any desire to ask for more.

"When's that Mullins s'posed to get here?" Byrd asked.

"He cain't get here afore tonight. He won't know that we got hold o' these two till we don't show at the cabin at noon. He'll be along right smart after that," concluded Yancey dryly.

"An' what'er we s'posed to do with these two brats? Why don't we jest find out 'bout them papers now an' be done with it?"

"Go right on ahead," commented Yancey. "Long as ya don't fix it so's nobody else can ask more questions later."

"All right, Nigger!" Byrd faced Mont, sticking his nose near his.

"Where'd that master o' yours hide them papers?"

Mont gulped before answering. "What papers, suh? I don' know nothin' 'bout no papers."

A powerful backhand caught him on the side of the head and sent him sprawling to the floor.

"Ya see, Yancey, I tol' ya we'd have trouble with 'im. His memory ain't workin' too good, but I expect I can help 'im along some."

He dragged Mont back roughly into the chair and continued. "Now 'bout them papers, boy. Didn't ya see that colonel you was with hide somethin'?"

At the shake of Mont's tiny head, another cuff landed on his other ear and knocked him into the table. Nathan jumped from his seat, shouting, "You leave my friend alone! He doesn't know anything about any old papers! Stop hitting him!" Byrd turned to grab Nathan by the throat when a voice from the lower outlet of the cave commented, "Yes, you'd best stop hitting him for now, Byrd. You might succeed in killing him before I find out what I want to know, and that would not make me happy." It was Robert Mullins!

"Boss, how'd ya get here so soon? I mean, how'd ya know already that we had 'em?"

"Apparently you two incompetents not only succeeded in making off with one child too many, but you left enough marks that the Dawson child's uncle could follow you in the dark! It took all my persuasion to see to it that there wasn't a posse on your trail last night!"

"But, Mr. Mullins," Nathan blurted out, a shocked expression on his face, "what are you doing here?"

"I might well ask the same thing of you, young Master Dawson. But I think I'd be addressing the wrong person." He fixed his stare on Byrd.

"They was together. I mean, we didn't think it'd be smart—"

"Guidett, your problem is that you *never* think. At least for once you didn't leave a gory corpse beind to mark your passing. If you had, I don't think even I could prevent the fools who inhabit that miserable little town from tearing this mountain apart with their bare hands until they caught you."

Here he turned to address Mont and Nathan again. "Which is not to say that anyone would ever find two very small corpses if they were hidden inside this mountain. Perhaps you can persuade your little friend there to tell us what we want to know. What ails you, boy? Can't you stand up straight?"

"I . . . I . . . don't know. I feel real strange all of a sudden," said Nathan in a shaky voice.

"Come, come, boy, you'll have to do better than that! Shall I let Mr. Guidett resume his intended action at the moment I arrived?"

"No, please. I feel better now, just a little woozy is all. But please, sir, let Mont alone. He don't know anything about any papers."

"Is that so, boy?"

"Yassuh. I din't see no papers, an' Colonel James, he din't tell me 'bout none, neither."

"Hmmm. All right. Suppose for a minute that I believe you. Why don't you tell me where you stopped the night before Colonel James's unfortunate death?"

"I don' rightly 'member de man's name, suh. But it were a fine house next to a riber. Kinda on a island-like."

"What's that, boy? You mean to say you stayed *with* someone? You weren't just camped?"

"Oh no, suh. Dere was even a fine barn for me to sleep in, an' dey give me a real nice supper."

"Jehoshaphat! Think, boy, think! What was the name?"

"Shall I see if'n I can jog his memory some?" offered Byrd, but Mullins waved him back impatiently with his fleshy hand.

"I'se real sorry, suh. I spects I din't hear no names. Dis house was by a riber on one side, like I tol' you, an' had a slough on de other. An' jes' 'cross o' dat slough dere was a big field, an' folks was acampin' dere fo' de night, but we—"

"Stop!" shouted Mullins. "That's Baker's house and his field. Listen carefully, boy. Did the man you saw there look like this." Mullins gave a brief description of Colonel Thomas Baker.

Mont's eyes brightened, "Yassuh, dat's de very man! Can we go home now?"

The storekeeper squinted his piglike eyes, and a most unpleasant expression crossed his face; then it passed, and his usual ingratiating smile returned. "No, I'm afraid that won't be possible just yet. You see, we have to recover something from that house that belongs to me, and just in case we have trouble locating it, I might want to ask you some more questions. You just stay here as our guests for a while and behave yourselves, and I'm sure you'll be treated all right. Won't they, Yancey?" A look went between the two men, but nothing was said.

"Guidett, you come with me. Take good care of our guests, Yancey. Even young Dawson may have some bargaining value." Mullins and Byrd exited down the tunnel up which the fat man had lately come.

16

"**H**OW COULD THEY be so spiteful?" questioned Emily. "Those two little boys, out there alone, or worse. How can people be so small?"

"It isn't that they're altogether hateful, Emily," corrected Mrs. Swift gently. "You must remember that they're terribly afraid for their own families as well. Most of them have lost kinfolk in the war, and lots of people want to raise their families out here in peace, just like you. Now that peace is threatened. Byrd Guidett is just a big bully, shooting up the church like he did, but he has made these folks see violence up close, and most of them would rather shut their eyes or run away. Still, may God forgive them for not going out to search at least. I'm praying that God will put a terrible weight on them until they do what's right."

"Can't we track the riders any farther?" the parson asked Tom, who was seated with his head bowed in sorrow and exhaustion.

"No, Parson, the little dab of snow we got last night was just enough to hide the tracks. If we had more help, maybe we could comb the whole canyon down to below the snow line and pick up the trail again, but I just can't cover all that ground myself."

"Then, what will we do?" sobbed Emily again. "We can't just leave Nathan and do nothing."

"I'll help you, Uncle Tom," suddenly voiced a pale, thin figure in a long nightshirt. Jed stood in the bedroom doorway looking weak but resolute.

"Bless you, Jed, but no, you get back to bed," Tom replied. "The best thing you can do is get your strength back and stay here and look after your ma."

"I'll go out with you, Tom," Parson Swift offered.

"All right, Parson. There's nothing else to do but try. Let me get some grub together and some bedrolls, and we'll go. Maybe we'll get lucky and run onto the trail easier than I expect."

"We can bring something with us more powerful than luck, Tom. God loves those boys—and you, Tom, Emily, and Jed. We need to hold on tight to our faith and expect God to lead, even when there isn't a trail we can see with our eyes."

There was a knock at the door. When Emily rose to answer it, she swayed, overcome by fatigue and worry. The parson's wife gently but firmly seated her again and went to the door instead.

Standing on the porch was McKenna, owner of the Bella Union. "Is Tom Dawson nae aboot?" he asked. Then seeing Tom in the room, he addressed him. "I was nae in town last night or I would have been with ye sooner. When I heard what had happend, I coom straightaway. These others here have coom on, too."

"What others?" inquired Tom, coming to the door and peering out.

Outside in the yard, bundled up in heavy coats and looking sheepish, was a group of riders. Among them were Bill Gardell, Red Burton, Bob Davis, and a few others. "Hello, Tom," began Gardell. "Me an' some o' the boys . . . well, we figgered we didn't do right by you last night, but we want to make amends."

"Tell him the whole truth, Bill," urged Red. "When we got home last night and told our wives what went on at that meetin', an' how Mullins talked us inta not doin' nothin', me and Bill an' Bob here got lambasted real good. We was in Alex's havin' coffee this mornin' and kinda comparin' bruises when Alex got the gist of what happened, an' he allowed as how he'd horsewhip us if we didn't get over here right smart. Ain't that the size of it, fellas?"

A chorus of "and how" and "you bet" chimed agreement, and Davis added, "Truth is, Tom, I didn't sleep too good last night anyways. I figger we let Byrd Guidett bully us jest far enough. An' as for Mullins and his slick talk, well, you see neither him nor Pettibone is here now. We figgered we couldn't wait on them to lead no more, so here we is. That is," he added respectfully, "if you'll still have us."

"You bet I'll have you! Parson and I have just been sitting here trying to figure out how we could cover four hundred square miles between the two of us. Come in, fellows, and fill up your canteens with hot coffee; we've got some hard cold riding to do."

They went out in pairs to scour the hillsides. They took a bearing on the approximate direction the tracks were heading when last seen, then fanned out in a half circle before riding down to the snow line, so as to give themselves the broadest possible chance to pick it up again.

It was late afternoon when Red Burton spotted the deep tracks that emerged from the snow on the gentler slope of the canyon-side that led down toward Tailholt.

Three rifle shots fired in close succession brought Tom and the others riding over. "Look here, Tom," said Red. "These tracks is fresh, and they come out headin' in the right direction."

"But that's the track of only one horse. Where did his partner go?"

"We figger they split up at the head of the canyon, plannin' on meetin' up later," replied Red. "An' Bob here agrees it's likely this one was up to no good, or else why'd he be ridin' over here on the hill with a good road no more'n a quarter mile away?"

"All right. It makes sense to me. Part of us'll follow this trail, but the others need to keep working their way down the opposite side, just in case the second rider turned off another way. Parson, you and Bob and Red come with me; Alex, if you don't mind, I'd like you to lead the other group."

"Whatever ye say, Tom. Coom on then, boys, we're nae followin' naught by sittin' here."

Tom's group followed the hoof prints down toward Tailholt without difficulty. They found where the rider had apparently waited for some time, and saw marks on the ground to indicate that something had been thrown there. Another set of tracks rejoined there, but Tom decided not to call the other group immediately, thinking they might come across some clue that would be helpful. He did send Bob and Red into Tailholt to ask if anyone had recently seen Byrd Guidett or two small boys. By the time they returned with negative answers to both questions, Alex's group had completed their search and joined up again.

"They didn't leave the boys anywhere along the trail, and no one's seen them in Tailholt. Let's figure that they went on from here and we'll follow this track up Shadow Ridge."

"They've hoodwinked us for sure," said Bob Gardell. "They rode up on this shale, then doubled back, dustin' their tracks as they went. Shucks, if they come this far in daylight, they could've chanced goin' back on the road by night an' be most anywheres by now."

Tom rose in his stirrups and looked anxiously up the mountain. "What about farther up? Couldn't they have crossed the slide rock and gone on up?"

"Naw, you can see for yourself there ain't nothin' up there," remarked Red. "Why, even a squirrel would stand out, no more brush than there is up there. Besides, what'd they do up there anyway but come back down?"

McKenna turned to Tom in apology. "I ken he's right, Tom. We're wastin' time on a cold trail."

"Are you all for giving up, then?" asked Tom quietly.

"Nay, nay, dinna misunderstand. Let's split up again. Some will ride through Tailholt an' doon the mountain, inquirin' of all travelers if they've seen aught of two men and two young lads, and others to do likewise up yon Jack Ranch way. Never ye fear, they canna stay hid for long."

Tom looked down at his saddle horn for a long moment before nodding slowly in agreement to this plan. All the riders turned their mounts then, making their way back down the hillside in single file. Tom was the last to leave. He turned his horse around, then turned in his saddle to look up at the bleak summit of Shadow Ridge. He raised a clenched fist toward it in anguished helplessness. Something close to hatred was in his eyes as he turned again to follow the others.

It was five days before Byrd returned to the cave. When he did he was in a foul mood, and Yancey as well as the two boys shrank back from him.

"Five days hidin' out in that stinkin' swamp in a cold camp. Not even coffee, that fat pig says, we don't want to give away our presence."

"What about them papers?"

"Who knows? We ain't even got inside the house yet."

"Why not? Don't them folks ever leave?"

"Naw, it's worse than that. He's got a mess of Yankee officers stayin' with 'im!"

"Yankees! What we s'posed to do now?"

"Mullins went on back to his store—his nice, warm, dry store, an' left me to watch. 'Wait till day after tomorrow,' he says. 'If you haven't gained entry by then, go back and trade places with Yancey,' he says. 'I'd stay myself but my continued absence would be noticed.' That lousy, stinkin'—"

"What's the matter with him?" Byrd continued, indicating Nathan.

"Don't know exactly. He's been acting real poorly since right after you left. First I thought he was fakin', but I felt of him an' he's got the fever all right. Says his head hurts an' his throat, and he's breakin' out in some rash or somethin'."

"Well, I ain't gonna wet nurse no sick kid. Be just too bad if he hauls off'n dies, now wouldn't it? Save us the trouble."

"No! No! Home! Mama, Mama, Mama! Jed, look out . . ." Nathan's voice trailed off, but he continued to thrash around.

"Listen here, boy, you'd best keep yer friend quiet. I'm gettin' powerful tired of his carryin' on," ordered Byrd ominously.

"Yassuh," replied Mont. "But he's burnin' up wid de feber, an' now dem spots is 'most all over his body."

"Yeah, well, give him some more water, but keep him quiet!"

"Yassuh." Mont tried to get Nathan's attention, but to no avail. Mont took off his own jacket and used it for an extra cover over Nathan's trembling limbs. He moistened his pocket handkerchief and used it to cool Nathan's fevered face.

Nathan continued to shiver all over as if he were in a freezing snowstorm without a stitch of clothing on. Mont looked anxiously at his friend, and then, making up his mind, got all his courage together and went into the larger room to address Byrd.

"Mistuh Byrd?"

"What is it now, Nigger?"

"My frien', he need to be next de fire, an' he need some hot food."

"Why ya little . . . I'll . . ."

"If'n he dies, Mistuh Mullins gonna be powerful upset. You'd best stop an' think on dat!"

Surprised that such a small person could stand up to him so forcefully, Byrd laughed. "All right, then, fix him a place by the fire, an' let's see if ya can cook. I'm almighty tired of my own cookin', anyways."

Almost as soon as Mont assisted Nathan to stretch out by the fire, the sick boy began to calm down. His contorted muscles relaxed, and he ceased muttering to himself and fell into a peaceful sleep.

Mont used this break in his constant attention to his friend to fill the cleanest pot he could find with fresh water from the stream and put it on a hook over the fire. As it began to heat, he got grudging permission from Byrd to use a small pocketknife. With it he shaved pieces of jerky into small bits, which he dropped into the pot.

Byrd dipped himself a cupful of this soup just as soon as it began to boil, but Mont continued to heat and stir the mixture until it had reduced to about a third of its original volume.

Nathan began to show signs of awakening as Mont poured out a small amount into an empty tin can to cool. As Nathan's eyes opened and he looked around the room, Mont aided him in sitting up halfway, and then held the can to his lips. At first Nathan sipped slowly, but little by little he ate more eagerly until he had consumed all that remained in the pot. He smiled gratefully up at his friend, then lay down and returned to a relaxed sleep.

"Nothin'—not a blessed sign of 'em!" reported Red. "Me an' Bob went clean to Tulare. We met up with drovers, an army patrol and even a band of Tuolomnes. None of 'em have seen Byrd, or two men with two kids, or even one black kid, for that matter. You have any luck?"

"Yeah, tons of luck, an' all of it bad," said Bill Gardell. "McKenna an' me went to Jack Ranch, Sugarloaf, even busted our hump gettin' over Portagee Pass, an' nothin' to see nor nothin' to hear about. It's like they dropped off the world. One thing's certain, though, Byrd must be mixed up in this, else it's right queer of him to disappear at the same time as those two kids."

"Where's Tom and the parson?" asked Bob.

"Parson went back to check on Mrs. Dawson an' give 'em the report, such as it is."

"And Tom?"

Bill and the Scotsman exhanged rueful glances. "We couldna get him to coom back with us and rest a spell," said McKenna. "When we could nae mair ride nor walk, he made us give him the rest o' our kit, and he rode out Howling Gulch way."

"Howling Gulch? That windswept hellhole? There ain't even water nor wood for fires up that rock-choked gully. What'd he think to find up thar?"

"Do ye nae ken, mon? Tom is near crazed with grief, and what's mair, he canna think on what will coom to Miss Emily if he canna find her lad."

"It's sure enough true what Alex here says," added Bill. "He's aclutchin' at straws."

Tom rode Duncan around a pile of rubble that had fallen from the heights of the narrow gorge into its narrow throat. The boulders and gravel completely filled the canyon to a reach of twenty feet up the walls. For the third time in the past hour Tom had to dismount from Duncan and look for a way to scramble around a dusty obstacle.

The sides of the gully were treeless, even brushless, in their barren disarray. It appeared to Tom that the only thing growing there was a fine crop of decomposed granite that flowed down the walls as if determined to prevent even the tiniest plants from ever taking root. The bottom of the canyon was dry, a stranger to any regular flow of water, though it showed the unmistakable marks of flash flooding. The gorge was a tremendous runoff channel when the storm clouds broke over the heights of Sunday Peak, but the swift passage of water did no more than aid the crumbling rock avalanches in keeping the sides scoured clean.

But it was neither the sliding gravel flows, nor the boulder-strewn gully, nor the violent passage of a temporary river that gave the canyon its name. Howling Gulch took its designation from the fact that the tiniest gust of wind reverberated down the plummeting walls, shrieking in exit at the canyon's mouth like demons being cast into everlasting torment. And the wind blew all the time.

It was blowing particularly hard today. A week of fruitless searching had brought Tom to the point of being alone in the search, and the rising volume of the canyon's howling heralded the approach of another wintry storm that had mercifully held off through much of the search for the boys.

Gravel blew into Tom's face, assaulting his eyes like red-hot sparks from the blacksmith's forge. He ducked his head down to his chest, and soon found that he could not lead Duncan and hold on to his hat with the other hand and keep his balance all at the same time. Leaving the horse to stand ground-tied for a moment, Tom made several attempts to fasten his bandanna over his hat's crown before he finally succeeded in bringing the ends together under his chin.

When he could next clear his vision, Tom looked upward at the rock slide he was trying to lead Duncan around. This pile of rocks seemed even more jagged, heaped up higher and the canyon sides even steeper than those he had crossed to get to this point. Tom considered trying to retrace his steps to the bottom of the gorge and try the other wall, but momentary glimpses across the rubble showed no more promise than what he was already facing. "I guess this is as far as you go, boy," he commented to Duncan. Tom retrieved a rifle from its scabbard on the horse and thrust a box of cartridges into the pocket of his heavy coat. He loosened Duncan's girth, but left the saddle in place. He was glad Duncan could be trusted to remain ground-tethered, for there wasn't anything he could be tied to, anyway. "Be seein' you," Tom remarked, to which the horse only made answer by turning about and placing his broad rump into the wind. *Fine send-off,* thought Tom with grim humor. *Even the horse turns his back on me.*

He struggled upward for the next twenty minutes before reaching the top of the rock dam. He was right to have left the horse behind, he reasoned, or he would not have made it this far at all. The wind was really howling now, a blast so fierce that Tom could not stand erect for fear of being blown back down the slope he had just climbed. The screech noise increased, sounding like a steam boiler about to explode.

Tom stumbled down the other side, heedless of the path he took—anything to get off the exposed ledge where he felt like a fly in the path of a descending fly swatter. Halfway down, his feet went out from under him on a patch of loose gravel. As his boots shot forward with increasing speed, Tom flung his arms out to the sides, grasping for anything that might offer a grip to stop his plunge. The rifle, flung against a quartz ledge to Tom's right went off on impact, but its roar was completely masked by the wind.

Tom fell heavily on his side against a boulder; the ribs broken in the fight with Byrd cracked painfully. This time it felt as if an even greater fist had slammed into Tom's body, and his breath was expelled in an agonized "Ooof!" Tom lay still, panting, trying to draw air back into his lungs.

He looked around in a daze, unable to see the rifle from where he lay, and anxious to locate it—not because of its firepower, but simply because he felt that he would have to have it to lean on if he were to stand up. For the moment he had completely forgotten why he came to be in such a place. As he crawled up the side of the rock against which he had fallen, each breath was like a spike driven into his side. His face was raw and bleeding from the gravel driven into it by the force of the gale. His hands were stiff and aching, and when he looked to see why, he saw that on one hand three fingernails had been ripped out by his scramble to find a hold on the rock face. The palm of the other hand was bloody with fingernail marks where he had clenched his fist in the agony of bruising his ribs.

"God!" he cried, "what am I doing out here? Why don't you help me?"

17

"**W**E IS CLIMBIN' Jacob's ladder, we is climbin' Jacob's ladder, we is climbin' Jacob's ladder, sol'jers of de cross," sang Mont to Nathan. The two were sitting in the small cave where they had been sent by Byrd while he went to feed the horses.

"An' don't even poke yer noses out till I get back an' tell ya to, un'erstan'?"

So the two sat in the dark, and Mont sang softly, much to the delight of his friend.

"Mont, how long have we been here, anyway?" asked Nathan.

"I don' rightly know" was the reply. "An' when you was mos' outta your head wid de feber, dem days did drag on so. Bes' I can figger, we done been here 'most ten days since we was catched."

"Do you think they'll ever let us go, or is anyone ever gonna find us?"

"Shore we's gonna get outta here, you jes' wait'n see!"

They heard noises coming from the other cavern, but thought only that it was Byrd returning from feeding. There was a shuffling sound, a pause, and then another shuffling noise. It sounded as if some heavy sack was being dragged across the floor of the tunnel. Mont stopped singing so they could listen, but neither boy made any move to go see what it was.

Presently they heard a flop as if that same imagined sack had been carelessly thrown onto one of the cots. A long, drawn-out groan followed, then silence.

Their heightened senses anticpated Byrd's return from the upper tunnel even before they heard him enter the adjoining cave. When he did enter, they heard him say, "Yancey! When in thunder did you come? What ails ya, anyway?"

A hoarse croak that in no way resembled Yancey's voice replied, "It's the fever an' the pox. I'm like to die with it, Byrd. I couldn't watch no more, so I come up."

The boys heard and understood the clumping footsteps that followed this announcement. It was Byrd backing up rapidly away from Yancey's bed.

"Well, ain't this fine! How're we s'posed to watch them kids an' Baker's if ye're alayin' here sick?"

"I'm cold clean through, Byrd Guidett, an' I ain't been dry since I left here. I can still watch them brats. You get on out to Baker's an' leave me be!"

"All right, all right, jest don't let them two put nothin' over on ya."

Some time later there was no sound from the other room, and no one had come to tell the boys that they could come out, or when it was time to eat. So they went silently to the juncture of the two passages and peered carefully around the corner. Yancey lay on his bed, breathing heavily. His hair hung in matted streaks across his face, and one arm trailed limply to the floor. Mont and Nathan looked at each other, and each knew what the other was thinking. Remembering how quickly Yancey had awakened on their last escape attempt, the boys decided to test him. Nathan called out softly, "Mister Yancey, is it time for supper?"

To their great disappointment, Yancey sat up immediately and regarded them with sunken, red-rimmed, bloodshot eyes. He stared at them, saying nothing and swaying slightly back and forth. "You two—" he began, but got no further as a racking cough shook his whole frame, bending him almost in two with the spasm of it. When he could speak again, it was to gasp, "You two get back an' keep still. Leave me alone!"

How long Tom had been lying stretched out across the rocky ledge, he didn't know. What finally roused him from his stupor was no new pain or another moment of violent activity. Instead, his conscious mind struggled to awareness because of a lessening of the storm's frenzy, a gradual slackening of its voice.

Tom took stock of his injuries before trying to move. His hands were stiff but no longer bleeding. All his fingers worked, though unwillingly. His face felt burned as if polished by the wind, but his vision was clear and undamaged. As for his side, he drew a cautious breath and was almost surprised that no sharp pain resulted. He sat up carefully and noted with gratitude that his rifle lay where it had landed—just on the other side of the rock on which he was lying. He turned his gaze around to look at the gravel pile on which he had fallen in order to begin calculating a path around it, but it was not the marks his boot heels had made that drew his horrified attention. At the point where his side had been crushed up against the rock, at the precise location where his next step would have taken him, there was an abrupt drop-off that fell straight down into the gorge. Leaning out, Tom could just barely see the bottom some hundred feet below.

He crept on forearms and knees over to the rifle. It was undamaged. Tom used it to pull himself upright, where he stood, shakily surveying the canyon. "God," he said aloud, "you are here with me. You were helping me even when I thought you'd left me all alone. Wherever Nathan and Mont are right now, won't you hold on to their hands like you did mine? And Emily too, Lord. Help her see that you know all about lookin' for lost children."

When Tom had struggled painfully back to where he had left Duncan, he found the horse patiently waiting. Taking a canteen from his saddle, he drank a swallow, then poured some water into his hat for the grateful beast. With another handful he bathed his face, then he took another long swallow. "Let's go home," he said to Duncan.

Not until late the next evening were Tom and Duncan able to get all the way back down to the area of Greenville. Though exhausted and sore, Tom felt an unexplainable calm.

When he arrived back at the Dawson ranch, he was received with exclamations of joy and made to sit next to the fire while Emily tenderly bathed his face and hands and put ointment on the deep scrapes.

Tom listened as she related to him that all the other searchers had again reported in, with no greater success than when Tom had last seen them. In turn, he told her what he had experienced. He didn't try to conceal his disappointment at not being able to locate Nathan nor the extent of his anger and frustration that had driven him up Howling Gulch.

"But, Emily," he added, "something happened to me up there. I haven't found the boys yet, but I know we're going to. And this isn't just false hope to make you feel better. I really believe God promised me he'd bring them home if I'd just trust Him."

"I know, Tom," she responded. "I've been praying for your safe return, and look what God brought you back from. Everyone has been here praying for you and the boys, especially Victoria Burton. She stayed with me all night last night."

"God bless 'em," he replied. "Now I just need some sleep; then I can go out lookin' again."

She brushed her lips against his. "I know you will, Tom, and God will be leading you every moment."

Back in his room, Tom fell instantly into a deep sleep. He awakened once to drink a small bit of soup, then slept again clear into the next night.

Tom was having a confused dream. In it he was trying to swim up a rockslide. He heard a shot and then a shout. It was his brother's voice. No, it was Nathan's high treble. Something was pulling him down. The air was thick like mud as he tried to come to the surface of Shadow Ridge, but the syrupy air didn't slow the rocks and boulders that went bounding past him—each one narrowly missing his head. Another shot and another shout. What was holding him back? He squirmed around to see. It was a silver chain, its links twined around his legs. The links glinted dully in a shadowy afternoon light. The chain wound around his boot tops and tightened around the cuffs of his trousers, the end of the chain dropping off down the hill. Someone was tugging on it, but Tom couldn't see who. Then came a shot followed by an agonized shout!

Tom sat bolt upright, covered with sweat. He rubbed his hand over his face and shook his head. What a nightmare! He had relived his brother's death, but with himself as the intended victim, and the unknown fate of his nephew thrown in as well. How vivid that gunshot, how lifelike the scream—

Tom stopped himself in mid-thought. Deliberately he forced himself to reexamine the confused scenes. What was it that bothered him so about the two sounds which were so deeply implanted in his consciousness? Tom forced his mind to return to the actual scene on the mountainside that tragic afternoon, comparing its events to his dream.

There was no sudden flash, no leap to an instantaneous understanding, but rather a gradual realization. Tom thought it through carefully, tested his conclusion, found it sound. He remarked out loud to himself, "The shot came before the shout. That means that Jesse's gun didn't go off in the fall; he was shooting at something before he was struck. Something, or *someone.*"

"If that's true," he reasoned, "then somebody wanted his death to *look* like an accident. They wanted to keep us from finding something, but they didn't want to let on that there was anything anybody would want to find."

He debated whether he should wait until morning to tell Emily, but he couldn't sleep, so he dressed quickly, deciding that he would walk around a little and think.

When he got outside his room, he noticed a thin sliver of light coming from under the window shade in Emily's room. Perhaps she was still awake. He went to the front door and tapped gently, not wanting to disturb her, yet willing her to be awake. His quiet knock was rewarded with a shuffling noise followed by a gentle "What is it?"

"Emily," he called, "can I come in and talk a minute? I think I've figured something out."

"Of course, Tom. Just a moment."

He waited as she drew back the bolt and stepped aside to let him enter. Her hair was down on her shoulders, and she was wearing a dark blue dressing gown. She didn't appear to have just awakened, but Tom asked, "Did I wake you?"

"No," was the reply. "I couldn't sleep, so I was up reading the Ninety-first Psalm and praying for Nathan and Mont. What's this you've figured out?" she asked eagerly. "Do you know something of the boys' whereabouts?"

"Maybe. Maybe," he said slowly as this new aspect of his dream entered his mind. "Listen to me. I'm sorry," he said awkwardly. "Can we sit down?"

"Come into the kitchen, Tom, and I'll make us each a cup of tea."

While he sat at the kitchen work table, she stirred up the wood stove with a few pieces of oak wood, then put on the kettle. She sat down across from him and looked expectantly at him.

"Now, this may be nothing at all, so don't get your hopes up," Tom cautioned, "but the dream I had . . . I think it means something."

"Tell me from the beginning, as much as you can remember, and don't try to explain it till you're all done," she instructed.

His dream, which had seemed to last for hours at the time he had had it, took only moments to tell. He went slowly and carefully, trying to recall every event, every sight, and every feeling. "You see, it was the order of the two noises that bothered me up there that same night on the mountain, but I was too dazed to figure out what it meant. Later on, there was you and the boys to see to, and I guess I sort of blocked it out, just not wanting to think about it. But now," he resumed firmly, "I'm certain that what I heard was Jesse getting off a shot at whoever was pushing the rocks off the rim at him, and the shout just before the—" He stopped, unwilling to cause her more pain.

But Emily was all business now, the mother bear scenting the air for danger and preparing to defend her cubs. "Yes, I see. Whoever killed Jesse did so in order to prevent you two from either finding a route over, or discovering some secret about Shadow Ridge, *without* causing further investigation. That must mean," she continued, "that you and Jesse were right about the stage robberies and Byrd Guidett being linked with a hidden way to cross. And perhaps," she concluded, "it may mean that Nathan and Mont are being held there now!"

"At the very least," Tom pondered aloud, "there may be a clue to their whereabouts up there. And I aim to find it." He made as if to rise, but Emily stopped him. "Wait," she said, "there was more to the dream; let's not run off without working it all out while it's still fresh in your mind." The kettle was whistling on the stove, and Emily poured its contents into her blue china teapot.

"But it was all so confused and tangled," Tom protested. "How can it help us any?"

"Tell me the last part again," she urged. "About the chain."

"It was a silver chain that led down into a dark hole, and someone I couldn't see was trying to drag me backward into the path of the rockslide. It was all wrapped around my legs. I remember especially that the links were around my cuffs, heavy silver links twisted around my cuffs, and—"

"What, Tom, what is it?" Emily asked as Tom got a faraway look in his eyes.

"Cuffs and links, Emily—cuff links! I'm sure that's it! Now I know why Mullins didn't want anyone to go up Shadow Ridge, or to get a posse to chase after Byrd."

"Wait, Tom, you're not making any sense. What cuff links? And do you mean Robert Mullins, the storekeeper? What about him?"

"Pour us some tea, Emily, while I explain," Tom said confidently. "I even know now how we can check to see if I'm right."

18

A SOLITARY DOG barked in sudden alarm, and Tom froze in his tracks. He listened intently, every sense tuned for the banging door or creaking hinge that would indicate someone coming to investigate. Two anxious minutes passed with Tom pressed against the side of the hardware store; then the dog lapsed into silence, apparently satisfied that he had successfully repelled the intruder.

When another minute's silence went unbroken, Tom breathed a sigh and resumed creeping toward the store's rear door. He was struggling not only with the worry of being caught but also with how he could explain his actions. He doubted that anyone other than Emily would put as much credence in his dream as he did. Even in the midst of this exploit, which Tom felt driven to perform, perfectly reasonable objections kept asserting themselves. How could a man of such recognized standing in the community as Robert Mullins be a party to the crimes of murder and kidnapping? Could such a pompous but ingratiating manner conceal such sinister intentions? Tom's agony at uncovering the fate of his nephew and Mont drove him to believe the answer was yes; not only was Robert Mullins a mass of flesh but a heap of duplicity as well.

And that, Tom reasoned, *is why I can't go to Pettibone or any one else with this suspicion without something to back it up. Even if I could convince them to investigate, I might only succeed in giving Mullins enough warning to get away or cover his tracks some other way.*

So here he was, on a bitterly cold and thankfully dark night, preparing to break into Mullins' store. He knew what he was seeking, but even Tom wasn't sure why. He intended to retrieve the silver cuff link that had come from the body of the man slain by Byrd Guidett. For some reason Mullins had chosen to appropriate the cuff link and squelch any further reference to it. Tom's gut feeling told him the cuff link had some bearing on the whole mystery.

Tom wore his Colt Navy strapped to his side. He didn't expect to be using it tonight, but he wouldn't have felt safe without it. Tom wasn't certain how he intended to enter the store. He had chosen the rear because the front bordered the two main avenues of travel through the little town and made discovery much more likely.

Tom located the outline of the door and began to explore it with his hands. A quick investigation of the frame left Tom completely disgusted with himself for coming out on such a fool's errand without having found some pretext to check out this entrance first. His rapidly numbing fingers found that the rear door was completely set into the frame. It closed from the inside only and was apparently bolted from within, leaving neither bolt nor hinge on the outside. There was no lock to be broken, and the fit was so tight that there was little chance that a prying tool would work.

Now what? Tom wondered. *I've come this far; I'd best not go back without checking for some other way in.*

He circled the store cautiously, checking all the windows on the off chance that one had been left ajar. No such luck. He had almost reached the front of the building when he heard a noise from the road. No dog this time. Instead, it was a steady, measured footfall. Tom crouched down at the corner behind a scrawny lilac bush just off the porch that ran across the front. He hoped he would blend into the other dark shadows and not be noticed. The footsteps turned off the gravel of the roadway and went unhesitatingly across the small yard with its two hitching rails. The un-known person stomped heavily up the wooden steps to the porch and paused in front of the door. The jangling sound of a ring of keys came to Tom's ears, and he realized with a start that the bulky figure was Robert Mullins himself.

Tom's mind whirled at this complication. Should he wait until the shop-keeper had entered, and then make his own getaway? Should he step up and boldly confront the man, hoping that the shock of his unexpected presence would surprise Mullins into revealing something? The hesitation caused by these two conflicting plans settled the issue for him, for as Mullins located the correct key and proceeded to unlock the door, he began to mumble aloud. Tom leaned forward to catch what was said.

"Should have thought of this before. Can't depend on that rattle-brain and his shifty-eyed sidekick . . . Think of some pretext to get into Baker's . . . Delivering something . . . Show him the recognition to-kens. Ha! We can . . ." His words trailed off into inaudibility as he snapped the bolt back and threw open the door. He closed it behind him but did not latch it on the inside.

Casting aside most of his caution, Tom moved quickly up onto the porch. He pushed the door open just slightly, hoping to hear more of the monologue without alerting Mullins. Tom peered carefully into the store through a window just beside the entrance.

At first he couldn't make out anything inside; then a spark of light flared as Mullins struck a match and lit an oil lamp on his counter. The hulking form fumbled with the key ring again before selecting another one with which to unlock his cash drawer. Suddenly Mullins threw the ring of keys down on the counter. "Can't get too excited," he murmured. "Know they're in the safe where they belong. Can't be too careful. Oh, but we're close." He turned his massive body around with some difficulty in the narrow space behind the counter and made a wheezing sound as he bent over to reach his safe.

Silently praying that the hinges were well oiled, Tom eased the door open and slipped inside. He tiptoed almost up to the counter. From behind it a mixture of grunting noises and the soft click of the combination lock could be heard. On the wall an ugly shadow-beast—half pig and half bear—played and stretched. A final click and the clank of the handle, and then Mullins gave a snort of satisfaction. He tossed something over his shoulder to the counter. No, it was *two* something: a pair of silver cuff links like the one bearing the initials J.D.!

Robert Mullins rose ponderously to his feet with the lamp in one hand and turned around to find himself looking into the cold, murderous gaze of Tom Dawson.

"Why, Mr. Dawson!" sputtered Mullins, "whatever are you doing here at this time of night?" Then, as if he realized that was not the proper tone to use, he added, "I'll thank you to leave my establishment immediately. If you have business to transact or something to discuss, come back tomorrow."

When Tom said nothing but continued staring into Mullins' startled and apprehensive eyes, the shopkeeper struggled to regain his composure. He put the lamp down on the counter. "I mean to say, why are you sneaking in here like this? Is something wrong? Is there an emergency?" His hands, like two fat spiders, began crawling across the counter top toward the cuff links.

At last Tom spoke. "Leave 'em right there, Mullins. I wouldn't want want one of 'em to disappear before Colonel Mason had a chance to ask you how you came to be in possession of the twin to the cuff link found on a corpse!"

"Why, I can't think how it came to be here. I mean, I was looking for something else when—"

"It won't wash, Mullins. I heard what you were mumbling about recognition tokens. Let me take a guess. J.D. wouldn't stand for Jeff Davis, would it? Now, unless you want me to partly settle accounts with you about my brother before I turn you over to the army, you'd better tell me quick where the boys are."

A crafty smile played across Mullins' features. "Well now, that is the problem, isn't it? If you want to see you nephew safe, I suggest that you let me go. You understand the character of the two men who are holding them, don't you? If I'm not able to call them off, well, let's just say I couldn't guarantee how long those boys would remain healthy."

"I'll healthy you, you!—" shouted Tom, lunging across the counter. With a sweeping motion of his arm, Mullins knocked over the lamp, intending to plunge the room into darkness. Instead, it hit the floor with a crash and spread a pool of fire over the wood floor.

Reaching under the counter, the shopkeeper yanked out a .44 caliber Derringer. Tom, who was sprawled across the counter, rolled to the side, but not before Mullins' shot took him on the side of the head. Tom rolled heavily to the floor and lay still. Mullins paused only long enough to sweep the cuff links into his fist before lumbering heavily out the front door of the store.

The stirring sounds of the community told him that the gunshot had not gone unnoticed. Cursing to himself and moving as rapidly as his bulk permitted, he made his way home to where his buggy was already hitched up and waiting. On the way out of town, he noted grimly that flames could be seen through the store windows, and as he rounded a curve shutting out the view, he heard the church bell begin to give the alarm. "I hope he fries," he muttered as he drove off.

Tom was dragged from the fire by the hotel proprietor, McKenna. Ignoring the frantic activity of men scurrying about trying to save the building, he noted that Tom was still alive. The wound, which had knocked him unconscious, had just grazed the side of his head. McKenna and Parson Swift carried Tom to the parson's home, as it was nearer than the hotel. The parson's wife held a cold compress to Tom's head, and soon the wound stopped bleeding.

Tom began to come around as Mrs. Swift bathed his face with cool water, and all at once he gave a jerk and cried out "Mullins! He!—"

"Easy, Tom," urged the parson. "You've been shot, so lie still and rest."

Tom gathered his wits and then spoke again. "Did Mullins get away? Did someone catch him?"

"Do ye mean to say 'twas him as shot ye, lad?" inquired McKenna. "He hasna been seen by me this night. Have ye seen him, Parson?"

"No, but give the man a chance to tell us what he means, Mr. McKenna."

"To be sure," agreed the Scotsman. "Just take yer time, lad, an' tell us what this is all aboot."

Tom opened his eyes, then grimaced in pain and shut them again. Slowly, through gritted teeth he gasped, "Mullins . . . rebel spy, or . . . something. He and Byrd. Got the boys. Killed my brother. Got to follow."

As if even this effort was too taxing for his battered brain, Tom fell unconscious again.

Parson Swift looked at McKenna. "Go get Deputy Pettibone, would you, please, Mr. McKenna. I think he should hear this when Tom is able to speak."

"Ay, ay," agreed McKenna. "An' there'll be some others who'll take an interest in his tale as well, I'm thinkin'."

Robert Mullins' mind was whirling faster than the buggy wheels were turning. His first thoughts were of escape only. If he stayed behind, there would be questions—too many questions. How did the fire start? How did Tom Dawson come to be there, shot in the head? Mullins wondered briefly if he could have convinced the town that Dawson was a burglar suprised in the act of rifling the store's safe. But no, no one would believe that. What if Dawson lived?

Mullins knew his bullet had struck Dawson, for the storekeeper had seen him fall heavily to the floor; but in his bolt for the door, Mullins hadn't even considered stopping to see if the man was dead. Cursing his panic, Mullins thought, *If the man is truly dead, then perhaps I could have sold the burglar idea. Well, no chance of that now. But what if Dawson lives and tells what happened?*

That thought made Mullins snap the reins on the back of his horse and push him to greater speed. What must be done now was a desperate gamble. He must go instantly to Baker's home. The papers must be there; they *must!* Then he remembered the gold stored in the tunnel from the stage robberies in anticipation of the arms purchases. Right now, no one was pursuing him, but that fact might soon change. He might not be able to get back to Shadow Ridge to get the gold. Better to retrieve the gold first, then go and get the papers. He'd take Byrd from the cave as a guard, pick up Yancey at Baker's. Those two could be used to create a diversion if need be, or he could sacrifice them to fight his way clear. Even if he just delivered the gold to the Confederacy, he'd still be a hero, be recognized, be given his rightful place of honor. And, he reasoned, he needn't deliver all the gold. Some of it would compensate him for the loss of his store and his home in Greenville. Maybe there was a way to avoid paying Byrd and Yancey, too. He'd have to think about that.

And what about those two rats in the cave? Too much trouble to take along. And if the papers weren't at Baker's? If the Negro child wasn't telling all he knew? There was still the gold. And the two boys? Leave them tied up in the cave to starve? No, it would be better just to kill them now. The end result was the same anyway, but with no chance of their escaping or being found. Yes, that was all of it. Leave no loose ends. Get the gold, dispose of the two witnesses, go to Baker's, if only briefly, then move on to . . . to where? San Francisco. Of course! He'd have no difficulty hiding in that booming town. Surely he could find someone to contact, even without the papers. But to live in luxury—ah, that had an attraction all its own.

Mullins had already reached the bend of the road marked by a big oak tree with a huge bare limb that protruded some fifteen feet above the ground. The hanging tree, it was called. Mullins pulled off the road onto a patch of rocky ground. He got out of the buggy and led the horse down a depression bordering Poso Creek and around some brush to a point out of sight of the road.

He retrieved a lantern from the buggy and lit it. Tying the horse to a fallen tree, Mullins clambered awkwardly over it and climbed a steep bank to where some elderberry bushes grew up in front of an overhanging rock. At one time a stream had flowed here, but its course had since shifted underground to join the Poso at a lower point, leaving this concealed tunnel entrance.

Some years ago Mullins had discovered this connection with the summit of Shadow Ridge and all the useful caves and passages in between. Actually, Byrd Guidett had located the upper opening on some occasion when he was fleeing from the law; but after a conversation with Tommy Fitzgerald, Mullins himself had explored the depths of the cave and come upon the lower exit exactly where it was most needed. By leaving his horse at the top of Shadow Ridge, walking downward through the passage and picking up a previously arranged fresh mount here near the road, a man could cut a full day's travel off riding around the circumference of the peak—the way the roads actually went.

Mullins had carefully cultivated the notion that the mountain was haunted, that it was dangerous, that it was impassable. So far these stories and the natural barrenness of the western slope, together with the difficulty of climbing the eastern approach, had kept the mountain's secrets intact. Once or twice it had been necessary for some unfortunately curious folk to get "lost" or have "accidents," but until Jesse Dawson, no one had tried to ignore the danger and live right beside old Shadow. Well, Jesse had been rewarded for his curiosity, all right; maybe now Tom Dawson had been taken care of, too.

Byrd Guidett threw his canteen down in disgust. *Cold water and cold beans! I'm sick of this waitin' around here. There's more blue-bellied Yankees hereabouts than fleas on a dog's back*—he paused to scratch vigorously. *Or on me! An' for what? What if them papers ain't even in this here Baker's house? What if he don't know what I'm after? What if he tries to save his own skin by turnin' me in?*

Each round of Byrd's thoughts grew more and more angry. "An' even if I get them papers," he muttered, "Mullins'll jest take 'em without so much as a say. An' he'll be takin' the gold to spend on guns, which he'll try an' give to them crackers up in the hills. Huh! More'n likely they'll turn 'em on him! General Mullins! Governor Mullins! What a laugh!"

"Now that gold! In the jobs we already pulled there must be . . ." His shifty eyes got a faraway look, and he squinted up at the sky. "Thar must be close on a hundred thousand dollars! Man, I could live like a king in Frisco with that!"

The thought was more than he could stand. "What do I care who wins the war? I ain't seen 'em hang no medals on me, but if I stick around that fat fool Mullins, they'll be hangin' somethin' else!" He jumped to his feet.

"I'm for the gold," he declared to his horse, "an' right now!"

19

TOM SHOOK HIS head and tried to clear it. He sat up, over the protests of the parson and McKenna, and put one hand up to his now-bandaged skull. "Mullins. Did you catch him?"

"Na, lad, he's nae been seen, but the deputy is here now. Do ye feel able to tell him yer tale?"

Tom was able to repeat his story to Pettibone, giving more details about the cuff links. The deputy listened, his eyes wide with astonishment. As Tom recovered somewhat from the grazing wound, his explanation became clearer and all the pieces of the confusing puzzle fell into place.

"Then you believe Mullins masterminded the scheme to hold up the stages and use the gold for some plot?"

"Yes, but something got fouled up when Byrd killed that stranger. The only thing I can figure is that the dead man had something Mullins needed, so he had Byrd kidnap Mont to see if the child knew anything about it. He must think that whatever it is could be hidden in Colonel Baker's home, 'cause that's what I overheard him mumbling about tonight. He's bound to be desperate, because he must know that Baker's being guarded by the army."

Tom paused, and though he sat silently thinking, no one interrupted to voice an opinion. Finally, he began again. "That means that the boys, if they are still alive now, are in terrible danger. Mullins must have decided that they are no longer needed. Anyway, we can't delay. We've got to follow Mullins right away if the boys are to have any chance at all."

"But follow him where?" asked Pettibone. "We don't know which direction he went out of town, or if he's goin' straight to Baker's, or where his hideout is."

"Yes, we do! Don't you get it? Mullins kept you from searching Shadow Ridge for Guidett right after the killing at Granite. My brother was killed up there when we went looking for a trail, and I don't believe any longer that it was an accident."

"But there is na trail on the Ridge; ye said so yerself," observed McKenna.

"That's right, but there is a cave *under* it! I saw one entrance the day my brother was killed, but I didn't know it for what it was, and afterward I forgot about it till my dream. It must go all the way through and connect up the Tailholt road with this side of the mountain."

"All right, Tom, you've got it ciphered out for sure," said Pettibone. "What'll we do?"

"Parson, you and McKenna should ride to Baker's and alert the soldiers. Have them hold Mullins if he shows up, and get them ready for an attack in case Guidett and some of his kind try to break in."

"Pettibone, take Red and some men and hurry over to Tailholt. When you get there, go up the slope of Shadow. Even if we don't know exactly where that entrance is, they won't be expecting that bolt-hole to be watched, and you can block their escape."

"And what about the lower entrance, Tom—the one you say you saw on the Poso?" asked the parson.

"I'm counting on Mullins wanting to take his stolen gold with him. He must be going up that way right now. I'm going in after him."

Tom held up his hands to silence their protests. "There aren't enough of us to go around, and we've got to cover the other possibilities in case I'm wrong. But after all he's done to my family . . . just leave him to me; he's my meat."

"Death come aknockin' on dat gambler's door; said, 'O Gambler, are you ready to go?' " sang Mont.

"He said, 'No, no, no, no, no, 'cause I ain't got on my travelin' shoes," responded Nathan enthusiastically.

Neither boy heard the snorting and rustling sounds coming from the other cavern.

"Said, 'O Liar, are ya ready to go?' "

Even louder this time Nathan replied, "No, no, no, no, NO!"

An animal sound went unheard. If either boy had noticed, it would have reminded them of a hawk's diving screech as he swoops to kill.

"O Sinner, are ya ready to go?"

"No, no, no, no—AHHHH!"

The abrupt end to the song and the drawn-out scream from Nathan were caused by Yancey's sudden appearance in the entrance to the prison cave. His eyes were sunken and red-rimmed, which by contrast with his normally ashen skin color made his face appear skull-like. He had his boot knife in his hand and he moved it across in front of his body in slow, downward stabbing arcs.

His words, when they could be understood at all, were slurred and crazy. "No. NO! It won't take me. No! Jest one small death will do."

"Mistuh Yancey, we din't hear you. We'll be quiet now. You—"

"Run, Mont!" yelled Nathan. "He's plumb crazy!"

As if to punctuate Nathan's words, Yancey turned one of his stabbing motions into an outward flip of his wrist. Had not Nathan jerked Mont aside at that instant, Yancey's knife would have been imbedded in the black boy's chest. As it was, it bounced ringing off the rock wall.

"Come on, Mont!" Nathan yelled again, and the two made a dash past Yancey toward the passage. Yancey lunged at them as they went by, catching Nathan by the shirt collar. Nathan twisted in his grasp, crying, "Lemme go! Lemme go!"

Holding the strangling Nathan up by the throat, Yancey twisted the boy around so that they were at eye level. Yancey reached behind his collar with his free hand to draw the other knife that hung there.

Before the man had completely drawn it from its sheath, Mont threw himself at Yancey's legs, and all three tumbled down together. Yancey's cry rose again to a screech, "I've got two for you. Two! Not me; I ain't ready. But here, come and take these!"

Mont scrambled up on the man's chest and flung himself on the arm holding the knife. "Let 'im go! Nathan! Nathan!"

Nathan broke free from Yancey's clutch and struck the outlaw in the face as hard as he could with his two hands doubled together. He and Mont jumped up and dashed into the other cavern.

"Which way'll we go?" cried Nathan.

"Grab de lamp!" yelled Mont, "an' le's go down befo' he can get another light."

Snatching the lamp from the table, the boys jumped into the opening that led to the downward passage, just as Yancey picked himself up and came out the tunnel after them. He threw himself across the table at Nathan, but missed him and sprawled across its top.

Down the boys plunged, on a steeply slanted narrow rock path. Here the floor was slick with moisture coming from the nearby underground stream. With no time to pick their way, the boys skidded around corners and slammed into rocks. From behind them they could hear a keening sound: "I'll find 'em for ya. Just you wait here a spell. I'll bring 'em back."

They came to a place where the tunnel branched. One fork led downward, the other crossed the stream and went upward again. "What'll we do now?" asked Nathan. "He's still followin' us, like he can see in the dark!"

"No, dat ain't it," replied Mont. "He's jes' done dis trip enough so's he knows de way. But he can't foller de other path in de dark. Le's go up!"

The two plunged into the stream. It was icy cold and swifter than they expected. In an instant they were spun around. Mont collided with Nathan and both juggled frantically with the bobbing lamp. It fell against a boulder with a crash and was immediately extinguished.

Nathan jumped for the other bank and was rewarded with a handhold on the far side. Pulling himself up from the water, he turned and offered his hand to Mont. Mont climbed out on the bank, and they began crawling farther into the tunnel, judging their direction just by the upward feel. Behind them they could hear the water rushing down the narrow bed, but above that they could still make out Yancey's strange crooning monologue: "It won't be long now. Oh no, 'most any minute we'll be aknockin' on their door . . . knockin' on their door. Will they be ready? Le's go see, le's go see."

As the crying voice came closer, it was all they could do to lie still in the absolute darkness. Both boys were afraid that Yancey would decide to cross the stream. Nathan and Mont hugged each other and trembled with fear and cold.

Robert Mullins bustled up the tunnel. His thoughts were all of gold and San Francisco, of opulent comfort, culture, and attentive service. Every few steps he paused to wheeze at the labor of the climb up inside the mountain; then he resumed a panting pace, impatient now that his mind was made up to get his hands on the wealth stockpiled there.

He was sweating, partly with exertion and partly with the flush of anticipation. He'd decided that he could convince Byrd that it was time to transport the gold to buy arms; and after enlisting Byrd's help in loading the gold into Mullins' buggy, he'd make off with all of it. With a smile he patted his huge belly at the top of his trousers. Abruptly his smile faded as the handle of the pistol he expected to feel wasn't there. He tried to remember what he had done with the Derringer after shooting Tom. He could have sworn he'd thrust it into his waistband. Frantically he patted his vest and trouser pockets, then, with a relieved sigh, his outside coat pocket. There was the pistol. Mullins recalled that the thought of climbing over the rocks at the cave's mouth with a loaded pistol bound against his gut had made him uneasy, so he had transferred the small weapon to the deep pocket on the outside of his coat. He drew it out to examine it in the lamplight and remembered that he had fired one of its two shots but hadn't reloaded it. "Better safe than sorry," he muttered, and his pudgy fingers squirmed into a vest watch pocket until closing on another .44 cartridge. He broke open the breech and, discarding the spent casing, replaced it with the new one before returning the gun to his coat pocket.

The next part of his hike was Mullins' least favorite, for it involved his girth in a most unpleasant way. The passage he was in continued on past a crevice in the floor some hundred feet farther before coming to a dead-end. The true route lay down through the opening in the floor of the tunnel. A short drop would land him in another parallel passage, from which the journey up continued. A limestone ledge was only four feet below, but the process involved setting down the lantern, fitting himself into the opening and groping with his feet for the ledge. There he could stand and retrieve the lamp before stepping on down another three feet to the passage floor.

He put the lantern down close to the edge and eased himself into the opening. His small feet began pawing at the rock in search of the ledge as his weight transferred to his arms. The moment's effort made him puff, but his toes located the spot and he moved to grasp the lamp and continue down. But he couldn't move. He had grown so fat that, with the addition of the heavy coat and the presence of the Derringer pushing against his hip, he was unable to slide any farther down. Standing on his boot tips, he tried to raise himself back up to the space above, but his arms could not support his poundage and overcome the friction of the tight fit. With his arms stuck above the hole and his legs straining sideways to maintain contact with the small ledge, he made a most effective cork in a bottle.

"Where did ya go, little travelers? Come out and meet a friend," crooned Yancey. "Are ya ready to go?"

He scraped on down the tunnel, past the side branch that the boys had chosen as a hiding place. Feeling his way along the limestone passage, he slowly waved his knife back and forth in front of him. Occasionally he would rub it against his shirt sleeve as if wiping it clean of blood.

He came to a place where the passage widened out and then split into a maze of smaller channels woven among a thicket of limestone columns that reached up to the roof. For some reason, Yancey decided that the boys were playing hide-and-seek with him in this room, so he began to creep softly around each corner, thrusting ahead of him with the knife. He lowered his monologue to a whisper, but continued chanting, "No, no, no, no, ain't ready to go, 'cause I ain't got on my travelin' shoes."

Nathan and Mont were petrified. They had heard Yancey pass their escape route and could not bear the thought of his attempting to cross over. They feared that they could not cross the stream again without making so much noise that he would hear and return to catch them, so they decided to crawl farther into the side tunnel and hope for a way out.

Mont crawled in front, with Nathan coming along behind, one hand grasping Mont's ankle. They stayed down on all fours because in the total blackness they were afraid that they would fall over an unseen drop-off.

After crawling some distance, they felt rather than saw the passage widen around them. They had reached another good-sized room, but had no way of guessing its extent, the height of the roof, or where it led.

"What if we're crawlin' straight for a dead-end?" whispered Nathan.

"Does you want to go back?" returned Mont over his shoulder.

Nathan thought about the tunnel they had left behind with Yancey and his knife and shuddered. "No!" he whispered urgently. "Only, let's get on out of here." Then he added, "Please, God!"

To which Mont just as fervently replied a whispered "Amen!"

Mont put out his hand to move a bit farther and drew it back in horror. "Nathan!" he breathed, "dey's a dead body here! Ah can feel his trousers, an' his leg is cold an' stiff!"

Nathan jerked backward and wanted desperately to run, but a supreme effort made him hold still, deciding that a dead body was less of a threat than a live Yancey. "Are you sure?" he asked.

"Well, ah thinks I is. Here's his one leg an' here's another. My, dey do feel hard!" Gritting his teeth, Mont gingerly knocked his knuckles against the leg.

"Whooee!" he breathed. "It ain't a dead man; it's jes' a pile of sacks or somethin'."

"Sacks?" whispered Nathan, curious in spite of the recent scare. "What would a heap of sacks be doin' here?" He crawled up past Mont's side and reached out to touch the objects in front of them. "You're right. It's a whole mess of canvas bags. What do you suppose is in 'em?"

With these words he began to poke around the sacks, feeling the heavy oblong objects contained in them. After a moment's thought, he said excitedly, "Mont, it's the gold—the stolen gold! This here is the loot stolen from the stage holdups. I bet there's even a reward for findin' this!"

When Mont made no comment to share his friend's enthusiasm, Nathan asked, "What's the matter, Mont, ain't this excitin'?"

"Nathan, it's *too* excitin'! Don'cha see? Dis here is de gang's loot! Dis ain't no secret tunnel; dey knows jes' where it is. An' sooner or later, dey's gonna think to look here!"

20

"**W**AL, WAL, WHAT have we got here? An ol' hog stuck in a gate? My, don't he squeal!"

"Byrd, thank God you're here. I'm stuck in this cursed hole. Pull me up, and be quick about it!"

"Now hold on a mite. I seen yer buggy asettin' down to the bottom. You musta come here in the middle of the night. That ain't like you fat boys, what likes yer soft beds. Now, why d'ya s'pose a fine citizen like ol' Robert Mullins'd be out here this time of night?"

"Pull me out!" Mullins swore at Byrd, but could move neither up nor down.

"Tut, tut! Such speech to be acomin' from a church-goin' feller." Byrd was clearly enjoying Mullins' predicament, and the storekeeper was about to be overcome with rage when a thought struck him.

"Why are you coming from outside the cave? Where's Yancey? Why aren't you guarding those two brats? And who's watching Baker's house? Baker's," he said again. "Did you get the papers? Is that why you're here?"

"Naw," replied Byrd with a grin. "I'm here for the same reason as you, I reckon. I been wet, an' I been cold, but I ain't agonna be poor much longer."

Mullins suddenly shivered all over. "You've got it all wrong, Byrd," he soothed. "I was coming up here to divide the gold with all three of us. Yes, that's what I came here for."

"Ain't that mighty white of you, General Mullins? Wal', the way I figgers, two shares is better'n three. An' one is even better yet. Ain't that the way you got it figgered?"

Before Mullins could utter a word of protest or plea, Byrd drew his Walker and shot Robert Mullins between the eyes. Mullins feet slipped from the ledge and the weight of his body caused him to fall heavily through the opening.

"Ain't that somethin'?" remarked Byrd wonderingly. "He weren't really stuck any of the time."

"We are climbin' Jacob's ladder," crooned Yancey, "sol'jers of the cross." Around the maze of limestone byways he glided, stabbing his knife into corners and into side passageways before entering them himself.

"Climbin' Jacob's ladder, gonna climb them golden stairs. Golden stairs," he repeated. "Gonna climb right up to the sun. All kindsa light up on that golden stair."

"Gold," he repeated. "Up the ladder to the gold."

"My, my, my," he said, a crafty grin playing over his features, "what have we got here? Lights to light the night, right on up the golden ladder."

So saying, he produced a box of matches from his pants' pocket, which his fever-ridden brain had not remembered till now.

Striking one, he turned about to face back up toward the passage he had just descended and sang to himself, "Are ya ready to go? They said, 'No, no, no, no, no . . .'"

Tom halted Duncan beside Mullins' buggy and Byrd's horse. Not knowing exactly where to look along the banks of Poso Creek for the tunnel entrance he expected to find, Tom had ridden slowly along the road. His pace had been much quieter than Byrd's pounding ride, so it was easy to get off the road to watch without being spotted. Tom didn't know Byrd for who he was, but he reasoned that few people up to any good would be out in the middle of the night, and fewer still would have a reason to turn off at this spot.

He had allowed Duncan his head, and the canny horse, like a huge bloodhound, had followed Byrd's track as it wound down to the stream bed. Tom had watched as Byrd lit a lantern and climbed up and into the entrance to the cave. What with Mullins having such a long head start, Tom had been convinced that to tackle the unknown rider would delay him further or in some way warn the fleeing storekeeper.

Now Tom tried to decide what to do next. He thought briefly of returning to town for help since his idea was correct and he had run Mullins to earth, but he was afraid they might leave before he could return. He also couldn't stand the thought of the boys being held captive one moment longer. Tom waited a couple of minutes; then taking a bull's-eye lantern from a saddlebag, he lit it and proceeded to enter the cave.

Just inside the tunnel mouth, he heard a gunshot. Tom's heart sank. "Oh, God," he prayed, "let the boys be all right! Don't let me come this close and not rescue them."

He carried his lantern in his left hand and his Colt in his right. Even though his lantern might betray his presence, Tom hoped that anyone he might encounter would not be climbing around this secret place with his weapon at the ready; so he felt he would have the advantage.

Now his insides were twisting. He didn't know whether he should run ahead toward the sound of the shot or continue his cautious stalk. When no further shots were fired, and no other sounds indicated another person's location, Tom decided to continue moving quietly.

Up ahead, just around a bend of the tunnel, he suddenly saw a light. Tom dropped to a crouch. Setting his own lantern down behind him, he drew as far over to the other wall of the passage as possible, keeping close to the shadows and advancing with the Colt leading the way. Carefully he peered around a corner.

He saw Mullins' lantern still sitting in the middle of the cavern floor. Tom wondered if it could be a trap. Reaching down with his left hand, he picked up a small chunk of quartz. Preparing himself to fight, he hurled the rock at the lamp. He missed, but the resulting clatter sounded as loud as an avalanche to his ears. When nothing happened and no one appeared, Tom decided to chance going on forward. He slowly approached the crevice, scanning all around as he did so.

After another quick glance around, Tom looked downward into the opening. There lay Robert Mullins, his jowls sagging limply. He seemed to have grown a third eye in his forehead. Tom guessed at what had transpired, but wasted no more thoughts on Robert Mullins. Instead, he made a quick examination of the hole and spotted the ledge for stepping down. He swung his legs into the opening, aware that he was going to be completely helpless for a moment. With this thought, he skipped stepping to the ledge, but allowed himself to drop through the hole in one motion, just missing Mullins' body as he did so.

Almost without thinking, he bent and scooped up the Derringer that had fallen from Mullins' pocket, and thrust it through his belt. Looking around quickly, Tom guessed that he would have already drawn a shot if there were a sentry, so he stepped back up onto the ledge and retrieved the lamp from beside the hole. He then proceeded to advance up the passage as before.

"Oh, Gambler, are ya ready to go? Go up Jacob's ladder?" Yancey was moving rapidly back up the tunnel, striking matches as he went and walking quickly with the help of the light. He moved purposefully now, his knife carried blade upward in his fighting stance. No longer did he wave it around or stab it into corners. He clearly had a destination in mind, and he was heading there.

The boys had climbed over the sacks of gold, reasoning that the best they could do now was to try to get still deeper into the side passage. They were still crawling, but now Nathan was leading. Mont was praying aloud, "Oh, Jesus, he'p us, Jesus, he'p us get outta here."

Byrd could hear some sounds up ahead of him, but he couldn't quite make out the words. "Blast!" he said, drawing his Walker, "what in blazes is goin' on up here?"

"Yancey?" he called out. "Yancey, is that you? Where are ya?"

Yancey stopped lighting matches as he heard Byrd's yell. He had just reached the point at which the side tunnel branched off to reach the gold. Yancey lit one more in order to get his bearings; then he stepped into the stream and crossed over. Just on the other side he stopped, his back pressed against the wall of the passage and waited. "Death come aknockin' on that sinner's door," he muttered.

Upward went Byrd. He noticed the trail of burned-out matches. "Those kids musta run off, an' Yancey's tryin' to find 'em. Why ain't he got a lantern, though?"

When Byrd reached the side tunnel, he raised his lantern high over his head so as to illuminate the far bank. Sure enough, he could just make out the wet tracks where someone had crossed. "Yancey!" he yelled, "C'mon back out here, an' we'll hunt 'em together. C'mon, ya cussed snake, I ain't gettin' my feet wet less'n ya tell me what's up!"

There was no reply. "You don't s'pose ol' Yancey got to hankerin' after that gold hisself?" mused Byrd aloud. "You cain't trust nobody!" As he stepped into the stream, he saw a flash reflected from Yancey's knife as Yancey lunged from the shadows. Byrd's foot turned on a rock, his sideways sprawl saving him. Yancey's thrust was intended to catch Byrd in the stomach just as he emerged from the crossing, but instead it caught only air.

Byrd's revolver leaped into his hand, and he fired. Byrd saw the first bullet strike Yancey, but in twisting around and firing, Byrd dropped his lantern into the water. He fired twice more in quick succession—once into the body he saw starting to topple and once more into the blackness of the floor where he believed Yancey to be.

All was still. "Yancey?" Byrd called softly. "I sure hope you is dead, but if ya ain't you better talk nice an' sweet to me less'n my finger gets to jumpin' again." There was no reply—not even a groan. "I reckon I'm done with you," he concluded, pulling himself up out of the water. Carefully he kicked Yancey's body, holding his Walker ready. He kicked again—harder this time.

"Yup. I don't know what got inta ya, but I figgered it'd end thisaway anyhow, iff'n that's any comfort to ya."

He rummaged through the corpse's pockets till he found the matches.

"Jest a handful left? I guess ya won't be needin' 'em, ol' cuss, so I'll jest mosey along an' check on my gold."

The boys froze at the sounds coming from the tunnel behind them; they heard Byrd's yell echo down the passage. "We'll hunt 'em together." When the shots came, the boys didn't know what to make of it. They waited silently, hearts pounding like a blacksmith's hammers as they waited to see what would happen next.

Back toward the sacks of gold they peered, straining to see something through the darkness. Presently they could see a flicker of light, and once they heard Byrd swear as he held a match too long and burned himself. They saw him illuminated in the scratching hiss of another match as he crouched over the gold, his face an evil mask of gloating delight, made hideous by the strange play of shadows around his beard.

Nathan gave an involuntary gasp, and instantly clapped his hand over his mouth. But Byrd had heard. He looked into the darkness where they lay and called out, "Is you kids there? Come on out. I ain't gonna hurt ya. Yancey done went crazy, but I've fixed him, an' the ol' fat boy, too. Come on out now, I say."

When neither child moved or uttered another word, Byrd gave an exasperated sigh. "You'uns is determined to make this tough, ain't ya?" He shook out the match and lit another while counting to himself. "Lessee, one bullet for Mullins an' three for Yancey. Why, that leaves me jest enough, don't it?"

"Don't count on it," said a voice from behind him. Hearing the gunshots, Tom had blown out his lantern and had been watching as Byrd crossed the stream, following by the flashes of Byrd's matches. He had arrived just in time.

Byrd whirled, dropping the match and plunging the cave into darkness as he did so. He fired a shot in the direction from which Tom's voice had come, then threw himself to the floor of the cavern and found shelter behind the gold. His bullet caught Tom's gun barrel and spun the revolver out of Tom's grasp.

"Whyn't ya shoot, Dawson? Could it be I've killed ya jest like we did yer brother? Like I'm fixin' to do with them two brats?"

Byrd reached into his pocket and drew out another match. Holding his cocked pistol across the canvas sacks, he struck the match on the cave's floor and held it aloft in his left hand.

Lying just a few feet away was Tom. Byrd noticed the shattered Colt Navy lying against the far wall and the bandages swathing Tom's head. "Why, shoot, Dawson," said Byrd, rising to his feet, "you was 'most dead already. But, since I got this here bullet, I'll use it on you, an' then I'll take care of yer brats. An' then," he added, leering, "I aim to pay a little visit to that Emily lady."

At these words, Nathan rose up behind Byrd, shouting, "No! no! You can't hurt my ma!"

"What the—?" was all Byrd got out of his mouth before Tom snatched the Derringer from his belt and put a .44 slug straight through Byrd Guidett's heart.

"Keep still, boys," called Tom. "Let's wait to see that this isn't a trick."

A moment later he called, "Say, where's that light coming from?" A faint silvery glow was coming from the far end of the tunnel. By it, Tom could see Nathan and Mont come out of their concealment, and could make out Byrd's body slumped over the sacks of gold.

"Uncle, Uncle! Mistuh Tom!" came the glad cries as the boys ran to Tom.

After a moment of embracing, Tom observed, "That's got to be daylight, boys. Let's go see where it leads."

Around the next corner, the boys drew up against Tom in sudden alarm. Daylight was pouring into the cave through a hole in the roof, and lying at the bottom of a ramp of dirt leading up and out was the skull of Tommy Fitzgerald's gigantic grizzly.

Tom laughed as he hugged the two boys again, and putting his arms around the boys' shoulders, he climbed up the incline to stand in the morning light. He stood looking down the eastern slope of Shadow Ridge toward where the ranch and Emily were waiting. "Come on, boys," he said. "Let's go home!"

RIDERS
OF THE
SILVER RIM

To the memory of Jesse Dodson Wattenbarger,
Potsy . . .
accomplished blacksmith,
skillful stage driver
and master storyteller . . .

PROLOGUE

HE WAS NOT sure when he abandoned the blanket roll. He probably parted company with it some time after discarding his coat and before losing the empty water bottle. He had continued to carry the bottle long after its contents were gone, hoping against hope that he would soon locate a spring. Later on the loss did not seem to matter.

Even with a derby on his head, the sunlight beating down on him seemed to be a physical weight on his neck and shoulders. His back and legs ached from supporting the burden. His head felt swollen to the point of bursting, while his body seemed shrunken, aged and frail.

The sun reflected off the sand into his face, hitting him mercilessly on both cheeks as wave on wave of heat rolled over him. It was like walking into an oven. His features were baked like overdone bread, his eyes swelled to blurred slits, his lips cracked and blackened. His enlarged tongue felt like an old, dried-up stick.

He no longer perspired. His body had no more moisture to contribute to the Mojave afternoon. What sweat had dried and darkened into salty rings on his flannel shirt now gritted and chafed against his parched skin. But he did not notice anymore.

How he continued to move forward he could not have said. The trail stretched clearly into the heat-swirled distance, but he saw only the space of his next three steps. A nagging voice in the back of his mind told him that to stop moving was to die. For a time he argued with the voice, favoring a rest, a short break, a chance to sit down. Now the effort of disputing it seemed greater than the plodding on. He was resolved to walk until he found water—or until night fell and he could no longer keep to the path.

One step became two, then three, then another and another. There was no feeling in his tormented feet; perhaps their ache just blended with the rest of his misery. Despite his constant motion, he might as well have been simply marking time. The mountains ahead came no closer, and the hills he had descended to reach the desert plain had receded to merge with a brown horizon. The salt pan which he had been crossing for what seemed like weeks now appeared bowl-shaped, curving upward all around him.

Maybe the desert really *was* beginning to curve upward; or maybe he was just losing the strength to step over the grains of sand in his way. In either case, his constant tread became a lurching shuffle, his body bent forward from the waist. As if he were walking into a gale-force wind, the heat would not let him fall. He leaned into it, embraced it, as if to straighten up would push him over backward.

He continued staggering forward until something besides the heat worked its way into his thoughts. The sound had been there for a long while without his notice, and when he did notice it, he ignored it. Finally something demanded that he seek the source of the whispering, sighing noise. He peered about him, moving his head painfully from side to side— cautiously, as if he feared it would topple from his body. Nothing around for miles seemed to have the capacity for sound, yet the sighing had moved in closer; had become a rustling.

He blinked, then stopped stock still. The dull realization dawned that he *hadn't* blinked—a shadow had passed over his path. He forced himself to lean back, painfully straightening his neck, willing his chin from his chest, sending hammer blows of pain into his back.

His face sought the sky, and through the tiny slits of his tortured eyelids he saw it momentarily darken, then brighten again. He had the fleeting thought that he was grateful for even an instant's respite from the intense rays of the sun.

Then he saw it: a buzzard flew in lazy circles over his head. Higher still, two of its feathered companions soared, banked, and spiraled. The wings of the nearest bird made the slightest whispering sound as it passed directly overhead; otherwise the three were silent.

The man bared his teeth, even though the grimace made his lips split and crack more. He raised a clenched fist over his head. A guttural croak escaped him, more from his chest than from his burning throat.

He swayed, moving in an arc counter to the circling birds. His chin, once stuck to his chest, now seemed impossible to lower. He saw rather than felt his arm fall heavily to his side. He attempted to turn his head, surprised at the involuntary action, but his whole body twisted instead, and he fell awkwardly on his side in the sand.

A shadow crossed his face, then returned to hover directly above, and something rustled close by. He struggled, attempting to flail his arms to ward off the vultures. *My eyes* he thought, *they're after my eyes!* His convulsive heave produced only a shudder of his frame. *Roll over,* he pleaded with himself.

Then the stirring came again, a soft fluttering. When it stopped, a soft voice out of the shadow spoke. "You poor man! Just lie still, here's some water."

Water! Like rain the words splashed on his soul. *Water! Saved!* A delicious coolness soothed his lips. He pursed them in a sucking motion; the moisture trickled down his throat—shocking, as if he had swallowed ice.

Tiny sip followed tiny sip. Some of the cool liquid spilled over onto his eyelids, and a hand as gentle as a feather's touch soothed his ravaged cheeks. He jerked his head, trying to shout not to waste a single drop.

The voice came again, "Don't worry, there's plenty and to spare. Your poor eyes—your poor, poor eyes."

Another splash on his lips and then another on his eyes. His body began to wake up, as if missing parts were getting reattached.

"More," he managed to groan, "more."

"Yes, of course, there is more. But slowly, slowly." The voice sounded like distant, gentle chimes.

This time he felt the touch of the bottle on his lips. A moment of panic struck him. He must have the water bottle! His arms responded to his brain, flinging awkwardly together over his chest. His clawing fingers found a sleeve, an arm, then lost it. There was a startled half-cry, and the shadow over his face retreated. The water bottle dropped onto his chest, sprinkling his face even as he grasped it eagerly and upended its contents into his mouth. His eyelids parted momentarily, and he saw the most delicate features framed in a ghostly shimmering light.

Half the contents of the bottle crashed into his stomach at once and hit his wracked and twisted insides as if he had swallowed a rock. The rock became a bomb that exploded in his brain, and consciousness fled away, leaving his punished body in peace.

1

FROM THE HIGH vantage point of a rock-strewn bluff, the old Mojave Indian chief watched the struggle of the tall white man in the strange hat against the sun and the vultures.

The old chief could see what the white man could not: the town of Garson was only a short walk from where he had fallen. He knew the miners of the Silver Rim also could look up into the sky and see the black dots of the turkey-buzzards as they swooped and circled overhead. Perhaps they would come to the sunlight from their dark hole in the ground and think a wild horse had fallen to die in the desert. Later, they would hear that one of their own had fallen. They would wag their heads in wonder that anyone had tried to cross the desert of the Mojave without water, without a horse, in headgear that wouldn't keep the sun off a prairie dog.

For a long time the Indian watched as the body of the fool was slung across the back of the mule. Perhaps the man was dead. He would be taken to Garson and buried, then. If he was still alive, it would not be long before he died. *These white men do not belong in our land,* the chief reasoned. *The spirits take revenge beneath the sun.*

As the mule was led away, the old chief turned his eyes back toward Garson and then to the west, where his own village nestled between the cliffs of Wild Rose Canyon.

Once, his people had been fierce and proud. They had contested dominion of the western lands with the Navajo and the Apache. The coming of the white man with their repeating rifles had broken them. Now the soldiers thought so little of them that the Indians were left to fade away in the desert.

The chief knew his white neighbors would not even consider their little camp a village. A migratory band, his tribe traveled from the Sierra peaks, where they gathered pinyons for grinding into flour, to these desert canyons where they obtained maguey for making *pulque,* a venomous, fermented brew that whites would not drink. Wild Rose Canyon was more a favorite campground than a permanent settlement.

Chief Pitahaya sighed deeply. *I am only half a ruler now,* he thought with sorrow.

They had a miserable existence, their old glory gone. The whites despised them, and they were an easy prey to white diseases and vices. Some Indians would even barter their squaws for whiskey, which they much preferred to pulque.

Chief Pitahaya argued, threatened and railed against the growing depravity of his people, but without the authority to force compliance. The white man's Indian Agents offered no assistance, and the Army said it was no business of theirs. There was no law in the desert.

The Chief watched the dust stirred by the little mule while he thought what must be done. He closed his eyes and considered the frailty of these white intruders. *What we need,* he whispered to the spirits, *is a good war. What pride we had in the days of my youth when a call to punish the Membreno horse-eaters would be answered by two hundred strong warriors! Even when the whites came to our sands, we made them go everywhere in companies of fifty for safety. And many were the fifty who never reached their stone lodges.*

Now look at us! the old chief mourned. *Faugh! We are too feeble to fight a determined gang of lizards. Nothing seems to stir us enough to shake off this sleep-with-open-eyes. Perhaps I was wrong when the white soldiers grew so powerful that I counseled Sihuarro to give up war. Perhaps I should have told him, "It is a good day to die."*

Joshua Roberts sat bolt upright. His heart was pounding so hard that with each beat it threatened to burst out of his chest.

"Easy there, young fella," ordered a gruff voice. "You'd best lie still a mite longer."

"Longer? How long . . . ? Where? Who?" Joshua was trembling all over like an aspen in the breezes of the Sierra passes.

"For a fella pretty much cooked, you're plumb full of questions, ain't cha?" The voice was amused. "Lie down 'fore you shake the bed apart."

Joshua obliged. It wasn't difficult to see the wisdom of the advice, especially since he had to squeeze his eyes shut to make the room stop spinning. When he opened them again, he found himself staring at a patched canvas roof strung over a frame of mismatched wooden slats.

He was lying on a cot in someone's tent, but he could not remember how he had gotten there. He touched his face—gingerly—and noticed that the skin felt thick and leathery. The swelling around his eyes had gone down, and his tongue seemed to be in working order again.

A round, bearded face leaned into his view. Bright blue eyes peered out from lines and crevices which mirrored the desert landscape. The old man looked to Josh as if he had been carved from the desert floor and brought to life. Curly gray hair escaped from a crushed and shapeless felt hat and blended into a curly gray beard. The beard was clipped short around his jaw. He was dressed peculiarly in red flannel long-johns, stained with sweat. He was caked with a layer of dust from his hat to his toes.

Joshua was trembling with cold. How had he come to be in a place so cold, when the last thing in his memory was the searing heat?

"Who are you?" he managed to ask. "And where am I?"

The old man spread another blanket over him. "More questions, eh? Why don't cha save them questions for later and concentrate on breathin' first?" The dusty face split into an enormous grin. The leathery skin folded into a thousand fine lines, as if life here had eroded away his youth.

Again Joshua touched his own face. He wondered if he looked like the man.

"Please," he whispered with a shudder. "How long have I been here?"

"Well, for three days you been out of your skull, boy. Ravin' on 'bout this 'n that—now and then you'd haul off and yell, *My eyes! They're after my eyes!*"

Joshua nodded grimly as waves of the horrid memory flooded through him. "It was the vultures. I thought they were going to pluck my eyes out."

The old man shook his head. "It like to clabber my blood the way you was goin' on. Plumb loco."

"There *were* vultures. And then the lady. . . ." He stopped abruptly and struggled to sit up again. "Where is she?"

The old man stepped back warily. "Are you fixin' to rave some more, boy? There ain't nobody here but you 'n me."

Joshua let his head fall back. "I'm sure of it . . . there *was* a woman, a beautiful woman . . . just after I pitched over in the sand. Thought I was a goner, but she gave me a drink. I'd like to thank her."

"There ain't nobody here besides us two, unless you count Jenny out yonder." He jerked a thumb toward the open tent flap. "She's a gal all right, but she ain't no lady."

Joshua carefully propped himself up on his elbow. Through the flap he could see a little mule with her head drooping and her eyes half-closed in the early morning light.

"But I saw a lady—I even touched her arm." The vision in his mind was strong.

The old man shrugged and reached for a pair of mud-caked trousers that probably could have stood alone. "When I found you, I thought you was dead. Propped up against a rock like you couldn't go no further and had give up. Ain't no fine lady gonna be out in this outpost o' hell, boy."

Joshua lay still, struggling to reconstruct how he had gotten here . . .

wherever *here* was. He hadn't the strength to ask more questions, and the old man set about his morning chores without offering further explanation.

Presently his host returned with a tin plate. "Sorry it ain't more, boy. I ain't much a hand at cookin', and I ain't had time since comin' across you to get no Mexican strawberries on the fire." He thrust the plate into Joshua's hands. Two rock-hard, over-sized lumps of dough that Joshua recognized as yeast powder biscuits sat in a puddle of bacon grease.

Joshua dipped a biscuit in the fat and took a tentative bite. He was surprised to discover how good it tasted. Between mouthfuls and sips from a canteen, he listened as the old man launched into an account of himself and the last few days.

"My folks hung the name of John Springer on me. But where I'm known in these parts, folks call me Pickax. *Pick* for short. This is my digs, for now. Course, I might be forty mile away after breakfast, if I've a mind." Pick waved a stubby arm toward a lumpy sandstone rise visible across the dry wash. "You was just over that ridge yonder. Town of Garson is just up that way a piece. Fact is, I was comin' back from there with my grub when I seen you. You didn't weigh no more 'n a sack of potatoes, you was so dried up. I slung you over Jenny and brung you here."

Josh's eyes suddenly narrowed and his expression turned grim. "You meet anyone, coming from Garson? I mean—did you see a man dressed in dark clothes? Dark hat. Swarthy skin?"

"Is this another dream, boy? Ain't nobody crazy 'nough to be out in the heat of the day 'cept you and me. And I can't figure why you was out there without water."

"I *had* water. I may be a tenderfoot—" Joshua shrugged ruefully at the accuracy of this statement. "But even I knew not to start out without water. I met up with a man in Mojave who said he knew the way to the mines, and we traveled together. He said he knew a short-cut, so we turned off the road. Slept out that night. Next morning, he was gone—with both water bottles and every cent I had in the world."

Pick made a noise low in his throat like a dog walking stiff-legged toward a fight. "And then what happened, boy?"

"I figured I could follow his tracks. Figured he would head for more water. I finally struck the road I was following when you found me, but I never saw the man again."

Pick's face grew dark as Josh told him the story, and his outrage exploded. "He ain't nothin' but a murderer! Ought to be strung up pronto for doin' you that way. D'ya think you'd know him again?"

"Anywhere."

"Know his name?"

"Called himself Gates."

Pickax nodded solemnly, then after a few minutes' pondering the tale, he looked curiously at Josh. "Well, you know *my* name, and I know *his* name. But you ain't give me *your* name, boy!"

Joshua extended his hand with some effort. "My folks gave me the name Joshua Roberts," he said. "And that's what I go by. My friends call me Josh."

After two more days in the care of the old prospector, Joshua was able to move about again, but slowly.

On his walk across the desert, Joshua's feet had burned and blistered inside his boots. Pickax had cut away the leather and soaked his raw flesh in a bucket of precious water. In this way, Pick explained, Joshua absorbed two quarts of fluid while still unconscious.

As he regained his strength on biscuits, bacon and the beans which Pickax called "Mexican strawberries," Joshua had time to ponder the strange vision of the woman who had given him a drink. And, during the long, cold nights, he considered the thief named Gates who had left him to die.

Pickax said that the robber must have taken one look at Joshua's size and strength and known he couldn't take him any other way than by stealth. "You got the hands of a blacksmith, boy," the old man had commented.

When Josh confirmed that blacksmithing had indeed been his trade, Pickax grinned and shrugged as if he knew all along.

This last matter troubled Joshua. What might he have said about his past when he'd been out of his head? Did the old man know about the dead teamster back in Springfield? Had he pieced that part of the puzzle together?

"Men ain't got a past when they come out here," Pickax told Josh one night as he blew out the lantern. "Your life. My life. It ain't between nobody but you and the Almighty. There's no laws out here, boy. And nobody needs to know your business."

And so the terrible accident which had driven Joshua from his home and led him to this desolate land remained unspoken. The colors of his old life had been abandoned to bleach away in the sun of the Mojave. Yes, he was still Joshua Roberts, but when he looked into the cracked mirror in Pick's tent, he could find only hints of the man he'd been in Illinois.

Perhaps he had finally run far enough to escape his memories. Maybe this place was close enough to hell that just *being here* was his atonement! With its freezing nights and searing days, the desert offered a man no comfort, no real peace.

There was no past here, Pick said. Only *Now* and the *Future.* Joshua Roberts had three things he wanted to do. Work again, find the woman who had given him water, and find the man named Gates who hadn't bothered to waste a bullet on him but who'd left him most certainly to die in the desert sun.

2

JOSHUA'S STILL-TENDER feet were sheathed in an old pair of the prospector's boots—mercifully, a size too large. He had not shaved in two weeks, and what precious water remained did not allow for washing his clothes. He wanted a bath more than anything, and although Pickax did not himself approve of baths, he informed Josh that such luxuries were indeed available in Garson.

On this morning, without warning, Pickax announced, "Goin' to Garson. Grub and water. Grab your hat if you're comin' along," he said, eying the derby a tad dubiously.

Joshua pulled on his hat and lent a feeble hand loading the empty water barrels onto Jenny's back. It was fourteen long miles to Garson. Fourteen miles to water. Joshua suddenly realized what a sacrifice the old man had made to share water and food with a half-dead stranger. And Joshua didn't have a penny to repay him.

"I'd like to find work, and pay back what I owe you," Josh said as they led the mule away from camp in the pre-dawn light.

Pick looked back at his ragged tent. "It don't matter none. I enjoy the company. You talk better'n ol' Jenny here. I'll put in a good word for you with Mister Morris at the Silver Rim Mine. Maybe you can grub-stake me someday."

As they trudged over the desolate countryside, Joshua could not help imagining that he would find Gates in Garson and recover what had been stolen from him. Then he would be able to repay Pickax, buy himself some clothes and have a bath. Pick told him that he should buy a gun and learn to use it. He had never felt the need to carry a side-arm before.

Back in Springfield, few men had dared to challenge the strength in his six-foot-three frame. He had used his size to wrestle down horses protesting a shoeing. But out in the West, Pick insisted, it was prudent to carry a gun.

"There ain't never been a sheriff in Garson," Pick explained. "It ain't likely one would live too long, anyway."

He then proceeded to spend the hours of their journey telling Joshua the history of the little town. After all, he had been here looking for *The Lost Gunsight Mine* long before Garson was anything but a couple of tents and a well. It was hardly more than that now, according to Pick.

Still an hour's walk away, the little town became visible in the distance. It looked to be a ramshackle collection of wooden and canvas buildings shimmering in the heat, some more permanent than others but none very substantial. Pickax claimed you could throw a Chinaman through any of the walls, and the truth of this had been demonstrated more than once.

For all its flimsy construction, Garson performed the necessary functions to be called a town. About half the population consisted of hard-rock miners. The other half were there to sell their wares to the miners—or was it to prey on them? Shopkeepers, saloonkeepers, bankers and card sharps, cooks, seamstresses, and ladies of easy virtue made up the citizenry that was not mining.

Garson had a chance to become a town twenty years earlier than it did, Pick explained, owing to an unusual circumstance. A French prospector named DuBois had passed through the area hoping to locate gold. He had arrived in California too late for the rush of '49 and ended up wandering through the Panamint and Argus mountains, hoping to make his pile. When he discovered that his rifle sight was borken, an Indian guide from the local band of Mojaves offered to repair it. Reasoning that if the firearm was never returned it was useless anyway, the prospector agreed. To his surprise, it was returned in perfect working order with a new bead of pure silver!

When pressed to reveal the source of the silver, the Indian became frightened and fled. DuBois searched the canyons unsuccessfully until his water ran low and forced him to a more hospitable area. He never returned—partly because of the harsh landscape, but more probably because the lure of gold was so much stronger than silver.

Pick recalled that over the years the legend of The Lost Gunsight Mine was told, retold and embellished, or scoffed at. Occasionally it was searched for, but never successfully.

Then the gold began to play out. The placer mine's heyday was done in California, and mining began to be run by the big money moguls who could afford the equipment for underground operations. It seemed that lone prospectors had lost the chance to strike it rich—lost it, that is, until the wealth of the Comstock lode was trumpeted around the camps. Then *"Silver!"* became the cry.

The fact that fabulous wealth could be found in parched, arid lands like

those of Virginia City, Nevada, miles from running water, gave the tales of
The Lost Gunsight new credibility. When Pick prospected in the area, he
found silver-bearing ore even if he didn't find lumps of silver sticking out
of the walls of an ancient Indian tunnel.

Just as important, the returning prospectors found water! Drilling a test
hole, they were startled to find a water table at only twenty feet. Without
ever coming to the surface, an underground stream was gurgling its way to
the salt flats of the desert floor.

Overnight a tent city sprang up, and soon after came a parade of merchants to see to the miner's needs. How the town came to be called Garson, Pick did not know for certain, but it's likely that it was an attempt to
call it Garçon, in honor of the Frenchman DuBois. By 1875 it didn't matter what anyone called it; fifteen hundred souls called it *home*.

Even if their clothing was the same, the miners were distinguishable
from the merchants by the speed of their activities. The miners were either
in a hurry to spend their money, lose it at the card tables, or drink it up.
The clerks, bartenders, and the town's undertaker were much more deliberate and methodical in their approach to life. Maybe the difference was
in their knowing that wealth would come to them in someone else's pockets.

Garson's main street required no name because it was the only street in
town. Josh noted that most of the buildings were grouped along either
side of the wagon road that served as highway. The other structures com-
prising the town were set amid the creosote bushes just as their builders
saw fit, without regard to straight lines or intersections. The businesses
along the road had more semblance of permanence only by leaning together in what appeared to be mutual intoxication. The Red Dog Saloon
leaned against the Tulare Hotel, which leaned against Jacobson's Hardware Store, which leaned against (and was leaned on by) Fancy Dan's
Saloon and Faro Parlor.

Across the rocky street the scene was repeated, with the Kentucky Gentleman Saloon and the Chinaman's Chance providing rather alcoholic
bookends to an office building housing a lawyer, a doctor, a dentist, and
the Golden Bear Mining Company.

The livery stable and corral stood alone at the bottom of the dusty slope
upon which the town was spread. At the top, dead center, was not a
church or school but Freeman's Mortuary. Pickax explained that the saloons flanking the business district were the pillars of society, and that
Freeman's commanding position at the head of the town showed how well
the results of society's practices were provided for in Garson—or words to
that effect.

Around these businesses, in random disorder, stood the tents and cabins of the population. The most elaborate of these consisted of two twelve-by-twelve rooms separated by a roofed open space or dog run. At the other extreme were canvas awnings covering cots and bearing grandiose names like *Sovereign of the Sierras* Hotel.

But Garson was definitely growing, and more importantly, families were starting to put down roots and a few children could be seen running through the streets.

Into this scene Pick led Jenny and Joshua. After turning Jenny into a corral, Pick and Josh unloaded the wooden water casks and filled them from the well that stood outside, then rolled them into the barn to keep them cooler. The essential job done, Pick turned and remarked, "What say we go see who all's in town t'day boy? Maybe we can find you some work, like you been wantin'."

Joshua nodded, and the two walked up the slope through town. Pick pointed out the various establishments, passing judgment on the quality of their liquor and food and greeting several other miners pleasantly with his ready grin.

Joshua's city clothes and derby hat caused some second glances, but the costumes to be seen in Garson were so varied Josh soon gathered that his very presence with Pick caused as much curiosity as his dress. Josh returned their looks, searching each face for the man called Gates, but to no avail.

Pick guided him past all the businesses on the main road and turned aside into the mesquite just before Freeman's. The brush had been cleared off a space just big enough for a canvas tent to be erected.

"This here's the No Name Saloon, Josh. Pard o' mine by the name of Jersey Smith owns it. He came here as a miner but couldn't take the heat. So, he brung in a case of Who-Hit-John and set up this here tent. Somebody asked what the place was called, and he allowed as how it weren't fancy enough to have no name. Well sir, that hit the fella's funny bone, so it kinda stuck." He gestured broadly and waved Joshua through. "Welcome to Garson and the No Name."

Four tables, all of different ancestry, and fifteen assorted chairs completed the furnishings—except for a wooden counter along one wall. There were no windows, let alone mirrors or paintings. In fact, everything, including the patrons, seemed to be a uniform shade of dust. Everything, that is, except the proprietor.

"Great Caesar's Ghost!" erupted a voice from behind the counter. "Pickax, what's the meaning of this? Is it true you've found the old Gunsight after all? You're here to celebrate and share your wealth with your old friend and bosom companion?"

"Naw, Jersey, put a cork in it. If I tumbled onto that treasure vein, I sure wouldn't tell you—leastwise, not till it was registered proper and guarded."

At Jersey Smith's hurt expression Pick hurried to add, "Not that you'd jump it, understand. But you sure as shootin' couldn't keep a secret, and I don't want ever'body from the Trinity to Sonora knowin' my business."

"Ah, but I'd only wish to rejoice with you, my friend. To help you celebrate your good fortune."

Jersey Smith eyed Joshua for a brief moment, noting the tall, strong, and so-far quiet young man, while Joshua returned the gaze at an equally tall but thin man, a shock of white hair combed straight back and a small pointed white beard. Jersey's leaping green eyes seemed to be constantly moving; Joshua assessed him as a man of quick wit to match his glib tongue.

Smith broke the silence first. "And who might this strapping fellow be? Don't tell me, Pickax, you've finally parted with your hoarded wealth and hired an assistant to do your work while you supervise."

"Now, Jersey, this here is Joshua Roberts, late of Illinois. He and me run onto each other out by my place, and I brung him in to look for work. He ain't no actor fella like yourself, nor broken down old rock-hopper like me. He's skilled in the smithin' trade."

Joshua glanced at Pickax for the way he had glossed over the circumstances of their meeting, but did not offer to elaborate.

Instead he stuck out his hand and grasped that of the bartender. "I'm pleased to meet you," he said.

"The pleasure is mine, I assure you," responded the carefully modulated baritone. "Men as good as Pick are difficult to discover, and if he vouches for you, then your credentials are impeccable. What's your pleasure, gentlemen? The first is on the house in honor of a new acquaintance."

Before either Pick or Josh could reply, a slurred growl interrupted. From a table back in the shadows, a fleshy figure dressed in denim and flannel and packing a Colt Peacemaker stood and swayed slightly, then advanced to stand before Jersey Smith.

Of medium height, he wore his coal-black hair greased down to a bullet-shaped skull. Three days of black stubble grew on his face, and from the half-open shirt front, a tangled thicket of coarse black hair bristled.

At the sight of this intoxicated, menacing figure, Josh thought instantly how much like a bull he appeared. From his beefy arms to his thick neck and powerfully compact build, the man seemed a perfect image of an Angus in human form.

"What do you mean, on the house?" he slurred out. "What're you playin' up to this ol' dusty lump o' brokendown trash for? Las' time I asked you, you wouldn't even allow me the price o' one stinkin' bottle. Me! Mike Drackett hisself! Now set 'em up, you pasty-faced ape. You kin have the pleasure of buyin' a real man a drink!"

"Mister Drackett," replied Smith quietly, "I've told you before that I don't extend credit, and that if you don't care for my house rules, you may take your business elsewhere. As for my guests, I'll give them a drink if I choose to, and I'll thank—"

Jersey got no further with his little speech because Drackett shouted, "Shut your gob! I'll just help myself," and lunged across the countertop. Smith tried to dart out of the way, but Drackett's powerful right hand grasped the proprietor's shirt and dragged the thin man back over the bar in one jerk. "Where's the key to your good stuff, beanpole? I ain't gonna drink no more rotgut, neither. I just bet that key's 'round your neck. Lemme see." Suspending Jersey on his toes with his right, Drackett made as if to grasp Smith's neck with his left.

But before he could get his fingers around the bartender's neck, he was astonished to find his left wrist caught in a grip like a steel manacle and a second later bent up behind his back.

Dropping the white-haired man to the earthen floor, Drackett swung around but found himself confronting no one. Joshua had danced around behind him, all the while wrenching upward on Drackett's wrist.

"Hey, what the—? Come here, you, an' fight." Drackett attempted to reach Josh with his right, but stopped abruptly with a howl of pain so intense that everyone in earshot thought he'd been knifed.

"You're breakin' my fingers," he screamed, as Josh coolly bent Drackett's fingers backward. "Stop! I didn't mean nothin'. I was just havin' some fun."

"Your fun, as you call it, is not to my liking, nor to Mr. Smith's. Now, you apologize to him."

"Apologize? To that fancy—Stop! All right, I'm sorry! Sorry, you hear? Lemme go now!"

"Just you hold on to him another minute, Josh, whilst I relieve him o' this here piece." Pick slipped up and drew Drackett's Colt from the holster he wore tied low on the left and stepped back. "Right, now I reckon he's harmless enough. Let'm go."

Joshua released Drackett's arm, and the brawny man whirled around as if to resume the fight but stopped at the sight of Pickax casually waving the .45 back and forth. Drackett abruptly changed to rubbing his injured left hand and wrist, but it was plain he was controlling himself with difficulty.

"As I was saying, Mr. Drackett, in my establishment, I'll buy drinks for whomever I choose. And as for you, you need not bother coming in here again. Henceforth even your *cash* is no good here." Jersey regained some of his ruffled dignity.

Drackett looked angrily back and forth between his Peacemaker in the hands of Pickax and the haughty Jersey Smith. In transit his gaze stopped and moved upward to lock eyes with Joshua.

"Who're you, anyway?" he asked sullenly.

"Name's Roberts. Joshua Roberts. Now, don't you think you'd better do as Mr. Smith says and take your business somewhere else?"

Drackett spoke no further word, but turned his head slightly toward the side and gave a quick jerk of his chin. Without a sound, two men rose from the corner table where he had been sitting and followed him out through the tent flap.

Pickax moved to the entrance and watched as they made their way down the slope and back into town.

"By gum," he chortled, returning to stand by Josh, "ain't nobody *never* put a stopper to Mike Drackett afore, and without a gun or even an axe handle!"

"I'm genuinely grateful, Mr. Roberts," Jersey added. "That ruffian and his kind are all too ready to cause destruction and are not usually to be dissuaded."

"No matter," said Josh modestly. "Besides, he was all liquored up and didn't know what he was doing."

"Don't you believe it," offered Pick. "They's a rough string of hombres that's been hangin' about lately, an' Drackett's as bad as they come. You'd both best watch your backsides. Drackett'll not like bein' showed up. He's one who'd drygulch a fella. Now hold on to this Colt—after all, you won it fair and square."

"No, thanks, Pick; it wouldn't do me any good. I never learned how to use one. Why don't you keep it, or give it to Jersey here?"

"Tarnation, boy, don't they have no learnin' where you come from? Ain't you never heard of self-defense?"

"Joshua, let me offer you a gift and some advice," put in Jersey Smith.

"What's that, Mr. Smith?"

Reaching under the bar, he pulled out a sawed-off shotgun.

"Ever use one of these?" he asked in a whisper. Joshua and Pick moved in closer.

"Not on a man," Josh answered. "I've hunted pheasant and grouse some."

"Well, then, take it with my compliments. If you want to swap the Colt, that'll be all right too, but I'll make you a gift of the greener in any case." Jersey carefully removed the shells and reversed the stock to hand it to Josh.

"That's real nice of you, but I don't think I could drop the hammer on a man. Maybe you'd better just keep it and the pistol, too."

"No, my boy; when you think of this in the future, remember I offered not only a present but some advice as well. Here it is: A well-prepared man doesn't have to fight as often as one who is not prepared. Just the fact that you go about armed may convince some ruffian to avoid tangling with you. It's amazing how persuasive these two barrels can be, especially if one is looking into them. Remember, the evildoers we're speaking of have no qualms about shooting an unarmed man just to rob him, let alone one who they feel has shamed them. Please accept this weapon and practice with it. Then perhaps you'll have no need of it."

Joshua reflected an instant, then nodded his acceptance. "All right, then, what you say makes sense. I'll take it—the greener, you say—and thank you."

"Good. Now promise me you'll practice until you are proficient and—" He raised his voice so that all the customers looking on this scene could plainly hear. "No one will bother you unless they want to be chased out of town by a load of buckshot. You'll have to control that violent temper of yours, or it and these hair-triggers will get someone killed."

Dropping his voice again, he added with a conspiratorial wink, "Dramatic effect. It won't take long for word to get around. Before nightfall, you and this shotgun will be the terror of the county."

3

PICK ESCORTED JOSHUA over to the offices of the Golden Bear Mining Company, owners of the Silver Rim Mine. The Golden Bear was the largest mining company operating in Garson, which didn't say much for the others. Despite its proud and rich-sounding name, the Golden Bear was struggling, Pickax told Josh. The quality of silver ore recovered from the mine was tolerable, but since Garson had no stamp mill, the ore had to be shipped to Turbanville, a hundred miles away, to be processed.

Pick explained that the costs of shipping and processing and the increasingly difficult task of removing ore from deeper and deeper in the mountain kept the Silver Rim on the edge of closing. At the time of Joshua's arrival, the mine was producing $2000 per week in silver bricks. A third of its profit went to pay for the shipping and processing. Since the miners were paid $25 per week, this left very little earnings for its superintendent, Mr. Morris, to report.

Morris, Pick told Joshua, was an interesting man. In a rough country of shaggy, unkempt men, Morris was clean-shaven and kept his hair neatly trimmed—"a real gentleman," was Pick's assessment. He had experienced all the ups and downs of mining life, having struck it rich in '49 only to be swindled out of his claim by the collusion of a trusted partner and the claims recorder. Never one to give himself over to bitterness, Morris had struck out again into the canyons of the Mother Lode.

Pick said he'd heard that Morris had again located a rich gold claim, and this time he saw to it that his work was duly registered in his name. He remained partnerless. Later on he had sold out to the Golden Bear Mining Company, in exchange for cash, Golden Bear Stock, and a seat on their Board of Directors.

Morris had thought himself settled into a life of ease when the mining company dividend payments began to drop off. Upon investigating, he had discovered that none of the other Board members had any actual mining experience; assessments for mine improvements were eating up the profits.

Morris, according to Pick, demanded the chance to improve the situation and so was dispatched to oversee the Silver Rim Mine. He had succeeded in reducing expenses, and he still believed in the value of the mine, but it appeared that for once his luck had failed him. He hadn't yet made enough difference in production for the mine to turn the corner to prosperity.

Pick and Josh waited respectfully for Morris to finish giving instructions to one of his foremen.

"Now, Dub, I want you to see to it that the new face on the third gallery is cleared tonight. I want that drift to make twenty feet this week, so as to intercept the vein coming off of two."

"Yessir, Mr. Morris. Is that new shipment of timbers here yet?"

"No, blast it, but it will be by tomorrow if I have to go get it myself. Now go on with you." The foreman departed and as Morris looked up, a pleasant smile replaced his frown.

"Well, Pickax, come in, come in. What brings you to my office? Don't tell me you've finally decided to take me up on my offer of a position!"

"No, sir, Mr. Morris. I thank you right kindly for settin' such store by me, but the truth is, I got this here young man to see you about it."

Morris rose to his feet and stuck out his hand. "Pleased to meet you, young man. What did you say your name was?"

"My name's Joshua Roberts, Mr. Morris. I'm a smith by trade. I just came here from Illinois, and I'm anxious for work."

"Smithing, eh?" Morris stopped and appeared to be sizing up Josh much as one would choose a draft animal. "Are you a drinking man, son?"

"No, sir, I'm not—" began Josh.

Pick interrupted by snorting, "I'll say he ain't! Why, he even turned down a drink after the offer of it 'most got him killed. He disarmed Mike Drackett slick as you please and still didn't take no drink to celebrate!"

"What's this? Are you a brawler then, young man?"

Josh opened his mouth to reply, but Pick again saved him the trouble of answering. "A brawler? Shoot, he ain't no brawler, he's a genuine iron-corded set o' human manacles!" Pick proceeded to recount the events in the No Name Saloon with great gusto, while Morris nodded, raised his eyebrows and smiled occasionally.

When Pick finally subsided, Morris turned to Joshua and said, "If you are half as good as Pickax here claims, you can have an immediate position with me as a security guard. I'll pay you twenty-five dollars a week."

"No, thank you, Mr. Morris. I'll tell you what I tried to tell Pick and Mr. Smith. I'm no hand with a gun, and fighting's not my line. They seem to think I should practice up with this old scattergun, but I wouldn't care to be a guard. Don't you need a smith, sir?"

Morris shook his head as if disappointed but replied, "As it turns out, we do. Even though I've known him a long time, I've had to discharge our blacksmith just yesterday for being drunk at work. He has ruined four-hundred-dollars-worth of drills by his inattention. You can have the job, but I'm afraid the pay is only twenty dollars a week. Are you certain you wouldn't consider the guard's position?"

"No, thank you anyway, Mr. Morris. That blacksmith spot suits me right down to the ground. What time do I start?"

"Come tomorrow at seven. I'll have Dub Taylor, the general foreman who just left here, line you out."

Josh found lodgings in the modest but clean Tulare Hotel. Its proprietor, Mrs. Flynn, as Irish as her name, took an immediate liking to the young man and saw to it that his cot in the dormitory-like room he shared with seven other men had a clean Navajo blanket rather than the old army-issue wool blankets which served the others. "Ten dollars a week, and two square meals a day goes with it. Leavin's can be taken for your work meal. No drinkin' nor fancy gals in my place, an' I'll have no smokin' or chew in the sleepin' room, if you please. Smokin' and chewin' is permitted in the parlor, except on Sundays."

Josh replied to each of these pronouncements with a respectful "Yes'm" and "No'm."

"Breakfast is at six and supper is at four. Look sharp, or you'll get naught. Unless," she said, softening a little, "you come to be workin' graveyard, then I'll be savin' you some biscuits for when you come off shift—but no," she remembered, "the smith works morning tower except at need. If I want some repairs done, likely you can work out some costs, if you've a mind."

"Yes, ma'am."

"An' one mare thing," she said, her flattened "o" betraying her County Cork origins, "I run a quiet house, so's men can get their sleep. My dear departed Clancy, God rest his soul, was a miner, and he swore by good food and good rest."

Joshua lay awake in the dark room of the Tulare Hotel and listened to the night sounds of Garson as a cool breeze passed through the open window.

He hoped that the good food promised by Mrs. Flynn was better than the good rest she held in such high esteem! The hoots and whistles of Josh's seven snoring roommates kept sleep far from him.

The sound of a dance-hall melody emanated from Fancy Dan's Saloon. Then the sounds of hymn-singing, of all things, began to rise and fall in a strange counterpoint to the honky-tonk music.

Shall we gath'er at the Riv-er. . . .

Thar's a yel-low rose of Tex-as! I'm go-in' there to seeeeee. . . .

Among all the saloons and gambling houses there was not one church to be seen in all Garson. Yet Joshua was certain he heard church music—women's voices!

Yes! We'll gather at the Riv-er. . . .

No-body else could love her, not half as much as meeeeee. . . ."

Joshua sat up, careful not to bump the little miner from Cornwall who slept beside him. The man stirred.

"Seems the Crusaders are at it again," muttered the little man.

Josh was glad someone else was awake. "The music—" he began.

"Aye, they'll stop soon enough. There's a group of 'em. They've taken the pledge."

"The *pledge?* You mean there's a Women's Christian Temperance Union in Garson?"

"Aye," replied the weary voice. "They'd close down every saloon and bawdy house in town if they had their way. Every night a different shift of 'em sings until Fancy Dan's closes down. His place is the only saloon with a piano." He yawned. "You'll get used to it."

Joshua was smiling at the image: members of the Temperance Union singing hymns in the dark outside the town's biggest saloon. He was, him-self, a man of temperance where whiskey was concerned, although he was not religious and made no attempt to awaken the conscience of a drinking man.

"Are there miners singing with them?" he asked, hearing a male voice in harmony.

"Some. And she's *even* managed to save the souls of a few of the Calico Queens!"

"*She?* She who?"

Now the Cornishman chuckled. "You haven't met her, I see. Do your utmost *not* to meet her, Mister Roberts." He rolled over. "Aye. She's tough as iron! Spotted me for the sinner I am, right away." The voice became sleepy and faded into a soft snore.

Now the music shifted to *The Battle Hymn of the Republic* as Joshua envisioned the town battle-axe leading the chorus. He would do his utmost to avoid her—*whoever* she was! Like Pick commented, his past was his business. Between him and God, he'd said.

But Pickax had not warned him about *the battle-axe*. No doubt such goings-on was one reason the old prospector chose to live fourteen miles out of town!

Joshua finally fell asleep, an amused smile on his lips, as the members of the Garson Women's Christian Temperance Union continued their musical showdown late into the night.

Fancy Dan's Saloon and Faro Parlor were operated by Fancy Dan McGinty. So called because of his flashy manner of dress, it was an image he not only enjoyed but fostered.

McGinty was a little over middle height and stockily built. Despite his last name, his olive skin and wavy black hair owed more to his mother's Mediterranean forebears than to his Irish father.

Early in his life, McGinty had discovered that living by his wits was preferable to using his muscles, and that it was easier to part others from their hard-earned money than to earn his own.

He lived by two mottos: *You can never have too much of wealth or power,* and *No one should be allowed to stand in your way of increasing either.*

McGinty had amassed a significant amount of capital by fleecing the miners of Virginia City, Nevada, with a crooked faro game. When he heard of the silver strike in Garson, he decided the time was ripe to invest on the ground floor of a new opportunity. This decision to relocate was motivated in part by a disgruntled group of miners who had threatened to stretch McGinty's neck. He concluded that a change of method as well as venue was required.

Since arriving in Garson, McGinty had risen in both wealth and popular opinion. His saloon, if modest by the standards of a more civilized part of

the world, was opulent for Garson. A real wooden building, its plank
floors were kept swept, and the genuine mahogany bar was polished to a
dull sheen. Behind the bar were signs advising miners to enjoy the free
lunch and admonishing them to write home; paper and ink supplied, gra-
tis.

McGinty's employees were the best. He tolerated no obvious cheating,
relying instead on paid schills who encouraged both immoderate drinking
and excessive betting. He also maintained a group of strong-arm types
who not only maintained order but saw to it that the house got its proper
share of the profits. No one working for Dan McGinty went independent
and stayed healthy in Garson.

But for all his success, McGinty was not content. He was steadily increasing his fortune, but what was there to spend it on five hundred miles
from nowhere? He dreamed of returning to his hometown of San Francisco in regal style—building a mansion on fashionable Russian Hill and
mingling with the Hopkins and the Crockers. This dream could not be
realized, however, without his becoming *really* rich, even fabulously
wealthy. He calculated that owning a top-producing silver mine would do
it.

Fate certainly seemed to be smiling on Dan McGinty. In his clandestine
recruiting efforts among the miners, he had not hired all of them away to
become schills, card sharps and bouncers. Some he conveniently left in
place as informants and for other purposes as the need arose.

None of these confederates was more valuable to him than Beldad, the
graveyard-shift foreman at the Silver Rim. A small, bitter man with a
much-inflated opinion of himself, Beldad believed that he should have
been made the general foreman of the Rim, and when he was passed over
for this position he made his displeasure known around Garson.

A few dollars and the promise of elevation to his rightful place had
more than won Beldad to McGinty's side. He was angry at the whole
world; Mine Superintendent Morris became his convenient target, and he
eagerly encouraged griping among the miners. McGinty's grand strategy
called for the work in the Silver Rim to be slowed to a virtual standstill in
every way possible. Fancy Dan reasoned that when Morris was shown to
be a failure and the Rim near insolvency, the rest of the Board of Directors of the Golden Bear Mining Company would be pleased to unload the
whole boondoggle for a very modest price.

All had been going according to plan until Beldad had brought some
unexpected news to Fancy Dan. Beldad came to the back stairs leading to
the second floor of Fancy Dan's Saloon. There was no reason why he
could not enter the front to drink and gamble with the rest. No reason

except that tonight two dozen Temperance members were singing on the sidewalk outside the saloon.

Two raps in quick succession, followed by two more, and the door was opened by McGinty himself.

"What is it, Beldad? I've got Dr. Racine, Freeman, and the new Wells Fargo agent coming over in about twenty minutes for a little card party. Make it quick."

"Boss, you won't be thinking about cards when you hear what I've got to tell. It's bigger 'n anything.".

"All right, spill it. What's this great news that can't keep?"

"You know that new gallery we're opening in the mine on level five?"

"Yes, what of it?"

"After we shot the south face last night, I was the first one back in there. Boss, we've hit it—I mean, really hit it! There's a silver vein there as wide as this room and so rich it almost glows!"

"Are you certain? Morris was positive the best chance was on three— you told me so yourself."

"I know, I know, but Morris is wrong. Five is smack spraddle of the sweetest ledge you ever saw, perfectly cased in clay and running down into the mountain. Morris could stay on three the rest of his life and never lay eyes on this."

"Have you tested a sample yet? I mean, you're not getting the 'fever,' are you?"

"Boss, listen. This ledge is shot through with blue threads—blue cables, more like! I chipped out a piece for the fire assay—and mind you, I was in a panic to get out before the men came in to see what was keeping me, so I didn't pick and choose. Boss, that bit assayed out at two thousand dollars per ton!"

"Two thousand the ton! Are you positive?"

"Absolutely certain."

McGinty grabbed the smaller man's shoulders and held him, frowning in deep thought. When at last he spoke he looked squarely into Beldad's eyes. "Not a word of this to anybody, or I swear I'll give you to the vultures piece by piece myself."

"No, no. Not a word."

"Also, this changes things. We've got to work faster. We can't take a chance on Morris discovering the ledge. If he did, Golden Bear'll never sell out and he'd have all the financing to develop a mill right here.

"We've got to speed our plans up. Do what you can to delay any further work on five while I figure out what's to be done. We've got to keep Morris so busy with everything else that he won't even have time to think about mining. Nothing must interfere now. Nothing!"

Beldad exited McGinty's office by way of the back stair. He could still hear the strains of "In the Cross of Christ I Glory" competing with a raucous version of "Sweet Betsy From Pike."

A short looping walk in the darkness brought him back onto the road at an angle that suggested he was coming directly from his cabin. He was still early for the change of shift, and he saw no one on the way to the Silver Rim.

Beldad acknowledged the hoist operator with a curt, "Goin' down to three." As the wooden floor of the lift began to drop down into the blackness of the shaft, he flicked the butt of a cigarette into a mound of sand. He watched overhead as the gallows-frame, which supported the great block through which the cables ran, was briefly silhouetted against the stars. As the lift dropped further, it disappeared from his view.

Stepping off when the platform halted on the third level of the mine, Beldad glanced around. As he expected, no one was yet approaching the lift to return to the surface. He had arrived unseen.

He could hear the clang of the double-jack and drill and the sing-song cadence of the miner's picks working the face of the ore on level three.

The rumble of an approaching ore car was just becoming audible as Beldad turned sharply to his right. Near the lift was an unused *winze*—a vertical shaft that connected different levels of the mine by ladder.

Elsewhere, the winzes were in use, but this one was so near the hoist that it seldom had traffic. Beldad was able to descend by its wooden rungs all the way down to the deepest part of the Silver Rim.

Pausing at the opening of a connecting passage, Beldad listened for any human noise to accompany the clanking sound of the pump. When he judged the way to be clear, he stepped out into a chamber where a fitfully flickering lantern marked the location of the pump laboring to remove water from level five.

Nearby, on wooden skids, sat a replacement pump ready in the event that the first failed in some way.

Glancing around once more, Beldad took a wrench from one pocket of his long coat. He quickly removed the cover from the pump; then, from another pocket, he retrieved a sack of iron filings. He poured these into the mechanism and replaced the cover.

By the time Beldad repeated this process on the spare pump, the first was already making strained, complaining noises.

4

AT 6:30 THE next morning, Josh was waiting outside the foreman's shack near the entrance to shaft number one of the Silver Rim Mine. The foreman, Dub Taylor, was just exiting from an ore car which he had ridden to the top of the shaft. He was addressing a short, stocky, bald-headed man who had come up with him.

"How do you explain that pump breaking down so fast, Win?"

"It was no breakdown, sir; it was wrongly installed, I'm thinkin'."

"Wrongly installed? But how can that be?"

"Well, sir, I canna rightly say."

"All right, then, I'll have a word with Beldad, and I'll see that Parker hears about it. He'll have to stop the work on three until we get gallery five cleared, otherwise we'll lose it."

He turned to see Joshua waiting, then pulled a Rockford dollar watch from his pocket and examined the time. "Come early your first day, eh? I like that. Mr. Morris sent word to expect you, Roberts. I'm Dub Taylor."

"Pleased to meet you, Mr. Taylor. It sounds like you're having some trouble?"

"That we are, indeed. What do you know about mining, son?" At Josh's shrug he continued, "Well, no reason why you should, blacksmithing being a lot the same for farming or mining, I guess. Anyway, these mines are deep—" He waved his hand toward shaft number one. "And the deeper we go, the more we have to fight to stay ahead of the water.

"Mr. Morris thinks the vein we're following on three is fixing to widen out into something worthwhile," he continued, "but now I've got to jerk my crews off of three till we get five pumped dry and the damage repaired." He shook his head, then smiled briefly at Joshua.

"Anyway, it's no concern of yours. Come on with me to the smithy."

Taylor led Josh up the hill a short distance behind the foreman's shack; Josh identified the smithy by the heaps of iron lying around and the glimpse of a forge through the half-open door.

Dub nudged a pile of drill bits with his foot, then said in a disgusted tone, "I don't know how much Mr. Morris may have told you about the man you're replacing."

"Well, he said he was drunk at work," Josh replied quietly.

"Drunk at work is right! And not the first time, either. But this time it wasn't a bolt cut too short or a shoe not fit properly, it was hundreds of dollars of drill bits just brought in to have the edges put back on them. Now look at them: Every one bent out of true and absolutely useless!"

Josh nodded and leaned over to look at the obviously curved metal spikes. "I can fix these," he said.

"If you can, it'll be a miracle. We need those bits sharpened to replace the ones we're using now, otherwise it brings everything to a stop to re-edge the one set. If we sent for more, it'd take two weeks for them to get here, and it's an expense we can't afford right now."

"Just let me get to it," Josh said.

Dub shrugged doubtfully but shook his hand and turned to go. "No harm in trying," he said.

"If you need anything, see Parker," Dub called over his shoulder. "He's the day shift foreman. I'll send him over to meet you."

Josh inspected the smithy with a critical eye. The slag had not been cleaned from the forge any time recently, and the floor appeared never to have been swept. Since straightening the drill bits would require a pre-cisely-controlled fire, Josh decided to attend to the forge first. He cleared it out completely, then restacked it in a careful pyramid shape of coke built over charcoal and kindling.

A shot of coal oil, and the forge was blazing cheerfully. While Josh waited for the blaze to subside before working the bellows, he located a broom and swept out the place. Next he rounded up a variety of hammers and tongs and cleared a work bench of debris. As he was filling the tem-pering keg, a tall red-haired man walked up.

"I'm Parker," he announced. "Best luck with those bits, Roberts. I hear there's a peck of trouble on five, so I've got to go. I'll see you at the end of the shift." With no more conversation than that, he was gone.

Joshua worked steadily all morning. His pace was unhurried as he gave attention to each bit in turn, judging with his practiced eye when each was the exact shade of cherry-red to be reformed. His hammer made a rhyth-mic sound as it bounced from steel rod to anvil in a precise cadence.

As he completed the straightening of each bit, he returned it to the forge and heated the cutting tip to the white heat required to form the edge for splitting the silver ledge a hundred feet below where he stood.

The morning was heating up after the cool of the desert night. As each rod was finished, Joshua allowed himself a moment to stand in the shade of the doorway and catch a moment of breeze. From where he stood he could gaze across the valley floor west of the mining camp. Sometimes it would be obscured by dust-devils and made hazy by waves of heat. At other times it cleared for a moment—long enough for him to see the bright white reflection of an ancient, dry lake bed.

Most often his eye did not linger on the desert floor but would be drawn upward to the gray mass of the Sierras beyond. Though they were far enough away to be indistinct, an occasional peak thrust up into the morning light radiated a glistening shine off its snow-covered summit. In his mind's eye, Joshua could see an eagle turning lazy circle over those peaks, gazing down at majestic pines and redwoods reaching heavenward from rocky slopes.

Josh shook his head and sighed, then returned to his forge. By noon he had completely reshaped and sharpened all the drill bits and turned his attention to other projects he found lying about in obvious neglect. He repaired several buckets and welded the broken stem of a windlass handle. He was just debating whether to repair a broken wagon spring or straighten a pick head when a shadow fell across the work bench. Someone was standing in the doorway behind him.

Shading his eyes against the gleam of the westering sun, Josh walked toward the door to see what was wanted. A blast of whisky-laden breath almost knocked him back a pace.

"What you doin' theah?" demanded a slurred and angry voice.

"I'm the blacksmith," replied Joshua. "What can I do for you?"

"The devil you say! I'm the blacksmith heah—Big John Daniels. Now get outta my way," the man demanded, roughly shouldering his way in.

Josh had moved to the side as Daniels entered. Now that he could see better, he could tell what an enormous man Daniels was: six-foot-six, three hundred pounds, and black as night. Daniels' shiny, bald head seemed his only part not able to grow with complete success.

"Daniels, Mr. Morris told me you were let go. I'm the new smith here," said Josh simply.

"Says who?" sneered Daniels. "You gonna put me out, you little pipsqueak? Ain't nobody fires Big John. I'll go when I've a mind to, an' not sooner. Now you better skedaddle, or I'll crack yo head like an egg!"

"Listen here, Daniels, you've not been doing your job around here, and being drunk like you are now almost cost this—"

Joshua never finished the sentence, for with a roar that was probably heard in Mojave, Daniels grabbed a hammer from the work bench and charged at Josh.

Josh ducked under the blow, and a good thing too, because the descending hammer and the force behind it knocked a hole completely through the west wall of the smithy.

Josh put the forge between himself and Big John as the giant lumbered around in a clumsy circle. "Stand still an' fight, you little rat," Daniels bellowed, "or I might jes' wreck this place so's *nobody* works here." At this

he seized an iron bar and, with a round-house sweep, he took out the
bellows chain, dropping it crashing to the floor.

"That's enough!" shouted Joshua, and he leaped to catch the bar at the
end of its swing, pinning it against the ground.

Big John struggled for a moment, attempting to free the bar from Josh's
grasp. He was startled at Josh's strength and even more surprised that
Josh stood up to him.

When his fuddled brain finally understood that he could not wrestle the
bar away from Josh, he dropped the hold he had on it with his right hand
and drew his fist back for a swing aimed at the back of Josh's head.

This was exactly what Josh had expected, and he was ready for it. Even
before the blow began, Josh gave a sudden shove on the bar directly
toward Daniels.

The move caught Daniels off guard; pulling on the bar with his left
hand, he was not prepared to stop its sudden plunge into his mid-section.

His breath exploded with a convulsive burst, and he began panting in
short gasps.

Despite his heaving, he put his head down and charged Josh. The reach
of his arms and the force of his rush propelled Joshua back into the opposite wall. With a crash and a clatter that sounded as if the mountains were
falling, tongs and hammers and blanks of iron for horseshoes flew from
their shelves.

Big John's eyes lit up with unholy glee, and he raised both fists over his
head, ready to smash them down on Joshua.

Josh threw a hard right that caught Daniels on the jaw and rocked his
head back. A left drove into the big man's rib cage just above his massive
stomach, and Daniels staggered.

He lunged forward again, intending to catch Josh's neck in the crook of
his arm. He knew he could squeeze until Josh's neck broke. But Josh flung
both arms up quickly, threw off Big John's grasp with an upward motion,
and in the same move grabbed the giant's head behind both ears.

Josh threw himself back violently, at the same time yanking Daniels'
head downward with all his might and raising his right knee to meet it.

A sickening, crunching sound resulted, like the noise of a rotten tree
when it falls. Daniels' nose and mouth burst like a watermelon dropped
from a wagon bed, and he slumped heavily to the floor.

Josh backed up, breathing heavily, and took stock of his injuries. His
shoulders and the back of his head felt like they were on fire from being
jammed against the wall, but otherwise he was unhurt.

He picked up a ballpeen hammer and moved cautiously over toward
Daniels. As he approached, Daniels moaned and stirred slightly, and Josh
raised the hammer. Then a hissing, bubbling sound escaped the fallen

giant as he exhaled a lengthy sigh from his ruined mouth and nose. Josh shuddered at the thought of further violence, and threw the hammer to the floor.

A noise at the doorway made him glance in that direction. There stood not only Parker, the day foreman, but Mr. Morris and a crowd of miners.

"Are you all right, Roberts?" asked Morris.

"Man, it looks like an earthquake hit here," commented Parker. "How did you keep from being slaughtered?"

"I just got lucky, I guess."

"Lucky, nothing!" said Parker. "Nobody has ever bested Big John in a fight, drunk or sober. Half the miners off shift came running to tell me Big John was coming with blood in his eye to wreck the place. The other half are laying odds on how many pieces you'd be found in!"

"Not *all* the others; several came to warn *me* that Daniels was on his way up here," commented Morris. "I came as fast as I could to see if we could subdue him, but here you've done it all by yourself!"

"Mr. Morris, maybe God is just looking out for me." Josh was uncomfortable with the obvious respect on the faces peering at him.

"That may be, my boy, that may be; but you were brave enough to stay and look out for mining company property when a lesser—and more sensible man, perhaps—would have run away. I want you to reconsider working as a guard for me. I'll make it thirty dollars a week."

"No thank you, Mr. Morris. I said before, I'm a smith, not a guard or a lawman."

"Well now, say, Mr. Morris," began Parker, "what are we to do with Daniels there? I mean, we don't want him to be loose when he wakes up."

Morris reflected a moment, staring at the hulk on the floor. "Say, that's right. We could . . . maybe in the . . . perhaps the basement of . . ." He stopped in consternation. "Where is there a place strong enough to hold him? We don't have a jail in this town, and if we weighted him down with enough iron to hold him, we couldn't move him ourselves. Besides, he'd tear down any place we confined him, weighted down or not."

"All right, Parker," he continued, "detail off some men to guard him." He stopped as Parker and the others who were crowded into the doorway began backing up. "Well, what is it? Are you all afraid of him? Come, come, where's your courage? Can't you put some guns on him? He wouldn't charge a hail of bullets, surely."

"It ain't just that, Mr. Morris. Sooner or later he'll have to be let go, an' he'll remember every mother's son who guarded him. Big John ain't much on thinkin', but ain't nobody can hold a candle to him for gettin' some of his own back!"

Morris paused a moment to look around the circle. "Do all of you feel that way?" he questioned. A vigorous nodding of heads was his reply.

Morris turned to Josh and found him gazing speculatively around the smithy. "And what about you, Roberts? Do you have any ideas?"

Everybody expected Josh to reply that he'd done his part already.

"Have you got a length of ore car track to spare?" he asked.

Morris glanced at Parker, who replied, "Sure, we've got a whole stack the other side of shaft number three. So what?"

Josh addressed Morris again. "And that level space that's cleared down there—" He motioned toward a vacant patch of ground behind the fore-man's shack, out of sight of the road from mine to town. "The one with the pit in the middle—is that to be used for anything?"

"No," Morris answered. "It was an exploration shaft, only five or six feet deep; the clearing is to be the site of a new mine office, just as soon as we bring in the big vein, right men?"

A chorus of half-hearted affirmatives responded, but Morris ignored the lack of enthusiasm. "What have you got in mind, son?"

"I think I'd better show you. Mr. Parker, how long is one of those rails?"

"Twenty feet."

"That will work just fine. Could you get some men to bring a rail to that cleared space?"

Parker looked puzzled and glanced at Morris for approval, who nodded. Then he addressed the group of miners. "Jones, take nine men with you and bring back that rail, double quick now. All right Roberts, what next?"

Josh selected a piece of metal rod about four feet in length and handed it to Parker. "Have someone bolt this through the tie-flange of that T-rail." The men glanced at each other dubiously.

"All right," he went on, "help me drag him down to the clearing." There was a general movement backwards, which Morris attempted to stop with threats of firing. But Josh was even more convincing: "You don't want him to be loose when he comes to, do you?" There was a rush forward, and soon ten men were dragging Daniels down the short slope to where the rail rested with the cross-bar already bolted in place.

When the pit had been filled in with rocks and leveled under Josh's direction, the rail was standing upright in the center. Josh was about to ask the men to drag Daniels' still-unconscious bulk to the rail. But the miners had already guessed his intent, and in a flash Big John was seated on the ground with his legs straddling the rail and his battered face leaning up against it.

It took no time to fashion manacles and leg irons from chains, hammering the bolts so that the chains could not be released without being cut free.

When the last stroke was completed, Josh stood and addressed Morris. "There's your jail, Mr. Morris. Even Daniels can't pull that rail free of two tons of rock, and he can't climb fourteen feet of rail trailing those chains, either."

"Brilliant, my boy, brilliant!" Morris spouted jubilantly.

Parker spoke up, "There's just one thing, Mr. Morris."

"What's that?" said Morris, who was beaming in satisfaction.

"Well, sir, I expect you'll be sending for the deputy sheriff to take charge of Big John and, well, sir, seeing as how it'll take three or four days to get him here, who's to care for Daniels meantime?"

"I thought you, or your—"

"No, sir, I don't think so. I mean, we didn't sign on as no guards, and anyway, we got some mining to do. Ain't that right, men?" This time the chorus of assent was loud and enthusiastic. No one wanted to be remembered by Big John as having been the cause of his confinement.

Joshua sighed and shook his head ruefully. "I guess it's up to me, Mr. Morris. After all, it was my idea, and here he is right in my front yard, so to speak. I'll see to him."

A relieved murmur went through the crowd, and Morris grasped Josh's hand eagerly. "Well done, my boy, well done! Now listen you men, this is the kind of spirit that will make this mine prosper and all our livelihoods will be secure. Roberts, I'm upping your pay as blacksmith to the thirty-dollar-a-week figure anyway.

"And—" He groped in his pocket and displayed a gold double-eagle. "Here's a twenty-dollar bonus!"

Later that evening, Josh went back to the mine property with a jug of water and a plate of beans. He told no one what his plans were and spoke to no one as he went.

Over his shoulder he carried a Navajo blanket. The sun was setting as he stopped by the foreman's shack. No one was inside, but he borrowed a lantern anyway, and when he had it burning cheerfully he stepped outside and went around the back.

Big John was still leaning against the T-rail, but a stirring let Josh know he was awake.

Josh stepped up to the edge of the filled-in pit and said, "I've brought you some supper and a blanket."

Through bruised and swollen lips, a garbled voice replied, "What makes ya think I wan' anythin' from you? All I wan' ri' now is ta git my hands 'roun yo neck and pop yo head off yo body like a cork outta a bottle."

"I figured you'd be feeling that way about now," Joshua replied evenly. "But even so, I said I'd be responsible for seeing to you, so here's food and bedding. What you do with them is up to you."

He set the plate, bottle and blanket down within reach of Daniels, but on the opposite side of the rail. Joshua then backed up slowly, taking the lantern with him. Once out of the small circle that made up Big John's cell, he turned to go.

"Hey!" shouted Daniels after him. "Ain't cha gonna leave that lantern here?"

"What for?" asked Josh. "You aren't going to be walking anywhere, and you said you didn't want anything from me, remember? Anyhow, it's company property, and I've got to return it."

"How long you gonna leave me like this? I mean, how about turnin' me loose?" he whined.

"No, I can't do that. You put yourself in this fix, and I can't get you out of it. As to how long—well, I think they've sent for some judge or other."

"A judge? That could take mos' a week! Say, don't cha know they's rattlesnakes and scorpions out here at night? What'm I s'posed to do about those?"

"Well, now, I'll tell you. If it was me, I'd wrap up good and tight in that blanket, and I'd lay real still all night and roll over real carefully come morning."

"What?! Why, you—I'll break ever bone in yo sorry carcass. I'll string yo intestines up like sausages and use yo guts for garters. I'll—"

But Big John was shouting imprecations at empty space. Josh had taken the lantern and departed.

5

THE NEXT MORNING Josh carried a plate full of biscuits and sorghum and a jug of buttermilk with him to work.

He found Dub in the foreman's shack. Dub eyed the food and shook his head with a wry smile. "I don't envy you, even if I am sorry I missed seeing what happened yesterday. How'd you get stuck feeding that wild bull? Didn't anybody tell you he never forgets and never forgives?"

Josh grinned. "Back home my daddy taught me to break horses by keeping them tied short, and giving them fodder and drink by my own hand. That method never failed to bring around the most cantankerous, rough stock you ever saw, so I thought maybe it'd work on the same kind of human stock."

"You'll pardon me if I don't go with you to watch," said Dub. "I don't even want to be associated with you in Big John's mind. Just leave me an address of your next-of-kin so I can deliver your remains."

Josh stepped around the building, unsure of the reception he'd receive but not wanting to voice any of his own doubts.

Big John was standing upright, the blanket around his massive shoulders barely reaching around him against the morning chill. The plate from the night before was clean, the empty bottle on top of it.

"Good morning," greeted Josh. "I won't ask if you slept well, but I don't see any dead rattlesnakes laying around, so you must not have had to wrestle any of them. Are you hungry?"

Big John started to snarl a reply but a long look from Josh seemed to get his attention. In a less belligerent tone he said, "Man, I can eat six times a day and still be hungry. Can I have the plate of biscuits, or are you fixin' to torment me?"

"No, no, I was just testing to see what kind of mood you were in. Here you go," Josh stepped directly up to Daniels and extended the breakfast.

Big John looked down at the food, then at Josh standing less than three feet away, then at his shackled hands. He shrugged, and reached for the plate.

"You're welcome," said Josh meaningfully.

"Right—yeah, thanks," Big John mumbled.

"Nothing to it," said Josh. "I came early today so I could rig a little tarp for you before I go to smithing. I figure today's gonna be a scorcher."

"I can't understand how that second pump could have broken down so quickly." Morris was speaking to the men assembled in his office.

Dub Taylor squirmed uneasily in his chair, and looked around at the others to see if anyone else would offer an opinion. When none did, he cleared his throat roughly and began. "It sanded up real bad, I guess, and when it froze up, nobody caught it in time. The shaft is bent all to thunder. Even Josh Roberts says he can't straighten it to where it'll run true."

"How did it happen that no one was watching more closely?"

Again there was some shuffling of feet and spitting of tobacco juice into spittoons before Taylor continued. "Near as we can figure, it happened on the change of shift. Beldad's crew was comin' off, and Parker's hadn't moved in yet. Beldad here thought I was sending someone down to watch it and I thought he had detailed off somebody to stay with it." Taylor looked miserable, Beldad defiant, and Parker and the other foreman, Sexton, concerned.

"Well, this really tears it. I don't have to tell you men how far off the pace we are now. The only thing to do is abandon five for the time being. It'll take probably two weeks to replace that pump. We'll press ahead on three and hope we get a break soon."

Parker finally spoke up. "Are you gonna keep us at full crews, Mr. Morris? And if so, what'll you want the boys to be doing?"

Morris looked unhappy and stared at his desk blotter before replying. "There's no way we can absorb the expense of keeping a full roster now. Only a few at a time can work on three, the others will be laid off." There was a low murmur at this news, but no one spoke.

"Emphasize to the men that the situation is only temporary, and will be corrected as soon as five is workable again, or as soon as we make the breakthrough on three."

Sexton, the evening tower foreman, spoke up. "How'll we pick who goes and who stays? Can I keep my best men?"

Morris's reply was firm. "No. I feel an obligation to this town and those who are raising families here. We'll keep the married men and let the singles go. A man without dependents can move more easily to another job—or town, for that matter. I don't want to impose that on wives and children if I can help it."

"The men won't like that, Mr. Morris," Beldad interrupted. "It isn't fair unless it's by experience or time in the Rim. We're liable to have more trouble."

"Trouble? What sort of trouble?"

"Well, I can't say exactly, but we don't need any kind of problem with the men right now, do we?"

"I'm sorry, Mr. Beldad, but my mind's made up. I *will* support families first. We'll just have to bring the rest back as soon as we can."

Four nails dangled from Joshua's lips as he hefted the rear hoof of Pick's little pack mule.

" 'Bout done?" Pick asked as he leaned against the door jamb of the blacksmith shop and gazed down at the forlorn figure of the prisoner.

"Hmm-mm. You in a hurry to get somewhere?" Josh muttered through the nails.

"Yup." Pick scratched his beard thoughtfully. "I aim t' be on the other side of the Sierras when you get around to unchainin' Big John." He grinned broadly, showing his nearly toothless gums, and turned to pat the mule on her rump. "Ain't that right, darlin'? We saved this here fool so's he could catch hisself a grizzly and get hisself killed proper!"

Joshua tapped in another nail and crimped the sharp point, bending it down on the outside of the hoof wall. Every nail entered the hoof at the proper angle—deep enough to hold the shoe securely, but not deep enough to nick the tender quick. It was a good job. Joshua picked up the rasp and carefully filed the rough edges of the hoof until the iron shoe blended perfectly with it. He deliberately ignored Pick's jibe.

The old prospector leaned against his mule and tried again. "I ain't but half-way jokin', boy," he sniffed. "I reckon the minute you turn Big John loose and turn your back he's gonna get hisself another gallon of ol' tangle-leg and drop an anvil on your head when you ain't lookin'."

"Then he'll find himself hugging another iron rail when he comes to, won't he?" Joshua let go of the mule's stout leg and straightened slowly.

"He can be a mean'un."

"When he's drunk."

"When he's sober, too." Pick narrowed his eyes in warning. "I reckon he's sittin' down there right now listenin' to you clangin' around here in his territory, an' he's figgerin' jest what it'll take to make you git!"

Josh retrieved his tools and shrugged as the mule stretched her neck and bared her teeth, braying loudly.

"That's right, darlin'!" Pick nodded agreement. "You tell 'im! He's a durn fool if he—"

The mule's bray was answered by the whinny of a horse from the road below the shop. Pick peered out the door and in an instant forgot what he wanted to say.

"What in tarnation!" he exclaimed, stalking out of the building and raising his hand to shield his eyes against the sun.

Josh wiped his hands on his farrier chaps and followed. Behind them the mule brayed again and was answered by a dappled gray mare pulling a buggy. An ancient Chinaman, complete with pigtail and black silk cap, was driving the buggy. In the seat behind him sat a young, dark-haired woman in her early twenties. Even from this distance, Joshua could see that she was lovely. *Elegant* was a better word. She wore a blue dress and carried a parasol to shield her fair skin against the sun. She sat slightly forward in her seat, and her head was tilted upward as if searching the sky for something. Her eyes were hidden by round, smoked glasses. To Joshua she looked like the very picture of the fancy ladies who rode in their carriages through the city park back home. The Chinaman driver and the bleak surroundings of the Silver Rim did not do her justice.

"Who is she?" he asked as the muttering of Pick broke into a full-scale tirade.

"Why, that good-for-nothin' . . . ! That old laundry-totin' prune of a Chinnee! I told him not t' bring her up here! Her pa is gonna hang him up by that pigtail of his!"

Josh laughed involuntarily at the image spun by Pick. It would be easy

enough to hoist the tiny Chinese driver by his long gray braid. The man
was not more than five feet tall and probably weighed less than a hundred
pounds.

As the horse trotted smartly up the road, Josh took Pick by the arm and
held him back for a moment. "Well, who are they, for goodness sake?" he
demanded again.

"The one drivin' the rig—the little shriveled-up one with the droopy
whiskers and the funny silk shirt—his name is Ling Duc Chow. Lean
Duck, we call him around here. He's Chinnee . . ."

"I guessed that much." Joshua's eyes were riveted on the young woman.

"Says he's the oldest human on earth! An' by gum, he just about makes
a feller believe it! He looks at you with them Chinnee eyes and slaps your
hand like you was a kid, when all you was doin' was tryin' t' taste one o' his
biscuits! Why, he told Mr. Morris I was stealin'!" Pick looked like a
rooster scratching the ground before a fight. "An' now look at him,
bringin' Miss Callie right up here, when I said to Mr. Morris that she
ought not come!"

"Pick!" Josh spun him around in frustration. "You're not making
sense!"

"Oh yes, I am! That Chinnee might a' been cookin' for Mister Morris a
hunnert years longer than I been prospectin', but this time he's gone too
far!"

"Pick!"

"Bringin' Miss Callie up here to feed the grizzly bear! She told me she
was gonna bring supper, an' I told her—"

"Who is she?"

"Are you blind, boy?" Pick gestured angrily as the buggy pulled to a
stop near the makeshift prison where Big John sat scowling toward
Joshua. "That is *Miss Callie Morris!*"

"The wife of Mister—?"

"*Miss!* Are you deaf? His *daughter.* Head of the Temperance Union,
Lord help us all! She's got no business comin' up here. It ain't no act of
mercy, neither. Pure foolishness! That Lean Duck oughta be . . ." Pick's
words degenerated into an unintelligible mumble as the Chinaman tied off
the reins and hurried to take the outstretched hand of the young woman.
Her chin was still slightly upward, and she seemed to grope for the little
man's hand.

"It ain't proper, I told her!" Pick continued. "It ain't right for a blind
girl to be feedin' a black man like that!"

Blind!

Ling Duc Chow helped the lady from the buggy. She was several inches
taller than he, slender and well-proportioned. As the driver retrieved a

large basket from the buggy, she waited with her hand poised expectantly. She smiled as her guide took her arm and led her over the uneven ground toward the iron rail.

Ignoring the prating of Pickax, Joshua found himself moving swiftly down the hill toward the rail and Big John. Two dozen miners, just off their shift, also gathered just beyond the perimeter of the tarp and out of sight of Big John. Pickax scurried indignantly after Joshua. Now voices and laughter floated up.

"Miss Callie!" called a dirty-faced miner. "What do you want to waste all that good food on Big John Daniels for?"

" 'Specially since he seems to want to bust up your Daddy's blacksmith shop so bad?" said another voice.

She laughed upward at the sky. "Is that Mr. Crawford there?"

"Uh . . ." He would just as soon not be identified in front of Big John.

"Well, if you remember your Bible," Miss Callie continued, "you'll recall that we are told by our Lord to feed the hungry!" She raised her voice a bit over the laughter of the spectators. "Are you hungry, Mr. Daniels?"

More laughter. Big John Daniels squirmed at the rail. A hulk that enormous was in need of vast amounts of food. Certainly a few biscuits were not enough. He lowered his chin. "Yes, ma'am. I is very hungry."

"Why don't you throw us some of that 'stead of wastin' it on a drunken black man," scowled a young miner. Someone nudged him when the young woman stopped in her tracks and snapped her head in the direction of the comment.

"God has seen to it that you are all black to me," she replied, anger in her voice. Ling Duc Chow looked first at her, then at the men, and finally at Big John. The laughter stopped abruptly. Seconds ticked past. "Now go home to your own suppers," Callie Morris said.

Joshua watched the stand-off with admiration. Here was a display of the iron-toughness the Cornish miner had warned Joshua about.

One by one the men backed up a step, tipped their hats to the sightless daughter of their boss, and left. Only Joshua and Pick silently remained at a distance. Joshua kept his fingers securely clamped around the old prospector's forearm, warning him not to interfere.

Big John sat with his back to Joshua and Pick. Callie and Ling Chow faced him. The withered little Chinaman looked directly at Joshua, but he did not mention their presence to the young woman who now took one step closer to the iron rail.

"Are they gone?" she asked quietly.

Ling Chow met Joshua's gaze again. "Yes. They are gone."

"Good," she answered. "We aren't here for a show. Where is it?" She extended her hand and Ling Chow guided it to the rail. She touched it gingerly and winced. "Horrible. Horrible to be put on display like this."

Joshua recoiled. *What else could he have done with Big John?* he thought.

"But you deserve it, Mr. Daniels," Callie continued.

"Yes'm."

"You have brought yourself to this shame."

"Yes'm."

"You were a free man, and you brought yourself back into slavery to the bottle. That's worse than being chained to this post."

"Yes'm."

"Whiskey. Who-Hit-John, they call it. Now look at you, John Daniels! Somebody hit you. Somebody bigger than you . . ."

Josh smiled slightly. Actually, Big John was a lot bigger than he.

"And I'll tell you who it was that hit you," Callie finished. "It was the *Lord!* Brought you right here in the dust. They call your whiskey *old tangle-legs.* Now look at you. Your legs all tangled around this iron rail. And you deserve everything you got because you gave up your freedom. Gave up a fine job. You did not drink like this when you shod the horses of General Grant. And now look at you!" She raised her chin. "I don't have to see you. I can *smell* you—smell the stale whiskey. You should be ashamed!"

The shiny bald head of the prisoner sagged in remorse. "That I am, Miss Callie," his voice small and sounding genuinely penitent.

Pickax jerked his head back in unbelief at the words. He stared in wonder at the bald dome and scowled when Ling Chow shrugged at him.

"I was told not to come to visit you—you, who cared well for my father's horses for so many years—but I had to see for myself. Yes, I said *see.* My soul can see quite clearly, you know, Mr. Daniels. And the Lord has told us to visit those who are in prison. He is not speaking always of walls and bars or iron rails in the ground. Sin is the prison you have chosen for yourself." The words were still direct, but her tone was compassionate.

The big man sagged in misery against the rail. "Yes, Miss Callie. Lord help me!"

"Ling Chow will feed you now," she said in a matter-of-fact voice. Then she turned to the Chinese cook. "Big John has some praying to do, Ling Chow. I shall wait in the buggy while you pray with him. Some things are not for a lady to meddle in." She turned slightly. "Read the Scriptures with him, man-to-man, when he has eaten."

Big John was weeping in earnest now. Ling Chow escorted Callie back to the buggy and helped her in. With that, the pint-sized Chinaman retrieved a small wooden stool from the buggy and placed it beside the shackled giant. He removed a well-worn Bible from the food basket, handed a plate to Big John, and filled it with food. Before he could take his first bite, Ling Chow placed a restraining hand on his arm. "Thankee God for food," he suggested, and Big John meekly bowed his head. "All good things come from your hand. We thankee you."

With that Ling Chow opened the Bible to the sixth chapter of the book of Romans, and began to read. Big John continued to nod and clank his shackles as he cried, "Amen! Yes, Lord," between bites.

Joshua and Pickax exchanged wondering looks as they retreated back to the safety of the blacksmith shop to watch the strange spectacle out of earshot. They were even more amazed to watch Big John stop eating and bury his face in his hands.

Pickax's amazement mellowed into a philosophical amusement after a few minutes' observation.

"Yep, my ol' ma used t' say that when a feller wakes up feelin' half-ways between *'Oh Lord,'* and *'My God,'* he knows he overdid it!"

"Looks to me like Miss Morris and the Chinaman have moved Big John closer to *'Oh Lord,'* " Joshua commented dryly.

"Shoot, yeah. That pig-tailed Temperance man learned the Good Book from them Boston missionaries in the Sandwich Islands! He come as a coolie workin' the sugarcane fields." Pick spit a stream of tobacco into a ground-squirrel hole and wiped his mouth on his sleeve. "Then he come to 'Frisco on a sailin' packet in '48. Worked on the railroad as a cook for the coolie crews. Did more preachin' than cookin'. Don't ask him about it. He'll tell you more'n you want to know!"

Joshua was not as interested in Ling Chow as he was in the young woman who waited quietly beneath her parasol in the buggy. He let his gaze shift to her and linger there. Beautiful. Strong-willed. "What's a woman like her doing in Garson?" he asked Pick.

"Her pa's here. And she says one place looks the same as another to her. Since her ma passed on, she figgers her pa needs her, this bein' his last chance at makin' the Silver Rim pay off."

Joshua did not take his eyes off the slender figure. She shifted the parasol, leaving her face in shadow while the sun glinted on her thick black hair. "But she's blind. How can she be of help to Mister Morris?"

"She can't play poker or checkers, that's true enough. But she's smarter'n ten men put together. She ain't always been blind, neither. Some quack doctor put a poultice on her eyes when she was a young'un. She remembers colors and critters and just 'bout everything, I reckon. And in a way, she sees a whole lot better'n folks with two good eyes. She was one of them Christian Temperence workers in Boston, and a teacher at a blind school." Pick nodded with authority. "Yep. Readin' little bumps on paper with her fingers. She showed me—like readin' a map in the dark, I figger. 'Course I can't read a-tall, and you know I got the eyes of a brush wolf . . . spot silver from ten miles off!"

Joshua viewed the girl in the buggy with a mixture of curiosity and respect. He turned back to his work with a half-smile and the comment, "Strong woman." Retrieving a cherry-red metal bar from the fire, he placed it on the anvil for shaping beneath his hammer. He could not help but wonder about the fires and the hammer which had shaped the life of Callie Morris.

Beldad addressed the group of miners assembled in the Chinaman's Chance Saloon. "It's not right, I tell you. It's not fair. Some of us been bustin' our hump longer'n anyone else for the Silver Rim, and now his highness, King Morris, up and decides to play favorites."

"Yeah," a voice responded. "You tell 'em, Beldad."

"He can't run us off."

"We'll show him he can't work the Rim without us!"

"It won't even come to that. He ain't man enough to look us in the face and tell us we ain't wanted!"

Jan Svenson, a burly Swede who normally preferred to listen rather than talk, now spoke up. "Yust a minute, Mr. Beldad. How can you be shoor Mr. Morris goin' to lay anybody off?"

"Haven't you been listenin', Swede? I'm a foreman. I tell you, I was there when Morris up and said so. He said, 'We'll send the single fellows packing—there aren't any of them worth a plugged nickle, and they're drunk all the time besides.' "

"What? That no-good polecat!" someone burst out.

"An' what about you, Mr. Beldad?" Svenson interjected. "If you are such an important fella, you must not be worried about your job. Why are you tellin' us all this?"

"Because I'm on your side, man. I aim to see everybody treated fair and square," responded Beldad.

"What'll we do, Beldad? What's the plan?"

Jan Svenson stood up, and his massive size called for respect even if his opinions didn't. "I say you are all about to give Mr. Morris a good reason to let you all go. He's been fair and straight with us all along. If I had a family here to care for, I'd be glad he gave that some weight. Besides, as long as I've got these," he declared, raising two fists the size of hams, "I can find work. After all, I was looking for a job when I found this one. Don't cross Morris, men, he's played fair with us."

Beldad glared down at the Swede, but it was a short angle even from where Beldad stood on the tabletop. Svenson looked directly back into his eyes without wavering.

Finally Beldad spoke. "Swede, there ain't no more pleasure in your company than in a wet dog's. Why don't you go on and shine old Morris's boots?"

Svenson scowled at Beldad for a moment, then spun on his heel and exited the saloon.

As he went, Beldad caught the eye of Mike Drackett, who had been standing in the shadows at the back of the meeting. As he did so, he gave Drackett the smallest of nods, and Drackett went out just after Svenson.

Joshua worked silently while Pick watched out the door of the smithy and muttered to himself. After a time he exclaimed, "Well, sure as my name is Pickax you're in for somethin' now!"

Joshua continued to shape glowing metal into a horseshoe without reply. He had learned that sooner or later Pickax would explain himself.

"My pa always said you could tell what a mule was thinkin' by watchin' the way his ears pointed. Now, I'll tell you—Miss Callie's got them little ears of hers pointed right up here where you're bangin' and clangin'! I bet my last nugget she's fixin' to come up here with that Lean Duck."

The thought of meeting Callie Morris pleased Joshua. Here might be opportunity to at least satisfy some of his curiosity. He imagined that she might have a word of congratulations for him since he was the only man in town who had been able to stop the rampage of Big John.

"I told you, boy! Here they come! Right up the path like they was out for a Sunday promenade in 'Frisco! It'll give me a chance t' give that Chinnee a piece of my mind! Bringin' Miss Callie out here t' feed that grizzly—"

Pick paused. "She ain't lookin' none too pleased, neither! I seen that stubborn look on her face afore, an' I know—"

Now Joshua laughed as the brash courage of Pickax seemed to fade away the closer the two came. "My daddy said, 'What you can't duck, welcome.' You afraid of a lady?" he asked, poking yet another iron in the fire and pumping the big bellows a few times. But Pick didn't reply.

Joshua was smiling when Callie Morris entered the shop with Ling Chow. His smile, like the bravado of Pickax, soon disappeared.

"Your name is Joshua Roberts, I am told?" she said, her pretty features set with indignation.

Joshua cleared his throat. Her face turned toward him as if she were staring at him. "Yes, ma'am," he answered with respect. "And your name—"

"Callie Morris. And this is Ling Chow." She paused. "And I can tell Pickax is in the room as well. What are you doing here?"

Pickax shuffled forward, now completely docile. "Why, Miss Callie, I was jest here gettin' shoes for Jenny." He glared at Ling Chow. "Me and Josh saw that you brung supper to that ornery grizzly down there, and I was just sayin' I'll bet your pa wouldn't like you mixin' with that no-good—"

Callie raised her hand to silence his protest. "You know Big John has been a faithful employee of my father's for many years." Her tone invited no argument. "He's been trussed up like some sort of animal."

"Hold on just a minute, Miss Morris—" Josh argued.

But before he could continue she inclined her head. "No, *you* hold on. Perhaps Big John Daniels fell into bad ways, but he is not a steer to be bound hand and foot for branding."

"But Miss Callie!" Pick protested. "You ain't never seen such a mean drunk!"

"He is sober now," she said. "He needs to be released."

"I can't do that." Joshua narrowed his eyes. "Not until I'm sure—"

"I will speak to my father," Callie replied evenly, as if the matter was already settled. "In the meantime, please put up a tent for Big John."

"I did put up a tarp," Josh defended.

"Over his head." She raised her chin slightly, and her voice trembled. "But what about his—his personal, private needs? No human should be put up to public ridicule."

"Ain't nobody laughin' at Big John to his face," Pick said quickly. "Only a fool would laugh at him out loud."

She was adamant. "He needs privacy. Even in jail, there is some privacy. It doesn't matter what he has done."

Joshua now regretted his curiosity. He looked at the stack of cold iron shoes and then at Callie Morris. She was, indeed, strong. Strong-minded. Strong-willed. Too strong, to his way of thinking. "Ma'am, he has not been sober for weeks. You know that as well as I know it, and I am a newcomer here. I have done only what I needed to do in order to restrain him."

Her face softened just a bit. "Well, that may be so. But he does need a tent. Provide him with a chamber pot, and water with which to wash. In private. Away from the eyes of the miners, Mister Roberts. That is only common decency."

She was right; Josh hadn't thought of it. He did not like being ordered around by a woman, but she spoke the truth. He stared at her for a moment, considering how strange it was that a woman who could not see was so aware of what it meant for Big John to be totally without privacy.

"Yes, Miss Morris," Josh replied. "Common decency."

"Thank you," she said abruptly, turning to reach for Ling Chow's arm. "We are agreed," she continued. "Ling Chow and I will be back with breakfast for him in the morning. I hope this matter will be taken care of before then." Her tone indicated that Josh probably wouldn't want to be around if she found anything different than that.

Josh and Pickax exchanged looks as Callie Morris and Ling Chow drove away from the blacksmith shop.

"Well, Pick," Josh said dryly, "I purely admire the way you gave them a piece of your mind."

6

JOSHUA AWOKE EARLY for a moment not certain what had interrupted his peaceful sleep. He lay on his cot, glancing out the window toward where the faintest of predawn gray was beginning to brighten the eastern sky. He looked around the packed room; none of the miners were awake. Listening to the chorus of snores, snorts, and wheezes, Josh couldn't imagine that any outside sound had penetrated even these thin walls.

Then he heard it again: the call of a horse, answered by another, and the clattering of hoofs on the rocky slope leading upward toward Garson from the desert below. Josh swung his legs over the cot and sat up, drawing on his Levis and thrusting his stockinged feet into his boots.

Joshua clumped downstairs. On the way he heard the banging of pans in the kitchen, indicating that Mrs. Flynn was getting the day in order, but he saw no one.

Out to the board sidewalk he went, leaned over a rail, and looked down the slope. Now he could hear human voices mixed in with the horse whinnies. One said, "Get up there," and another called, "Whoop, whoop." A couple of sharp whistles and the sound of a coiled rope smacking against a leather-covered thigh accompanied the voices.

Presently the first of the herd of horses came into view. They were scruffy, wild-looking creatures, with flaring nostrils and tangled manes and tails.

A rider galloped up alongside the herd to unlatch and open the corral gate. He did this all from the back of his horse, a beautiful glossy-coated bay. At a slight urging from the reins, the horse backed up to block the road.

The rider then removed his hat and stood in his stirrups to wave the leading horses into the pen. As he did so, Josh got a good look at this tall man who rode with such assurance. He was flamboyantly dressed in a bright yellow shirt with a bright red bandana knotted at his throat. But the most amazing aspect was the man himself: he was black.

The herd of wild horses needed little urging from the black cowboy. As they came within sight of the corral, they could smell the watering trough, and into the gate they turned.

A second cowboy had come up along the left side of the herd. He was white, similar in size to the first rider, equal in horsemanship as well as age. Both men looked to be in their early twenties.

Josh counted fifteen horses as they paced into the corral. The black horseman moved his bay back up to the gate and shut it quickly behind the last mustang. The drag rider was older than the other two and had a slightly shorter and stockier build. His sun-browned face broke into an easy grin as he slapped the back of first one cowboy and then the other in mutual congratulations.

Josh strolled down toward the pen, curious about the obviously friendly group. As he approached, the three were just dismounting and preparing to lead their horses into the livery stable.

"Howdy." The older rider spoke to Josh as he passed by into the barn. The other two touched their hat brims and nodded politely, but said nothing.

Josh could overhear the instructions the older man gave the livery man regarding the care and feeding of the saddle horses and the rough stock. "Grain these three up good. We had planned to be here last night but ran out of daylight up the trail apiece, so we turned 'em into a box canyon an' come in this morning."

The three riders strode back out into the brightening morning light. Garson was beginning to come to life, and the sounds of the awakening town filled the air.

"Wonder where's a good place to put on *our* feed bag, Pa?"

"I don't know, Nate, but perhaps this gentleman can tell us," the older man said as he approached Joshua.

"Yes, sir," replied Josh politely. "I think you'd find the food at my hotel, the Tulare, to your liking. Mrs. Flynn's cooking isn't fancy, but she doesn't stint on the portions."

"Sounds just like what we need, eh, boys?"

"You bet," the younger white man responded.

The black cowboy replied, "Sounds good to me, Pa," to Josh's surprise.

"Lead the way, young man," said the man to Josh. "And perhaps you'll join us and give us some information about this town."

The introductions which followed Josh's agreement revealed that the older man was Tom Dawson, a rancher from Greenville on the other side of the Sierras. "Up in God's country," Dawson said, "where the land grows grass and trees instead of rocks and cactus."

Tom gestured to the younger white man and indicated him to be his nephew, Nathan. He referred to the black cowboy as his son, Mont James.

Mrs. Flynn was pleased to have three more paying customers for breakfast, and when Tom indicated that they were interested in a room as well, she was even more generous in ladling out gravy for their biscuits.

"What brings you to Garson, Mr. Dawson?" inquired Josh.

"We've been rounding up wild stock out of the desert and breaking them for the army," Tom replied. "But the army's interests of late have moved quite far from California, what with the Sioux troubles and all, so our market's dried up some. Anyway, Mont here had an idea. Tell him, Mont."

The black cowboy finished swallowing a mouthful of biscuit and washed it down with a quick swig of coffee before answering. "I thought maybe we could find some takers in these mining towns who were in need of desert-bred stock. Plus I figured if we rounded them up and did the breaking here, instead of driving them home and back again, it'd save some expense and wear and tear on us."

"Anyway," broke in the one named Nathan, "we thought we'd make this a trial run and see how it turns out. Would you be interested in purchasing a fine broke horse, Mr. Roberts?"

"I don't think I can afford one just yet. And I should tell you that I'm probably not the one to ask for information about Garson. You see, I'm pretty new here myself."

"You didn't steer us wrong about the food," said Tom. "Why don't you just fill us in on what you do know?"

Josh described the town's situation as best he could, including the troubles besetting the Silver Rim and Mr. Morris's efforts to make it pay. "I don't know that you'll find many buyers among the mine workers. They don't have anywhere to go and not much money to spend. But the storekeepers and merchants sure might be interested."

"I guess we'll sound them out directly," concluded Tom. "Anyway, we plan to put up here for a month or so while we're putting some school on these cayuses."

Chief Pitahaya regarded the two young Mojave Indians before him. *Sotol and Turtleback have shown some courage,* he thought. *Perhaps their smoldering hatred of the whites can be fanned into flame.*

"Sotol," Pitahaya said to the taller and brighter of the two, "have you had any word of Yellow Plume since she ran away with the white man?"

Through gritted teeth Sotol replied, "As you know, Pitahaya, her brother here and I tracked them to the white village of Dar-win. But the whites there laughed at our demand that she be returned."

"Indeed," Turtleback added. "They called us *dirty Injun* and drove us out of their village with rocks."

Pitahaya eyed them both. "How is it that you let such insults stand, my brothers?"

Sotol and Turtleback exchanged looks. Sotol replied, "They have guns with which to give their taunts force, Pitahaya. Pistols and long-guns which shoot many times, while we have none."

"So," mused Pitahaya thoughtfully, "you do not lack courage, only guns. Is that so?"

At the nods of the two younger men, he continued, "Here is what should be done. In the white village of Gar-son they sell the guns which shoot many times—" Pitahaya raised his hand to cut off the protest he saw coming. "What we must seek are the whites who newly come to this land and who would not be sought after should they lose their way in our desert. Do you understand?"

Sotol and Turtleback grunted in reply. They agreed to take turns watching Garson, exchanging places from Wild Rose Canyon by night.

"Good day, Mr. Jacobson," called Callie to the proprietor as she left the hardware store.

"Yah. Und tank-you, Miss Morris," replied the portly little shopkeeper.

Callie felt the stares of two men she had heard enter the store after her. *They must be new in town,* she thought.

"Und what can I do mit you, gentlemen?" Jacobson asked.

Their full reply was cut off by the closing door, but not before Callie heard, *"Do you have ammunition for Winchester . . ."*

"Come along, Ling Chow, don't dawdle," chided Callie Morris over her shoulder.

"No, Missie, I comin' plenty fast," puffed the little Chinaman over the basket he carried piled high with groceries.

Callie strode briskly along the boardwalk in front of Jacobson's Hardware Store. Her familiarity with the limited business district of Garson enabled her to walk with all the assurance of a sighted person.

She paused when her hand encountered the gap in the rail indicating the front of Fancy Dan's Saloon. Here she turned and prepared to cross the road to her carriage, which was tied up in front of her father's office.

Callie listened carefully for a moment, preferring to judge for herself if the street was clear for crossing rather than calling on Ling Chow's assistance.

While she waited, a carefully modulated voice spoke from behind her. "Good day to you, Miss Morris. May I offer you my arm in crossing the street?"

Callie recognized Dan McGinty's voice and replied, "No, thank you, Mr. McGinty, I can manage just fine."

"But I insist," he said, stepping up in a flourish of brocade vest, and what was to Callie a wave of bay rum. He gently but firmly placed her left hand on his right arm and prepared to step out across the street.

"May I say how lovely you look this morning, Miss Morris? You certainly add a note of classic beauty to our humble surroundings."

"You are a flatterer, Mr. McGinty, and a rather forward one at that," Callie responded tartly, lifting her hand from his forearm.

"If I cannot be of service, then I certainly don't wish to impose," said McGinty, with a quick fan of breeze that indicated a sweeping bow. Then he was gone with a light step and a creak of new leather boots.

Callie paused a moment, her cheeks burning. *I must like his flattery a bit,* she admitted to herself. *But he is not a man I can trust,* she thought as she walked determinedly to her carriage.

"And you are certain, Sotol, that these two white men know no one in the white village on the rocky slopes?"

"No one, Pitahaya. I was outside the Place of Iron Tools when I saw them leave and heard them ask directions of the prospector known as Pickax.

"The man pointed them toward the north and told them of water to be found at such and such a place. Then they told that they were from the land of the Utes and were newly come to this place."

"We think," said Turtleback, "that the meaning is clear: they are so newly come as to need directions to water. When they obtained food, they left again quickly without being much regarded."

Pitahaya nodded slowly. "And what have they of use to us?"

Sotol glanced at Turtleback before replying. "That is truly the best part, Pitahaya. Each carries a shining Colt six-shooter and a Yellow Belly. We saw them load boxes of bullets for these on their two fine, strong horses."

"You have done well, Sotol, and you also, Turtleback. Now, let us plan what is to be done. Will they camp near Three Kill Spring tomorrow night?"

"Yes, Pitahaya. We believe we can meet up with them in the canyon that lies before Three Kill Spring."

7

"**H**EY, SOMEBODY BETTER come here, quick!"

"What's the matter, what is it?"

"I dunno—is somebody snakebit?"

"Could be—I just heard the hollerin'."

There was a flurry of activity around the first dry wash north of Garson. Someone had spotted something at the bottom of the little canyon and gone down to investigate. Immediately afterward came a series of yells until a stream of miners had scrambled down the rocky slope, around the jutting overhand of rock, and into the bottom of the draw.

"It's Swede Svenson!"

"Sure enough is. Is he hurt?"

"I'll say so! He's dead!"

"Dead? What happened to him?"

"Don't be thick! Look up there at that drop and then where he's layin'. He musta got drunk and walked off that cliff in the night and broke his fool neck."

"Powerful shame. I liked ol' Swede—he was a good'n. And I never knew him to be much on drinkin'. But he'd have to be drunk to end up down here."

The lead horse, a tall, long-necked bay, pricked his ears forward again. His rider took no notice and neither did his partner, riding a few paces behind and leading a pack animal.

But the second rider's horse, a smaller and better-proportioned, apron-faced sorrel did catch some of the other horse's agitation. Neither horse stopped, shied, or snorted an alarm, however, and the riders were too inexperienced to catch the subtle signs.

The canyon through which they were riding was narrow and winding, the sandstone walls rising thirty to forty feet on either side. Yucca and creosote bushes grew on the plateaus, but the canyon walls and floor were almost without vegetation. A blue-bellied lizard skittered out from between the lead horse's feet and disappeared into a crack in a low ledge.

The two men knew where they were headed, but not how long it would take them. Their destination was Three Kill Spring, where they had been told they would find water.

Both men suffered from the worst malady that could befall a desert traveler—overconfidence. Even though both men realized that they were new to the desert and its ways, neither was smart enough to feel the least apprehensive or even cautious.

The two young men, easterners out for an adventure, had come west intending to prospect for silver and gold in the Comstock Lode. When they reached the Great Salt Lake, they met up with a returning party of discouraged prospectors. They were told all that was left was hard work for poor pay.

The two were considering going straight on to San Francisco before returning east by ship when they heard some interesting news. Silver had been located in the Panamint Range and the Argus Range of eastern California. They began to hear names like Death Valley, Lone Pine and Darwin.

By train they got as far as Carson City, Nevada, then turned south and took the stage for Independence, California. At Independence they parted with some of their stake and proceeded to outfit themselves.

They bought horses, packs, mess kits, and boots, picks and shovels, flour and coffee. Most exciting of all to their spirit of adventure were their firearms—brand-new, six-shot Colt revolvers and lever-action Winchester rifles nicknamed "Yellow Bellies" because their brass receivers gleamed golden yellow in the light.

Their choice of weapons happened to be a good one; both pistol and rifle fired the same .44 caliber ammunition, making it unnecessary to carry two different loads. Unfortunately, neither knew how to hit anything that wasn't stationary, and neither had ever had occasion to fire a shot in self-defense.

The man on the lead horse turned in his saddle to inspect his companion's progress. "That pack saddle is slipping again, William."

William also turned around and regarded the mound of gear loaded on the last animal. The canvas-covered bundle of supplies was leaning precariously to the left. In their travels so far, the supplies had never been carried for more than two hours without a stop to readjust and tighten the ropes.

Their concern about the pack was caused by an experience they'd had early after leaving Independence. After a lengthy spell of inattention, the gear had slipped completely under the pack horse, and the lead rope had come loose. Two miles later they finally caught up with the horse, but it took another half day to recover all their belongings, strewn over a thousand acres of sagebrush, granite boulders, and ground squirrel holes. They never did find the package of chewing tobacco, but neither of them chewed, so it wasn't much loss. They had only bought the tobacco on the advice of the storekeeper, who told them that all salty prospectors chewed.

"You're right, Lawrence. I suppose we'd better stop and fix it right now." William pulled his red horse to a stop.

He struggled with the girth that secured the pack frame. When he first tried to right the load by yanking on the offside, it refused to budge. He loosened the cinch that secured the pack frame, but it began to slip before he got around the animal again. He returned to stop its slide and succeeded in pushing it back upright, but the ineptly tied load had shifted under the canvas and so continued to lean.

Frustrated, William looked up at his partner who, still mounted, was staring intently up the canyon. In an exasperated tone William said, "Aren't you going to help me, Lawrence?"

Lawrence gestured for silence without turning around, and as his angry partner moved up beside him, he said in a hoarse whisper, "Did you see him?"

"See him? Him who?"

"An Indian, I think. I didn't see anyone when we were riding or when we stopped, except just out of the corner of my eye. I thought I saw someone stand up, and as I turned to face him, he disappeared."

"You're imagining things. Or perhaps it was a mirage."

"Why would a mirage suddenly appear and then disappear?"

"Who can explain what a trick of refracted light may do? Come on, give me a hand with this pack animal, or we'll never make the spring by nightfall."

Lawrence stood up in his stirrups and surveyed the trail ahead before shaking his head and stepping down from the animal.

Together the men spent twenty minutes untying, rearranging, and resecuring their belongings. The load looked no more secure than before, but at least it perched mostly upright. Both men remounted the horses and prepared to continue forward.

"Don't you think we should at least have our weapons handy?" asked Lawrence.

"I can't think that we'll be needing them, but if it will make you feel better, all right."

Both men drew their shiny new Winchesters from leather rifle boots and chambered rounds of ammunition. Following instructions, they carefully let the hammers down to the half-cock safety positions. They were sure they were ready for any trouble.

They topped a ridge of sand in the canyon's throat, a formation that would have been an island in time of flood. Before them the canyon opened out wider on either side and the steep walls leveled out at the bottom.

"You see, Lawrence?" insisted William, "there's nothing in sight for miles. Besides, if Indians were lying in wait for us, why wouldn't they have attacked us back in the narrow part of the canyon?"

"I suppose you're right," replied Lawrence, attempting to urge the bay down the sand bank. But the horse was suddenly uncooperative. He shifted his weight from one foot to the other and swung his head from side to side, as if being asked to make a dangerous leap. His rider didn't help matters by pulling reins counter to each movement of the horse's neck until both came to a confused stop.

"What's the matter now?" called William.

"It's nothing; he's just being fractious. Come on, fellow, come on," replied Lawrence, and he administered a kick to his mount's ribcage with both heels. The bay jerked forward, blundering between two sand piles on the short slope.

Instantly the heaps of sand erupted. Sotol jumped up to grab the startled lead horse's bridle, while on the other side, another Mojave jumped to his feet and seized the .44 rifle.

A more seasoned man would have instantly given up his hold on the rifle and drawn the Colt at his side, but such experience was not available to Lawrence, and he struggled to retain the Winchester. With the horse being pulled one way and the struggle for the yellow belly taking place on the other, rider and horse parted company and Lawrence was thrown to the ground. He had only a moment to experience the pain of an arm broken underneath him in his fall, for the successful Mojave spun the captured rifle in a flashing arc that brought it smashing down on Lawrence's head. After that he felt nothing at all.

Sotol let the bay prance around in a circle as he held on to the bridle and watched the end of the tug-of-war for the rifle. Then he turned to see what had happened to the other white man.

Turtleback and a fourth Mojave had also been disguised as mounds of earth forming a line just below the rim of sand. Their simple strategy had been to arrange themselves so that Lawrence had to descend the slope between two Indians. Turtleback and his companion had also jumped up when Sotol struck, but they ran immediately toward William and the pack horse.

Willliam's reactions were no quicker than Lawrence's, but he had a moment longer to think. He saw the struggle for possession of the rifle, and as the other two Indians ran toward him, he threw down the lead rope of the pack animal and raised the Winchester to his shoulder. By sheerest good fortune, his first shot took Turtleback in the cheek, shattering his face and taking off a considerable part of the back of his skull as it exited.

His second shot missed the other Mojave entirely, and in that same moment the Indian threw a razor-sharp hatchet that hit William just below the knee and neatly sliced down his shin bone. William cried out and almost dropped the rifle, but his horse showed greater presence of mind; the sorrel spun around to bolt back into the canyon. William saw in a whirling glimpse the descent of the rifle butt on Lawrence's head.

William reeled in the saddle and almost fell. He held both reins and rifle in his right hand as with his left he clutched his bloody leg and bent low over the horse's neck.

Through eyes almost squinted shut against the pain, he could see the pack horse racing ahead of him back the way they had come. An oddly detached part of his mind noted with chagrin that the pack had once again slipped and the supplies were being distributed over the landscape.

He had just had time to notice this when the remaining two Mojaves, who had remained hidden to cut off such an escape, jumped up to block his path. Their sudden appearance made the already panicked pack animal rear and swing broadside to the on-rushing sorrel. In the collision William went flying over both horses, the spinning rifle sparkling golden in the sunlight.

One of the Mojaves caught the Winchester in mid-air and waved it in triumph. The other rushed to stand over William, only to discover as he bent to slit the white man's throat that William's neck had snapped; he was already dead.

Tom Dawson had asked Josh to see to the shoeing needs of their three mounts, and so Josh was working beside the corral after his smithing duties at the mine were done for the day.

The three cowboys were finishing their own day's efforts, sacking some horses who were still pulling back against lead ropes, putting weighted saddles on others, and tying still others up to stand with bits in their mouths.

Josh had already completed the shoeing of Tom's mount, a horse named Duncan, and was fitting a second shoe to Mont's. After clenching the nails and ringing them off, he allowed the hoof to slip to the ground and straightened up with a creak of backbones.

"Hey, Josh," called Nate Dawson, "which of these plug-uglies do you like best?"

Josh let his eyes rove over the herd standing in varying degrees of submission. All were lean and scraggly in appearance, but one caught his attention. The animal Josh admired was taller than the rest, a buckskin with a dark mane and tail and four black stockings. He stood with his head held high and his body turned along the length of the rail to which he was snubbed. He appeared to be watching the proceedings in the corral with an intelligent and interested eye.

Josh waved toward him and replied, "That buck there."

Mont looked over from the roan he was sacking and commented, "You got a good eye, Josh. I figure he ran off from somebody; he's mostly broke already. Not like this fleabag." He indicated the roan which had begun plunging and straining at the lead rope even *before* Mont had waved the saddle blanket.

"Well, I'll be hogtied and horn-swoggled!" Mont exclaimed. Josh followed the line of the black man's outstretched arm past the buckskin, beyond the corral to the mesquite-covered hillside beyond.

Down the trail slanting away from Garson rode Pickax on Jenny. Behind him, at the end of a lead rope, was a stylish gray mare, and seated on that mare was a very erect young woman wearing smoked-lens glasses.

"That is Miss Callie Morris," Josh explained, "the daughter of mine superintendent Morris. I didn't know she could ride, and I'll bet her daddy doesn't know she's doing it, either."

All four men stopped to observe the progress of the two riders across the field. Apparently Pickax was calling out instructions over his shoulder, for he kept turning in his saddle, first one way and then the other, to watch Callie's ride.

And then it happened. As he was turned to watch her, a rattlesnake must have buzzed across the path in front of them. Jenny was a desert-wise creature who didn't buck or bolt, but her sidestep and twist off the trail was enough to tumble the backward-facing Pick into the dirt.

The gray was neither desert-bred nor very bright. At the first nervous activity by Jenny and Pick's clumsy sprawl right in front of her, the mare reared and bolted off across the hillside.

By sheer grit and determination, Callie kept her seat, but whether this was good fortune or bad remained to be seen. The mare, sensing the inability of the rider to gain control, plunged headlong through the mesquite and creosote, occasionally leaping over clumps of brush. And, of course, with every stride the horse was in danger of dropping a leg into a ground-squirrel hole or coming to grief on the uneven ground.

Josh took in the unfolding disaster at a glance. Without a second thought he threw himself at Duncan's lead rope. With a yank on the quick release that spun the startled horse around, he vaulted onto Duncan's back.

"Dear God, help Miss Callie!" came unbidden to his frantic mind as he felt the cowpony gather his haunches under him and spring away from the rail. He desperately hoped that the horse would respond to leg pressure, for he had only the free end of the lead rope in one hand and a handful of mane in the other.

Josh immediately discovered just how well-trained Duncan was. Tom Dawson's jug-headed horse was nothing special to look at, but he was smart and quick to pick up what was needed in the situation.

Almost as if he knew without being told what Josh wanted, Duncan galloped after the bolting mare. His great muscled neck stretched out front. His ears were pricked forward, and it was obvious that he was enjoying the chase.

The same could not be said of Josh. The blood was pounding through his heart like the hammer on his anvil. His breath caught in his throat with each leap and pivot of the gray mare, and he was filled with dread for the moment when he would see Callie flying off the mare's back to be broken against the rocky slope. The thought that this uncontrolled, desperate flight was happening to a blind girl made him full of unspeakable horror and dismay.

He urged Duncan to even greater speed. For what seemed like an agonizingly long time, the gap between the racing horses remained the same, until at last Duncan's greater muscle and length of stride began to tell.

As Josh and Duncan began to overtake the mare, Josh shouted ahead to Callie, "Hold on, Miss Morris, I'll get her stopped for you."

Over her shoulder, blown to him on the wind of the rushing horses, he heard, "I—have—no—intention—of—letting—go!"

Gradually, Duncan drew up alongside the racing mare. Lathered with exertion and fear, the gray rolled a wild eye sideways at Duncan before spurting away again. A quarter of a mile ahead, Josh could see the line of mesquite shrub beginning to dip into a boulder-strewn ravine.

Josh leaned far out over the horse's right shoulder, holding with great difficulty to both lead rope and mane clutched in his left hand.

He had to trust completely in the sureness of Duncan's pace and in the horse's sense of what was at stake. He urged Duncan on to the limit.

His fingertips stretched out toward the bridle of the mare. Another inch closer, and Josh glanced over at the blind girl. Though she had not screamed, her clenched fists on the reins and her face, completely drained of color, spoke of her fear.

Now his fingers touched the bridle, grasped the cheek strap, and pulled the mare alongside Duncan as Josh straightened himself upright. Still apprehensive that the mare would pitch Callie off, he did not try to bring her to an abrupt stop. Instead, he turned Duncan and the gray in a wide circle around to the left, back toward Garson. "It's all right, Miss Morris, I've got her now. Just another moment," he assured her as calmly as he could.

Slowly slackening Duncan's speed, Josh brought the mare under control. At last Josh turned them through the deepest sand he could find, and the gray gave up the race and shuddered to a stop.

Josh slid off Duncan wrong-sided, afraid to give up his grip on the bridle. When he stood alongside the mare, he shoved his left shoulder up under the gray's chin; only then did he reach up to assist Callie Morris down from the side-saddle on which she had perched for two terrifying miles.

"Here, Miss Morris, let me help you down. It's Josh. Josh Roberts. I've got you."

"Thank you," she gasped, "oh, thank you. I'm quite all right, Mr. Roberts—" she began. Then she collapsed into his arms with her face buried against his chest, the two horses snorting off steam and pawing the sand. Josh couldn't help but notice that she smelled like wildflowers.

"You there! Yes, you, Indian. Come here." McGinty gestured emphatically toward Sotol, who had been squatting unobtrusively around the corner of Fancy Dan's Saloon out of view of the street.

Sotol looked up, then away, staring out at the mesquite as if he hadn't heard a word.

McGinty walked over to the Mojave and stood, eyes squinted, regarding him. "I know you speak English; I saw you look up when I first called you."

Sotol grudgingly agreed, "I speak."

"Yes, and you understand even more than you speak, curse you. Now get up, I need you to carry a message to your chief."

Sotol looked up slowly and returned McGinty's stare.

Looking into those hard dark eyes, McGinty almost changed his mind and turned to walk back into his saloon. He swung back, trying to give as much smoldering hatred to his gaze as the Indian was giving him but found himself looking away.

Angrily he reached in his vest and withdrew a .44 shell from his watch pocket. He threw it down at the Indian's feet. "Go show that to your chief. Tell him I want to talk to him about it. Tell him I'll be at the old shack by Poison Well tomorrow night at moonrise."

Sotol looked at the shell lying on the ground, but gave no indication of agreement, not even a grunt. McGinty was inwardly relieved at the break in eye contact, so he didn't press the issue. He turned around and went to the outside staircase leading to his office.

As he reached the corner of the building he glanced over his shoulder.

Sotol and the cartridge were gone. Though the plain around had no brush taller than three feet for miles in all directions, the Mojave had disappeared as completely as if he'd never been there at all.

8

JOSHUA SOAPED UP again as Pick dumped yet another bucket of steaming water over his head.

"Somehow it just don't seem right usin' precious water for washin' all over." Pick shook his head in disapproval. He kicked the small tin bathtub where Josh sat folded up like an accordion. "And what's gonna happen to this water after you get out of it? Why, it ain't good for nuthin'. Can't cook in it. Can't drink it." He sniffed thoughtfully. "S'pose a feller could water his mule with it, 'cept the soap would make it sick."

"Well now, Pickax," Josh said as he scrubbed his neck, "we might be able to stretch the use of this water. You can take a bath after me."

"No, thanks. It ain't natural, a man gettin' wet all over. Don't know why you want to do it. Miss Callie ain't gonna see if you've got clean ears or dirty."

"No, but she has a fine-honed sense of smell. She recognized you by odor the other day in the blacksmith shop."

Pick aimed at the spittoon and let fly with a bullet of tobacco. "And I wouldn't think of deprivin' the lady o' that clue, neither. Why she's gonna think Joshua Roberts skedaddled and sent a well-oiled Mississippi gambler over to eat supper in his place. She ain't gonna know you, all sweet smellin' like lye soap an' lavender water! You better sleep in the livery stable tonight when you're done, or one o' these drunk miners is likely to mistake you for one of them Calico Queens!"

With that, Joshua dipped the tin cup into the water and drenched the old prospector. "Take your own gol durn bath!" Pickax roared. "Now I'm gonna smell like a wet dog!"

"That's some improvement, anyway," Joshua howled as Pickax hurled the bucket at him and stomped out of the small room.

The truth was, Joshua had no explanation as to why he now stood in front of the washstand mirror and worked to straighten the part in his hair. Pick was right. Callie Morris couldn't see him, so why had he taken a week's earnings and spent an hour at the general store picking out a new shirt and trousers and a celluloid collar? Why had he stood scowling down at the too short sleeves of the only Sunday-go-to-meetin'-coat in the place? Why had he washed his socks and dusted off his derby hat like some city slicker greenhorn from St. Louis?

Indeed, it was a mystery even to him. But when she had collapsed into his arms, when she had leaned against him, showing she was made of much softer stuff than he had thought, he had forgotten that she could not see him. As he had lifted her onto Duncan and escorted her back, he'd had the fleeting thought that in the future she should not meet him on the street and recognize him by the same method she had identified old Pick!

She was truly a beautiful woman—as fine and mysterious and strong— yes, and soft and sweet—as any woman he had ever seen. That kind of beauty deserved to be in the company of a man with a straight part and a clean shirt. After all, she hadn't invited a mule to supper, so Joshua reasoned he ought not smell like one!

Garson had no flowers for Joshua to bring to her, so after he had bought his new duds, he spent his last two bits on a bottle of lilac water. He hadn't forgotten that her skin smelled like a flower garden. He would bring her the scent as a token of the flowers he did not have.

Joshua had not counted on Pickax's ability to provide an instant crowd of grimy spectators. As he emerged from the boardinghouse, a chorus of hoots and yelps and hurrahs greeted him.

A group of two dozen laughing miners swelled to four dozen as he strode, red-faced, down the street. The No-Name Saloon emptied out when customers mistook the cheering, jeering uproar for a brawl.

"Ain't never seen a blacksmith so clean!"

"Kin you *smell* him? Hey, Josh! You fall into a barrel of eau de toilette or somethin'?"

"He's either died or he's gettin' hitched!"

"What's the difference?"

"He smells too nice to be dead!"

"Naw! That's the new embalming fluid!"

"It shore beats ice!"

"So does a warmhearted woman!"

At that, Joshua stopped in the center of the street and turned around to face the audience. The last comment had pushed the fun too far. After all, Miss Callie Morris was for sure not one of the girls in the town bordello.

The men nudged each other playfully as they saw Joshua's obvious irritation. He clenched and unclenched his fists and stared down the rowdies.

The laughter died to a nervous twittering.

"Who said that?" Joshua's voice was low and menacing.

Silence fell over the crowd. *This is the man who beat Big John Daniels. This is the man who . . .*

The men gulped and stepped back, their smiles apologetic. They knew they had gone too far.

Pickax shrugged. "We didn't mean nothin' by it, Josh. The fellers wasn't talkin' about Miss Callie disrespectful. They was just meanin' that women in general was better than ice."

Josh considered his words. He scowled deep and mean at a young fella who seemed to have developed the shakes. "You think women are better than ice, do you?" Josh growled. *"Well, I say . . .* that just depends on how hot the desert is!"

With that the group once again roared with laughter. Grimy hands reached out to clap Joshua on the back as he yelled above the boisterous tumult, *"Now quit following me before I take you on one at a time!"*

Content, the group turned back to the saloons of Garson, leaving Joshua to walk the last quarter mile to the Morris house in peace.

Joshua had hoped that the invitation to dine at the Morris home had been Callie's idea. Now as she sat silently across the table from him, Josh was certain that the invitation had been Mr. Morris's plan.

The small, tissue-wrapped bottle of perfume seemed to mock him from his pocket. *What were you thinking of, Josh Roberts? Even if she could see your face, she wouldn't look twice at you. You're a blacksmith, not a gentleman.* The new collar seemed suddenly too tight. The starch in his shirt made the fabric rustle when he reached out for the bowl of mashed potatoes. He wondered if word had gotten back to Callie that he had bought himself new duds for the occasion. He wondered if she could sense his embarrassment.

Ling Chow placed a heaping platter of fried chicken in front of Callie as Mr. Morris laid the purpose of this meeting on the table.

"I'd like to appoint you town constable, Joshua. Marshal of Garson, if you prefer that title," Morris announced as though it was already accomplished.

Joshua ducked his head slightly, and after letting the words sink in, he chuckled carefully. "I prefer blacksmith. Just . . . blacksmith, Mr. Morris."

Now it was Morris's turn to chuckle, and he glanced at Callie, who did not respond. "You were right, daughter." He turned back to Josh. "She told me you wouldn't want the job."

"She was right. I . . . I thank you, Mr. Morris, for the honor—if it is an honor. But I've no desire to get near anything hotter than my forge."

Morris stuck out his lower lip and again glanced first at Callie then back at Joshua as he considered the refusal. "You're a good man, Joshua. Good with your fists, and good with this." Morris tapped his forehead lightly. "Any fool can pack a sidearm. I could hire two dozen gunslingers tomorrow and pin badges on them, but they'd still just be trash behind tin stars. No. The Silver Rim . . . Garson . . . we're in need of a man who can think on his feet. You're our man."

"I've had little choice in any of the circumstances. It's not that I—"

"Nonsense!" Morris interrupted his protest. "If you had not done what you did, Callie would be dead. Tom Dawson said as much, and I believe him to be a man who speaks the truth."

Joshua shrugged. He had lost his appetite. The thought of keeping the peace in a town like Garson was the last assignment he wanted. "Anyone would have—"

"And then there is the matter of Big John." Morris cleared his throat authoritatively. "Not easy for you to say that anyone would have stopped *him*. But you found another way. I've been out in the West long enough to know that plenty of men have used the law as an excuse for killing. You had plenty of reason to pull the trigger and put Big John permanently into a hole in the ground. No one would have blamed you."

Callie still did not react to her father even though Josh was quite certain she would have had plenty to say if Big John Daniels had been killed. "I might have killed him," Josh admitted, "if I had thought of it." He looked quickly at Callie, trying to judge her expression.

Again Mr. Morris raised his hand to silence Joshua. "Tom Dawson tells me you were admiring that big lanky buckskin they're breaking down there." Was Morris changing the subject?

"He seemed the best of the remuda," Joshua nodded, relieved that the conversation had taken a different turn.

"He's yours, then."

"But—"

"It would not be proper for the Constable of Garson to go around on foot."

"But, Mr. Morris—"

"You'll need a saddle. Pick out something down at the livery stable and send the bill to me. Tom Dawson and those boys of his will finish breaking the buck and then choose a second horse from the herd. You might need a spare."

Joshua glared at the oblivious mine-owner. Now he could see where Callie Morris had acquired her obstinate nature. He waited until he was certain that Mr. Morris had finished speaking.

"I am just a blacksmith, Mr. Morris. Every day of my life since I was a boy, I've wrestled with horses and mules and pounded hot iron. It's no miracle that I could wrestle down John Daniels, no great shakes that I could pound him into submission. He is smaller than a horse and less ornery than a mule. There is nothing unusual in what I have done." He paused a moment, the said as firmly as he could, "I am no lawman."

Callie now smiled softly. She turned her face slightly away from him and said almost coyly. "Come now, Mr. Roberts. Some men have the law written in their hearts. My father has taken you for one of those."

Morris nodded. "That makes you lawman enough for me."

"Steel," Callie said in a voice that touched on admiration, "tempered with the gentleness of mercy." Her face shone in the soft glow of the candles in their silver candlesticks. Joshua saw his own reflection in the smoked glass of her spectacles. He felt trapped, unable to refuse her words or the tone of her voice. "My father is right, Mr. Roberts. You are quite ideal for the position."

"Except that I don't *want* it," Joshua replied incredulously.

Morris looked toward his daughter as if appealing for help. Although she could not see her father's face, she seemed to understand his feelings instinctively.

She smiled as if coaxing a reluctant child. "Joshua," she said, using his given name for the first time, "often we are called on to do things we do not wish to do. But we do them because there is simply no one else." She laid her hand palm up on the table. Instinctively, he responded to her gesture and placed his fingers against hers. It was as if their eyes had met.

"But there must be someone else," he said lamely.

"No," she replied, "there is no one else. You're the man for the job."

McGinty paced around inside the tumbledown shack, absently kicking a broken chair leg. Mike Drackett, who was leaning against the door frame, grinned at his boss's discomfort and remarked, "If you'd set down a spell you wouldn't be raisin' so much dust."

"Shut up!" said McGinty abruptly. "They aren't coming after all. Look there—" He gestured toward the almost-full moon which had risen over the starkly outlined cinder cone to the east. "We've been here since an hour before moonrise, and now it's an hour past. Let's get out of here; maybe this was a dumb idea all along."

Drackett was surprised to hear Fancy Dan admit to having second thoughts. *'Course, it's not like I wasn't havin' no jitters myself,* he thought, then said, "You was gonna give them Mojaves rifles to stick up the stage, is that right?"

"Certainly. Only *we'd* tell them which ones to attack so as to cause Morris the most grief over lost payroll and people."

A sigh, softer than a breath of air, sifted into the cabin. Outside, the shadows of the cat's claw bushes reached gnarled talons toward the cabin, retreating reluctantly before the rising moon. A nightjar twittered softly.

Drackett blinked, then rubbed his eyes. *Was that shadow that large a moment ago?* he wondered, a stab of fear quickening his pulse. Almost of itself, his left hand eased his Starr revolver a little higher in his holster.

From behind him a voice with the age and gentle power of a shifting sand dune spoke. "You will remove your fingers very carefully from the pistol."

Drackett and McGinty both had the good sense to freeze where they were. Drackett's hand slipped up across his stomach. Making no sudden movements, both turned slowly around to see Pitahaya standing in the deepest shadow of the room. *How did he get there?* both men thought in unison, but their attention was more intently focused on the muzzle of the rifle Pitahaya held.

"Why have you called me to this meeting? I know you to be a seller of the water-that-burns-with-fire, but my people have no money with which to buy. And what means the little-death-carrier you sent which is now in the fire stick pointed at your belly? I have done speaking."

McGinty explained to the chief his plan to help the Mojaves know which coaches would be carrying the payroll shipments. With that much money, he explained, Pitahaya's people could buy rifles, whiskey—anything they wanted.

"And when the pony soldiers come against us, what then?"

"It won't last that long. Two or three times at the most, and your people can go to your mountain camps with enough money for supplies to stay a year. By then this will be forgotten."

"And why do you make war on your own people?"

"Because others have what should belong to me and I want it," Mc-Ginty said cautiously.

"Bah! You are no man of honor, Mig-In-Tee. But we will fight this fight, and we will go to the mountains to live better than we do now. I want fifty of the golden-sided rifle-that-shoots-many-times and twice ten hands of bullets for each."

"Fifty rifles and a hundred rounds of ammunition each?" exploded Mc-Ginty. "I don't want to make war on the whole state, I just want you to knock over a couple of stages!"

At the angry tone in Fancy Dan's voice, Drackett's hand crept back down toward the butt of the revolver. His fingertips had barely touched the wood of the grip when he felt the prick of a steel knife point on his neck and a chill of fear down his spine.

"I know, Mig-In-Tee, that you wish us to be blamed for doing evil for you. You say the army will not come before we have gone. This may be true, but still we will be ready to fight them or we will not walk the war trail with you."

"All right, fifty rifles and the ammunition," McGinty agreed. "But," he warned, "it will take some time; I can only give you ten rifles now."

Pitahaya grunted a reply which McGinty took for assent, and he continued, "Also, you must only attack those whom we say. I know about the two prospectors you killed. That's where you got the Winchester you're holding."

Pitahaya shrugged as if the matter was of complete indifference to him. "It may be so, who can say? The desert claimed them for its own, that is all. They were not wise in its ways."

"If we're agreed, then tell your friend there to take the knife out of Mike's neck," commanded McGinty, proud of himself for having noticed the Indian behind Drackett. The pressure of the knife point was withdrawn and Drackett, who had been holding his breath, sighed with relief.

"Now about those first ten rifles . . ." McGinty, who had turned to look with amusement at Drackett's wide eyes gleaming with fear, was startled to discover that Pitahaya was gone as soundlessly as he had come.

Nearly everything had been settled by the time Ling Chow cleared away the dishes and poured coffee into the fine china cups. They were not made to fit the finger of a blacksmith. They were made for the delicate hand of a woman.

The observation gave Josh determination to speak out. There was something that had troubled him ever since Callie's mare bolted with her on its back. Josh knew more than a little about horses, and he was certain that the flashy gray was not made for the young woman who sat across from him now.

He cleared his throat. "That's a fine-looking mare you've got, Miss Callie—" His voice trailed off. After all, the choice of a mount was a very personal thing, like the choice of a friend.

"She was a gift. I brought her with me," Callie said abruptly, without a smile. Did she guess where he was leading?

"A fine animal for a bridle path in a park, no doubt." Josh glanced at Mr. Morris who understood completely and encouraged him with a nod.

"Yes. I spent many afternoons on her, with a friend at my side. I can ride as well as a woman with sight. What happened last Tuesday was just a fluke, Mr. Roberts. It might have happened to anyone."

"It *would* have happened to anyone, on that horse," Josh plunged ahead.

"There is nothing wrong with the horse. She was frightened by the snake, and—"

"And she almost got you killed," Josh interrupted.

Callie's voice quavered slightly. "It could have happened to anyone," she repeated. Defensive and frightened by the experience, she made an effort to convince herself.

"Not with the right mount," he said firmly. "I know a little about horses. That mare is too high-strung for this part of the country." He was careful not to add that the horse was too high-strung for Callie Morris.

"I am used to her," Callie argued with lifted chin.

"She'll get you killed," he repeated, determined to see the discussion through by the hint of helplessness in her voice. She did argue, but certainly she understood that he was telling her the truth.

"But I love riding; it is the only real freedom—" She faltered.

"Look, I watched those Dawson boys break a whole string down there." Excitement edged his voice. "They've got one little bay mare—a pretty thing, she is. Black mane and tail, black stockings and good feet. And she's the kind of horse that just *wants* to please. Miss Callie, I trimmed her feet, and she was just the sweetest thing—practically turned around and said thanks! I said to myself, 'Now, this is a horse a man could ride from here to Mexico and never feel it!' And she's careful. Watches where she's going. Mont James rode her all over these hills, and her ears were perked and listening to every word he said. And I told him, 'There's a horse for Miss Callie.' "

She sat silently as he paused and waited. A slight smile curved her lips. "Then . . . you aren't saying I should never ride again?"

"No, Miss Callie. You've just got the wrong animal for the territory. But there is a right one for you . . ."

Now she inclined her head toward her father, who had chosen not to enter into the discussion with his strong-willed daughter. "Papa, could you arrange . . . I mean, if I am going to be riding again in the desert, perhaps Shadow is *not* suitable. If Mr. Roberts says there is a horse which will be better . . ."

Now Josh pretended to convince Mr. Morris, who was relieved down to the ground. "She's a three-year-old. Mont James says he'd be happy to put a bit more time on her and then give your daughter a hand until they're acquainted. No two horses are ever broke alike, but I never saw a horse so willing."

"Well, then," Morris eyed Callie. "It's rare to find a filly so well-tempered. I'd be a fool to pass her by."

A smile of genuine relief filled Callie's face. "May we go now and see her? I could use a little walk after Ling's dinner."

"Now? After dark?" Josh was surprised by her eagerness, and pleased he had pursued the offer.

"The dark does not hinder me, Mr. Roberts . . . *Joshua*. I can lead if you like." She laughed lightly, at ease with her handicap. "And please call me Callie."

And so Callie Morris took Joshua's arm and strolled slowly toward the corral where the new horses milled around. Josh liked the warmth of her small hand on his arm, and so he did not tell her that the sky was lit up with stars that illuminated the world from one horizon to the other. Instead he let her guide him.

"This is going to be a real town someday," she said quietly. "Thank you, Joshua, for agreeing to be the constable. My father really needs your help with this. I wasn't just trying to 'sweet-talk' you into doing something you didn't want to do."

His smile forgave her and he quipped, "Just so long as I don't have to do it forever!"

"You see that knoll over there?" Callie pointed and, indeed, there was a knoll to her right. "I told Papa that as soon as the mine pays off we are going to have a church there. You can't have a town without a church."

He chuckled. "In this town we'd better have a jail built first. You can't have a town without the law."

"No. First the church, so that the jail will more likely be empty." In the distance the low nicker of a horse was heard. Callie stopped and turned to face Joshua. "Thank you for what you did in there." Her voice was full of gratitude. "Pick had taken me riding before, but we didn't want to worry my father, so we kept it a secret. Even the time we found you dying in the desert . . ." Her face flushed. "I didn't know who you were then, of course."

Josh's mouth fell open. "So it was *you!*"

"After what happened this week, my father told me I would not be allowed to ride here again," Callie continued. "He said the incident occurred because I am blind, and—well, I almost believed it myself. Anyway, thank you for—" She did not finish.

Josh placed his hand over hers lying lightly on his arm. "I reckon you can do almost anything better than any other woman I know." Could she tell he was smiling at her? Did she know he wanted to kiss her?

She raised her face slightly as if to look at him, and he leaned toward her, smelling the fresh scent of lilacs. She smiled gently and lifted her chin toward him. He kissed her tenderly, and after a long moment she squeezed his arm.

"We'd best get back to the house now, Joshua," she said quietly. "But thank you—thank you for everything."

9

"**B**IG JOHN," SAID Josh to Daniels, still chained to the post of his improvised jail, "aren't you about ready to get loose from there?"

"You got that right! I been here a month, seems like, an' I keep thinkin' 'bout them creepy-crawlers, so's at night I don't sleep much."

"You know, they told me they were gonna send for a judge or deputy for your case. But now I hear tell they've got some kind of inquest going into the death of two prospectors found over by Three Kill Spring. Nobody seems to know what to do about you, much less care, but I personally don't like the idea of leaving you tied up. Now if I cut you loose, are you gonna take out after my hide again?"

"Ah, *naw,* Josh! Shucks, you been right good to me. Feedin' me and fixin' this here tent an' all. I figger as off my head as I was, I coulda wound up shot and throwed to the coyotes. I only gets mean like that when I mix it up with the tangle-leg. Then I wants to mix it up with ever'body."

"Yeah, I figured that out. You ought to stay away from that rattlesnake juice."

"I try to, Josh, I really do. But when I'm a'workin' the forge, an' he comes by an' says, 'Come on, Big John, come and wet your whistle,' why I just natur'ly did what he said. An' he kep' sayin', 'Drink up, plenty more where that come from,'—shoot fire, I'se too far gone by then to see straight, much less stop."

"You keep referring to 'he,' Big John; who is 'he?' Who gave you the whiskey?"

"I thought you know'd, Josh. It was Beldad, the night foreman."

Before they'd reached a final agreement, Josh had given Morris two conditions for accepting the job of constable. The first was that Big John Daniels be reinstated as blacksmith. Morris agreed only after Josh assured him he would take full responsibility. The second was that Josh be given a week with Pickax to learn the ways of the desert.

As the two approached Pick's camp, the old man made a wide sweep with his arm in a gesture of welcome. "All right, boy, if you've a mind to study the desert, just remember that she don't take foolin' with. You gotta go with her, not agin her."

With no more preamble than this remark, the lessons had begun. Pick started by asking if Josh knew why the camp was located in this spot, and why the tent flap opened in the direction it did. The miner nodded his approval when Josh explained correctly that the campsite was shaded from the afternoon heat by the shadow of the overhanging bluff, and that the tent opening was such that it kept the prevailing wind from filling the tent with sand.

The two reached the tent and unsaddled their mounts. Josh gathered some dry mesquite branches, then collected some of the fleshy bulbs of prickly pears, as he had been instructed. "What do you want these for?" he asked curiously as the miner got a fire going.

"Lot's of good in a cactus, boy. Look here." Pickax proceeded to singe the barbs off the plant before tossing it to the ground. Jenny eagerly began to nibble the cactus shoots before they were completely cooled. Then Josh's horse Injun followed suit.

"Desert-bred critters can usually forage for themselves," commented Pick, "but sometimes we help 'em out a mite."

The next few days passed quickly with Pick proving an apt instructor and Josh an eager pupil. He learned which trees indicated the presence of moisture beneath the sand, and how to keep himself and his horse fed.

Pick told Josh to gather mesquite beans, which could be eaten, and pointed out the value of lizards for roasted meat. Josh also learned of a good poultice for snakebite—chewing tobacco.

"You gotta watch out for them little sidewinders and Mojave greens," warned Pick. "They hide in the sand with just their eyeballs out. And they don't give no warning before they take out after you, neither."

The one topic Pick laid the most stress on was the need for preparation and planning. "I seen people come to grief out here who shoulda knowed better. Like they was countin' on findin' water at a certain tank, and it was dry. They shoulda planned for that! They shoulda kept back enough water to get them by to the next spring."

"But what if that hole was dry too, Pick; what then? How can you plan for that?"

"Why shoot, boy, in that case they better be planned up on how they's gonna meet their Maker, 'cause they shore nuff will be seein' Him pronto. The trick, though, is doin' your plannin' so you don't see Him too soon!

"I seen men crazy fer water drinkin' sand, an' I seen men drink horse blood so's they could make one more sunset.

"Just remember, a man with a mount an' water is home safe. A man with only his horse or only his water can tough it through. But a man with neither horse nor water is a *dead man!*"

Whenever Pick saw that he was dishing out information faster than Josh could take it in, he'd call a halt to their classroom time. Then they'd retreat up the draw behind Pick's camp for a little shotgun practice. Josh had not carried the greener around town, but in his new job as constable, he agreed with Morris and Pickax that he should carry a weapon.

"No, boy, no, ya gotta clamp that scatter gun tight against your side, less'n you want to be missin' some teeth when she goes off!"

Josh quickly concluded that there weren't many fine points to blasting away with a sawed-off shotgun. The idea seemed to be to point the greener in the general direction of the target and keep a good hold on it so it wouldn't leap out of your hands when fired.

"This here rig is a whole sight better'n them old cap-fired models. Why, a man can load an' fire these little paper cartridges faster'n you can holler, *I quit!*"

Pick walked over to Josh's target area. "Looky here at this heap of prickly pear you just blasted. Throwed pieces out in all directions an' ain't any of them pieces too big, neither!" He laughed and shook his head.

"Remember son, a six-gun'll give you a scratch, but buckshot means buryin'."

10

JOSH TOOK TO his new duties with sincere interest, if not enthusiasm. He practiced the frontier proverb, *You play the hand you're dealt;* only he would have said, *You shoe the horse they bring you.*

The merchants and townspeople were, for the most part, supportive of his appointment. They saw the establishment of a full-time peacekeeping position as one more step toward civilization, respectability—even permanence. Jacobson, the hardware store owner, was especially agreeable.

"Yah, dis a great day for Garson. We haf ben mit out a lawman long enuff, und de riff-raff is gettin' too big mit der britches, yah?"

"*For* their britches, Mr. Jacobson," Josh corrected. "But I hope you don't expect the town to change overnight just because I'm around. As long as there's drinking and miners mixed together, there's always a match to the dynamite, I think."

"Yah, but you are de strong breath to blow out dis metch. You, und dat cannon you have der—" He gestured toward the shotgun that Josh carried muzzle downward by a sling around his right shoulder.

Josh reached over with his left hand and grasped the greener around its stock. "You're right about that. Even folks who'd argue with me don't care to get into a dispute with this."

Their conversation was interrupted by the sound of gunfire. A man Josh recognized as an employee at the Red Dog Saloon burst out of the swinging doors and ran up to him. "Hey, aint'cha the new constable?"

"That's me. What's the trouble?"

"You better come with me, pronto. There's this Texican shootin' up the place!"

Josh moved cautiously toward the saloon while Mr. Jacobson dashed inside his store and bolted the door.

"Whoopee! Ah'm the original, double tough, quick as a rattler, death-dealer! Whoopee!" With the second yell came another gunshot that shattered the Red Dog's front window and made curious citizens across the street run for cover.

Josh had unslung the shotgun and held it at ready as he crouched beside the building, but his mind was racing, looking for some way to avoid a shootout.

"Barkeep! Barkeep, I say! I don't like the looks of that lady's pit'cher up thar. She's lookin' at me funny. Turn her face to the wall, Barkeep, and be quick about it."

Josh peered cautiously around the corner through the broken window, and saw the drunken man holding a six-gun on the trembling bartender as the latter tried to reach a painting hanging over the bar. When he still could not reach it after climbing up on the shelves of liquor, the Texan said, "Let's see y'all jump for it," and he fired another round, just barely missing the bartender's foot. The bartender fell sideways in a crash of bottles, smashing three shelves down to the floor.

Josh knew it was only a matter of time before somebody started shooting in earnest. Hanging the shotgun back over his shoulder, he stood up and called loudly into the saloon.

"Where you at, you old cuss? Hey, don't be bustin' up all them bottles, save some for me!"

The Texan whirled around and stood swaying slightly as if pondering this interruption.

Josh gave him no time to respond. "Where you been keepin' yourself? Why, I ain't seen you since Waco. How ya been?"

The cowboy's eyes squeezed shut, then opened slowly and focused on Josh with difficulty. A gambler was hiding under a table by Josh's feet as he stepped over the window sill and into the saloon. He called out, "Shoot him, shoot him quick!" He was silenced by Josh's sudden kick into his midsection.

Josh continued to address the drunk in a loud voice. "Still usin' that same ol' Colt, ain't you? Danged if it ain't a fine piece. Is your eye as good as it was when y'all shot twelve bullseyes runnin' at that turkey shoot on the Brazos?"

The Texan considered this question by looking down at the Colt in his hand, then back at Josh. He nodded slowly, then yelled, "Wanta see? Prop up one of 'em tin-horn gamblers. I'll shoot out his gold fillin's!"

"Naw, old hoss, now that ain't no contest. See if you can shoot the flies offa the top of that wall there." Josh waved toward the side wall of the saloon, away from the street and the rest of the town.

The Texan squinted his eyes and then remarked with confidence, "Ah'll take the one on the left first!" and he fired another shot that hit high on the wall.

"Dogged if'n you didn't nail him. Can you catch his friend there, too?"

Without further comment, the cowboy fired again and with evident satisfaction, yelled, "Whoopee! I kin lick my weight in wildcats, an' shoot faster'n greased lightning, I—"

Josh added quickly, "Hey, hoss, that little one up there's gettin' away."

"No, he ain't!" shouted the Texan, and "click" went the hammer on an empty chamber.

"Grab him, boys," ordered Josh, and the cowering drinkers and gamblers wasted no time in subduing the cowboy.

"Don't hurt him," cautioned Josh. "Tie him up and bring me his rig. Take him upstairs and let him sleep it off, then let's see about cleaning up this mess."

"What about that Roberts fellow?" McGinty asked Beldad.

Mike Drackett leaned forward in his chair and grinned. "Lemme take care of him, Boss. I been itchin' for the chance."

McGinty spun his office chair around to face Drackett. "No, you ignorant lunk, do you want to really unite this town against us? I don't mean *eliminate* him, I'm talking about *recruiting* him!"

Drackett snorted, "Him? He's Morris's right-hand man after savin' that blind gal. What's more, I hear tell he's sweet on her. I can take him, Boss, I know I can. Lemme just solve this problem once and for all!"

McGinty wasn't so quick to reply this time. "Not now, not yet," he muttered. "Not while he's riding so high and has those friends in town. The Dawsons are no folks we want to cross. We'll give Beldad a chance to sound Roberts out, and wait for those cowboys to get out of town. All right, Beldad?"

"Sure, Mr. McGinty, anything you say. But Mike here is right. Roberts can't be bought, I'm thinkin'."

"Everyone has his price," murmured Fancy Dan softly. "We just have to find out what his might be."

At twilight Josh was leaning against the wall outside Jacobson's Hardware, watching the progress of traffic up and down the road. Despite rumblings from the working men of Garson about the upcoming layoff, no violence had broken out, and the town seemed calm.

Beldad approached Josh from across the street. "Hello, Roberts," he said.

"Beautiful evening, Mr. Beldad. Are you headed up to work?"

"Directly, directly. Time enough for a drink first. Thought I'd ask you to join me."

"No, thank you, Mr. Beldad. I believe I'll just stay here and enjoy the evening."

Despite this refusal, Beldad gave no indication of intending to move on. Instead he moved closer to Josh and dropped his voice.

"You know, there's something I've been meaning to speak to you about, having to do with the welfare of this town and the mine and all."

"Yes, Mr. Beldad. What might that be?"

"The men are not going to stand for this unfair treatment by Morris. You can see they'll be able to prevent any work from being done at all if Morris doesn't change his mind. Anyway, it's important for us to know where you stand."

"I'm curious about who *us* might be, Mr. Beldad, but then you haven't been exactly keeping your sentiments quiet. Even though you're a foreman, you belong to the so-called Working Men of Garson, don't you?"

"There is no shame in being connected with a group who are standing up for their rights and demanding fair treatment."

"No, that's correct as you have described it. But what I see of these who style themselves Working Men is a group of loud-mouthed bullies. Your group, Mr. Beldad, seems to contain a high percentage of men who were already discharged for drunkenness or loafing or being general troublemakers. I'll bet the actual number of single miners who wholeheartedly support you is very small indeed."

"And you, Roberts? Aren't you single? Or are you special since you been sparking that blind girl? It don't hurt your standing with—"

Beldad's words were cut off mid-sentence as Josh lifted the man by his shirtfront so that only his boot tips touched the planks.

"Beldad, I'm going to tell you this just once: your opinions about me are of no interest to me. But let me hear tell of you bad-mouthing Miss Callie—just once, and not only will I thrash you within an inch of your life, but I'll tie a can to your tail and stone you out of town like the miserable cur you are! Now get out of my sight!" Josh let Beldad drop so abruptly that instead of landing upright, Beldad missed his footing and landed heavily, seat first, on the boardwalk.

"You better watch yourself, Roberts," snarled Beldad. "You'll be sorry you didn't listen to me. You'll see you can't treat me like this!"

Roberts turned slowly to stare down at Beldad, who for all his tough talk had not risen to his feet to speak his piece. "Should I consider that a threat, Mr. Beldad?"

"A warning, call it. You'll be sorry!"

"Beldad, I'm already sorry I didn't run you out of town before now! Get out of here before I change my mind and start looking for the can and string!"

Beldad scrambled to his feet and made a quick exit in the opposite direction, cursing and muttering all the way.

11

JOSH PATROLLED GARSON'S street for a few uneventful days. Then he looked up one morning to see Mont James sauntering toward him with a cat-that-got-the-canary grin on his face.

Before Mont could speak, Josh held up his hand. "Don't tell me; let me guess. You've unloaded all those spavined, jug-headed death-on-four-feet critters on some poor, unsuspecting greenhorns."

Mont's grin grew still wider, his eyes dancing with merriment. "All right; you're so all-fired smart, you tell me the rest."

Josh mused a minute, then continued, "And instead of making a down payment at Freeman's Mortuary, like they ought to before forkin' one of your widow-makers, they paid in cash!"

Mont's smile fairly reached from ear to ear, but he only replied, "Now you're with it, brother; preach on, preach on!"

"And, and . . . what else is there?"

Mont raised his eyebrows expectantly.

"You don't mean—you got more buyers than you had horses!"

"You can put a big 'Amen!' to that, brother Joshua!" Mont dropped his exaggerated accent. "We sold every head out of this string and we're heading back out for more!"

"That's great news, Mont. Will you and Tom and Nate be leaving right away?"

"Yes, but we're going home first. Tom's been missing Miss Emily something fierce. We've been on the dry side of those peaks for better'n a month now, and some things up yonder need tending to. We figure to be back in two or three weeks and get another roundup and breaking done before the snow flies."

Josh stuck out his hand. "I hate to see you go, Mont. You and your family have been about the only ones in this town who aren't either crazy or scared or angry about something."

Mont grasped Josh's hand and looked directly into his friend's eyes and replied, "Josh, you and me, we work around horses and we know how tricky they can be and how ornery and how powerful. But sooner or later, they all come around to being broke to ride. How is that, do you figure?"

Josh wasn't sure where this twist in the conversation was leading, but he found himself nodding thoughtfully and answering, "I guess some horses figure out sooner than others that you're going to feed them as well as break them, and that for a little cooperation they can get a lot of care."

Mont nodded. "And do we try to take all the spirit out of 'em?"

"Naw, no way. You just try to break their will to fight back, not destroy their spirit. Why, a horse with no spirit is as worthless as a nag that's never been broke, only in a different way."

"Exactly." Mont smiled.

"What do you mean, *exactly?* I don't know what you're getting at."

"You said everybody in Garson is angry or fretted or crazy. The truth is, they've never been broke; they're still fighting the bit and kicking the saddle to flinders."

"Broke? Broke by who?"

"Come on now, Josh. You told me your mama raised you in the church. You know what I'm driving at. The Lord Jesus is just waiting for a chance to care for them and teach them and take the fret out of their lives, but first they've gotta get their muliness broke down to size, so He can build up their good qualities from there."

"Yeah, I see what you mean. Just like breaking horses, huh?"

"Yep. Except for one little thing."

"What might that be?"

"When I go to break a horse, I don't ask his permission. But when God wants to make someone over, He can't even begin till they ask Him."

"Are you saying I need to ask Him?"

"Well, Josh, only you and the Lord Jesus know about that. But I know you're headed His way. God's got big plans for you, Josh Roberts, and He isn't through putting the school on you, yet!"

Mont pumped Josh's hand again and added, "You be extra careful, Mr. Constable. I want to see this town prosper and get civilized so they'll buy more horses. I figure the town needs you to guide it along." He slapped Josh on the shoulder. "If you need us sooner than a month, just give a holler and we'll come running. Be seeing you, Josh."

The stage from Mojave was running late. The connecting stage from San Bernadino was delayed, and the driver from Mojave had no choice but to wait. The connecting stage carried the payroll, some two thousand dollars in gold coin, for the Silver Rim in Garson.

The driver was a five-year veteran of this desert run. A short, stocky man with a loud voice and a swaggering walk, his name was Hurry Johnson. He enjoyed the task of guiding the four-up team of mules through the arid country. Much of the terrain was flat, allowing many opportunities for speed, and speed was what Hurry Johnson lived for.

Hurry was a great admirer of the exploits of Hank Monk and other line handlers whose daring—if not insane—driving had made them legendary. For all that he imitated of their style, Hurry didn't care about achieving fame; the chance to drive fast as often as possible was reward enough.

In spite of his emphasis on speed, Hurry was a skilled professional, constantly asking questions of the other drivers to improve his knowledge of the conditions of the road. But he was not given to worrying about what he considered idle speculation, so when he heard talk of Indian activity, he was skeptical.

"Them Mojaves ain't got grit enough to attack a stage with a armed driver and guard. Their style is more pickin' on lonely old dirt-poor prospectors an' toothless dogs," he said.

He was told that some stretches of the trail toward the silver mining country were watched by Mojaves. It was not uncommon to see small clusters of Indians making their way from place to place, but they had never seemed to be concerned about the passage of the red and yellow coaches that spattered them with gravel and left them in the dust.

"Lately they been watchin' us, but it ain't like them to be movin' much in the heat of day," he was told.

Hurry discounted all this talk. He knew stage drivers craved adventure. The plain fact was, most of the present bunch had grown up too late for much of the excitement in the West. Now the really long trips were all made by train, and even little out-of-the-way one-horse towns were getting civilized. Hurry figured that any talk of Indian trouble was a result of wishful but fanciful thinking. Anyway, speed was where real adventure could be found. "Aah," he snorted, "I can outrun a Mojave any day."

His guard for this trip was a young man, Oliver de la Fontaine by name. Folks around said Oliver was too short by half for such a long name, but if they did make that observation they did so out of his hearing. Oliver was a slight young man of nineteen, but he had "killed his man" when he was only seventeen and was known to be a practiced hand with the Smith and Wesson he brought west with him from Boston.

For this trip he was carrying a shotgun, as stagecoach guards often did, but he still wore the S and W at his side. Hurry was impatient to be off, so when the inbound coach finally did arrive, he barely grunted in greeting before throwing the mail pouches and the payroll bag into the boot. He snapped its cover down and had it half secured when he was told that he also would have a passenger with some luggage.

Hurry ripped back the canvas with a violent yank that indicated how irritated he was. When the trunk had been deposited, he wasted no time in tightening the leather straps and buckles, then vaulted into his seat.

A kick to the brake lever and a slap of the reins and they were off, with Oliver making a quick grab at his hat and their solitary passenger being seated somewhat more abruptly than he had intended.

This was a good stretch of road to make up time, and Hurry proceeded to take advantage of it. The road skirted the mesquite and yucca-covered foothills east of the Sierra Nevadas as it ran northward. The land was not flat, but the rises and washes were gentle enough to cause little loss of speed. Behind the coach rose a dust cloud twenty feet high that trailed them for a quarter of a mile as they sped along.

To reach the first stop at Weidner's was only a matter of an hour or so. The team was not changed here; they were just given a little water and a chance to breathe before the run was resumed.

The next hour contained both faster and slower passages. The road crossed deeper washes that flooded when the thunder crashed over the Sierra peaks. These canyons not only had steeper sides, but sandy bottoms that slowed the team as resistance to the coach's wheels increased.

Slowing down was something Hurry did relunctantly, but he knew a driver who had dumped a coach in an attempt to use too much speed in one of these arroyos. Hurry hadn't particularly thought the wreck was a tragedy; what bothered him was that the driver had been fired and had been forced to leave this area to get work. So in the plunges into the canyons, Hurry used more caution than he really wanted.

These periods of slower travel were compensated by the times when the stage road ran through the alkali flats. Formed when the occasional flood burst out of the confining arroyos, the flats could be as much as a mile wide. The mineral-laden water which pooled in these areas was either absorbed into the soil or evaporated, leaving behind a crust of alkali salts which formed a hard, shiny surface on which almost nothing grew.

On these stretches Hurry was really in his element. He urged the team to greater and greater speed, and they responded till the coach fairly flew over the ground. A grin would break out on Hurry's features as if the force of the wind itself had pulled the corners of his mouth back toward his ears.

Oliver had ridden with Hurry enough to be nonchalant about this breakneck charge across the desert. Passengers, on the other hand, were so often unprepared for the intensity of the rush that they remained unable to speak or relax their white-knuckled grips on their valises for several minutes after reaching Red Rock Station.

There the team was changed, and sometimes mail and passengers exchanged. The road also split at this point, turning aside toward Garson from the main track that continued on north to Indian Wells.

From the station eastward through Red Rock Canyon, Hurry's face resumed its normal, uninspired look. The twists and turns of the road as it followed the wash through sandstone ledges never allowed for the velocity Hurry craved. Passengers might enjoy the orange and pink formations and comment on the colorful bands stretched on either side of the road, but Hurry took no pleasure in sightseeing.

As the coach turned into the third in a series of S-shaped curves leading through the canyon, Oliver leaned over and observed, "You know, Hurry, I think I saw an Injun up top of that rock. Isn't this the stretch where Murchison said he saw those Mojaves?"

"I reckon. I never paid him no mind, anyways. What d'ya figger the Injun was doin'?"

"I don't know, but let me get Betsy here limbered up anyway," said Oliver as he took the shotgun out of its rest beside his seat and checked its loads.

"Hey, in there!" Oliver called to the passenger. "Look sharp! There may be some trouble up ahead. If you got a piece, get it ready." The message produced more than just startled consternation, for in a moment a hand protruded from the driver's side window holding a .45 caliber Colt.

The stage entered the next turn, slowing to a cautious pace, then speeding up as the corner was made and the way shown to be clear. "Twern't nothin' to it, after all," grunted Hurry. "Mebbe you had a speck o' dust in your eye."

Oliver was about to agree when a rifle shot struck the seat between the two men, splintering the underside of the board. Oliver whirled around to catch a glimpse of a Mojave on an overhead sandstone ledge just as he directed another shot at them. He returned one barrel of the shotgun at the attacker, more in hope of spoiling the Indian's aim than of hitting him, then immediately emptied the second barrel at another Mojave on the opposite canyon wall. This time the blast made its mark as the Indian clutched his chest and tumbled forward off the rocks.

Hurry snapped the reins and cursed the mules into a sudden burst of speed. They needed no urging as they caught the nervous excitement of rifle fire popping around them.

The passenger was firing now also, taking deliberate aim as well as he could from the pitching and careening coach. The sandstone walls seemed to have sprouted Mojaves; half a dozen were firing from either side of the arroyo. The passenger's last shot took out an Indian who was firing down on the coach, but not before a .44 slug tore behind Hurry's left shoulder and dug a furrow down his back.

From the sudden curse that burst from his lips and clenched teeth, Oliver knew Hurry had been hit. "Shall I take the lines?" he shouted.

"I can drive with my teeth if I have to. Just you keep 'em offa me, an' I'll get us outta here." Other shots hit the coach as he spoke.

The fact was, the coach had already swept past all but the last pair of Mojaves. Although the occupants of the stage couldn't have known it at the time, the Indians had been unsure of their strategy and had relied too much on new weapons with which they were not yet very familiar.

Oliver fired his S and W at the last Indian on his side when both Mojaves leaped from their rocky perches toward the speeding stage coach. One landed on top of the coach, but was slung over the side as they jolted around a curve. The Indian caught himself just before being thrown off and began to pull himself back up over the side. Oliver leveled his pistol at the Indian's head, but the hammer snapped on an empty chamber as he pulled the trigger. He instinctively reached for the shotgun which lay at his feet. Swinging it by the barrel, his gun stock's blow swept the Mojave backwards and off the coach, bouncing him against the rocky wall and onto his face in the sand.

The other Indian, landing further back on the stage's roof, did not attempt to attack either driver or guard. He had made his leap with a knife clenched in his fist, and he used it now to slit open the canvas covering of the boot.

After knocking the one Mojave clear of the coach, Oliver had crammed two more shells into the shotgun and clambered to the roof. He was surprised to see the Indian crouching in the boot, throwing out the passenger's trunk and mailbag, then raising the payroll pouch to throw it off. At Oliver's involuntary shout, the Indian looked up, poised to throw his knife. Oliver's shotgun, no more than four feet away, blew him right off the back.

Hurry never let up on the mules until they had exited the canyon and put some miles of open space between themselves and the attack. Then he pulled up to rest the lathered and trembling team and allowed Oliver to examine and bandage his wound. The bullet had torn the flesh clear down to Hurry's hip where it had glanced off a bone before exiting.

"Looks to me like this'll be more trouble to your sitting back in a chair than it will to your driving," observed Oliver.

"I coulda told you that," said Hurry, through gritted teeth. "Ain't nothin' keeps me from drivin'.'"

"I can't imagine where the Mojaves got those rifles, but it was lucky for us they weren't too good at using them!"

"More'n that, it's lucky they didn't hit the mules. Likely they was tryin' not to hit 'em, so's they could drive 'em back to their camp and make a meal of 'em."

"Did you ever know these Indians to attack a stage before?"

"Never. Mostly they stay clear of folks that can fight back, but this bunch had a plan to take us out."

"Suppose they knew about the payroll shipment?"

"How in tarnation could an Injun know about that? That last 'un was likely trying to get whatever he could, since they couldn't stop us."

"You know, we were downright lucky. Helped to have that passenger shooting on your side of the coach."

"Ain't that the truth! Say, why haven't we heard from him?"

Oliver and Hurry looked at each other as the same thought struck them. Neither were surprised when Oliver opened the stagecoach door to find the passenger's lifeless body sprawled across the seats. Two of the Indians' .44 slugs had made their marks after all.

12

CALLIE WAS SITTING in her carriage, waiting for Ling Chow's return, when Fancy Dan walked up beside her.

"Miss Morris, a word with you, if you please?"

"Yes, Mr. McGinty, what is it?"

"It never ceases to amaze me how you can tell in an instant who a person is by their voice alone."

"Is that what you wanted to tell me, Mr. McGinty?"

"Why, no, no it's not. I actually wanted to say—well, what I intended to ask was . . ."

"Come now, Mr. McGinty, bashfulness is hardly your style," remarked Callie dryly. "What is on your mind?"

"You certainly are a direct person, Miss Morris; I like that. All right, I'll be direct as well. I'd like to call on you at your home, to get to know you better. You are a lovely and well-spoken woman, and I'd like to—"

"Thank you, Mr. McGinty, I believe I understand your question. To be equally straightforward, your interest does not interest me. No thank you."

"Ah, but, Miss Morris—may I call you Callie?"

"I'd rather you didn't, Mr. McGinty."

McGinty continued smoothly, as if he hadn't detected the snub, "Miss Morris, I believe that I can offer you refined, intelligent conversation. What's more, I am a man of ambition. I expect to own a fine home in San Francisco; perhaps enter politics."

"And then what, Mr. McGinty?"

McGinty's smoothness wavered. "What?" he demanded. Then catching himself, he said soothingly, "Pardon me, I didn't quite catch what you asked?"

"Then what?" she repeated. "What are you doing that will outlast your saloon in Garson, your fine home in San Francisco, and even your ambition?"

In what was a most unusual circumstance for him, McGinty was momentarily speechless. He decided to ignore this baffling discussion and try a different approach.

"Your friend Roberts may style himself a constable, but he's really just a sweaty blacksmith. He won't ever be able to treat you to the kind of genteel life you deserve."

This may have been straight talk, but it was entirely the wrong tactic to take with Callie Morris. She stiffened noticeably, and whether intentionally or not, she managed to turn so that the brilliant sunlight reflected off her smoked glasses directly into McGinty's eyes. He blinked and fidgeted uncomfortably, but she tilted her head to follow the sound, so that the irritation continued. "That is not even remotely any of your business, Mr. McGinty. Now, good day to you."

"Miss Morris, you shouldn't be so hasty. After all, my attention might benefit your father. You do care about your father, don't you? Indeed, one might say that a disregard for my attentions could be, shall we say, *unpleasant* for your father."

Callie's remaining patience snapped at this poorly veiled threat. She stood in the carriage, her hand finding the buggy whip that rested at her side. She snatched the whip up and snapped it into the air. McGinty leaped back out of its way, but not before the stinging lash caught his ear. "Mr. McGinty," she said slowly and deliberately, "do not threaten me or my father. And if you know what's good for you, never speak to me again."

At that moment Ling Chow hurried out of the hardware store. "What going on here? Miss Callie, what you do?" He climbed in beside her and took the reins.

"Ah, Ling Chow, Mr. McGinty asked my opinion of something, and I was *giving it to him.*" Callie flung the whip down on the leather seat.

McGinty, now that he was safely out of range, had recovered his aplomb. Holding a silk handkerchief to his bleeding earlobe, he sneered, "You shouldn't be so high and mighty, Miss Morris; and you *won't* be soon. If you're lucky, I might give you a job in my casino making change for gamblers. I guess even a blind girl could do that."

Callie turned her face from him. "Drive us home, Ling," she said through stiff lips. She could hear McGinty's mocking laughter behind her as the team stepped out smartly and drew the carriage up the street.

"But what did he mean, Papa? How can he hurt us?"

"Hush now, child, he can't hurt us. He's just a no-good, rotten bully and a cheap crook with a two-bit way of talking."

"Papa, you're not telling me everything. How can he even think to turn us out?"

Morris sighed heavily, and taking Callie's hands in his, led her over to the settee. "All right, Callie, you deserve an explanation. Sit down here."

"First of all, McGinty has nothing on us, and you mustn't fret about it. But he has made an offer to the Golden Bear Company to purchase the Silver Rim."

"Buy the Rim? But Papa, you're a Director of the Golden Bear."

"Yes, Callie, that's true. But I'm only one of many. You know the Rim's been losing money, and—well, McGinty's offer was substantial enough that the other directors have voted to consider it."

"Just like that? Without even thinking of us and all the work you've done?"

"Now simmer down, California. No, it's not just like that. The directors have agreed to give me a little more time to prove my belief in the quality of the ore the Rim can produce. Unfortunately, they're not willing to give me very long, and you know the setbacks we've been having."

"Yes, and I bet McGinty's behind them, too!"

"I'm sure he's encouraged the talk of unrest among the men I laid off. But, Callie, he can't have been responsible for the loss of the payroll in the Indian attack. No, even McGinty wouldn't stoop that low."

"All right, Papa. You know, you shouldn't keep things from me. Anyway, I can always tell when you're upset. But how can I pray for you if I don't know what to pray about?"

"Lord love you, child, you're right. Let's both do some praying right now. If God is willing, we won't have any more trouble, and the Rim will make this town bloom—but it won't be by the likes of Fancy Dan McGinty running things!"

13

HEADING BACK TO town on foot after another evening with Callie, Josh tried to analyze how he felt. Warmth flooded him, like the instant sense of heat when gray clouds part and sunshine bathes your face. The sensation felt unfamiliar, like waking up in a new place and not knowing for a time where you are. And it felt scary, like having the responsibility to care for something precious beyond measure. He was in love!

"Injun," he spoke to his horse, which he was leading behind him, "do you suppose everyone who's in love feels like this all the time? How do they ever get any work done?"

The horse nickered softly as if to reply, *Who knows? Wait and see, and enjoy the waiting.*

Josh shut his eyes and stood still, absorbing the night sounds, senses, and smells. He continued on down the road toward town, still walking and leading Injun. Riding would cut short the time he wanted to spend thinking.

He had just passed the turn in the trail which hid the Morris home from Garson when the buckskin whinnied again softly, then louder.

Off to his right, another horse answered! Josh couldn't have said why, but instinctively he knew something was wrong, and in that knowing he reacted.

Josh swung Injun around on the lead rope, the horse prancing nervously. He slipped the straps of the greener and the cartridge pouch off the saddle horn, and as he thumbed back one hammer, something whistled just past his ear, and a muzzle flash and report of a pistol came from the darkness.

Josh swung up the greener and fired from the hip as Pick had taught him, directly back toward the unseen attacker. Then he flung himself to the ground as Injun pounded off, back up toward the Morris home.

A second shot and a third went over Josh's head as he lay on the ground. From the two flashes Josh could see that his attacker was circling to the left, apparently moving to get a clean shot at Josh's side.

Josh pulled back the other hammer, pointed the shotgun's muzzle along the road, and lay very still. An instant later his guess was proven correct as a boot crunched the gravel of the road not ten yards away.

Josh didn't wait for his assailant to fire, but blasted off the second barrel, immediately rolling to the other side of the road as he did. His fire was met with an agonized scream and a wild return shot that ricocheted off a rock beside the road and went singing off into the dark. An instant searing pain, like a hot iron, leaped across Josh's forehead. A second later, Josh heard the sounds of feet running clumsily and a continuous string of curses.

Joshua fumbled in the cartridge bag. His nervous fingers spilled three shells on the road, then closed on two more as he broke open the shotgun's action and replaced the spent ammunition with fresh.

Lying still in the slight depression beside the road, Josh could hear the retreating footfalls stop, and then more cursing and shuffling as his attacker tried to get a spooked horse to stand still. The sound of saddle leather creaking suggested that the man, whoever he was, had succeeded. This was confirmed a moment later; hoofbeats retreated rapidly toward town.

Joshua stood up slowly and felt himself grow dizzy. He put his hand up to his forehead, and it came away wet and sticky to his touch.

From up the road came Morris's voice, "Joshua, are you there? Joshua, answer me! Ling Chow, have that rifle ready!"

"Ready, Mistah Mollis! Let Ling go fust!"

Josh called out to them, "It's all right. I'm here. Someone shot at me, but he's run off now."

Morris and the Chinaman hurried up, and as Morris stooped to light the lantern he carried, Josh could see a six-gun in his hand. The Chinaman was armed with a Henry rifle.

Morris stood up. "Are you hurt, my . . . good *grief*, your face is all bloody! Sit down, or, or . . . lie down! Ling, fetch the wagon. No, we'll carry you."

"It's all right, Mr. Morris, it's only a scratch; I'm just a little dizzy. There, that'll do for now," said Josh, as he clamped a neckerchief over the wound.

Morris and Ling Chow walked on either side of Josh as they returned to the house. Callie was standing in the doorway, her face a mask of worry and concern. She called out as she heard the returning footsteps, "Is he all right, Papa?"

Mr. Morris and Joshua exchanged looks that said, *She really cares* and *Let's not worry her.* Morris replied, "Yes, Callie, Joshua chased the other man off, and he's coming back with us."

Once inside the house, Josh was forced to admit to his forehead wound, and Callie immediately took charge. Leading him to the kitchen where she could get warm water, she sat him down on a short stool. Bathing his forehead, she instructed Josh to hold a clean compress on it while she washed the rest of his face. With strong, steady fingers, she gently traced the edges of the wound and announced with relief that it was, indeed, only a grazing.

Josh nodded thoughtfully. "I don't even think it's a bullet wound. A chunk of rock must have flown up from his last shot."

"Maybe—but, oh Josh, *who* would want to *kill* you? It *could* have been a bullet!"

Josh reached up and took her slender hand in his. "God watches out for me, Callie; you told me that yourself this very evening. As to who did it, that's exactly what I aim to find out!"

The next day Josh made his way around Garson with his forehead bandaged, asking questions. He wanted to know who had been seen coming back to town with a fresh wound.

Among the merchants, no one knew anything or had seen anything unusual, and there was no reason to think they would cover up for anyone. Doctor Racine examined the patch job Callie had done on Josh's forehead, but vowed he'd had no late-night patients with gunshot wounds. "I'll sure let you know if anyone shows up. Any idea what sort of wound I should be looking for?"

Josh instinctively rubbed his forehead, which had a dull ache. "Whoever it was made it back to his horse all right and rode off, but his last shot was wild and he didn't fire again. I'd say it's good odds he's at least hit on his gun hand side."

"Good enough; I'll be looking out for him."

Josh was hesitant to tackle the saloons. There he expected a less cheerful reception. If the attack was connected with the growing dispute among the miners, members of the so-called Working Men were less likely to be helpful.

Might as well start off with the place I know will be the least troublesome, he told himself. Turning his steps up the brush-covered slope, he entered the No Name Saloon.

"Welcome, my friend, welcome!" burst out Jersey Smith, his pointed beard bobbing as he spoke. "What have we here? I perceive some jealous female has attempted to scratch out your eyes!"

"Something like that, Jersey," remarked Josh, laying the greener on the bar top. "Can we visit quietly here for a minute?"

"Of course, my boy," agreed Jersey, lowering his voice. "Tell me what you need."

Josh recounted the story of the night before and ended by putting the question to Jersey about any man with a newly wounded right side or arm. Jersey thought carefully before answering, then shook his mane of white hair. "No— I've seen some wounds, but nothing of the sort you describe. Perhaps the ruffian has left town by now."

"I don't think so. I'm pretty certain he was acting on someone else's orders. They may try to get him out of town, but I was watching the road last night, and Dub Taylor's keeping an eye out today."

"He must be in hiding somewhere."

"That's what I think, too. I'm hoping that where I find him will tell me who's behind this."

"I'll be happy to be of service any way I can, but I really doubt that he'd show up here. As you know, I'm opposed to the group of hoodlums calling themselves Working Men, so they don't frequent my establishment."

"I figured as much, but I don't want to jump to conclusions and overlook something."

Josh turned around slowly and surveyed the small saloon. The men were all quietly talking or playing cards. Most of them were married, and those who were single were not known as troublemakers. Josh turned back to Jersey with a wry smile. "What I really mean is that I put off going into the lion's den long enough. Thanks for your help." Taking the shotgun from the bar top, he left through the tent flap.

Josh squared his shoulders and took a deep breath. It was time to get down to serious business. He went first into the Chinaman's Chance. Immediately he felt some hostility in the sidelong glances and whispered comments that passed among the miners. Even though Josh had been well-liked by all the miners, his position as constable with the full backing of the Silver Rim owner put him on the opposite side of the fence from the Working Men. Besides that, the fact that he was still employed while being a single man made for even more resentment.

No one knew anything about a wounded man, or if they did, they weren't saying. Josh located a few friendly faces to have a moment's conversation, but these men were subjected to intimidating stares for even giving the time of day to the constable. In any case, they added, they were moving on in a day or so to look for work in the mines around Independence.

That's just great, Josh mused, soberly shaking his head as he headed across the street toward Fancy Dan's. *Pretty soon the only single men left in Garson will be the ones who would rather drink and fight than do an honest day's work. I sure hope Mr. Morris is right about that bit vein opening up soon. This town needs some good luck before it boils over.*

Josh thought he saw Beldad looking out the door at the front of Fancy

Dan's, but the face disappeared too quickly for him to be sure. One thing was certain—McGinty had been warned about Josh's approach. He stepped up to shake Josh's hand before he was completely through the door.

"Well, Constable Roberts, what brings you in this time of day? Say, I'll bet you're looking for information about that drunken sot who took a shot at you last night. How is your head, anyway?"

"My head's fine, Mr. McGinty. I'm looking to find whoever that was last night all right, but how do you know he was drunk?"

McGinty scratched absently at his smooth-shaven cheek. "Heh! Well—I don't know for a fact, of course, just guessing. But it must have been someone who'd had more than was good for him. Perhaps it was some cowboy nursing a grievance against you."

"Mr. McGinty, what happened last night was an attempt at cold-blooded murder. I've Divine Providence to thank that I'm alive today. Drunk or not, an ambush is not the ploy of an angry cowboy. This was more like the move of someone following orders."

"Perhaps you're right," agreed McGinty hastily. "In any case, how can I be of help?"

Josh was aware of the same hostile glances he had been subject to in the other saloon. There was an undercurrent of animosity which seemed to be directed at him personally—almost as if someone had been talking about him when he walked in.

When Josh spoke again it was in a calm, quiet voice. "I'll just have a look around, if you don't mind."

"Not at all, not at all. Help yourself."

Josh made a slow circuit of the room, getting angry looks and muttered half-hearted curses, but seeing no one with the kind of recent injury he sought. He returned to McGinty, who was standing at the bar, sharing a private word with the bartender and smiling at something.

Josh stopped and took a good look at the slick saloon-keeper, then remarked casually, "Guess I'll take a quick look upstairs."

McGinty reacted immediately. "Now, why would you want to do that? You can see I have nothing to hide. Besides, the activities upstairs are no concern of yours, if you know what I mean." He gave Josh a broad wink and a leering smile.

"I believe I'll have a look, just the same." Josh started for the stairs, and at the same moment the bartender, who had been arranging the bottles on a shelf behind the bar, knocked one over. It fell with a crash, amplified by its collision with a brass spittoon.

Josh whirled around, but the bartender merely lifted his palms and shrugged. Josh had his foot on the bottom step when a door at the head of the stairs opened, and one of the girls of the line came out, followed by Mike Drackett.

Drackett's voice boomed down the stairs, but it sounded somewhat strained. "What was that racket? Oh, it's you, Constable. Fall in the gaboon, did ya?" The sneer with which Drackett addressed him made Josh bristle, but he forced himself to stay calm.

"Where were you last night, Drackett?"

"Last night? My, my, ain't we gettin' nosy? Guess you could ask Irma here, ain't that right, Irma?" Drackett waved his right arm in a sweeping gesture.

The girl only nodded, her pale skin ashen against her bright red dress.

"Are you through pokin' in my private life, Constable?" This time the sneer was accompanied by his teeth gritting.

Without waiting for Josh's reply, Drackett hooked his right arm through Irma's elbow and began to tug the girl back into the room behind them.

"Just a minute, Drackett," called Josh sharply. "I seem to recall taking a Colt off you over at Jersey Smith's."

"Yeah? Well, what of it? I ain't forgot, you little—But you can see I ain't wearin' one now." Drackett moved his right hip and side into Josh's view, and once again started to back up into the doorway.

"But, Mike," Josh corrected softly, "my recollection is that you are left-handed."

The girl called Irma screamed, as if some restraint had suddenly snapped. She pulled away from Drackett's grasp, stumbled, and fell to the floor, propelled by a rough push from her companion.

As he turned involuntarily, his blood-stained left side and bound up left arm came into view. So did the Starr revolver he wore in a cross-draw holster on his left side.

Dracket reached for the pistol as Josh fumbled with the stock of the greener. The upward angle was awkward for the sawed-off shotgun. It was a toss-up which man could bring his gun to bear first, but Drackett's side was stiff and he was not that good with his right hand.

The Starr hadn't even cleared leather when the twelve gauge's deafening roar sent all the patrons of Fancy Dan's diving for cover. Eight of the nine double-aught pellets found their mark, and Drackett was hurled backward through the doorway behind him and into the bedframe. His torso folded back onto the bed, his legs draped on the floor.

"Lower away," hollered Dub Taylor, shouting to make himself heard over the ringing sound of single jacks and the puffing donkey engine whose cables drew the ore cars.

Taylor was on his way down to gallery number five to inspect the condition of the working face. The lowest level of the Silver Rim had finally been pumped dry, and just last night Beldad had personally set the charges to begin the excavation.

As he rode deeper into the mine, the heat increased noticeably, and the walls became slick with moisture. *This sure enough reminds me of the Consolidated in Virginia,*he thought. *Now there was a bonanza—three or four levels of good assay that anyone would be proud to work, and then wham! Right in the middle of the hot, steamy water, the sweetest vein you ever saw. To think what they'd have missed if they'd never gone that deep!*

Far overhead, the operator of the cable saw the red painted stretch of steel cords appear that marked the level of the opening to gallery number five. Slowing the descent of the platform, the operator brought the moving floor to a stop even with a rocky ledge.

Taylor stepped off and walked forward in the curious step-pause-step gait of the long-time hard-rock miner. Underground, men didn't rush about, or the candle in the tin reflector mounted on their heads would blow out. Moreover, many a man had lived through a narrow escape by listening to the sounds of creaking timbers and rumbling earth in that brief delay between steps.

Taylor patted the sixteen-inch square box timbers that formed the framework of the mine's tunnels and shafts. Bending over, he paused to inspect the base of the timber which had been immersed in water the day before. It didn't appear to have been damaged, but for safety's sake it would need to be replaced. Dub wanted to see if work could continue on gallery five while new timbers were being put in. Beldad's blast the night before was intended to test the trustworthiness of the giant beams.

Beldad's shot, loaded and fired by him alone from much further away than the miners usually worked, was also expected to reveal something else. If level five showed promise, then Morris could begin rehiring additional miners. If, on the other hand, it showed poorly, then work would continue on three alone, and the single men would still be without jobs.

The flickering light of Dub's candle-lantern began to show pieces of rubble from the blast as he got nearer to the working face. As he turned a bend into what should have been a wider and higher gallery with a sloping mound of rubble ready to be cleared from the face, he stopped in consternation. The space was choked with debris. Boulders of all sizes blocked the passage and kept Dub from even seeing, much less reaching, the far wall. "What in blazes is this?" he demanded of the heap of stone. "It looks like Beldad shot the roof instead of the face! He's completely blocked the gallery. We'll have two more weeks of work just to get it cleared."

Taylor turned, still muttering to himself, angry to the point of distraction as he thought about how quickly he'd like to fire Beldad and then wring his neck, or maybe the other way around. He was still disturbed as he kicked first one loose stone and then another. Why would Beldad do something so patently stupid and which benefited no one? Absentmindedly, Dub bent to pick up a chunk of rock.

He didn't even hear the hissing, crackling sound until he turned to see the flame moving up the cord to the ceiling of the tunnel ahead of him.

"Hey!" he shouted, "Hey! I'm in here!" He realized even as he yelled that the fuse was already burning too close to the charges to be pulled out in time.

A series of short, sharp concussions went off like brief claps of thunder. Dub was thrown against a rock wall, but wasn't knocked unconscious. He had just time enough to raise his hands to his bleeding ears before twenty-five tons of ceiling fell on him.

14

"I SAY WE lynch him—string him up."

"What cause did he have to blast old Mike thataway?"

"It was Mike who bushwhacked Roberts the night before; that's how he got that wound on his left side."

"Yeah? Says who? That's what Roberts wants you to think, ain't it? He's had it in for Mike ever since he came to Garson. Besides, who said Roberts got bushwhacked? Did anybody see the other feller? And don't be handin' out that swill about Roberts bein' shot in the head an' all. A little bandage don't account for a head wound. How come *he* ain't dead?"

"But Drackett *was* shot in his gun arm—that's the only way Roberts could beat him at the draw."

"Who you gonna believe anyway, Mike or that bootlick Roberts? Mike told me that somebody shot *him* from ambush."

"Hey, it coulda happened that way. What about the fellers who died suddenly? Like Swede—with his neck broke. In his whole life he never drunk so much he couldn't walk straight. How could he end up walkin' off a cliff?"

"Yeah, an' how about Dub Taylor? Mighty peculiar, that rock fall catchin' him all by hisself."

"Why would Roberts want to kill a foreman? I mean, they both work for Morris, don't they?"

"Yeah, well, maybe Roberts wants to run this whole town *and* the Silver

Rim. I hear tell that since that blind gal is sweet on him, Morris'll do anything he wants."

"McGinty won't let 'em push us around. McGinty's as big a man as Morris, and he'll stand up to Roberts, too."

Beldad smiled contentedly and listened, while rolling a homemade smoke as he leaned back in his chair. He hadn't even had to stir this pot to make it boil. The out-of-work men were ready to believe the worst about Roberts. He was a handy target, since he represented both the management of the Rim and the law. All Beldad had to do was drop the suggestion that Roberts was looking for an excuse to murder Drackett, and the fuse of mob action was ignited.

McGinty will be pleased, Beldad thought, *and that spot as General Foreman is as good as mine. You did good, Mike. You didn't amount to much alive, but you made up for it in your death!*

"I think," remarked Fancy Dan McGinty with evident satisfaction, "that we've got everything coming our way now. Don't you agree, Mr. Beldad?"

"Yes, sir, Boss, it sure seems that way—except for . . . except . . ."

"Oh, yes, the loss of your job at the Silver Rim. Think nothing of it, Beldad, uh, *Mr. General Foreman.* How does that sound to you?"

"Sounds great, Boss. But are you sure everything's been taken care of?"

"Second thoughts at this late hour? All right, Beldad, let's review: One, gallery five is buried under enough rubble that Morris and his men won't stumble on the big strike. But we can get it in operation in, oh, a week or ten days, since we won't waste any time on level three. Two, the Working Men are disrupting even the little production that the Rim still has, hastening the time when its stock will fall into my lap. Three, Pitahaya and his savages have gotten their promised rifles and will be able to take the next payroll shipment, no matter how well armed it is. That will be the finish of Morris, because none of his precious family men will continue working if unpaid. He'll be forced to concede defeat."

"Haven't you forgotten something, Mr. McGinty?"

"I don't think so. What's that?" McGinty replied easily, pulling out his watch to examine its polish.

"What about Roberts?"

"Didn't I tell you, Mr. Beldad? I'm sending up to Jawbone Canyon to bring back Logan."

"Miles Logan?"

"The same. The man they call 'Gates of Hell.' And that, Mr. Beldad, should put a finish to any concern we have with Joshua Roberts, once and for all."

"Josh, I've something I need you to do. I'll tell you now that I don't feel good about asking you, and I'll understand if you refuse."

"Mr. Morris, I never went looking for this constable's job, but once I took it, I never figured to turn down something because it looked hard. Tell me what you need."

"As you know, we've got to get the next payroll shipment here at once, or the Rim is finished. McGinty will certainly own it, and he'll be able to run this town as he sees fit. I don't think either of us wants that." At Josh's emphatic shake of his head, he continued. "I'm certain that the Mojaves are watching the line closely, and waiting to attack again when they know the gold is there. So even if I could get a party of armed men to guard the stage, that would only be a signal to the Indians that here was a coach worth attacking!"

"But they wouldn't try to hit a well-armed party, would they? I thought a quick raid against no defense was more their style," Josh interjected.

"Up until the last attack on the coach, I would have agreed with you. But some things have changed. The Mojaves have figured out that the army is occupied elsewhere. They may be trying to get enough gold to retreat across the border to Mexico in between Apache-style forays. Even worse, they have gotten hold of some repeating rifles."

"Yes, so I hear. They must have stolen them from the prospectors they ambushed."

"That's what I assumed, but the stage driver and guard both say that as many as a *dozen* Mojaves were using them—poorly, I might add, but we can't trust poor marksmanship to continue. Besides, if someone is trading Winchesters to the Indians, the next coach may be facing twenty or thirty rifles!"

"What's the answer, then?"

"I've sent an urgent message requesting a detachment of cavalry be sent here at once. I have some friends in San Francisco with enough connections in Washington to get some prompt action. But 'prompt' in army terms means a couple of weeks, anyway. Right now we need to pay these miners, or all work on the Rim will stop."

"What does all this have to do with what you said you had to ask me?"

"I want you to ride as scout for the next coach. There will be just the driver and guard on board. With you riding ahead to look for signs of ambush, you should be able to give the stage enough warning to turn around, avoiding a fight altogether.

"The Mojaves won't expect us to ship gold without a string of guards, so a second coach will be hitched up and surrounded by as many men as I can hire. It will proceed to the edge of the most dangerous stretch, then fake a breakdown. If the Indians are watching as closely as I think they are, they won't want to give away their position by attacking you when they think the gold shipment is following close behind."

Josh nodded pensively. "Sounds like it might work. When do you want to try it?"

"Just as soon as possible. Hurry Johnson and his guard have agreed to drive if you're the scout. Seems they've heard about your reputation for coolness. Said they'd agree to it, if you would."

"And we'll be leaving—"

"Tonight. Under cover of darkness, going *away* from Garson, there'll be little chance of trouble with the Mojaves."

"All right sir. I'll go make ready. Oh, one more thing. Do you think I could say goodbye to Callie before I go?"

A smile broke through Morris' weariness, and there was a twinkle in his eye. "I thought you might ask, son. She's waiting in the other room."

"Boss, that stagecoach pulled out last night," reported Beldad to Mc-Ginty, who was shaving with an ivory-handed straight razor in front of a brass-framed mirror.

"So, what of it? We're not interested in coaches leaving Garson, only those coming in. Anyway, I've told the Indians that the next gold shipment will undoubtedly be heavily guarded. Now that they have the rest of the rifles, they're ready to attack at the first sign of valuables being shipped."

"Right, Boss. Uh— By the way, Roberts isn't in town neither."

McGinty turned around with his face still half-lathered. *"What?* How do you know?"

"Remember you told me to keep an eye on him on account of what we got planned for the Rim? Well, I had one of the boys ask if Mr. Roberts was at breakfast yet, and that old potato-eatin' biddy—sorry, Boss—that Mrs. Flynn said he wasn't in the place and hadn't been there since yesterday afternoon."

"What? Hold on, Beldad; let me think." McGinty turned back to the mirror and absently resumed shaving.

"It must mean something," he observed to his reflection in the steamy glass. "Old Morris may be more subtle than I give him credit for. He wouldn't part with Roberts just to send him to hire some guards. He must know that Roberts's presence has been keeping the lid on things here."

Beldad knew better than to interrupt McGinty's reverie. Besides, he was inwardly cursing his stupidity for making a disparaging remark about the Irish. He was so involved with hoping McGinty hadn't noticed that he missed it when McGinty addressed him again.

"Huh? What did you say, Boss?"

"Pay attention, Beldad. I think the time is ripe for all our plans to bear fruit. With Logan coming to town tonight, we're ready to shut down the Rim. By the time you get back, we'll have it all."

"Get back from where?"

"Didn't you hear anything I said? I want you to ride to Red Rock Canyon and tell the Mojaves not to be fooled by any guarded coach unless Roberts is with it. Tell them he'll be riding a buckskin horse and carrying a shotgun!"

15

"**I**'M SURE SORRY we had to let on to those men that they weren't really guarding a gold shipment. I'm afraid some careless word might get back to the Mojaves." Josh voiced his doubts to Hurry Johnson as they hitched up his teams at Weidner's.

"Naw, it ain't likely. Gettin' in two nights ago, and jest hirin' them last night, and leavin' this mornin'—I figger it ain't had time to get to them savages. Besides, you can't blame them for not wantin' to face Injuns totin' brand new Winchesters for no twenty dollars."

"I guess you're right. But I wish we hadn't been here a day already. Are they ready to roll?"

"Same as us. They're gonna be just enough behind us that them Injuns will be watchin' both coaches. We don't want them to be hittin' us by mistake on account of not seein' the play-actin'."

Hurry's voice held a sad and regretful note. Josh caught it and asked, "What's the matter? Don't you think it'll work?"

"Yeah, it'll work, I reckon. But to keep from gettin' ahead of them fellers, I'm sure gonna have to drive slow!"

"What do you mean, stopping these miners from going to work? By what right are you trespassing on Silver Rim property?" Morris was shouting at a group of men who were milling around in front of the mine entrance. They included a line of men carrying weapons and led by a man dressed in black.

"Well, I represent the Working Men of Garson, and they have picked me to be their spokesman—"

"You?" interrupted Morris. "You're no miner, and neither are these others with you. I see some *behind* you who used to work for me. You men, what are you doing with these hooligans?"

The man in black laid his hand on the butt of his pistol with a confident air. Several others in the line did likewise, but with less bravado. "I said I'm the spokesman, old man, so you'd best speak with me."

"All right, whoever you are, what do you want?"

"Are you prepared to give these single men, unfairly relieved of work, their jobs back?"

"Certainly not! Not only is it impossible for the Rim to support them now, but I would never give any man holding a gun on me a position in my mine—now, or ever!"

"Then we, the Working Men of Garson, are prepared to see that no one else works either, until we are treated fairly."

"We'll see about that! You just get—"

Morris's push forward and his brave words were cut short when the man in black drew his pistol and slammed its barrel into the side of Morris's head, knocking him to the ground.

"Tote his carcass out of my sight," the gunslinger ordered, "before I get really mad. And don't bother comin' to work until he either changes his mind or there's an owner with more sense at the Silver Rim. This mine is closed."

Just outside the mouth of Red Rock Canyon, Hurry pulled his team to a halt. Oliver got down off the box to check the rigging as Hurry stepped around for a word with Josh.

Josh had been riding inside the coach, with his horse, Injun, tied on and trailing behind. He and Hurry had decided to travel this way to keep the weight off Injun's back and keep him fresher for the time when his speed might mean the difference between life and death.

"Right here's where that other bunch will have their breakdown," observed Hurry. "I figger there's a Mojave watchin' us right now, but all he'll see us do is put out an outrider." Hurry squinted back across the alkali flats to where an approaching swirl of dust could be seen. "In about five minutes, that Mojave'll be talkin' about a whole mess of men and a coach with a busted wheel gettin' fixed, right here outside the canyon. Soon as the guards get in sight, you can saddle up and go to scoutin'."

Josh limbered the greener and checked its loads, thrusting some more shells into his shirt pockets from the cartridge pouch hanging from the saddle horn. He put the bit in Injun's mouth and flipped the bridle over the buckskin's head. Tightening the girth on the saddle, he untied the lead rope from the coach frame and mounted.

"I'll ride as far out front as I can so you can still see me. That will give you the most time to get turned if we've guessed wrong."

"Look sharp, boy. Them Mojaves ain't likely to show themselves, so you'll have to be right good. Just don't come back toward the coach for a chaw or nothin', 'cause if I see you turn around before we get through this canyon, you'll be eatin' my dust clean back to Weidner's!"

When Morris came to he was lying in the parlor of his own home being tended by Callie. A concerned and watchful half-circle around him was made up of Ling Chow, Pickax and Big John Daniels.

"My head," groaned Morris. "What happened?"

"Easy, Papa, just lie still," urged Callie.

Morris grimaced with the pain and clenched his jaw as if steadying himself. When he opened his eyes again his expression told them he now remembered what happened. "What are the miners doing about this?" he demanded.

Big John shifted his great bulk uneasily, hoping Pickax would speak. When he didn't, Daniels replied, "They ain't doin' nothin', Mr. Morris. They's scared. Scared of them hired guns."

Now Pickax broke his silence. "Scared is right! Especially by that black-dressed snake, Gates of Hell Logan. He's a cold-hearted killer if'n ever there was one."

"But surely we can get enough men together to outnumber those thugs!"

"Yessir, we kin," said Big John slowly, "but—"

"But what?"

"There ain't nobody the miners will follow, leastwise not against Logan."

"I'll lead myself. I'm not afraid of Logan."

"Oh no you won't," said Callie firmly, pressing her father's shoulders back down on the sofa. "I won't let you go and get yourself killed. No mine in the whole world is worth that."

There was a tap at the front door. Ling Chow shuffled out to answer it, returning in a moment with his face set. Almost without moving his mouth he announced, "Mr. McGinty here." Fancy Dan stepped quickly into the room, doing a poor job of concealing the smirk on his face as he looked at Morris' prostrate figure.

"What do you want, McGinty?"

"I heard about your unfortunate labor problem, Mr. Morris, and I came to offer my assistance."

"Your assistance? You swine, you're behind all this if I know anything!"

McGinty held up a cautioning hand as Big John took a menacing step toward him. "Don't be hasty, Morris; hear me out."

"All right, John, let's hear what this . . . this swindler has to say."

"It's plain that you cannot operate the mine. Your own people won't attempt to cross the line of the Working Men. Why, they're down in town right now, talking about how they haven't been paid, and asking why they should risk their lives for you."

"They know they'll get paid. There's a replacement payroll on the—" Morris silenced himself abruptly.

"On the way now? Well, let's hope they don't run into any Indian trouble like the last time, eh? But even *if* they should get here with that payroll—" The heavy emphasis on the *if* made Callie shudder—"these miners aren't going to challenge armed men for the sake of a few dollars." He smiled briefly, coldly.

"Look, here's what I'm willing to do," he went on blandly. "I'm so confident that I can run this badly managed mine better than you that I'm willing to buy your shares of Golden Bear Stock right now. That'll give me a place on the Board, which I will happily relinquish to the other directors in exchange for clear title to the Silver Rim. How's that for fairness? To take over a failing operation in the midst of a labor dispute, at a time when the town may be surrounded by hostile savages! You may call me crazy, but how does twenty-five thousand dollars sound, eh?"

Morris wavered for just a moment, weighing the offer. Then abruptly he made up his mind: "McGinty, get out of my house this instant!"

It was Callie who spoke next. She stood erect, facing McGinty as if her blind eyes nevertheless could see into his soul. "My father has poured his life into making this mine work and making this town a respectable place to live, to bring up families. Neither you nor your hired murderers will ever make us abandon the Silver Rim! Big John, show Mr. McGinty to the door!"

McGinty was already backing up as the giant black man advanced. "You'll regret this," Fancy Dan snarled; then he was gone.

"All right, Papa, now we know for certain who the enemy really is. What should we do now?"

"God bless you for your courage, child. Thank you for speaking out at just the right time. Now we need to pray for God to show us what is to be done."

"And pray for Josh's safe return?" asked Callie in a small voice, as if all the air had gone out of her slender frame.

"Yes, Callie, for that, too."

The plan must be working, thought Josh to himself with grim satisfaction. *Either that, or I have to suppose those Indians have given up their taste for stagecoaches after one try. And that I just don't believe.*

The sandstone walls rose plain and barren into the windless afternoon. Their pace through the canyon had been steady but unhurried, Hurry reasoning that to race through its snakelike turns might result in a spill that could prove fatal in more ways than one.

If Pick is right about the fighting Indians—and he is about everything else in this desert—then the prickles on the back of my neck mean we're being watched right now. Josh was watching the buckskin's ears closely, but while they were in motion, flicking back and forth, the horse's attention seemed more on the route up the canyon than toward the rocks on either side.

In a few moments Josh understood why. He reined Injun to a halt as the echo of hoofs coming toward him rebounded off the walls of the arroyo.

Josh glanced back over his shoulder; the coach was still coming along steadily. The guard was alertly scanning the cliffs to the sides and behind the coach, while Hurry watched ahead. *Nothing to do but keep on going,* thought Josh. *If I stop here, Johnson will think something is wrong even before I know what this is all about.*

Pressing the buckskin close against the side of the canyon that had a slight overhand, Josh cocked the greener and went warily forward.

Around the next bend came a lone rider. He too studied the canyon walls, twisting nervously in his saddle. Paying so much attention to the sandstone cliffs, he failed to notice Josh's approach.

When he did look up and recognize Josh, he nearly spun the dun horse he was riding around. Mastering himself with great difficulty, he held up a trembling hand to halt Josh's progress.

Josh exclaimed, "Beldad! What are you doing here? Don't you know there's an Indian war on in these hills?"

"I . . . I . . . I came to find . . . find you," stammered Beldad.

"Came to find me? Since when have you—"

Just then the coach came into Beldad's view from around the last corner of the canyon before its walls opened out.

Beldad stood up in his stirrups and shouted, "It's here! It's here, you fools—this is the coach you want!"

Sotol had planted his ambush near the mouth of the canyon closest to the Garson side, hoping to lull the guards into falsely believing they had come through safely. He had let the first coach pass through without attacking it, so as to not give any indication of the presence of his band. When Beldad approached from the Garson road Sotol hadn't recognized him, and Beldad hadn't yet gotten up enough nerve to call out to the Indians he knew must be lurking nearby.

Across the canyon from Sotol's position, a young brave jumped to his feet and began firing wildly. One of the first shots knocked Beldad from his saddle; he hit the ground calling out miserably, "Not me, you idiots! Not me!"

Josh fired up at the cliff face, knocking down the Indian with a blast of buckshot. Over his shoulder he saw Hurry snap the reins to make his break through the canyon, now only a short distance away.

Confusion reigned among the Indians. They had been advised not to fire until the band of guards arrived and to remain completely still.

The Mojaves began firing their rifles, but the Indian Josh had killed was the last brave before the mouth of the canyon; the coach had, in fact, passed all but two of the ambush positions.

The stage raced ahead, and Oliver began firing with good effect, his booming shotgun forcing two Indian ambushers to take cover behind the rocks. The other braves had only the rear of the speeding coach for a target.

Josh spurred Injun ahead, then jerked him to a stop beside Beldad. Instinctively, Josh leaped from the saddle to drag Beldad out of the road just before the coach thundered by. Then he draped Beldad across the saddle, and leaping up behind him, encouraged his horse after the stage. A few badly-aimed shots rang out from the rocks, but they were soon out of range and danger.

At last the coach came to a halt, and while Oliver stood on the roof of the stage to watch their back trail, Hurry helped Josh load Beldad into the stage. He had been hit in the chest, and his breath came in short gasps.

Hurry looked at Josh, and shook his head. As they laid him on the passenger seat, Beldad's eyes fluttered open and he spoke to Josh with difficulty, "You . . . tried to save me. . . . I was trying to get you . . . killed!"

"By the Mojaves?" burst out Josh.

"McGinty . . . he and the Indians . . ." Beldad's back arched in a spasm of pain. His eyes widened, then glazed, and he was gone.

"You heard him, Hurry." Josh's voice was bitter, full of determination and anger.

"I sure did! I'd say we get on to Garson. McGinty's got a heap to answer for! And . . . look there!" Josh whirled in the direction Hurry was pointing and exhaled a long gasp of air.

16

"**I** SAY WE can't wait no more," Big John Daniels declared. "The longer we lets them gunmen stay, the tougher it's gonna be to get anyone to go up agin 'em. Besides, them mining company folks is liable to take McGinty's offer to buy the Rim just to get shed of all this mess."

"How many of them hired guns you figger there is?" Pick asked Big John.

"Well, we seen ten, counting that Logan, but three of 'em ain't really gunfighters. There could be more in the mine, but I doubt it. I ain't sure how many more Working Men there are in Garson, but they's just loudmouths an' out-a-work miners. They ain't killers."

"All right, then, let's go see what we can muster for our side. Lean Duck, you stay here with Mr. Morris an' Callie. Big John, you an' me best split up an' spread the word. Tell 'em to meet at the No Name in one hour."

At the prescribed time, at least fifty miners and townspeople were gathered at Jersey Smith's place. Two of the side canvas flaps had been tied up and back so as to accommodate the crowd.

Most already knew the situation, but at Big John's call for action there was an uneasy silence. Finally a burly miner spoke up, "I'm right grateful to Mr. Morris for all he's done. But the reason I was still workin' is cause I have a family. And that family would rather leave here than have me dead. I ain't no hand to be facin' up to Miles Logan."

"Besides," said a single man, "I belong to the Working Men. I'm not sayin' hirin' those gunslingers was the right thing for McGinty to do, but this dispute's between him and Morris, right? I don't wanta get killed for either one of them."

When the man mentioned his connection with the Working Men, Big John started toward him with an upraised fist. Pick stopped him. "Easy there, Big John. We don't want to start any fightin' here—that won't get no mine back."

"An' you so-called Workin' Men," Pick said, "you listen up an' listen good. That's your side up there blockin' the road. Most of your group's up there now, herded together like so many cows. You'd best choose up sides pronto. This ain't no time to be watchin' which way the wind blows."

A few men backed out of the group and, with furtive looks behind them, skulked off up the road toward the mine.

"All right, here's the plan. We'll divide up into groups. Big John here'll lead one into the arroyo and up the wash behind where them fellers is blockin' the road. The second group'll go up the road and spread out along either side."

"Who's leadin' the second bunch, the ones goin' right into the teeth of them guns?" shouted a voice from the back of the crowd.

"Well," drawled Pick slowly, "It looks like I get that pleasant duty."

Shouts of "No" and "Sit down, old timer," erupted from the group.

"Some of those men are friends of ours," said a tall man with close-cropped brown hair, "and the others are hired killers. How can we fight that? I say we try to parlay with them."

There were murmurs of agreement and nodding heads.

"It won't wash," Pick replied. "Fancy Dan McGinty wants to keep the Rim shut down until he can take it away from Morris. I don't aim to let him do it."

"Then you'll get killed, Old Man," shouted another miner. "I haven't even been paid lately. Maybe McGinty could manage it better."

"Why don't you leave with them other skunks?" retorted Pick. "Sittin' here jawin' ain't getting work for nobody. I may be old, but I ain't yella!"

"What do you say, Big John?" asked the tall man who'd spoken earlier.

"I say we got to be men an' stand up for what's right. If talkin' would fix it, then talkin's jes' fine, but I say we go ready to fight!"

"Enough said," rejoined Pick. "Nobody's twistin' your arm, but if you're comin' with us, get your guns and let's go!"

Logan was lounging in the foreman's shack smoking a cigarette. A hired gun rushed in to warn him: "You better come, Logan; we got trouble."

Logan took another drag on his cigarette and tossed it through the open door before leisurely getting to his feet. "Sonny boy," he replied, "we don't got trouble; we *make* trouble. Ain't you figured that out yet?"

"Yeah? Well, there's a bunch of armed men comin' up the road right now."

Logan drew his six-shooter and spun the cylinder, then replaced it loosely in its holster. He casually checked the leather thongs that tied it down to his leg before sauntering after the nervous young gunhand.

"Well, well, what *have* we here?" Logan spoke to Pick, who had halted with twenty others about thirty yards from the mine property. "You're an even older old coot than the last old coot who came up here. Ain't there any young folks who know how to talk in this town, or are you all played out?"

"Logan, we come to tell you to get outta here. You ain't wanted in this town."

"Is that it? And if I don't choose to go—how do you propose to make me?"

"Me an' these—" Pick began.

Before he could finish, Logan shouted, "Let's open the ball," then drew his Colt and blasted point-blank, putting a bullet through Pick's stomach and another into his side as the old prospector collapsed. Logan continued firing, joined by the other hired guns, until the miners and townspeople scattered to find hiding in the gullies and brush.

When the gunfire had ceased, Logan spoke again. "You men out there! Go on home, and there won't be any more killin'. Just don't cross me no more!"

A single miner came up behind Logan, who whirled around on him, the Colt pointed at the man's chest. The young man put both hands in the air, and swallowed hard. "We didn't want no killing, Mr. Logan. Not old Pickax, he—"

"Shut up before I plug you too! If you ain't with me right now, then I'll shoot you down where you stand."

"But I'm not even armed," sputtered the miner.

"Then you best run on back to that mine so's I can protect you, little squally brat. Now git!"

Rifle fire from circling miners and townspeople began erupting from the brush. The young Working Man needed no further urging; he and the other unarmed dupes of McGinty crowded into the mine entrance.

"All right," yelled Logan, dropping to cover behind an ore car, "give it to them!"

The armed thugs who began firing had chosen their protection better than the attackers. From behind the walls of the mine buildings and heaps of timber and mounds of ore, hired guns fired with deadly effect.

One of the attackers rolled over, wailing and clutching his shoulder. Another staggered up, holding his face in both hands, and fell over dead without making a sound. A third was hit in the hand.

None of the hired guns received so much as a scratch. "Go on home— all of you!" Logan called out again, "Unless you're itchin' to die. That we can oblige."

A crackle of rifle fire mixed with the popping of smaller caliber pistols came from behind Logan's position. One of his men grabbed his leg and rolled on the ground cursing. Big John's group had succeeded in getting up the wash unseen and began another attack.

"You five—" ordered Logan, waving his pistol in a sweeping motion toward his gunmen on the front line. "Keep those rock-grubbers out there from moving up while the rest of us take care of the others."

Members of Big John's party were shooting steadily from the lip of the arroyo, but Logan's men still had plenty of cover from which to return the fire. Logan dashed from the ore car to a stack of timber. He fired three times over the shack, then retreated to calmly reload while a few shots struck the beams in reply.

Moving around the other end of the timbers, Logan dropped a miner who had just raised a rifle to his shoulder, then turned his aim toward Big John, who was brandishing a long-barrelled ten gauge shotgun. Logan's first shot clanged off Big John's shotgun as he brought it up across his face. The huge black man fell heavily to the ground, trying to conceal himself behind mesquite scrub one-quarter his size. Logan was aiming another shot at Big John's head when the ten-gauge blasted, and Logan dropped quickly to his belly.

General firing continued on all sides. The miners and townspeople had the greater numbers, but the skill of the gunfighters was winning the day.

The sound of pounding hoofs and the rolling, continuous creaking of a stagecoach at full speed drifted up from Garson between shots. Then the sound slowed but didn't stop, and the rushing noise continued right through town and up the hill toward the mine.

Hurry Johnson's rig rolled with such speed up toward the entrance of the Silver Rim that men from both sides of the fight had to throw themselves out of the road to avoid being trampled. When Hurry pulled the team to a halt, the leaders reared at the sudden stop. Behind the coach rode Josh on Injun. He was shouting and waving his hat, but no one could understand what he was saying.

When the team had quieted and the crowd stilled, those who heard him were taken aback by the authority and urgency with which he spoke, "Stop this nonsense at once! Return to your homes; retreat to the mine buildings. Our only hope of survival is to band together."

"What? What are you talking about, Roberts?" One of Logan's men spoke up. "Is this some kind of cheap trick?"

"The Mojaves are preparing a full-scale attack on the town. At least fifty of them—maybe more!"

"That won't play, Roberts. Them Mojaves ain't got sand enough to make a try for a whole town!"

"That may have been true in the past, but now they're carrying Winchesters, and they're on their way here."

"Winchesters!" several gasped. "Where'd they get rifles from?"

"McGinty," was Josh's simple reply. "McGinty supplied them with all they'd need."

"My family! They're alone!" a miner cried out.

A single man from the entrance called out, "I'll come with you, Jim." A stream of men exited the mine, running for their homes and weapons to defend the town.

"What about us?" asked one of the gunslingers, shifting allegiance to the constable.

"Stay here and keep the road to town open. If necessary, we may have to all retreat back to the mine."

Before Josh could continue, he noticed Pick's body lying face down in the dust beside the road. His breath caught in his throat and he leaped from the buckskin to cradle the old man's head in farewell.

When he looked up, he asked bitterly, "Who's responsible for this?"

"Logan. Gates of Hell Logan."

"Gates! Where is he?" Joshua demanded.

Not even his own hired guns knew. In the sudden confusion at the entrance of the stage and Josh's announcement of the Indian attack, the man in black had taken the opportunity to escape.

McGinty pulled a .32 caliber pistol out of his desk drawer at the sound of footsteps pounding up the outside stairs to his office. He held it leveled at the entry.

The door burst open and Miles Logan almost fell in, panting. "The jig's up, McGinty. We've had it."

"What do you mean, 'had it'? Do you mean to say that you let this rabble of town clowns and dirty grubbers run you out?"

"No," gasped Logan as he struggled to catch his breath, "they're on to us—*you,* I mean. They know about the Indians and the rifles."

"What? How can they possibly know that?"

"Because," sputtered Logan, gesturing toward the sound of running feet pounding along the board sidewalks,"the Mojaves are coming to visit, and they're bringin' your calling cards with them!"

"Josh," Big John Daniels spoke quietly, "leave him for now. We gots a town to defend."

Josh made a pillow of his own hat and placed it gently under Pick's head, then he rose slowly to face Daniels. "All right. Let's go check on the Morris home."

"Good idear," Big John replied. Then he told Josh how Logan had beaten Mr. Morris with the butt of his pistol. Josh's jaw set grimly, the news giving him fresh determination to stop this madman.

At the Morris home, the two men hadn't even reached the front step when Ling Chow came rushing out. He held a shotgun under one arm, but the other dangled at his side, blood soaking his wide sleeve.

"Mr. Josh! God be thanked, you here!" the Chinaman burst out.

"What is it, Ling Chow, what's happened?"

"McGinty and man in black come here. They say they need . . . they need . . ."

"What? *Why* did they come? What did they say?"

"They say they need trade to buy freedom. They say no one follow till they send word or they will kill."

"Kill? Kill who, Ling Chow. You are making no sense."

Agitated and confused, Ling dropped the shotgun and grasped Josh's arm. "Why you not *understand?* The take Callie. *Callie!* They ride off in desert!"

"Callie!" Josh whirled Injun around, then stopped briefly to talk hurriedly with Morris before instructing Big John and Ling Chow in the defense of the house.

Morris himself lay on a couch with its back against an upstairs window, ready to defend the yard below. "Godspeed," he called hoarsely to Josh. "Please bring her home safely."

Josh nodded and was gone, pushing Injun to the limit up the winding trail that led past the Silver Rim and down through the canyons and washes to the desert floor below, even as the first sounds of gunfire drifted up from the town of Garson.

17

AS JOSH RODE furiously, his brain tried to sort out what he knew of tracking and what Pick had taught him of the desert trails. The thought of Callie's abduction and Pick's senseless death made him fearful and angry and his heels dug into Injun's side, spurring him on to greater speed.

What's happening to Callie? pounded through his brain. He hardly dared think of the danger she might be in. He could think only of finding her, making her safe again. He forced himself to watch the trail left by three horses—two side by side, and what seemed likely to be the prints of Callie's mare being led behind. If he thought of other things he feared he would miss a turn or mistake a sign.

Scanning the trail ahead, Josh was aware that Logan was too experienced a man to leave his back trail unwatched. So far, the kidnappers seemed to travel straight as an arrow. Intervening brush-covered hillsides blocked more than half-a-mile's view at a time. With each approach of the crest of a sandy hill, Josh skirted its rim so as to approach the backside from an unexpected direction. With no sign of any movement about, Josh regained the trail and rode on.

He knew they must go to water within another day; they could not be carrying a greater supply than that. He trailed them until darkness forced him to stop for the night.

Josh hobbled Injun, and had a cold supper of jerky and hard biscuits from his saddle bags, washed down with water. He didn't want to take the chance of a fire revealing his position on the trail.

He could hear Injun contentedly chewing and rustling just outside the range of his night vision. Apparently the horse had found something to his liking, not returning to look for supper from his rider.

Josh took mental stock of his camp. His shotgun was at the ready and close at hand. Canteen and provisions were wrapped tightly in canvas, and stowed beneath his saddle, secured against marauding pack rats. The saddle served as his pillow. Calling goodnight to his horse, and breathing a prayer for Callie, Josh turned over, pulling half the tarp up over his muscular frame.

The faintest gray in the east told Josh of the approach of dawn. He had slept fitfully and was eager to be off. Rubbing his eyes, a quick glance around revealed Injun standing not far off. In seconds he'd gathered his belongings together in a pile, and was striding toward his horse, bridle in hand.

As he walked, he observed that the stems of thin grass which his horse had been grazing were supplanted in places by clumps of a gray, hairy plant with long, spiky leaves. Here and there stalks of white flowers stood above the gray-green foliage. This must have been the plant agreeable to Injun, because he had chewed it down to the ground in places.

At his call, Injun lifted his head, and Josh approached the horse and stroked his nose and head. "Come on, boy, let's get movin'." The words, though spoken without urgency, had an unexpected effect.

Injun snorted violently and jumped sideways. "Easy, boy, easy. What's wrong with you? You got the jumps about something? Here now, easy."

Josh reached out again to stroke the horse's face and the animal appeared calm. *I wonder what that was all about?* Josh thought.

He flipped the loop of bridle over the horse's ears and began to place the bit in his mouth. Injun was trained to drop his head to allow the bit to be inserted, but he seemed to have forgotten this. He stood with his neck out-stretched and his head held unnaturally high.

Josh returned to camp and poured water into his hat for the horse to drink. After taking the water eagerly, the horse was more agreeable, letting Josh put the bit in his mouth. Leading him again to camp, Josh smoothed the saddle blanket on his mount and secured the saddle. Then he tied his blanket roll behind the saddle and looped the strap of the greener over the horn on the offside. Tying the two canteens together, he hung them on the left side of the horn.

After a quick inspection, Josh jumped into the saddle and resumed the trail, hoping that Callie would be able to delay her captors as much as possible.

As Josh rode, the dawn breaking over the eastern hills began to light up the canyons and ravines to the west. From gray shadows, streaks of pink and orange began to appear as bands of brilliantly colored sandstone reflected the early morning rays. But Josh hardly noticed in his concern for Callie.

Soon the disk of the sun burst over the peaks. The warmth felt good on Josh's face, but it promised to be a very hot day. The night chill was nearly gone, and the sunlight had reduced the pale frost on the ground to white westward-pointing streaks shielded by the clumps of brush. In between the bushes, the ground was drying and beginning to steam.

Injun was still unusually agitated. His ears were constantly in motion, as if searching for danger nearby and confused at not finding it. His easy, ground-covering lope was interrupted frequently by sudden shifts to a bone-jarring trot. He could be urged back to the lope, but would again break its gentle rhythm without warning.

After about an hour of this annoying pattern, Josh stopped the horse to inspect his feet. Even though he had not been limping, Josh thought perhaps a hoof was giving him trouble. He soon located and dislodged a pebble from the hoof, and when he mounted again, Injun seemed to have a smoother gait. Josh fretted over the delay, regretting the time lost from his pursuit.

Then all at once Injun shied violently, sending Josh sideways in his saddle, almost dislodging him. The horse made three jumps over clumps of mesquite before Josh hauled up on the reins and shouted for the horse to stop. With the halt, Injun stood shuddering in place.

Josh patted the horse's neck and spoke soothingly to him. The horse's shuddering subsided, and Josh urged him back on the path once again.

Suddenly something white caught Josh's eye on the trail. Drawing up alongside it, he recognized it as a woman's handkerchief. *Good girl, Callie!*

With another pat to reassure his mount, Josh climbed down to retrieve the scrap of linen, keeping his fingers entwined in the bridle.

As Josh breathed in the scent of Callie's perfume, the horse gave a lurch backward, tumbling Josh to the ground. He cried out in pain as his elbow struck a sharp rock and he lost hold of the reins.

Rubbing his elbow, he reached for the trailing reins, but at the same moment Injun whirled, lashing out with both feet and nearly connecting with Josh's face.

"Hey! Calm down!" Again the animal was quiet, but as soon as Josh reached for the reins, Injun moved off, trotting a few more yards and stopping again to look back at Josh.

Josh mused. The stop-and-go game continued for three more attempts, but no amount of coaxing, wheedling, or threatening would make the horse stand still for Josh to grasp the reins.

Josh stood in the middle of the trail at a loss to figure out the problem. Then he used another tactic. As soon as the movements of the horse's ears and tail momentarily stopped, Josh made a rush for the trailing reins. But at the exact moment his fingers touched the leather, he stumbled over a rock on the trail and fell face-first in the dirt.

The fall was fortunate, however, because Injun had at the same time aimed another kick at Josh, which whistled over the top of his head. Then the horse was gone, running flat out down the trail, and disappearing over a small knoll about half a mile ahead.

The full horror of the situation washed over Josh. Not only had he lost all hope of overtaking Callie, but his bedroll, shotgun, and canteens of water were disappearing along with his horse, out of sight and out of reach!

The horse's abrupt departure left Josh some thirty miles from the nearest water. It would have been a hard day's ride; now it was going to be a punishing hike.

Josh could only hope the horse would stop to graze, enabling him to catch up somehow. At least he appeared to keep to the trail.

Nothing was to be gained by waiting, so he started off down the faint path. As he went, Pick's words echoed in his ears: *A man in the desert without horse or water is a dead man.*

When Josh topped the next rise he could see Injun, not a quarter of a mile away, grazing just to the side of the trail. He plodded on toward the horse, trying to plan his strategy as he went. *I need to come up on his left to have the best shot at grabbing those trailing reins,* he reasoned. *And I can't spook him before I get that close.*

He decided to mimic the horse's own actions as a means of putting the beast at ease. Each time the horse lifted its head to gaze around, Josh stood still and bent to the ground, even plucking a handful of the thin grass. Moving forward only when the horse grazed, and stopping when it lifted his head, he was able to approach within a few yards of him. The next time Injun raised and turned his head, Josh shook a handful of the grass, and called gently, "Look here, boy—see what I have for you."

The horse flared its nostrils suspiciously, and when Josh didn't move, stretched its neck toward him.

Injun had been standing sideways to Josh's approach, but now he turned to face him directly. Stretching out his neck again he sniffed at the grass, deciding whether to investigate the offering.

Josh took a step closer and the horse snorted, but didn't move. Extending the bouquet without moving another muscle, Josh stood completely still, silently praying.

Injun nudged the grass with his nose, and took another step forward. Josh held his breath. If only he could wrap both arms around its neck, then secure the reins. The whole scene was so incredibly bizarre.

The horse pulled away again, as if reading Josh's thoughts. Slowly, agonizingly, Josh began to inch forward again with the bundle of drying weeds, willing the horse to lean closer. He arched his left leg, fearing to step forward, lest he frighten the horse away.

At six feet apart Injun stopped. Josh gingerly pushed the fistful of drooping grass stems out. The horse stretched his neck to its greatest length, and then as if this were not safe enough, proceeded to nibble the weeds with only his lips. Injun's ears flicked nervously back and forth. A tremor began in his withers and ran down through his flank. *He's getting ready to bolt,* thought Josh anxiously. *It's now or never.*

As if reading his thoughts the horse exploded into motion, whirling to its left, and pulling the reins out of Josh's reach.

Lunging for his neck, intending to hold on for all he was worth, Josh stumbled forward and Injun reared. A flailing hoof glanced off Josh's shoulder as he ducked to the side.

Josh leaped for the horse's side, thinking he could perhaps drag himself into the saddle. His hand felt the shotgun hanging from the horn, and he grasped it. The horse reared again, lashing out with iron-shod hoofs and twisting again to the left.

For a moment Josh could feel the horse being pulled toward him. Seconds later, the leather sling on the greener parted from the stock with a crack like a whip.

A wild flurry of flying hoofs was followed by a buck that brought Injun's head completely to the ground. One murderous kick aimed at Josh's face, and the horse was gone, pounding away to the west. Josh was alone again, holding the greener with its dangling, broken strap.

18

FOR TWO HOURS he tracked the horse into the relentless afternoon sun. Once he came within a hundred yards, but that was the closest point before Injun made another dash away.

Dear God, help me, Josh pleaded. He continued to trail his only hope for survival into the dusty, still, desert afternoon. His mouth was dry and the skin on his face became stiff and taut. The moisture was leaving his body. As lack of water in the blazing heat took its toll, his mind began to wander and his steps faltered.

He began to pick up small pebbles from the trail to put in his mouth to start the saliva flowing. In his delirium he found himself spending a long time choosing the stones. Hours passed, and Josh could feel his life ebb away with the moisture. A thick, pasty film formed on his palate, causing him to gag and retch.

The shotgun trailed over his shoulder by its broken sling, and the stock bumped against his back causing increasing irritation. At one point he was tempted to whirl it around his head and fling it into the brush. He interrupted his frustration in time to allow the weapon to swing to a stop.

Then he tried to tie the end of the leather strap through the trigger guard to make a loop again, but found that his brain would not communicate the necessary steps to his fingers to tie a knot. He wandered aimlessly down the path, his feet keeping to the trail while his mind and hands fiddled with the problem.

A dry wash cut across the landscape in front of him. Its drab brown and ashen color blended in with the surrounding plain, and he didn't see it until almost too late. Half-sliding, half-swinging around a Joshua tree saved him from falling.

There, just below him in the wash and pawing anxiously at the sandy bed, stood Injun. They both caught sight of each other in the same instant.

The horse whirled again to run but was slower now, awkward and struggling. The relentless sun had taken its toll on his mount as well. The greener was already in Josh's hands. He instinctively brought it to a tight grip against his side and his right hand thumbed back the hammer. There was a deafening roar and a cloud of bitter gray smoke.

Josh dropped the gun and ran into the gully, tumbling head over heels as he went. He came up next to the still form of Injun. A quick look told him that the double-ought had done its work—the horse had dropped down dead and never moved again. But in spinning, rearing, and falling, Injun had come down heavily on his left side. The double-yoked canteens had been crushed beneath him, and as Josh wrenched them free from beneath the carcass, the last drops were being swallowed up by the thirsty sand.

Flinging himself face-first into the dust and gravel of the gully, Josh tried to suck life-giving water from the moist sand. He came up sputtering and retching as the harsh alkali soil burned his mouth and throat. The earth must have been even drier than Joshua, because it leeched the last moisture from his mouth, leaving him worse off than before.

Joshua knew he was in the most desperate situation possible. It was best that he act in anxious haste, because otherwise he might not be able to act at all. Reaching into his pocket, he drew out a small, folding knife. With a crushed canteen held as a bowl under Injun's neck, Josh stabbed downward fiercely and slit the horse's throat. Bright red blood gushed out, flooding the canteen, Josh's hands, and the ground. After a moment's hesitation, he drank. Forcing down his rising gorge with difficulty, he swallowed and swallowed again, until the bowl was empty. The blood flowing from the dead horse was now only a trickle, but he refilled his improvised bowl. When it was full, he drank it all down again, every drop.

Josh looked at his gore-covered hands. Then he looked at the crimson pool shrinking rapidly into the sand and clotting into blackening clumps. His mind flashed a picture of how his face must look—mouth ringed with blood, and chin and shirt spattered with it. He dropped the canteen and threw his hands up to his face in horror and revulsion.

Josh had to rouse himself from the desire to lay back and rest. He had to continue on in search of Callie. *Callie!* Her face flashed across his brain like lightening leaping to a peak in a Sierra thunderstorm. He had pursued the horse and the canteens for a whole afternoon, gradually forgetting why he was out in the desert in the first place.

God, he thought, *I'm going crazy. I think I hear her voice calling my name.*

"Josh, is it you? Josh, answer me!"

Callie! Then he heard McGinty and Logan. He *had* found them. Or was it the other way around?

"Ain't you a sight?" chuckled Logan. He casually drew his Colt.

At the rustling of the gun from its leather, Callie pleaded, "No, wait! Please don't hurt him!"

"Well, now, pretty lady, just since you ask. I just wish you could see your hero, gettin' hisself a fine drink of horse blood."

Turning to McGinty he added, "Shall we jest leave him out here to find his own way back? Maybe someone will rescue you, like the first time I left you in this predicament," he sneered at Josh.

"Gates," Josh groaned hoarsely, trying to make his brain, fuzzy with dust and sun, to work. *How can I get Callie away?* he pondered.

"Let's get going, Logan. Bring Miss Morris and come on," ordered McGinty.

"You know, Roberts, it wasn't too smart of you to go blastin' off with that cannon yonder. Not with us sittin' just the other side of this gully. Not smart at all."

"I wouldn't be too sure about that," came another voice from the edge of the wash.

Rather than waste time looking to see who spoke, Logan spun on his heels and fired the Colt in the general direction. Such a move may have worked had there been only one man to deal with. But *three* men stood on the rise. Before Logan made a full turn, Nate Dawson's .45 cut him down and Logan's shot went wild. Callie Morris screamed.

Tom Dawson never flinched. He kept his gun on Logan a moment longer, gesturing for Nate to walk cautiously down from the opposite side of the gully. He approached carefully in case the gunman was shamming, but Miles Logan was dead.

"Miss Morris, Tom Dawson here. Don't worry; everything's under control. Mont is holding a gun on Mr. Fancy Dan McGinty."

Callie didn't wait any longer. She cried out as she ran toward Josh, calling his name.

"Here, Callie! I'm here, love!"

She flew to him, throwing her arms around his neck. Holding each other was enough.

Josh tried to hold her back, saying, "No, Callie, I'm all over blood!"

Callie stopped only a fraction of a second and, as Josh wiped his face on his sleeve, she scolded, "Joshua Roberts, what's a little blood as long as it isn't yours?"

"Come on, you two," Tom called after he figured an appropriate time had passed. "We'll take Mr. McGinty with us while Nate and Mont bury Logan."

"I guess I can take Logan's horse," Josh commented. "He won't be needing it any more."

"Sounds good," said Tom. "The others are a mite frisky, even for a salty old desert hand like yourself."

"Others?" Josh asked, looking around.

"Just up ahead," Tom indicated. "This wash leads up to the box canyon where we round up the mustangs before driving them to Garson. There's water there, but none of that loco weed for the horses to get into. Drives 'em crazy, you know."

EPILOGUE

"YES, PAPA, I'M just fine. Better than you, I think," Callie assured him.

"If you feel up to it, sir," urged Josh, "tell us what happened in the Indian attack."

"Wasn't anything to it at all," said Morris, his head wrapped in bandages. "Those Mojaves weren't expecting a whole town full of armed folks, and mad besides! For all their Winchesters, they couldn't stand up to the citizens pulling together and fighting it out like real soldiers. The only real damage done was by a fire. Quick work saved the other businesses, but not before Fancy Dan's place was gutted. Anyway, I've heard that the army detachment is on the Mojaves' trail and will chase them clear to Mexico if need be."

"And the mine, sir—can you save it from being closed permanently?"

"That's the best part. I sent Sexton into the Silver Rim to see if those hooligans had damaged any equipment. He brought up a specimen of rock from gallery five's collapsed roof. You won't believe what he found."

"What's that, sir?"

"The sample assayed out a thousand dollars a ton! Sexton says it probably gets richer behind the rockfall. Of course McGinty knew about the rich vein, and Beldad was working to keep it a secret till McGinty owned the Rim. I've already telegraphed the news to the other directors, and they've agreed: everyone goes back to work."

"That's wonderful, Papa!" exclaimed Callie. "Now the town can grow— be a place to raise families and—" She stopped, blushing suddenly.

Both men laughed, and Callie joined in. "But you have to promise me one thing, Papa," she continued. "That the Rim will donate land and money to build a church."

"Whatever you say, my dear. Sounds like a very good idea to me." He turned to Josh. "Seem reasonable to you, constable?"

"I think we still need a jail, first," he countered.

"Why, Joshua Roberts, how can you say such a thing?" Callie protested.

"Well, actually I was just quoting what Fancy Dan McGinty is probably saying."

"McGinty? Why do you say that?" Morris questioned.

"Because he's out there right now, chained to that T-rail," gestured Josh, pointing out the window toward the bustling activity of the Silver Rim.

GOLD
RUSH
PRODIGAL

In memory of
Shelly Nielsen
and Brian Wilson,
two of Glennville's own
who are Home.
Ora loa ia Iesu . . .

1

WILLIAM DAVID BOLLIN stood on the deck of the schooner *Wanderer.* Ten days out of Honolulu and bound for Panama, his ship lay becalmed like the whaler across the way, whose roaring night fires were the beacon of her trade. The two ships had drifted within sight of each other just at sundown and had not as yet acknowledged each other's presence.

The orange fires leaping beneath the whaling ship's try pots threw gleaming streaks across the swells. In the moonless night the reflections of the twin blazes reached out and withdrew, then stretched toward the *Wanderer* again. To Bollin the light seemed like a forked spear probing for the heart of the ship on which he stood.

Even in the gloomy darkness of midnight, the contrast between the two vessels was evident. The *Wanderer* lay silent, waiting. Only a few of her crew were awake on this watch, hoping for a rising breeze that would fill the sails and carry them southeastward. The decks of the unknown whaler bustled with activity. The flames beneath the huge cast-iron pots made a rushing, crackling sound that carried clearly over to where Bollin leaned on the rail. Above the roar could be heard the rattle of chains and the dull clank of metal on metal. Punctuating the mechanical noise was the occasional muffled shout of some order being delivered.

The same sinister orange glow that reached out toward David Bollin also illuminated the deck and lower rigging of the whaler. Against this gleam the distorted shapes of men moved, grotesquely elongated and seeming to leap from canvas to canvas.

Unbidden, an image leaped to David's mind from the recesses of his childhood—a picture of hell, bathed in red sulphurous light, with figures of the condemned writhing in eternal pain. He shuddered inadvertently and glanced over his shoulder, then, angry with himself, consciously squared his shoulders and tightened his jaw muscles. His father would have seen the same vision of demons and hellfire, but he would have made it an image for his next sermon.

The thought of his father broke the eerie spell of the night. David shook his head in derision as he considered his father's life and work—twenty-five years pastoring a church in backwater Kohala, with only an occasional invitation to preach in the great Kewaiahao stone edifice in Honolulu. He had buried a wife, three children, and most of his life in the Hawaiian Islands. It didn't seem like much to show for twenty-five years.

Back down in his cabin, staring moodily into the dark rafters, David thought again how his father had hoped—no, *expected* him to follow in his footsteps. "Not likely," he muttered aloud. Even the disquieting spectacle of the whaler had more allure than the prospect of living and dying in some village, preaching to an all native congregation in exchange for a cramped house and second-hand clothing sent in barrels from far-off New England.

David's resistance to his father's expectation had made him jump at the opportunity for this sea voyage. The death of his maternal grandfather back in Boston had made it possible. The old man had willed a substantial sum of money to David directly, perhaps harboring a grudge against David's father for his daughter's death ten years earlier.

The news of the windfall inheritance had been accompanied by a letter of credit. David also received the promise of a high-placed introduction to Boston society if he should "return to civilization."

He could still see his father's face reflecting deep disappointment and sorrow as David had made it clear that he would invest none of *his* money and no more of *his* life in Hawaii. David now shook his head in angry self-righteousness. How could his father have expected him to stay on when the means were present for him to escape?

Since the *Wanderer* had been in port at the time, booking passage for the Isthmus of Panama was a simple matter. Once there, a short overland trek would take David to another sailing vessel headed for Boston.

His letter of credit easily secured him first-class accommodations and much forelock-pulling by the officers and crew. Settling down to sleep, David's thoughts drifted back to the whaler still clanking and roaring nearby. David had once considered escaping the islands by signing on such a ship. He'd heard stories about how rough the life was, and now he was glad he'd waited.

David idly wondered if any of the whaling men now working through the night had ever been in Honolulu. Probably they had—drinking and carousing and pitching rocks through church windows. David's father had often used whalers as the perfect example of what drink and lawlessness could produce in men. David smiled to himself as slumber crept over him; he need not choose between the life of his father and the life of the whaling men. He would be a gentleman, a man of means.

It was still dark outside the mission house. Pastor William Bollin sat on the edge of his bed and looked impatiently out the window toward the west. Earth and sea and sky blended together in deep lavender hues still flecked with stars.

By now the sun would be bright over the ship that had carried David away. The thought made Pastor Bollin close his eyes, imagining his son bathed in sunlight on the deck of the schooner *Wanderer*. David would not be looking back toward Hawaii. William Bollin was certain of that.

The thought tied a knot of grief around his heart, making it difficult to breathe. He shook his head and opened his eyes, defying the waves of sorrow and the anger that threatened to drown him.

He looked down at the pages of his open Bible. The letters were too dark to read, and yet he knew them by heart. He spoke the words in the soft language of the people of Hawaii.

"Pomaikai ka poe e u ana." Blessed are those who mourn, for they shall be comforted. . . .

For twenty-five years, William Bollin had proclaimed those words; lived and walked in that truth through the death of a wife, two sons and an infant daughter. In the end, only David had been left to him. Now David was gone, and for the first time William found no comfort. Once again he murmured the prayer, the plea, that the hurt would fade and dissipate like the clouds that clung to the towering *palis* of the island he called home.

To his small native congregation, Pastor Bollin was known as *Kapono*—The Righteous. His son, called Kawika to his face, had earned the whispered name, *A'a*—Rough Lava. Just as lava cuts the feet of the traveler, young David cut the heart of his good father.

The saying was true, and yet nothing had cut so deep as this final parting of father and son. Days and nights had passed, but the grief had not diminished for Kapono Bollin. The people saw it clearly in the eyes of their beloved teacher, and their pity somehow made it more difficult for him to hide the ache.

Kapono Bollin had learned another side of the story of the Prodigal. The father had mourned for his son and had not been comforted.

When David awoke the next morning, he could tell that the *Wanderer* was still becalmed. He started up on deck, but checked himself and forced his feet into the unaccustomed pair of shoes. A gentleman never went barefoot.

No breeze was stirring, but the captain cocked an eye at the horizon and ventured the opinion that they would see a change soon.

The whaler still lay off in the same position relative to the *Wanderer*, and the activity on its deck continued. David made his way to the spot on the stern where he had watched the previous night, and again he leaned on the rail. In the clear morning air he could make out the forms of two men with long poles warding off sharks from a huge strip of blubber being hoisted on board. Of the whale, little remained but a carcass, except for its gigantic broad head.

The fires of the try pots didn't gleam as brightly by day, but their baleful glare was replaced by an oily column of thick smoke. The smoke rose in a perfectly vertical shaft like a fourth mast, only much taller and blacker than the others. It ascended over the whaler until it reached a certain level in the air, then began to spread out in a layer of haze. The whaling ship seemed to be laboring under a cloud of its own making.

While David watched, the two men standing at the rail of the whaler took up the end of a rope that was tied around the waist of a third man. This man stepped over the side and stood on the whale's head, while a large iron hook was lowered to him on a chain.

Fascinated, David hopped up on the rail to get a better view. He clung to the rigging with one hand while with the other he shaded his eyes against the glare of the morning sun.

The man standing on the whale's head bent over and seemed to be doing something around the whale's jaw. A moment later he motioned for the iron hook to be lowered down to his feet. David guessed that he was inserting the hook through the whale's jaw before cutting the head free of the body. Sure enough, David could see the man reach up and receive a long, thick-bladed instrument, like a saw. The man began wielding this tool right behind the whale's head.

David strained to see even better, certain that there would be a dramatic moment when the head would be severed and would swing free of the carcass. In that instant, the man using the saw would be totally dependent on his shipmates holding the rope to stop him from plunging into the sea with the sharks.

A moment more passed. The man gestured for the chain to take up some slack. A few more deft strokes. Forward of David on the *Wanderer* came the cry, "The wind is rising. Now she fills!"

David tried to look three places at once: up at the sails no longer hanging limp overhead, over his shoulder at a cloud mass rushing down on them, and back at the sailor who was even then leaping for the railing to reboard the whaling ship. The *Wanderer* gave a lurch forward, then heeled sharply to starboard. David jerked once, then a second bounce sprung his grip loose. His new shoes, with their slick leather soles, accelerated his slide. Over the side he went.

Down he plunged into the dark blue water. Down he sank as the sea closed over his head. He kicked off his new shoes and struggled out of his new dress coat. It had so quickly filled with water that it threatened to carry him to the bottom.

Up he struggled and up, feeling as if his lungs would burst. At the last moment, when his tortured lungs could take no more, his head finally broke through the surface. He coughed, then breathed frantically, sucking in a huge breath before a swell broke over his head.

David raised his arm to wave to the *Wanderer;* he opened his mouth to shout and got a throat full of saltwater. Kicking as hard as he could, he thrust his body up above the surface. Incredibly, the *Wanderer* was already two hundred yards away and increasing its speed. Had no one seen him fall?

"Wait!" he yelled. "I'm here!" He saw no move to slacken sail; heard no shouted order to come about.

For an instant, David panicked. He saw himself alone, abandoned on the face of the deep. Then he remembered the whaler. He spun himself around, catching another wave in the face as he did so.

The whaler had been lying with its sails furled, willing to remain becalmed while it completed its industry of turning the whale into oil. Now that its task was nearly complete, it would return to the hunt—but leisurely, not racing ahead like the *Wanderer.*

David addressed himself to the whale ship, waving and shouting again. After an eternity, it seemed to David, a figure at the rail pointed in his direction, then called to another and another. Soon the rail was lined with men pointing and shouting.

David struggled to keep waving. His legs were tiring and he wanted to rest from the constant kicks upward, but was afraid he would disappear in the swells and be lost from view. He quickly stripped off his new linen shirt and flung it back and forth over his head. From around the opposite side of the ship came a whaleboat. As if already returned to hunting whales, it came on with the harpooner standing in the prow. Six men were pulling at the oars while an officer at the tiller shouted first to pull to larboard and next to give way as he followed the hand-signals of the brown-skinned harpooner.

The whaleboat had closed half the distance between them when David saw the harpooner stoop down and take up the eight-foot-long tool of his trade. The sunlight glinted off the razor-sharp edge.

What's he doing? screamed David's brain. *What's happening?* A moment later from the whaleboat he heard the exclamation of the oarsmen mixed with shrill cries from the watchers on the ship's deck. "Mano! Big shark! Big shark! Look at that fin!"

David's mind refused to accept this new information. Nearly drowned, and now a shark? It wasn't possible! Then he saw a scythe-like fin cutting through the water on a line directly toward him.

He began flailing wildly, slapping his shirt from side to side in a frenzy of terror. As if it were frozen in time, he saw a picture of the distance that still separated him from the boat, saw the shark's cold, lifeless eye stare into his, saw the harpooner's weapon drawn back, poised in his hand.

A frozen moment, but no longer—all was a rush of motion again. The shark's jaw closed on the shirt David slapped in its face as he jerked aside. The harpoon flashed forward, burying itself in the shark's body and making it curl on itself suddenly. David's plunge to the side had thrust him down in the water, and he choked, strangling and fighting, then lapsing into unconsciousness.

The whaleboat pulled past the thrashing shark. Strong hands lifted David into the boat and pounded him between the shoulders, but he couldn't see or feel them; he lay senseless in the bottom. As they pulled back to the whaler, all hands wondered if they had rescued a corpse.

David heard the distinct flapping of sails and then felt the warm sun begin to penetrate his wet clothes.

A broad, nut-brown face leaned into his view. A deep, resonant voice spoke in fluid Hawaiian tones, "Kawika. Kawika. You are safe now."

David tried to draw a deep breath, as if to prove that he was indeed still alive. Instantly, he was racked with coughing and retching as the remains of the sea water he had inhaled and swallowed tried to come up at once.

"Kawika!" said the voice again. Strong and gentle hands raised him to a seated position and thumped him on the back.

Trying again to focus his eyes and his thoughts, David was momentarily blinded by the sunlight. He still could not speak, but he raised one hand, palm outward, in a gesture of thanks—and to stop the pounding on his back.

David's mind raced as he turned to look at his benefactor. Who would know to call him by the Hawaiian version of his name? Who on this whaling ship could know him at all?

The man behind him moved around David and squatted down in front, blocking the sun's glare. A thatch of white hair crowned a large tan face with an enormous growth of side whiskers. The face split apart in a huge grin, revealing radiantly white teeth. The image of a coconut being suddenly cracked open flashed through David's thoughts. "Keo. Keo Kekoa?"

"Hey, Kawika," said the Hawaiian, "you pupule, or something? Crazy? What you go swim with old Mano for? You want end up in his opu?" Keo laughed exuberantly and patted his own ample belly.

"Keo," began David again. "I haven't seen you in five or six years, and now you save my life. That was you with the harpoon, wasn't it?"

"Sure, sure, Kawika. I been harpoon-man all this time here on Kilikila." He waved his hand to indicate the whaler. "The *Crystal.* Good whale ship."

A gravelly voice interrupted. "Stow it, Kekoa. Have your reunion later. Who is this wharf rat?"

David stood up to face the speaker. He found himself looking down on a thin-faced man whose eyes appeared to have a permanent squint to match the perpetual sneer on his lips.

"I am not a wharf rat, Captain. I am a man of property *en route* to Boston, and if you'll put me back aboard—"

"Belay that guff. Have you got money?"

David shook his head. "No, of course not. Not with me. You can see I barely escaped with my life, but not my clothing. Back on the *Wanderer* is my letter of credit."

The sneer widened. "You talk fancy for island scum. Like enough you are a runaway cabin boy who jumped ship in Owyhee."

"Captain, I assure you, I have means."

"Avast that sea foam. Don't I have eyes to see you there all burnt brown like Kekoa here? You are no gentleman."

"But I . . . just recently I—" protested David lamely.

"You, Kekoa," addressed the captain to Keo, "you know this fella. Who is he now? Sail a straight course, or I'll pin your ears to the mast."

"Aye, Cap'n," said Keo, throwing a reluctant glance at David. "I speak true. Kawika here son of preacherman Kapono Bollin."

"Aha!" shouted the captain, his sneer fairly playing all over his face. "I mighta know'd. He was a stowaway, no doubt." The captain dismissed Keo curtly by gesturing aloft and ordering, "You heard the cry to make sail; now up the foretop with you."

"Aye, Cap'n," agreed the native. With a regretful look at David, he left to ascend the rigging.

The captain moved very close to David. "Preachers are useless spawn, and the spawn of a preacher is worse. You may think fancy words make you better'n me, but look sharp! The *Crystal* is carryin' no cargo but oil— so less you want to fetch up shipped home in a cask, or thrown back to the sharks, you'll work for your keep, or my name isn't Captain Greaves."

The towering green peaks of Nu'uanu Pali were bathed in sunlight. Below, a blue mist hung, enfolding the valleys at the foot of the mountains. The dew sparkled on the short, crisp grass that carpeted pastures surrounding the village. Surf pounded on the shoreline a hundred yards from the white frame church of Kapono William Bollin.

How very close to paradise this place seemed! The laughter of brown-skinned children filled the air. In front of a small grass house, an old man labored to make fishing line from the fiber of beaten hemp. It was not hard to imagine the voice of the Lord as he looked upon this small corner of creation, *"Maikai, maikai; it is very good. . . ."*

Yet this morning, the beauty that surrounded Kapono Bollin only served to sharpen the depth of his grief as he read the contents of a letter from the captain of the schooner, *Wanderer*.

"And so it is my sad duty to inform you that your son was lost at sea, presumed drowned. There is some small hope, perhaps . . . a whaling vessel nearby . . . ."

The church bell pealed over the peaceful land, calling all the villagers to assemble. While Kapono Bollin retired to mourn in his house, assistant pastor Edward Hupeka stood before the congregation and translated the letter into Hawaiian.

The drone of insects accompanied the announcement in the packed room. Men and women, small children looked at one another in sorrow for the tearing of Kapono Bollin's heart. With a trembling hand, young Edward Hupeka placed the letter on the pulpit and looked out over the silent faces of his people. Tears filled his eyes. David had been like a brother to him once, yet David had not chosen the path of righteousness. He had rejected the truth his own father had taught. He had turned his back on the way of *Aloha*.

Edward turned his gaze onto the sad eyes of his sister, Mary. The small children of her class clung to her skirts. They looked worried. Mary was crying also. After all, she had loved David more than anyone.

Edward cleared his throat and began to speak. "Our brother is lost," he said, and his voice cracked. "What do we learn from such sorrow? *E imi oukou ia Iehova*—Seek the Lord while He may be found; call upon Him while He is near!" Heads bowed in thought and prayer as the voice of Edward rang out the warning. "Let the wicked forsake his way, and the unrighteous man his thoughts; let him return to the Lord, that He may have mercy on him, for He will abundantly pardon!"

"But perhaps Kawika still lives," said an old man near the pulpit.

"There was the whale ship nearby," cried another.

"We should pray that this is so. For Kapono Bollin, we should pray the boy still lives!"

"No ka mea, o ko'u mau." For my thoughts are not your thoughts, says the Lord. Edward raised his arms and all the people began to pray together for their lost brother. For the lost son of dear Kapono Bollin.

2

THREE MONTHS LATER found David still aboard the *Crystal*. David's already tan body was burnt to a deeper brown, his blond hair bleached to a paler gold. His six-foot-three frame had filled out to a lean-muscled twenty from a boyish nineteen. His light green eyes reflected that he was stronger, more confident. Although he had acquired skills in the whaling trade, he still hated it all.

He had soon learned that life aboard a whale ship divided into only two categories: relentless boredom and punishing work. For days on end the *Crystal* cruised the whaling grounds with no quarry in sight. David's watches were usually spent hollystoning the decks. His knees and palms became thickly calloused until they felt like the soles of the shoes he had lost.

But even four hours at a time on hands and knees was preferable to being confined in the cramped forecastle. There, with little light and less air, those who knew scrimshaw engraved shark teeth and pan bones with fanciful scenes, while the others watched.

The only other recreation seemed to be griping. There was plenty to gripe about, too. The sailors warned David that it was well that they ate in the dark forecastle so as not to see the number of weevils in the bread.

David learned to swallow and keep down a drink called *switchel*. Compounded of water dosed liberally with molasses and vinegar, it was less putrid than plain water that had stood in moldy barrels for forty days at a stretch.

David, like all the others, hoped and waited for the cry from the mast-head, *There she breeches! There go flukes!* A sighting meant an injection of excitement into their boredom. It was soon ended, though, for the whale either escaped and the whaleboat crews came back to face Greaves' derision or else they towed the dead hulk back to the *Crystal* and their work began in earnest.

David was assigned to the "reception room," where huge blankets of blubber were cut into smaller pieces for the try pots. With malicious irony the captain had seen fit to require David to use the two-handled knife that cut the fat into thin squares called Bible leaves. Aside from the rough humor, it was a dangerous place to work. Razor-sharp blades were slicing in all directions in the cramped space, and sharp-spiked staves called blubber hooks gouged into the masses of fat without regard to legs or feet. David was the only man with all his fingers and toes working in the reception room.

Just as the flurry of activity was pushing the crew to the point of exhaustion, it ended. Back to the dull routine went the men, except that David's life was worse because all the surfaces he had just finished hollystoning were now covered again with a layer of grease. Grease that coated deck and rail, windlass and mast, whose removal was David's special duty. Very seldom did the *Crystal* resemble her name.

Greaves would not put David ashore until the *Crystal* returned to Honolulu for her semi-annual refitting. David dared not protest, because the only thing harder than the work of rendering a whale was the discipline. Insubordination was punished by example: Greaves had not been joking when he threatened Keo with ear-pinning; David had seen a sailor pinned to the mast by a spike through his earlobe. The choice was to stand up for twenty-four hours in blazing sun or bone-numbing fog, or to pull out the spike and be lashed to unconsciousness.

Keo would pass David on the deck and whisper, "Ho' omanawanui. Be patient, Kawika." But he could seldom say more. The harpooners were considered to be a class above the common seamen, and for Keo and the young man to be openly friendly would mean trouble for both.

Many was the time David wished he had never left Hawaii, his self-pity often supplemented by anger. Then, perversely, he would blame his father for his predicament, unreasonably thinking that if they had returned to New England together, this would not have happened. At other times he missed his father and hoped that his father was praying for him.

Three months of this pattern went by, and the *Crystal* was coasting along the shores of California, far from the familiar beaches of Hawaii. She had put in for water at a wild stretch of the Baja Peninsula and was following the track of the gray whales north for a time.

Captain Greaves ordered the ship to lay in the lee of Santa Rosa Island until sundown. The *Crystal* would be heading windward to round Point Conception, and Greaves hoped the nighttime passage would make for calmer seas.

David was off-watch and below decks when the order came to make sail. As the canvas stretched and caught the wind, he could feel the *Crystal* shake herself like a dog getting up from sleep.

Once outside the shelter of the island, two things became clear to David: the wind had not died down as expected, and the ocean swells were running from behind the ship, as if opposing the wind.

In order to progress to the northwest against the wind, it was necessary for the ship to zigzag across the intended course. The ship ran well enough on the leg in toward land, but each time the *Crystal* put her helm over to move west she came almost to a complete stop. David experienced a sense of helplessness as he felt the ship slide backward, pushed by the wind and overtaken by the swells. Tension gripped the pit of his stomach as he remembered a bit of sailor doggerel about a following sea and a wallowing ship.

He overheard the mate Nelson being urged to query Captain Greaves about breaking off the attempt and running back to shelter. Mentally he agreed. But when he heard Greaves tell the mate to stop acting so childish and return to his place, David felt his uneasiness return even more.

Greaves ordered the steersman to put the helm over once more and bring the ship up on the port or westward tack, away from land. As he did so, David, who was stationed by the foremast, saw an unusual movement of the timber. The mast not only bent and shivered, but seemed to revolve part way around.

David's sense of danger increased to a certainty. He tried to call this occurrence to the mate's attention, but was curtly ordered back without a chance to explain. At that moment the *Crystal* was passing to the west of Point Conception and was no longer even partly sheltered by the cape. The wind, which had been blowing at eighteen knots, jumped up to forty. The tops of the onrushing swells blew back into the faces of the *Crystal*'s crew.

"Captain!" shouted the mate over the roar of the wind and the whine of the rigging. "Let her give way and run downwind. We're making no headway at all!"

Greaves refused. He reasoned that if they held to their present course long enough, they would round the point. To give way now would drive them miles out to sea, just when the worst of the passage must be ending. What he did not know was that the south swells were being pushed out from a hurricane hundreds of miles away that was only beginning to gather its force. Outside the island channels, the swells were already increasing in height and force as if to compete with the wind.

David watched six-foot swells become twelve, then twenty. The ship became a plaything of the opposing forces that batted her back and forth. Shrouded by black skies in which the stars appeared to whirl like tiny candle flames about to be puffed out, the *Crystal* slid from crest to trough. Poised on the brink of a forty-foot hole in the ocean, blacker than the night itself, the ship, lifted by the onrushing swell, hung from the lip over a cavern into which thousands of tons of sea water were about to fall. Then the swell crashed past, while the *Crystal* slid backward into the trough. David looked up at a solid wall of water ready to fall on him.

Childhood prayers came to his mind. In a panic of gut-wrenching fear,

he prayed for deliverance, prayed to be spared, offered bargains of refor-
mation in return for life. He expected each moment to be the ship's last—
and with it, his own end.

Now the mate was imploring the helmsman to keep her up into the
wind. An instant's inattention could swing her broadside, to be rolled over
and crushed.

"I can't hold her!" the steersman cried. Two burly sailors and Keo
jumped to his aid. Together the four men struggled with the wooden
spokes of the wheel to keep her nose up into the gale.

At that instant David saw the foremast revolve. "The mast is going!" he
yelled, throwing himself back and out of the way. The starboard rigging
parted with a sound like a dozen pistol shots and the foremast toppled
over the portside of the ship.

Lines and yardarms snaking across the deck flipped men over the side
like a giant flicking matchsticks. Two sailors were flung away without time
to make a sound, while a third gave a horrible, drawn-out scream that
followed his high arc into the sea. David shuddered as his mind told him
that he might be next.

One of the try pots broke free of its brick oven and slammed a sailor
against the gunwhale. Then it spun off, as if seeking others to run down.

"Secure that cursed pot!" shouted Greaves, "and chop the foremast
free!"

The foresails, and the jib which had been carried away with the mast,
were hanging over the portside of the *Crystal.* The added drag threatened
to spin the ship sideways into the canyon-like troughs.

Transforming panic and fear into frantic chopping, David snatched up
an axe and began to cut at the rigging that still secured the foremast to the
ship. His breathing was rushed and his arms rose and fell with the speed of
a steam-driven piston. Other whaling men began to hack at the lines with
their knives.

Presently the cry went up: "She's going!" The men jumped to get clear
when the massive pole and acres of canvas fell free of the ship. The *Crystal*
bounded to the starboard as the strain of the sails fell away.

Past the tip of Point Conception, the wind's direction shifted. While not
letting up in force, it backed around to the northeast. Now the ship's
motion toward the west came easier and she stood out from the land and
rocks that had been waiting to tear out her keel.

As the *Crystal* limped along, the ship's crew were able to reef some sail,
tying it down to take some of the strain off the rigging. The captain and
the mate inspected the damage. The foremast was gone completely, and in
the confusion the maintop had been carried away without anyone noticing.

The rudder was damaged as well, making the *Crystal* very difficult to steer to starboard.

David experienced a strange welter of mixed feelings. He felt embarrassed for his time of panic and wondered if anyone had noticed him. He felt overwhelming relief at still being alive and a guilty shame because he was so glad that he was not one of those sailors lost overboard. He even associated his prayers in that time of fear with the foolishness of panic.

Below decks the scene revealed by cautiously lit lanterns was one of jumbled confusion. Several casks of oil had burst and the entire hold was soaked in a slippery coating. Fortunately, the barrels had not shifted or the *Crystal* would certainly have capsized.

As dawn broke over the coast range, the sailmaker was set to work stitching together spare canvas, and a juryrigged boom was added to the stump of the mainmast. Greaves assured the crew that the *Crystal* could still be controlled in this way. What he did not report was how badly sprung the ship was, nor the fact that he was not sure how long she would hold together. A constant rotation of men kept the pumps going. David saw some of the more experienced sailors exchange knowing looks, but they made no comment. David did not even want to ask for explanation. He wanted no emotion except relief.

Where could they go for repairs? Clearly, they could not return the way they had come. The run northeast to the port of San Luis Obispo, which was the next closest shelter, was not possible either.

Monterrey seemed the logical choice. Captain Greaves was counting on the wind returning to the prevailing northwest direction in order to move the ship back toward the coast.

The following day was spent watching the beautiful but desolate central California coast slide by. The cleanup and repair work—but not the pumping—were suspended only briefly while the body of the man crushed by the try pot was consigned to the Pacific. The captain read no service and spoke no words. He merely stood in bareheaded silence for a moment before his curt nod caused the plank to be raised and the canvas-shrouded body to splash into the sea. David was standing next to Keo. Glancing over at the native, he saw that Keo's eyes were shut tightly and he was murmuring the words of the Lord's Prayer to himself in Hawaiian. David tried to force himself to follow suit, but his happiness at not being dead kept intruding. He'd just been lucky, that was all. The dead man had been unlucky.

By the middle of the next night, it was clear that the *Crystal* could not make port in Monterrey. She was now too far out from the coast and too damaged to move northeast against the wind. Their next—perhaps last—

hope would be the tiny settlement of San Francisco, if the ship could be turned to make the narrow entrance into the bay.

Just after dawn on the second morning after the storm, the wind from the northeast died and the swells from astern shrank in size. The *Crystal* had at last outrun the effects of the Mexican hurricane.

3

IT WAS FLAT calm from six o'clock till nine. David paused in his work of splicing lines to gaze eastward at the yellow orb of the sun rising over the bank of gray fog that blocked his view of the coast.

Gently, almost imperceptibly at first, a breeze out of the northwest came up. The crippled whaling ship was being wafted in toward shore.

David's attention was caught by two cone-shaped masses that rose higher than the fog bank. He pointed them out to Keo, who was seated cross-legged on the deck nearby.

From the sling rigged to replace the vanished crow's nest, the lookout called, "Headland! Headland! Off the starboard beam!"

"Then we've made it?" asked David happily. "We're safe?"

He turned to find Keo looking serious rather than elated. "Not yet, Kawika, not yet. You feel how late *Kilikila* turns? I have been this Frisco place before. The tide moves very fast. If it falls we cannot enter, and if we catch the rise, then like the swiftest tuna we will swim. Only—" He paused and added soberly, "We cannot steer good."

Greaves had decided that there was no choice. He directed the helmsman to hold a course between the headlands. Presently they entered the fog bank and were steering by compass alone. The fact that they were in the channel soon became apparent; the *Crystal* once again began to pick up speed. The tide was on the rise and they were committed.

A rocky cliff loomed up to port, and the *Crystal* was urged by the steersman's touch and the combined wills of all the crew back to the center of the channel. The fog swirled about the deck and through the makeshift rigging as the mist was also funneled through the mouth of the bay.

Every man aboard the *Crystal* seemed to be holding his breath. When would they make it through the narrows into safety? Would the fog break before they smashed into some unseen obstacle? David's eyes were strained to bulging as he tried to pierce the clammy curtain; his ear was keenly tuned to catch the sound of breakers on the unseen shore. He wanted this voyage to end, wanted desperately to be safe on land again.

No human sounds were heard for a time, and then a collective sigh went up. From the ruined prow of the *Crystal* to her battered stern, exhaled breaths of relief worked their way aft. As cleanly as parting a curtain and stepping from darkness into a lighted room, the *Crystal* sailed into the sunlit broad expanse of San Francisco Bay. The warmth on David's face was like a welcoming hug of safety and rest.

Even Greaves' shoulders relaxed a bit. "Let her have her head, helmsman. I'll have her run southeast around the point."

"Aye, sir," came the reply.

Passing between the rocky island shown on the 1847 chart and the peninsula containing the settlement still listed as Yerba Buena, the *Crystal* shaped her course toward the anchorage. The drifting fog still obscured the waterfront. Backslapping, congratulations, and a strange brew of profanity and prayers of thanksgiving erupted from the crew.

"Captain," came the call from the lookout, "ease her off a point. We'll have to pick our way through the ships ahead."

"Eh?" replied Greaves, his thoughts interrupted. "What ships? How many?" Even as this question echoed up the mast, Greaves' own eyes were supplying the answer, but his crew came to conclusions of their own.

"Forty ships! I count forty!"

"No, I make it seventy-five. See, there's another row over yonder."

"It's closer on a hundred!"

"What is it, Keo? Why are all these ships here?" asked David.

"I don't know, Kawika. War, maybe? Some angry storm coming, maybe? And something scare men away."

"What do you mean, Keo, scare the men away?"

"Look, Kawika," replied Keo, his muscled brown arm outstretched, "ships all malukia, too quiet. Sailors all gone!"

It was true. The ships appeared to be derelict. The harbor showed none of the expected activity—no loading or unloading of cargo, no ships preparing to weigh anchor, no small craft carrying men between the anchored ships and the shore. It was all eerie and ghostlike. Unpleasant memories of ship-born plagues and mass graves came to David's thoughts.

His gaze wandered to the shore, following the line of his thoughts. The fog, already blown from much of the bay, still clung to the steep, knobby hills that made up the settlement of San Francisco. As he watched, the haze began to clear from the waterfront. At last the mystery of the deserted ships became clear—at least as far as the whereabouts of their crews. The waterfront was a bustling mass of activity, as busy with milling throngs of people as the ships were deserted. Past a line of larger, two-story shops, stores, and hotels, row upon row of haphazard-looking cabins climbed the hill behind the harbor.

As the *Crystal* slowed to a position at the end of a line of unmanned ships, David saw smoke rising from a hundred chimneys and stovepipes. On the muddy thoroughfare along the wharf, he caught glimpses of men passing with tools on their shoulders. He saw two men pulling the lead rope of a reluctant donkey while a third man pushed the animal's rump. A group of men passed, covered in blanket-like garments that reached to their knees. These same men were wearing wide-brimmed, low-crowned hats. David looked an inquiry at Keo, who merely shrugged and remarked, "Ha'i mai 'oe, Kawika, you tell me."

The anchor was let go and Captain Greaves, first mate Nelson, and one whaleboat crew prepared to go ashore. The others were ordered to remain aboard. There was some grumbling amongst the crew at this pronounce-ment, but no move toward open rebellion.

David was hopeful. "Perhaps one of these ships is the *Wanderer* with my letter of credit," he remarked to Keo. "Or perhaps at least someone has news of her. At the very least, I can work my passage back to Hawaii. Maybe my things were returned there."

David began scanning the rows of moored ships for the *Wanderer.* Be-hind him, back toward the mouth of the bay, he heard a signal gun boom. Another ship was entering the harbor.

Presently, out of the fog bank she came, looking clean, efficient and healthy, especially compared to the bedraggled *Crystal.* It was the side-wheeler *Fremont,* as the gold-lettered bow proclaimed. Her paddlewheels churned the waters of the bay as she steamed into view. Pennants were streaming from every masthead and an oversize American flag flew over the stern, its thirty stars gleaming proudly.

Even more remarkable to the sailors left on board the *Crystal* were the men lining the rail. The *Fremont*'s upper deck was crammed shoulder to shoulder with men waving their hats and cheering. Keo and David ex-changed questioning looks and waited as the *Fremont* blew a long whistle blast and drew up alongside. The crowd on the *Fremont*'s deck could be seen picking up bundles and suitcases piled on the deck beside them.

"Some kind of hurry these haoles in, eh, Kawika?" commented Keo.

David nodded, "And look there, Keo. See how many of them have their bundles tied to picks and shovels."

David waved to a tall, frock-coated man carrying over one shoulder a pick from which hung a carpetbag. The man was wearing a stovepipe hat. Raising his voice to carry above the murmurs and rustles of the *Fremont*'s passengers preparing to disembark, David yelled, "Ahoy! What's all the commotion about?"

"Don't you know?" shouted the tall man in reply. "Gold! Gold has been found upriver from here. We're all going to be rich as Croesus!"

"What?" yelled David. "Where's this gold?"

But the man could not be bothered to converse further. He was busy pushing past others who were still gathering their things. Soon his stovepipe hat could be seen in a lighter, dangerously overloaded boat, bobbing its way toward shore.

"Gold, Keo!" David exclaimed. "The stories I heard in Honolulu last winter were really true. There *is* gold in California. I can make my fortune here! What do I need Boston or a letter of credit for? I'll make my own riches."

"Kali iki, Kawika. Wait a little. Let us find out more." The news spread like wildfire through the men on board the *Crystal*. The word was on every tongue; visions of wealth swirled through each brain. *Gold!*

Some of the sailors on the *Crystal* were as impatient as David. While he and Keo were still watching the *Fremont* and discussing the exciting news, a group of whaling men piled into a boat and dropped away from the ship.

"Come back!" shouted the man Greaves had left in charge. "Be hanged," returned a sailor named Branch. "We'll no more sail with the reek of blubber, nor 'Squinty' Greaves. When next we sail, it'll be as kings and princes on our own yachts!"

David saw the whaleboat pulling toward shore meet up with Captain Greaves returning from the dock. Too far away to hear, David could only guess at the furious argument taking place as Greaves stood in one boat gesturing angrily. David watched as Branch rose in the other boat to reply. A moment later Greaves reached quickly inside his coat pocket, then withdrew his hand and extended his arm to point at Branch.

A puff of grayish-white smoke obscured Greaves' hand, and an instant later the report of a pistol cracked in the ears of the watchers. David could see Branch grasp his midsection with both hands before toppling suddenly backward into the water.

Three other men in Branch's boat leaped into the water, but no one had the idea of rescuing him. Instead, Keo and David saw them all strike out for shore, swimming as rapidly as they could.

Greaves gestured with his other hand. It must have contained another pistol, for soon both whaleboats and the remaining men could be seen pulling back toward the *Crystal*. As the boats tied up alongside, David could see that both Greaves and the mate were armed. The crewmen clambered aboard, closely watched by the two men with guns. David looked into each sailor's face as they climbed over the rail. He read there mixtures of fear, sullen anger, and greed, and he knew his own face reflected these qualities, too.

Greaves ordered the men onto the foredeck. When they were assembled and standing under the watchful guns of the officers, he began to address them.

"All right. You've heard the tales. While we were at sea, some madness about gold has set in. This port is lined rail to rail with lubbers thinking to make their piles." Greaves went on to explain how the gold seekers were all fools and how the real wealth lay in profiting from their madness.

"This whale oil that sells for 21 or 22 cents a gallon back in the States is fetching five times that much here! I intend to profit by this foolishness, and so shall you, but only if we get the *Crystal* refitted and get back to hunting whales!"

Greaves gestured angrily with his pistol at the hulks of abandoned ships. "These ships are mostly merchant vessels, derelict because their crews deserted. Well, by all that's holy, it won't happen to the *Crystal!* The master of the *Hartford* and others clapped their crews in irons to keep them from runnin' off. I won't do that, but you all are confined below decks till this madness settles and you see the wisdom of my thinking!"

An angry rumbling went through the crew at this, and some jostling forward. The mate looked frightened and backed up a pace, but Greaves merely waved his pistol and warned, "You saw how I served Branch. So shall all mutineers be served. All right now, speak up. Who wants some on their plate?"

No one spoke. "I thought not. All right, Mr. Nelson's watch is confined to the fo'c'sle. Get below there, now. The rest of you men, down in the hold with you."

David descended into the dark, greasy, evil-smelling hold, followed by Keo and the others. When the last one entered, Greaves clapped the hatches shut and ran the bolt home.

A man named Hughes called out then, "Hey, there's two feet of water in here, and oil on top of that!"

Greaves could be heard chuckling on the deck. "If you don't like the accommodations, then pray I strike a quick bargain for the cargo so's we can lighten ship before she settles right here at anchor."

David heard him call to the mate, "You have the watch, Mr. Nelson. I expect to be back shortly."

The men crammed into the hold could just barely make out the sounds of the oarlocks creaking as Greaves began to row back to shore. Suddenly everyone in the hold was talking at once.

"He can't do this!"

"That old pirate, who does he think . . ."

"How we gonna get outta here?"

"Let's rush him when—"

"Not me, brother! I don't want to be shot in the face. He'll do it, too. Look at poor old Branch!"

David took no part in these discussions, but his mind was racing. Certainly for the kind of money Greaves could obtain for the cargo, he'd be back with hired guards. If Greaves made good on his plan to force them to repair the *Crystal* and put to sea again, it could be another three months or longer before they had another chance at making port. And the gold! What about the gold? It must be real, and available in great quantity, to bring so many people so far from home!

David had seen his fortune, which had flown away on the departing sails of the *Wanderer,* come suddenly back within his grasp. If only he could get off this stinking ship! But how? What would make Greaves let them out at a time of enough confusion that he could slip over the side and swim to shore?

"A fire," he said aloud.

"Eh? What's that? Where?" remarked a startled sailor next to David.

"No, no. There's no fire. But listen, I have an idea."

Keo, who had heard those comments, called out in a booming voice that silenced the babble in the hold, "Be quiet, Kawika has an idea."

The other men gathered around and listened. David explained in quiet tones so that there was no chance of his plan reaching the ears of Nelson. The mate's footsteps could be heard echoing hollowly overhead as he patrolled the deck above.

When David was finished explaining, there was silence for a time, then nods of approval. "Is good, Kawika," Keo summed up. "We will follow your plan."

Greaves was gone a long time. The mate's worried pacing kept up all afternoon, describing small circles, then larger ones, then a circuit of the deck, and finally a pause at the landward rail to look for Greaves' return. Then the whole process began again.

On one of these circuits, David called out, "Mr. Nelson, how about letting us out of here?"

"I can't do that. Greaves would hand me my own head, right enough."

"But Mr. Nelson, we could take to the other boats and be lost in the city before he ever came back. Besides, what about the gold—gold enough to make all of us rich?"

In the gloomy shadows of the hold, the men could see reflected on all their faces the same eager, calculating looks they were sure appeared on the mate's face. For a long time he said nothing, and then responded, "No, it won't wash, men. You might escape, but he'd hunt me down for certain. Better we just wait and see what happens." David was disappointed and a little worried now that his plan would have to be used.

Enough curses to light the hold a sulphurous blue followed the mate as he resumed his stalking around the deck. Many a sailor promised himself to even the score with Nelson at the first opportunity, but David was fretting about Greaves.

It was evening before the splash of oars indicated Greaves' return. This timing was all the better for David's plan, and he went over it again with the sailors in hurried conference.

"All quiet, Mr. Nelson?" they heard Greaves inquire.

"Aye, sir," was the response.

"Now, you swabs hear me," shouted Greaves. "I've three armed men with me to see we have no more trouble. When I open the hatch, come up easy and I'll see you get fed. I've sold the whole cargo, and we'll all celebrate."

The bolt was thrown back and the hatch crashed open. Greaves stood and backed slowly away, gesturing with the pistol he held for the first man on the ladder to come up.

Keo and the other sailors first on deck saw that Greaves had spoken truthfully. Three grim-looking men circled around the hatch, each armed with a rifle and each carrying pistols and knives thrust into their waistbands.

"That's it, everybody come up easy like," instructed Greaves. "I'll unlatch the fo'c'sle now, and we'll all be one happy family again."

By this time, some fifteen men had exited the hold and were milling about, encircled by the guards. At that moment, still in the hold, David carefully ignited a greasy rag in a pan of oil and called out, "Fire! Fire in the hold!"

Others took up the cry, "Fire! The ship's on fire!"

The trick seemed to work. Greaves whirled about and ordered, "You men! Back down there double-quick and get the pumps going. Lively now!" Fire in the hold of an oil ship was a disaster all whaling men dreaded. David had counted on Greaves making an instant call for action without thinking that it could be a ploy.

The men really did turn back toward the hatch, which by now was venting dark, acrid smoke. The curious guards stepped in closer, not noticing that two whalers had moved particularly close to each of them.

Keo shouted, "Wela ka heo! Strike them now!"

Instantly, three wrestling contests began as two sailors grappled with each guard's rifle. Peering out of the hatch from the ladder, David saw a sailor shot at point-blank range as he grasped a rifle muzzle in an attempt to help. As the sailor fell back, the guard regained control of the rifle, and reversing it, swung it by the barrel in an arc that felled another whaler.

David gasped as one of the other guards lost the struggle for his rifle, and went down with a sailor's dirk protruding from his back. Greaves shot one sailor in the face, then began using his pistol as a club on anyone within reach, shouting for the mate to help him.

As David struggled upward on the stairs, Keo charged toward the mate, thinking to take him out before he could go to Greaves' aid. Nelson saw the Hawaiian rushing toward him, a belaying pin in his upraised fist like an ancient war club. The mate shrieked, discharged his pistol ineffectively into the air, and turned to throw himself over the side before the Hawaiian's blow could descend.

David sensed that the struggle could still be lost as the third guard released his hold on his rifle after shooting a sailor through the arm. He pulled a pistol from his belt, and brandishing it in front of him, waved the sailors back. He began to move, crablike, toward the rail, when his feet came within an arm's length of the hatch.

A sailor lunged out of the hold, grasping the guard around both ankles. Startled, the man discharged his pistol down into the deck, then toppled over backward, carrying both himself and the sailor down the steps into the hold. They tumbled over several others, including David. The pistol fire struck the oily casks, and they began to burn furiously.

A renewed, and this time, frenzied cry of "Fire! Fire!" went up, and there was a rush for the companionway. In the struggle for the stairs, the guard was trampled underfoot, drowned in the pool of muck in the hold.

David fought his way up the steps to find the remaining guard and Greaves fighting back to back on the deck. At the sight of flames shooting out of the hold and roaring up into the rigging, the guard and several of the whalers abandoned the struggle and threw themselves over the side without a backward glance.

Suddenly David stood face-to-face with Greaves. The captain was completely out of his mind; the crazed look in his eyes went everywhere, but focused on nothing. He snatched up a still-loaded pistol that had fallen to the deck and aimed vaguely at David. In the instant before firing, the captain found himself encircled from behind by Keo, and the belaying pin crashed down on his forearm. His shot caught David across the cheek— just grazing him, but raising a great, bloody welt from below his right eye to his ear. David's heart beat wildly; Greaves' face had taken on the coldly murderous expression of the shark.

Greaves just had time to fix David with a look of unutterable hatred before Keo picked him up. Two steps to the rail, and the native unceremoniously dropped Greaves into San Francisco Bay.

By now the fire was past extinguishing. The center section of the ship was engulfed in flames, and the stump of the mainmast was burning. Men all around were jumping into the water. David was preparing to leap also, when Keo laid a restraining hand on his shoulder.

"Wait, Kawika. You hear something?"

Above the roar of the flames devouring the *Crystal,* they heard cries for help. Agonized screams of terror were coming from the forecastle.

"Sailors still locked in fo'c'sle!" Keo cried. "Come on, Kawika, we must save them."

David looked at the flares of orange light erupting from the ship's deck and felt the heat on his wounded face intensify. He glanced at Keo's eyes and, for an instant, thought he read sorrow there. Then David swung his legs over the rail, and dropped into the bay.

4

DAVID GASPED WHEN he hit the water. Even in midsummer, the bay's temperature was icy. He struck out strongly for the shore, his direction plainly marked by the increasingly brilliant light thrown out by the blazing *Crystal.* A momentary shame at the thought of his cowardice made his face flush even in the frigid water, but he shrugged off the thought by the remembrance that he could still drown if he did not reach the shore soon.

David swam through a line of deserted ships. He thought of seeking shelter on one of them, but there was no one aboard to help him, and his increasingly numb fingers would not sustain his weight for a climb up the steep sides. He caught an anchor line and rested for a moment, panting from the exertion and shivering uncontrollably.

Up ahead he could see lights in the windows of a building. It was much nearer than he had supposed the shore to be, just behind a ship that was docked across a narrow channel from him.

David struck out again with renewed strength, anxious to get to land. When he was ten yards from the dock he began calling for help, but the noise and music from the lighted windows of the nearby building drowned out his cries. He clung to a piling, oblivious to the damage being done to his hands by the rough barnacles and mussels. David looked briefly for a ladder, but found none.

He resolved to pull himself piling by piling around to the shore side of the dock. Soon he reached the hull of a ship that he thought rested between him and the building on the shore. The ship *was* the building!

Above its decks rose a makeshift three-story structure. Surrounded by docks and permanently fixed in the San Francisco Bay, it had been turned into a floating gambling hall, still fifty yards from shore.

A bumboat ferrying passengers out from shore to the gambling hall was arriving. Its occupants heard David's calls and assisted him from the water.

"Bit cold for swimmin', ain't it, young feller?" remarked the boat's skipper. He brought David a blanket to wrap up in.

Through chattering teeth, David explained about the fire onboard the *Crystal.* Several of the new arrivals strolled around the plank walkway to observe, but no one seemed very excited or made any move to get help. Now safe himself, David tried to urge these men to assist the *Crystal.*

"We don't get too excited about ship fires here, boy," explained the bumboat's operator. "Most of these ships is abandoned an' rottin' away. Shoot, Frisco has at least one fire a day—an' that's on a slow day. Why, we can't be runnin' off to put out no burnin' boats where they can't hurt nothin' by burnin' anyways."

"But there may be men trapped on that ship!" exclaimed David, feeling remorse now and worried about Keo.

"I'm sorry son, but you just take a peek at that blaze. She's burnt 'most to the waterline already. We're fixin' to put out again to pick up swimmers like yourself. Don't worry none. You go on in the *Bernice* here and warm yourself up."

David took the skipper's advice and, still wrapped in the blanket, made his way up a gangplank and into the converted ship-saloon.

Inside lay a scene of mammoth confusion, both of sight and sound, not to mention the smell of liquor and the all-pervading smoke that filled the room like a low-lying cloud.

The entire lower floor was one large room, filled almost entirely with tables crowded by gamblers, except along the wall opposite the entrance, which was occupied by a bar. David was stunned to see a portico of marble pillars behind the bar—until he realized that the scene was painted on the wall.

Near the center in front of the bar stood a group of bearded men with long, shaggy hair. They wore high-topped boots that reached to their knees and talked animatedly, between puffs on cheroots, about the good prospects of a place called Little Rich Bar.

On the left, as David faced the counter, stood three men dressed like those he had seen from the deck of the *Crystal.* They sported pointed beards and carefully groomed mustaches, and were covered front and back by a blanket-like garment through which their heads protruded. They were speaking a language David took to be Spanish, although he couldn't understand a word.

At the opposite end of the bar stood a pair of Chinese men. Their pigtails hung down below broad, flat straw hats with small pointed crowns. Apparently they could be understood by the bartender; as David watched, one of the Chinese reached inside his green silk jacket and retrieved a small bag. The barkeeper helped himself to several pinches of something from the bag, which he deposited carefully in a similar pouch behind the bar, then took down a bottle from the shelf behind him and set it and two glasses in front of the Chinese.

Dripping wet, barefoot, and penniless, David was unsure how to proceed or what to do with himself. He decided to address the bartender as being the only one present in any kind of official capacity. To approach the bar, David picked his way through intent circles of gamblers, stepping over a drunk lying full-length on the floor snoring, and carefully skirting a pile of shattered glass.

"Save your breath, friend," anticipated the bartender. "Drinks for gold either pinch or coin. No greenbacks and no credit."

Before David could even respond, the loudest of the bearded prospectors whirled around and confronted the white-aproned saloon man. "Say, barkeep, that weren't neighborly. Not neighborly a'tall. You must be tryin' to ruin this town's repute for friendliness."

"Strawfoot, are you willing to vouch for this fellow?" quizzed the bartender. "He's wrapped in a blanket like some Indian, he's been in a knife-fight or somethin', and he's almost without pockets to put money in—*if* he had any money, which I strongly doubt."

The man addressed as Strawfoot reached into a deep outside pocket of his faded blue knee-length coat and drew out a leather pouch like those David had already seen. "Here, young fella," he said, pitching the pouch to David. "I imagine that'll earn you a little respect." With no more comment or attention than this, he turned back to his interrupted conversation and instantly resumed arguing the respective merits of something called long-tom versus something else called rocker. He might as well have been speaking Spanish—or even Chinese—for all David understood of the debate.

David was astounded, and it must have shown on his face, because he looked up to see the bartender grinning broadly at him. He glanced away quickly and furtively loosened the drawstring on the pouch, half-expecting Strawfoot to snatch it back.

Reaching in with thumb and forefinger, David drew out a fine-grained, flaky powder that glinted dully in the light of the oil lamps. Leaning over the bar, the saloonman said, "That's enough to buy you a drink. Five like that, and you can keep the bottle."

Nodding slowly in bewilderment, David deposited the pinch of gold dust in the bartender's outstretched hand and accepted a glass of whiskey in return. David tossed down the fiery liquor, choking back an urge to gag. He swallowed hard twice, then unclenched his eyes and teeth.

David held the pouch up and felt its substantial weight. He looked questioningly at the bartender, who gestured for David to hand it over. The bartender weighed the sack in his hand and considered briefly, then remarked, "Eight ounces, I judge. Worth, oh, a hundred and twenty dollars or so."

With that he passed the bag back to David and turned to answer a call for "Mo' whiskey" from the Chinamen down the counter.

David was flabbergasted. He started twice to tap Strawfoot on the shoulder and twice drew back uncertainly. Finally he collected himself and said in as firm a voice as he could manage, "Mr. Strawfoot—"

The bearded miner turned and regarded David with a smile. "Just Strawfoot. No Mister to it."

"All right, Strawfoot. My name is David Bollin, and I . . . I don't know quite what to say. I mean, we don't know each other, and yet the bartender tells me what you've handed me is worth over a hundred dollars in gold. Sir, you should know that I can't say when I'll be able to repay you, or how."

"Forget it. It weren't a loan, anyway." The hairy miner looked David over. "Appears that you are a mite down in your luck. Well, I been down, an' folks has helped me before. I just like to return the favor. Besides," Strawfoot continued, "it ain't so much. I come to this town with five thousand dollars to spend, an' I ain't leavin' till she's gone. You just helped me out a scooch."

Strawfoot seemed willing to continue the conversation, but he must have noticed something about David's wounded face or a waver in David's stance that concerned him, because he stopped abruptly. Leaning closer he asked, "You feelin' all right, son?"

"Just a little weak, is all," David replied.

"Shore, shore. Ice cold bath, somebody playin' merry ned with your cheek, and then a glass of this rat poison they serve for liquor. Fine doctor I am. Like to kilt you, no doubt."

Strawfoot called the bartender over. He gave instructions that David was going to use his room, and that the barkeep would please see that David got upstairs safely.

Over his protests, David was escorted upstairs and put to bed. As he fell asleep, his mind was a whirl of blazing ships, icy water, Keo, Strawfoot, and gold. Gold! Gold by the bagful, in shiny glittering heaps!

When he woke up the next morning, David couldn't immediately place where he was. At first he wasn't sure that the events of the day before had been real and not some unbelievably complicated dream. Then he put his hand up to his face and winced as his fingers touched the puckered wound that stretched five inches across his cheek. The fingers of his other hand closed around a small leather pouch, its drawstring still looped around his wrist just as he had placed it the night before.

A long rasping snore from close by interrupted his thoughts and made him clutch the pouch of gold even tighter. Cautiously David raised up from the pillow to look over the side of the bed. There, still fully clothed and stretching his six-foot length on the floor, was his benefactor, Strawfoot. Every time the miner breathed, his bushy black beard rustled like palm fronds in a high wind.

David's stomach growled, reminding him that through yesterday's confinement in the hold of the *Crystal* and all that followed, he had had nothing to eat. There should be more important things to think about, but David's hunger asserted itself, and his stomach growled again, louder this time.

This new noise had a curious effect on Strawfoot. His snoring stopped, replaced by a slurred mumbling. "Dang grizz. After that haunch a' venison. Bang some pans, somebody."

Apparently Strawfoot decided that no one was going to follow his instructions, so he sat up abruptly as if intending to see to it himself. He blinked widely three or four times, then added an enormous yawn and a stretch to his waking-up motions. He turned to regard David equably, without any of the confusion that had plagued David's waking.

"Good mornin'. You awake, too? You're looking some better—least you're gettin' some color back. Last night you was so pale, that cut on your cheek looked like somebody writ with red ink on white paper."

David explained that he was indeed feeling much better, and that he was sorry to be occupying Strawfoot's bed while the miner slept on the floor.

"Think nothin' of it," was the prospector's reply. "Just bein' indoors with a roof over my head is a whole lot better'n other places I've slept.

"Say," Strawfoot continued, "are you hungry?" David's stomach growled again in reply. Addressing himself to the noise just as if David had spoken, Strawfoot agreed, "Well all right then, let's get goin'."

David vaguely remembered the bartender helping him out of his soggy shirt and dungarees the night before. Now he found them hanging over the foot of the bed, dried, if not any improved in quality. In a single moment David, with all his earthly possessions, was ready to travel.

"Where can we get breakfast?" inquired David.

"We could feed here on the *Bernice*," commented Strawfoot, "but I've got a hankerin' for oysters an' eggs, an' there ain't no better place for that than the Atlantic Hotel. Let's get goin' an' see if we can roust out that scoundrel of a ferryboat skipper."

Strawfoot's comments reminded David that he was still in the bay on a ship of sorts. This thought made his worry for Keo surface again strongly.

"Strawfoot, I need to go look for a friend. He . . . he was in the same ship fire as me last night and I, that is . . . We got separated . . ." His voice trailed off.

Strawfoot tried to cheer him up. "Why, we heard all about it. A bunch of your sailor friends was pulled out of the water here last night, an' a bunch more got picked up an' taken ashore. You needn't worry, I'm sure your friend is all right."

"Really?" asked David hopefully.

"Shore," came the reply. "An' what a grand fire it was, too! Some a' that burnin' oil spread over to a couple other ships. We was makin' bets on which one would burn the quickest!"

"I can't believe it!" exclaimed David, alarmed to find just how far his original plot had gotten out of hand.

"Nothin' to be upset about. The *Fremont* got up steam and moved out of the way. Whatever burned was just rotten hulks anyway. Come on, let's go eat, then we'll have a go at huntin' up your friend."

Outside on the dock David and Strawfoot found an arriving bumboat loaded with men eager to drink and gamble even though it was only mid-morning. "I ain't headed for shore just now," the boat's operator explained. "All these fares is comin' from the steamer anchored over yonder that's just in from Sacramento."

The pilot suggested that they go down to the end of the dock. "There's a boat tied up there with a feller sleepin' on it. Likely you can hire him to take you to shore."

As the small boat came into view David commented, "That looks like one of the whaleboats from the *Crystal*. And that man lying across the seats looks like—it is! Keo! Keo, wake up!" David ran the rest of the length of the dock shouting and waving.

Keo bounded up out of the whaleboat and grasped David in a hug that would have crushed several ribs had he not stopped when he did. "Kawika! you safe. I paddle all over looking for you."

Another pang of shame went through David. While he had been inside sleeping, his friend had been out searching for him!

"But the fo'c'sle, the men there—" stammered David.

"Oh, everybody get off all right," reported Keo. "I even have time to lower last boat and help sailors out of bay. I keep looking for you but not finding."

David hung his head. "I know, Keo. I was already here, safe."

"Is good!" shouted the native. "Now everything is maika'i. All just fine now!" Keo looked at Strawfoot and the miner returned the gaze.

"This new friend, Kawika?" asked the Hawaiian, indicating the miner.

"What? Oh, yes. Strawfoot, this is the friend I was telling you about, Keo Kekoa. Keo, this is Strawfoot. He sort of took me in last night."

"Is good you help Kawika," said Keo sincerely. "Keo be friend to you, too. Say, Kawika, Pololi au! I am very hungry. Is food near here?"

"That's just where we was headin'," offered Strawfoot. "In fact, if you can get this boat goin' again, we'll go tie into some breakfast right now." Strawfoot paused as a thought struck him. "Unless, a'course, you're one of them cannibal fellas. I don't know where they cater to that whim!"

Keo laughed and thumped the miner so hard on the shoulder he almost knocked him off the dock. "No worry. I not hungry for tough haole covered in wire brush!"

The Atlantic Hotel turned out to be another ship converted into building, this one up on the shoreline and hemmed in on either side by more conventional structures. To reach it, the three companions had to slog down a planked road that was more mud than planks. Anyone who stepped off the planks sank to the knees, so most passersby resorted to jumping from board to board in a curious kind of hopscotch.

"I hear tell there's a whole freight wagon down under this somewheres, an' a Irish teamster still tryin' to get his mules to goin'," commented Strawfoot.

"I think I believe it," puffed David, pausing between leaps. "What do they call this triumph of engineering?"

"This highway is known as Market Street," replied the miner, leaping over to the ladder that rose from the mud to the deck of the Atlantic Hotel.

The foredeck of the Atlantic still had its mast in place. A sign tacked up near the gangplank read, "Here Laundry Done. You Wait," as an industrious group of Chinese scurried around scrubbing clothes and running them up the rigging to dry. Somewhat less wordy, but more enticing to David was a large sign reading simply "EATS," with an arrow pointing aft.

Over a meal in which the men consumed three entire skillets of scrambled eggs and oysters, they exchanged stories about past lives and future plans.

David said little about leaving Hawaii. Instead, he focused his attention on the gold fields, bombarding Strawfoot with a string of questions.

Strawfoot related that he had already been in California when the gold strike was first reported. He had been in the army, he said, and had elected to stay in this new country when he mustered out. He owed his unusual name to his army experiences as well. Soldiers who didn't know left from right were taught to march with a wisp of hay tied to one foot and a twist of straw on the other. The drill sergeant kept time by shouting, "Hayfoot, strawfoot, hayfoot, strawfoot." Most learned to march properly, but the bearded miner reported sheepishly that he never had quite gotten the hang of it and had received a permanent nickname as a result.

"I was headed for Coloma when I learned about a new strike a ways south of there. Seems some fellers named McCoon and Daylor took out, oh, seventeen, eighteen thousand dollars in one week. 'Well sir,' I said to myself, 'that's good enough for me.' "

"And did you strike it rich right away?" inquired David eagerly. "Is it really that easy?"

Strawfoot leaned back in his chair, clearly enjoying the rapt attention of his audience. "Hold on a minute, while's I wet my throat." He called the waiter and requested a "stone fence." When he explained to David that it was a mixture of whiskey and apple juice, David opted to try one also, but Keo declined.

When the drinks had arrived and been partly consumed, Strawfoot resumed his narrative. He explained that he had gone directly to an unoccupied section of a stream that was "no wider than this here table," which he had selected completely at random. He told how he had begun digging in the dry soil of the creek bank, shoveling out loose soil and stones to get down to bedrock. It had taken him four hours to get down four feet.

"I seen there was a crack in the rock face running alongside the creek. It were a space about as big across as my three fingers together." Strawfoot held up a gnarled and calloused hand to demonstrate.

After another swallow of his stone fence he continued, "That crack was packed with pea gravel and clay, so I taken my knife and went to scrapin' out that crack." He drew a broad-bladed knife almost ten inches in length from a sheath at his side and tossed it on the table.

"When I got to the bottom of that crack, what do you suppose I found?" Again Strawfoot stopped, and looked back and forth between his listeners with snapping dark eyes.

Slapping a meaty hand down on the table, Keo demanded, "H'ai mai! Tell us what!"

"All along the bottom of that space were a whole row of gold! Little kernels of gold, 'bout the size of apple seeds." Strawfoot fished an apple seed out of his drink, and laid it in his palm. The other two men leaned over to inspect it as carefully as if it were really a gold nugget.

"That first day's work weighed up to be close on fifty dollars, an' that was just the beginning."

David's heart was beating so fast that his voice sounded wavery when he asked, "And is there more left?" He tried to not breathe, so as to hear the reply clearly.

"Shoot, yeah. Most all prospectors plan to make their piles and skedaddle for home. I got no family and no home to go back to, so after I prospects a piece I come to town to celebrate. After all, what good is it if you can't spend it?"

David's heart wrenched at the words "family" and "home," but he quickly shoved those sensations aside. He wanted no sloppy sentiment to interfere with his becoming rich.

"How does one come to the country of gold?" asked Keo. "Is it far?"

"It's a pretty fur piece upriver," acknowledged the prospector. "Most fellas with money goes by boat as far as Sacramento. Them that can't afford passage gets across the bay here anyway they can, then they goes to walkin'!"

" 'E!" exclaimed Keo. "We already have a boat. Since *Kilikila* burn, I do not think Captain will be paying my six months' share. I think I keep whaleboat."

"Say, that's right. Strawfoot, would you like to travel with us? That's the least I can do for your kindness," offered David.

"Fair enough. Fact is, I was fixin' to ask you two to partner up with me," responded Strawfoot. "Unless," he added suspiciously, "you think I'm gonna help *row* all the way up to Sac."

"No, no! Keo can rig a sail, can't you Keo?"

"Pono! You bet!" agreed the Hawaiian.

Strawfoot advised David to buy supplies in San Francisco rather than wait to get them upriver. He explained that a $25 barrel of flour would cost $50 in Sacramento and climb to $100 at the diggings. They reviewed together the items needed and the quantity of each—flour, sugar, coffee. Picks, shovels, pans, stout knives, and at least one firearm for providing camp meat. Strawfoot headed back to collect his things and spend one more night "whooping it up" on the *Bernice,* while David and Keo set out to gather their supplies and see a little more of San Francisco.

5

SEVERAL HOURS OF shopping later, David and Keo had all their equipment and provisions purchased, wrapped securely in canvas, and stored aboard the whaleboat. Out of Strawfoot's gold dust, they had just enough left for dinner, one night's lodging, and breakfast before sailing.

"It doesn't matter, Keo," commented David confidently. "By the time this store runs out, we'll be as rich as King Kamehameha."

More out of a sense of curiosity than either the ability or the desire to participate, the two friends entered the Eagle Saloon and Gambling Parlor. Their attention was first captured by the barker who stood out front chanting, "Here's the place to win it all back! Step right up, gentlemen, find the lady and win two ounces. Yessir, you heard right. Wager one ounce and win two!"

From outside, the Eagle looked no more substantial than any of the other hurriedly built wooden structures forming what was euphemistically called the business district. It was sandwiched between a building with a sign proclaiming "Cheap Publications" and a structure announcing itself to be the headquarters of Epic Fire Company #1.

David was intrigued by the shoddy construction of so populated a city. Honolulu was a much more substantial place, with several imposing stone structures and a sophisticated society—even if he, as a preacher's son, had never belonged to it. San Francisco felt like an extension of the wilderness, pretending to be a city. For all the saloons, shops, and other establishments, he had not seen one school. Honolulu had three.

He was snatched from this reverie when the barker addressed him directly. In his new flannel shirt and canvas pants, tucked into still-shiny new boots, he looked like a man of substance.

"Come in sir, come in. Finest establishment of its kind in the world. Come in and sample our Queen Charlottes—the best anywhere. The first is on the house. Yessir, right this way."

David looked at Keo, who shrugged agreement and the two made to enter. Seeing this, the barker dropped his loudspeaker voice and caught David by the arm. "Hold on a minute there, friend. Your partner here. He's not Indian, is he? Or Negro?"

David looked startled for an instant, then replied, "No, he's Hawaiian, and so—" He stopped midsentence and choked off the words, "am I."

The barker looked relieved. "Well, that's all right then," and added doubtfully, "I guess."

David and Keo went on into the saloon. David looked at Keo out of the corner of his eye to see if the islander showed any reaction. David thought perhaps Keo's jaw looked a little tighter than usual, but then decided he was imagining it. *Why didn't I finish saying that I was Hawaiian, too?* wondered David to himself.

In an attempt to change the subject of his thoughts, David said to Keo, "What is a Queen Charlotte, do you suppose?" When Keo did not reply, David shifted his attention to the gambling table just inside the entrance.

"Find the lady, gentlemen. That's the name of the game." The three-card monte dealer kept up a running patter while slapping three red-backed cards around in rapid motion. Over, under, under, over, the cards flew past each other, while an occasional flick of the wrist revealed the location of the queen of hearts before it rejoined the shuffle with the two jacks.

There were plenty of other games of chance operating in the Eagle. A large wheel of fortune was set in motion with a practiced hand, while miners placed bets on a hand-lettered board. Several faro tables were in use as well, but David didn't understand the game and soon drifted up to the bar.

"I'll have a, what do you call it? A Queen Charlotte." "Yessir," the bartender responded. He picked up a large tumbler and began pouring into it from two bottles at once. David saw that it was compounded of red wine and raspberry syrup. "On the house," the bartender confirmed, setting the drink in front of David.

David took a sip. It was amazingly sweet, and so heavy with syrup as to be gagging. David set the drink down and said for the bartender's benefit that it was very good, but he guessed what he was really thirsty for was a stone fence.

The bartender obligingly set up the requested concoction, then accepted a pinch of gold dust from David's dwindling supply. Aside to Keo, David remarked, "I can skip breakfast tomorrow and eat some of our crackers on the boat."

"Come on, Kawika, let's go now," advised Keo.

"You go on, if you want to," remarked David. "I'm not through looking around here yet."

Keo murmured something about still needing to rig the sail for the whaleboat and turned to leave.

David felt a kind of relief when the native was gone. He didn't stop to think about it, but he wanted to get over his embarrassment. David downed the rest of his drink and called for another. Picking it up from the bar, he began to inspect the gambling tables again.

David's attention was particularly caught by one dealer who appeared flashier than the rest. This man was clean-shaven. He wore his receding dark hair long and combed back from his face; four of his ten fingers gleamed with rings, and he wore a shiny stickpin.

The dealer continued weaving the three cards in their rapid and intricate pattern, then stopped to place each one carefully in a box drawn for it on his green felt working surface. He took a moment to cover each card with his hand and straighten it so that its edges were exactly aligned with the box.

He then called for the bettor's decision as to the location of the queen. In contrast to the continuous flow of instructions, encouragement, compliments, and other patter that had come from the dealer, the opposing gambler was a silent man. He was studiously inspecting the backs of the cards as if he could read their identity through the pasteboard.

At last he reached a decision and placed a gold half-eagle in front of the center card. With a careless flick of the wrist and a small smile, the dealer turned over the chosen card to show that it was, in fact, a jack. Before collecting the money, the dealer took a moment to cover each card as before, carefully aligning the edges. He then turned over the card on the gambler's left, revealing the location of the queen.

The miner swore softly but acknowledged the dealer's right to pick up the coin. David saw him reach into his inside coat pocket and draw out another coin, this time a twenty dollar double-eagle. The man held on to the coin for a moment, eyeing it thoughtfully. At last making up his mind, he placed it on the edge of the table.

The dealer's patter began as before, and the cards resumed their mesmerizing flight. David had to force himself to avoid either listening to the dealer's words or looking at the flashing rings. Instead, he tried to concentrate on the cards alone. Each time the queen was turned up, David checked to see if his guess would have been correct, and he concentrated entirely on following that one card.

When the shuffling ritual was done and the cards again perfectly aligned, David was certain he knew the location of the queen. He and the man gambling apparently agreed, for the miner staked his double-eagle on the right-hand card without any hesitation.

For a bare moment, a flash of white from the dealer's palm caught David's attention. The dealer turned up the required card with practiced assurance, revealing that the miner had lost again. The miner shrugged, and prepared to stand and leave.

Almost without thinking, David interrupted. "Before you straighten the cards again, could I see the one in your hand?"

The dealer stiffened and made no move to bring his left hand up to the table. Instead, his right hand moved across his chest, reaching toward his coat. The miner who had just lost his money was paying close attention and moved faster than either the dealer or David.

The miner yanked a Bowie knife from his boot top and pinned the dealer's coat sleeve to the table. From the dealer's other hand a card floated free. The queen of hearts landed face up and smiling on the floor. There were still three cards on the table top. All three were jacks.

A brawny hand clasped around the dealer's throat and he stopped trying to free his imprisoned coat sleeve. As David watched, fascinated at the scene being played out in front of him, the prospector reached inside the dealer's coat. Thumb and forefinger lifted a single shot .44 caliber derringer from the coat pocket. The sight of the pistol made David's face twitch. He put up a hand and gingerly touched the crease made by the bullet wound—was it just the night before?

A crowd of gamblers had gathered around the table to watch, and as the proof of the cheating was revealed they began to murmur, "String him up."

"That's it, hang him."

"He was goin' for his gun, too. Lousy cheat!"

The owner of the Eagle came rushing over. "Gentlemen, please," he requested, "let's not have any bloodshed here. Right, sir?" He addressed himself to the miner who still held the dealer off the ground by the throat.

The prospector shook his head in disgust. "Turn out his pockets," he growled.

Several others jumped to obey this instruction. Like a chicken being plucked, the man was swiftly stripped of coat, vest, and pants.

When the dealer was left standing in his underwear and boots, a money belt he wore strapped around his middle was added to the pile of gold dust pouches and coins on the table. The humiliated dealer gasped out a feeble protest, "Most of these winnings were fair!"

"So, how about it, boys?" the miner addressed the crowd. "This cheat says he's bein' robbed. Do we believe him?"

A chorus of, "No. No way a'tall," and a renewed demand to hang the man rang out from the crowd.

"He's too scrawny now that he's plucked," concluded the prospector, echoing the same image that had occurred to David. "Just don't ever let me lay eyes on you again," said the miner, and he roughly threw the cheater to the floor.

The man started to stand up, but a well-placed kick stretched him on the floor again. Once there, he decided that crawling toward the exit would be safest. He did make it out the door, but not before a few more boots had connected with his posterior.

The miner turned to David. "I'm obliged to you, son. I imagine that I lose more than I win, but even so, I don't like bein' cheated."

David refused the miner's offer to split the money with him, but accepted the derringer. The prospector examined the money belt and seemed to find it to be fair compensation. He swept the odd change into a pile on the table and called out, "Drinks for everyone till we use it up." With whoops of delight the crowd expressed their agreement.

Fortunately for David, the Eagle was only a few blocks from his hotel. Several stone fences later, David had to have two new-found friends help him back to his room. There he found Keo waiting for him, and he was soon asleep.

Even though he had been caught cheating this time, Owen Barton, the dealer, was a clever man—too clever, some folks said, and sharper in his business dealings than was good for his trading partners. The news of the strike in California had been truly a golden opportunity for him. The gold rush wasn't exactly the deciding factor in his leaving Saint Joe, Missouri. His neighbors had decided that for him when they concluded they'd been swindled enough. But the gold rush did decide the direction of his departure, a destination full of promise for a man who made his living cheating other people out of theirs.

Barton was a tall man, his stature accented by a high forehead and straight nose. He was vainly proud of his looks, despite his receding brown hair and his pockmarked face. He oozed persuasion as a maple tree oozes sugary sap. He could pretend to be a sharp-tongued Yankee or an aristocratic Southerner—whatever the circumstances called for.

Selling land he didn't own, hocking shares in fictitious businesses, or touting marvelous inventions that hadn't been invented yet were all part of his portfolio, but his day-to-day subsistence came from gambling. He was a cardsharp of the first water. Barton knew faro, fantan, monte, and poker, which he despised. Poker allowed a degree of skill to be made use of by Barton's opponents. He wanted only chance, greed, and his own subtle influences to affect the outcome.

He had gambled his way down the Mississippi and cheated his way across Panama. Once on the Pacific side, he had duped the skipper of a schooner into carrying him to San Francisco for free, courtesy of a rigged hand of three-card monte.

He had gone no farther toward the gold diggings than San Francisco, because he saw no reason to chase gold already coming to him. A few months raising capital with his gambling, and he would be all set for something more profitable and refined. San Francisco was ripe for a land scheme of some sort. After all, real estate values were already starting to soar.

But a moment of inattention on his part, together with too much attention by a sharp-eyed busybody, and Barton's plans had come unravelled. He had made a really stupid blunder with the monte game in the Eagle Saloon. Barton upbraided himself savagely for his slip. For a man who had been palming cards all his adult life, he could not believe how clumsy he had been.

Reaching for the derringer had been another stupid mistake. He should have distracted the miner somehow and rearranged the cards. If only, if only . . .

Yet Barton knew that he was lucky to be alive. The brand of justice served up in San Francisco was to hang men from lampposts—except that there were no lampposts yet. But he had seen men hanged from ships' masts and cargo cranes.

With the perverse logic of the chronically criminal and habitually lucky, Barton felt that he had been abused. To have all his gold hijacked was a terrible blow to his plans. To be stripped of his clothes and kicked into the street was an indignity past bearing.

Barton frowned and shook his head as he reviewed his circumstances. It was *almost* past bearing. The threat to his life was real if he remained in San Francisco: a new scheme would have to be developed—and quickly.

He ducked into one of the shabbier establishments. Shabbiness was relative in San Francisco, but the Weathereye Tavern catered to seamen who had no gold to speak of and preferred their liquor potent and cheap. There were no Queen Charlottes in the Weathereye. Captains in need of replacement crews had been known to furnish rum in quantity for men who would wake up miles from land the next morning.

The bartender glanced up at the sight of the normally dapper gambler crossing the saloon in his underwear, but said nothing. Not only was the bartender naturally cautious, he had also been in Frisco long enough to know that much more unusual sights were possible.

Barton took the stairs to the second floor two at a time. He pushed into a room and shut the door quickly behind him. The slam of the door brought the tenant of the room to partial waking.

Lying on the rudely framed wooden bed, for which a salvaged sail served as both mattress and blanket, lay a man. He started up with his hand already grasping a Walker Colt. His saggy, jowled face was puffy with too much drink and too little sleep.

"What the—? What's the idea bustin' in here, Barton? I coulda shot you."

It had not yet registered with the occupant of the bed that Barton was only partially clad. The man laid the gun back down and brushed a hank of stringy black hair out of his eyes. He swung his stockinged feet over the side of the bed and inserted his arms through the loops of suspenders that lay in tired circles on the canvas bedding.

From a tin can on the floor the man withdrew a crooked black cigar. He lit the cheroot and drew a long drag before turning his head sideways to regard Barton.

"What happened to you?" he asked.

Barton explained the mishap in the salooon that had resulted in the loss of his clothing and his money belt. "Moffat, I need you to fetch my trunk from the Eagle and bring it here," he concluded.

"Only the trunk?" asked the large man with the greasy dark hair.

"No, the trunk *first*," Barton explained, "so I can dress properly to reserve our passage upriver on the morning steamer. After you retrieve the money belt from that miner who did me in, we'll want a sudden change of scenery, I think."

Outside the Eagle Saloon the street was dark. Fog broke from its tether on the knobby hills and drifted through the streets. The noise of raucous laughter echoed out of the tavern, and occasionally a miner, having exhausted his last pinch of dust, would stagger out and wander up the street.

Moffat stood leaning against the corner of the Epic Fire Company #1 building. He was smoking another cheroot and casually flicking the ashes onto the board sidewalk. He glanced up as each departing customer left the Eagle, but each time the features and dress were not those he had been instructed to single out.

At two A.M. he considered going back in to make sure the man he sought was still playing faro. Moffat decided against it for the time being. He had been noticed enough when collecting Barton's trunk, and he didn't want to stir up any suspicion.

Fifteen minutes later his patience was rewarded. The miner Barton had described to Moffat stepped out of the Eagle and paused before setting off, as if obligingly allowing Moffat to confirm his identity.

Moffat saw the man pat his belly. Undoubtedly it was not dinner that the man's gesture showed appreciation for, but rather Barton's money belt.

Moffat fingered the coil of rope in his coat pocket. The man took a deep breath of the cool air and then elected to walk up the street away from Moffat. Moffat began to follow him, in no hurry to close the gap until they were both well away from the entrance to the Eagle.

A short distance up the hill the fog closed in to darken the night even further and muffle the sounds of gambling and revelry. *Now,* Moffat thought, lengthening his stride to overtake the miner.

Moffat was five paces behind, then four, then three. His right hand started to produce the rope, and then a board creaked underfoot.

The miner whirled around and bent to place his hand on the knife handle protruding from his boot top. "Who's there?" he demanded.

Moffat dropped the half-drawn rope back into his pocket. He spread his hands wide in a gesture of harmlessness, and walked slowly up to stand in front of the man he had been following.

"Please, sir," he whined, "can you spare a bit for a poor, starving man what ain't eat for two days?"

The miner stood up, drawing his knife from its sheath as he did so. He patted the flat of the blade against the palm of his hand as he replied, "You don't look like you've missed too many meals yet. Be off with you."

Moffat ducked his head and backed away one step, then another. Just at the moment when it seemed he would turn to go, he stretched out his left arm and pointed over the miner's shoulder.

"Look there! Another big blaze is breaking out!"

The miner turned to look and swung the knife around away from Moffat. This was all the opportunity Moffat needed. He drew the coil of rope and quickly shook it out, holding one end in each hand. Moffat stepped up behind the prospector, and before the man could turn around again, had flipped the rope over his head and around his neck. The attacker crossed his hands and began pulling with all his strength, tightening the loop of hemp.

The victim tried to turn to face his attacker, but Moffat put his knee in the man's back and kept him tightly crushed against the rope.

The prospector slashed backward with the knife, but Moffat saw the blows coming and swung his victim around in a small circle. The blade flashed down once and then again; on a third missed stab, it fell from the miner's hand.

The prospector's fingers went up to his throat, attempting to get a grip under the coarse fibers to pull it away from his neck. His nails scrabbled on the line, his body beginning to stumble awkwardly as his brain clouded.

The miner's eyes protruded from his head. He tried to scream for help, but could not make any sound pass his tortured throat. The pull backward on the rope and the push forward in the small of his back made him feel as if he were breaking in two.

He was almost right. Moffat twitched the rope sideways with a sudden jerk of both hands, and a cracking noise like the sound of a tree branch breaking under a load of snow echoed up the deserted street. The prospector's body slumped to the boardwalk. His tongue protruded from his lips and his dead eyes still bulged from their sockets. This was one gambling miner who would never catch Barton cheating again.

Moffat looked up and down the deserted street. Then, reaching into the man's shirt, he removed Barton's money belt with a yank that rolled the corpse over. The dead man came to rest face down in the muddy San Francisco street, while Moffat strolled away, whistling to himself.

6

STRAWFOOT, DAVID AND Keo met up at *Bernice*'s dock as planned. They had a beautiful clear morning to cross the bay and an onshore breeze to push Keo's lobster-claw shaped sail. All in all, it would have been perfect, if David hadn't had such an abominable headache.

Christened the *Gold Seeker* by Strawfoot, who had romance in his blood but no seamanship, the little whaleboat bounced across San Francisco Bay. On the way they passed other Argonauts in all manner of crafts, including homemade rafts that spun and turned with each whim of the current. The men aboard these and other frail-looking boats paddled mightily with their makeshift oars. David could tell by their irrepressible grins that they were on course for the gold fields and even pleased with their progress.

They passed the first night at the port of Benecia. A United States customs official briefly examined their cargo and asked a couple of questions about their origin, destination, and purpose. He nodded wearily as if to say, "I knew that already," when they relayed their intent to prospect for gold. He passed them through with a tired wave of his hand and turned instead to a more thorough search of the cargo vessel *Milwaukee*.

The next day found them entering the Sacramento River, and the propelling breeze failed them. Over Strawfoot's protests that he had been hornswoggled, they took turns hiking along the shore with a length of cable. The two men on board the *Gold Seeker* would row while the one on shore would wrap the cable around a tree trunk and pull for all he was worth. In this way they made substantial, if painful, progress.

Hiking through the muck and tule marshes and enveloped in a swarm of mosquitoes, David was reminded of the rain forests of his home island.

Except, he thought to himself, *the mosquitoes at home were never this many or this big.*

The second night up the river they tied the whaleboat to an overhanging limb of an oak tree that jutted out over the waterway. David was so tired that he voted to eat cheese and crackers from their supplies and then turn in. The other two agreed, and soon all were fast asleep.

The following day went much the same, except that when daylight began to fail, there was no oak tree nearby. In fact, there was no tree of any size in sight. The tule bog that bordered that reach of river stretched uninterrupted for miles.

"We can't tie up to these reeds," complained David. "The current will break us loose for sure, and we'll be way downstream again by morning."

"Don't this here boat have an anchor or somethin'?" inquired Strawfoot, rubbing his neck.

"Whaleboat no need anchor," explained Keo. "Maybe we can find something."

He rummaged around in their store of goods and came up with a large cast-iron kettle. "Will work, yes?"

Cast-iron kettles just like this were used by the prospectors for all manner of duties. Strawfoot recounted for David how this pot would cook meals, wash clothes or render fat. David shuddered, remembering his recent experience around the try pots on the whale ship. Strawfoot concluded that he had never heard of one used as an anchor, but he didn't see why it wouldn't work.

They filled the kettle with mud and dumped it into the river. It dragged with the current for a moment or two, then successfully entangled itself in the matted tule roots. The three weary men settled down to sleep.

The next morning, David was the first to awaken. There had been a change in the level of the river during the night. That fact, coupled with some trick of the morning light, made the normally murkey water extremely clear. Gazing around him and rubbing his eyes, David could follow the line of the rope connecting the boat to the kettle. The cast-iron pot was still faithfully holding the bow of the *Gold Seeker* into the current, even though the wash of the stream had cleaned the thick mud from its insides.

As David watched, a shaft of sunlight refracted into the kettle's dull black interior. Tiny glittering sparkles appeared, then disappeared, as a swirl of water obscured the bottom. David blinked hard and rubbed his eyes again. *Could it be?* he wondered. He had heard that the California streams were full of gold, but could it be literally true? He peered intently into the water. In a moment the river cleared, and immediately the inside of the kettle could be seen to glisten as if a tiny blacksmith were plying his trade and showering sparks around.

David's first few pulls drew the boat up to the anchor, but failed to break it free of the bottom. He called for help, and Keo began heaving on the rope as well. David excitedly explained about the flashes in the kettle, how it glinted just like gold, and how fortunate they were to have anchored in that spot.

Keo caught the excitement that David was generating. He leaned over the rail of the boat to grasp the handle of the kettle as it broke the surface, and with a mighty heave pulled it into the boat. Bucketfuls of water splashed over both David and Keo, spreading a stream of tiny, metallic flecks across the whaleboat's decking.

"Save it, save it!" shouted David. "Don't let those little flakes get away!"

Tiny particles were hastily gathered up. Keo transferred the little fragments from the tip of his right forefinger to the palm of his meaty left hand.

"Maybe cast iron attracts gold or something," spouted David. "Maybe we've found a secret method—or else just a real rich spot!"

"Or else two pair of new boots with greenhorn prospectors in 'em."

In his excitement, David hadn't noticed that Strawfoot had taken no part in gathering up the glittering particles. Now David turned to see the bearded man standing in the stern of the boat with his arms folded and his head cocked to the side.

Completely misunderstanding Strawfoot's meaning, David hurried to explain. "We weren't going to keep this gold separate. Honest, we were going to share everything we found. We were just hurrying because we got excited and didn't want to miss one little speck of this gold."

"Gold?" the prospector repeated. "I don't see no gold."

"But . . . but . . . right here," stammered David. "See how it shines?"

"Shade it in your hand," suggested Strawfoot. "Is it still gold color?"

"No," responded Keo, "is like black sand."

"Try and bite it," the prospector suggested to David. "And you," he said to Keo, "hammer it with somethin'."

They reported that it was gritty like sand and shattered when hammered. Strawfoot explained that real gold was soft when bitten, soft enough to hammer flat without shattering.

"But what is this stuff if it's not gold?" demanded David.

"I disremember what it's called for real," replied Strawfoot, "but it flakes out of the granite rocks up in the mountains. Most folks calls it 'fool's gold'."

David and Keo looked at each other's wet clothes and the eager way they clutched the tiny fragments of worthless rock, and both began to laugh. "Pretty well named for such as us, isn't it, Keo?" said David, brushing his hands off on the seat of his trousers.

"You bet," responded the Hawaiian. "Maybe better we rename this boat LōLō."

"What's that mean?" asked Strawfoot.

"He says," answered David, "we should call it the *Stupid.*"

Two more days of travel upriver brought the three partners to the confluence of the American and Sacramento rivers and to the settlement named for the latter.

"When I first come by here, they weren't but a half-rotted boat fetched up on the bank yonder and a tent store for a tradin' post. Now look at it." With a sweep of his arm, Strawfoot indicated the sprawling expanse of Sacramento. Three sailing ships and a number of smaller craft were tied up to the wharf. A commercial district of shops and warehouses lined the docks. David could see that the buildings became simpler and shabbier as one looked farther inland. Just past the town on some cleared land nearby were acres and acres of tents, their occupants busily engaged in loading and unloading wagons.

"Where did all these people come from?" asked David. "We didn't see that many on the river."

"Bunch of these folks come here overland," explained Strawfoot. "Crossed the prairies and the Rockies and the deserts and the Sierras, and here they is." He added with an uncharacteristic note of surprise, "And they's lots more than when I was here last, too."

Strawfoot explained that they would have to go ashore here. Even though they could travel farther by river, this was the last opportunity to trade the whaleboat for overland transportation, namely mules. David reflected that he was sorry to part with the *Gold Seeker,* but the change meant that his voyaging had finally come to an end. Thousands of miles of water now lay between him and his home, but any regret was lost in his realization that only a few more miles stood between him and gold.

They pulled ashore past the wharf on a muddy bank near a solitary water oak some sixty feet tall. The riverbank rose to a plain twenty acres in expanse, crisscrossed by every conceivable wheeled, hoofed, and footed conveyance—men and their trappings off in the pursuit of wealth.

David saw a man pushing a wheelbarrow on which rested a chicken coop. The red rooster caged in the coop loudly proclaimed his independence and noisily challenged all comers to dispute his superiority. A team of six oxen pulling a high box freight wagon crossed the wheelbarrow's

path by way of no discernible road. Around the base of the oak tree a
string of mules were tethered, tended by a Mexican muleskinner wearing a
serape and leather moccasins with leggings that reached up to his thighs.

A man galloping by on horseback scattered a disorganized group of
miners who were walking across the muddy plain. David stared at the
view—not because of the confusion, but because something seemed missing. What could possibly have been left out of a setting already so jumbled
with men and their belongings? Then it struck him: there were no women
anywhere in sight. It could have been a street scene at the waterfront of
any number of busy port cities, except that Sacramento had no women at
all. David wondered if the absence of female influence made men coarser
and less civilized; then he mocked himself for unconsciously echoing one
of his father's sermons.

Satisfied that he had resolved the mystery of what seemed wrong with
Sacramento, David leaped ashore and plunged one of their crowbars into
the clay bank, then tied the whaleboat securely.

Two hours later, Keo, David, and Strawfoot were headed upriver again,
walking and leading a pair of mules. Strawfoot had successfully traded the
whaleboat to one of Captain Sutter's lieutenants, and the supplies were
loaded in short order.

As they traveled eastward, David noted the change of both scenery and
climate. The low, marshy grassland gave way to foothills of oak trees, and
the summer heat became drier.

"Strawfoot," David asked at one of their rest stops, "all this way you've
just called your claim 'the diggins.' Does it have a name?"

Strawfoot gave a sideways glance at Keo, then allowed his gaze to rest
on David, as if deciding whether or not to reply. Finally he launched in.
"Well, it were mostly always called Old Dry Diggin's on accounta the first
strikes was found up a ways from the creek. We had to carry the paydirt
down to the stream to pan it, you see."

Strawfoot stopped, as if hoping that this account was satisfactory. David
prompted him to continue by asking, "You say it *was* called that. What's it
called now?"

The reply, when it came, was much lower in volume than Strawfoot's
usual boisterous conversation. David leaned over toward the miner and
caught the reply clearly: "Hangtown."

David rocked back upright, more startled by Strawfoot's dramatic manner than by the name itself. "Why did you hesitate to tell us?" he asked.

Strawfoot drew a deep breath and sighed heavily before continuing.
When he did, it was in the same subdued tone. "Just after the turn of this
year, three men was hanged up in the diggin's. They was part of a gang of
five what had robbed a man and got caught."

"They were hanged for robbing?" interrupted David. Strawfoot waved his hand for silence and continued. "No, they was whipped for that. But whilst they was bein' lashed, three was recognized as having kilt a man up Stanislaus River way."

Strawfoot proceeded to explain that over a hundred miners formed themselves into a jury and convicted the three in the space of half an hour. He recalled that a man named Buffum, a former Army lieutenant, was the only man to speak against the lynch law.

"But twarn't no use. Buffum was told to shut up or he'd be hanged, too. The boys was all likkered up, and nothin' would satisfy them, exceptin' . . ."

Strawfoot shook his head sadly and wiped his forehead with a red bandana.

David could sense how deeply painful this account was for Strawfoot, so he tried to sum up by noting, "But they had a fair trial, right? Only one man took their part? And nothing they could say would prove their innocence? Seems to me your miners taught a harsh, but correct, lesson."

Strawfoot stared into David's eyes with the look of a haunted man. It made David shudder, and the icy trickle of fear down his back made him stammer, "They were guilty, weren't they? Did they beg for mercy?"

Strawfoot's eyes looked through David to some recollection only he could see, but from which he could not turn away. "No, they didn't beg for mercy; they didn't speak no English, an' they couldn't even understand what they was charged with!"

Beside David, Keo exhaled a long breath through pursed lips, making a whistling, sighing sound. Very gently the big Hawaiian asked, "You vote for their death, too?"

Strawfoot nodded slowly and added, "An' when Buffum said that he would interpret, them bein' French an' him knowin' the language, I—me, Strawfoot—I shook a busted bottle in his face and told him to keep still or I'd cut his tongue out."

David unconsciously backed up two steps from the miner's side. The prospector noticed the unspoken reproof and added, "I sobered up next day and kept to myself ever since, minin' all alone. I got so lonesome, I went to Frisco for a spree. I figgered on pickin' some new partners, and then you come along. I didn't figger you for foreign till I saw Keo there. By then I didn't know what to say. See, I liked you right off. Anyways," he concluded sadly, "I guess you can make up your minds about me now."

David couldn't think of anything to say. He knew he'd never be so craven as to send men to their deaths without a word for their side. In his mind David cast himself as Buffum, the gallant, if unsuccessful, voice of reason. David watched with surprise as Keo moved toward the miner and put his bronzed arm around the prospector's shoulders.

"You feel grief for your part, yes?" David heard Keo ask. At Strawfoot's short bob of his head in agreement, Keo continued, "You Christian man? You know Jesus?" Again the brief nod. "Jesus speak no word to save Him from cross when all bad men say for Him to die. But He ask Father God not to crush them for killing His Son. You think maybe God forgive for Jesus, maybe God forgive you too?"

This was more than David could stand to hear. An ignorant native sailor was speaking words of redemption and forgiveness learned from David's father. And this bearded miner was actually responding, visibly brightening! David stalked off to be by himself for a while.

Later on, Keo approached David to report that Strawfoot was feeling much better and was ready to proceed. "Do you believe all that Bible story stuff you were handing him?" quizzed David gruffly.

"Kawika," responded the harpooner firmly. "I tell Strawfoot how God in his heart already forgive all his sins more than just one which make him so sad. I tell him God forgive me for worshiping stone gods in dark time." Keo stopped and looked thoughtfully at David, "He ready forgive you too, Kawika."

"Forgive me?" snorted David. "I don't need forgiveness. I haven't done anything wrong."

David's first glimpse of Hangtown was not what he expected—or, rather, more than he expected. The trail crested a low rise topped with pine trees, and suddenly the town lay immediately below him, nestled in a bowl-shaped depression. From the ridge he could count over forty buildings, and saw smoke rising from other chimneys hidden around a curve of the hill.

He turned to Strawfoot to ask if this was the right place, since it seemed so much bigger than the one he had described. Strawfoot responded that it had, in fact, changed a great deal since his departure. " 'Bout doubled, I figger."

For all its size, Hangtown did not seem overly busy or crowded with people. The prospector explained that the population of miners was spread up and down the creek working their claims until nightfall brought them to town.

"When I first seen the place," Strawfoot continued, "there wasn't but two log buildings hereabout. Everything else was tents and wickiups."

"When do we start mining gold?" asked David, unconsciously rubbing his hands together in anticipation.

"Hold your horses. My place is just upstream a ways. We'll go unload our gear and maybe dig a bit before dark."

The procession of three tired men and two very weary mules picked up their pace in expectation of arriving at camp. They skirted the edge of Hangtown by hiking around the rim of the valley, because this was a faster approach to Strawfoot's claim.

"It's just through this gap here," said Strawfoot, pointing to where the path led between granite boulders. In his excitement to be home he raced ahead of the others.

When he reached the space between the rocks where the path began to descend toward the creek, he stopped stock still. David saw him stiffen, almost as if he had been slapped in the face. David and Keo hurried up to stand beside him.

"My cabin's gone," the miner said in a harsh croak. "It were just yonder by that pinyon tree. Now there's three tents there."

"And my claim!" he shouted, waving his arms. "Somebody has gone and wingdammed the creek and backed it up over my bar." With that he took off at a run down the hill toward the stream, all thought of partners, mules, and supplies left behind.

David and Keo followed him down the path to stand beside the pinyon pine. Twenty Chinese miners were working beside the stream. Some were digging down to the bedrock in the stream bed uncovered when the wingdam diverted the water. Others were transporting the sand and gravel to a long tom set up beside the stream, while still others were walking along beside the wooden frame, turning the muddy contents with shovels. A few glanced up at the new arrivals, but none left off working.

Presently a tall man, dressed like all the rest in high boots and baggy pants, but white and armed with an unmistakable air of authority, came over to where they stood.

"Can I help you men?" he asked. "Are you looking for work?"

"Work!" exploded Strawfoot. "I'm looking for my claim! And while we're about it, where'd my cabin get off to? Who are you, anyway?"

The man seemed unruffled by the flurry of questions. He scanned Strawfoot up and down and spared a glance or two for David and Keo before remarking, "You must be Strawfoot. We heard you were dead, but obviously it isn't true."

Strawfoot snorted, a sound David thought closely resembled a bull in a dangerous mood. "No, I ain't dead! Not by a long shot. But some others 'round here may be right soon if I don't hear why all these folks are messin' around my claim!"

"Calm down, Mr. Strawfoot. My name is Foster. I'm the foreman here with the Amalgamated Mining Company."

"The what? I've never heard tell of your outfit. Where do you get off damming the creek and covering up another man's claim?"

"Your claim's played out, Mr. Strawfoot. We took every foot of gravel off and swept the bedrock of your claim before we diverted the river. We put up your gold in a jar—in case your heirs turned up to claim it."

"All played out," puffed Strawfoot, suddenly deflated like a bellows with a ripped out seam. "But I took thousands out of that claim."

"I've heard that. By sheerest good fortune you hit the only pocket on your stretch. Two feet either way, and there was nothing. We scraped up every flake we could find, but it didn't amount to more than, oh, another pound or so."

"All played out?" Strawfoot repeated, clearly struggling with the thought of how much gold he'd blown on his spree in Frisco.

"For what it's worth," Foster continued, "you can have your claim back soon. We've about exhausted the stream bed here also, so you can tear down the wingdam if you've a mind to."

"What about his cabin?" asked David, with the sinking feeling that his dream of instant wealth had taken wings and flown away.

"That cabin, I'm sorry to say, burned down. I don't know what possessions you may have lost, but we can provide you with a tent to use."

"Is it your company that's made the town grow so?" inquired David.

Foster explained that Hangtown's growth was mainly due to its place on one of the main routes over the Sierras from the East. "Ever since the passes cleared, they have been coming—first by the tens, but lately by the hundreds. All gold seekers in search of El Dorado. Well, they'll need to search elsewhere. We're about done here, except for fluming the river to use it in a dry canyon that shows promise. A company of Chinese is going to buy this stretch—more fools they. Now I've got to get back to work. Good day to you, gentlemen."

"What'll we do now?" said David to Keo, ignoring Strawfoot. The miner was staring so grimly over the scene in front of him that David was almost afraid to interrupt his thoughts.

"Maybe we can work for these folks for a time," commented Keo. "They hire Chinese, so maybe they take Kanaka and haole."

That comment got a rise out of Strawfoot. Bristling all over he declared, "Work for these Amal Gee Mates? Not on your tintype. I'd ruther be shot in the rear with a pint of hornets! I found this here claim, didn't I? I'll just find another one!"

7

THE THREE PARTNERS crossed a high ride northeast of Hangtown and struck out for what they hoped would be unexplored territory, rich with gold. For two days they travelled, rejecting location after location because of the astounding number of other prospectors already working claims. At last they reached an expanse of steep canyons covered in fir trees, and Strawfoot declared it was time to begin prospecting.

At the first of these stops Strawfoot directed David and Keo to dig out a pile of gravel from the foot of a massive boulder. This rock sometimes lay in the path of the creek, but the lowered water level had left it dry. Strawfoot explained that when the flood water washed against the rock and turned the current to the side, pockets in the bank could trap gold washed down from farther up.

They dug down until Strawfoot was satisfied they were below the surface soil. Taking a pan and a shovelful of earth from the hole, he squatted beside the stream and began swirling the dirt away.

David and Keo stood looking over his shoulder. David held his breath with anticipation. He saw the miner squint his eyes, frown, purse his lips and stare off into the distance.

"What is it?" asked David eagerly, "Is there gold? Not fool's gold, I hope."

"Why shore, it's real enough," began Strawfoot, when his explanation was cut short by David almost knocking the pan from his hand.

"Show me!" demanded David. "These flakes here? Is this gold?"

Strawfoot straightened up and stretched his back and legs. "Shore am out of practice for setting by a pan all day," he remarked.

"Why aren't you more excited?" questioned David. "You said it *is* gold?"

"Oh there's gold, right enough. I count eight specks in this here pan."

"Eight specks—is that good?"

"Not less'n you want to eat beans the rest of your life. I calculate if we worked here from sunup to sunset, we might make ten dollars a day."

"But that's not enough to feed the three of us!" David cried, shocked at the news. "What do we do now?"

"That's why they call it prospecting," replied Strawfoot. "We've gotta keep looking somewheres else."

Two more days passed this way. Strawfoot would lead them to a likely spot, where they dug a test hole. A few swirls of the pan, and the contents would be dumped back into the creek, the few tiny flakes left to lure other gold seekers.

Finally Strawfoot's examination of the gold pan lasted longer than usual. Weary from a day of tramping over steep hillsides and climbing in and out of narrow ravines, David hardly paid any attention. His thoughts were wandering back to San Francisco, to the fancy hotels and sumptuous meals that gold could provide.

Keo, his usual stoic self, was watching closer than David. "Is good color?" he asked, combining his Hawaiian inflection with prospector jargon.

"Yup, I'm satisfied," announced Strawfoot.

This startled David out of his daydream. "You mean we've struck it? This is a worthwhile spot?"

"See for yourself," responded Strawfoot, extending the pan toward David.

The ridge where the slanted side of the pan met the bottom was a solid line of gold flakes around half of the circumference. In the center of the curve was the real prize: a nugget the size of the last joint of David's little finger.

"What do you figure? I mean, how much can we make here? A day, I mean?"

"Well," began Strawfoot, pulling his beard into a bushy handful. "If this pan's showing holds good for this stretch of creek bed, we can do, say, a hundred dollars a day betwixt us."

"Three thousand a month!" exclaimed David. "What are we waiting for?" and he began attacking the sandbar with as much enthusiasm as if he'd been starving and a roast pig lay underneath the ground.

"Simmer down," advised Strawfoot. "Now that we've located, we'll fix us a proper camp. I'm tired of sleepin' in a bedroll with no tent between me an' the crawly critters. Plus I got to knock together that rocker we been carryin', so we can get serious. Here," he added, handing David the nugget from the pan. "Keep this for good luck." David accepted the gold lump and tucked it into his shirt pocket, buttoning the flap down to keep it safe.

By the following afternoon they had "got serious." All three attacked the stream bed until paydirt was uncovered and a pile of it dug out with pick and shovel. Keo kept the wooden box called a rocker in motion, swirling the water around the pailful of earth David dumped in the top. David followed up the load of dirt by carrying pail after pail of water to be added to the mixture. Strawfoot collected the gold flakes and a few nugget from the riffle bars in the rocker's insides and processed the fine sand and gold with his pan.

The routine produced $120 worth of gold their first day. David was elated. He was really a prospector now, and on his way to being rich. Amazingly, even after all the calluses he'd acquired scrubbing the decks of the *Crystal,* David's hands still found new places to blister. He grimaced as the handles of the heavy pails of water cut into his fingers, but he was satisfied that when he escaped from this pain, he would be wealthy.

The next day's work produced $100, and the day after, $90. Each evening the three would work until dark, then gather around the lamp for a weighing process that became a solemn ceremony. Strawfoot would unpack a pan balance and a set of brass weights and tally up the day's results. The flake gold was poured into a leather pouch and the pouch tucked beneath the bedrolls. Lumps of gold were divided up among the three men, each man taking turns selecting until all were gone. David rarely thought of home any more; he went to bed each night exhausted, but happy, thinking of all his new-found wealth could buy.

A shaft of sunlight arcing through the tent flap struck David in the eyes. On one side of him, Keo was sleeping peacefully, while on the other, Strawfoot sounded like he was sawing timber for a few thousand rockers.

Through the opening David could see the creek and a pile of their tools. The trunk of a fallen cedar lay partly in the stream, and the uphill side was covered in a layer of ladybugs. As David watched, one detached itself from the mass and flew almost directly toward the tent, striking the canvas with a tiny but audible thump.

What a peaceful morning, thought David. *It reminds me of Sunday mornings back home, before Father would yell at me to hurry up or I'd be late for service.*

David wondered drowsily why the morning seemed so peaceful. His brain turned this thought over while he watched a blue jay swoop down from a redwood to land on a rock that was part of their cooking ring.

Something finally clicked and he sat up, saying out loud, "Hey, why are we sleeping so late?" Strawfoot always got them up in the gray light, before dawn. Now it was full light and still the prospector let them sleep.

Strawfoot mumbled, "Sabbath. Day of rest," and turned over again.

"But say," objected David, "what about the gold?"

"Still be there tomorrow," breathed the miner through his whiskers.

"But it's my day to have first choice of the nuggets, and I feel lucky today," objected David.

"You can have your turn tomorrow," explained the prospector, now fully awake. "Me and Keo talked this over after you'd already dropped off last night. We want to give the Almighty his due, so we figger on reading some scripture verses and bein' grateful for a day of rest."

David turned over to find Keo also awake and propped on one elbow regarding him with liquid brown eyes. "Is Lord's Day, Kawika. He let us keep gold, we let Him keep one day. Long time whale ship no different Sabbath Day from other day. Is good idea."

"Well I don't think it's such a good idea. You two lie around camp if you want to, but I'm going to run some pans, if nothing else. And I'm going to keep what I find, too."

"Okay Kawika, you go. Maybe get out of camp do you good. God show His work all around here," added Keo, extending his broad palm toward the sunlit creekside. "Maybe you talk to Him some, too."

David took off away from camp to prospect. He rationalized that he didn't want to make Keo and Strawfoot feel bad because he was working and they were having a day of rest. The truth was, he felt uncomfortable staying in camp when they were reading from the Bible. An unnamed irritation came over him—they believed him to be in the wrong, even though no one had tried to force anything on him. He threw the shovel he was carrying into a sand bar with more force than was necessary.

David dug beside the stream and turned a few pans of gravel in the clear water, but found no color. He found himself unable to concentrate on what he was doing and reproved himself for being stupid. How much concentration did it take to dig a hole?

In any case, he trudged on upstream, trying to recall all the signs that Strawfoot had suggested looking for.

Another sandbar, another two feet of gravel, and the same result. Digging down to bedrock seemed like too much work. After all, David felt that the gold should be calling to him, practically jumping into his pan.

Something was calling to him—not audibly, but persistently, in his head. For the third time he stopped to try to determine what was bothering him. As he paused to consider this elusive annoyance, he noticed that he had dug his test hole too near the course of the stream and the hole was filling with water. Throwing his pan down in disgust, David settled on this interruption as a good excuse to lean against a nearby boulder and think.

Sunday morning in the mountains of the Sierra Nevada. He squinted up at the sun shining down through the branches of a willow tree growing across the stream. It was about ten o'clock, he judged. Just the time at home when his father would be ringing the handbell that called his flock to worship.

David closed his eyes and let the warm sunshine bathe his face. It wasn't nearly as intense as the sun would have been at home. On the other hand, the breeze in this Sierra canyon was clean, but it carried none of the heady sweet aroma of the Ilima and Pikake blossoms that grew outside his bedroom window.

When the islanders decorated the church altar with fragrant bouquets, David's father would always make a point to draw a deep breath of jasmine or the scent of gardenias, then spread his arms as if to embrace the whole congregation. He would thank those who had brought the flowers for blessing the very air with their gift, and then remind them that the fragrance of the blossoms was like the enjoyment God receives from the prayers of His people.

David's eyes popped open with a snap. They were praying for him! He knew it with a certainty, and in that same instant understood what had been nagging him all morning. It was Sunday morning, and they were praying for him!

David looked at the gold pan lying at his feet and put a hand to his buttoned shirt pocket to touch the gold nugget there. *If they only knew how little I need their prayers,* he thought. *I'm well, getting rich and having an adventure. In their entire lives they'll never be twenty miles from the village where they were born.*

David stretched—an expansive, relaxed stretch. He was relieved to have figured out what had been on his mind. *Let them pray for me,* he thought, *even if I don't need it.*

David decided to relax a moment longer there on the warm slab of granite. He put his hands behind his head and began to lie down on the rock. Halfway down he stopped and turned over to brush the pine needles and ladybugs from his wilderness bench. Mid-motion, he froze.

Right behind him, also taking advantage of the morning sun, was a coiled snake. David sat up slowly, inspecting the resting reptile with curiosity but no fear. Hawaii had no native snakes, and David saw no reason to be afraid of this one tht was so amiably sharing the boulder. Strawfoot had warned David and Keo about the poisonous snakes called rattlers that inhabit these mountains, but he had told them about their warning rattle and their belligerent striking. This snake hadn't offered to do either. It was small, dark brown in color. Its scales were dull and drab, and it had a squat, unattractive head.

As David watched, the snake tested the air with quick pulses of its forked tongue. The reptile moved his head from side to side as though looking for something; although at two feet away, David was the only thing that could possibly be in sight. He was stretching out his hand to touch it when he heard the music.

Very faint, echoing off the canyon walls, was the sound of singing. This was no church music; David could hear snatches of lyrics like *My dearest*

Sally . . . I'll go to Californy . . . and she threw a dozen in! A mining camp, without a doubt—and just one canyon over, by the sound of it.

David decided he had dug enough dirt for one week; he would hike on over to that camp and see what it was like. He glanced back toward the snake, but in the moment when his attention had shifted, so had the serpent. He caught just a quick glimpse of its tail as it disappeared down a hole. *That's strange,* David puzzled. *Those little buttons sure look like I'd expect rattles to look.* Shrugging, he gathered up his pan and shovel and set out to hike over the hill.

As David crossed the ridge line and began to descend the canyon on the other side, the music grew louder and the words more distinct. He heard a mixture of voices, some good and some bad, some old and some young, but none female. They were singing, "I fed him last at Chimney Rock, that's where the grass gave out; I'm proud to tell we stood it well along the Truckee route. . . ."

Apparently Sally was a popular name for the girl left behind, for the next song also had a Sally handing out advice: "Here take the laud'num with you Sam, to check the diaree." It didn't seem that any of these travelers needed the mentioned remedy, for all were dancing in a lively manner. They would have benefited from the presence of Sally and her sisters; however, the dancers were all male. Some partners wore bandanas tied to their arms, but in the stomping and whirling, it was impossible to tell who was leading anyway.

David approached the outskirts of the ruckus and leaned his shovel and pan against a tree. He found a tall, bald man who was neither dancing, singing, nor playing fiddle or banjo. The bald man, who *was* smiling and tapping his foot in time to the music, looked over at David as he arrived. "Welcome, stranger. Where are you from?"

"My friends and I have a claim downstream on the next creek over," David answered. "I followed the music, and here I am."

"Yessir, good for what ails you. Dancing and music and kicking up your heels. This is the Washington Company, son. We've been four months on the way here from Michigan. Lost half our stock before we ever saw the South Pass of the Rockies and had more stolen by Digger Indians. We buried a few of the company, too. Some from cholera back in Missouri, and one just about your age, just last week."

Startled by this flood of words from a complete stranger, it took David a moment to realize that the pause after the last statement showed the expectation of a question.

"Um, uh, what did he die of?" asked David, finally catching on.

"A wagon fell on him. We were hoisting our equipment up by ropes, just like it says to do in *Hasting's Guidebook,* when a rope broke and he

couldn't get out of the way in time. But we're here now," the man continued, "and we aim to celebrate before we go to mining."

"Did you say you had a *guidebook?*" asked David incredulously.

"You bet. Lansford Hastings. Of course, he had some of the landmarks
wrong, but on the whole his was better than the others."

"The others? Is there a regular business in guidebooks?"

"You can say that again! And not surprising, either; I think the whole
country's coming west. There were times when we could see a line of
wagons stretching to the horizon in both directions. Just look around
you," offered the man. "We've only been here two days and we've started
to build cabins and a dam to divert water from the creek bed. We've got
carpenters, engineers, blacksmiths. Why, we'll be a regular settlement in
no time at all."

The man gestured toward a tent building that stretched along one side
of the dance floor. "That's our store. Already open for business."

"You mean you brought trade goods all the way across the continent?"
David was clearly ready to be impressed.

The man looked momentarily embarrassed. "Actually, most of the stuff
got thrown out coming across. But—" He paused for effect. "We do have
whiskey. Twenty-five cents a glass."

Several samples of trade goods later, David made his way back across
the ridge to camp. He explained to Keo and Strawfoot about the nearness
of the other camp and talked at great length about the vast numbers of
miners, who were apparently just beginning to arrive.

Strawfoot seemed to shrug off the news as being of no concern.
"There's still plenty for everybody," he said, "and plenty more places to
look, too."

Their claim continued to pay well enough for several weeks. David still
left camp on Sundays, but he did no prospecting and he took no long
walks just to think. Instead, he went directly to the neighboring mining
camp, now big enough to be called a settlement. David showed some luck
at the faro tables, but he was quick to notice that the man acting as the
"bank" was the only sure winner.

Members of the Washington Company drifted over to the canyon where
Keo, Strawfoot, and David were working. Their camp had proposed some
rules for fair play, they said, and they considered the side stream as part of
the same mining territory.

David listened as the rules were explained. Each miner's claim was to be
limited to ten yards of stream frontage. No man could hold more than one
claim, and work had to be done at least one day out of seven for the claim
to be valid.

There was no discussion of these rules, nor were the three partners asked for their opinion. Their "company" was allowed one additional claim for the right of discovery, but that was it. Soon a hundred miners were working up and down the creek where once only Strawfoot's solitary tent had stood. Strawfoot seemed to think that the rules were just and proper, but David frowned and turned surly whenever a prospector announced a rich find or displayed an especially large nugget.

Eventually the return dropped off considerably. They were processing larger amounts of gravel each day, but finding less gold. When their take had fallen below thirty-five dollars for three weeks in a row, they decided it was time for a change. David felt as if he had personally dug up every rock on half a mile of stream, so he had no regrets about moving on.

They decided to continue moving upriver. Strawfoot told them about the "mother lode," a ledge of pure gold somewhere in the mountains that was supposedly the source of all the flakes, grains, and nuggets found in the streams.

Despite Strawfoot's sense that there was "plenty for everyone," for several days they saw no opportunity to test a likely spot, for every one they came to was already staked. They passed one stretch of creek where all the miners were from Mexico and spoke only Spanish. Another day brought them to another area populated by Chinese immigrants. The Chinese were working a bar already examined by other miners and rejected as showing too little promise. But the "Celestials," as the Chinese were called, methodically sifted the sand so that not even the finest particle of gold escaped their search.

Obtaining supplies became increasingly difficult. Even walking as rapidly as possible, one man could not lead a mule down to the trading post, load up, and complete the trek back upcountry in less than three days. Sometimes it took even longer if the trading post was out of flour, bacon, or other essentials. The man hauling the freight wouldn't dare to leave before being resupplied, or the store might run out before he got back again.

Prices were outrageous. Flour sold for a dollar a pound, and eggs, when they could be had at all, for a dollar each. The level of gold dust in the partnership sack began to diminish instead of increase.

Finally the morning came when David, sleeping next to the wall of the tent, rolled over into it, shaking the canvas. A shower of ice crystals shattered down on his face and neck, waking him up instantly. He lay in the dark for a minute, trying to figure out what had happened, and discovered that his breath was condensing and freezing inside the tent. They would have to decide what to do, and soon. Clearly winter was not far away.

8

"**I** SAY WE head for town for the winter—Hangtown, at least, but Sacramento would be even better." David vigorously pushed for the three partners to get out of their mountain camp.

"If we skedaddle now while there's still another month of working weather, other folks will move in on our claim. Come spring, this whole stretch of country will be shoulder to shoulder with miners." Strawfoot was just as determined to stay, unaware that he was now arguing that there was *not* unlimited gold.

"Let's just sell this claim, then," responded David. "We're not making but an ounce a day, most days, sometimes less. Why don't we sell out, find some cozy spot to hole up, and prospect some other place in spring?"

"Didn't you hear anything I said? There won't be anybody *buying* claims this close to winter, but they'll sure take over one that's been abandoned."

"Why don't we let them have it, then?" shrugged David. "If we stay here any longer we may have to winter over, and that doesn't appeal to me. What about you, Keo?"

Both miner and young man turned to the native for his opinion. Keo tugged on his bushy side whiskers in thought before replying. "I think Strawfoot is right, Kawika. If we stay here now, others will be the ones leaving. Perhaps we better our claim. If we all work, we can have a fine cabin before snow comes. Then spring will find us already at work, not looking for a place."

"So that's how it is, eh Keo?" said David with a sneer.

"Why you sound so full with HuHū, so angry, Kawika? Did we not say if two agree, the third will say aye?"

"Did you know that you only speak Hawaiian when you're trying to convince me about something, Keo? Well, it won't work this time. I'm tired of being cold, I'm tired of working twelve hours a day just to get enough money to feed us. I'm tired of the lousy food, and I'm tired of both of you. That's it! It's all pau! Pau, Keo. Finished!"

"Now hold on a minute, Bollin," protested Strawfoot. "We said this partnership had to stay together till we come out of the hills. We need your share of the dust to have enough for supplies to see us through the winter, and we need another pair of hands to help build a cabin that's snug. You can't leave till we all do."

David turned to rummage through a knapsack. "I thought it might come to this," he announced. He pulled out the derringer taken from Barton back in Frisco, and calmly cocked the hammer. "Now weigh out my share, and let me get out of here."

"Do not do this, Kawika," begged Keo.

"You won't miss me," replied the young man. "You two can just go on having your prayer meetings without me like you were anyway. I'm through grubbing in the dirt." With that, David helped himself to a third of the gold, shouldered his knapsack, and turned to leave. "If you think I've taken out more than my share," he added, "remember that I let you keep both mules. I don't expect to need them again." Then he was gone.

It was only a rumor, brought to Honolulu by a whaling ship refitting for the season. A passenger from an unnamed schooner had been swept overboard and picked up by the whale ship *Crystal.* Those who heard the rumor, which had passed from ship to ship, were uncertain if the young passenger had been alive or dead when he was fished from the deep. Common sense dictated that he was dead.

But the heart of Kapono Bollin chose to believe that David was alive. *Here at last was hope!*

The warm Kona wind brought a perfect, drowsy stillness to the air, and yet the congregation of Kapono William Bollin was stirring this afternoon.

Clean woven mats were spread out beneath the trees. A pig had been killed and roasted to succulent perfection in a pit behind the church.

Sweet voices were raised in joyful hymns as the people gathered to feast one last time with their beloved teacher. Although the voices were light, hearts were heavy today. Many had grown to adulthood never knowing any other teacher but Kapono Bollin. What would they do without him?

"Why you want to go there, Kapono Bollin?" asked a tall, brown-skinned young man who had learned to read in the class of the *haole* preacher-man.

The pastor dipped his hand into a large calabash filled with poi. The curious brown eyes of the other villagers turned to consider Kapono Bollin as he answered.

"Many hearts have been won here." He spoke so softly that all the others fell silent to hear him. "But I have lost my own son, and if he is still alive, I must find him."

The wife of Edward Hupeka frowned. "But California is such a terrible place, Kapono Bollin. Dangerous and wild. We hear there is no law there. No king. No God."

"I am not afraid," answered Kapono Bollin. "Hawaii was once a place with many gods and a king who sacrificed his people to idols. And yet we came here."

"But we were waiting to hear of Iesu," replied Hohu, a very old man whose tattooed body had once bowed down before the altars of human sacrifice. "We longed to hear the word of Iesu and true Aloha. *Ora loa ia Iesu!* Endless life by Jesus!"

"Yes," agreed another, "in California the white men do not wish to hear. They have run from the churches and the laws of the East."

Quietly Mary added, *"But perhaps David is there!"*

All eyes turned toward her. There was small hope of such a miracle. Only Mary and Kapono Bollin believed it could be so. And everyone knew they believed and hoped because they loved too much. They loved even though David had rejected them. Such love was a heavy burden.

"Dear Kapono Bollin." Old Emma Ipo put a gnarled hand on the arm of the preacher. "What if David is not? I am *Iuahine*—an old woman. When I was young my husband was killed in battle with King Kamehameha. They tell me, but I do not believe. Every day I look and wait. I bear his child—" She waved a hand toward her son at the far end of the mat. "I still believe my *kāne* not dead. I live in false hope for many year." She pursed her lips in thought. "Why you not stay here with us who have great aloha for you?"

The soul of William Bollin wrenched at the thought of leaving this place and these people after so long. He inhaled deeply and searched for the right words. "Once we were all lost, Emma, and the Good Shepherd came to find us." He frowned. "If David still lives, I must look for him."

"There are no churches in California. Maybe you will not come back, Kapono Bollin," said the young man sadly.

William Bollin answered in Hawaiian. *"Ku'u Kahu no Iesu!—The Lord my shepherd is.* I am not afraid."

They all understood. Kapono Bollin had no thought for his own safety. Everyone knew that Kapono Bollin did not care so much for dying since the day news had come that David was swept away. Perhaps that was the real reason he now wished to travel to such a terrible and wild land as California.

Much later that night, when the lamp in Kapono Bollin's house went out, the people still spoke of it among themselves as they cleaned up from the feast.

The elders of the village remembered what life had been before the missionaries had come. They had seen much. They had witnessed many miracles. *"Ka'a mau ke akua!"* declared the old man as he raised his tattooed arm. *"God moves in a mysterious way!* He sometimes leads men to walk where they do not wish to walk. In the end, sometimes men turn into the arms of Iesu. Sometimes they run from God and fall into the belly of old *Pele* who eats them with fire. Jesus is the Shepherd of our Kapono. Kapono Bollin is more safe on that narrow path with God than anywhere without God. As for us, we have only to pray. The rest is not for us to think on."

The people listened to the old man and felt much better. They sang softly as the moon climbed to a silver crescent above the village.

Barton shuffled the cards with an expert flourish and offered them to a small dark man seated at his left. After the cut of the cards, the gambler reassembled them in a neat pile. With a snapping sound audible over the clinking glasses and the hubbub of the saloon, he flicked over the first card.

"Ace of spades, gentlemen. A bad luck card already turned. Place your bets. Who feels lucky?" With a practiced forefinger he pushed one ball up the row beside the ace on the card counter.

Three other miners sat around the faro table with the little dark man. Moffat hovered behind them, a glass of whiskey in his hand. The four players studied the layout of the betting board, on which painted figures of each of the thirteen cards could be seen.

"Next card's the winner and then the loser, gentlemen. Court the one and avoid the other. Place your bets."

The short man wagered an ounce of dust on the queen, and the others made their selections. When the bets were down, Barton flipped over the cards in rapid succession. The first revealed was a ten on which no one had bet, the second the queen. Barton reached over and casually removed the small doeskin pouch of gold dust and smoothly deposited it in a box by his feet.

When Barton had moved the counters for the ten and queen, he announced, "Three down, gentlemen. Who can guess the order of the next two? Place your bets."

The play continued this way for thirty minutes or so, with Barton paying off on an occasional lucky guess, but winning more often than not. Once he turned up a pair of jacks and another time two fives appeared; each time he accepted half the wagered amount as the house percentage. When the deck was exhausted he declared, "Let's all take a break for drinks, gentlemen. Who's thirsty?"

While the players moved to the bar, Barton held a quiet conference with Moffat. "How'd we do?" asked the killer.

We're up about two hundred dollars on the night," replied the gambler. "All the luck is coming our way, too. I haven't had to pull a second so far. What have you heard? Anything interesting?"

"Nah. These miners don't give a rip about owning property. All they care about is their stretch of creekbed. You want me to put together a gang so we can push some of them out of the way?"

"Moffat, you have no subtlety at all," Barton growled. "Haven't you heard any griping about anything? Some complaint we can play to?"

"These rock-hoppers grouse about everything, but nothing that'll turn us a nickel. They're down on the cost of food, the price of shovels, the Chinks, the lousy whiskey, the greasers, the lack of women, the—"

"Hold it!" ordered Barton. "What did you say?"

"I said they're looking for camp floozies, but what—"

"No, before that. Never mind, Moffat. I need to think a little. Chinks and greasers, you say. Tomorrow we may need to travel to improve our knowledge. Come on, it's time to start the game again."

"I tell you it's the truth. Them Chinese can see at night! They ain't human, I tell you. Sifting through a ton of sand to find specks of gold as fine as flour dust," spouted a pot-bellied miner with red hair.

"But where's the harm in that?" needled Barton. "If they want to work harder or longer, shouldn't they be allowed to?"

"Friend, I can see you haven't been in this country for long. I hear tell there's a hundred million of them Celestials, and more coming all the time. Pretty soon they'll be spreading out all up and down this country, and then where'll we be?"

"And it ain't just the Chinks," asserted another miner, a skinny man with a bulbous nose and wandering Adam's apple. "You can't trust nobody what don't know good English. Why, how can you tell what they's thinking, if you can't even understand them when they talk? Greasers and them other Spanish talkers hang together pretty thick, too."

Barton let the conversation run on without pressing the issue further. He'd already gotten the information he sought: there was growing anti-foreign sentiment in the prospecting community. Of course, it was mostly confined to men who did more talking than prospecting and more complaining than working, but that suited Barton's purposes all the better.

All up and down the streams, the pressures of thousands of gold seekers competing for space was beginning to be felt. Already some prime locations were known to be in the hands of the Chinese, the Mexicans—even miners from Peru and Chile. *But,* Barton thought to himself, *not for long.*

David ambled down the trail toward Hangtown, whistling to himself. He carried a pound of gold dust and nearly another pound in nuggets. It wasn't a lot, but David knew what he would do to get more. He planned to buy a second-hand faro outfit and set himself up as a professional gambler.

He shook his head in derision as he passed knots of miners working along the streams, and laughed to himself when some hopeful prospector hiked by, eager to get to the diggings. His mind was occupied with thoughts of gambling halls, and hotels with real beds and decent food. He licked his lips at the memory of his last drink of whiskey, and pictured himself decked out in a new suit of clothes.

It's San Francisco for me, he mused. He expected to earn enough at each stage of his descent from the mountains to finance a move to the next larger and more elegant setting.

David stopped off in the tent saloon at Washington. He didn't intend to stay there long or to gamble with any of his precious stake of gold. Even though Washington had grown in size as predicted, it was still a ramshackle collection of tents and bark shelters and shanty hovels.

What he really wanted was a drink. He stepped up to the counter to discover that the tall, bald man he had met on previous visits to Washington was now tending bar.

"Well, if it isn't David Bollin, back from the wars. Where you been keeping yourself, Bollin? We haven't seen you since Methuselah was a pup."

"Prospected clear to the moon and back, nearly," replied David. "But now I'm through."

"You don't mean you've made your pile, do you?" asked the bartender.

"No, but I've figured out how I'm going to, and it isn't by prospecting." David tossed his sack of dust up on the bar. "I figure this'll get me started into gambling in Hangtown."

The substantial thump of the sack hitting the counter made several men turn and look. If David had turned around, he would have seen two men seated at a rough log table who continued to stare at him when the others had looked away. The heavier, coarser of the two, he wouldn't have known, but the one with the receding hairline and pockmarked face might have looked familiar. The two men exited the bar while David was still conversing with the bartender. David bought a pair of drinks for himself and the tavern man.

"You be careful, Bollin," advised the bartender as David prepared to leave. "You'd do well to wait till daybreak to travel."

"Sleeping on the trail tonight gets me that much nearer to Hangtown tomorrow. Besides, who would hold up a poor, beat-down prospector like me?" asked David, gesturing at his faded shirt, run-over boots and patched trousers. "Be seeing you."

At twilight David came to one of the numerous crossings of the stream his trail was following. A wave of tiredness compounded with the whiskey he had drunk, and David decided to make his camp for the night in a meadow just across the creek.

The water plunged through a narrow gorge at this stretch of the canyon. The bank on which he stood remained high and steep for some distance downstream, but opened out flatter on the opposite side. A fallen log rested across the gorge. The night promised to be cold, and David surveyed the log carefully. The idea of staying dry held definite appeal. He stepped up onto the log and began carefully placing one foot in front of the other as he made his way across. The tree lay not very high above the stream, and David had no fear of being injured by a fall, but the risk of losing his gold was frightening.

He watched the log for projecting stumps that might throw him off-balance. Midway across, one remaining branch poked up, offering a temporary goal and a chance to survey the remainder of the crossing.

The log rested securely on the opposite bank, caught between a large boulder and the trunk of a pine tree. An overhanging branch made the end of the log disappear in a pool of shadows, but David thought he could remember two smaller rocks by which he could climb down. He was glad to have the limb to hang on to, because he seemed a little unsteady.

Only two steps separated him from the end of the log. The branches of the pine tree stretched out toward him, beckoning him on. Another step and David reached out a hand toward the pine, expecting to grasp a branch and pull himself to the boulder.

Instead, the tree reached out toward him. A vise-like grip grasped his right wrist, and in the time it took him to shout "Hey!" it pulled him off the end of the log. He slammed headfirst into the granite rock, with an impact that caused cascades of lights to explode in front of his eyes. For a fraction of a second the exploding stars reminded him of the fireworks at the newest Kamehameha's coronation; then the lights went out.

Moffat relieved David of both pouches of gold and passed them to Barton, who stood on the ground below the rock face. Moffat rolled David over to examine the contents of the knapsack and produced the derringer. He handed it to Barton, who exclaimed, "You see! I told you this was the same busybody who interfered in Frisco. Taking his gold is like getting the rest of my own back again."

"What do you want me to do with him?" inquired Moffat.

"Bash his head and dump him in the creek," responded Barton, with no greater concern than he would show for discarding a heap of garbage. Barton leaned out from the shadows to scrutinize his derringer in the failing light.

Moffat bent over to look through a heap of stones around the base of the boulder. He spent some time selecting a rock the size and shape of a melon, and then grunted as he strained to heave it free of the thick mud.

"What's that?" Barton said sharply. The sound of shuffling footsteps came toward them on the trail.

Moffat had not heard the sound because of the rush of the creek, but he straightened up abruptly at Barton's cry.

"What's what?" he yelled back, even louder than Barton.

A voice called up the path, "Who there? What going on, please?"

A sudden oath burst from Moffat and he shouted, "Someone's coming!" The two men turned at the same instant and collided with each other. The derringer flew out of Barton's hand and he went to his knees to scrabble in the blanket of pine needles.

"Leave it! Leave it!" hissed Moffat. "Come on!" Without waiting to see if Barton was following, he plunged into the creek, not even trying to walk the log.

Barton delayed only a moment longer, then he too splashed into the stream, tightly clutching the sacks of gold. Both men were soon across and into the woods on the other side.

A tiny frail-looking figure in a dark blue coat cautiously advanced onto the rock. It was a Chinaman with a long silver braid. The little man bent slowly and exclaimed over David, who lay moaning softly.

The Chinaman turned to face the last waning rays of light. He tore a strip of cloth from the lining of his coat, then bandaged David's head with gentle, nimble fingers.

He kicked something in the dirt as he maneuvered around David and bent to pick it up. It was the derringer; he placed it in David's pack.

The little man's nursing had not even awakened David; he merely groaned. The Oriental bent his back until his head nearly touched the ground, then with unexpected strength lifted David onto his own shoulders. When the large young man was slung across his back like a deer carcass, the smaller, older man picked up David's pack. He began to move off down the trail, plodding slowly back the way he had come.

"Now you men are clear on what's to be done?" Barton addressed a scruffy group of unsuccessful prospectors who were moderately successful drinkers.

"Shore enough, Mr. Barton," responded a beady-eyed little man whose pointed nose and bristly mustache made him look remarkably rat-like. "We're just 'sposed to ease into conversations, like about how the Chinks are taking over claims us Americans oughta have."

"That's right, and any time someone volunteers that sort of sentiment, encourage them. I'll keep you in liquor and if we are as successful as I plan, there'll be better pay later."

9

DAVID GROANED AND started to put a hand up to his injured forehead, but even the start of that motion sent a stab of pain through him like a bolt of lightning. *What was I drinking?* he wondered. Once when David had sneaked out at night from his father's house, he had experienced a potent native brew called *Okolehau,* which the sailors nicknamed *Oh Holy Cow;* but even it had not left him feeling this clubbed.

Clubbed, he thought suddenly. *I've been robbed!* Despite the pain he began thrashing around, trying to locate his gold sacks, but someone was holding his shoulders.

"Easy there, young fella. You've taken a nasty blow to your head. Don't try to move so fast."

"But my gold," stammered David. "Where is it, and where am I?"

"You're in a hotel in Hangtown. I should know, I run this place. As for your gold, the guy who brought you in said you'd been robbed. Said he found you up the creek a ways. He paid for the two days you've been here—"

"Two days?" interrupted David.

"Yes, and one more's paid besides. Plus," said the hotel owner, nodding toward a table beside the bed, "he left a sack of dust for you there."

David turned to regard a small leather pouch resting beside him. "Where is this man? I need to thank him. I mean, isn't he staying here too?"

"Course not. We don't allow—" A bell jangled in the background, causing the man to start up toward the door. "Got to go. Glad you're awake young fella." He left without completing his sentence, and the identity of David's benefactor remained a mystery.

David stretched out his hand and grasped the leather bag. He felt very weary, but he clenched his fist tightly around the gold before falling back to sleep.

The next morning David's head felt two sizes too large for his shoulders, but he was awake. The fingers of his left hand were stiff from clutching the pouch all night, and he wondered again who had befriended him without staying around to introduce himself.

The contents of the bag looked to be about two ounces of extremely fine gold dust. The sight of this small pile of shining metal reminded David of how expensive the Hangtown accommodations were and how quickly he had better make arrangements for earning more money.

But the first order of the day was breakfast. He dressed as quickly as he could, trying to keep his head motionless while he pulled on his clothes; even the slightest motion made his temples feel as if the spike that killed Sisera was being pounded home.

It was almost daybreak in Honolulu. The small guest room in the mission house, where William Bollin had spent the night, faced the huge gray outline of Kewaiahao Church and the churchyard where William's wife and children were buried.

Built entirely of hand-hewn blocks of coral, the building stood as a testimony of the spiritual changes that had come to these islands in only twenty-five years.

William sensed that he was viewing this place for the last time. He pulled on his boots and wrapped his Bible in a fresh change of clothes, then placed the bundle into his leather rucksack.

The mission family still slept upstairs. William walked softly over the wood-planked floor and stepped out onto the veranda.

With a sigh, he embraced the memories of his life one last time. At this hour, this island paradise seemed almost perfect. Life and work had grown comfortable, and William had hoped he would live out the rest of his years here.

All of that seemed of little importance now. Any price was worth it if he could only find his son alive.

William inhaled deeply. The scent of gardenias and pikake lingered in the air with a thousand other scents that drifted down from the pinnacles and up from the deep valleys of Oahu. He gathered an armful of blue flowers that tumbled over the fence and walked across the deserted yard toward the graves of his wife and children. He would say his goodbye quickly. He wanted to board the ship early, before the city awakened.

Flowers dripped in an untidy pile onto the grave of his wife.

MARTHA ELLEN BOLLIN
b. 1801
d. 1838
Ora loa ia Jesu: Endless Life by Jesus

He cleared his throat and fixed his gaze on the name carved in the black granite pillar. The stone was 5′4″ tall, the same height Martha had been. It had been shipped around the Horn from her family in Boston.

"Martha," William whispered, "I would not wish you here with me this morning. I . . . I have lost him, Martha. I have won many, but lost my own son. Our son." He looked at the graves of Samuel, aged 9, and Daniel, aged 4. Tears clouded his vision for a moment. "At least you left still loving. Loving Jesus. But David loves no one, Martha. He left us without ever learning that love."

At last the sky began to lighten. The air was rose-tinged, the grass wet with dew.

He had stayed too long. Wiping his eyes, he raised his head as the morning sounds of Honolulu drifted up the road. Backing up a step, he turned to find a silent crowd gathered to wait for him beyond the stone fence of the churchyard. He had not heard them come, and even as he faced three hundred of his congregation, they did not utter a sound.

Kapono Bollin stepped carefully around the graves and nodded at Edward Hupeka, the young Hawaiian who would take his place. Edward swung back the metal gate for Kapono Bollin, and the crowd parted for him.

Murmurs of farewell rippled through the crowd, *"Aloha, Kapono Bollin . . . God go with you, Kapono Bollin!"* The small brown hands of children reached up to touch their beloved Kapono one last time. Tears traced the wrinkled faces of those who could remember the day Kapono had first brought word to them of Iesu Kristo. *"Aloha! Aloha, Kapono Bollin!"*

He bowed his head as leis of fragrant flowers were draped around his neck. "Do not forget us, Kapono Bollin! Forget not your children, Kapono!"

He had not expected this. Indeed, he had hoped to slip away without another word of farewell. But now he was glad the people had come. Looking over the sea of faces, there was not one among the crowd whom he did not know from the heart out. Births and deaths and baptisms, marriages, and twenty-five years of Sabbaths played through his mind in a moment. Moving through the crowd, he spoke their names and reached to touch outstretched fingers.

At last he stopped before the small figure of Mary.

She and her brother Edward had been abandoned at the church nineteen years before. Kapono Bollin and his wife had taken them in, cared for them, seen to their education. Now, Mary, in turn, cared for half a dozen unwanted children gathered from the villages.

Her wide-set brown eyes brimmed with tears. William took her hands in his. She spoke softly, in perfect English, "So you really are leaving, Kapono?"

"Only for a short time. Perhaps a few months."

"He has broken my heart as well, Kapono. But where shall I go? I must stay, but my heart and prayers will go with you."

William straightened to his full six feet and looked away toward the wharf and the waiting ship. He did not reply, but squeezed her hands. She was still just a child.

"Aloha, Mary."

Then he turned his back on her and raised his hands for silence as he prayed one last time with the congregation.

After a meal of flapjacks and bitter coffee that removed another dollar from his dwindling supply, David moved his things. He arranged to stay at a flophouse that would give him floor space for one dollar a night.

David reflected on his meager finances and shabby dress, and decided that his future as a professional gambler depended on getting some working capital—and quickly. He entered the Empire Saloon as if to do battle. He intended to start a faro game, take Lady Luck captive, and crown himself king of the gamblers.

This romantic-sounding pipedream was a sad contrast to the bleak reality of gambling at the Empire. Its wood-plank floor was covered with sawdust that was almost unrecognizable because of the liberal amounts of mud, tobacco juice, and spilled booze. The proprietor, a portly German named Finster, deliberately left the footing as unattractive as possible, to discourage miners from trying to retrieve gold dust spilled onto it. He paid a helper to shovel up and pan the debris whenever the saloon was closed. On the morning following a busy night, he might reclaim between fifty and a hundred dollars of dust.

David entered the gloomy saloon and surveyed the gaming tables. It was early in the day, and only one half-hearted game of faro was in progress. Through the thick air that smelled of stale smoke and cheap liquor, David crossed to the faro table and asked if he could join in.

The other two players and the dealer glanced at his bandaged head but nodded their acceptance, and David seated himself on an upturned half of a barrel that served as a stool. Studying the card counter, David could tell that this particular deck was about half run. He noted that no ten had yet been turned, so he placed his pouch on the pointed betting board and announced, "In for a dollar."

The next card turned was the ten of diamonds, and the dealer made a pencil mark on a scrap of paper to show one dollar in David's favor. David played steadily, never risking more than one dollar at a time and reviewing the card counter intently between plays. David was ahead by five dollars when the dealer summoned a drink for him.

David sipped the drink with evident satisfaction, studied the tally sheet, and increased his bet to two dollars. This time he backed the queen to come out next, but lost. David returned to risking only one dollar, but after winning three times in a row, he raised his stakes to five dollars.

A second drink appeared at his elbow. The five-dollar wager won, and David's spirits began to rise. *I can really do this,* he thought. *I have a sense for these cards. They speak to me.* He downed the rest of that drink and raised his bet to ten dollars.

When the ten-dollar bet was made and won, David's savings had reached almost fifty dollars and he had nearly doubled what he started gambling with. A third drink arrived and David reached out and took it without even considering why he was being kept so well-supplied. He was finding it harder to concentrate, and the drafty room began to feel oppressively warm.

The faro dealer asked for the amount of David's wager. For a moment his drink-fuddled brain refused to work, then at last he mumbled, "An ounce."

This was a sixteen-dollar bet. David indicated that he wanted his pouch of dust moved to the painted likeness of the seven card at the end of the board. David saw the dealer's eyes flicker to the back of the deck before flipping out the next card.

The oiled hides that served as window coverings at the Empire allowed in very little light. David couldn't be sure, but he thought that the dealer had made some extra motion of his ring finger before revealing the card that showed that David had lost.

David was aghast. He saw tally marks being removed from his column. His brain refused to do calculations; he couldn't determine how much of a stake he had left and wasn't able to concentrate on what card to back.

When the dealer asked for the amount of his wager, he slurred, "All of it." The dealer was pouring the contents of David's gold pouch into a hand-held pan balance before David even understood that he lost.

David's bandaged head had begun to throb. He stayed sitting dumbly, staring first at the faro table, and then down at the empty pouch that the dealer had tossed into his lap. "Will you be making another wager?" asked the dealer.

"You—you cheated me. Give me my money," David mumbled, stumbling to his feet. The other two players jumped back out of the way, knocking over their stools as they went. The dealer also rose, coming up with a gleaming knife in his right hand.

Before anything further could happen, the beefy arms of the proprietor,

Finster, pinned David tightly against the white apron, which the German wore tied clear up to his chest. Finster carried him outside and deposited him in a heap in the street. "Yank man," said Finster, "I gif you some advice, no charge. Don't call no man a cheat unless you can back your play. Unt don't play no more cards mit a busted kopf." Finster dusted his hands off with authority and returned to the Empire Saloon. David staggered back to the flophouse and passed out on the floor.

"Gentlemen, I appeal to you on the basis of fair play and right thinking for all Americans," declared Barton to the assembled group of miners and hangers-on.

"It is our destiny to subdue this land and wrest from it the treasures for which so many now labor. Many benefits of civilization have already been bestowed on this land and much wealth produced. But I ask you, is it right that foreigners, Popish greasers, and heathen Chinese come here and take what rightly belongs to Americans? Should they be allowed to send America's treasure out of this land to benefit foreign governments?"

"Hang dem!" shouted German-born Finster.

"Let's burn 'em all out right enough," contributed Downs, whose grandparents had come to America from Yorkshire.

"No, no, gentlemen. Civilization must flourish here, and the rule of law prevail. The code of the mining community specifies how much size each claim may hold and how much work must be done to maintain it, isn't that so? We must have a meeting to amend the rules, specifying that foreigners may not hold claims. Now, who shall we have as chairman?"

The next morning found David more miserable than he had been since awakening to the truth of his condition on the whaler *Crystal*—worse in fact, because at least there had been food. Here he had no food, no money, and no answer in sight.

He thought briefly of begging enough food to hike back to Keo and Strawfoot, but decided against it. He reasoned that his head injury made it impossible to return to them. The truth was, he imagined himself having to explain to them what had become of his money and his ambition. He might have to admit that he had been wrong, and he couldn't bring himself to do it.

He wandered around behind the saloons and hotels, hoping to find a cook who would take pity on him, but soon discovered that he could not bring himself to beg. When he finally did get hungry enough to overcome his pride, he found that no one would give him anything. Food, like everything else, cost money to have freighted into the mines. Nothing was given away, and nothing wasted. Even the garbage was used to feed the hogs being raised for meat and lard.

After two days of starving, David found himself headed upstream, toward Strawfoot's old claim. Once there, he roused himself from his stupor enough to notice a gang of men working. They were mostly Chinese laborers, moving the stones from the wingdam that had flooded Strawfoot's diggings. As David watched, each Chinese filled a wicker basket with rocks, picked up a leather strap and, stepping inside the loop of the strap, hoisted seventy-five to a hundred pounds of rocks up onto his back. The strap rested on the worker's forehead. David thought to himself what incredibly strong necks these wiry little men must have. The largest of them could scarcely outweigh the burden being carried by more than twenty pounds.

A white man in a leather vest and a white shirt with his sleeves rolled up was overseeing the work. He apparently spoke no Chinese, but instead transmitted his orders through a rotund Chinaman dressed in a brocade coat and silk slippers. The white foreman would give instructions to the Chinese overseer, who then relayed the order to the workers by means of much clapping, shouting, and hand-waving, and a torrent of Chinese.

David approached the line of workers. A steady stream of men in baggy trousers and matching dark blue baggy shirts toted rocks upstream to a destination David couldn't make out, returning with empty baskets for another load. With their straw hats and pigtails, the workers looked Oriental in both features and garb—except for their boots, the single concession they made to life in the Sierra gold fields.

While David looked on, the foreman consulted a pocket watch and made some comment to the overseer. With an imperious clap of his hands and a shouted command, repeated up the line of men until the message went out of earshot, all the workers shed their baskets and sat down. This was a meal break; other workers quickly began distributing paper-wrapped parcels from a hand cart. All labor ceased.

In the silence that followed, the growl of David's stomach sounded as loud in his ears as the ocean breaking on Makapuu Point. Both supervisors looked around at the sound. The Chinese man put a handkerchief to his nose as if David were as disgusting to smell as he was tattered in appearance. The white foreman rumbled, "You there—what do you want?"

David could scarcely deny that he was hungry. "Please, can you spare me some food?"

"This chow is for the coolies only. Now beat it on out of here."

"Can I have a job, then? I can haul rocks."

The Chinese supervisor laughed delicately behind his handkerchief. To laugh at a white man, even one this bedraggled, was unwise, but for a white man to ask to do coolie labor was just too droll.

"You can't be serious," said the foreman. "Why aren't you out panning for gold like everyone else? These human mules are moving rocks to make the footings for a bridge up yonder. You want to carry rocks for twelve hours a day to make a dollar?"

"And you'll feed me?" David asked.

Startled, the foreman realized that David was indeed serious. He made a quiet remark to the portly Chinaman, who shook his head and whispered something back. The white man looked David over and asked, "Isn't there anything else you can do? Don't you know anybody in town who can give you a job? What skills do you have?"

"I don't have any profession. I've been a prospector and a gambler, but right now I need food." David's stomach rumbled at that moment, as if in agreement.

"Where'd do you learn words like 'profession'?" inquired the foreman.

"I did get a good education from my father. He's a preacher," David explained.

The last comment caused another flurry of whispered comments from the overseer.

The foreman listened, then said to David. "Ah Sing here says you'd be trouble. He says you'd be disruptive and a bad influence. He says he doesn't need a white man. But I am telling him now," the foreman said loudly, "that he doesn't have the final say on hiring and firing. As the chief engineer for these Celestials, I do. And I don't want to see a white man starve while these Celestials get fed."

The foreman paused to consider, then offered, "All right, if you want food, help yourself. We're back to work in—" he stopped and considered his watch again—"ten minutes. Be ready."

He turned away from David's thanks and only grunted when David tried to tell him his name. The Chinese overseer spun around with a swirl of brocade coat, as if highly offended. David stood, uncertain who would show him where to go to get food and one of the baskets for carrying stones.

A small, thin Chinese man detached himself from the seated line of workers and approached David. With a twinkle in his eye he said, "I speak English. You come with Ling Chow. I get you food." Soon David was seated cross-legged on the ground eating rice balls mixed with pinyon nuts and a piece of broiled salmon. It was odd fare for a California Forty-Niner, but not so unfamiliar to a Hawaiian, and David devoured it eagerly.

When he was finished, David looked up from inhaling the meal to find a number of his new co-workers watching him with curiosity, and Ling Chow regarding him with a smile. He licked the last morsel of rice off of his fingers and David asked the man who had helped him, "Do many of you speak English?"

"No," the little man replied. "I speak. Not many others. All English talk-talk come to Ah Sing," he said, gesturing toward the overseer.

"Then how does it happen that you speak English?" Before the Chinaman had a chance to explain, Ah Sing clapped his hands, and another shouted order worked its way up the line. The workers replaced their baskets on their backs and began moving in their monotonous circle again. Because David had received an empty basket while Ling Chow's was filled already, the two men were soon parted and walking in opposite directions.

Once at the wingdam David soon discovered what strong necks these Chinese workers really had. When he loaded the basket to the top with stones, David could barely lift it.

Another man helped him balance the load on his back and he started walking. David found that he could not stand the pressure of the strap on his injured forehead, so he was forced to use both hands to hold the strap away from his head. In this awkward position, he was unable to use his arms for balance as did the coolies and he staggered from side to side. David tried to engage his closest co-workers in conversation, but the one ahead only turned and scowled, and the one behind grinned and giggled.

David examined the faces of the workers passing by in the opposite direction. *I hope I can remember what he looks like,* mused David. When the moment came, David didn't recognize Ling Chow again, but it didn't matter, because the friendly Chinese spoke first. He spoke as if David's question had just been asked, instead of ten minutes before. "I taught by missionaries in Sandwich Islands."

David just had time to respond, "I'm from Hawaii!" when the two men were parted again. Another ten minutes passed as David reached the building site to dump his load of stones and returned halfway back with his empty basket.

A scrap of conversation, a shouted response, and ten minutes of plodding. This cycle continued into the dizzying afternoon. Ling Chow managed to convey to David that he had been converted to Christianity in Hawaii by Hiram Bingham, a member of the original New England Missionary Company and an old acquaintance of David's father.

It took David several baskets of rocks to decide whether or not to mention his identity. Finally the desire to establish some link with someone friendly overcame his wish to hide his background, and he mentioned his name to Ling Chow.

To his surprise, the Chinaman responded, "I know you already. I heard you tell name to boss-man. Your father Bollin a good man."

At the close of the tedious day, David received fifty cents and was dismissed until the next morning. The Chinese all bunked together in their own encampment, but David was not invited to share lodgings with them.

He went back to his flophouse and collapsed. He would have to get more money somehow, or choose between a place to sleep and eating more than once a day. At the moment he was too tired to care.

10

WHEN DAVID AWOKE the next morning, his arms ached unbearably. From being held in such an awkward position the previous day, they refused to straighten out. Compounding this misery, he discovered that his flop-house bedding had been infested by "quicks"—fleas. He was bitten all over, but he couldn't make his arms reach anywhere to scratch. The decision was made for him between housing and food. Another such night, and he might also be visited by "slows"—lice. He decided to sleep out in the open, or build himself a bark shelter like the early prospectors had done. In the back of his mind lurked an awareness that winter was fast approaching, but he pushed this thought away.

David's morning improved immensely when he found that Ling Chow had brought him a tin cup of noodles, still warm in the chill air. The slight Chinaman also arranged to walk immediately ahead of David in the line, so that they could converse all day.

Ling Chow explained over his shoulder that he had wanted to return to his homeland as a missionary, but was denied that privilege. He had worked for a time with his countrymen on plantations in Hawaii, but had felt led to join the large numbers who were moving to work in California.

David did not know how to respond. How could he explain that he was running away from the same values that Ling Chow was enduring much hardship to promote?

At last he decided to say nothing about the way in which he'd left home. He referred instead to seeking his fortune in the gold field, making something of himself, and improving his prospects. He used all the phrases of a young nineteenth century gentleman. Ling Chow listened without comment, nodding as if accepting David's statements at face value. Suddenly David was struck by the irony of his attempts to sound self-assured and in control. Here he sat, eating rice among Chinese laborers, plagued by fleabites and unable even to scratch himself, with no place to sleep and no future to speak of. Who was he kidding, anyway?

That evening David found a new shelter. Ling Chow had told him about an abandoned miner's shack called a "Yankee house." It was about the size of a dog kennel and had no more comforts than one, but it had neither human nor obnoxious insect inhabitants.

David claimed squatter's rights to the place, wondering how much food he could buy for his dollar. While still considering this question, Ling Chow arrived with another pot of noodles and a small jar of some strong-smelling paste.

"What is this?" asked David, eyeing the pungent goo and wondering how he could politely refuse to eat it.

"Old Chinese remedy for bites," grinned Ling Chow. "Anyway, I am old and Chinese, and I make ointment, so is truth. Juniper berry juice and goose grease. You try."

David felt both grateful and resentful at Ling Chow's arrival. He wanted to be self-sufficient, successful, and he resented being beholden to this old Chinaman. On the other hand, he had felt so depressed and lonely that he was pleased to see someone take an interest in him. His life seemed to have taken a turn for the better since meeting Ling Chow.

The Chinaman paused at the door of the hovel, and in a kindly voice said to David, "I come this country seeking my countrymen. You come seeking something too, David Bollin. Maybe what you seek is not gold in streams like you think. Maybe you just turn around and find what you seek." No word of criticism, no demand for appreciation—just this calmly delivered cryptic advice, and he was gone.

What am I seeking? David asked himself when Ling Chow had gone. *What was it I left home to find? And what did he mean about turning around? I've come so far from home.*

The soothing ointment did its work; his spasmed muscles even began to relax, and his injured head stopped throbbing. He told God that he was not yet certain what he was seeking, but he hoped he was on the road to finding it, whatever it was. David briefly reflected that it was the first time he had prayed in years—really prayed, anyway. Then he fell asleep.

"Ching, chang Chinaman," chanted Moffat at the frightened little Oriental who was running up the alley trying to get away. "Hey, where you off to in such a hurry? Catch him, Jim, Sandy."

A pair of miners stepped out of the shadows, blocking off the line of retreat. The Chinaman glanced over his shoulders, decided the odds were better against one than two, and bolted back the way he'd come—straight into Moffat's arms.

A moment later Moffat was holding the little man off the ground by his pigtail. As the Oriental struggled and kicked, Moffat pulled a huge knife out of his belt and laid it across the Chinaman's throat. "I'd hold right still, if I was you," he hissed, "and I wouldn't make no noise, either." The smaller man complied, and Moffat lowered him until his tiptoes touched the ground, but Moffat kept a firm grasp on the queue.

"Look what I caught, boys," he remarked to the other two who had closed in around the scene. "What are you doin' outta your warren, little Chink?"

"He was prob'ly thievin'," remarked the one called Sandy.

"Up to no good, that's certain," added the other.

"Hear that, little man? I think maybe we should just go ahead and cut your throat. What do you think of that?"

The man made no response and eyed the three men in terror but made no plea.

"He don't even understand plain lingo," sneered Sandy. "He's too dumb to even remember how polite we warned him."

"He'll remember this," remarked Moffat abruptly, and he slashed the man's pigtail off short behind his head, dropping him unexpectedly to his knees. The man was up in a flash, running again down the alley, and this time they let him go.

The next day David talked cheerfully to Ling Chow while loading the first basket of rocks for the day, and smiled at his co-workers, who grinned uncertainly back at him.

"I've decided to go back upriver," he told Ling Chow. "I can own up to being wrong about leaving my partners when they needed my help. In another week I'll have enough for supplies for the trip—if," he added with a wry smile, "I keep on eating rice for a while."

"Is good you do what is right," said his Chinese friend. "God watching you all time. He help you know what to do."

"Ling, you must be right. Do you know, I never till right now thought of selling a pistol that I have. I'll never use it—why, maybe I could even leave tomorrow."

David could hardly wait for the end of the workday, and the time did seem to go by quickly. He asked Ling Chow to stop by the supply store later to tell him goodbye. After setting aside the straw basket, he hurried to his shack, retrieved the derringer, and set off for the Empire Saloon.

David felt ill at ease going into the saloon. He had not had a drink since the night he gambled away the last of his rescuer's gold. For a time his sobriety had been enforced by his lack of money, but now it was automatic.

He was not certain whom to approach with his request to sell the derringer, so he walked up to the only person he recognized, the German proprietor, Finster. "Mr. Finster," he began, "I'm sorry about the ruckus the last time I was in. I hope you'll accept my apology. Anyway, I'm also hoping you can help me with something else. Do you know of anyone who might be interested in purchasing this derringer?" David deposited the small pistol on the bar, and Finster leaned his bulk over to look at it.

"Maybe so," he breathed in a voice made hoarse and short by a recent consumption of a large quantity of beer and fried potatoes. "But you'll haf to vait till after our meeting. I'm busy right now."

David was disappointed. He had hoped to raise some cash on the firearm and get over to the general store across the street in time to buy supplies. David was excited at the idea of seeing Keo and Strawfoot again and wanted to make an early start of it.

Without any particular interest he asked, "What meeting is that?"

"Our committee is meeting tonight to propose a change of rules to the assembled miners. You should attend and vote. Of course there is no doubt about the outcome."

David had heard of these meetings of miners' committees, even though he had never attended one. He assumed that the rule changes concerned some issue like how many feet of creek frontage were permitted in one claim. As gold was disappearing from the streams, claims were being extended up and away from the water line. In following the twists and turns sometimes these dry land claims overlapped. Maybe this meeting was to resolve that sort of difference.

Evidently, interest ran high about whatever these rules concerned; a large number of miners arrived at the Empire Saloon for the meeting. The gambling stopped and tables were pushed closer together to allow later arrivals room to stand at the rear of the space.

Finster assumed a dignified air, puffing up his chest. He had changed his dirty apron for a clean, white one, and David thought the German moved behind the bar in a fair imitation of a heavily loaded ship under full sail.

"Mine friends—" He laid his fleshy hands palm down on the bar. "I ask you to gif attention to our chairman, Mr. Barton. I gif you Mr. Barton."

As David watched from the fringe of the crowd, the assembly parted and a tall, balding man stepped through toward the bar. He was neatly dressed and, according to the cut of his clothes, apparently well-to-do. The man shook hands with Finster across the bartop, then turned to face the group. *That's funny,* thought David, *he looks familiar to me.*

"Gentlemen, it's been my privilege to act as your chairman in this matter, and I believe we have properly discharged our duty as a committee when we issue this report for your vote. It is the committee's belief that it would be in the best interests of the Hangtown Mining District to adopt a new article, number seven in fact, to the District's bylaws."

David was bored at these proceedings. He assumed that the committee chairman was a lawyer seeking to drum up business or perhaps angling for an appointment as a justice of the peace. He decided to go on over to the store and size up the merchandise, then come back and try again to sell the pistol.

David was pushing his way through the crowd between him and the door when he heard Barton announce, "I will read you the text of the resolution, before we put it to a vote." David was carrying the small pistol by its stubby stock, the hammer upright and the barrel pointed downward.

David had reached the last ring of men between him and the door when Barton continued, " 'Be it resolved that only native Americans, which phrase shall not mean Indians, shall be permitted to hold claims or transact business for claims.' Is there any discussion?"

David stopped in his tracks, uncertain if he'd heard correctly. Only native Americans could own claims? That would mean that Ling Chow and all the Chinese could be thrown off their hard-won claims! It even meant that Keo, perhaps David himself, would be barred from owning the land they'd staked and worked and sweated over.

Barton continued smoothly, "Hearing no discussion, the chair will entertain a motion to vote—"

"Just a minute!" David cried, hopping up on a stool. "I have something to say. What gives you, or any committee, or this whole group for that matter, the right to say that people who have already been working their claims for months now can't own them?"

A voice from behind him jeered, "Ain't you the fellow that's been working with them Chinks? I know'd you was loopy when I see'd you hauling them rocks on your back like a coolie. Pay him no mind, boys, he must be half-Chinee himself."

"But the Chinese are working claims already abandoned by other miners. What harm does it do if they can make a go of some place just by working harder at it?"

Barton was dismayed to see that a low murmur from the group showed that there was some agreement with David's point. Quickly he spoke up, "Ah yes, but what about those of their fellows coming after them? If the door, which is open a crack now, is allowed to swing wide, how many millions of slant-eyed heathen will follow? I say we should slam it shut while there's still time."

A growing rumble told David that an even greater number of miners accepted Barton's position. Shouts of "Sit down!" and "No heathen Chinks gettin' our gold!" drowned out the few who said, "Let's be reasonable, let's not be hasty."

At least I tried, David thought to himself as he stepped off the stool. After all, he could pass for American easily enough. No one need know he wasn't born in the States. He shrugged and headed for the door of the saloon.

"Look here," David heard a gruff voice shout from the saloon steps. "Them lousy Chinese even sent 'em a spy to our meeting. Look what I caught outside here, snoopin' around. What say we hand him back his pigtail?"

Moffat was holding Ling Chow aloft by the queue in one hand while his other hand encircled the little Chinaman's throat.

At that moment something snapped in David Bollin's mind. This kindly little man who had done no one any harm was about to be injured, perhaps killed.

"No! Let him alone!" David shouted. He pushed two miners out of the way and rushed out onto the wooden sidewalk. Moffat saw him coming and threw Ling Chow to the ground. Moffat stooped to draw the knife in his boot and came up with it in his hand, intending to stab David at the end of his rush.

The light of the oil lamps gleamed on the blade at the last second before David ran on it. He threw himself to the side and brought the pistol butt down on Moffat's head, striking the bigger man on the temple.

The gun discharged with a roar that echoed under the wooden overhang. David's hand was seared from the powder blast against his palm. All movement stopped. David and Moffat stood no more than two feet apart.

Moffat was struggling with the knife. For some reason, he could not make his arm bring the point upward in the killing thrust he had planned. He watched with a stare of disbelief as his hand and arm dropped downward against his will. A dark red stain overflowed the waist of his trousers. His knees began to buckle. His mouth formed the words, "I'm shot," but no sound came. As if seeing the event in slow motion, David watched as Moffat crumpled to the ground and lay still.

David felt someone pushing him on the shoulder. He turned to see a miner trying to shove him in the direction of the street. David's ears were still ringing from the gunshot, and he saw rather than heard the man saying, "Run! Run!"

He began running up the dirt street toward his shack. The prospectors who had been in the saloon crowded the doorway so that it was several seconds before they reached the street. Once there they stood over Moffat's body. Nobody seemed anxious to face the weapon that had killed Moffat.

"Shot him clean through from stern to stern," said a grizzled miner in a slouch hat.

"Yup," agreed another. "Slug went in behind his collarbone and came out below his ribs."

"Get a doctor! Carry him in and put him on a table!" suggested one in the back of the group.

"What for?" replied his friend. "Can't you see he's stone dead? We don't need a doctor, we need an undertaker and a hunk of rope!"

11

SAN FRANCISCO.

William Bollin had not been prepared for the filth and squalor of the teeming city. He gazed over the jumble of tents and wooden shacks that merged at the water's edge with the hulks of once-proud ships which now served as hotels and brothels and saloons.

The discordant sounds of an off-key piano drifted over the muddy street. Smells of sewage filled the air.

Not one church steeple could be seen amid the shanty-town buildings that clung precariously to the hills. The ship's captain had been right in his description of San Francisco. Within a few square miles, the very best of every bad thing could be found. The best bad women. The best bad whiskey. The best bad gamblers. The best bad men.

Somewhere in all this, William Bollin hoped to find David. He trembled inside as he considered what his son might be involved with in such a place.

"That thar burned-out hulk is the whaleship *Crystal*," explained a saloon keeper as he pointed to the charred remains of the ship. "If yer lookin' for anyone who sailed that vessel, you'd best be lookin' up in the hills. They're all long gone. Sold their souls to the golden calf, jest like the rest of us!"

His mind reeling from the sudden events, David ran up the street. Several miners called out to him, "What is it? Is someone shot?" but no one tried to stop him. David made no reply to the questions, but ran on into the night toward his shack.

An accident, he reasoned to himself. *That's all it was. I didn't mean to shoot him.* He thought about going back and giving himself up, but his legs refused to slow down.

When he reached his cabin, David sat in the darkness for a moment, not even willing to light his lantern. He had his belongings all packed and was ready to bolt out the door, when he remembered that he had not had a chance to buy supplies. He wavered between running on anyway and going back into town to explain.

As he was still trying to decide what to do, he heard a shuffling of footsteps outside the shack. He held his breath, listening to the movement outside, then a low voice called, "David, you there?"

It was Ling Chow. David burst out of the dark cabin to hug the China-man. "Ling Chow! Are you all right? Is that man dead? Are they coming after me? How'd you get here? Should I go back?"

Ling Chow waited for the torrent of questions to subside, then replied firmly, "Is plenty time to make decision. Is not enough time to panic."

David drew a deep breath and forced himself to slow down and listen.

Noting the way David got himself under control, Ling Chow nodded his approval. He then began to answer David's questions. Ling had left the scene of the shooting while all the miners were still gathered around Moffatt's body. Ling had heard enough to know that a lynching was being discussed, and he had brought a packet of food for David. "Is best you go away for a while," he said. "You know some place?"

David indicated that he would try to reach Strawfoot and Keo to seek their help. After that, his plan depended on the law and the mob. Ling Chow agreed. He would send word upstream in a few days to let David know how things stood.

"You good man, David Bollin," added the Chinaman in a benediction. "Maybe you save my life. God take care of you, take you home."

Stumbling up the trail in the darkness, David fell more than once over unseen rocks and roots. On one of these plunges he heard a commotion behind him, and he crawled off the trail to lie in the chaparral. A few minutes later, four men with a lantern came up the trail from town, muttering among themselves, "He wouldn't go this way."

"Naw, he'd make better time heading downstream."

"Still, he might have come this way."

All this discussion took place not ten feet from where David was lying in the dirt and sharp spines of the thicket. He lay face down, afraid that the lamp's glare on his pale face would give him away. Even when he felt some crawly thing drop onto the back of his neck, then skitter off his shoulder to the ground, he gave no sound or movement.

"Now, a fugitive wouldn't keep to the trail," one of the voices said.

David's heart skipped a beat, then resumed thumping wildly when he heard, "Let's search off on the hillside over there."

After a few minutes' discussion, the group decided to go back to report their findings and obtain more lamps. David lay still a while longer, listening to their voices retreat down the trail, then cautiously raised his head to watch their lantern light dwindle to a pinpoint before disappearing.

When he rose from his hiding place, he figured that the way ahead must be clear, and he kept to the trail with as much speed as he could manage. He opened the packet of food Ling Chow had brought, devouring the rice and smoked fish as he hiked and carefully stuffing the wrapping into his pocket so as not to leave a trail. Ling Chow had also included a small leather pouch; David figured it for gold from the weight of it.

At daybreak he was on the outskirts of Washington City. Even though he knew that the trail he had followed was the only one connecting the upstream camps and Hangtown, he was afraid to be seen in town. David figured that word of the shooting would reach there later that day, and he didn't want anyone hearing his description to put the pursuers on so close a track.

As he was debating whether to stay near the town till nightfall in the hopes of obtaining more supplies or circling it in the brush and pressing on, the matter was decided for him. Up the trail from Hangtown galloped a pair of horses. From his vantage point behind a gnarled oak trunk, David couldn't see the men's faces. But from the speed of their travel, he knew they rode like men with news to deliver, and that news could only be about him.

As David proceeded, his travel involved tougher walking, even slower at times than the previous night. He climbed through chaparral-covered hillsides so thick with brush that it took all his strength to push forward. At times the slopes were so steep that David had to climb them on his hands and knees. He regretted having eaten all his provisions already, for it seemed unlikely that he would get more soon.

He drank water sparingly from his bottle: his path would be over the ridges and not down near the streams. As he climbed higher, he encountered piñon pines and located some cones from which the squirrels and jays had not yet removed all the nuts. He eagerly pried them open and popped the seeds into his mouth, scouring the brush to locate more.

When night fell he rolled himself in a tarp and tucked himself as best he could into the hollow at the base of an oak tree. He tried gnawing on some fallen acorns but found them too bitter to eat, so he tossed them away in disappointment and tried to sleep.

Of course he dreamed about food. His mind painted a picture of a luau in his home village on Oahu. His nose twitched in his sleep as if smelling the fragrant steam rising from the uncovered mound of earth in which the pig had been roasting. His mouth watered as his subconscious remembered baked yams and fresh mangoes.

The chill air made him hunch more closely into his bedroll. The scene in his dream mind shifted, transporting him to the Nuuanu Pali, with its sheer six hundred foot drop. He saw himself in the role of a Hawaiian warrior opposing King Kamehameha the First, being driven back toward the precipice. The sides of the Pali were closing in and there was no place to scale them or to circle around the oncoming forces. At the last moment, David's dream figure hurled a spear at his opponent, then leaped, screaming, over the cliff. He woke with a sudden start, his body rolling abruptly against a tree root and his stomach still refusing to give up the notion that he was falling through air.

A rim of frost covered the ground, and the dull gray sky held no promise of warmth for the day. David was debating whether to stay in his canvas cocoon until the sun was full up, or unroll it and build a fire. A movement in the brush froze him in place, half in and half out of the tarp.

It was not the noise of a man walking; indeed, no man could arrive at David's sleeping place without a lot of crashing of brush and snapping of twigs. The sound that accompanied the motion sensed by David was a padding sound, a weight pressed carefully against the earth in an unhurried rhythm that seemed to flow up the hill toward him.

An instant later a mountain lion stepped through the chaparral into David's view. Man and lion regarded each other from a distance of a dozen feet.

The lion was sleek and well fed, with powerful muscles that rippled beneath its tawny hide. Its yellow eyes locked on to David's in an embrace of mutual fascination. The man had to tear his eyes away from the cat's before he noticed the limp form of a rabbit hanging from the lion's jaws.

David bolted upright, struggling with his canvas covering and thrashing around to free himself. The cougar, startled by the sudden movement, lashed its tail and leaped across the clearing into the brush. With a parting snarl, it dropped the rabbit before disappearing up the slope.

David blinked at the spot where the lion had been a moment before. For an instant he wondered if anything could actually disappear from view so quickly. Perhaps the lion had been another part of his dream, just before he was fully awake.

Then he saw the rabbit, lying on the hillside just beyond the circle of leaves shed by the oak tree. He struggled again to free himself and this time succeeded.

A few minutes later, the rabbit, minus its fur and entrails, was impaled on a forked branch and roasting over a small fire. He tore off a half-cooked hind limb and began devouring it, while continuing to roast the remainder.

David was pleased at the lucky accident that had brought the lion up the hill by this path at this time. If he had still been sleeping, the lion would have passed unseen. A few moments later, he would have been up, making enough noise for the lion to have heard and chosen a different path. The odd coincidence that the predator had recently killed but not yet devoured its prey also entered David's mind.

Finally Ling Chow's promise that God was interested in David's well-being broke into his conscious thoughts. He wasn't sure what it meant, but the idea that God was watching him made David uncomfortable. Somehow David's picture of God and the memory of his pastor father were mixed up together, and he felt a surge of remorse.

Hangtown buzzed with a discussion of Moffatt's death for about a week. Riders dispatched to the neighboring mining communities carried David's description and an account of the crime, but the mob's interest in tracking him dissipated after the first night.

The shooting had interrupted the vote on the issue of the mining rights of foreigners. Try as he might, Barton could not get the discussion started again. He tried to press the notion that the shooting had been a deliberate attack in which the Chinese were conspirators, but nobody bought it.

What really caused the interest of the town to shift away from Barton's proposal was not any change in attitude toward foreigners, but the arrival of a new immigrant—a woman from Missouri, and the first woman many a miner had seen in almost a year.

She had been coming overland to California with her husband and their small child, a girl, when the man had been taken ill with cholera and died. Now she and her daughter had arrived at the destination for which they had planned, but without the husband and father to build their cabin and prospect for gold.

She sat in the back of her wagon, numbly pondering their future, when a grizzled miner approached. His beard was bushy and black as coal and his wiry hair was smashed flat by the slouch hat he wore, only to escape around his neck and shoulders like an immense scrub brush. He wore two revolvers in his belt, the handles reversed for a cross-draw. The hilt of a bowie knife protruded from his boot top, and his fierce eyes gleamed out from the thicket of hair, adding to his savage appearance.

He approached the rear of the wagon and stood glaring at the canvas flap through which the woman was watching his arrival with some misgivings. She was uncertain whether a call for help would scare this menacing figure away or rouse him to violence.

Presently he swept off the slouch hat, and in a loud voice remarked, "Ma'am, if you're at home, may I speak with you?"

The woman made no reply, but timidly drew aside the canvas. The miner stepped up to peer into her face. He seemed to be in a trance as he drew several deep breaths without speaking. At last he said, "I have a family back in the States. I came to California so as to make enough money to buy land to go to farming. I've been cold, wet, hungry, scared, disappointed and dejected. I'd almost forgot what I was working for, till I saw you and . . . is that a child there?"

The woman nodded that it was indeed. Her daughter lay asleep with her head resting against her mother's knee. The fierce-looking prospector stepped up closer to the wagon, stretched out his hand, then stopped, lifting his eyes to meet the mother's. She smiled and nodded briefly. The miner continued to reach out his hand until just the tips of his rough, scarred fingers brushed the little girl's hair.

His hand began to tremble and he drew back, fearful that his nervous shaking might awaken the child. He replaced his slouch hat, and with one hand loosened the rawhide ties that connected a small leather bag to his belt. The miner laid the pouch on the tailgate of the wagon and stepped back, gruffly murmuring "much obliged," as he turned to leave. One gnarled and hairy fist gouged at his eyes as he sought to clear away the tears coursing down his cheeks. Ten yards away he stopped and looked back toward the wagon. "Mrs.—?"

"Parker," the woman replied, looking straight into the miner's eyes. "Mrs. Parker."

"Thank you, Miz Parker," he finished. "Thank you for coming."

The woman examined the pouch curiously, pouring out a small pile of gold into her palm. Breathing a prayer of thanks, she carefully returned the precious dust to its bag, then raised her eyes to look across the clearing. There, in a silent, respectful line, stood a hundred miners, waiting for a glimpse of her and the child. At each belt was tied a small leather bag.

Barton watched this scene with an amused and cynical eye. He saw no way in which he could profit from the miners' sentimentality. In fact, he felt vaguely threatened by the notion that civilization and a gentler spirit might be arriving in the hills.

Above everything else, Barton knew that to recapture the attention of the town and rekindle interest in the scheme to drive out the foreign miners, he would have to show his leadership. He would have to take public, personal charge of bringing Bollin in to face trial and hanging. It might be even better if Bollin put up a fight and was killed resisting.

The day Pastor William Bollin arrived in Hangtown, rain was falling in sheets. The runoff coursed down the main street in such a torrent that one could almost believe that the town was built with a creek in its middle. Pastor Bollin lifted his face to the cold, gray skies and felt very far from Hawaii, indeed.

He had walked all the way from San Francisco. His congregation had given him a generous gift, but between the cost of passage to California, at Gold Rush prices, and his new outfit of gear suitable for a Sierra winter, there wasn't much left.

From the brow of the hill that hung over the town, Pastor Bollin got occasional glimpses as the wind swirled the curtain of rain aside. It was not a very inviting scene. Behind what must have been the livery stable, a few mules stood in companionable misery with their heads drooping and rain dripping from their soaked hides. An occasional human figure could be seen, but only making a dash from one doorway to another.

Pastor Bollin had not fixed his destination as Hangtown because of any definite news of David. Instead, he had decided to start his search in this soggy outpost because its name had been mentioned more often than any other in overhead conversations in San Francisco. Now that he had arrived, he was not at all sure where to begin inquiring.

Through a break in the storm, Pastor Bollin could make out one sign on top of a building at the far end of town. *Empire,* it said. The preacher fixed his bearings on this target and began descending the muddy slope. The main street was a more direct route, but travel there seemed to require hipboots at least, if not a rowboat. The side streets were a little less water-logged, but they zigzagged so much that Pastor Bollin lost his way and spent thirty minutes covering the last half mile.

Once under the Empire's wooden awning, Bollin took off his heavy coat and shook it out, then removed his felt hat and wrung what seemed like a pint of water out of it. He ran his hands through his graying hair to restore it to some sort of order before stepping inside.

The Empire was clearly a saloon and a gambling parlor, full of disreputable-looking characters. Pastor Bollin shuddered at the thought that he felt led to such a place to ask about David's whereabouts. The smoky room was only slightly less muddy than the street outside. Behind the counter, a large man with a dingy white apron tied high up on his chest wiped up spilled whiskey with a bar towel. As the reverend watched, the man took the same rag and rubbed it lazily over some glasses, which he then placed upside-down on the shelf behind the bar.

"What you haf?" asked the bartender in a guttural accent. "Whiskey?"

"No, thank you," replied the preacher. "I'm really in search of information."

"Dis iss not a libarary," replied Finster curtly. "Conversation iss only free for customers."

"All right then, what have you got to eat?"

"Beans iss what vee got. A dollar a bowl. You vant some?"

"Sure," agreed William Bollin, laying a coin on the bar.

"What iss that? I never see a dollar or a peso like that before."

"It's a Hawaiian coin. In San Francisco they took it as fair exchange for a dollar."

The big German eyed the coin suspiciously. "Unt where did you come by such a piece?" he asked.

"I'm from Hawaii," the preacher replied. "Actually, I'm not a miner. I'm here looking for my son."

"You don't look like no Kanaka fella," said the bartender, shaking his head in disbelief.

"No," responded Pastor Bollin with a chuckle, "but I've been there long enough to think like one. I'm a missionary, you see, a preacher. As I say, I'm here—"

Finster interrupted with an explosive guffaw, and then in a loud voice that rolled over the murmured conversations around the gaming tables, called out, "Guess vot ve got here, boys! A preacher-man! What brand of preacher iss you? Ve had a Methodist kind here but ve gave him a ride out of town, didn't ve, boys?"

"Look," said William Bollin with dignity, "I didn't come in here looking to preach at you. My name is Pastor William Bollin, and I'm looking for infor—"

From a large table in the center of the room rose a well-dressed man with a receding hairline and an air of self-importance. He strode up to the preacher and stopped the noise of the room by holding up his hand in an order for silence. "What did you say your name was?" he demanded.

"My name is William Bollin, and I'm looking for my son, David. Do you know his whereabouts?"

"Not yet, but I will soon. Your son is a wanted man, preacher, but I aim to bring him to justice."

"Thank the Lord he's alive! But wanted for what? What's he done?"

"Done? Just cold-blooded murder, that's all. He got drunk and killed a business associate of mine who was just enforcing some of the rules we have around this town to keep out riffraff and foreigners."

"I don't believe it," maintained Pastor Bollin stoutly. "David may be in trouble, but I want to hear his side before I'll believe that he's a killer."

"You'll get hear his side all right—right after my men bring him in, and right before we hang him."

"You won't hang him until we've heard from other witnesses," said the preacher grimly. "I'll make it my job to dig out the whole story."

"I knew you'd be a troublemaker, soon as I heard you were a preacher," said Barton, appealing to the gamblers with outstretched arms. "Isn't that right, boys?"

Barton's extended left hand curled into a fist, and he swung it around in a short arc that connected with the preacher's nose, knocking him back against the bar. "Jim, Sandy, throw this foreign gospel sharp out into the street."

Two men rose from a nearby table to comply. They dragged William Bollin through the muck and trash of the saloon floor, his nose gushing blood. At the doorway they paused only long enough to swing him back and forth twice before heaving him into the muddy street.

Barton stood in the doorway rubbing his bruised knuckles. "I'll give you some advice, preacher. We don't want your kind in this town. Being kin to a murderer doesn't endear you to our hearts, either. If I was you, I'd head straight back to wherever I came from." With that, Barton turned on his heel and went back inside the Empire Saloon.

Once back inside, he called Sandy and Jim and two others over to him. "Rain or no rain, you get out there and get on Bollin's trail now. I want him found before anyone else comes around talking about witnesses and justice, understand?"

Pastor Bollin lay in the muddy street, momentarily stunned. He shook his head to clear it, and raised his chin to let the rainwater wash away the blood from his face and restore him to clear thinking. He was puzzled by the fact that he did not feel more distressed about the news of the murder accusation. Then it came to him with a thudding awareness more substantial than Barton's fist: David was alive!

Kapono Bollin lifted his hands toward the stormy sky. "Thank you, Lord," he whispered as tears of joy began to choke back his words. "My son, who was dead, is alive! Dear God, David is *alive!*"

After months of anguish and grief, Kapono Bollin had proof at last that David still lived—at least as recently as the shooting. But how to find him? And how to protect him from the lynch law in this place?

A pair of muddy boots walked into Pastor Bollin's view, and a hand reached down to help him to his feet. The preacher looked up into the ruddy face of a man of medium height who wore his hair neatly trimmed. "Friend," the man said, "I don't know who you are, but you look too respectable to have been thrown out of the Empire for not paying your tab, so you must have found some other way to antagonize them. If a man is known best by his enemies, you're the right sort for me. Come along."

"Where are you taking me?" asked the pastor with understandable concern, given his Hangtown welcome.

"There are some upstanding folks in this town. Most of them gather at Widow Parker's eating place. My name is Morris," added the man with a firm handshake and a pleasant smile. "We'll see about getting you a hot meal and some dry clothes, and you can tell me how you came to be on the cross-grain side of Barton."

12

OLIVIA PARKER DID not fit Pastor Bollin's image of the kind of woman who would run a restaurant in a place like Hangtown. Tall and slim, with a ready smile and a homespun kind of attractiveness, Mrs. Parker brought a welcome ray of grace and gentility to a rough and hostile environment.

"I guess she did most of her grieving on the trail after her husband's death," Morris had told Bollin as he filled the pastor in on the woman's history. "By the time she got here, she was pretty determined to pick up the pieces and get on with life—maybe as much for her daughter's sake as for her own."

Morris stood aside and held open the door of a low, pole-supported building of rough-sawn timber. It had been a storage shed before Mrs. Parker bought it, he said. In the short time since receiving the donations from the miners, she had purchased the building, had some windows cut in the sides, and put down planks to cover the bare earthen floor. All the labor involved crowded out her sorrow and grief with practical concerns.

Mud still squished up between the planks, but the inside was clean, cheerfully lighted by oil lamps. Widow Parker served no liquor and allowed none to be consumed on the premises, but the miners did not seem to mind. Her wholesome cooking and kindly disposition attracted them.

She welcomed the man named Morris as a favored customer, and clucked with sympathy over the injury to Pastor Bollin's nose. She bustled around, directing the preacher to a side room in which to get out of his soggy gear. She brought him a set of dry clothes—a barter struck a week before in exchange for a meal—and fixed a chair for him close to the fire.

When Bollin was settled comfortably, Mrs. Parker brought him a steaming bowl of soup. "Oxtail soup," she announced. "Very nourishing. Now, no questions until he's drunk every last drop," she instructed Morris firmly.

When he had consumed the pleasantly fragrant broth, Pastor Bollin thanked his hostess, and pronounced himself ready to tell his story. Mrs. Parker, Morris, and a group of others gathered around. Bollin explained who he was and the events that had led up to his untimely departure from the Empire Saloon. At the mention of the pastor's name and his search for his son, a bearded man with a shock of black hair looked up abruptly, glanced over his shoulder, and left the restaurant.

"So you see," Pastor Bollin was concluding just as the bearded man returned, "now I know that I haven't come all this way for nothing; David really is alive. God has brought me directly to this place to find him and help him."

"And we will help you, Kapono Bollin," announced a voice from the doorway. The burly, white-haired form of Keo Kekua entered Mrs. Parker's, accompanied by Strawfoot, who had gone to fetch him.

"Keo! Keo Kekua!" Pastor Bollin stammered. "What—what are *you* doing here?" The shock of seeing a familiar face was almost too much for Bollin, and he started to sink back down in his chair.

Keo, however, never gave him the chance to sit. He grabbed the pastor and lifted him bodily off the ground in an enthusiastic hug. Tears filled the big Hawaiian's eyes as he laughed, "Kapono! Kapono Bollin!"

"Put him down, Keo," Strawfoot insisted. When Bollin was safely deposited in his seat, Strawfoot recounted the events leading up to David's part in Moffat's death.

"We were all partners after we met up in San Francisco," Strawfoot finished, indicating Keo with a nod of his head. "David—uh, left the partnership, and we kinda lost track of him. When we got word of the trouble he was in, we came down to help."

"Kawika good man," Keo put in. "He in trouble, but he not murder nobody."

"I'm just glad he's alive," Kapono Bollin said softly. "Whatever trouble he's in, we'll find him—before that man Barton does."

"Excuse me for butting into this reunion," interrupted Morris, "but I want to help also. A friend of mine was killed in San Francisco, shortly after catching Barton cheating at cards. David is known to have been a witness. I have obtained a writ requiring Barton to return to Frisco for questioning, but here I find him practically running the town. In fact, I felt it necessary to send the Chinese who witnessed Moffat's death away to Sacramento for safety."

"That's where I come in," added Mrs. Parker, "I was received here with

such kindness that I cannot believe that the majority of miners want anything to do with Barton's brand of evil and lawlessness. And—" She
stopped to retrieve a folded poster from a pocket of her apron. "Look at
this."

The poster displayed a likeness of Barton and the words *WANTED FOR
FRAUD*. Underneath, the small print added that Barton was known to be
a cheat at cards, and was often in the company of a suspected murderer
named Moffat. "I picked this up accidentally with some dress patterns at a
dry goods counter in St. Joe," explained the widow. "It wasn't until I was
unpacking my things here the other day that it came to light. Don't you
see the hand of God in this, Reverend? This paper came all the way across
the plains with me, and I didn't know anything about it until it was
needed."

All the men were speechless for a minute, then Pastor Bollin asked,
"Since this Barton is clearly not the man to be running a town, how is it
that he remains in charge?"

"He's surrounded himself with a group of strongarm types," Morris answered. "They have the support of a group of malcontents and complainers looking for someone to blame for their own failures. The crowd would
desert him quick enough if he didn't have his crew of self-appointed shoul-
der-strikers pretending to be policemen."

"Is there enough sentiment among the decent folks to arrest Barton and
hold him on the various charges if his bullies weren't around?" asked
Pastor Bollin.

"There certainly is," agreed Morris. Mrs. Parker nodded vigorously.

"Well then, friends, we must pray that God sees fit to separate Barton
from his henchmen, and protect my son David at the same time."

David traveled as far as he could toward Strawfoot's claim, but he struggled through thick brush and up rocky slopes. The trail itself went through
such rocky gorges and along such treacherous dropoffs that it was impossible to try to travel it at night. That left David moving in daylight to avoid
breaking his neck, but increased the likelihood of his being captured and
having his neck stretched. He continued trudging over steep ridges and
following rocky ravines, only to find that he had to climb out of them
straight up granite walls. His hands were torn and bloody, and the sense of
well-being he'd had after eating the rabbit had long since disappeared.

The wind that began to whistle down from the Sierra summits had a bite
to it, threatening that the night would be bitterly cold. David recognized
that he'd better use the daylight that remained to locate a sheltered place
to spend the night. Up ahead he spotted another narrow ravine like the
ones he had been climbing into and out of all day; this one seemed to

beckon with the promise of a safe haven from the wind and a place secluded enough to build an unnoticed fire.

From the lip of the canyon, David saw that it was a steep climb down, not appearing to have running water at the bottom. Both factors made it unlikely that it was occupied by humans, or that his pursuers would seek him there. David examined his swollen and aching fingers, then flexed his hands and felt how stiff they were getting. He could not delay any longer, or the descent would be impossible.

The first part of the climb he made from handhold to handhold, bracing himself on the trunk of a cedar tree while looking for the next rocky ledge. Then his feet slipped on a thin patch of gravel that concealed a smooth rock face, and he began to slide downward. David threw himself backward against the cliff, flat on his back, with a jolt that jarred his head. Momentarily stunned, he flung his arms out in a desperate attempt to stop the motion toward an even steeper part of the cliff that dropped off into space.

His arms found nothing to grasp, and his boots skittered over the slide-rock as if they had a life of their own and were determined to throw him off the cliff. He tried to find something to catch a heel on, but encountered nothing. *No one will ever find my body,* he thought briefly as his legs shot out into the air over the dropoff.

All at once his movement stopped. With a twang like a bowstring, his body hit the end of its slide, and an unseen hand seemed to yank him back from the edge. David hung there, suspended over a fall whose height he could not even guess, much less see. His backpack had caught on some tiny unevenness in the rock, but how securely he could not tell.

David lay completely still, pressing himself tightly against the rock. He was afraid to raise his head to look around and afraid to move his arms to hunt for a handhold, fearing that even the slightest movement would dislodge whatever held him and throw him over the edge. Even the prayer he breathed was delivered cautiously, as if too vigorous an exhaled breath would become his last. He tried to think what to do by picturing himself as an onlooker trying to coach someone out of this predicament.

A voice in his head told him to bend his knees. They had been locked, holding his lower legs out straight over the void. Gently and carefully, he allowed them to fold downward. His heels bumped into the rock. There was a ledge, just above where his feet were hanging. Ever so slowly he raised one boot until the heel bumped in to rest on a narrow seam of rock. Carefully he repeated the process with the other foot so that both feet were resting on a two-inch lip of stone.

David pushed downward on first one foot and then the other, testing to see if the ledge would bear his weight. Even after he felt that it was secure, he hesitated. Finally, he raised his body until he was sitting on the edge of the cliff with his boot heels supported by the tiny rim of rock.

Peering over the edge, David could see that it was a forty-foot drop to the canyon floor. He might have survived the fall, only to die of starvation after breaking every bone in his body. Despite the chill in the air, sweat trickled off his forehead into his eyebrows.

The ledge angled downward into the gloomy shadows that already filled the ravine, but David could follow its path far enough to know that it led to safety. Just a few feet to the left of his heels the rocky step widened out into a narrow path. Scooting his body gently along the edge, David reached the point where his heels would no longer touch. Holding his breath again, he stoop upright. The ledge held his weight, and the increased width gave him room enough to spin his body around and press his stomach against the rockface. Once this was accomplished and he was breathing again, he began to creep down the angled verge of the cliff.

David was trusting his feet to feel their way along. His face rubbed against the stone and his eyes darted from one tiny handhold to the next so that he would have a secure grasp if the ledge gave way. His face pressed into the rock and the shadows increasing, he didn't see the rope hanging down the rocky slope until his nose ran into it. Even then it took him a moment to grasp the significance: if there was a rope hanging down this canyon, then humans had been there before. They might, in fact, still be there.

David leaned backward, out from the wall, and turned his head slowly to look around. The path on which he stood led all the way down to the ground, but his eyes had to adjust to the darkness before he could make out the cabin. It was actually just the front of a cabin, a wall of hewn logs set into a recess in the rock with a door of rudely split planks in the middle.

David hung there, trying to decide what his next move should be. Clearly, he could not go back up the way he had descended. The cabin's builder had hung the rope to assist his entrance and exit, but David's battered hands and shaking legs would not support such a climb. He listened for the sounds of human activity, but didn't hear, see, or smell anything that betrayed the presence of another.

The final few feet to the canyon's bottom proved an easy crossing, and in a moment David stood outside the door. "Hello?" he called, hoping anxiously that he would get no answer, and not at all sure what he would do if one came. Silence continued in the dark ravine, and David pushed open the wooden door. By the waning light he could make out a candle stub on a tin holder in the middle of a rough table. Alongside the candle, in readiness for the owner's return, lay a handful of matches. David struck one of these on the tabletop, and lit the candle, then began to peer around the room.

Only the front wall of the structure was made of wood. The rest of the cabin was a natural alcove of the rock, roughly boxlike in shape with the stone ceiling about eight feet high at the front, but sloping downward toward the rear. A heap of rocks formed a partial wall joining floor and ceiling, forming a ledge along which the owner's belongings were laid.

A duffel bag such as a common seaman used was lying there, but of much greater interest to David was a partially full sack of flour. There seemed to be no other food around, but even this looked enticing. A charred ring of stones and a gap in the wooden wall directly above it indicated the builder's cooking facilities.

David soon located a frying pan, but hadn't yet found any water. Poking around the rear wall again, he discovered another reason for the built-up ledge of stone: a seep of moisture oozed out of the rock face, and a catch basin had been made to hold a small pool of the cold, clear water. The basin was full, and the surplus ran downward again through cracks in the rocky floor; no one had been at home here for some time.

David went out to gather some small dead branches and brush and soon had a cheerful fire blazing. He mixed flour and water and cooked a flap-jack the size of the skillet. It was burned in places and raw in others, but he ate it happily before falling asleep beside the fire.

"Hey, where is everybody? Pastor Bollin, Mrs. Parker, Morris, hang it all, are you all deaf? Wake up!" The excited voice of Strawfoot broke the stillness of the dawn at Mrs. Parker's restaurant, and he pounded on the door for good measure.

From behind the hanging blanket that partitioned off Mrs. Parker's sleeping area, the sleepy voice of a child could be heard asking, "What is it, Mommy?"

"Just a minute, Sugar, I'll go see." Mrs. Parker belted a dressing gown around herself, and went to the door, stepping around the form of Pastor Bollin, who was sleeping by the fire, and past the bench that held the recumbent outline of Morris.

Opening the entrance a crack, she peered out. "Yes, Mr. Strawfoot, what is it? And what time is it? Everyone is still sleeping."

Strawfoot looked surprised. "Why, I beg your pardon, Ma'am, but it's well past five. I just figgered everybody would be up and anxious to hear the news."

"We're certainly up now, Mr. Strawfoot," the widow agreed, gesturing over her shoulder at the stirring men. "What is this news?"

"After last night's discussion, me and Keo decided we oughta keep an eye on Barton and his gang. Well, not thirty minutes ago, they rode out."

"Who rode out?" asked Morris, now wide awake. "How many of his men are gone?"

"Ain't that just what I've been tryin' to tell you? All of 'em! That sandy-haired feller, the one they call Jim—the whole lot of them."

"What? You mean to say Barton is in town without any of his close associates?"

"That's exactly what I do say," replied the prospector.

"Did you hear that, Pastor?" asked Mrs. Parker. "Your prayer has been answered. We can get a group of concerned citizens together and arrest Barton today. We'll have this town cleaned up in a week."

"What you say is sure enough true, ma'am," continued Strawfoot, "but we'd best keep on a'prayin' for David."

"Why yes, but—"

"Don't you see, ma'am? The reason they skedaddled in such a hurry is to hunt down David. I heard Barton as they was leavin'. 'Bring him back,' he said. 'Alive if you can, but dead is all right with me!' "

The next day dawned gray and cloudy, and a light rain started falling. Through gaps in the ridgelines around, David looked up the mountains toward the higher country and the passes he would have to cross to reach Keo and Strawfoot. As he watched, the became obscured in a swirling haze that at first dulled and then veiled the stretches of hillside forest. David had never encountered it before, but he had heard enough about snow to recognize the first storm of winter. If it continued falling and the weather stayed cold, he would have to give up the idea of rejoining his two companions.

For the time being he was content to remain where he was. He felt secure, convinced that not only was the cabin's builder absent, but he was never going to return. He gave some thought to the lack of food, but decided that he could trap rabbits or quail, given the time to remain in one location safely. In any case, he was optimistic about his immediate future for the first time since the shooting.

For breakfast he cooked another flapjack, then used more flour and water to form a crude lump of dough which he nestled among the heated stones of the firepit to bake for later. This accomplished, his curiosity finally caused him to dump out the contents of the seabag onto the stone counter.

The duffel bag seemed like a treasure trove. Out of it tumbled a heavy sweater, an oilcloth jacket and matching trousers, long underwear, heavy socks, a waterproof hat and a pouch containing gunpowder, percussion caps and shot. David was still carrying the derringer around in his backpack, though he had never had but the one charge for it.

Eagerly David discarded his worn-out clothing and after bathing with handfuls of water from the small pool, dressed himself in his newfound gear. The pants were a little short, but in general the fit was not unmanageable.

David reloaded the pistol and went out to explore the ravine. Just as he had seen from above, the canyon's walls were sheer everywhere except for the place he had descended. The canyon floor was only wide for a couple of hundred yards, then it pinched off again at both ends, becoming almost too narrow to pass through. In addition, the upper end was blocked by a rockslide, so only the downslope direction offered any possible exit, and it seemed to plunge into an even more precipitous stretch of ravine.

Exploring done, David returned to the cabin. He removed the baked crust from the stones and munched on it thoughtfully. The prospects of trapping anything on the canyon floor did not seem so good after all, but in another day or so his hands would be recovered enough to be able to make the climb out using the rope. The surrounding hillsides would certainly provide some game, especially now that he had a usable firearm.

David imagined himself hunting with the derringer, drawing a bead on a squirrel and carrying it home to cook. He thought of himself as Robinson Crusoe, making a home in the little canyon as if it were a deserted island.

Remembering how his father had read Defoe's book to him when he was ten or eleven years old made him miss his home in Hawaii. He thought of his father with real longing, and his storybook sensation dissipated. The reality of his situation hit home: he was alone in a wilderness with winter coming on, and he was being hunted outside this narrow little world as a murderer.

I'll go home, he thought. *I don't know why I didn't think of it before. If I can get back to Frisco without getting caught, I can work my way home on a sailing ship. I'll say to my father that I'm sorr—*

His thoughts were violently interrupted as the door to the cabin burst open. For an instant David thought that a freak gust of wind had caused it: then he saw the form of a man standing in the gray rain. "What are you doing in my place with my belongings?" demanded a strangely chanting voice. When David made no reply, the man advanced into the room and threw off the sodden hat that had hidden his features.

A thrill of fear burst up David's spine and raised the hair on the back of his neck. It was Greaves! David had last seen the captain of the *Crystal* being dumped into San Francisco Bay by Keo, right after his pistol shot had creased David's cheek. Instinctively, David's hand went up to the location of the old wound, now faded to a thin scar. He pulled his hand back down, but not before Greaves had seen the gesture.

Greaves took another step into the shelter. He leaned forward to peer at David. His eyes widened and his face became a mask of hatred. "It's you!" he panted. "How I've thought about this day! You, who burned my ship, stole my life, ruined me! Now I find you here, stealing from me again!"

"Captain, I . . . the fire . . . I didn't . . ."

Greaves gave him no opportunity to explain about the ship. "I'll strangle you with my bare hands!" Greaves lunged forward across the room, seeking David's throat.

David jumped aside, pulling the derringer from his belt as he did so. He leveled it at the sea captain and warned him to stay back. "You lily-livered swine!" Greaves yelled. "You haven't got the courage to pull the trigger. You only work by stealth. Fire and flame. Blazing destruction! The *Crystal,* my *Crystal!*" Specks of foam began to appear at the corners of Greaves' mouth. His eyes unfocused, and a second later he charged David again.

Greaves had been partly right. David couldn't say what had stopped him from pulling the trigger, but he let Greaves crash past him again. He had already planned his next move: he made a grab for the pouch of shot and powder, and ran out the door into the rain.

Down the canyon he went, leaping over boulders and racing toward the narrow exit from the ravine. He pulled away from Greaves, whom he could hear pounding after him, and went sliding over a huge rock. He landed heavily, but got up and continued running. The crazed captain apparently stopped following at the rock, but his voice echoed after David down the twisting defile, "I'm on to you now! I'm on your trail again! I'll never rest until you're dead! Dead, do you hear me? Dead!"

The last word echoed and bounced off the rocky walls of the canyon, and seemed to chase David for a long time before finally dying away.

13

DAVID LEANED AGAINST a rock and breathed heavily, his sides aching and his chest on fire. He tried to take stock of his situation while watching up the canyon to see if Greaves was following. He held his breath to listen for the sounds of pursuit; otherwise his own rasping was all he could hear.

He recovered enough to move on again, but more slowly, trying to think as he went. He regretted the loss of his backpack and bedroll, but he had gained the warmer clothing and waterproof covering. In addition, he now had a supply of ammunition and still possessed Ling Chow's pouch of gold.

Instinctively, he thanked God for the new clothing and for delivering him from Greaves without the necessity of killing the captain, astonished at how radically his attitudes had changed. And now that he had decided to go home, he was also grateful for his new sense of direction.

David chuckled hoarsely to himself that he could find things to be appreciative for his present situation. Ling Chow would approve; Keo would be amazed.

Eventually the canyon he was descending became too dangerous for him to follow, and he looked for a way to climb out. But the rain had made the rocks slick, so he located a flattened bench of stone on which to rest. Against the wall of the arroyo, a slight overhang offered some protection from the downpour, and into this crevice he pressed himself.

He had intended only to rest a short while before continuing, but the combination of fear, excitement and relief overcame him. When he awoke it was pitch black, and even though the rain had stopped, David decided against continuing upward before dawn.

When morning came again to the Sierra Nevadas, David woke up feeling as if something were wrong with his ears. It was too quiet, unnaturally still. When he opened his eyes, he saw why: the snow which had been falling at the higher elevations the previous day had moved lower. Everything around him was covered with a thin white blanket that muffled noises as if nothing were stirring at all, as if the whole world, except David, still lay asleep.

He shook off the little bit of snow that had landed on his back and legs and stood up. The air was crisp, but not too frosty, and the sun rising over the line of peaks promised some warmth later in the day.

David had never seen snow before, and he scooped up a handful. He marveled at its coldness and the way it could be pressed together. He tossed his first snowball into the canyon below and made another.

David amused himself by making the snowballs smash on a large rock at the base of the canyon wall. He tried an experimental mouthful of the glittering substance and wished that he could have seen it falling.

The fully risen sun now burst into his sight, its rays illuminating the snow-covered hills. The glare lit up the stretch of canyon before him. By the sharp contrast between dark rock walls and brilliant snow, David could see a long way back up the ravine. Very far up, but coming toward him, he could make out a solitary figure. It had to be Greaves.

David threw his last snowball away and turned to climb up the rock face. Once out of the canyon he began to run down the snowy slope on the other side, occasionally sliding and having to catch on to the branches of oak trees to keep from falling. Each time he grabbed a tree branch, a shower of snow fell on his head, and his progress downhill looked like a series of crystalline explosions. Rolling hills lay before him, their tops covered with snow, as far as he could see.

After crossing several of these hills, David saw smoke rising from a hollow ahead of him. Smoke meant another mining camp, another danger to be avoided. But smoke also meant food and he'd eaten nothing since the crust of burnt dough a whole day before. He tried to put that thought out of his mind and moved to circle the rim of hills that bordered the little community.

When he was directly above the camp on the slope, a breeze caused the smoke to drift toward him. Instantly his nose reported that the smoke was not just campfires, but a hundred miners cooking their bacon and boiling their breakfast coffee.

It's early yet, David's mind suggested. *I could go in and grab supplies and get out while everybody is rustling their grub. Nobody will give me a thought.* David's stomach rumbled its agreement, and suddenly it was easy to ignore the part of his mind arguing for caution. *It might be risky,* he thought, *but it's better than starving.*

David descended the last hill in front of the little settlement so as to come out on the road leading into it. It would look less suspicious for him to be seen arriving from a normal direction, rather than overland. When he reached the first of the tents and shacks that were the miners' dwellings, it seemed that his stomach's point of view was correct. No one paid him the least attention, and those who did look up as he passed looked back to their fry pans just as quickly.

David located a log struture that grandiosely proclaimed itself to be the "Emporium of the Golden West." In crudely lettered script it offered "Fine Merchandise and Choice Provender." The building was crowded with miners who were devouring plates of flapjacks in sorghum and clamoring for more. Scraps of overheard conversation informed David that this camp was new, only a month old at most, and owed its founding to a new gold strike.

A short, fat man wearing round spectacles on his round face was delivering orders in a high-pitched voice to a line of waiters carrying the heaping platters. David took him to be the owner, or at least the manager, and approached him to ask about supplies. He waited patiently for the torrent of instructions to subside.

"Jed, watch out for that jug."

"Seth, mind that you collect another dollar from that party by the door."

"Mose, bring some more coffee."

"No need to ask about a place, sit down anywhere and you'll be served."

David didn't even realize that the last comment was directed toward him till he saw the round little man waiting for him to be seated.

"No, no, I'm not interested in breakfast. That is, I am interested, but what I came in for is supplies," David stammered.

The proprietor looked him over and shook his head. "No time till after this rush subsides. Sit down and eat, if you've a mind to—dollar a plate and free coffee. I'll see to the rest presently." Before David could reply, he was back to shouting orders at the waiters.

Eventually the pace of flapjack consumption slowed, and David, who had never stopped glancing over his shoulder, had managed to eat a plate as well. Here and there a few individuals were still finishing breakfast, but only one table full of men remained, calling loudly for more.

The rotund little man bustled over. "Now sir, what supplies were you wanting?"

"I want to get outfitted with as much in the way of staple goods as this will purchase," said David, standing and removing the pouch from his belt.

"To be sure. To be sure. You are just newly arrived, then?" David thought he saw one of the men at the crowded table looking at him. "No, no, been here right along. Doing well, too."

The proprietor puckered his eyebrows above the round spectacles. "Curious that I haven't seen you before. This is the only store in these parts."

"Yes, well, can you get on with it?" David asked. The man who had been staring at him leaned over to whisper something to his neighbor. David couldn't decide whether it was best to turn away from their view or to continue standing so as to keep an eye on them.

"Let's just see your purchasing power," said the storekeeper, setting up scales. He poured David's pouch of gold into one pan, then began adding brass weights to the other.

"Say, where did you get this?" he asked in what seemed to David an unnecessarily loud voice.

"I told you, I've been in the diggings for a while," said David nervously.

"But this gold didn't come from around these parts. This is real fine gold and everything we've seen here so far is coarse stuff. Where'd you say your claim was located?"

David saw the four men who had been seated at the table push back their chairs and start to stand. Hastily grabbing the pan, David poured the gold dust back into the leather pouch, spilling some on the counter. "That's all right. I've changed my mind."

"What's your rush?" asked the storekeeper.

"Your name Bollin?" growled a voice behind him.

David reached his hand under his sweater to grasp the butt of the der-ringer. When he made no reply, the man who had stepped up behind him laid a rough hand on his shoulder.

"I said, what's your name, stranger?"

David couldn't wait any longer. He spun around with the open pouch of gold dust in one hand, spraying its contents into the face of his challenger, and drawing the pistol with his other hand as he turned.

The startled ruffian put his hands up to his face as the glimmering pow-der hit him in the eyes, blinding him. "What the—?" he demanded, falling back a pace.

The sunlight streaming in through the slit windows of the log building turned the shower of gold into a cloud of shimmering sparks. The other three men stood transfixed for a moment, then froze as they noted the .44 caliber opening of the derringer pointed at them.

"I want a horse and I want it now," demanded David, glancing at the proprietor.

"Out back, tied to the tree. Take it, take it," the man stammered ner-vously, holding his pudgy hands in plain view.

"First one who tries to stop me will have a hole big enough to put his fist into," announced David, backing out the door. As soon as he set foot on the ground outside, he turned and ran for the rear of the building. A jumble of voices and a stamp of boots told him they were coming after him.

The storekeeper had told the truth. Tied to a limb of an oak tree was a short, dark-coated horse. David pulled on the rope to release it, just as the first pursuer rounded the corner of the building. He fired the derringer. The pistol, now loaded with birdshot, sprayed the side of the structure and peppered the man, who fell back yelling, "I've been hit!"

That single shot gave David the time he needed to jump on the horse's back and yank it around by the lead rope. He had no saddle or bridle, but David clung desperately to its mane and pounded away up the street.

The leader of the pursuers, still trying to rub gold dust out of his eyes, was shouting for the others to bring their horses around. His partner was pleading for someone to help him pick the bird shot out of his cheek and neck.

Ignoring them both, the storekeeper rushed behind the bar and picked up a dustpan and brush. Methodically he began to sweep up the golden specks scattered across the floor.

The horse David was riding had surely been born from the marriage of a mule and a sledgehammer. It was a good thing that the little black horse was headed up the road that led out of town, because no amount of pulling or sawing on the lead rope could turn the animal one inch. All David could do was hang on as tightly as possible; the horse seemed determined to stamp each leg down with as much force as possible.

The road led up an incline to the face of a steep hill, then began to circle the slope, still gaining in altitude all the time. David and the horse left the mining town behind, flashing past the last of the tents and huts. The ground to the right dropped off into another boulder-choked canyon. When David found that he was looking down on the tops of oak trees, he leaned over the left shoulder of the horse, pressing as close to the canyon wall as possible.

The black horse dug up chunks of earth from the trail without showing the least sign of becoming winded. As David looked around for a path or gully that he could use to escape the main trail, the sound of a shot echoed up the canyon and reverberated off the granite walls.

Throwing a quick glance around, David could see three riders coming up the trail after him. Even as he watched, the man on the lead horse extended his arm and a puff of smoke arose. A second crash resounded in the arroyo, then another.

David ducked low over the horse's withers, hugging as close to its compact neck as he could and wrapping his arms around its throat. A shot whizzed past, drawing a spark and a handful of dust from a rock just to the left of the trail.

He had almost reached the crest of the hill. The trail was flattening out, and David could see the area opening up into a small valley scattered with snow-covered oak trees and gooseberry bushes. If he could top the rise without getting shot, he stood a chance of getting into cover before the pursuers had time to finish their climb.

The trail made a sharp hairpin turn just a few yards from the top. David looked back over his shoulder again to see how close the followers were getting.

Just in the middle of the turn, some shale rock was hidden under the thin snow. As the black planted a pile-driver foot and began to turn his body, the hoof slid out from under him, and he lurched to the left.

The horse hit hard on his left shoulder. As the horse stumbled and its rear pitched up, David lost his grip. He executed a perfect somersault in the air, turning completely over and landing heavily on his back with a thud. The blow was cushioned by the layer of snow, but it still knocked the wind out of him and left him dazed.

The black rolled completely over, but came up again a dozen yards away, apparently unharmed, trailing its lead-rope in the snow. David shook his head as he rose shakily to his feet. He stumbled over the snow toward the black, hoping to grab its rope and swing back aboard.

As his hand reached out to grasp the rope, another shot was fired that threw up snow beneath the horse's belly. The beast plunged sideways, and the three riders galloped around the switchback as David's horse skittered over to an oak tree and stopped again.

David drew himself up and turned to face the pursuers. Two split off to circle him, cutting off his escape. The third halted with his horse facing David. He was the leader, still blinking furiously, his eyes watering from the gold dust.

"Bollin, we can take you back alive or slung over the back of that black horse. It makes me no never-mind."

"Why don't you shoot me, then?" said David with more calm than he really felt.

"Don't rush me. You'd be a whole lot less trouble thataway, but Barton says he'd prefer you alive."

His hands tied together, David was placed back on the black horse and his feet bound underneath its belly. If he slid off again, he would certainly be trampled to death.

The posse started back down the slope at a walking pace. The man who had spoken was in the lead, and the other two rode flanking David and slightly behind.

"Where are you taking me?" David called to the leader.

"Back to Hangtown, of course. Barton aims to see that you get a fair trial before you're hanged. Ain't that right, boys?" This blunt jest sent the other two men into gales of laughter.

"Barton'll prob'ly figger to sell tickets," returned one.

"You bet," responded the leader. "Why, shoot, Bollin, if you dance real purty on the rope, Barton'll no doubt cut you in on the take!" More howls of laughter erupted from the three.

"You know I didn't mean to kill him," said David. "It was an accident."

The leader turned to look over his shoulder at David as he spoke. "It don't matter. Ain't nobody misses Moffat anyhow. You just stuck yore nose in where it din't belong. Why'd you try and help that old Chink, anyways?"

David was silent for a long time, and the leader continued to look at him curiously. "I guess it was just time for me to start doing what I knew was right."

"Well, savin' that short Chinee is gonna help you to a real long neck," returned the man, and he straightened back around in his saddle. At that moment the four riders were passing beneath a twelve-foot granite boulder that loomed over the trail like a stone idol brooding above the canyon. A gunshot erupted from the top of the rock, sounding as if a clap of thunder had burst right above their heads. At the same instant, David's horse gave a sudden scream that cut the morning stillness with such pain and terror that David felt as if a knife had been plunged into his chest.

The black horse fell over on its side and lay still for a moment. Its corpse then began a slow slide down into the canyon, dragging David's bound form along with it. Lying on the uphill side of the horse, he did not have his leg pinned beneath it, but the rope connecting his ankles still prevented him from being able to get away from the carcass.

The skid began to pick up speed as the slope increased; ahead lay the lip of a dropoff into a hundred-foot crevice. David hadn't even glanced toward this rapidly approaching danger. All his attention was focused on hugging as tightly as possible to the body of the horse. Gunshots tore into the ground near him, and one struck him in the thigh, making him cry out.

The other three riders had drawn their guns and were returning fire toward the top of the rock. They had not yet caught a glimpse of the attacker. As they began shooting back, the unseen marksman seemed to notice them for the first time. One of the riders, shot through the neck, fell dead from his horse. His animal bolted down the canyon trail, causing the leader's horse to rear and spin. The leader was thrown from the horse's back, and as more gunshots turned his way, he lunged over the edge of the path to shelter himself behind some small rocks lining its border.

The third member of the posse had prudently stepped from his mount, keeping its body between him and the source of the gunshots. He fired across his horse's back, his shots throwing up rock splinters from the top of the boulder and drawing a cry of pain from the attacker.

There was a lull in the firing. The two remaining men on the trail kept their Colts aimed toward the location from which the shots had come. The leader called out to the other, "Try to flank him! I'll make him keep his head down."

"Who's up there?" returned the other. "If he was trying to rescue Bollin, he came near to killing him right off instead!"

David was in a precarious spot. The black horse's body was resting right on the edge of the dropoff, on the verge of plunging over. Trying to get free of its dead weight, David crawled carefully backward over its rump, pulling the rope that tied his feet along the body in little jerks and bumps. The young man gritted his teeth against the pain of the leg wound. He was hidden by the steepness of the slope from any more shots from the rock above the trail. But looking upward toward the gun battle, David could see that the leader of the posse was watching his efforts to free himself as if debating whether to shoot David himself.

The rope hung up on something under the horse. David was completely behind the body, but couldn't free himself. He could feel its weight starting to shift again, moving almost imperceptibly toward the drop. In desperation, David threw himself backward with all the force he could achieve. The movement was too great for the remaining balance, and the body of the black horse plunged into the canyon.

In the moment of falling, its head and withers dropped over a split second before the hindquarters followed. The corpse slightly pivoted, and at the point when its eight-hundred pound weight should have carried David into the abyss, its legs pulled through the loop of rope.

David lay clutching two handfuls of gravel, his eyes screwed tightly shut. He had expected to be whizzing through the air to be crushed against the stony bottom of the arroyo. He lay completely still for a moment, not believing that the danger had dropped away and left him alive.

When it dawned on him that he was not lying in the depths of the canyon, he sat upright and began working with jerking motions of his bound hands to untie the rope from around his legs. Dark blood slowly seeped through the leg of his pants. Looking up toward the trail again, he could see the leader of the posse watching him intently. Suddenly, the man made up his mind.

"Bollin's gettin' loose!" he shouted, rising to his feet. "Hold it, Bollin," he ordered, "or I'll plug you right where you lay."

At the shout of David's name, the figure of Captain Greaves stood up on top of the monolith. A bullet from the second man's .45 hit Greaves squarely in the chest, and a flower of bright red blood blossomed instantly on the front of the sea captain's shirt.

As he crumpled to the ground, the pistol in Greaves' hand discharged one final time. He had risen to his feet, seeking to aim another shot at David, but his shot found a different target. His bullet hit the leader of the posse right between the shoulder blades, and the man pitched forward over the slope. He rolled past David, tumbling head over heels down the rocky hillside. For one terrifying second it seemed that this additional falling body would strike David and carry him over the edge after all, but at the last instant, the rolling corpse veered aside and dropped like a stone into the canyon.

David succeeded in freeing himself from the rope around his ankles. He stood up, testing his leg, and began stumbling along the edge of the drop-off, limping down the canyon. His hands, still bound, were clasped in front of him as if in a continual attitude of prayer for deliverance. That was, in fact, what David was thinking.

The sole remaining member of the posse saw him running down the canyon. "Hold it, Bollin!" he shouted. When David didn't stop, the man leveled his pistol at David's retreating back and pulled the trigger. It clicked on an empty chamber. He thumbed the hammer back and tried again, without success.

By now David was out of sight along the bends of the arroyo. The man swung up on his mount and rode along the path. He caught one more glimpse of David, now far below him, angling down the slope. The man looked over the shale of the slope below the trail and considered the distance to the bottom of the canyon. "I'll be hanged if I'll risk my neck going down there," he muttered to himself. "Come on horse," he observed out loud, "let's go back to town."

The surviving member of the posse returned to the settlement known simply as The Forks. He went back to the general store and eating house that had been the scene of their early morning encounter with David.

Outside the store he found the comrade whose face had intercepted the birdshot fired by the derringer. The man's head was bound up in a bandage that ran over his hair and around his chin. This wrapping, along with the puffy, inflamed flesh that protruded from the bandage, made him look like a child with the mumps.

The bandaged man waved to his friend, and even tried to call out to him, although the effort of moving his face evidently caused him great pain. "Sandy, come here quick."

"What is it, Jim? Be glad you weren't along on this ride. Ned's dead; so's Billy. Some crazy man shot us up, and Bollin got clean away."

"But Sandy, Sandy, listen!" mumbled the other. The cloth wound around his face muffled his words.

"Yessir," Sandy continued, "killed 'em both stone dead. I nailed him, or he'd a prob'ly got me too."

By now the bandaged man was fairly jumping up and down in his efforts to make his friend listen. "Shut up, you fool!" he fairly shouted, then groaned and put a hand up to his jaw as the stretched cheek had a sudden spasm.

Three men stepped out the front door of the store, all armed and wearing serious expressions.

"Are you Sandy Sullivan?" demanded a tall brown-haired man, laying a hand on the butt of his revolver.

"Well now, maybe I am, and maybe I ain't," answered Sandy with a sneer. "Depends on who's askin'."

The brown-haired man drew his Colt and held the barrel against Sandy's chest. "That's good enough for me," he replied. "I'm Cobb, newly elected sheriff of the Hangtown Mining District. These are my deputies," he added, nodding toward the others who also stood in poses of readiness for battle. "I've got a warrant for your arrest, as an accomplice of Barton."

Sandy's jaw dropped and his mouth hung open. "I tried to tell you, Sandy," mumbled Jim. "Tried to warn you."

"What do you mean, 'accomplice'? Barton is the head of the committee that runs Hangtown!"

"Not any more," continued Cobb smoothly. "Not since Widow Parker recognized Barton from a wanted poster back in St. Joe. Man name of Morris is head of the committee now. Seems he knew Barton from Frisco, where Moffat and Barton were both wanted in connection with a murder."

"That's got nothing to do with me," blustered Sandy. "We was just followin' orders to bring in Bollin for murderin' Moffat."

"Yeah, and it's good thing you didn't kill him, because you'd be looking at a murder charge yourself."

"How do you figure that?" asked Sandy, glaring sullenly.

"The new committee has brought in a verdict of death by misadventure; Bollin is innocent!"

14

DAVID STRUGGLED UP the steep slope on the opposite side of the canyon from the gun battle. Pausing to gasp for breath, he scanned the hillside below him and the trail across from him for signs of renewed pursuit. Seeing no indication of anyone close behind, David took the time to work on the knot of the rope that bound his hands. He tugged the coarse hemp with his teeth, forcing himself to keep trying even as the rough fibers pulled and cut into his wrists.

Once his hands were free, David examined the damage to his leg. He winced as he pulled the fabric of the trousers away from the wound. The bullet had passed completely through without shattering the bone. The holes had not bled much, in spite of the exertion of climbing out of the gorge. David continued to stagger on toward the top of the ridge.

He had a destination in mind. He had seen Greaves at the moment the captain was shot. There was no mistaking the leaping gush of blood from Greaves' chest. Since civilization was closed to David, he would go back to the dead man's hideout and remain there until he could come up with another plan, some way to get home.

He stumbled over the crest of the hill. Looking back at the little settlement, David felt a sense of regret and longing. He knew that he would find no aid in any of the mining towns. Nor could he endanger Keo, Strawfoot, or Ling Chow, even if he had a way to get a message to them. He would have to go it alone and survive as best he could in the secluded arroyo camp.

David made his way back up the stream bed he had followed when leaving the hideout. The snow had melted, and treacherous muddy footing remained in its place. He crossed the stream several times in an attempt to cover his trail, leaping from rock to rock. The impact of each landing made him clutch his leg in pain.

David was still wearing the waterproof raingear he had taken from the hideout, but he had lost the faithful derringer.

Afternoon stretched into evening before David managed to reach the narrow, boulder-choked length of canyon marking the lower end of the creek's outlet from the hidden valley. He knew he would have to climb out of the canyon again and descend Greaves' secret cable to return to the cabin. This was all too much for his exhausted condition and the early darkness. Finding a sheltered place in the rocks, the fugitive curled up and went to sleep.

Torrential rains and a bitterly cold north wind swept over the high Sierras, obscuring the blue peaks from view.

William Bollin, accompanied by Keo, strode into the log shack that now served Hangtown as jail and sheriff's office. The sheriff looked at them from his bunk. He did not attempt to rise.

Sullivan and Barton were imprisoned with half a dozen other men in a space ten-by-ten feet square. The new sheriff made his office in the outer area. There was room for a small stove, a bunk, and a chair. An upturned crate served as both desk and table, and a deck of cards sat ready for a game of poker played between prisoners and the sheriff.

Through a narrow slit in the heavy wooden cell door, Barton mocked, "Well if it isn't the holy saint Reverend Bollin and his Kanaka dog out for a stroll!"

The sheriff responded by hurling a boot at the slit, which sent Baron momentarily ducking from his peephole. A great round of laughter and curses resounded in the tiny prison.

"You'd best shut up, Barton." The sheriff sat up slowly. "These fellas are bringin' your supper, and I wouldn't blame 'em if they et it theirselves." Now silence fell behind the door.

Keo placed a large cloth-covered box on the floor beside the stove. The aroma of biscuits and beans and fried chicken was unmistakable.

"Widow Parker says this supper enough for ten men. You eat first. Mince pie for you."

The sheriff was already pawing through the basket and making smacking noises with his lips as several pairs of eyes now crowded to stare through the slit.

William Bollin cleared his throat, but the sheriff did not look up until he found the pie and held it up for all to see.

"Keo and I would like to go with you to retrieve the bodies of the dead men. And to look for my son," he said quietly. "When will we leave?"

Sheriff Cobb inhaled the aroma of the chicken and rummaged for a drumstick. "We won't be goin' anywheres until the weather clears, Parson. It ain't worth dyin' of pneumony to fetch a load of dead men."

"But my son—" Bollin protested. "Barton's man said he was still alive."

The sheriff bit off a mouthful of chicken and shook his head. "He won't be alive when we find him, Parson. Not meanin' to discourage you none, but he ain't gonna live through the night. Not with weather like this. He was all trussed up, scramblin' down a path no wider than chicken tracks. And no food. Give it up, Parson. Say your prayers for him and get on with your life. Your boy ain't gonna be found alive."

Keo and Kapono Bollin exchanged glances of indignation and concern at the sheriff's disregard for David. A chorus of hoots and laughter emanated from the cell. Someone howled out, "When the roll is called up yonder, he'll be there!"

Keo looked as angry and dark as the storm that raged outside. Kapono Bollin put a hand on his arm to calm him.

"Keo and I will bring back the bodies of the dead men. Save you the trouble, Sheriff." William Bollin's voice was amazingly matter-of-fact. "We will need a map showing the exact location. And horses."

The sheriff shrugged. "Sure. Whatever you want." A fresh gale of wind moaned over the little building. Sheriff Cobb looked up toward the rafters as if beseeching God. "But you ain't gonna find your boy alive. If I thought different, I'd go with you. But it ain't likely."

"Don't let them go, Sheriff," wailed a prisoner in mock concern. "You'll end up picking up two more dead men!"

A chicken bone bounced against the door. "All right, Sandy Sullivan! These gentlemen'll be needin' a map. A good map, if you please, or you ain't getting none of this fine supper!"

Silence fell over the group behind the door. "Sure," came Sandy's muffled reply. "But don't blame me if these fools freeze to death and don't get back!"

"I'll blame you!" shouted Sheriff Cobb. "And you ain't gonna eat ever again if you don't draw the exact map." He shoved a scrap of paper beneath the door and dropped a pencil through the slot. "Make it quick and be warned!" he menaced.

What had been a trail before the rains was now little more than a faint track fit only for mountain goats.

Keo rode a stout black mare that had belonged to one of Barton's men. Two sure-footed pack mules followed behind him, then William Bollin on a mountainbred bay mare, leading another mule at the tail of the procession. "This path bad as Waipio, eh Kapono Bollin?" Keo called over his shoulder as the track all but disappeared along the steep canyon wall.

William nodded and looked up at the sheer rock face that rose another five hundred feet above them. Not a single tree or shrub clung to the sides of the gorge. Only a series of sharp switchbacks marred the nearly perpendicular wall that climbed to a dizzying height above the bottom of the gorge.

When they had climbed three quarters of the way along a path, measuring a mere thirty inches wide in places, the ledge grew even more narrow and dangerous. One wrong step meant certain death for men and animals. William looked down at the barren trees on the floor of the gorge. After half a lifetime in the perpetual summer of his island home, the pastor had forgotten the barren landscape of impending winter. He shuddered involuntarily as he prayed for his son, who had never known the bitter winds of this season. Could David survive?

Sheriff Cobb had offered a fourth pack mule. "You may be carryin' home one more over the saddle, Parson," he had said.

William had simply shook his head and told the pessimistic lawman that David could ride back to town behind him.

Rocks and gravel slid away beneath the hoofs of Keo's mount as she scrambled and strained to gain footing on the switchback corner above William. The sand pelted William, and for a moment he thought that Keo's horse would fall over and wipe all of them from the ledge in one sweep.

Keo looked fearfully over the edge and called down, "Very bad, Kapono. You pray plenty!"

William nodded. *The steps of a good man are ordered by the Lord, and he delighteth in his way. Though he fall. . . .* Keo's horse jumped forward over the loose shale. A fresh downpour of gravel pelted the end mule, causing it to balk momentarily and pull back on William's lead rope. *He shall not be utterly cast down.* The bay mare scrambled upward, attempting to gain footing on the upper level of the switchback. The earth fell away beneath her rear legs, and rocks ricocheted off the wall of the gorge.

"Kapono Bollin!" Keo shouted and urged his own horse farther forward to give the struggling bay more room. Her neck bowed forward, straining against the pull of the valley floor. William prayed for help as he felt the horse losing the battle. He stood forward in the stirrups until his head was over hers. Forelegs pawed and dug in the sliding ground. Back legs struck at rock and soil, finding no hold. Could the search end this way?

"YOUR HAND, LORD!" William cried out. "GIVE . . . US YOUR . . . HAND!"

In that instant, the horse lunged forward while the pack mule screamed and fell away into the abyss. Within seconds the mare stood trembling on the narrow ledge. Shaken, but safe.

Somehow Keo had managed to dismount. He peered wide-eyed around the black mare, then he looked down and down to where the end pack mule finally tumbled onto a boulder. Keo did not speak. He could not. Death was very near them now. Above them three bodies lay still and cold. Below them a terrible force seemed determined to drag them to their deaths.

"I am all right," Kapono Bollin said in a calm and quiet voice. "Do not be afraid, Keo. I felt His hand. He is with us. He is with us."

At that, William swung carefully off his frightened mount, easing his way forward until he stood in front of her. "Easy now," he soothed her, stroking her foamflecked neck. "We must lead them on foot, Keo," he called. "And the Lord will lead us!"

If the trail up the crumbling switchback was frightening, the scene that awaited the travelers beside the monolith of granite was stark, grim horror. Rain had mingled with the blood spilled on top of and around the rock's base, until the stone resembled an ancient altar of human sacrifice. The man shot through the neck was lying face up in the trail, exactly where he had fallen. The blood that had drained his life away had pooled under his body. Sheltered there from the rain, it formed a ghostly image of the man's form that remained even after his corpse had been loaded onto the pack mule.

Leaning carefully over the precipice and looking far down into the gorge, Keo could just barely make out a flash of red from the bandanna tied around the throat of another body.

"Kapono Bollin," said Keo, "I can work my way down to body there." He pointed over the edge. "You stay here and check for man on top of rock?"

"Of course," replied the pastor. "And you be careful, Keo. There are enough bodies in this canyon already."

Keo removed a coil of rope they had brought for this purpose and tied it securely around a rock. Then he began to make a sliding, cautiously controlled descent.

William Bollin worked his way around the standing stone. He discovered a way to climb to its high side, then picked his way over a heap of rubble till at last he came out on its pinnacle. Face down before him lay the body of a man dressed in the dark blue dungarees and foul weather gear of a sailor. The corpse looked curiously flat, crumpled into the rocky surface as if it had tried to melt into a crevice of the stone with only partial success.

Swallowing hard, Pastor Bollin rolled the body over. The shirt, which should have been white, was dyed a deep reddish-brown, much like the color of the soil of the hillside from which the boulder thrust.

The preacher stood for several minutes, searching for some sign of David on the hills. Keo struggled again to the lip of the arroyo. He had a third body slung over his shoulder, which he held there with the pressure of one hand, while with the other he kept a tight grip on the rope. The Hawaiian lunged forward for one more pull and staggered onto the trail. He rolled the body from his shoulder onto the ground, then sat down panting for a minute.

When Keo stood up, he called to William. "Kapono Bollin!" He paused to catch his breath before resuming, "Kapono Bollin, you all right?"

"Yes," came the reply from above. "There is another dead man up here, just like that outlaw said."

"You wait," called the native. "I come help." He scrambled up to join the pastor on the summit of the rock.

"Hey," Keo puffed, "I know this man. This Captain Greaves, whale ship captain for Kawika and me."

William Bollin straightened up and looked grimly over the unending series of mountains and valleys that fell away from this place. David was somewhere out there. But where? The highest peaks were already white with snow. The spruce and pine of the lower mountains were dusted white. The pall of winter death seemed everywhere.

These three dead men were just a small remnant of a multitude whose lives had been shattered by the lust for gold. Bollin remembered the words of the bartender in San Francisco: *"They sold their souls for the golden calf. . . ."* He glanced at the three bodies. What good were all the riches of the Sierras to them now?

William sighed and shook away the ominous thought that it might also be too late for David.

The lifeless forms were tied securely to the remaining pack animals. Only then did Kapono Bollin share his thoughts with the Hawaiian.

"I am staying here, Keo," he said in a low voice. "David was here, right here, not long ago."

Keo glanced doubtfully at the lowering sky. "Big gale coming, Kapono Bollin. I see such storms on the ocean. Big wind. Plenty snow to freeze off a man's fingers on the rigging. You come back now. You not find Kawika in this world."

William put his hand on the broad shoulder of Keo. "I must search for him, Keo. If he is alive, he will need help. If he is dead . . ." His voice trailed away and his eyes lingered on a single shaft of sunlight that broke through the clouds and rested on the bald dome of a distant peak.

Keo pulled a thick canvas tarp from one of the bodies, then unstrapped a saddlebag full of provisions. "One week, Kapono Bollin." Keo furrowed his brow and narrowed his eyes as if he were speaking to a child. "You stay here one week. If you don't come back, Keo come back here. Iahova take six days to make all this, and then he rested. So. You look. I come for you on the seventh day."

William Bollin nodded his agreement, grasped the hand of Keo in farewell, and began his search even before the sound of hoofbeats had died away.

It had been three full days since David had eaten. His wounded leg ached. The world shimmered in his fevered vision. He had traveled less than four miles, and now he wandered in hopeless confusion. Once David had fallen down to rest, and when he had awakened he thought he was in Hawaii again. Pitifully, he called out for his friend Edward, and then for his father. *"I have fallen from the Pali, Father,"* he breathed, raising his face from the gravel. *"And I am lost."*

He lay weeping, like a child who had wandered from home. Would no one come for him? Would no one find him until it was too late?

With that thought, David jerked his head up. *Now he remembered!* If they found him they would kill him. And if he remained here for one more night, he would certainly die from the cold and the hunger that ravaged him.

He squeezed his eyes tightly shut and shook his head to clear his vision. He said his own name aloud. He wanted to pray, to ask God for help, but words seemed beyond reach.

Suddenly, he heard his own voice whisper a verse he had memorized years before as his father had taught him the story of another David who had fled to the wilderness from King Saul. *"When my foot slippeth, they magnify themselves against me. For I am ready to halt, and my sorrow is continually before me."*

He lifted his eyes to the silent rocks and trees that surrounded him. Was someone watching him? Someone just beyond his blurred vision who stood behind the trees to watch and wait? David propped himself on his arm and looked desperately around for the presence he felt so near. "Where are you?" he shouted hoarsely. "Then, once again he repeated the words of the Psalmist, *"I will be sorry . . . for my sin. . . .* Oh God, help me," he finished quietly, bowing his head in exhaustion and grief. And then he slept.

David was uncertain how many hours he had passed in sleep. Or was it days? His head was clearer now. He pulled himself to a sitting position and looked around. Suddenly he recognized a dozen landmarks he had etched in his memory before leaving the hidden canyon. He was very near; he was certain of that now.

His eyes traced the down slope of a familiar ridge until it disappeared behind an enormous boulder. Yes. The canyon was just beyond that point. Safety and refuge was within walking distance. No longer confused, David wiped his dirt-caked face in relief.

David's leg had stiffened up considerably and the young man had to massage the muscles for several minutes before the limb felt flexible enough to walk on. Locating a forked branch to use as a crutch, he leaned heavily on it while moving toward the rim of Greaves' hidden canyon. In the gray afternoon of drifting mist, David could not find the rope that would let him enter the shelter he was so anxiously seeking. Crossing an expanse of slick shale, the tip of his improvised support slipped out from under his weight, dropping him heavily onto his injured leg.

David ground his teeth together and rocked back and forth, holding both hands over the throbbing wound. When at last the pain subsided, David raised up and spotted the crutch stuck in a clump of brush a little way down the slope.

Crawling forward to retrieve the stick, he slid down to it and found the tree stump that was the anchor for Greaves' lifeline. David laughed out loud. This was no coincidence. Had he not fallen, and had the crutch not lodged just where it did, he would have stumbled past the hidden cord and perhaps never found the way down. He breathed a silent prayer of thanks and felt the kindly presence of the Watcher once again.

Descending the rope was a great struggle. Taking a loop of cable around his hands, he let it slip slowly through his fingers, while the boot-tip on his good leg groped for a support. More than once he hung suspended over the edge of the cliff before finding a tiny crack in the rock with the toe of his boot. His mind went back to the day he had dropped a knife over the edge of a high *Pali* on Oahu. Edward Hupeka had held the rope with his strong brown arms while David had descended to retrieve it. Now the laughing words of encouragement seemed to echo audibly in the canyon. Somehow he felt as if Edward stood above him, helping him safely down the granite wall an inch at a time.

When at last his feet touched the firm ground of the canyon, he called up, "Thank you, Edward! Thanks for your prayers!"

Was the momentary flash of a smile and the upraised arm only imagination? David squinted up to the rim of the canyon, his vision blurred again. He winced. Edward was not there, of course. *Imagination. Wishes.* David was alone.

He turned away and staggered painfully toward the little shack. Falling through the door, he threw himself on the rough cot and lay there until the world stopped spinning around him.

He eyed the cold hearth longingly. There could be no fire for warmth or cooking or light tonight. He dared not give in to such a luxury. A single wisp of smoke could lead his pursuers to this place.

His gaze wandered to the rock shelf where Greaves had stacked provisions. Tins of hardtack and crackers were there, along with coffee, beans, and flour.

"Maikai," David whispered as he closed his eyes to sleep. "It is good."

Something roused David at midnight. He had been having a dream of home, the little church where he had grown up. He saw the figure of his father standing at the pulpit, his arms spread wide to embrace them all.

In his dream he saw Mary seated across the aisle, giving him a shy smile before turning her pretty features back toward Kapono Bollin.

His father was asking them to stand and sing, and as they did the booming voice of the preacher led out, "All Hail the Power of Jesus' Name." In the vision, David could hear the words clearly, *"Po-ni ia Iesu ke 'Lii mau.* Crown Jesus Lord of all."

Flushed and confused, David walked outside into the chilly night air, trying to clear his muddled brain. The air seemed to carry a faint echo of the refrain from his dream. *I must be feverish,* he thought.

Far off in the night sky and low against the horizon, an orange star suddenly appeared. It grew in brightness and intensity. David stood in wonder at the sight until his brain finally sounded the alarm. *It's a watch fire,* he thought. *It means they're still after me.*

David went quickly back inside the cabin and shut the door. He lay shivering in the tarp, but sleep refused to return.

Suddenly his aching stomach reminded him that he was hungry. His need for food was stronger than his fear of being heard by some phantom pursuer in the dark.

Trying not to put weight on his wounded leg, David crawled from beneath the tarp and groped his way across the hard-packed dirt floor toward the rock shelf.

Pulling himself up, he reached toward a heavy tin, his hands trembling as he took it from the ledge. He fumbled to open it and reached in eagerly. Then he cried out in disappointment as his fingers closed around a small rock. He sat down on the floor and dumped out the tin. It was filled with stones and rocks! David wept in frustration as he ran his fingers over the cold pebbles in the darkness. Captain Greaves seemed to mock him from the grave. *Which of you, if your son asks for bread, gives him a stone?*

It was a cruel joke from one dead man to another. Greaves had his revenge: David would also die if he did not eat soon. Weary and nearly overcome with despair, David clutched a handful of the stones and gritted his teeth in anger.

But something was wrong. The stones were cool and smooth, not hard and jagged like rocks. Still clutching the pebbles, he made his way to the cabin door and flung it open, letting in a blast of cold air.

In the dim light of the stars, the pebbles glinted. He opened his fist and held the handful of rocks close to his eyes. *Gold!* David laughed bitterly. So Greaves had struck it rich and had hidden his wealth in a hardtack tin!

But what good was any of it now? David could not eat it. It could not keep him warm or heal his wound. It could not give him life.

He closed the cabin door and let the nuggets slip through his fingers to the floor. Returning to the ledge, he reached for a second time. It, too, was heavy.

He pried open the lid and stuck his fingers in—it was full to the brim with nuggets. With a cry of desperation, David let it fall with a clatter to the ground. He reached out for the third tin with the plea, *"Father? Just one slice of bread. Oh please!"*

The third tin was lighter. He shook it hesitantly; it rattled. David carefully opened the lid and reached in. *Crackers?* He raised it to his nose and inhaled reverently. *Soda crackers! Bread!*

He laughed and cried in gratitude as he raised a small, salty square to his lips and held it between his teeth for a moment before biting down.

Had he ever tasted anything so good? He took two more squares from the tin and returned it to the shelf, then carried his treasure back to the tarp.

For the remaining hours of darkness, David huddled beneath the canvas and nibbled on the crackers. When daylight came he would check his meager stores of food and calculate how long he could remain here and survive. The gold nuggets still lay scattered across the dirt floor.

15

PASTOR WILLIAM BOLLIN had claimed all the mountains of the High Sierras for his King. For six days he climbed peaks and descended wild valleys in search of David.

He did not cry out the name of his son, but his booming voice resounded through the forest hymns and praises in the Hawaiian tongue.

Ho'o-ka-ni ke 'Lii mai-ka'i . . .
All hail the power of Jesus name!
Let angels prostrate fall . . .

If David were still alive, he would hear and recognize the voice of his father!

Song followed song. As drops of freezing rain clung to his beard and numbed his hands, he scrambled over slick rocks and cheered himself with song. *Come, Thou Fount of every blessing! Iesu E, Kumu Nui!"*

The cold did not seem to pierce him. The chilling fear that time was running out for his son did not cause him to despair:

"All the way my Savior leads me! Iesu mau Ku'u . . ."

Every daylight hour was filled with searching and singing followed by a time of silent prayer and waiting for the voice of his son to call for him. But only the hushed whisper of the wind through the pines answered William Kapono Bollin.

At night he built a fire on the rock that towered over the maze of valleys. *Surely David will see the light and be drawn to its warmth,* he thought.

And so the six days and nights of hoping passed away without an answer. William ate a small morsel of hardtack, then wrapped the remaining supply tightly and placed it inside the canvas shelter as the sound of Keo's horses drew near the camp.

He left enough food behind to sustain a man for three days. Kapono Bollin had fasted for that length of time, in hopes of having food left to care for David.

Now, as the sky spit out a stinging snow, Kapono Bollin left his hopes and his heart and rode wearily down to The Forks.

For a week David ate and slept well. In his waking hours, he distracted himself from the pain in his leg by rigging snares for birds and other small animals. These traps he constructed by pulling fibers from ropes. The pattern his fingers followed was learned in his childhood from Hawaiian acquaintances who used such devices in the mountainous valleys of their island home.

David's hands may have automatically carried out the braiding of the snares, but his conscious mind was carried back to island days spent with Edward and with Mary—and to memories of his father. David's father had always encouraged him to learn as much as possible from his Hawaiian friends. For a long time, David's boyhood had been an exciting life as the blond-haired child had played and learned with his darker companions. David found himself wondering when the life of the islands had ceased to satisfy him. He remembered the importance he had attached to the ambition to be wealthy, to be respected, to have a fine cultured home back in the States. How foolish that all seemed now.

When the day came that he felt he could give his wound no more time to heal, he set the snares in the woods on the top of the cliff. Catching no game that day, he put himself on half rations. Two more days passed until he finally caught a rabbit in one of the traps. He gave in and built a fire, and that night he splurged in celebration, devouring the rabbit and treating himself to another biscuit, baked rock-hard by the edge of the fire.

Two weeks passed with nothing in the snares. David's precious supplies dwindled away. Each day he allowed himself to eat less than the day before.

One morning David awoke at dawn to the sound of an icy rain falling in earnest. He wanted to ascend the cliff again to inspect his trapline, but could not. The cable and rockface were too slippery to support his climb. Reducing his rations still further, he waited out the storm by braiding more snares.

When the rain finally stopped, twenty-four hours had crept by. The feeble sunlight had barely changed the canyon's blackness to a gloomy gray before David was clambering up the rock wall. Once he slipped and almost fell, hanging on grimly while his toes groped for footing on the slick surface and his injured leg protested the abuse in a scream of pain.

David had inspected all the traps but the last two; all of them were empty. Then he came upon the remains of another rabbit. As if to taunt him, the fox that had beaten him to the kill left only the rabbit's head behind.

When the last trap also proved to be empty, David returned to the cabin and fixed himself a scanty meal of two scraps of fat bacon and another lump of flour. Then he lay down to sleep and tried to ignore the complaints of his stomach.

It was raining again; the storm was even stronger at the higher elevations. The trickle of water into the hidden chamber had filled the stone
bowl until it overflowed, flooding half of the floor. David moved his meager provisions to a sheltered location, then began stacking his supply of
firewood on the drier side of the cavern.

An hour later the rain slacked and stopped. He peered out and up
toward the threatening sky. He would have to inspect his trap line. If he
waited, the storm might begin again, perhaps isolating him in the cave for
several days.

Bitter disappointment filled him as he went from snare to snare, finding
each empty and untouched. It seemed as if David himself were the only
living creature in the canyon. And without food he would die soon
enough.

It started to rain again. The clouds lowered over the arroyo until the
morning was almost as dark as night. David nearly broke off his examination of the remaining snares; to delay longer might trap him outside his
shelter. *Besides,* he told himself, *there isn't going to be any game. This is a
waste of time.*

But his stomach drove him to complete the circuit of the traps. The last
snare was a tiny net of hemp, rigged from the leftover remains of the other
traps and set in a low elderberry bush almost as an afterthought.

David shrugged as he passed the bush and turned back toward the canyon. The snare was empty, just as he had thought. He started to walk
away, then turned again toward the bush. There was something caught in
the trap! A shape a little darker and a little bulkier than the bush itself
was hanging in the center of the fibers.

David moved cautiously toward the shrub. Even though there had been
no movement, David's anxiety rose; he feared that whatever was caught
there might break free and escape. He moved to stand beside the bush,
then bent down to peer into its shadowed recess. Upside down, suspended
from the woven snare, hung a quail.

Gently, even tenderly, David untangled the strands of hemp from the
bird's legs. As he held it in his hands he was struck with the desire to tear
it apart and stuff its flesh into his mouth. He struggled with this desperate
compulsion for a few moments, then forced himself to place the bird inside the pocket of his raincoat.

He started to run back toward the shelter, but made himself slow down
and walk for fear that he would fall on the rain-slick hillside and lose his
prize. Every few steps he would pat his pocket to check that the tiny body
was still in place, and twice he stopped and took the little carcass out and
turned it over and over in his hands, marvelling at his good fortune.

Before starting down the cable he took a length of rope, cut it with his pocket knife, and looped it around the outside of his coat. He tied it in place over the pocket that contained the quail as extra protection against it somehow falling from the pocket as he was descending. The rain changed to lazily spinning white snowflakes and descended with him.

When he reached the cabin, David took the quail's tiny form and laid it on the stone sideboard. With his knife he began to whittle shavings to form into a pile in the fire pit. He started to rake out some live coals from the previous night's blaze to get his fire going again, but stopped to run over to the rocky ledge to check to see that the quail was still there. Then he returned to the fire, digging out the embers and piling on the shavings. He blew gently until the kindling sprang to life with a cheerful blaze.

When the fire was burning to suit him, he whittled a sharp point to the end of a long stick. He pictured himself reclining beside the fire as he cooked the bird to a golden brown, and his mouth began to water at the thought.

He retrieved the bird and settled himself by the fireside to pluck it, carefully pulling off each downy feather so as not to harm the skin beneath. When the tiny form was bare, he took his pocket knife and gutted the bird, then skewered it onto the stick and began to roast it over the flames.

Drops of fat began to ooze out and fall sizzling on the coals. David stopped cooking long enough to get a skillet in which to catch the drips. He took the skewered bird with him, afraid that it might fall into the fire and be ruined while he was away momentarily.

At last he couldn't stand to wait any longer, and he laid the tiny form into a puddle of its own grease in the skillet. With utmost care he began to dismember it with his knife. He took a minute slice of meat and popped it in his mouth, shutting his eyes and letting the morsel rest on his tongue before he began to chew.

Soon he was pulling off bigger chunks, and at last he thrust the entire ribcage into his mouth and started to chew it up bones and all. He tried to slow down but couldn't. He was devouring the bird, crunching its bones, swallowing sharp fragments that scratched his throat as he choked them down.

Soon it was all gone; all but the clawed feet. David picked up the fry pan and began to lick its surface, sucking every drop of grease from the metal. When he had finished, he put the skewer in his mouth and chewed the end of the stick to draw the last flavored drops from it.

His eye fell on the minuscule claws. He picked them up and nibbled on one speculatively. It was like eating wire or coarse brush. He decided that he would cut them up into small pieces and force himself to choke them down. He picked up the knife to hack at the tiny feet, when the gleam of firelight off the blade caught his eye.

David brought the knife up nearer to his face. Reflected in its shiny surface he saw his eye, but it was like no human eye he had ever seen before. It was bloodshot and sunken, and his eye sockets seemed to overhang his eyes as if his soul had retreated far inside his head. He turned the blade this way and that, catching glimpses of hollow cheeks, scraggly beard with patches missing, and unkempt strands of hair that hung down all around.

From the bed David stared woefully at the empty tins of provisions and the useless containers filled with Greaves' gold nuggets.

How he resented those tiny gold lumps which filled up space that might have held hardtack, crackers, or flour! David rolled over and stared at the moss-filled chinks in the cabin wall. He remembered the smooth hewn timbers of his father's house, the clean sheets, the fragrant warmth of the breezes that lulled him to sleep at night.

All the gold in the mountains could not buy those things for him now. And if he loaded his pockets full with the stuff and trekked back to The Forks to buy himself a meal, he would be captured and strung up.

As the penniless son of a missionary, David had been wealthier by far than he was now with handfuls of gold within his grasp. All those years he had been rich, but he never knew it until now. Tears stung his eyes as he thought of his father and those dear friends he had turned his back on. He longed to see them just one more time. He ached to tell them how wrong he had been.

Perhaps a letter? But there was not even a scrap of paper in the cabin. David frowned. He could remain here only a short time. His scant provisions would be gone by the end of the week and then he would have to rely on his trap line. Death by starvation seemed a certainty. He wondered if anyone would ever find this place, find his body and wonder at the horde of useless gold.

They would not even know his name. They would not care enough to bury him.

He sat up slowly and reached for his knife and a smooth bit of firewood. He would carve his own name, the name of his father and their address in Hawaii. Perhaps a verse—some message that might be sent home that his father might know that David had died loving him.

For hours he worked, carefully carving out his name and that of his father:

DAVID, SON OF REV. WILLIAM BOLLIN
MISSION BOARD,
HONOLULU, OAHU

What message could he leave so that his heart would be somehow read and understood? How could he say, *"Like the Prodigal son, I would have come home . . ."?*

David winced as the pain of longing filled his heart. He could not remember the scripture reference for the story of the Prodigal. He had never liked the story or even understood it until now. He wished he had paid more attention. He wished he had a Bible to read. But such wishing was useless, and so he carved out the sweet words that had comforted him when he stood before his mother's grave.

ORA LOA IA IESU

Endless life by Jesus. Even as he etched the words, he found comfort in them. He was carving his own epitaph, and suddenly he was no longer afraid to die. He had died here already. All the empty things he once thought important now seemed foolish—as foolish and useless as the gold nuggets in the hardtack tin.

David smiled for the first time in months. He was free. He could see his father clearly, and he loved what he saw.

In that moment David also saw clearly what he must do. Somehow he must leave this place and find a way to tell his father what he had discovered in his heart. He could not trust such a message to a carved piece of firewood and a chance that someone might someday discover his remains.

David closed his eyes. Tomorrow morning he would head back to The Forks and turn himself in. Surely they would let him live long enough to write the words . . .

16

SNOW FELL ALL night, and morning only changed the swirling gray curtain to one of white, a wet snow that blew against the sides of trees and rocks and clung there. The storm was blowing in out of the west, on a rising wind. Anyone who had spent a winter in the Sierras would have instantly recognized the signs of a blizzard. But David had never spent a winter in the Sierras, never seen a real snowfall.

The thin dusting of powder through which he had hiked on his earlier trip to The Forks was nothing like this. Whole clumps of icy dampness struck David squarely in the face. The snow stuck to his beard and the hair that protruded from his hat. He had to tuck his mouth down into the collar of the coat so as not to get a mouthful of snow while trying to breathe.

David had to wipe the snow from his eyes every few paces so he could peer ahead into the billowing particles. When leaving the canyon hideout, he had firmly fixed in his mind the direction of the watchfire he had seen. He told himself that to go there in as direct a line as possible was best. To find where men had been was to find men, and the food he desperately needed. What he had not counted on was that once outside the narrow confines of the little arroyo, even the smallest distances became vast. David's goals shrank from the next ridgeline, to the next tall pine, to the next boulder, dimly seen only a dozen feet away.

In a partly sheltered hollow David saw the tops of some plant stalks. From some hidden corner of his mind he pulled out the knowledge that these were lily stalks, and that at their roots he might find a bulb that could be eaten. Eagerly he kicked aside the snow, dug into the earth, and probed with his hands. He pried up a handful of tiny bulbs and crunched on them. He could not have said if they had any flavor, just as he could not have said whether he had learned of them from Strawfoot or Keo or Ling Chow or his father.

The small patch was soon exhausted, and David plunged on again, out of the protected place into a drift five feet deep. He floundered there for a while, trying to push his way straight ahead into a snowbank that seemed to get higher and higher until it rose above his head. At the same time it seemed to grow softer underfoot, as if the whole world had turned to snow and he was swimming in the middle of it.

At last he could go no farther forward. He turned around to try to retrace his steps, only to find that the passage he had forced with such great effort had already closed in behind him. He turned round and round in place, unable to go forward, unwilling to fight the same battle over again to go back. *Will I freeze to death standing up here?* he wondered. He started to climb up over the snowbank. At its rim he lay down on his stomach and crawled like a great wounded beast. When his outstretched arms encountered a tree trunk, he clung to it, feeling like the snow would suck him back down if he let go.

After a time he pulled himself around to the other side of the tree. He had reached a hillside that sloped upward away from the swale where he had nearly smothered in snow. He began to pull himself up the slope from branch to branch. How high above the ground he was walking, he could not say, but he stepped gingerly, testing each foothold, expecting at any moment to fall through into a final resting place in a column of snow.

His strength was failing. He was badly in need of food. Shelter would be wonderful, warmth would be paradise, but food was a necessity. The fires of his body's furnace were burning low. Without food soon, the machinery that place one aching foot in front of another would cease to function.

David could not have known by sight or any difference in the feel of the snow underfoot that he was on the crest of a hill. Instead, that sensation came to him as snowflakes suddenly seemed to be blowing upward into his face. There was a lifting quality to the wind, almost as if he and the snow might be lifted up and blown back skyward.

He fell over a mound of rocks, picked himself up, and immediately fell over another. As he fell, he rolled sideways into a slanting expanse of snow-covered stone. The white-draped wall he took to be stone yielded under his weight. It gave beneath him, and when he rolled off, it sprang back.

Rubbing the snow from his eyes and shaking loose the wet clumps that had found their way down inside his coat, David put out a tentative hand. The slanting wall was made of canvas; it was a tent braced up against a rock. David threw great handfuls of snow into the air, hunting for the buried flap that would give him entrance. All at once, he found it, and he flung himself into the dark embrace of the tent's interior.

Inside, he explored the corners and folds of canvas, coming up with a wrapped parcel. He tore it open. Pieces of hardtack biscuit flew all over the lean-to, and David eagerly pursued and devoured every one.

While he was crunching the bread, the snow abruptly ceased. When David emerged from the shelter, he knew with a sudden clarity where he was: he had come full circle to the giant rock from which he had been shot. Below him, far down the slope, he could just make out the lights of The Forks.

Christmas Eve. The snow lay deep around the settlement. Blue smoke from two hundred fires and stoves curled lazily upward in the early evening sky.

The tracks of three hundred homesick gold hunters led straight to the door of a stout log building on the edge of town. Native Hawaiians and Chinese coolies mingled with men from England and Maine and Virginia and Missouri. This evening there seemed to be no notice of race or accent. Men from every place on the globe turned their faces toward a memory of home, a vision of family.

With one yearning heart they trudged through the snow toward the newly constructed church of Pastor Kapono Bollin. The Reverend had pitched his tent and staked his claim at The Forks. It was the last place his son had been alive; here he would live and preach and wait for spring thaw when he could begin the search for his son's body once again.

The miners talked about it over bad whiskey in the saloon. It was a sad story, the kind of story that made them think about their own fathers. A few even made the connection between some nearly forgotten Bible school story and the gold rush prodigal, David Bollin. In the original story the prodigal son had come home. But David Bollin was long dead. He would not be coming home.

Still, as men tramped up the steps of the new log church, they could not help but notice the way Pastor Bollin shook their hands and looked away up into the Sierras as if he were looking for someone else. Perhaps he was remembering some long-ago Christmas. Maybe he was seeing his boy opening a present or singing a Christmas carol. Ah, well. This was a hard winter. A hard Christmas for everyone in the Sierras. And this little church was as close to home as anyone was going to get.

The night lay in perfect stillness. Tiny crystals of snow drifted down from the pine boughs above David. His breath rose in a labored, steamy vapor from his cracked lips and then froze into icicles on his beard.

His legs continued to move mechanically, lifting first one foot forward and then the next. Always he stumbled toward the lights in the valley. The Forks. A town with people. Warmth. Food. He had long since stopped thinking of the gallows that awaited him. He had lived and died a hundred times since he had fled from his captors. To eat and sleep and be warm for the first time in weeks! To hold a pen in his hand and write his father a loving farewell, a plea for forgiveness for the grief he had brought on him! Death at the end of a hangman's rope seemed a small price to pay.

David stumbled and fell, tumbling headlong into a drift that covered him completely. A weight pressed down on him, a weariness that urged him to sleep a while. *Sleep tonight. Stay here. You can walk better in the daylight.*

He felt strangely warmed. His leg did not throb. He could almost feel his father's hands tucking him in to bed. And there! Behind him in the doorway . . .

"Mother?" David cried with a start, and the image evaporated. Suddenly he knew. He could not sleep, or he would never awaken again.

He forced his eyes open and struggled against the comfortable pull of death. The snow bound him, but he kicked up, searching for the cloudless, star-flecked sky through the treetops. An inch at a time he freed himself from the drift.

Managing to stand at last, he reached out to the trunk of a tree and leaned against it as he tried to clear his mind. Which way to go? The fall had muddled his sense of direction. To walk even a short distance the wrong way was as much a threat as if he lay down in the snow and did not rise. His strength was failing.

He raised his head and inhaled deeply. *Woodsmoke!* But where was it coming from?

Leaning his back against the tree, he sniffed again. The scent of smoke was strong before him. He circled halfway around the tree and drew another breath. On this side he could not smell the smoke.

Moving back to the front of the tree trunk, he fixed his sense on the smell of cooking fires. He moved from tree to tree, pulling himself through drifts that threatened to swallow him whole until spring thaw.

He did not want to die. Not yet. Not this way. The face of his father loomed before him, urging him on. He imagined the warm kona winds blowing over his island home. It must be nearly Christmas. The people of the village would be gathered in the little white frame church. They would be praying for him.

"Yes!" he cried out to the silent forest. "Pray for me!" He stumbled forward to the next tree trunk and the next. In his mind he could hear the sweet strains of mellow voices singing:

Silent night, Holy night!
All is calm, All is bright!

The voices drifted on the cold wind. Like the wood smoke, the music drew him ever forward, one hard step at a time. *To falter was to die!*

Suddenly the music stopped. David clung to a tree and cried out, "Please! *Please!* I am lost! Please don't stop singing!" Sobs half-choked him, and his knees began to give way to the weeks of starvation and the days of walking. Still his arms held him up. Encircling the rough bark of an oak, he kept himself from falling for the last time.

"Please," he whispered, "pray for me, Father. Mary. Edward . . . please. I'm right here. Here. I want to go . . ."

His words trailed off as once again he heard a faint refrain through the trees. He fought to quiet his labored breath. To hear words distinctly . . .

Could it be?

Once again the melody of *Silent Night* was clear. But now the faint words came to him in a familiar and dear tongue. Was he dreaming, or simply dying with one last sweet memory of home playing out in his fuddled brain? *"Silent night . . . ,"* the voices called. The refrain was followed by an answer in Hawaiian. *"Pola'i e, Pokamaha'o . . ."*

David stretched out his hands towards the voices as if they could hold him up; pull him safely home. He stumbled forward, crying out the words he had sung every Christmas since he was a child.

His words slipped from English to Hawaiian. *"All is calm! All is bright! Ka makua-hi-aloha. . . ."*

He stumbled and fell, rose, and pitched forward again. Once more he fought to rise, to move toward the music. To move nearer toward home.

David coughed and brushed the snow from his face. His legs had failed him. He lay at the edge of the forest. A clearing opened up just beyond him. He could see lights twinkling below like bright warm stars. The drifts of snow around buildings glowed golden.

Men, bundled against the cold, walked toward a large log building. They opened the door, and light and warmth and music glowed out, then re- treated as the door closed.

"As close to home as a man can get," David muttered. Then he willed himself to rise again. He stood on the edge of the clearing and reached toward the building. It was a church. It was home—or at least as close to home as he would ever be again in this life.

Once more he moved toward the slope. He stumbled and slipped, roll- ing over and over down the hill. At the bottom, in a lane deep with mud and rutted with wagon tracks, David lay still for a moment, then sat up and measured the distance to the church.

The voices began to sing again, loud and bright: *"O come all ye faithful!"*

David stood swaying in the road. He pulled his shoulders erect and raised his chin as he took first one tentative step and then another. His thoughts flew toward home and all those who had loved him, those he now loved in return.

He would write. He would tell them. He would live long enough for that, at least. Nothing else seemed to matter as he staggered toward the church. He reached out to grasp the rough pole banister and pulled him- self up the steps. The music was strong, filled with promise, hope, and joy!

David halted before the door and listened. Light seeped through the cracks and touched him. And now a clear, familiar voice resounded from the pulpit:

"Fear not: for behold, I bring you good tidings of great joy, which shall be to all the people!"

In those words, David Bollin heard the voice of his loving father. It was impossible, he knew. His father could not be in such a place as this. Yet his heart raced with joy as he groped toward the entrance.

In his mind he could see them all there. The pews crowded. Hands reaching heavenward and swaying with the music. Smiling faces. The arms of his father reaching out. He was home again! Home!

"Thank you, Father," he whispered. *"I've come home!"*

Then he opened the door and entered.

PO LA'I E
Silent Night, Holy Night

Joseph Mohr, 1792-1848
Eng. Tr. John F. Young, 1820-1885
Haw'n Tr. Stephen Desha

STILLE NACHT Irregular
Franz Gruber, 1787-1863

1. Po - la'i e, Po __ kama-ha'o, Ma - lu - hia, Ma - lama-lama, Ka ma-kua-hi - ne a - lo - ha, e, Me ke kei - ki He - mo-lele e, Moe me ka ma-lu - hia la - ni, Moe me ka ma-lu - hia la - ni.

2. Po - la'i e, Po __ kama-ha'o, O ni na Kahu-hi - pa e, I ko ka la - ni, na ni no, Me le na a - ne-la Ha-le-lu - ia, Ha - nau ia Kris-to ka Ha-ku, Ha - nau ia Kris-to ka Ha - ku.

3. Po - la'i e, Po __ kama-ha'o, Kei - ki hiwa - hi - wa a - lo - ha e, Ka la - ma la -'i mai lu - na mai, Me ka loko-ma -i-ka'i ma - ka-mae, Ie - su i kou ha-nau a - na, Ie - su i kou ha-nau a - na. A - mene.

"Silent Night, Holy Night" Hawaiian translation from *Na Himeni Haipule Hawaii,* © 1972 by Hawaii Conference, United Church of Christ. Used by permission.

SEQUOIA SCOUT

"For Penny and Woody Watson,
with blessings and thanks . . ."

1

WHEN WILL REED came to his senses, he looked up into the low ceiling of the tiny brush shelter and knew immediately where he was. But when he tried to leap to his feet, he discovered that both his hands and legs were bound with rawhide thongs. His lunge upward accomplished only a clumsy lurch, and he fell face forward on another man.

"Get off me," screamed Aubrey, "my leg's broke!"

Outside the hut, the rhythmic chanting of the Mojave Indians was accompanied by eerie dry clicking of gourds and punctuated by increasingly wild yells.

Will rolled off Aubrey as gently as he could and came to rest face up beside Forchet who was still unconscious. The Frenchman's breathing was ragged, and a raspy gurgle brought to memory the arrow that penetrated Forchet's chest just before a club had crashed into the back of Will's head and everything went black.

Aubrey, nearly hysterical, sobbed and repeated over and over again, "I don't want to die . . . don't kill me . . . I don't want to die . . . ."

No help there, Will decided. He forced himself to think rationally about the spot they were in, what he knew about the terrain and the possibilities for escape. His heart pounded faster as the rhythm of the gourd-accompanied chants gained in tempo. Aubrey changed his moan to, "They skin folks alive. They're gonna peel us. . . . Why can't they just kill us and be done with it? Why'd I ever come on this trip?"

Outside, another yell went up from the dancers as more brush was thrown on the fire, blazing up instantly in a thunderous roar. With the sound, Will wondered if the Mojaves intended to set fire to the brush shelter that served as their prison cell. Aubrey could be wasting his breath fretting about being flayed; roasted alive might be their sudden fate.

Forchet stirred momentarily and rolled half over on his side. The light from the brush fire outside illuminated the open flap of his buckskin shirt. Under the shirt, tucked in a leather strap that Forchet wore over one shoulder was the concealed sheath of a skinning knife. Had the Indians searched the French trapper and found the knife?

Will's glance flew toward the uprooted creosote bush that served as the doorway. No movement there yet. He heaved himself up to a sitting position, frightening Aubrey.

"What—what are you doing?"

"Shh!" Will hissed.

He scooted over toward the unconscious Frenchman by bunching his heels up under him and thrusting himself across the small rocky space. Two pushes and he was sitting upright beside Forchet's chest.

"What is it?" inquired Aubrey again, loudly.

Will shook his head angrily from side to side, silencing Aubrey, then gesturing with a jerk of his chin toward the barely visible knife handle.

Aubrey raised up on one elbow and his bushy eyebrows rose almost to the level of his hair. Like a fool he made as if to stand, then his face contorted with pain and he shrank back with a groan. He waved his bound hands toward his injured leg.

Will nodded grimly, then attempted to lean down sideways to reach the knife handle with his fingertips. Halfway down he over-balanced and fell onto Forchet.

There! Will's fingers just brushed the wooden handle of the skinning knife. The rawhide straps cut deeply into his skin as he tried to spread his tightly wrapped wrists. He could barely force his fingers far enough apart to grasp the handle. Only the last joint of two fingers had any purchase on the rounded wooden end.

Then from outside came a sudden glare, a crackling roar and a chorus of shrill howls as more brush was thrown on the fire. Will's attention was torn away from his goal. The end of the knife squirted from between his numb fingers.

Doggedly he set to work again, fixing all his concentration on the task of grasping the knife. He pulled it up toward Forchet's chin with a steady, tense draw, afraid that a sudden jerk would loosen his grip. Beads of sweat stood out on his forehead, gathering into large drops that rolled down into his green eyes.

Forchet stirred and heaved a deep sigh, rustling his coal black beard. To Will's horror the wounded trapper began to roll back again, carrying the precious tool away from his reach.

Every muscle in Will's body tensed, and his toes curled inside the leather moccasins he wore. He dared not yank or twist. He could only hang on desperately with his fingertips as Forchet completed a slow turn away, the motion of his body drawing the weapon from its sheath.

Will stared in stunned disbelief at the initials *GR* engraved on the blade. Flickers of light from the fire glinted on the steel. He pivoted slowly back upright, clutching the Green River skinning knife. The heavy blade came to rest on the topmost strap that bound his hands. Before attempting to saw at the rawhide strands, he threw a triumphant look toward Aubrey.

Aubrey had been holding his breath and clenching his teeth against the pain in his leg. His fears about the Mojaves' intentions were reflected in his terrified expression. By the dim light that penetrated the brush pile enclosing them, Aubrey could see the blade and the flash of a victory smile from Will.

Aubrey's pent-up breath exploded with a rush, "You've got it!"

At that instant there was an emphatic clap of hands to gourd drums and a resounding stamp of Mojave feet as their dance abruptly ended.

Aubrey regarded Will with wide-eyed apprehension. Had the Indians heard Aubrey's exclamation? Or did the sudden stop of the dancing and chanting mean that they were coming for the white men? Was it too late?

Then just as suddenly as the ceremony had ended, another one began. The pounding and shaking of the rattles resumed, and so did the chanting.

Both trappers sighed their relief, and Will grimly set to work sawing the leather thongs. Now the tightness of the bindings helped as he was able to steady the blade downward against them. Will blessed Forchet's attention to his equipment: The recently sharpened edge began to bite on the rawhide, although Will could only work it a fraction of an inch at a time with his fingertips.

Scarcely two minutes went by, but their passage seemed like hours. Finally the rawhide strip snapped apart. He was left with a loop still tied around each wrist and a length hanging down. But his hands were free. With one slash of the knife, his feet were loose as well.

He could see the pleading in Aubrey's eyes.

"Don't worry," he whispered into Aubrey's ear, "I won't leave you behind, or Forchet either. If the raft is still on the bank where they jumped us, we'll ride the river out of here."

Will cut through the thongs on Aubrey's arms even before he finished speaking. But he was afraid to meet Aubrey's eyes. Will knew that the chances of eluding recapture while trying to move an unconscious man and a cripple past half-a-hundred Indians were almost nonexistent. But he couldn't chance Aubrey starting into his moaning despair again. At least this way they could go down fighting, so he said no more.

Aubrey's bound hands sprang apart with an audible twang. Looking for a place to break out, Will turned his attention to the heap of brush that formed the back wall of their cell. He needed a spot that he could drag the other two men through without signaling their escape by too much rustling and shaking of the hut.

He spotted an arch in the yucca-palm branches that afforded an opening near the ground. The space was plugged with a clump of mesquite, which could be easily pushed out. Holding the knife at the ready, Will plunged headfirst into the brush, breaking out of the makeshift prison. With the hut shielding him from the fire, the deeper darkness beyond called him to save himself. Instead, he cleared the mesquite from the hole and prepared to rescue his compatriots.

Back into the hut he went, mentally urging Aubrey to be ready. Every second was precious.

He saw Aubrey's arms reaching out toward him, eager to be pulled to safety. Will stretched out his free hand, his fingertips finding Aubrey's trembling grasp. Aubrey had just locked his grip on Will's wrists when the brush doorway in front of the hut was pulled aside. A shaft of light from the Indian bonfire blinded both men.

Will sprang forward in a rush. His right hand pushed the knife point toward the intruder in a savage thrust, but he was off balance with his lunge and his vision was dazzled by the light. Instead of striking home, the blow was knocked aside. A forearm as lean and hard as a dried mesquite limb crashed into the side of his head, staggering him. Two dark hands as strong as steel traps closed over his wrists and shook the knife from his grip.

Will was on his knees, expecting the next instant to be his last. But the knife slash did not follow.

Instead, his assailant turned back to the doorway of the cell and rapidly pulled the brush shut. Will waited in the darkness to see what would happen next. He could not make out the features of the strong intruder, but the man was an Indian.

Will's eyes adjusted to the darkness again, and he could see the attacker kneeling and facing him only a couple feet away. The Indian spoke in a low but audible tone, and his words were in English.

"You must keep still. My name is Mangas. I am Apache. I tried to tell the Mojaves that you were not Spanish and to not attack you, but they would not listen.

"I have convinced two of the old chiefs to let you go, but the young warrior men will not listen. I cannot save you all, but if one of you will lead the war party away, I will put the other two safely on the river."

Even though the chanting and dancing outside continued unabated, the stillness inside the prison was suddenly absolute.

In a moment Will spoke. "It was up to me before, and I guess it still is now. How much time have I got, Mangas?"

"A few minutes only. You must hurry. I will try to put them on the wrong trail—this is all I can do."

"All right then, I'm ready." Will grasped Aubrey's hand. "Good luck. Take care of Frenchy as best you're able."

Mangas handed Will the skinning knife. Will accepted the weapon, then shook the Indian's hand and stared into his eyes. "Someday maybe I'll get to hear why you're doing this, but for now, thanks."

"Go with God," replied the Apache, and Will turned and dove through the opening and into the inky night of the Mojave desert.

Will crawled swiftly over the brush at the back of the Mojave camp. He had heard that these Mojaves drank a fermented brew made from cactus. He fervently hoped that they had been soaking in it this night.

Plunging through a screen of creosote bushes, he rolled down an embankment into a ravine and came up desperately clutching the knife. Shaking sand from his ears, he strained to hear a change in the sounds of the camp. Still no cry of pursuit.

Which way to run? he wondered. *The sand either direction along the river will leave too good a trail, so it's cross-country for me.*

He scrambled up the other side of the draw, then glanced over his shoulder at the glare of the fire. *Straight away from that is as good as any.*

Will climbed a sandstone bluff and stood just below its crest so as to not be skylined against the night. He was on the opposite side of the river from the trail he and the other trappers had been following when they were captured. The Indians had taken everything but the Frenchman's knife. Now Will was alone in the desert without map or compass, without food, and headed away from the only certain source of water.

A sudden clamor from the camp behind him replaced the chanting with cries of anger and outrage. From the bluff Will could see sparks rush outward from the glow of the fire as warriors grabbed flaming branches and began a hurried search of the camp.

Will watched just long enough to see the sparks gather together again in a body and race upstream along the river bank. *Good,* he thought. *This Mangas fellow knows his business. He's sent them away from me and away from the direction of the raft at the same time.*

Will remembered hearing Beckwith describe the land west of the river as flat plains, brushy and dry, rising slowly to meet the eastern slope of the Sierras.

He frowned as he remembered that tonight Beckwith was floating face down in the river with his skin full of arrows.

And unless I find some way to get off this plain by daybreak, that's what I'll look like. Come first light I'll stand out like a black cat on a snowbank.

For the next two hours he loped over the brush plain with the silent, ground-covering trot of a coyote, whose presence in the desert could be told from the barks and yips heard in the night.

Fixing his sight on the North Star, he kept it on his right shoulder as he ran. He heard the angry buzz of a rattlesnake's warning, but he never saw the reptile as he raced on into the night.

Pressing his elbows tightly into his aching sides, he forced himself to keep going. The Mojaves would be on his trail by now. At best he figured he had an hour's start on them, and within an hour it would be daylight.

Ahead lay his only hope: Though yet unseen, he believed a line of the Sierras reared themselves not too far to the west. Will's long legs had tramped many miles from his uncle's Vicksburg home, but they had never been called on for such an effort as this. Travel at night made it difficult to judge distances, but Will figured he had covered fifteen miles or so when the sky behind him began to noticeably lighten.

He threw nervous glances back the way he had come. Whenever he could, Will directed his path over rocky surfaces that would leave less trace of his passing, but finding a place to hide before full daylight was his main concern. Fortunately, a rising east wind was blowing dust over his tracks almost as soon as he made them.

There were precious few spots that offered any chance of concealment. The scrubby creosote brush was not over three feet high. In the thickest places it formed clumps big enough for a man to lie down in, but if he let himself get surrounded, the Mojaves would search an ever-decreasing circle till he was again their prisoner.

From the high mountain plateau, the old Indian's gaze lingered on the distant horizon. At the extreme edge of his vision flickered an orange star that pulsed and flared in time to an unheard rhythm.

He hunched his shoulders deeper into the rabbitskin cloak. An involuntary shiver reminded him of a nearby responsibility, and the old man bent over the sleeping form of a child.

The deeply etched lines on the weathered cheeks softened for an instant as he tugged another blanket of rabbit fur up around the boy. A drowsy, eight-year-old voice murmured, "Is it morning already, Grandfather?"

"No," replied the elder. "It is still some time yet before dawn. Sleep," he instructed.

Perversely, the mounded heap of rabbitskin and child stirred and sat up. "But why are you awake, Grandfather?"

"I keep watch, boy," replied the old man. "But now, since you are awake, look there."

The orange glow which the ancient eyes turned toward was no longer alone in the dark line which separated desert sand from desert sky. Both the young eyes and the old saw the flare multiply into many, as if the low star was dripping a cascade of sparks.

A deep, guttural sound came from the man, in words the boy did not catch.

"What did you say, Grandfather? What are those lights?"

For a time of silence which the child respected there was no reply. Then Grandfather spoke in measured tones, "There is evil about tonight, and you see its dance."

"But the bright lights are pretty," protested the boy. "They fly around like sparks from our campfires. Where is our campfire, Grandfather?"

"Hush now," urged the ancient voice with a hint of impatience. "These flickers hide wickedness behind their bright show. We have no fire because we do not want to attract such moths to our flame. Lights such as those are always ready to snuff . . ." The old man broke off his answer because his listener had gone back to sleep as abruptly as he had awakened.

Crouched down on a rocky ledge high above the desert sweep, the elder Indian studied the glints of flame rushing about. The pinpoints were slowly drawing closer to the mountains on which he and the child rested, and he dreaded to see them come. The east wind seemed to propel them along.

He watched until the finest thread of pale blue touched the easternmost rim of the bowl of night. As the dawn spread its gray hand, it pushed back the dark, so that the sparks dimmed and faded. But in each place, just as he had warned, Grandfather watched each light be replaced by a form of blackness, scurrying over the land.

Suddenly his eyes found what he had been seeking. At the near rim of the desert floor, appearing almost beneath his feet near a Joshua tree, was a lone dark insect-creature. It moved in a purposeful rush, seeming to look for a place to hide before the fast approaching light of day.

Grandfather stood once more. The surging wind was in his face, just as the rays of the sun glinted into his narrowed eyes. *Hurry,* he whispered urgently, without saying to whom he spoke.

The wind acted as if it had heard him, and obligingly raised its tempo. From the east flowed an airborne river of dust. Wispy at first, like smoke, the blowing sand soon formed a dagger-strike of black that competed with the sun for possession of the land.

The dust cloud knifed across the desert, blotting out the further horizon. It next overshadowed some of the black figures that had fallen behind the others. The partition of swirling dirt extended itself upward from the ground like a curtain that concealed by being pulled up instead of lowered.

The cloud of sand passed between pursued and pursuers. As Grandfather watched from his perch high above the scene, an enormous convul-

sion of the dust storm enveloped even the lone figure at the very base of
the mountain.

"Good," Grandfather nodded in approval. Then, "Come, boy," he
urged the sleeping child. "Day is here."

The change in elevation had grown more acute. From the flat plain
nearer the river, the land now had a noticeable rake to it. The increased
pressure on Will's legs took a toll on his lungs and strength, slowing his
pace. More than once he was thankful for the breeze that pushed him
from behind. He passed more Joshua trees, their contorted shapes looking
in the early light like tortured men frozen in moments of great torment.

His guiding star was gone, but in its place the elongated shadows of the
trees pointed him on toward the west. Ahead, the glimmering rays of the
sun were just touching the highest peaks of the southern Sierra Nevadas.
But Will did not see the arriving day as friendly. The spreading glow that
already sharpened the images of trees and rocks threatened to pin his dark
form against the dusty gray landscape. Should he halt his march, Will
knew a Mojave spear would complete the work the sun's rays had begun.

He set his course toward the tallest tree on the horizon. Will saw that
the rise in the desert floor broke sharply against a line of cliffs. No relief in
that change of elevation, the cliffs were sheer. Slick rock faces of sandstone offered no handholds. He was running into a horseshoe-shaped rim
of rock, but no direction in view offered any more hope of escape than
another.

Panting, he stumbled on over the uneven ground, aimed toward the
shadow cast by the tallest Joshua as it flowed up and into the cliffs.

This remnant of night shadow appeared unnaturally elongated, even
though produced by a tall tree. The shadow stood out against the pale
sandstone wall as if made of some darker, coarser material.

As he passed the tree, Will threw another glance over his shoulder. Far
behind him on a distant ridge he could make out dark moving dots, the
pinpoints of torchlight flickering out against the morning glare of the sun.
Racing on, he pushed his burning legs for more speed. Gasping the dry
desert air in great gulps, his throat felt like a parched corn stalk planted in
the middle of his chest.

When he reached the sandstone wall, there was nowhere left to run. An
unbroken wall of unclimbable rock stretched both ways from Will's perch
in the shadow of the Joshua tree's limbs. His pursuers moved relentlessly
nearer.

There was a crack in the rock face behind Will, but nowhere was it
wider than a handbreadth. As the sun climbed above the desert, the protecting shadow of the tree began to shrink. Will leaned against the rock.

For the first time all night, he faced the wind and gravel as it pelted his cheeks. In between breaths he prayed for a way out, prayed that all his efforts had not been wasted, that somehow, someway there was a way of escape.

And then, as if in answer to his desperate prayer, the veil of dust and sand howled into a blinding storm, drawing a thick dark curtain between Will and his pursuers.

Ten years of trapping had brought him to this moment. Ten years in search of fortune. Ten years since the mountain men had come east to the trading post of his uncle with their stories of the high lonesome—stories that had caused the young Will Reed to lie awake at night and dream.

He had been a young colt when he left Vicksburg, lean, gawky, but full of promise. The years had added bone, muscle strength and the sinew of endurance. Two dozen trips west with men like Jedidiah Smith and Jim Bridger had given him wisdom in the ways of the harsh and beautiful land. Two years among the Cherokees had made him more Indian than some Indians.

Will had never returned to Vicksburg, though he had never made his fortune or found his promised land. The restless spirit his uncle had cursed had brought him to this moment when all that separated him from death was a shifting curtain of sand.

He covered his face with his red kerchief and pulled his buckskin coat close around him. Turning his back to the wind, he let the hide clothing bear the brunt of the stinging grit. Like a lean brush wolf, he curled his body into a crease of the rock face and hoped that the storm that had saved him would not now suck the breath from his burning lungs.

2

THE EAST WIND swirled dust around the feet of Don Jose Dominguez as he stood in the hall of his hacienda. He stared at it morosely, then stomped his boots as if he could scare the dust away like he would a mouse.

He had forgotten that his new boots were too small even on his rather small feet. Stomping sent a wave of pain through already pinched toes. Characteristically, Dominguez swore at the bootmaker, but would not stoop to remove the offending articles. He also swore at his Indian housekeeper, although the dirt now dancing in the air around his head had come into the hallway when he pitched his filthy chapedero leggings onto the tile floor.

The picture of Dominguez's overstuffed body perched atop his tiny feet mirrored the relationship between his ambition and the quality of his soul: one was far too ponderously inflated to be supported well by the small stature of the other.

Dominguez, a bad soldier and a worse officer, was quick to take credit and unable to stand blame. But he had somehow managed to live to retirement. A threat to expose the misdeeds of a relative of higher rank had obtained him a pension in the form of a land grant. The relative, acutely aware of what an embarrassment Don Jose was likely to be, made sure that the rancho being offered was far away, near the dusty presidio of Santa Barbara.

Dominguez proceeded to make life as miserable for his ranch hands as he had for his troops. When the Indians he hired from the mission ran away, it was because they were "shiftless renegades," not because he disciplined them harshly for the smallest infraction. And if they refused to work the hours he demanded, it was because they were lazy, not because he fed them only two scanty helpings of beans and barley a day.

His cattle did not thrive because his land was not the best and there was certainly not enough of it. He whipped a vaquero until the man could not stand for suggesting that he might be overgrazing. It was the subject of land and how much he did not have that drove Don Jose Dominguez into his most frequent diatribe.

"It is the law!" stormed Dominguez. "It was supposed to happen ten years ago and more. Governor Figueroa is a weakling and a fool."

"Calm yourself, my son," soothed the short priest, Father Quintana. "Figueroa is a good Catholic and respects the church—"

"Figueroa is supposed to uphold the law. And the law says the missions are to be secularized and the land turned over to the Indians."

"But the heads of my order do not believe that the neophytes are ready to manage their own land," argued the priest.

This last comment brought a snort of derision from the bull-like nostrils of Dominguez. His barrel chest swung around with such momentum that the little father flinched in fear of being knocked over.

"Of course they cannot manage their affairs. The mission lands should belong to us, the soldiers who fought for it. So should the mission Indians. We need them to work the land." Dominguez's eyes narrowed and he peered down at the priest with suspicion. "Whose side are you on, Father?"

"Yours of course, I assure you," pledged Quintana, his open hands raised to placate the Don's anger. "There is a time coming when the church's lands will be forfeited to the state and redistributed, and I . . ." his voice died away.

The burly ranchero was without mercy and completed the sentence for the priest. "And you want to make certain that you are in line to receive some. Isn't that right, Quintana?"

"My order is headed by fine men. But they would actually *insist* on giving all the land to the Indians. Can you imagine? I would become a parish priest, living on the donations of dirty farmers."

"Instead of being a ranchero with a fine home and hundreds of Indios working for you." The thickset Dominguez turned on his thin legs, back toward the window overlooking his front pasture. "And I will be the leader I should be," he observed. Behind him Quintana obediently bobbed his head. "Instead of six thousand acres I should own ten, no twenty . . . even a hundred as much," Dominguez said. "And in the meantime, we will continue to supplement our income, eh, Quintana?" taunted the ranchero.

The little priest stiffened. He had buried much of his conscience, but he hated the reminder of how far he had fallen from his supposed role as pastor and shepherd to the flock of the mission Indians.

"We only ship off to the Sonoran mines those neophytes who prove to be renegades—the ones without remorse for their backsliding or chronic running away," the priest protested.

"And if we encourage their rebellious ways, or 'accidentally' capture a few wild Indios along with the runaways," Dominguez needled, "well, it is just 'God's will.' Isn't that right, Quintana?"

"I have seen no laws being broken," said the grayrobed friar primly.

"Bah! You are blind at very convenient times! A hypocrite of the first water!"

· For three days the warm Santa Ana wind had blown from the east and swept across the foothills of Santa Barbara.

Francesca Rivera y Cruz locked the louvered doors of her balcony and blamed her restlessness on that wind.

"It will wither the wild flowers before they have a chance to grow," she had complained to her father over breakfast just this morning.

Her brother Ricardo accused her of not caring for the health of the flowers at all. "You only care that the schooner of that pirate Billy Easton won't be able to come into the harbor in such a wind. Admit it, Francesca," he teased. "Bolts of cloth and lace handkerchiefs are the reason for your impatience with the Santa Ana."

Perhaps Ricardo is right, she mused when the winds had finally shifted and a cool ocean breeze wafted in from the west.

Throwing open her shutters, she stepped out onto her balcony and breathed deeply of the sweet cool air. The schooner of trader Easton had been spotted off the coast and would no doubt be making anchor in this gentle breeze. But this assurance did not drive away the restlessness in her heart.

She pulled the comb from her shining black hair and let it tumble down over her shoulders. The fingers of the sea breeze touched her face softly and she closed her eyes. What was it, this restlessness? Not the desire for a new dress or a few yards of fabric! What did that matter when there was no man she cared to impress?

White clouds scudded across the bright California sky. In the distance she could see the sea birds playing on the currents of wind. Those familiar sights did not give her peace. She felt the presence of *something* very near. *Nameless and frightening!* Like nothing she'd ever felt before. Yet she longed to learn the name of this fear and know its face.

A whisper of things to come had blown in on the Santa Ana wind and stirred her heart with the warning that nothing would ever be the same.

Captain Alfredo Zuniga believed in his natural superiority. He was born to command, to be recognized as a leader of men. He had been a junior officer in Santa Fe, New Mexico, when Manuel Armijo was the governor of that province.

Zuniga emulated Armijo, who was fond of remarking that "God rules the heavens and Armijo rules the earth." The young officer rapidly gained a reputation as a brave and ruthless Indian fighter.

If Zuniga was admired by his subordinates, he was also feared by them. He had the eyes of a shark; lifeless and deadly. With a small man's resentment of larger statures, he lost no opportunity to prove his superiority by the code "duello."

Zuniga killed men for slight or imagined offenses. He thought nothing of manufacturing offenses to eliminate rivals. One saber duel that ended another man's life was over a bad debt that Zuniga did not intend to pay. On another occasion he had skewered a man in order to possess his woman.

Most soldiers considered California to be a backwater, a dead-end posting, but Zuniga had requested the assignment to Presidio Santa Barbara. Civilized society did not tolerate the likes of Captain Zuniga, and he knew it. He found his heart's desire: a location where he was the only law, accountable to no one but himself.

He had no regard for anything except superior force. It was his way with enemies and women alike. And if he could project a cool detachment, it was only while gauging the opponent's strength, probing for the weakness which was always present somewhere. Once found, he would take full control.

Zuniga never offered to compromise unless at the bottom of the agreement the benefits were all his. It made him very suspicious of compliments.

"Captain Zuniga, you are a fine military man," observed Don Dominguez over a glass of brandy. "You are new here, but you have kept order exceptionally well. Why, I imagine that it is only petty jealousy on the part of your superiors that keeps you from rising to the position you deserve."

Captain Zuniga put down his glass with an audible clink, as if his every action required military precision. He leaned over the mahogany table, his piercing eye above the saber scar on his cheek boring into the ranchero's. "Don Jose," he said in clipped words, "you did not bring me here to compliment me or discuss my career. What is the purpose of this meeting?"

"You are very direct. I like that also." Dominguez offered the crystal decanter to the captain, who shook his head. The ranchero refilled his own glass and sipped it before continuing.

"I intend to own a much larger rancho than I do at present when the mission lands are secularized," began the Don.

"So," said Zuniga abruptly, "what has this to do with me? Figueroa decides when—if ever—it will take place, and his appointee will be in charge of the distribution."

"Just so," agreed Don Jose, "exactly my point. Don't you see that timing is everything? We must be ready to present claims for the newly available land and help the governor make up his mind."

"Why do you say 'we'? I am neither a ranchero nor a confidant of Figueroa."

"But you are ambitious, are you not, my good capitan? You would rise in rank and prestige?"

"And salary," added Zuniga. "I wish to own a fine house and be wealthy. I will not retire with a 'thank you' and a few hectares of land on which to grub out an existence."

"Of course not." Don Jose eyed the thin lips of the smaller man and knew he had judged Zuniga's greed correctly. "Let me pose a question to you: What would Figueroa do if there was a revolt among the neophytes?"

"He would order me to crush it, as was done here in '24."

"And if he were convinced that the padres' mismanagement had caused the revolt, what then?"

Zuniga studied the question for a minute, then smiled. "He would be convinced that it was time to complete the secularization of the missions, but not transfer the property to the Indios."

"Again, just so. And what better person to advise him on the proper distribution of the lands than the military hero who crushed the revolt?"

Captain Zuniga sat back in the finely carved chair, contemplated his glass, and then raised it in salute. "You may count on me," he affirmed.

Don Jose lifted his own glass and touched it to the rim of the captain's. "Your very good health, capitan. I was certain we would see eye to eye on this matter."

3

THE OLD INDIAN did not expect to find the man alive. What the desert covered with a mantle of sandstorm, it most often claimed for its own. Still, there was always a chance that a member of his own tribe, stolen by the Mojaves, had escaped. It had happened before that a woman or a child managed to avoid recapture and find their way back to the valley.

For this reason Falcon had descended farther into the barren landscape than his herb gathering normally took him. His grandson, Blackbird, riding easily on his grandfather's back, scanned the stony face of the cliffs with his sharp, young eyes.

"See, Grandfather, sitting against that rock."

Falcon's eyes followed the line of his grandson's thin brown arm and pointing finger. A figure in scuffed and dirty buckskins was resting against the shady side of a boulder. The knees were drawn up and a head could be seen lolling back on the curved surface of the stone.

"Stay here, Blackbird," said Falcon, setting the boy down. He added sternly, "Don't follow me unless I tell you to come."

Falcon approached the reclining form cautiously. He studied the man from a dozen feet away. What he saw was a powerfully built man with dark red hair and beard. The man's eyes, though closed, appeared sunken into his head and the skin over his cheekbones was stretched tight.

It was several minutes before Falcon detected the faint flutter of breath in the man's chest. He unslung his doeskin water bottle from around his neck and untied the rawhide thong that closed its neck.

Cupping his palm beneath the man's mouth, Falcon carefully poured a small amount of the precious fluid into his hand. At first the unconscious man seemed insensible to the moisture presented to his lips. In another moment the lips began to work, sucking the drips from Falcon's palm.

Falcon added another small amount of water to his hand, and the man drank it greedily. Strong throat muscles worked as if his gullet were trying to reach out and grasp the source of the moisture.

Falcon poured another handful of water, watching the opening of the container carefully as he did so. When he looked back at the man's face, Falcon was startled to find the eyes open and staring into his.

He controlled himself with difficulty, fighting the instinct to jump back. "Ojos verdes," he murmured softly, giving the Spanish for *green eyes.* Falcon's own language had no reference to eye color, since none of his people had any other shade than brown.

Will looked into the clear brown eyes of Falcon and read there concern and some confusion, but no animosity.

Will gestured toward the water sack as a plea for another drink. Falcon presented it without hesitation, letting Will drink his fill.

"Thank you," gasped Will, when he had finished swallowing half the bag's contents. "Thank you," he repeated, nodding his head and handing the water sack back.

"Español?" asked Falcon with a questioning tone to his voice.

"No, not Spanish," answered Will. "American."

"A-mare-can. Smit. A-mare-can."

Will shook his head to indicate that his fuddled brain did not comprehend. When Falcon extended the drinking sack again, Will gladly accepted and took another long swallow.

Falcon tried again to communicate his understanding of the word American. "Smit," he intoned.

Something clicked in Will's memory then, something he had carried since the trappers' rendezvous when Jedidiah Smith had shared his tales of California.

"Smith? You mean Jedidiah Smith?"

Falcon nodded, smiling, his prominent nose bobbing up and down. "Smit, yes. Trap-per."

"A trapper. Yes, that's what I am," agreed Will, pointing to his chest.

Both men sat in silent appreciation of their first clear communication. Then the old Indian seemed to decide something. He turned his head and made a short, birdlike sound. A moment later a small, round-eyed boy wearing only a breech clout stood beside the old man. He gazed at Will with frank curiosity and Will appraised them both with the same interest.

The child appeared to be eight or nine years old. His shoulder length hair was parted in the middle, and a headband of woven reeds braided with blackbird feathers encircled his head. He wore two strings of tiny round sea shells around his neck. His frame was small and skin color much darker than that of the desert Indians from whom Will had fled.

Will's eyes lingered on the shell necklace. Smith had spoken of Indians beyond the great Sierra mountains who used shells as money. These two must be far from home if that was the case.

The old man was unsmiling. Also dark and of small stature, he, too, wore a choker of larger shells around his withered neck. Falcon-feather ear ornaments hung to his shoulders. His headband was made from the down of an eagle. He had a deep scar on his upper left arm. *Probably the wound of an arrow,* Will thought. A longer scar across his left ribs had been made by a knife. The Indian lifted his chin and put a hand proudly on the shoulder of the young one.

"Chock," he said, then he touched the blackbird feathers of the boy's headband.

Chock sounded like the call of a blackbird. There was no mistaking the fact that the Indian boy's name was *Blackbird.*

Will pointed skyward and then back to the child. "Blackbird," he said the word in his own tongue. Then, "Chock."

The mouth of the old man twitched slightly as if this immediate understanding on the part of the white trapper pleased him. It did not surprise him, however.

Now he touched the falcon feather at his ear, then his own chest. "Limik," he intoned.

So the old one was called Falcon, a name of honor. Will raised his hand in the air and brought it down with the swiftness of a falcon falling upon its prey. "Falcon," he said, and then he repeated the Indian word as well. "Limik."

Will was pleased that the language of these Indians would be easy to master. Words seemed to take on the sound of the objects they labeled. The cry of a falcon did, in fact, sound very close to the name, *Limik.*

Now it was Will's turn, "Will Reed." He reached out to lay his finger against the child's reed headband. *"Reed,"* he repeated as little Blackbird ducked away from his touch.

Falcon grabbed the child by the arm and scowled at him. He pulled off the headband. *"Reed,"* he repeated. *"Español, Tule."*

Tule was indeed the Spanish word for Reed! So the old man understood some Spanish! "Si!" Will cried with relief. At least simple communication would not be a problem. Were they mission Indians far from the California padres? Will had only heard about such folk from the handful of trappers who had actually been there. These people with their shell necklaces and dark skin; were they from the ocean called Pacific?

Will was not alone in his relief. Both Blackbird and Falcon grinned as Will continued in Spanish, "Are you from California? Mission Indians?"

"No," Falcon put an arm protectively around Blackbird. "In Español we are known as Tulereños."

"People of the Reeds?"

"Si," Falcon nodded. "We are a free people. The reed people. Not mission Indians."

Will had heard from the staunch Methodist, Smith, of the proud tribes of California who refused the protection of the mission fathers. For over fifty years the Spanish missions had clung tenaciously to the coast line of the fabled western land, but seldom did anyone of white blood venture into the vast interior valley with its great waterways and thick reeds. Those Indians who ran from the Catholic missions fled to the tules. Fifty years of runaways had been enough time for the Spanish language to come in bits and pieces even to Indians like these, Will knew.

"What do you call yourselves? In your own language?"

Falcon's chest puffed out and he shook back his long graying hair. "We are *Yokuts.*"

"Yokuts," Will repeated the word once, and then again.

This again pleased Falcon. It was a sign of respect for this dusty white man to know there was a difference between the name the Spanish had given his people and the one they had always carried. It was a good thing, his expression seemed to say, that they had come in search of the one who ran from the dreaded Mojaves.

The headman of the Reed People gestured for Blackbird to produce a buckskin stuff-sack from around his neck. Reaching in he withdrew three pieces of jerked venison which the three companions gnawed on in thoughtful silence.

His strength returning, Will was able to get to his feet. He picked up the knife. The American saw both Yokuts glance at the weapon.

"Mojaves attacked my . . ." he groped for a word. "My group, my tribe."

Falcon let out a long hissing noise that his grandson mimicked an instant later. "Mojaves fight Yokuts too."

The three formed into a line and set off toward the west. At six feet three, Will towered over Falcon's five feet six. Blackbird tried to march as stoically as his grandfather, but kept sneaking sly glances over his shoulder at the red-haired giant now following behind.

Their path wound up through a rocky ravine. The creosote brush, boulders and Joshua trees looked no different to Will than countless other dry washes he had explored without result. The ground was parched and dusty.

When they returned into a canyon almost hidden from the desert floor by a low range of hills, Will could see that they were following a dry creek bed. Its meandering course led them to ever-higher elevations, where an occasional Yucca palm bloomed on the rubble-strewn slopes. The composition of the hillside changed to more rock and less dust, its uniform brown color giving way to streaks of red and orange.

The Indians showed no signs of weariness, but Falcon's consideration of Will was such that they paused every mile to let him lean heavily on a walking stick.

Presently, they filed into a cliff-sided arroyo where the climbing was even steeper. This passage soon gave way to a narrow grassy valley, dotted with oak trees. At the head of the valley the group paused and Falcon offered its name, "Te-ha-cha-pi." Was this the place Jedidiah Smith had told Will about as they shared the warmth of a campfire?

Clouds had piled up against the line of mountain peaks surrounding the little valley. As the three made another descent, again their path beside a trickling brook and the oak-tree-covered hillsides gave proof of how much moisture was trapped by the encircling summits.

Denser growths of oak trees appeared and Will began to spot larger numbers of animals. He saw a lumbering bear, momentarily glimpsed retreating over a ridge, and a herd of pronghorns flung up their heads in uniform alarm. A corkscrew motion of their tails and half-a-hundred white rumps disappeared into a side canyon. The land was thick with game and Will remembered the awe of Smith's voice when he had spoken of it.

The little procession stopped again on a rounded grassy knoll. Will made his way up from the end of the line to stand beside Falcon and Blackbird. He expected to see a winding descent to another brushy canyon.

Just as Will lifted his eyes to the west, a shaft of sunlight broke through the cloud cover. "Trawlawwin," gestured Falcon, swinging his arm in an arc that took in all the view from south to north. "In Español, San Joaquin."

Before Will lay the broadest expanse of green valley he had ever seen. From its southern terminus at the Tehachapis, Will looked west across to the distant range of coastal mountains. To the northwest as far as he could see was the unbroken sweep of a vast plain stretching onward until grayish-white clouds and rolling emerald vistas merged. *"The Promised Land,"* Jed Smith had called it. *"Or maybe a glimpse of what heaven looks like!"*

Beams of light performed a show for Will, dazzling his vision with scene upon scene of startling beauty. Here a patch of brilliant orange flowers painted a broad splash of color on a verdant hillside. The next ray of sun roved over fields of wild oats. Just-forming heads swayed with the rush of breeze like vibrant waves breaking against the rust-colored rocks. Beyond a chorus of nodding purple blossoms and past marching ranks of yellow blooms, the winding silver ribbon of a great river flashed a momentarily brilliant reflection. Following the river's course backward, red-helmeted flowers drew Will's eyes up to the mountains on his left hand. There the sunlight revealed that part of what he had taken for clouds was really a fringing mantle of snow lingering on the highest peaks.

"It's beautiful," he exclaimed. "A crazy quilt of color made by God Almighty." He quoted the phrase Smith spoke when he described this place. Indeed, there were no adequate words for it.

The Yokuts may not have understood all his words, but they had no trouble deciphering his feelings. In a tone of awe undiminished by years of repeating the experience, Falcon murmured, "We say tish-um-yu, ah, flower-blooming-time."

It was beautiful, yes. The kind of vision that made a man's heart ache, and yet . . . There were other things about this land that Will had heard. Tales of tragedy and brutality. When Jedidiah had described it, he had pulled out his well-worn Bible and issued this warning to the men who sat enraptured by his tale of the land beyond the Sierras: *"Beyond what a man can imagine, the place is. I cried out to God that I had found Eden once again in that great valley."* And then his eyes had locked on Will, as though he saw something in Will's future. *"Remember son, this warning . . . Even Eden had the serpent. It was in a place of perfect beauty that man brought Death to us all. . . ."*

4

"**Y**OU ARE MOST welcome, señoras y señoritas." Billy Easton swept off his straw hat. Bending over his white pantaloons and bare feet, he made a "leg" that was worthy of a French courtier.

The ladies coming on board the schooner-rigged vessel *Paratus* twittered behind their fans. All about the deck were spread the trade goods with which the *Paratus* was loaded: silks and laces from China, otter pelts from the Russians of northern California, exotic spices from Pacific islands with unpronounceable names.

Across one quarter mile of placid water from the schooner lay the presidio of Santa Barbara. The white-washed adobe walls and red tile roofs stood out clearly against the dark green hillsides. Further inland, but just as prominently in view, was the mission. The settlement bustled with activity on this fine spring afternoon and it was clear that all was well in the Mexican province of California.

Like a conjuror opening his program, Easton produced a silk handkerchief from out of nowhere and presented it to Francesca Rivera y Cruz. "A gift, so that we may bargain as friends, sweet lady."

Easton's courtesy earned him a blushing smile from Francesca, but a swat on the arm with a folded fan from her chaperon, Doña Eulalia.

"Aunt, you must apologize to Señor Easton," demanded Francesca, a slender young woman with darting black eyes and creamy pale skin. "He was only being polite."

"He should not be so forward," announced Doña Eulalia loudly, to the amusement of Easton's crew. "And you should not be so brash as to accept a gift from this, this . . ." Words failed the good aunt, but the word *pirate* came to everyone's mind, including Easton's.

It was an image he cultivated. Easton had long before discovered that while men bargained for hides and tallow with dour faces and closely watched ledgers, women preferred romance with their trade goods. From the gold ring in his ear lobe to the long hair pulled straight back from his face and gathered in another gold ring at the back of his neck, Easton looked the part of a privateer.

The truth was almost as fanciful. The son of a Yankee whaling skipper and his Hawaiian wahine wife, Easton had inherited his father's love of the sea and his mother's rich brown skin and easy smile. He had shipped with his father at the age of eight as a cabin boy and been first mate of a trading schooner at eighteen.

Now a muscular and solid five-foot-ten-inch man of thirty-five, Billy Easton sold his wares—whether "pirated" or bargained fair and square—up and down the coast of Spanish California, charming ladies of all ages.

He produced another silk handkerchief with a flourish. "A thousand pardons, most excellent Doña Eulalia. I meant no offense. Naturally I wished to offer a sample of my humble goods, poor and unworthy though they are, in comparison to such noble beauty as you yourself possess."

Now it was the aunt's turn to blush, which she tried to hide behind the ever-present fan. With a coyness not exactly suited to her age, she simpered, "You are quite forgiven, señor. I am most protective of my niece and sometimes speak abruptly."

"Understandable and commendable," replied Easton, the barest hint of a smile escaping below his drooping moustache. Extending his arm in its billowing silk sleeve, he offered, "Will you honor me by allowing me to escort you on a tour of my wares?"

Completely taken in by Easton's charm, Doña Eulalia quite graciously accepted the invitation.

5

WILL AND THE Yokuts made a cold camp that first night, high above the rim of Eden. The valley floor grew dusky purple in the twilight and fingers of smoke rose skyward, marking widely scattered Indian villages below. Falcon pointed to a distant plume. "Our village," he said.

The boy chirped, "They thought we would return tonight. They will think the West has taken us." At this remark, the old man whirled as if to strike the child. But Blackbird was far too fast, dodging and scrambling across the boulder out of reach. He had broken some taboo, Will guessed. The Mojave Indian raiders were east of the valley. And yet was there something in the West more terrifying to the People of the Reeds?

Will did not ask the meaning of this comment. He understood the ways of the Indian. Some things were only spoken of in hushed and reverent tones in the shadowy steam of the village sweat house. Two years of living among the Cherokee nation had taught Will not to ask questions but to simply live and wait. The answers inevitably came in their own time.

Tonight he did not question the wisdom of the fireless camp. They were still on the fringe of territory where the Mojave raiders might track them. It would be foolish to offer the enemy proof that they remained within reach of attack. And yet, it was the distant western mountains that the old man scanned now. He stood for a long time on the flat table of a boulder, which jutted out from the side of the mountain. Only when the last purple silhouettes were lost in darkness did he finally turn away.

Falcon tossed a rabbitskin cloak to Will and then gently took the remorseful boy under his arm. The three ate jerked meat in silence, and then Blackbird and Falcon curled up together beneath the old man's cloak to ward off the chill of the Sierra night.

Will's back was against the rough hide of the boulder that had been warmed through the night by his body heat. It now returned the warmth to him. The predawn air was sharp beyond the rabbitskin cloak. Will opened his eyes, surprised to see that the old Indian had resumed his post on the rugged granite table. He had left his cloak spread over the sleeping child, and now, dressed only in his breech clout, he searched the western horizon for sign of the talking smoke. He seemed undaunted by the chill, and yet his senses were so keen, it was as if he heard Will open his eyes. Turning away from the west, he strode quickly back the two dozen paces to where Blackbird slept.

Without a word, he yanked the warm cloak from the boy who sat up and then jumped to his feet in one movement. Will stood as well and rolled up his covering, tossing it to the old man.

"We have far to go," said Falcon. "We will eat as we journey."

The light of the sun touched the distant western mountain peaks before it seeped into the valley floor. The two Indians moved down the rugged trail like deer. Quick and agile, the old one moved with the same untiring endurance as the boy. It was plain to Will that the slow pace of yesterday's hike had been in consideration of the white man they traveled with. Now, after a night of rest, it was expected that Will would keep pace. His long stride and sure step did not slow them down.

The swiftness with which they covered the ground did not conceal the details of the country Jedediah had told him about. Men had doubted the tales of wonder as they listened, but now Will knew his trapper friend had reported truthfully.

The rest of the trek to the Yokut encampment was one of vision upon vision and wonder upon wonder. Coveys of quail scurried at the walkers' approach, and no fewer than two hundred quail topknots bobbed into the gooseberry thickets with every flock they scattered.

Ground squirrel mounds extending for literal acres spoke of vast underground rodent cities. Overhead, redtailed hawks dived and soared.

"Swoop, swoop," pointed out Blackbird, indicating the redtails.

"Yes, they are swooping," responded Will.

"No, no. No swoo-ping. Swoop, swoop," insisted Blackbird.

Will gathered that what he had taken for an English expression describing the hawk's hunting motion was actually the Yokut name for the bird.

A muted bugling sound echoed up from the swampy area just ahead of their path. Two dozen thick-bodied elk moved from their grazing with an unhurried, deliberate motion. When the herd had put the marsh between themselves and the humans, they stood gazing back at the intruders.

It seemed impossible to Will that Jedediah's serpent could have found this Eden.

In the moist soil of the valley floor, the height of the grasses increased. Now the wild grain stalks waved over the flowers, hiding the brilliant colors from view. A vagrant wind parted the stalks, allowing a flash of crimson to come to Will's eyes, then concealing it again. A moment later and another stray breeze uncovered an expanse of orange, and so on, until it seemed that the swirling puffs of air were playing a guessing game with Will: What color would be revealed next?

It was late afternoon when they came to the banks of a swiftly flowing stream and turned to follow its course northeastward again toward the mountains. For the first time since descending the pass, they followed a recognizably human trail. And for the first time, Will felt that he and his two companions were not the first people to see this paradise.

The breeze carried the faint odor of smoke to Will's nostrils and with it he caught the welcome aroma of roasting meat. Blackbird now broke from his place in the middle of the march, running ahead to announce their return.

Before the village came into view, Will could hear Blackbird's excited chatter. The scout guessed that a proclamation of the white man's arrival was something the small boy wanted particular credit for.

Around one more bend of the river and they entered the encampment. A semicircle of reed huts surrounded a clearing with a cooking fire in its center. Two small children squealed and ran to hide behind a young woman who was working near the water's edge.

An older woman was tending the meat Will had smelled. Green willow poles were fixed in the ground around the cooking fire. To each stick was tied a rabbit carcass, and the weight of the meat pulled the stick down to the perfect roasting height above the fire.

In front of one of the huts, a ponderously heavy man was chipping arrow points on a buckskin ground cloth. He rose slowly to his feet, leaving his tools and obsidian rocks on the ground.

When the squealing children had been shushed, Will could tell that he was being introduced. He heard Falcon repeat his name and the designation "A-mare-can." The rest of the speech was not understandable, but must have related the circumstances of his rescue.

But the introduction was short-lived. A sharp shout from across the stream drew everyone's attention. A Yokut man, a hunter about Will's age, came out of the screen of willows directly opposite the camp and forded the creek.

He called Falcon's name. The warrior sounded excited about something, waving his arms and pointing back the way he had come.

Falcon left Will's side to join the newcomer. The heavy man who left his toolmaking entered the discussion also. Falcon's voice was quiet and questioning, the other two loud and angry.

Will wondered if the Mojaves had raided the valley ahead of his arrival. Maybe that was what this unsettling report was about.

The women and children were silent and staring. No one paid any attention to Will at all. He stood awkwardly at the edge of the encampment, waiting for the noisy tirade to subside.

The toolmaker seemed to remember Will first. He stretched out a thick, muscled arm and leveled a calloused finger at Will's face. The tone of his

BROCK & BODIE THOENE

words was accusing and he was obviously blaming Will for whatever evil had just happened.

The toolmaker repeated the gesture, then accompanied it with a demanding slam of his fist into his hardened palm. Falcon's reply was a sudden emphatic cutting motion of his hand. In any language it meant "Enough!"

Falcon pivoted sharply on his heel and returned to the American. It seemed that now the entire camp was drawn up in a line confronting Will.

The old Indian explained, "Two hunters left our camp on the same day that I went east. They have not returned. That man, Coyote, says he followed their trail to the River of Swift Water, but no farther. He returned to bring word."

"Meho, the toolmaker, thinks you are the cause," Falcon added, "but he feels hate deep in his heart since his wife was taken by the West."

"I will help track the missing men," offered Will. He shook off Falcon's refusal. "I owe your people a debt and Meho must be shown how I will repay."

An hour later, Will was back at his profession—tracking. Falcon accompanied him, and the other two men went also, but they were not happy about Will's presence. The toolmaker, Meho, was openly angry, scowling at the scout whenever their eyes met. The other man was stoic but clearly suspicious. Each time Will looked in Coyote's direction, he found the warrior already watching him.

The tracks of the two missing hunters were not obvious, but clear enough to those who knew what to look for. A moccasined footprint showed occasionally in the dust. One of the two men was considerably larger than the other, as Will could tell from the greater length of his stride. The shorter man walked with a limp. His right foot made an indistinct track, as if he could not press the heel all the way down.

The trail ended abruptly at the bank of a river that was indeed swift flowing. Grass growing along the edges of the watercourse was stretched out flat against the bank by its force. When Will spotted a twig in the current, he got only a brief glimpse before it completely disappeared.

The two warriors tied their bows and foxskin pouches of arrow points into compact bundles, which they slung over their backs. Both men plunged into the water, pushing hard for the opposite shore. Falcon turned to the scout. "Do you swim, Will Reed?"

When Will responded that he did, the old man replied, "Good. Then we will not need to carry you."

The water was bitterly cold, and the current so powerful, that Will could make no headway against it. He wasted no time fighting it, but took a long angle toward a bend of the river downstream and let the water carry him there.

Will was the last to cross. The others had already restrung their bows and were prepared to continue the search. The big man, Meho, sneered at Will and said something contemptuous to Coyote.

A brief search of the shore located the spot where the two hunters had emerged from the river. Several tracks in the mud of the bank were evident. Will spotted a flint arrowpoint under a bush where it must have fallen from the hunter's pouch.

The three Yokuts became noticeably tense. The river seemed to mark a boundary between known and unknown, between safety and danger. There was no obvious sign of a greater hazard nor any indication that enemies had been near the two missing men. Still, Will scanned the rolling hills that marched along beside them. He kept a close eye on the treetops ahead for any unusual flights of birds that might betray the presence of others.

The trail was proving harder to follow now. It was obvious the two men had been hunting. They had separated and were travelling about one hundred yards apart. Will and Falcon were following the one with the limp. In about a mile, the tracks showed that the man had turned aside to stand on a rocky outcropping and survey the landscape.

When he did the same, Will noted a swampy area of thick grass just beyond a screen of elderberry bushes. It was a perfect spot for game, with plenty of cover to approach from behind. Will and Falcon headed that direction.

Will studied the area around the berry bushes till he found what he was seeking. A half moccasin print next to a shallow round depression in the soil showed where the hunter had knelt to take aim.

Looking across the clearing from this vantage point, the scout picked out a likely spot under an oak where he could imagine a deer to have stood. A dark stain on the ground just under the oak confirmed the accuracy of Will's guess. The trail of occasional drops of blood mingled with the curious halting steps of the limping man, and both led to the west.

When the two trackers heard a rustling coming toward them through the brush, they froze in place under the shadow of the oak. Falcon's gnarled hands fitted an arrow with a jagged obsidian point to his bow. He dropped to one knee and drew the bowstring back to his ear.

A moment later the Yokut chief and the white trapper both relaxed. The sound had only been Meho and Coyote. The man with the limp had apparently called his companion to rejoin him in following the wounded deer.

Together the four followed the track that was again plain to read. A vagrant swirl of air reached them. Death was on the breeze; the sick-sweet, metallic odor of decay. The three Indians instinctively fanned out across the trail, their bows at the ready. Will drew his Green River knife and moved from tree to tree, crossing open spaces with a rush, then stopping to look around. Overhead, a flight of vultures spiralled.

Ahead was an oak, seventy feet tall, with a large limb that jutted out a dozen feet off the ground. From this limb hung the bloated carcass of a deer, the deadly shaft of the arrow plainly visible just behind its shoulder.

And underneath the deer was the body of a man. Scavengers had already been at work on the flesh, but the twisted right leg told Will that this had been the man with the limp.

Falcon knelt beside the body, taking a handful of dust from the ground and sprinkling some on the corpse. The rest he poured on his own head. In silent mourning he lifted up his arms toward the sun, let them fall, then lifted them again.

Meho and Coyote stood as sentinels to this grief. They watched the surrounding area, scanning both near and far.

Will continued to search. Not far from the tree, a struggle had taken place, with torn up earth and uprooted plants testifying to its fierceness. Then at last a flattened space, where the uncoiling spirals of orange fiddleneck had been crushed by a man-shaped press. Two long streaks mutely bore witness that the other missing Yokut had been dragged away.

Will followed the drag mark to the edge of a tule swamp, where some horses had been tethered. One of the horses had shied violently, perhaps as an unfamiliar burden was loaded onto its back. The riders had then departed, heading west, skirting the outline of the swamp. There was nothing further to be learned here, Will thought. Or was there? He stopped and puzzled over something. One rider had been mounted on a mare. The position of the hoofprints where the animal had relieved itself made this clear.

But a mare was an unusual choice for a mount. Most riders believed stallions and mares were too much trouble and often unpredictable as saddle animals. Geldings were the usual selection. *Of course,* Will thought, *that logic only applies to riders who have a choice.* Indians thereabouts would have to make do with whatever runaway stock they could catch.

Returning to the place of death, Will found that the body of the dead Yokut had been wrapped in Falcon's rabbitskin cloak. The three Indians were preparing to return to their village.

"Wait," the scout said to Falcon. "The other man is alive. Or at least he was when he was taken. I found where whoever did this mounted up. We can still follow."

"Which way do the tracks lead?" asked Falcon mournfully.

"To the west," reported Will, "and just as plain as day. If we were to—"

Falcon shook his head, but before Will could say any more, Meho jumped between them. He waved his arms and shouted angrily again, then he pushed Will in the chest, hard.

"What is it? What's he saying now?" Will demanded of Falcon, who was trying to grasp Meho's arm. Meho roughly shrugged off the chief's grip and moved toward Will.

"He says it is a trap. He says you are here to lead us right into their clutches. I tell him to stop, not shame us, he . . . ."

Meho was in a blood rage, and like his namesake, the bear, he could not be called off easily. He drew a wicked-looking, curved-blade knife from a deerhide sheath that hung by his side and lunged at Will.

The trapper barely had time to throw himself to the side. The slashing knife missed, but Meho's massive shoulder crashed into Will, knocking him to the ground.

Will rolled completely over and bounced to his feet. His red beard brushed up fragments of wildflowers as he rolled.

The toolmaker rushed in again. This time Will stood his ground and let the anger-blinded man come. The American caught the upraised knife-arm in both hands, and the two stood momentarily locked almost face to face. Will wondered if he had made a mistake, because Meho was immensely strong in his forearms and hands. But before the stout Yokut could force the blade down toward Will, the taller white man used his Mississippi upbringing to good effect.

Will backheeled the Indian, setting him up by yanking the knife hand unexpectedly down, then pushing up suddenly. The off-balanced Meho toppled to the sweep of Will's leg. He fell with the American on top of him and the blade of his own knife pressed across his throat.

"Tell him," gasped Will, "tell him I could kill him now if I wanted to." After Falcon had translated these words, Will continued, "And tell him I am not leading anyone into a trap."

"He understands," agreed Falcon. "You may let him up now, Will Reed. He will fight you no more."

The two men stood up, brushing off the dirt and leaves. Will hesitated, then reversed the knife and extended it handle first toward Meho.

"Now," Will said to Falcon, "let's get after the raiders."

The Yokut chief still shook his head no. "The West has taken him, Will Reed. If we follow, neither our tribe nor yours would ever see us again. Let us go back to camp." He gestured toward the cloaked body lying on the ground. "I have a son to bury."

6

A STEADY STREAM of Indian women flowed uphill toward the mission. Each carried a single heavy adobe-brick building block. A second file returned, but these women were not empty-handed. The downhill stream carried bundles of straw to the mixing pits.

In groups of three, Indian men milled around in mud up to their knees, stamping straw, clay and water together to form the substance known as adobe. Another circuit of laborers piled the mixture into rawhide aprons, which they carried to the waiting wooden forms. There another set of men were smoothing off the blocks, turning bricks over to complete the drying process and stacking completed bricks.

There was no grumbling amongst the workers, but there was no enthusiasm either. For every team of nine workers, the object was to complete seven hundred bricks just as quickly as possible.

"You have gotten these miserios well organized," observed Don Dominguez to Captain Zuniga, "but I still object to your quota system. Letting these wretches quit when they have filled their allotment only makes my workers want to do likewise. I have heard that some groups finish work at midday and are allowed to do nothing all afternoon."

"It is not *my* quota system, as you well know," retorted the officer. "It has been the rule of the mission since these disgraciados were first coaxed into covering their naked bodies. Besides, I have already raised the quota twice, over the objections of Father Sanchez."

Dominguez snorted with derision at the name of the kindly priest. The noise he made startled the palomino horse on which he sat, and his gelding bumped into Zuniga's bay.

The bay reared slightly, and Don Jose's horse sidled away from it, stepping down into one of the adobe mixing pits. Dominguez shouted and swore, turning the confused horse around and around until one of the Indian workers grasped the cheekpiece of the bit and led the horse to firmer footing. The Indian muttered under his breath, "Gauchapin."

Dominguez overheard the phrase and slashed downward with his quirt, striking the man who had just come to his aid on the shoulder. The man actually drew his arms back as if he were about to leap onto the ranchero, but two of his comrades intervened and pulled him away.

"Did you see that impertinent scoundrel?" demanded Dominguez. "He was going to strike me! Zuniga, I want that man hanged! Gauchapin! Spur, he called me! Hang him, do you hear?"

The spectacle of the overweight ranchero having a tantrum while his agitated horse kicked up spatters of mud on the military commander brought all work to a sudden halt.

"Back to work, all of you!" shouted Zuniga. "Julio," he said to the native foreman, "bring that man to my office when you finish work today. That's an order." To the ranchero he observed, "Come, Don Dominguez. I will discipline that rebel personally."

The two rode on toward the shore. Dominguez turned around every few steps to curse and shake his fist at the Indians. Zuniga picked globs of mud from his uniform.

"What's the matter with you?" asked the ranchero petulantly. "We, gente de razón, were insulted! Why didn't you kill him right where he stood?"

"Calm yourself," the captain suggested in a quietly authoritative tone. "Should I kill a valuable worker? *You* of all people should know the *value* of every miscreant soul."

When Dominguez turned at the abrupt change in the quality of the officer's voice, Zuniga continued. "There is an important matter which we are going to discuss."

He gestured out toward where the *Paratus* was anchored in the bay. The ship's tender was coming ashore with some returning customers. "When I was last on board Easton's ship to review his cargo, he asked me about a certain cove a few miles north of here. He wanted to know if I had heard any rumors about any midnight loading of . . ." The rest of the sentence was allowed to flutter away on the sea breeze.

Dominguez froze, sitting very erect in his saddle. "I don't know what you are talking about," he muttered.

"Don't toy with me," threatened the officer coldly. "What you are doing is illegal. We both know that I could have you arrested and sent away in chains."

"But you wouldn't do that. We are partners," whined the ranchero.

"Partners must never have secrets from each other," said Zuniga flatly. "Never again. You should have told me, Don Dominguez. Now your avarice is going to cost you." Cold, black eyes turned fully on the rancher's face like a white shark out in the channel that had selected a seal to devour.

"Agreed! Agreed!" said Dominguez too eagerly. "I was going to tell you everything. Really. You must come to my hacienda and we can review the details. But what about Easton? How much does he know?" The ranchero was anxious to change the subject.

"Easton is not a problem. I am the only law that matters here, remember? I will take care of him if it becomes necessary," concluded the captain. Don Dominguez felt a shiver run down his neck as he heard these words.

The small boat from the *Paratus* was coming through the surf. Two sailors were rowing strongly, while the mate of the *Paratus* managed the tiller to keep the boat square to the waves. Timing the run perfectly, the boat shot forward on the mate's command and beached itself on the white sand.

The two caballeros watched as a group of women were assisted from the boat. Several bundles of their purchases were passed to them. The ladies waved cheerfully to the sailors who turned the tender around and floated it out to shove off. One of the women, Dominguez noted, was the beautiful daughter of Don Pedro Rivera y Cruz.

He turned to point her out to Zuniga, but found the officer already staring at Francesca. He continued staring as the group of women came up the beach and passed near them, the eyes of the shark still evident.

"Good day to you, ladies," called out Dominguez cheerfully. A polite murmur of greetings replied, except from Francesca, who walked with her eyes on the sand. She had seen his companion's hungry stare.

When they had passed, Dominguez remarked to Zuniga, "I do not think she cares for the way you look at her."

"All women desire a man's mastery," said Zuniga with a shrug. "Some conquests take longer than others, that is all. She will be mine."

"It would not be well to let her father hear you say that," observed the ranchero. "He would horsewhip you. Besides," continued Don Dominguez, "I now know how to cement our partnership."

7

THE CRACKLE OF the flames rising above the tule-thatched hut was deafening. A thick trunk of dense gray smoke sprouted from the fire like a seed germinating into a tree of pointless destruction.

No one made any attempt to quench the inferno. To prevent the fire from spreading, those Yokuts who lived on either side of the dead man's dwelling had taken the precaution of wetting down their homes, but that was all.

Will had seen this practice before. Other tribes also burned the homes of their dead. There was a finality, an absoluteness, to the end of Indian life that Will found unsettling.

As soon as the pyre was ignited and the first tendrils of smoke twisted skyward, the other Yokuts turned away. In fact, they did everything to make life appear as normal as possible. An ancient crone directed the grinding and leaching of acorn meal. Two hunters prepared to leave the camp in search of game. Only Will and Blackbird stood silently watching the hut being consumed.

In contrast to the morning's studied nonchalance, the dance for the dead had lasted the entire preceding night. For hours on end the women of the tribe jumped and swayed around a campfire, while the men chanted a funeral dirge over and over. The night was punctuated by the beating of log drums until all the listeners felt their breath and heartbeat become one with the rhythm. After hours of the monotonous pounding, Will noticed that even a temporary silence caused him to be filled with a sense of anxiety and foreboding.

Gifts of food, clothing, baskets and tools were all brought to the funeral ceremony, but not for the comfort of the bereaved family. Instead, as each dancer reached exhaustion, the gifts were tossed onto the blazing fire.

But now, the morning after, the savage excitement of the ceremony had worn off and was replaced by a blank numbness compounded by weariness. Blackbird stared into the dancing flames as the charred ribs of the willow framework crumpled into what had been the interior of his home.

Will walked up to the silent boy and put his hands on the thin shoulders. Blackbird's hands flew up to his face and small clenched fists ground into his eyesockets.

"I am not crying," insisted the child, though Will had asked no question. "It is the smoke that makes the water come from my eyes."

The scout said nothing, just stood quietly with his resting hands offering the comfort of a touch. Will was remembering himself as a young, red-haired boy with freckles, about Blackbird's age. A grieving child standing beside two mounds of earth back in the red clay hills of Tennessee.

The trapper shook his head, as if to make the image go away, but the hollow, empty ache remained. Will knew that the boy would be well cared for by his grandfather, but that would not lessen the anguish of missing both his murdered father and the mother who had died before.

Here was Eden, truly, but it was an Eden after Adam's fall. All the freedom to live, to hunt, to fish, to swim came to lie in the ashes of the now-smoldering hut. Evil walked in this land, and it brought death.

What was worse, Will knew that these people had no clear picture of a life beyond this patch of earth. Many Indians spoke in vague terms of a

Happy Western Land, but they did not know where it was or how to reach it. Sometimes their stories told that the beyond was a great forest in which a soul might wander forever without rest.

The Yokuts danced and chanted themselves to numbness. They tried as quickly as possible to put the reminders of a missing loved one behind them. It was their way of avoiding the awful question, "After this life, what?"

"Father," the boy suddenly cried. "Do not get off the path!"

Several adult Yokuts cast disapproving looks at Blackbird's show of grief. An elderly woman said, "Shh! Enough!"

"Do not get off the path," the boy repeated, unheeding. "It may be dark there. There may be thorn bushes and steep cliffs. If you fall from the path, how will you find it again?"

Will sat beside Blackbird and slipped an arm around the boy's shoulders. "I am not old enough," the boy exclaimed, "to know how to track well. How can I learn to walk where the trail is dim and unknown?"

The red-bearded scout spoke in a quiet voice, yet his words echoed with strength in Blackbird's hollow-feeling heart. "I know the path," he said, "—that is, I know the One who *is* the path."

"What do you mean?" asked the boy.

"Blackbird, all men everywhere are fearful about what lies beyond this life. We would *have* to be afraid of it, except for this fact: God, the one you call the Great Spirit, sent his son Jesus to scout the trail for us. You see, he not only took a punishment of death in place of us, but he came to life again, and he says he will show us how to walk beyond this life."

"Tell me some more about this man! He must be the greatest tracker who ever lived."

"And much more," the scout replied. "He will blaze a trail for you in this life also, if you will let him."

Will turned Blackbird to face him. "Listen. I need your help as well," he said.

The Indian boy rubbed his eyes again, then peeped out past one. "What do you mean?"

"I am going to stay with your people for a time," answered Will. "But I am ignorant of your ways. I need someone to teach me, to show me how a proper Yokut acts."

The boy straightened up and squared his shoulders. "I am the grandson of a chief. My fa . . ." his voice faltered. "*I* will be chief someday. I will teach you so you need not be ashamed."

The stillness of a soft, spring afternoon was interrupted by a messenger from another camp upstream. The man, Badger by name, brought news that a party of Mojaves had come over the pass from the desert. Badger had been surrounded while hunting, but had been allowed to go free in order to bring word that the Mojaves wanted a parley.

"What does it mean?" asked Will.

"Who can say?" shrugged Falcon. "The Mojaves raid the valley, robbing and killing. If they want to talk, they must want something that they cannot easily get by stealing."

The smoldering cooking fire was refueled. When it was blazing, a bundle of water-soaked reeds was placed on top to send up a thick column of white smoke that signaled the Mojaves to come down into the camp.

No more sound than the barest rustle of wind among dry leaves preceded the arrival of the desert people. Six warriors and a leader glided into Falcon's village under the watchful eyes of a dozen Yokut men. The women and children were out of sight, hiding in the tule huts.

Will stood inside the doorway of the hut he shared with Falcon and Blackbird. No one had asked him to help guard the camp, but no one had told him to stay away either. He felt a stirring at the back of his neck when the Mojaves came into view.

The desert tribesmen were taller than most of the Yokut men Will had seen. Their complexions were several shades lighter than the valley people, as if designed to blend easily into the sands of their home. They wore their hair long, down even below their shoulders. Unlike the Yokuts, who went barefoot or wore buckskin moccasins, the Mojaves wore sandals made of woven Yucca fibers.

The faces of the desert warriors were etched with ferocity and deep scowls. For men who supposedly had come to talk, Will noted that they had not come emptyhanded. Each had a short bow made of willow branches, and at his side was a short wooden club, shaped like a sickle with a round handle on one end and a flattened killing point on the other.

The leader of the Mojaves wasted no time on ceremony. He addressed Falcon in words unknown to Will, but conveying a tone of angry demands. His speech was accompanied by vigorous gestures to the south and the west, then with an exaggerated show of surprise toward the east.

The Mojave held up all ten of his fingers and displayed them to Falcon three times. Then, as if to prove a point, he reached into a rabbitskin pouch hanging around his neck and withdrew a knife. He flipped the weapon so that it stuck quivering in the ground between them.

Will could not help starting forward in horror—the knife standing upright in the soil of the Yokut village was a twin to the one Will had taken from Forchet.

As Will moved from the shadowed doorway of the hut, the Mojave leader took notice of the white man for the first time. The desert warrior first stared at him, then bent quickly and retrieved the knife from the ground.

Will pulled the other blade from his belt and advanced with coldly set anger toward the Mojave. The other desert Indians had nocked arrows to bowstrings, an action mirrored by the Yokut warriors. One wrong move and a fully pitched battle would break out.

Falcon shouted a command for Will to stop where he was. Without turning his back on the Mojave, Falcon continued calling out instructions.

"You will not come one step closer," Falcon ordered the angry scout. "You must put up your knife at once. You are not permitted to disturb the parley in this way."

"Ask him where he got the Green River knife," Will replied.

"He has already said he took it from a Mexican chief whose men attacked their village. He came here to propose that we join them in fighting against the Mexicans."

Will answered quietly, but his muscles were as tense as a coiled spring. "The truth is, he took that from Beckwith, another American and a friend of mine, after the Mojaves ambushed us without any reason!"

The two chiefs spoke together again. Turning toward Will, Falcon said, "Sihuarro says you were spying for the Mexicans and that thirty of you were killed attacking his people."

With icy calm Will responded, "There were only twelve of us and we never saw them till they jumped us. We traded peacefully with every tribe we met on the trail till these scorpions attacked. Tell him I said that."

"Do you know what may happen if I return your words to Sihuarro? If he chooses, he may fight you here and now to prove you have insulted him."

"Let her rip," replied Will calmly.

Falcon spoke to the Yokut guards, telling them to carefully let the tension off their bowstrings while the Mojaves did the same. Then, the Yokut headman said one word to Sihuarro, very quietly but very distinctly. It was the Mojave word for *liar*.

What followed was a smear of movement across what had been a painted scene. Sihuarro shifted the knife to his left hand and raised his killing stick with his right.

There was a whirring sound like an angry bee. Catching a glimpse of a blurred threat spinning toward his head, Will lifted his left arm to shield his face and nearly was too late: The killing stick smashed into his forearm, cutting a long shallow arc of a wound, then nicked his ear as it completed its murderous path.

Will pressed his injured arm against his chest and prayed that its instantly total numbness would quickly go away. From the corners of his vision he saw that the two opposing lines of warriors had closed into a circle around the fight. Then all his attention was focused on Sihuarro who rushed toward him brandishing the knife overhead. The Mojave intended to end the fight quickly with a killing stroke.

But the speed of the attack was his undoing. With a presence of mind born more of instinct than conscious thought, Will waited until Sihuarro was almost on him, then ducked under the descending blade. The trapper put his shoulder into the Indian's midsection and turned the attacker's momentum to his advantage.

With the same stretch and leverage used to hoist a hundred-weight of beaver pelts, Will propelled Sihuarro up and over his back. The Indian landed with a jarring thud, but rolled into a ball and jumped up again to face Will.

Circling each other warily, the opponents looked for an opportunity to strike. Blood from the cut on Will's arm dripped from his elbow onto the dark earth. Neither fighter looked up when a condor soaring overhead momentarily shadowed the scene. Again it was Sihuarro who could not wait, springing toward Will. This time the moment was more controlled, and the Indian's Green River knife was held low, blade upward. The blow was aimed toward Will's belly with a stab and a slash up.

But Will met the move blade to blade. Using the skinning knife like a short sword, he parried the thrust in a clang of steel. What he could not parry was a rake of the Mojave's left hand that tore across his eyes.

With a cry of pain, Will threw himself to the side away from the Indian's knife hand. One of his eyes began to stream tears and immediately began to swell shut. Sihuarro closed again, the knife straight forward.

This time there was no opportunity to meet the thrust and only an instant to duck out of the way. Will spun around and locked his hands on Sihuarro's wrist, but the injury to the trapper's left arm had left it still partly numbed and weak. Will used the butt of the knife handle to hammer on Sihuarro's hands.

Before he could make the Mojave drop the knife, a snake-like arm groped over Will's head. Long fingernails began probing for Will's eyes, making him squirm and duck.

The trapper smashed his skull into the Indian's face. The Mojave lost interest in raking the white man's eyes, reaching too late to cover his own shattered nose.

Putting his rough-and-tumble upbringing among river toughs to good use, Will snapped the chief's knife-arm upward, then yanked it down. With a mighty heave, he swung the warrior over his hip and to the ground.

"Two falls to none," he growled.

The savage had underestimated the white man's strength and fighting ability. Sihuarro sprang up before Will could press his advantage, but not so quickly as before.

Both men eyed each other, catching their breath. "I will enjoy giving your head to my dogs for their sport," hissed Sihuarro in English.

"I thought so," muttered Will. Then louder, "You'd best rethink that plan. I grew up wrestlin' Tennesseans, and the littlest one not so scrawny as you."

The Mojave moved toward Will's left, pressuring the trapper's injured arm and blinded eye. Another sudden lunge and a slash forced Will to circle quickly to his right.

Sihuarro repeated the move, trying to take advantage of Will's weaker quarter. A third time he made the same play, and Will stumbled, feigning a slip.

This time the chief came in farther and faster. At the last instant, Will ducked the opposite direction to the feint, leaping to his left. He slashed down hard with his own blade on the warrior's forearm.

Sihuarro gave a cry of pain, then spun away from Will, yanking his damaged knife-arm back toward his body.

The trapper jumped toward him. Sihuarro made a wild, backhand slash that Will only avoided by throwing himself flat. He lashed out with his right foot as he fell, kicking hard against the Indian's knees.

The Mojave chief tried to leap over the leg sweep, but Will's back foot caught and he heaved upward with all his strength. Sihuarro fell heavily on his side, plunging his own weapon into his side between the fifth and sixth ribs. He yanked the blade out of the wound with a shriek, then rolled face-down and was still.

The fight was over. Will dragged himself wearily to his feet. He felt no particular sense of victory, just gratitude at being alive. Sihuarro lay still in the dust of the Yokut camp. The spreading crimson pool widening beneath his motionless body gave mute testimony to the severity of his wound.

Will scanned the faces of the Indian onlookers. The Mojaves reflected sullen hatred, the Yokuts a stoic indifference. Falcon stepped forward from behind Will and stood silently at the trapper's elbow.

The Yokut chief offered Will the Green River knife that had fallen from Sihuarro's fingers. "Take it," he urged, "it is yours now."

Will accepted the knife, but still no one in the circle moved. "What's happening?" he asked Falcon. "What are they waiting for?"

"Are you going to cut off his head?" inquired Falcon earnestly. "The others of the desert are waiting to take his body back with them."

"Your people do this?" asked Will.

"It is our custom," returned the chief in a matter-of-fact tone. "Otherwise the warrior's spirit may return to the body and seek revenge."

"Well, it's not my custom," answered Will flatly. "Tell them to take him and go. He might still be alive. Don't they care?"

Falcon shook his head. "Even if he lives, he is a defeated warrior. He will have to fight many times among his own people to lead them again." He kicked dirt on Sihuarro's body and jerked his head toward the Mojaves as if to say, "Take this lump of earth out of here."

"Wake up, my friend," urged Falcon. "Come to the sweat house with me. When we are purified and bathed, your wound will heal faster and not feel so stiff."

Downstream from the camp was a willow and tule hut similar to the Yokut sleeping lodges, except that this hut was partly sunken in the ground and the exterior was covered with a plaster of mud. The inside temperature was already above a hundred degrees from an oak fire.

In no time Will's body cast off the morning chill and soon he began to perspire. Will wondered at the timing of this invitation—it was the first time since he had come to the Yokut village. The events of the previous day seemed to have gained him a new acceptance with these people. He picked at the moss poultice bound around his wounded arm.

"Falcon," Will wondered out loud, "have I brought trouble on your people with the killing yesterday? Will the Yokuts be blamed?"

"Put your mind at rest," answered the Indian. "There is no love between the Yokuts and the Mojaves. We would have listened to their speech, then sent them home. We do not trust them and we do not want their quarrel with the Mexicans."

"Then I may stay here longer?" asked Will.

"Of course," Falcon replied. "As long as you wish. But first," he commanded, "come into the stream and wash off the white man stink!"

The two men tumbled out the opening into the cool morning air. It was well that the sweat house stood just above the creek because it gave Will no time to consider the next action. As it was, he tumbled down the bank after Falcon without stopping and plunged waist deep into icy water.

"Phew!" Will sputtered to his Indian brother. "You do this for fun?"

"Every day," returned Falcon. "We spend half our lives in the water. It is our friend."

"Maybe so," replied Will, "but it sure doesn't like me yet!"

In the days following the fight, Will discovered that his relations with the Yokuts had changed in a subtle way. No longer their guest, now he was an accepted member of the clan. The early morning plunge into the stream never became a pleasure for the scout, but he adopted it as a part of the Yokut daily routine.

Another kind of adoption took place as well. Will went looking for Blackbird and found the boy sitting beside the remains of his father's hut. The child was idly picking up handfuls of ash and sifting them through his fingers, letting the east wind blow them away.

Will sat down cross-legged next to Blackbird. For a time neither spoke. Blackbird stared into the west as if watching the minute particles of dust float beyond the sight of mortal eyes.

"Blackbird," Will called softly, "I seem to recall your promise to teach me some things. It is time that I had a hut of my own. Will you show me the proper way to build it?"

The boy was short on enthusiasm, but he was agreeable. He and the scout tramped downstream toward the marsh to select reeds for the thatch.

Will stopped beside the bank of the creek to point out a clear footprint in the sand. "What is that?" he tested.

"Raccoon," replied the boy carelessly.

"And what was he doing here?"

The Yokut youth inspected the bank, noting the way the grassy turf overhung the water and was cut back underneath. "He was fishing for crayfish," replied the boy. Blackbird frowned in concentration, but Will could tell that the game was becoming enjoyable.

"Did he have a successful hunt?"

Blackbird was already scanning the banks as if he had anticipated this question. His gaze stopped, at last, a dozen feet downstream where a fallen tree stretched across an arm of the creek. The Indian boy scooted over to the branch and peered intently into the water.

"Ah," he said in triumph. "Raccoon sat here and ate his catch. Crayfish scales show where he picked apart and washed his food."

"Bravo!" applauded Will. "What a tracker you are."

The Yokut visibly brightened at this praise. He set to inspecting every inch of the trail for other signs that he could call to his friend's attention. "Deer. Coyote. Another deer. Skunk." Blackbird called the roll of every animal footprint he recognized. He looked at Will expectantly after each identification and smiled when Will gave him a nod of approval.

Up ahead, a thick patch of gray-green horehound surrounded the base of an oak, like a leafy collar around a neck of tree bark. Two does burst from this cover, sneaking off westward. They had jumped from their hiding even though the man and boy were still quite far and could not have seen them yet.

"Look!" exclaimed the excited boy. "Let's follow!"

"Hold on a minute," the scout warned. "Duck down behind this elderberry and watch . . ." Will inspected the surroundings, deciding at last on a buckeye tangle on a little knoll. "Watch the gully back of that knob."

A minute passed. Blackbird almost spoke, impatient with this unexplained lesson. With a shake of his head, Will cautioned him to remain silent. Once again the scout pointed toward the dry wash. A moment later, an old buck deer, hunched so low that he seemed to be walking on his knees, came sneaking out of his buckeye hiding place.

"That old buck sent those does out to distract us, while he sneaks out the back door," explained Will.

The shine of hero worship was radiant in Blackbird's eyes as the two gathered the reed bundles for the scout's hut. Together they cut willow poles and formed these into a travois to drag the tule bundles to camp. The boy assured the scout that this was proper Yokut fashion: the willow poles would be lashed together to form the framework of the hut.

They spent the next day building the dome-shaped dwelling. It stood in line with the rest of the Yokut homes, but at the opposite end of the camp from the ashes of the boy's former home.

That night as Will and Blackbird shared a small fire in front of their finished construction, Falcon greeted them and sat.

"You have done well," he said to Will in approval.

"I had a good teacher," the scout acknowledged.

Falcon nodded solemnly. "Blackbird," he addressed his grandson, "I see that you are taking your duty to our new brother seriously."

The boy did his best to return an appropriately adult nod of agreement.

"Therefore," Falcon continued, "I direct that you stay in Will Reed's lodge and continue to teach him the Yokut ways. To Will he added, "And we must give you a name. You say you met the great Cherokee Chief Sequoyah, who stood as tall among his people as the red-barked tree stands in the forest. You are tall and red-haired, so we will call you Sequoyah."

8

THE INDIAN NAMED Donato slumped on the cord binding his wrists. He was suspended at tiptoe level from an iron hook that protruded from a wooden beam.

"You are shamming, Donato," observed Father Quintana, "and it will do you no good. Let him have five more."

"But, Father," argued the Indian overseer wielding the whip, "he has received twenty-five lashes already." He pointed to Donato's bare back, already criss-crossed with cuts from the thin leather strap. Blood oozed from the mass of raw flesh and had spattered the wall by the hail of blows.

"Do not question me, Lazario, or you will hang there next," corrected the priest. "This one has carried the punishment pole, sat in the stocks, and still he persists in sneaking out at night. No more will I listen when he pleads he will reform. This will be a lesson he will remember forever!"

Lazario had raised his arm in preparation for another whistling stroke of the whip when the chamber door opened and Father Sanchez bustled in.

"What's this, Quintana?" demanded the little round priest of the lean one. "I thought we agreed to cease beating the neophytes for minor infractions."

"Minor!" spouted Quintana. "This little brother," he said with a sneer, "is disrespectful and willfully disobedient. He must be used as an example."

"Yes, but what kind of example will he be?"

"I will not discuss this with you in front of the prisoner and the mayordomo. We may exchange views later. . . . Why did you interrupt me anyway?"

"I came to tell you that Capitan Zuniga is here and wishes to speak with you immediately."

"Why didn't you say so at first?" stormed Quintana, pushing Lazario aside on his way to the door. "You may take over here, and do as you will with this . . . this . . . rebel!"

Sanchez and Lazario removed Donato from the hook and laid him face down on a rough wooden bench. "Bring me the salve from my cell—the blue tin on the shelf," the priest ordered.

When the mayordomo had gone to fetch the ointment, Sanchez sat on the bench beside the huddled form. He tried ever so gently to place a folded cloth beneath Donato's head, but even that slight movement caused a groan to escape the clenched teeth of the neophyte.

"Ah, Donato, my friend," murmured Padre Sanchez, "he will beat you to death next time. He is in charge of discipline, so who can stop him? Why do you persist in sneaking out?"

Bit by bit, in gasps expelled past shudders of pain, Donato told how he had visited the free-roaming Indians who lived in the Temblor range of mountains. There he had met a girl and fallen in love. But her people were preparing to move to their summer hunting grounds, much farther to the north.

"I must see her . . . convince her . . . marry me and remain here," Donato coughed.

"But why did you not tell us this before? If she is willing to become a Christian, we will welcome her among us."

"Quintana did not . . . believe me . . . said I ran away . . . to sin with the heathen."

"But if she returned with you, that would prove—"

"She would not. She says Christians are too cruel and not to be trusted."

9

ANOTHER MARK OF how much Will was accepted by the Yokuts came when he was asked to accompany the men on a hunting trip. Falcon's wife examined his wound and pronounced him healed and able to go, and Will was eager to give up the enforced inactivity. Besides, he thought it was about time to help replenish the Yokuts' stores that he had been consuming.

Awakened well before dawn by Blackbird, the boy excitedly informed Will that he was also invited on this hunt. Coyote had been selected to lead the group of four and Falcon would remain in camp. Will was without a rifle, of course, but he was a decent shot with a bow and had been honored to carry Falcon's for the purpose.

The hunters had sweated and bathed in the gray mists of predawn. More important than cleanliness, they wanted to reduce as much as possible the human scent they would carry to the hunt. The Yokus felt so strongly about this procedure that they would not touch their weapons until the cold plunge had been completed.

A hasty breakfast of cold acorn meal cake followed the bath and then the four headed northeast out of the village, crossing the stream by a shallow rocky ford. Their plan was to ascend a steep ridge of granite rock that ran down to the river.

On the bench of land about halfway up the ridge, the hunting party stopped for a brief rest. Climbing rapidly to the top of a huge boulder, Blackbird gestured for Will to join him. From this vantage point, Will could see back downstream and the Yokuts' village strung out along the banks. Looking upstream, the canyon was bathed in deep shadows as it pressed up against the wall of the Sierra Nevadas.

Will understood that Blackbird was proud of his home and showing off the Yokuts' domain. If the young boy grew to manhood, he would follow his grandfather to leadership of their clan. The future chief swept his arm in a semicircle from mountain shadows down to the tule bog where the stream disappeared into marsh.

Next he pointed his skinny brown arm toward different marks on the horizon and began reciting a list of names. Will was not certain if the names were those of Yokuts' rancherias or of neighboring tribes.

Apparently satisfied that he had passed his self-imposed test, Blackbird made a last stab of his finger. "Tubatulabal," he said as he hopped down off the rock.

The yellow disk of the sun was climbing above the Sierra, riding on the outstretched arms of the pines on the high ridges, when the hunters began their stalk. The breeze off the peaks was dying down, but its faint trace still bore the chill of the snowy summits and the tang of the mountain cedars.

Coyote and Meho were carrying their deer-head disguises. At a spot where two ravines met, the hunting party separated into two groups. The two Yokut men tied on their animal camouflage gear, explaining that a short distance up the left-hand draw was a spring and a small meadow. The Yokuts had often successfully hunted there before, but it required a painfully slow creeping approach.

Will and Blackbird were instructed to wait a few minutes, then begin moving up the canyon on the right. It was not as likely that deer would be found foraging in the right-hand fork, but Will would be in a position to get a shot if a deer was spooked and came over the ridge.

Will and his small partner squatted down to wait. Blackbird was doing such an intense job of scanning the brush ahead that Will took an opportunity to examine Falcon's bow.

The weapon was made of a stout piece of elderberry branch, smoothly finished. The front was rounded and the face toward the archer was flat. The flat surface was strengthened with an application of deer sinew glued lengthwise, and deer sinew was also used as the bowstrings.

Falcon had also presented Will with pouches of arrow shafts and heads to accompany the bow. Both of these were carried by Blackbird. Over one shoulder he wore a fox-skin quiver containing the feathered willow shafts. Around his neck, hanging on his chest, was a smaller buckskin bag that had different sizes of obsidian heads attached to short willow foreshafts.

In this way the Yokut hunter could quickly change the type of killing point to suit the game being sought, and if the arrowhead broke off in a wound, the main shaft could be recovered. When Will extended his hand toward the small boy, Blackbird immediately knew what was wanted. He carefully selected the straightest and best-feathered shaft and coupled it to a newly made obsidian head.

Will nocked the arrow and practiced bringing it to a full draw. He thought it wise to imitate the Yokuts' stance with the bow held at an angle to the left across the front of his body. The trapper nodded his readiness to proceed.

The tall, sun-bronzed white man and the short, dusky Indian child made their way up the right-hand draw. Will was amused to see the caution with which Blackbird took each step, placing his bare foot carefully and stopping after each pace to watch and listen.

There had been no sound from the direction the other hunters had taken, so Will was agreeable to the slow advance adopted by Blackbird. The trapper did not want to range past the location of the other two and let the quarry sneak out behind them.

A file of quail paraded across in front of them. Several birds took turns hopping up on a prominent rock to inspect the humans before proceeding. The Yokuts made a small arrowhead with projecting prongs for stunning birds, but they also had means of trapping quail in larger numbers.

When the last quail had scurried off into the chaparral, Will and Blackbird approached the stone perch. Above them on one side was a tangle of buckeye limbs and trunks. Several of the trees had blown down in the winter's storms, but with the enthusiasm always shown by buckeyes, the remaining twisted limbs were already covered in bright green leaves.

The hillside on their right was occupied with patches of gooseberry bushes. These thickets were showing the dark red buds that precede the outburst of the fruit. Higher up, the slope was dotted with oak trees sprinkled with a few faded green leaves that had neglected to fall the previous autumn.

Marking the open area between gooseberries and oaks were bands of poppies; brilliant orange in several places and sunshine yellow in others. Will struggled to keep his attention on the hunting and off the scenery.

A quail called from the gooseberry thicket closest to the bottom of the ravine. It was answered by another hidden in the mass of buckeye branches and yet another from the growth of oaks. Will's mind did a curious double-voiced response: half his brain was still glorying in the beauty of the scene, while another part was already screaming a warning.

It was fortunate that the warning voice overrode the admiration of the view. Will yelled "Get down!" and pushed Blackbird behind a rock just as a Mojave killing stick whirred past the little boy's ear.

The throw came from the clump of gooseberry bushes only twenty feet away. The desert Indian who had hurled it was already following up the attack, charging toward Will with an upraised knife.

Will knew that the single arrow now nocked would determine whether he lived or died. The little voice also reminded him that, depending on how many other Mojaves went with the quail calls, he might be dead anyway.

This added worry did not interfere with his aim or make him hesitate to release the arrow. The obsidian arrowhead, as sharp as a shard of glass, pierced the warrior's chest and passed almost completely through his body. His feet stumbled over a small tree limb, and he fell face forward on the grassy turf. The arrow point protruded two feet above his backbone.

There was not a second to be spent in self-congratulation. Two equally terrifying screams rose from opposite sides of the canyon. The Mojave high on the slope who had been in the cover of the oak trees broke into the open. The other attacker, waiting in the mass of buckeye branches, loosed an arrow without ever showing himself.

The downhill shot and the interference of the buckeye leaves deflected the arrow's path. It landed between Will's legs and the stone point shattered on the rock beside which Blackbird was crouched. Cooler under fire than many a grown man, the Yokut boy had fitted another broad point to a shaft and was handing it to Will.

Will grabbed the arrow from the child, but also shouted to him, "Run! Run!" and gave the boy a shove. The trapper was too busy lining up his next shot to see the reproachful look on the child's face. Blackbird slipped off the arrow pouches and made a dash back the way they had come.

Will had not fired his second arrow when another came whizzing at him from the buckeye clump. This time the Mojave's aim was true. In fact, it was too good. Directly in line with Will's chest, the arrow struck squarely on Falcon's bow. The arrow point stuck in the elderberry wood and the impact made the bow spring out of Will's hand like a wounded animal jumps when shot.

Will's second arrow discharged wildly into the air, passing high over the attacker's head. The white man knew that he could not survive another shot and he had no time to retrieve the bow. Instead, Will pulled one of the knives from his belt and charged the Mojave.

The startled desert Indian looked up to see Will leaping over a fallen buckeye trunk with a yell of his own and the gleaming knife flashing in his hand.

The Indian made a wild swing with his bow, trying to stop Will's rush or fend off the knife. The bow and the blade collided, forcing Will's hand wide of its mark. The power of his rush carried him atop the Indian and they tumbled over into the buckeye.

The native's hands closed over Will's wrist, intent on gaining possession of the skinning knife. Will drew back his left arm and drove a clenched fist into the Indian's jaw.

The desert-dweller's head snapped back, but his grasp of Will's knife-hand did not waver. The Indian twisted Will's arm inward, knotting the wrist joint. Again and again Will drove his fist into the Mojave's face. The round-house blows delivered in their tumbling struggle in the brush heap had little effect.

Will's inner voice reminded him of the desperate need to hurry. Only seconds remained before the remaining warrior came down from the oaks and finished the contest forever.

The Mojave was winning the struggle for the knife. The trapper's fingers were numbing and releasing their grip. Will tried again to drive his fist into the Indian's face, but the Indian ducked his head against the blow. Over they rolled again, coming to an abrupt stop against a fallen buckeye trunk with the Mojave uppermost.

A savage gleam of victory appeared in the eyes of the desert tribesman. He sensed that he controlled the blade, and he pushed it downward toward the trapper's throat.

From the direction of the other slope came the sound of running sandled feet. The other attacker was nearly down the hill. Suddenly there was the twang of a bow-string and a piercing cry. This scream was followed by an angry, outraged shout.

Without thinking, the warrior on top of Will spun his head around at the sound. It was just the opportunity Will had needed.

With his free hand the trapper grabbed a buckeye limb and swung it with all his strength against the Indian's head. The heavy branch crashed into the warrior's skull, and he crumbled much as the buckeye trunk had fallen in the winter's wind.

Will threw the Indian from him, and jumped the opposite direction into the thickest cover of the buckeye tangle. As he peered cautiously over the trunk, he saw an astonishing scene.

The last member of the desert-tribe's ambush was advancing to a kill, but not toward the trapper. The third attacker was dressed in a baggy shirt that hung to his knees. He was brandishing a killing stick at Blackbird, who cowered with his back against a boulder. The grimacing warrior was walking awkwardly, limping and halting.

The cause of his crippled movement was the point of a Yokuts' arrow-head buried deeply in his thigh, pinning the smock to his leg. Blackbird had disobeyed Will's order, retrieved his grandfather's bow and shot the enemy!

Will grabbed the fallen Mojave weapon and nocked another arrow.

Climbing out from the jumble of brush, the scout shouted, "Hold it right there!"

The wounded Indian did not understand the words, but the sudden English speech from a man he thought wounded or killed jerked him around. Disbelief, anger and pain competed on his face. He slowly dropped his hands to his sides, letting the killing stick fall to the ground. His features were flat, but more startling was the fact that his ears had been cut off next to his head.

"You're not Mojave. Why'd you jump us?" demanded Will.

In a growing stain from the barbed shaft, blood spread down the man's smock in a fan shape. He stood awkwardly, all his weight on his good leg.

"Please, señor," he said in clear Spanish, "you will help me remove the arrow?"

"First, I want some answers. Where'd you come from?"

"My name is Paco. I am—was a neophyte of the Mission Santa Barbara. I ran away from the mission and the Mojaves took me in. Please, sir, can you help me?"

"That still doesn't explain why you helped these sons of perdition attack us."

"But I did not, señor. I shot no arrow. I threw no club."

"You didn't come charging down the hill to wish me good luck. Blackbird here saved my life by nailing you."

The mission Indian hung his head. "It is true, what you say. But the fierce ones of the desert demanded I must prove myself true to them or they would kill me! They said a spy of the Mexicans was here and that attacking would revenge the wounding of their chief." The blood stain had spread to the hem of the smock and begun to drip on the ground. The man visibly paled and swayed.

"Wounding? He's not dead?"

"No, señor. Sihuarro is recovering his strength. His brother, the shaman, argues that Sihuarro was not defeated really. His spirit only sojourned in the land beyond, gathering power to return and defeat all Mexicans, all foreigners."

"So that is the reason for this raid? Sihuarro could prove it was true by having me killed?"

"Please, señor, may I sit down?"

Will made no reply, nor did he lower the arrow point from its aim at Paco's belly.

"Yes, yes," pleaded the man. "What you say is true. Sihuarro said that the raiders would kill you without difficulty and without causing war with the Yokuts."

At last Will gestured with a shake of the arrow point for the Indian to sit. Paco crumpled more than sat, catching himself only on his elbows before he fell completely flat.

Blackbird ran to Will and without saying a word grabbed the trapper around the legs and hugged him tight. Will was astonished for an instant, then reached down and tousled the boy's shaggy mop of hair.

"You did well, Blackbird. You saved my life."

"I was scared," the boy blurted out. "I thought you were getting killed, then I thought I was and . . . I never shot a man before . . ." his voice trailed off. He made no sobbing noise, but a silent tremor went through his body.

"But you did well . . . you were brave," encouraged Will. "Not many would have found the courage to return."

"I began to run," Blackbird said with a great sigh, "Then I remembered: I will be chief someday."

Moments later Coyote and Meho came over the ridge and descended to an amazing sight. They found Will bandaging the leg of an unconscious mission Indian while Blackbird gathered a collection of Mojave weapons from two dead warriors.

10

ON A SMALL knoll, clear of the surrounding willows, Falcon looked toward the west. He shaded his eyes against the glare of the westering sun, now turning an angry orange as it descended.

Will stood without speaking alongside the old man. At last the chief volunteered, "I look for sign of Meho's return."

"Yes," agreed the scout, "he said he would be back the same day he went to gather flint rocks."

That had been two days ago. When the toolmaker's lateness had first been noted, everyone said he must have found game to his liking. But now no one spoke of him at all. It was as if the Yokuts wanted to avoid thinking about what might have happened to him.

Falcon muttered something low, almost to himself. It sounded like, "The West has taken him."

Will observed quietly, respectful of the old man's thoughts, "Should we not search for him?"

Falcon rounded on him suddenly and spoke sharply, "No! The West has taken him. We will not speak of it further."

"I must leave you," Will said in his best Yokuts' speech. He was addressing a council of Yokut elders headed by Falcon. The men were dressed formally in their buckskin vests trimmed with fur and bits of shell.

Falcon spoke. "But why, our brother of the reeds? You have shown yourself to be truehearted and brave. Why would you separate yourself from us?"

"Because, Father," said Will with respect, "as long as I remain here, your people cannot have peace with the Mojaves. I endanger your families. Blackbird might have been killed for being with me. I cannot permit this."

Falcon stood erect on the side of the fire opposite Will and waited politely for him to finish. The Indian's hair was tied into two braids and laced with milkweed string twisted with eagle down. "I would say that I owe you the life of my grandson. You are welcome to live with my household forever. If need be we will fight the Mojaves together."

Coyote followed in turn, pleading with Will to remain. Others of the clan took turns expressing their willingness to face the threat of the desert tribe if the white man would remain.

Finally, Will alone stood before the silent, expectant group. A chunk of burning oak broke and crumbled in the fire pit, tiny sparks flying up. He shook his head gravely. "My father and my brothers and my friends . . . I owe you very much . . . but I cannot remain now. I came to this land for the purpose of furs. Now I have no means to continue *that* purpose, but I have not yet found another. What is more, I must seek news of my white brothers, if any of them still live. I must go."

Among the Yokuts, when a man expressed his decision after taking council, there was no more discussion, no continued debate. It was settled and Falcon rose to confirm the choice.

"So," the silvery-haired chief declared, "our brother Sequoyah will go from us. Let us smoke to bless his going." A short-stemmed clay pipe already charged with native tobacco was lit with a coal from the fire. Falcon blew smoke to the four points of the compass, and toward the sky. He then passed the pipe to Will who repeated the motion, then returned it. The small tube of fragrant embers was passed around the circle, and came back to Falcon again.

From around his neck, Falcon drew a string of the fuzzy red topknots of the mountain woodpeckers. It was one of the most precious things the Yokuts possessed and a mark of Falcon's status. "Take this, my son," he offered. "We know the Mexicans esteem it not, but should you wander among others of the Yokuts, they will know you for a man of honor and importance. Also, you must take my bow as your own."

Will thanked Falcon for this kindness and the meeting was over. The council began to disperse to their huts, but Coyote drew Will aside.

"There is yet one more matter to speak of," explained Coyote, tugging on a braid. "Since you spared the life of the man Paco, what do you wish done with him?"

Will had already considered this. "I would have allowed him to return to the Mojaves, but he was afraid. I know you do not trust him and cannot permit him to remain with you, so my way is clear."

"Good," nodded Coyote, "send him away to walk alone. His cropped ears mark him as a thief. Every hand will be turned against him wherever he goes."

"That was not my meaning," corrected Will. "I will take him with me. I have explained that he has no choice."

"You are wrong," Coyote argued. "He will knife you as you sleep."

"I think not," shrugged Will, "but I will be wary. Perhaps I will be back this way again soon and we will see who was right."

Coyote shook his head and snorted a mocking chuckle. "If you are wrong, my brother, you will not return this way ever."

11

THE MORNING CAME for Will to take his leave of the Yokuts and cross the great central valley and the coastal range of mountains. A three-day journey separated the Yokuts' nation from Spanish California.

The scout awoke in the predawn grayness to the faint flutter of a rising east wind. The camp was perfectly still. Far off he heard a jay scolding some other creature for waking him so early. Closer by, the creek laughed and gurgled as it lapped against the roots of a thirsty willow.

Gazing up at the reed-thatched ceiling took Will back to the hut in which he had been imprisoned by the Mojaves. The similarity lasted only a moment though; the Yokuts' village was too peaceful for such a disturbing comparison to last. The sense of calm and belonging carried Will's thoughts toward a dimly remembered childhood home on the Mississippi.

The trapper rolled over in the rabbitskin blanket. He was so wrapped up in memories that the fact that Blackbird was missing took a minute to register. The boy's sleeping cover was thrown in a corner of the hut and he was gone.

Will shook off the pleasant sleepiness and pulled himself awake. Where had the boy gone and why? Blackbird knew that the scout was leaving. Why would he choose this morning to disappear?

Exiting his hut, Will began a mental list of the more likely places to search. For a few steps Blackbird's footprints showed plainly in the cleared area around the huts. Will followed them quietly, not wanting to rouse the camp. The trail was lost after a few paces in the jumble of tracks around the village.

Down at the sweathouse? wondered Will. The communal structure next to the creek was deserted this early in the morning. Will did not need to feel the ashes; the cool temperature inside told him that the hut had not been used since the previous day.

The trapper searched the dark-green gooseberry thickets for signs that Blackbird might have gone in search of breakfast. He found no trace of the eight-year-old until he came to the trail that they had followed into the Mojave ambush.

Discovering the next footprint, he knew that he was on the right track. In fact, he already knew the destination.

Ignoring the faint traces of the young boy's passing, Will cut cross-country toward a rocky bluff that stood out against the skyline. It was the same spot where he and Blackbird had surveyed the Yokuts' world.

"Take me with you." Blackbird made the demand without any preamble as the scout joined him on the stony ledge.

"I can't do that," answered Will. "I don't know what I'll find or how I'll be received, and I sure won't chance your life to find out."

"But you are going west, and I will never see you again," mourned the boy, his brown eyes searching Will's face. "It makes my heart hurt. First my mother, then my father, and now you. Take me with you."

The scout gently explained. "But what about your grandfather? He needs you, and your people need you. Besides, it's not as you've said. I'm headed west, but I'm not going to die. I'll be back this way soon."

"How can I know that you are speaking the truth?" questioned the child. "No other one who has gone west has returned."

Will thought for a moment, then drew one of the Green River knives from the leather straps that crossed the front of his buckskin jacket.

"Look," he said, "I want you to keep this. I will hold its twin. Whenever you use it or see it, you must think of me and I will do the same of you. Keep it safe, because it and its brother-knife must be reunited before the snow flies in the passes." The scout gestured toward the high mountains to the east. "Learn all you can from your grandfather about the ways of the wilderness. Soon enough, you will be of an age to join me as a scout."

"Sequoyah," said the boy, "there is evil in the West. Come again soon, before it swallows you."

The child would not return to the camp. Instead, he remained at his post, gazing out toward the path that led toward the ocean, following his friend with his eyes and lifting him with his heart.

"I wish you would not do this, señor," asserted Paco for the third time in as many minutes.

Will had been trying to ignore the pleading mission Indian, but decided he could not stand listening to it for another minute, let alone days.

The scout whirled around, the fringe on his buckskin leggings twirling. "For the last time, Paco, you have no choice, unless you want me to let you wander off to starve. Why are you afraid?"

"You do not understand, señor. If I go back, they will beat me to death."

"Bah," snorted Will. "You're not serious. If you go back of your own free will, they probably won't beat you at all."

"Listen to me señor," begged the Indian, who was leaning heavily on a crutch made of mountain mahogany. "Perhaps you are right about the holy fathers, but they are not the ones who will punish me. They are not the men who did this." The short, stocky man stopped moving and forced Will to turn and look.

"Capitan Zuniga, he cut off my ears and this time he will cut out my heart."

"Paco, if you got your ears trimmed, it's only because you are a thief."

"No, no, señor. That is what Capitan Zuniga told the fathers so they would not trust me, but it is not so."

Will gestured impatiently for Paco to start walking again and the two men resumed their march. They were skirting the southern end of the great valley's tule bog. Over his shoulder Will demanded to know the real reason for their cruel punishment if Paco was not a thief.

"Ah, señor. It is what I heard Capitan Zuniga and Don Dominguez plotting. They intend to push the governor to take over the mission lands. I tried to tell the fathers this, but Capitan Zuniga said I was lying to cover up my thievery."

"It sounds pretty fanciful to me also," commented the scout. "Let it go for now and I'll speak up on your behalf if need be. Now fill me in on the mission. What's it like?"

They camped that night in Canyon de las Uvas. Will noticed the steep hillsides covered with wild grapevines, giving the canyon its name.

Over a supper of roast rabbit shot by Will and acorn meal cakes provided by the Yokuts, Paco gave the young trapper a sketch of life in Spanish California.

"I was born at the mission," he began. "My grandparents were of the Chumash people living at a rancheria right where Presidio Santa Barbara now stands. They lived off the sea, fishing and gathering. They made shell money and traded it with other people for things they needed.

"When the holy fathers came, everything changed. The Spaniards invited my grandparents' people to come to the mission. They were not forced to become Christian, but the holy fathers told them stories about how the Lord Jesus died for their sins and they listened. They were told that if they became neophytes they would receive clothing, better food, homes, be taught to grow crops."

"So they wanted to join the mission?" asked Will.

"Si, but they had to agree to many things. If they became neophytes, they had to work for the padres and no longer could they leave without permission."

"And runaways are forced to return and are punished?" Will inquired.

"That is right. Sometimes my people tried to revolt. My father died in one such attempt. But he was not a rebel, señor. He was killed protecting the mission from others who wanted to burn it down."

"Surely your people outnumber the Spaniards many times over," offered Will, remembering his grandfather's stories about the American Revolution against the British. "Why didn't they—what's that noise?"

A low rumbling sound could be heard in the distance. Very faint at first and harmless, like the drumming of rain on his cabin roof back on the Mississippi, the sound swelled until it resembled a continuous roll of thunder instead of a gentle rain. The noise seemed to be sweeping toward them, down from the high pass.

The rumble increased in volume and tempo, reminding Will of an avalanche heard in the heights of the Rockies. He jumped to his feet. "I know that sound," he exclaimed. "It's a buffalo stampede. I saw one when we were crossing the plains." Unconsciously he switched to speaking English in his excitement. "This oak here is good and stout. Quick, up . . ."

Paco still sat by the fire. "Calm yourself, señor," he urged. "There are no buff . . . what did you say, 'bufflers'? There are none here."

"Then what?" demanded Will.

A herd of horses swung into moonlit view. Their leader, a glossy black stallion of immense size, swept around a rocky outcropping two hundred yards away.

At the sight of the campfire, the stallion did not even break stride. He led his band in a great s-curve that carried them to the farthest side of the canyon opposite the two men.

Will caught brief glimpses of various horse hides—dark, light, pinto and spotted—as he stood watching the spectacle. Like the sudden release of a river hitting the rim of a waterfall, the horse herd spilled past the camp. Eyes flashing in the light of the moon, their hooves churned the sage into a piercingly sharp fragrance that filled the night air, and then they were gone.

Will stood staring after them. From behind him the still-seated Paco spoke, "There you see a part of the answer, señor."

"Answer—what answer?" said Will, who had forgotten his question.

"You asked why my people and the other Indios did not throw out the Spaniards. It is true that they came with weapons and armor of iron and with gunpowder. But most of all, they came with horses from whom these wild ones descend. With such beasts they can move men and supplies in great numbers and so quickly."

"Well why don't your people learn to ride—meet the Spanish as equals? You could catch that one herd and have mounts for seventy-five or one hundred men."

Paco looked furtive for an instant; the expression of a weasel surprised in the hen house. "Oh no, señor," he said quickly and shook his head, "only *gente de razón,* the people of reason, are permitted to become caballeros. It is forbidden for any of my people to even get on a horse."

12

DON PEDRO RIVERA y Cruz stood on the veranda of his hacienda and watched his gardener hoeing weeds. Don Pedro's thoughts drifted back some twenty-five years earlier to a tiny garden outside the adobe walls of Presidio Santa Barbara.

The Rivera y Cruz family was of noble blood, well-known and highly regarded in Spain. But notoriety and nobility, even combined with a Jesuit education, could not ensure wealth and position on the future adult lives of thirteen children. As the tenth in line, Don Pedro's military career in the Americas had been decided long before he wore his first beard.

The ranchero rubbed his hand over his now clean-shaven face, and then, by habit, up over his balding head. He thought ruefully how thick and black his hair had been when he was a young cuero, a leather-jacket soldier.

With his good looks and confident manner, there had been no difficulty convincing lovely Guadalupe Flores to become his bride. They were married in the Presidio chapel during the first month of the year 1801. She was the first to tend the scrap of garden outside the wall of the fort, and she was in his thoughts now.

Don Pedro's military service might have been without distinction had it depended on fighting battles. Garrison duty in California was almost always peaceful.

But in a different way, Don Pedro had earned the gratitude of Spain. In 1812 both the presidio and the mission were destroyed by a cataclysmic earthquake. Don Pedro put his studies from his youth to good use. Demonstrating an amazing skill at architecture and engineering, he soon had rebuilt both structures and it was recognized far and wide that the buildings were better than the originals.

At his retirement from military service, he had received a grant of land and set to work stocking it with cattle. At first there had been little profit in the sale of meat and tallow, but in time the demand for rawhide drew attention to California.

Within ten years, the first hesitant attempts at commerce with America's eastern states had grown into an active, thriving business. Valued at two dollars apiece, cowhides soon became known as "California banknotes." Their proprietors became wealthy men as the young and energetic United States continued to demand more leather for shoes, boots, saddles and harnesses.

There was only one sadness in the life of the ranchero: His wife had only had one year to share the hacienda built from the profits of his trade, and then she died.

Don Pedro was recalled from his reverie by the sound of creaking saddle leather at the front of the house. Turning the corner of the veranda, he saw that his son was mounted on the bay horse with the white blaze, and was awaiting instructions.

"Ricardo, I want you to ride out to the south pasture and see how the roundup, the rodeo, is going. The last two hundred hides are cured and stacked. It is time for us to prepare more."

"Si, Father," replied the slim young man. His features duplicated those of his sister Francesca, but in a chiseled, masculine way. He controlled the prancing bay horse easily and took the time to secure under his chin the strap of his flat crowned hat.

Don Pedro Rivera y Cruz looked at his son with pride. "Before your return tomorrow, ride up Canyon Perdido. I have had a report that some of our cows have been slaughtered there."

The son turned the bay in a circle back toward Don Pedro, the silver conchos on the tack flashing in the sunlight. "Should I take some men with me, Father?"

"No, not till we know more. It is probably the work of some travellers or Indios. Anyway, if it is only one or two dead animals and they have left the hides, it does not matter. We will not begrudge anyone meat, so long as they are respectful. Vaya con Dios, my son."

Ricardo had only to touch the bay's flanks with the tips of the five-inch rowels of his spurs and off they flew. Horse and rider merged into the fluid motion of water bubbling over rocks in a stream bed. In no more than a minute they were out of sight.

Don Pedro again reached up and wiped his work-thickened hand over his bald head with its fringe of short white hair. How proud his wife would have been of their two almost-grown children and how fine the rancho had become.

"Miguel," he called to the rancho gardener, "are the strawberries ripe yet? Ah, no matter, bring some anyway, the ripest you can find." To himself he sighed, "She could never wait for them to get really ready. Besides, she always said there was something magic about the first strawberries of spring." Don Pedro shook off his thoughts and turned to climb the steps back to his office.

13

WILL AND PACO worked through the mountains on a path that wound its way past forests of oaks and pinyon pines. On the trail they came to a deserted village in a hilly canyon.

Will stopped to examine the forlorn site. A circle of collapsed reed huts encircled by a mud wall was all that was left. On a bluff above the village were some grinding holes bored into a granite slab and the remains of a rectangular foundation.

The trapper called Paco over to him. "What about this? I never saw the Yokuts build anything that wasn't round."

Paco studied the ground for a moment. Next, he squinted down at a corner of the green valley that could be seen through the canyon's mouth. A sheen of silver reflected a large lake's presence in the valley.

"This place I have never been to before, but I have heard of it. There was once a great Yokuts' village here. The holy fathers came to this place and built a small mission. That must be the foundation. This was many years before I was born.

"Then some runaways passed through here, fleeing from Mission Santa Barbara. The military commander used this place as a fort to attack the tribes that were hiding the huidos, the runaways.

"When the Yokuts protested, he punished them also, so they all moved away and never returned. Soon the padres went away too."

Will nodded his understanding and tried to imagine what life might have been like here. "So the commander, by being so hard, chased away those that the priests had come here to seek. He made their work more difficult, not easier."

There was nothing to add to that. But it gave Will much to think about as the two pushed on upward through passes that led toward Santa Barbara. Eventually they faced a high rounded ridge covered in dark green grass and dotted with oaks.

"Just across those mountains, señor." The mission Indian directed Will's gaze to a zigzag path of red dirt, streaking the hillside like a faded scar over an old wound.

The next morning they were up before sunrise. Will was eager to cross the threshold of Spanish California. He had heard stories about the richness of the mission lands and their exotic Spanish culture from a handful of English-speaking trappers who had been there before him. He had seen nothing that resembled civilization in the usual sense of the word since leaving Missouri, a thousand miles and another lifetime ago.

The rounded ridge did not look threatening, but it was steep. The path they followed was long in reaching the top as it plunged in and out of canyons and gorges.

When the scout and the mission Indian finally reached the crest of the hill, Will was out of breath. Paco's leg was aching and he was ready to rest also.

Will looked back the way they had come, thinking how glad he was that the climb was behind them. He was not yet ready to look down the western slope. So many ranges had been crossed only to find another, and still another, and yet another looming ahead, so his enthusiasm to see what lay beyond had been tempered.

It was a shock past anything he had ever experienced to look out from his perch and see ocean! The land dropped away sharply below him, flattening out to a narrow coastal plain just in front of a line of white sand and foaming breakers.

The coastline made an arc, and Will could see it was a bay of sorts. The mountain range on which he stood curved to plunge abruptly into the ocean some miles south of him, while to the north it faded into a rocky point in the dim distance.

Will could see islands across a narrow channel of blue water. One especially clear lay directly before him. The length of its silhouette and the shape of its peaks and valleys showed that it was not inconsequential in size.

Paco tugged at Will's elbow when he saw the scout staring across the water. "My people once lived there," he said.

"There? You mean on that island?"

"Si. It is called Santa Cruz . . . the island of the holy cross. When the Spaniards came to this coast, one made a stop there. A priest lost a valuable silver cross while they were exploring. An ancestor of mine swam out to stop them from leaving so that the cross could be returned. The Spaniards were very impressed and grateful and decided to name the island to honor the event."

Will's first view of the ocean—in fact, of any ocean—filled him with wonder but was overshadowed by a sense of unease. There had never been a time when he had stood on the shore of a lake so vast that he could not see the farther shore. It strained his belief as well as his eyes that no matter how hard he peered into the distance, there was no trace of land. He had the same feeling of disquiet when he had left the little trading post outside Vicksburg: adrift with no farther shore in sight.

He was grateful for the islands on the near horizon. They were like a wall holding back the unutterable loneliness of the sea beyond.

"Come, señor," interrupted Paco. "Let us descend. Santa Barbara is just across these hills."

14

THE CALIFORNIA MORNING was perfect and young Ricardo Rivera y Cruz had enjoyed it to the full. His canter to the cattle roundup was made under brilliantly blue skies and billowy white clouds. He was pleased with the figure he made and with the performance of the horse he had trained.

Passing a group of Indians hired from the mission to repair an irrigation ditch, Ricardo was saluted respectfully. There was no hint of the sullenness that often accompanied their response to other masters.

Ricardo also met a carreta occupied by the daughters Gonzalez. The wooden-wheeled cart was creaking its way toward the market. Old man Gonzalez was not a great ranchero, but he was very successful at raising beauties for marriage. Ricardo touched the brim of his hat as he cantered by, pretending not to notice the giggling that erupted.

Ricardo wondered if one of the Gonzalez sisters might one day be his mate. He had known since he was little that his father had arranged a marriage for him, but he had not been told with whom.

At the age of nineteen, he was not expected to know his future wife. Indeed, decisions about his life were still his father's to make. He had not even been allowed to begin shaving until he was eighteen, and then only with his father's permission.

Thoughts about his own eventual wedding brought his sister to mind. Three years older than Ricardo, at twenty-two, Francesca was six years past the accepted marriage age. Her betrothed, a forty-year-old Don in San Diego, had died in a fall from a horse when Francesca was only fourteen. Some said he was drunk when it happened.

While a hundred other prospective sons-in-law could have been found, the death of Francesca's mother less than a year after her fiance had made Don Pedro reluctant to push her to marry. Don Pedro was proud of his son, but he doted on his daughter.

Ricardo shrugged, glad he was not responsible to find a husband for his sister, and rode into camp.

The roundup concluded smoothly the following morning. The ranch foreman and his vaqueros had gathered about two hundred of the rangy cows into a small meadow. With its surrounding thickets of brush and a rocky stream across one side, it was an ideal holding ground.

Some of the vaqueros were Indians. They were permitted to ride for Don Pedro only after he had applied to the government in Mexico City and was granted a special allowance. It had taken two years and much wrangling, but the prohibition against Indians on horseback had been partially lifted.

After a brief final talk with the foreman, Ricardo concluded that all was going well. By the next evening the cattle would be driven down to a section of the rancho near the ocean where the skinning would take place.

It did not matter that a few neighbor cattle had been rounded up with Don Pedro's. They would be skinned with the rest and the hides cured, then the finished product returned to the rightful owner.

This approach saved the effort of rounding up those cattle again later, as well as trying to separate out the strays. Since all the rancheros operated the same way, no one was cheated.

The ride up Canyon Perdido took Ricardo away from the ranching and farm operations and away from the travelled roads. The canyon's gnarled oak trees and tangles of brush had a wild, uncivilized appearance, though it was just beyond the sight of the grazing herds.

Ricardo had searched the canyon for strays many times. A path of sorts wound through a boulder-strewn gulch and up the slope toward the mountains. The path was said to eventually climb into the Santa Ynes Valley, but Ricardo had never ridden along it that far.

The bay shied suddenly and a moment later Ricardo caught the stench of rotting flesh. Around the next bend of the arroyo, he came upon the partially dismembered carcass of a cow.

It was lying next to a rock basin that held a small pool of water. The head and forequarters of the cow were partly covered with a pile of leaves and dirt. Someone had done a poor job of hiding their kill.

The horse's nostrils flared and it snorted violently twice, then pranced in a tight circle. "Easy," said the caballero to the bay, "easy."

Ricardo searched the rocks and the tree branches for a hide. Some wild beast had been feasting on the remains—that was certain. But the cow must have been killed and skinned for its hide.

He never saw the grizzly till it charged. The silver-tipped, hunch-backed bear thought the horse and rider were moving in on his larder, and he was having none of it.

The bay screamed as only a horse that has been frightened near to death can sound. It jumped straight up and lashed out with its hind feet, catching the bear on the nose and momentarily stunning him.

But the grizzly was not easily put off the attack. Lunging again, it closed its jaws over a scrap of the horse's tail and with that tenuous hold pulled the bay backwards.

The horse was truly panicked now, and stood almost straight up and down on its forefeet. The bay's rear hooves pounded against the bear's shoulders, but it hung on grimly.

On the third desperate plunge, Ricardo parted company with the bay and flew off forward. Arcing through the air over the carrion pile, he landed heavily on the rocky basin and was knocked unconscious.

When he came to, he lay very still, taking stock of his injuries before attempting to move. It was the wisest decision he ever made. Only an instant later, the hot, rotten-smelling breath of the grizzly blasted his neck.

In the tug of war with the stallion, the silver-tipped beast had come away with only a mouthful of horse tail for all his trouble. Knocked cross-eyed from the blow to his skull and smarting from the drumming his

shoulders had taken, the bruin was still spoiling for a fight. He swung his
slavering muzzle from side to side, his damaged nose having trouble sepa-
rating the strong man scent from the smell of the escaped horse and the
odor of the decaying cow.

Ricardo felt the bear snuffling along his legs. The young man's mind
was racing with horrifying possibilities. Even if he convinced the grizzly he
was dead, what if the bear decided to add him to the carrion pile?

That chilling nightmare became a bloody reality when the humpback
suddenly closed his jaw over Ricardo's head and sank his razor-sharp teeth
to the bone. Ricardo let out a yell almost equal to the bay's.

The bear dropped him, confused. A deep, angry growl rumbled like an
earthquake from the depths of the beast.

In the split second that elapsed between the grizzly's surprise and its
decision to tear the man-thing into bloody pieces, an obsidian arrowhead
sliced into its neck.

Ricardo scrambled for his life. Playing dead was now out of the question; he was only seconds away from the reality.

With one hand he held his pierced and torn scalp, bleeding from half a
dozen deep gashes. With the other hand he dragged himself over the
rocks, crying with terror and praying that he would not pass out.

Will Reed nocked another arrow as the grizzly sat up on its haunches,
roaring. It swatted clumsily at the painful barb sticking in its neck.

The shaft broke off and the bear drove the point inward, sending the
creature into a rage of pain. The second arrow struck low on the flank,
and the bear dropped its great head to bite at its own side.

Closing its teeth over the barbed shaft and ripping it free of flesh, the
silver-tip stood erect. Flashing eyes searched for the source of the cruel
flying things.

The grizzly spotted Will standing next to a tree at the edge of the clearing and bellowed at him, challenging him. "I am the master here," he
roared. "No one disputes the ground I own and lives to tell of it."

Will fumbled in the pouch for another arrowhead. His hand closed over
one, drew it out—too small! The tiny flake of stone was only fit for killing
rabbits, not this berserk hulk of killing ferocity.

He scrabbled through the pouch again, coming up with another only a
little larger. Across the stone basin Will could see Ricardo scrambling up a
rocky ledge to safety. Time to think about his own safety.

"Paco," Will called. "Paco, distract him! Throw a rock, something!"
There was no answer; the Indian was long gone.

The bear's claws rattled the granite as he dropped to all fours, ready to
charge. This contest was about to end!

A quick glance upward—no tree limbs near the ground—no time to run—no way to the safety of the rocks. Go down fighting.

Will drew out one last arrow shaft as the bear rushed, fitted the barb to the socket, nocked the arrow, and released.

The last arrow, a mere pinprick, also lodged in the thick folds of the bear's neck. The beast, on him now, seized the bow in its teeth, tearing it from him.

One more swat of an enormous paw at this latest nuisance, then the human was to be crushed. The grizzly batted hurriedly at the latest arrow, striking again the first barb whose shaft just protruded from the long, coarse hair, and driving it home.

The five-inch-long shard of razor-sharp black glass, pushed by a ton of angry grizzly, sliced through the bear's carotid artery. Blood burst from the wound, spraying the silver-tipped fur with crimson.

The bear collapsed like a huge fur sack full of air that had been suddenly punctured. The grizzly's lips were still curled back from his fangs, and on either side of the massive jaws lay shattered pieces of Falcon's bow.

The terror of the canyon lay silently in a heap at Will's feet.

But Will knew there was no time to relish this unlikely victory. Turning to climb the rock face Ricardo had crawled up, he found the horseman cradling his lacerated head in both hands. Blood streamed over and between his fingers, staining his hands and face scarlet.

The young man's breath was coming in ragged gasps, and he did not try to look up when Will approached.

"Can you hear me?" Will asked gently in Spanish.

"Si, and I think I owe you my life," Ricardo choked between gasps.

"Just sit easy until I find something to bind you up with. We've got to get you some help fast. You're losing too much blood."

Will tore a strip off the Spaniard's linen shirt. "Take your hands down now," he instructed.

Slowly, reluctantly, Ricardo did as he was told. Will saw why the injured man had been holding on so tightly: his scalp was bitten completely through in places. White bone gleamed dully against crimson streaks. The scalp was nearly detached around half the circle of the grizzly's bite. Ricardo's face visibly slipped, his features wrinkling grotesquely.

Trying to keep the wounded man from seeing him shudder, Will worked swiftly to wrap the scalp with linen. Searching for the least injured place he could find, Will knotted the bandage there and prayed the bleeding would stop.

Will had to guide Ricardo's booted feet into the cracks in the rock in order for the mauled man to climb back down. Reaching the bottom, the trapper brought the young horseman a drink of water from the pool.

"I'll fix you as comfortable as I can," said Will. "I'm a stranger here, so I need you to tell me the quickest route to get help."

"No need, señor," replied Ricardo, "just let me catch my breath and perhaps you can get me one more drink of that excellent water."

When Will had done so, Ricardo placed two fingers against his tongue and blew a shrill whistle. "Aiiee," he winced, "I never knew whistling to hurt before!"

A few moments passed and the bay horse trotted back into the clearing. Lather covered his neck and flanks and his eyes were wild, but he came obediently at his master's signal.

"Do you want me to walk and lead him?" asked Will.

"Not necessary. Lorenzo can carry both of us, and he knows the way home."

Assisting Ricardo into the high-cantled saddle, Will then mounted behind him.

"If you can take the reins, señor, I think perhaps I will concentrate on not falling off again," he said to Will.

Although it had slowed, blood was still flowing from the lacerations and dripping from Ricardo's matted hair.

"Señor, if it is far to your home, then we should seek help sooner," observed Will, keeping a tight grip on the reins to prevent the keyed-up stallion from racing down the faint trail.

A weak voice haltingly responded, "Turn the bay . . . at the fork . . . the mission is just . . ." Then Ricardo's voice faded out altogether.

But Will had heard all that was necessary. He settled himself firmly, gripping with his knees, and wrapped one arm around the now unconscious rider.

"Come on, Lorenzo," he urged. "Move out." The long-legged bay stretched out his neck and doubled his speed.

Just over the crest of a small hill, the horse broke free of the surrounding brush. Less than a mile below them to the west was the whitewashed mission. Its single bell tower glistened white against the green landscape and the blue of the ocean beyond.

Will rode directly up to the steps of the mission. Small adobe houses and thatched huts crowded the square in front of the great church. It was midafternoon and the square was nearly empty.

The clattering entrance of Lorenzo and the spectacle of the buckskin-clad stranger holding tightly to the bloodied body caused instant commotion. People poured into the square from every direction, then someone rang an alarm bell, as they did for a pirate attack or a fire.

A gray-haired man dressed in the cowled gray robe of a Franciscan padre hurried down the front steps of the mission. At the sight of Ricardo's waxy complexion caked with gore, the priest crossed himself and cried out, "What has happened? Who has murdered poor Ricardo?"

"A grizzly, Father. But he's still alive," explained Will. "Please help me ease him down."

The priest called two neophyte Indians to assist him and the three gently received Ricardo's limp body. As they moved quickly around the side of the building, the priest called back over his shoulder, "We have an infirmary. Follow us."

Will stepped from the horse and looked around for someone to hold the bay. A young boy approached and offered to care for Lorenzo.

In front of the mission was a fountain bubbling with clear water. Will decided that what he needed more than the infirmary was a quick wash and a long drink.

Stepping over to the pool, he washed Ricardo's blood from his hands and face with double handfuls of water. Once the filth was cleansed away, Will bent over the fountain and drank deeply.

When he stood upright, he saw that everyone in the square was staring at him with undisguised curiosity. Neophytes in short tunics like that worn by Paco were standing in groups, evidently discussing him. At a long tank fed by the outflow of the fountain, mission women stopped their laundry chores to gaze. Across the square, a mixed group of soldiers and men dressed in short jackets and tight pants were pointing at him and gesturing. A dark-skinned priest in a gray robe stared for a minute, then hurried away from the mission.

For the first time in a long while, Will was embarrassed. He was grateful when one of the Indians who had helped carry Ricardo returned and approached him. "Father Sanchez asks if you are wounded also? He wants you to come."

"No, I'm all right," responded Will. "But I would like to see how . . . what did the priest call him? How Ricardo is doing."

15

"PLEASE, ALLOW ME to pour you some more wine," Father Sanchez offered.

"No, thanks," responded Will. "It beats anything I ever tried before though. Did you have it brought by ship?"

The pudgy friar chuckled, "Only if you mean the rootstock. We made this wine from grapes grown on our own sunny hillsides." The priest poured himself another glassful and sipped with an appreciative pride. "We are trying other varieties of grapes as well, but I think this will rival any zinfandel in the world."

As Will sat back from the linen-covered dining table, an Indian servant whisked away his empty dinner plate and another removed the silver serving tray bearing the remains of a joint of mutton.

The trapper glanced down at his stained buckskin clothes. Even washed, wrung out and dried, they still smelled of woodsmoke and carried the stains of hunting, fighting and overland journeying. Since arriving at the mission that afternoon, Will had cleaned up and shaved, but his unruly thatch of hair and travel-weary clothing embarrassed him here.

"You live very well," observed Will.

"It is surprising isn't it, here on the edge of the world?" replied Father Sanchez. "Of course I am just the inheritor of great men of faith like Fathers Serra and Garces. When they arrived, they had to live in reed huts, just like the Indians. Can you imagine that? But look what has been achieved in less than sixty years."

"What about the Indians, Father?" prompted Will as a servant placed a china cup of fragrantly steaming hot chocolate before him.

"Oh, they are such children," laughed the priest. "We have all we can handle constantly checking on them to see if they have followed instructions. They are just as likely to run off and go fishing, but they are good-hearted, simple people.

"We have such a large neophyte population now that we can hire out the young men to the local ranchos for wages."

"What do the workers do with their pay?" inquired Will.

"Bless me," chuckled Father Sanchez. "You don't think such simple ones are responsible enough to handle *money?* Oh no! I meant that their wages are credited to the mission's account, of course, to balance what we purchase in supplies."

"Don't your workers resent giving up all their pay?"

Father Sanchez looked as if this were an astounding thought. "Why should they?" he remarked with surprise. "They receive all the necessities from our hands." He glanced down at his own soft, plump fingers. "No one forced them to become neophytes, señor, and we keep no secrets from them before or after they join our community."

"Isn't it true that most of those young workers are born to Christian families already attached to the mission?"

"That is correct," agreed the padre. "Sadly, the unbelievers of the interior are not as receptive as those of the coast."

"I'm not so sure that's true," responded Will. He reminded the Mexican priest of the interest in Christianity he had seen among the Yokuts. "But there is something else going on as well," he continued. "They seem very suspicious of your people, Father. I understand a very hostile tribe of desert-dwellers is already at war with you.

"You must understand this is a time of confusion," commented Father Sanchez. "We Mexicans have only been free of the yoke of Spain these past ten years. I am Mexican-born, but many of the highest-ranking families like that of Ricardo's father are highly suspect to the Mexican officials.

"Moreover," he continued, "there is much strife in Mexico itself. The military officials have so many conflicts that they have adopted harsh measures against many tribes. We hope to prosper here in California without such difficulties, but who can say?"

The padre's discussion was interrupted by an Indian servant announcing that Captain Zuniga had arrived.

The little priest's round face broke into a frown, the only time during the meal Will had seen him do so. "I wonder what he can want?" muttered Father Sanchez. Turning to Will, he added, "Excuse me a moment, please."

But before the friar could rise from the table, Zuniga's lean form and scarred face advanced into the room. He was accompanied by two soldiers wearing bullhide vests and carrying flintlock muskets. This did not look to Will like a friendly visit.

Sanchez tried to be gracious. "Ah, Capitan Zuniga," he began, "may I introduce my guest, Will Reed. He is the trapper from the east who rescued young Rivera."

"The American spy, you mean," said Zuniga abruptly. "Why was he not reported to me immediately? Where are his papers?"

Will answered the questions for himself, trying to smother the instant dislike and hostility he felt. "I only just got here, Capitan. The good Father allowed me to get cleaned up and treated me to a fine dinner. I'm no spy. I was part of a trapping party that was attacked by Mojaves. Captain Beckwith was our leader. He had papers from the governor of Sante Fe, but Beckwith didn't make—"

"Silence," shouted Zuniga. "I have heard enough. I arrest you as a spy. Take him away!" Will was immediately seized by the two soldiers. Zuniga grabbed the necklace of woodpecker topknots and ripped it from Will's neck. The captain ground it under his boot as he followed his captive out the door.

Sanchez protested, "But he saved the boy's life—brought him here to the mission. You can't do this."

The captain turned and remarked coldly, "You had better keep quiet, Father. Harboring a spy is treason and traitors are hanged." He paused to let the point sink in before adding maliciously, "Just like spies."

16

WILL'S ADOBE CELL was exactly eight paces long and eight paces wide. After twenty or thirty trips each direction, he could have walked blindfolded and stopped with the tip of his nose one-half inch from the wall.

He actually had been blindfolded and his hands tied behind his back for the march to the cell. These were removed when he was thrust into the prison. There was a tiny window in the stout oak door, but it was already night in Santa Barbara and nothing could be seen.

The tiny room contained a wooden bucket for a chamber pot and a moth-eaten blanket with which to cover the bare earthen floor. That was all.

Will found the blanket by feeling around in the dark, but its prior owners—thousands of fleas—found him the same way. Tossing it to a corner of the cell, he spent the night pacing, thinking, and scratching.

"So, Don Jose, now that we have him, what are we going to do with him?" inquired Captain Zuniga.

"For the time being, nothing."

"Nothing!" exploded the hot-tempered captain. "How long do you think it will be before Don Pedro blasts us from Monterrey to Mexico City for imprisoning the man who saved his son? He is still a powerful man and can hurt our plans with Figueroa—perhaps even get me recalled."

The ranchero rocked back and forth on his small feet, a smirk of smug satisfaction on his face. "So, when Don Pedro demands the American's release or else a letter will be sent to the governor, you will obligingly release him."

"But why antagonize Rivera first?"

Zuniga hated the condescension with which Dominguez spoke, but was forced to listen to an explanation that dripped with it. "My dear capitan, you will be at your most politically astute. You will say to Don Pedro, 'So sorry . . . just following orders . . . anxious to please you . . . completely understand.'"

He continued, "Don Pedro will accept your apologies and be mollified at your willingness to see reason, despite your having acted in accordance with written law."

"But what is the point of this charade?" demanded the blunt man of action.

"If we win the confidence of Don Pedro, all is well. If not, well, it gives us something to hold over him."

"You mean—"

"Of course. If need be, the American will be *proven* a spy. And who is it that demanded his release against standing orders? The traitor, Don Pedro Rivera y Cruz."

"Careful! Slowly now! Set him down gently!" Francesca Rivera y Cruz saw to it that her brother was carried safely upstairs to his bedroom. Then she took personal charge of tucking him in bed and changing his bandages.

Though she caught her breath at the severity of the gashes in his scalp, she bit her lip and said nothing. Ricardo protested that Father Sanchez had just renewed the compresses before allowing him to go home, but Francesca swallowed the lump in her throat and told her brother to hush and lie still or he'd be going back to the padre. He complied.

When she was convinced that Ricardo was properly attended to, she decided to ride to the mission to thank the good father and the American from the east who had teamed together to save her brother's life.

Francesca called the stableboy, Miquelito, to put her sidesaddle on the buckskin. She had always been too impatient to ride in a slowly creaking carreta anywhere, let alone all the way to Santa Barbara. Off she cantered, leaving her father and aunt to look after Ricardo.

The ride along the curving lanes was a familiar one. Once each week Francesca devoted a day to teaching mission children how to read. Mission policy stated that the children begin work at the looms at the age of nine. Francesca felt that if the neophytes were ever to become gente de razón, people of reason, they needed to be able to read and write.

Although Father Sanchez applauded her assistance, not everyone believed this was a good thing. Some of her father's friends said that education made the Indians think too highly of themselves. Others thought it beneath the dignity of a daughter of an important family to befriend the Indian children. Francesca ignored both opinions, and her father could only shrug his shoulders and reply, "In her heart, she takes after her sainted mother."

As she rode into the dusty plaza in front of the mission, several children were playing near the fountain. Seeing her, they dashed to greet her. "Doña Francesca," they called, "today is not the day for lessons, is it?"

"No, children," she smiled in return, "not today. I will be back on Friday as usual. Where is Father Sanchez?"

The brown-skinned children directed her along the arched colonnade, past the front of the church. Chico, the largest boy of her class, reported having seen the priest enter the mayordomo's quarters on the east side of the mission.

Francesca rewarded Chico by allowing him to hold her horse, which made him immensely proud and the envy of his friends. She hurried to the red-tile-roofed home that stood in the shadow of the bell tower. Reaching its porch, she met Sanchez coming out.

"Ah, Francesca," he called anxiously. "Your brother is doing well? No sudden turn for the worse? He insisted on going home this morning and I agreed against my better judgment. Is he all right?"

"He's fine, Father," she reassured the priest. "I came to thank you for attending him. I also want to thank the man Ricardo tells us saved his life. Where is he? We want to invite him to be a guest in our home."

The chubby padre looked embarrassed and awkwardly shuffled his sandalled feet. "I did not tell Ricardo this morning because I did not want to upset him."

Now it was the girl's turn to be concerned. "Tell him what?" demanded Francesca. "What has happened?"

"The American, Will Reed is his name, has been arrested. Capitan Zuniga came last night and took him to the presidio."

"For what?" exclaimed Francesca. "What has he done?"

"Nothing, to my knowledge. Zuniga says the American is without papers, or something. In fact, I was just going over the day's workplans with our mayordomo and then I intended to ride out to your home to explain this to your father."

"That will not be necessary," blazed Francesca, her eyes flashing dangerously. "I will go home at once and tell him myself!"

17

TOWARD DAWN WILL had dozed off. His weary body had slid down a wall to a seated position, and there he remained as gray light filled the tiny barred window, filtering around the cracks of the door.

The sound of the heavy door creaking on reluctant hinges brought him awake. Jumping to his feet, he found himself staring into the muzzle of a musket. The soldier aiming it told him to back to the opposite wall and not move until the door was shut again.

Will asked several questions of the soldier, but neither he nor his companion made any response. The second soldier set down a wooden bowl and clay jug, then slammed the stout door closed.

The bottle was full of water, for which Will was grateful, but he found it impossible to give thanks for the food.

The bowl contained a mixture of cooked beans and cornmeal with a greasy scum layering the thick mush and drowned weevils floating on the top. A rancid stench attacked Will's nostrils as well. He placed the bowl back down near the door, took the jug of water, and for the second time backed away from the entrance.

Could probably use that stuff to kill the fleas in the blanket, he thought. Once again he fell to brooding about his situation.

He had been attacked by the Mojaves for being an accomplice of the Mexicans. Now the Mexicans figured him for somebody's spy. He berated himself for leaving the Yokuts.

Did this happen to the Good Samaritan, he wondered. *Maybe next time someone's in trouble it should be every man for himself.*

Will had plenty of time to wonder how serious the threat of hanging might be. Of course, if the quality of the fare did not improve, he'd starve to death before they could hang him.

By afternoon, yellow light filled the hole of the door. Taking a deep breath, Will moved the bowl and its noxious contents to the same corner as the vermin-filled blanket.

The opening was only big enough for one eye at a time. Bending down a little, he pressed half his face into it.

He was looking across a dusty courtyard of what was evidently the military garrison. Two soldiers passed, one of them leading a mule. He made out the shadow of a tall pole, perhaps a flag pole, even though he could not see the staff itself.

"Zuniga!" boomed a voice in no-nonsense tones. "Zuniga, where is the American? I want him out now or heads will roll, starting with yours!"

Will could see that the dusty grounds of the presidio had suddenly been stirred into a flurry of activity. A balding man whose muscular size emphasized his obvious anger galloped into the courtyard.

The horse he rode was as black as midnight and he led a fine gray, but the newcomer's face was flushed a deep red that continued over his bald head. The veins of his neck bulged dangerously. Will watched him fling himself from the charger and contemptuously toss the reins to a startled soldier.

The man demanded something of the soldier. Will could only make out another booming, "Zuniga!" Shrinking back from the large man's fury, the soldier pointed a shaking arm over the man's shoulder.

Will glimpsed the captain who had arrested him at the mission advancing into the scrap of his vision. The officer was in full uniform, almost as if he had been expecting this visit.

The volume of the shouted demands fell as the officer made calming gestures. Next the officer nodded his head vigorously and pointed toward Will's cell. The two men turned toward the space where the scout was confined.

Will stepped back against the far wall. A rattle announced that the bolt holding the bar in place across the cell door was pulled free, then the door swung open.

The large man strode directly into the tiny space. "You are the American who saved my son from the grizzly." Don Pedro offered this as a statement, not a question, but Will nodded his head.

"I am Don Pedro Rivera y Cruz," stated the ranchero formally. "I am completely and totally in your debt and have come to see that you are immediately freed."

Don Pedro whirled around to face Captain Zuniga and repeated, "Immediately."

The officer shrugged. "Of course, Don Pedro. As you wish. We were simply following the standing orders for treatment of those who arrive in our country without proper papers. I am sure you understand that—"

The ranchero waved his large hand and raised his voice again. "Enough! I want this fine man out of your . . ." he wrinkled his nose in disgust, "your accommodations this instant."

"But certainly," agreed Zuniga. "You will accept personal responsibility for his whereabouts and behavior?"

"Yes, yes," snapped Don Pedro. "Bring my horses around now!"

Outside the gate of the presidio, Don Pedro's angry flush had faded and he spoke apologetically to Will.

"I cannot begin to express my sorrow at your treatment, Señor Reed. What must you think of our manners to take such a heroic gentleman as yourself and throw you into such a . . . such a . . . hole?"

The two men were riding side by side, Will mounted on the handsome gray. "The capitan's hospitality was less than cordial," he agreed, "but I've been treated worse. If he was just following orders, I guess it wasn't his fault."

"Ha!" snorted Don Pedro, the anger welling up again. "He's up to something, that one. Currying favor with his commanding general, no doubt."

"Your pardon, señor, but are you a military man yourself? You sit your horse like one, and a magnificent beast he is too."

Don Pedro's smile expressed his approval of Will's judgment. "You have an eye for horses and horsemen, eh young man? Yes, I am retired from the army. I received my land and El Negro here as recompense for my years of service. But the young officers today . . ." He gave a contemptuous gesture with his free hand.

"And how is your son?" inquired Will.

"Out of danger, God be praised. You will see for yourself soon."

"We are returning to the mission then?"

"No, no. You are going to be the honored guest of my humble home. Ricardo was allowed to come home and is anxious to express his gratitude. But now, tell me about yourself."

The two horses kept up an easy, slow canter that covered the ground in a fluid motion. Will related his experiences since joining the trapping party, the ambush, and his time with the Yokuts.

"That reminds me, señor," said Will, interrupting his story. "I came from the Sierras with a mission Indian named Paco, but he disappeared when the grizzly attacked. Do you know him?"

"Paco is a knave and a coward. You are fortunate he did not murder you in your sleep. Give him no more thought. He certainly ran away to save his own skin. If he appears, he shall receive the flogging he so richly deserves."

Don Pedro cast an appraising eye over Will's riding form. "You ride very well. What do you think of Flotada?"

"Flotada? Oh, 'massage'? Do you call him that because of his gentle rocking movement?"

Don Pedro laughed, a deep, resonant laugh that bounced off the green peaks and echoed through the oaks. "Now, yes! But you should have seen him when he was an uneducated brute. We called him Flotada because he *bucked so hard!"*

"My congratulations," offered Will. "He is well-mannered now and a real looker."

"He should be, young man. Flotada is a true son of Andalusian Torda, the Spanish grays. And," the ranchero paused, "he is yours."

18

"**T**HIS IS YOUR 'humble' home?" exclaimed Will at the first sight of Don Pedro's rancho. "It is magnificent!"

A flock of pigeons swirled like a cloud of white and gray smoke at the riders' approach. The whitewashed two-story adobe building was nearly eighty feet across its porticoed front. A veranda completely encircled the home, matched by a second-story balcony.

A trio of Indian servants ran to meet the returning ranchero and his guest. Two of them accepted the reins of El Negro and Flotado, while the third, bowing low first, led the way up to the main entrance.

Outside the front door was a bench. Don Pedro sat down, the servant kneeling in front of him. At Will's curious glance, he smiled and explained, "The floors in my home are polished oak. My dear wife, God rest her soul, made me promise to never wear my spurs into the house."

He gestured at Will's moccasin-encased feet. "You do not have that need at present; however, we will soon have you outfitted properly."

Don Pedro led the way. An enormously tall clock with a polished brass pendulum the size and shape of a banjo graced the entryway.

The ranchero gestured toward a formal parlor as they passed it. "My family and servants would all like to meet you, but first Ricardo wishes to thank you. He is confined to his bed upstairs."

The hallway terminated in a broad, elegant staircase leading up to the second floor. Dressed in his travel-worn buckskins, Will felt even more out of place here than at the mission.

Don Pedro brought him to the second doorway at the right of the stairs. Propped up in an oversized four-poster bed was Ricardo. His head was swathed in bandages and his color looked faded.

Seeing Will, he raised a hand in greeting. An attempted smile only brought pain to the already stretched skin of his face.

"You will pardon me, señor, if I cannot rise to greet you," murmured

Ricardo. "The good Father Sanchez, who is the only doctor we have in Santa Barbara, forbids me to move about yet."

"Señor, think nothing of it. To have met oso pardo face-to-face and live to tell of it! Your grandchildren will beg to hear this story over and over," commented Will.

"Yes, head-to-head even," corrected Ricardo ruefully. "And the living here to tell of it is solely due to your intervention."

Will shuffled his moccasins awkwardly. "God let our paths cross at just that instant, so your thanks are due to Him. Had you been armed and I the one attacked, you would have done the same for me."

Then to forestall any further expressions of gratitude, Will asked for more details about the young ranchero's recuperation.

"The good padre stitched my scalp back so tightly that I fear I may look more like a citizen of Cathay than of Mexico. He assures me that all will be well in time, even my left ear, which he at first despaired of saving."

Don Pedro, who had been listening from the doorway, added that Will's speedy actions had saved Ricardo's manly good looks as well as his life. "If he is to make me a grandfather, it is well if the young ladies do not run away in terror when he approaches."

Turning to Will, he added, "Ricardo must rest now, but we would like you to remain as our guest for as long as you wish. The room next to this is prepared for your use and . . . you may wish . . . you will find . . . There are some articles of clothing which should fit you," he concluded delicately.

Will looked from father to son and saw the same expectantly hopeful expression. "It would be my great pleasure to be your guest," he agreed.

"Good!" said Don Pedro, clapping his hands. He regretted his enthusiasm a second later when he saw Ricardo wince at the sudden loud noise. "Shh," he instructed unnecessarily. "Ricardo needs quiet for a time."

The two men closed the door as they exited the room. "Would you care to join me in the parlor in an hour's time?" asked the ranchero. At Will's agreement, he showed the trapper to the guestroom, then turned and went downstairs.

The room was the equal of Ricardo's. There was a finely made walnut armoire and matching dresser and a bed with a feather mattress that looked three feet thick. Trying to recall the last time he had slept on a bed, Will concluded that nothing he had ever slept on deserved to be called a bed compared to this. "Hope I don't drown in it," he chuckled to himself.

Neatly laid out across the silk coverlet was not just one set of clothing but multiple sets—dress pants, silk shirts, stylish jackets, undergarments. Will wondered what the correct dress was and if he could figure out what went with what. He determined to locate Don Pedro and ask for advice.

Opening the door to find his way downstairs, he bumped headlong into a young woman carrying a bowl and a pitcher of water. In the momentary jostle that followed, Will ended up catching the pitcher just before its contents went on the floor. "Excuse me," he said in English, then changing to Spanish, "I mean, pardon!"

The girl, dressed in a dark red skirt and a white scooped-neck blouse, had shining dark hair that fell softly to the middle of her neck and over smoothly rounded shoulders.

Completely caught off guard, Will lapsed again into English and stammered, "Say, you're really something!"

"Cómo, señor?" returned the girl, appearing not to understand.

Will watched as a rosy glow spread up the señorita's throat to her cheeks. Her complexion, like a fine porcelain cup held up to a firelight, set off her lovely dark eyes.

Finally collecting himself, Will said in Spanish, "No harm done, señorita. No need to be embarrassed. Were you bringing these for me?"

"Si, Señor," she murmured demurely, looking down at the floor.

"Gracias," said Will, taking the bowl from the girl. "Would you tell your master that I'd like his advice on proper dress?"

A curious expression flashed through the young woman's eyes as she looked quickly at Will's face and then away. She pointed toward a complete suit hanging over a chair in the corner of the room. "Not necessary, señor. Perhaps that one there?"

"Ah. Yes. Just right," mumbled Will as the girl departed.

Will dressed in his new California splendor. But he found his thoughts drifting to the beautiful maid of the Rivera household.

The white serge pants went on underneath. The second pair were of heavier dark green wool. They buttoned with silver barrel buttons down the outside of each leg. Will had seen Don Pedro wearing something similar and knew that the overbritches were left unbuttoned below the knee so that the white trouser legs would show.

A finely woven white linen shirt was intended to be worn under a short dark green jacket. The jacket also sported silver clasps to match the pants, but Will had noticed the clasps were left open.

White linen stockings and glove-soft buckskin boots accompanied the outfit. Also included was a flat-crowned, stiff-brimmed black hat trimmed with a horsehair hat band braided with silver beads. Will elected to omit the hat until something could be done with his hair: it would never fit under the crown now.

Shaved, smelling of lilac water and dressed in the fanciest apparel he'd ever touched, Will cautiously admired himself in the mirror. Around the high collar of the white shirt he knotted a black cravat. The last time he had worn a necktie had been at his uncle's funeral in Vicksburg.

Taken altogether, not half bad, he thought. *I guess that maidservant will approve.* He heard the clock in the downstairs hall strike the hour. *Now to see if the rest of the household agrees.*

Stepping onto the landing at the head of the stairs, Will saw Don Pedro awaiting him at the bottom. "Bueno, Señor Reed," encouraged the ranchero, "you look splendid. Please come along and meet my family."

The sitting room was already filled with people. Seated in the middle of the group was a gray-haired woman with a rather prim expression. She was introduced as Aunt Doña Eulalia. The household matriarch inspected Will closely before suggesting her approval by extending her hand.

Gathered around her chair were the household servants, the head foreman of the rancho and several godchildren of Don Pedro. Each acknowledged the introduction with a bow or curtsy of respect as protocol demanded for the savior of the heir.

When the formal introductions were completed, everyone seemed to relax, until Don Pedro remembered, "Where is Francesca? Why isn't she here?"

From the hallway behind Will a lilting female voice announced, "I'm over here, Father. Everyone was in such a hurry to meet Señor Reed that I was left to put up my hair by myself."

At the first sound of her voice, Will had been startled, then embarrassed. He had mistaken her for a servant! Now it was his turn to feel the heat of a flush rising in his cheeks as he tried to recall their exchange. What had he said? Had he been too forward? Was she offended?

Dressed in fine lace instead of the simple skirt and blouse worn earlier, Francesca entered the room adjusting a lace mantilla on a high comb. She looked the part of a Spanish princess. Her eyes seemed to have a mocking quality as they locked with Will's, as if to say, *The tables are turned now, aren't they?*

But she said nothing to give away the game. Advancing directly toward Will, she offered her hand in greeting, then called to the others, "All right now. Introductions are complete. Must we be so stiff?"

Taking the tongue-tied Will by the arm, she guided an instantly chattering throng into the dining room. Bustling servants soon laid on a feast of monumental proportions.

A steaming tureen of sopa de carne seca y arroz was placed before Doña Eulalia, who stood at one end of the table opposite Don Pedro. Will and Francesca were across from each other in the middle of each side, flanked by the godchildren.

Don Pedro recited a blessing over the food, then all were seated. When the tureen's cover was raised, the tantalizing aroma of spicy jerky and rice soup, filled the air. Doña Eulalia tasted the first portion, then allowed a maid to ladle a serving into each diner's bowl.

Will found himself staring down into the soup bowl, looking for the courage to raise his face to Francesca's. Since no inspiration came, he occupied himself by taking several mouthfuls of the soup. It was not until the fourth swallow that the chili seasoning took effect, causing Will to grab for his water glass.

He was afraid he had shamed himself again, until he heard Don Pedro praise the mixture by declaring, "Whew! This broth is capable of raising the dead! Pass the tortillas and the water!"

Roast lamb accompanied by beans, corn, and tortillas was seasoned by the spice of conversation. Everyone wanted to know Will's history and to hear his stories.

The children exclaimed over the tales of Will's wilderness wanderings and Indian ambushes. They all complimented him on his mastery of Spanish.

Finally gathering enough courage to look at Francesca, Will found that she appeared genuinely friendly and interested, with no trace of mocking. She said sincerely, "You may protest that it was Providence which brought you to meet the grizzly, but it was your decision to face the bear when you could have thought only of yourself. Gracias, Señor Reed, thank you."

"In two weeks," announced Don Pedro, "we will have a fiesta and invite all our neighbors to share in honoring Señor Reed." Excited squeals broke out from the younger children around the table.

After dinner, Will managed to find a moment alone with Francesca. "I want to apologize," he said quietly, "for mistaking you for a—for a servant, I mean."

"Doña Eulalia would have scolded *me* for not correcting you at once," she replied with a sincere smile. Offering her smooth white hand to Will again, Francesca said politely, "Let us say no more about it." Then she left Will with the memory of her hand in his.

19

"**M**OST ESTEEMED DON Pedro," began Don Dominguez.

Such formal speech coming from a neighbor, thought Don Pedro, *I wonder what is coming next?*

"For some time I have given careful consideration to a matter of great importance," continued Dominguez, "and I have decided that the time is correct for me to approach you."

"Go on," said Don Pedro cautiously.

"We are not getting any younger, you and I."

"This is most certainly true," agreed the ranchero. "Do you have a way to prevent it? Perhaps you have discovered a spring of magic water on your property such as the Indios say exists near the Paso de Robles?"

Don Dominguez looked offended at the jesting tone of his neighbor's reply. He ran his hands through his hair as if straightening his ruffled dignity before speaking again.

"As you are aware, I have no son, no heir to my estate. I am, alas, childless," he continued.

Aware that this matter was a difficult and socially delicate one for any ranchero, Don Pedro at once became properly subdued.

"You, yourself," Don Dominguez resumed, "almost lost, most tragically, the staff of your old age, Don Ricardo."

Don Pedro nodded his great bald head and felt again the stab of terror he had experienced when first hearing about Ricardo's injury. Dominguez had gained his complete attention.

"Fate has played with your future in a most devilish fashion. First, your lovely daughter loses her betrothed almost on the eve of her wedding, then you lost your sainted wife, and now almost your son. Do you not see how Providence has preserved you from the misery of Job?"

"I *am* very much aware of how blessed I am that I *still* have two strong, healthy children."

"Is it possible you have missed the divine warning within this blessing? Certainly you see that you must take steps to secure the future, even as I have?"

"What steps exactly?"

"I have decided to adopt Capitan Zuniga as my son and heir, and I would like to announce this important decision at your fiesta."

"I congratulate you. You are certainly welcome to make this announce-ment at our festivities, but wouldn't you prefer to hold one of your own for the purpose?"

Dominguez smiled at Don Pedro; a slow, easy smile that he must have practiced for days. "But for the second announcement, this would be the proper procedure."

"What second announcement?"

Speaking very carefully, Don Dominguez explained, "Times are very uncertain, are they not? The Mexican government, if it can be called such, changes almost daily, except in its disregard for us Californianos. We must be prepared to take charge of our own destiny."

Don Pedro looked surprised. "You wish to make a political speech at my fiesta?" he demanded.

"No, no!" corrected Dominguez. "You misunderstand me. My point is that you have been most understandably protective of your daughter. But it is time for you to secure her future and yours. My good friend and soon-to-be heir, Capitan Zuniga, has asked me to petition you for the hand of your daughter in marriage."

Don Pedro's first reaction was to be offended at what struck him as a very presumptuous proposal. But on second thought, maybe it made a thread of sense. Zuniga was a strong, though not especially likeable man, and was of a suitable age to marry Francesca. Though not a landowner, if the officer were Dominguez's heir, he would inherit sizable holdings. Moreover, some Rivera property bordered on Dominguez's rancho and if something should happen to Ricardo, while he was unmarried, at least Francesca could retain the land.

"I will not give you an answer at the present, but I will think on this matter," concluded Don Pedro.

"Gracias, Don Pedro. That is all I ask."

20

"QUIET, HERE HE comes now," cautioned Don Dominguez to Fa-ther Quintana. "Do you understand what to do?"

"Perfectly," assured the little priest.

The two plotters were seated on a low adobe wall that edged the plaza of Pueblo Santa Barbara. They had chosen their location well: just around the corner from the cantina where Don Pedro liked to enjoy a pot of hot, dark chocolate after an early morning ride into town.

Seeing the ranchero arrive and drop off his horse at the livery stable, the two had ample time to secure their position. Don Pedro was seated at his favorite table near the plaza and already sipping his favorite beverage when they began to speak.

In a voice just loud enough to carry to Don Pedro's ears, Dominguez began, "I just don't know what to do, Father."

"I am certain that you will do what is right, my son," soothed the padre.

"Yes, but which is correct? To carry a tale which may be only malicious rumor, or to warn my neighbor against what may be a snake in the grass?"

Don Pedro's ears had by now identified their voices and pricked up at the word "neighbor."

"Tell me all the particulars. Perhaps I can assist you in making up your mind. Rest assured, I will tell no one."

"I do not want to slander anyone, Father, you know that."

"Rest easy, Don Jose, tell me the worst."

"It concerns this American, this Will Reed. As you know, Father, he came here overland as a trader in furs . . . a so-called mountain man."

"Yes, my son, go on," encouraged Father Quintana. Don Pedro was thinking the same thing.

"It has been reported to me that this is a bloodthirsty man who has killed before and will undoubtedly kill again."

Quintana made light of the accusation. "But surely he has fought his way through territory held by savages. One must not judge—"

"Yes, Father, but there is more. He lived for a long time with the Indios . . . like the Indios. He has had Indian wives, and more than one, indulging in heathen and perverted customs I cannot speak of."

"Is this true, Don Dominguez? Can it be proven?"

"Oh no, Father. I heard it from . . . well, not matter . . . another wayfarer, who had no reason to lie. But tell me, Father, what would be best to do?" Dominguez stood, brushed off the seat of his dark blue trousers, and straightened his hat. Quintana stretched as he stood and smoothed out his coarse gray robe.

Though Don Pedro strained his ears, he could not make out any more of the conversation as the two men strolled off across the dusty, sunlit plaza.

He was still sitting, leaning his hand on one work-thickened palm, ten minutes later. A waiter finally stopped by to ask if the chocolate was unsatisfactory.

Don Pedro peered into his cup with as much distaste as if it contained vinegar. "No," he said, "nothing is satisfactory this morning."

From the window of his study, Don Pedro watched as his daughter strolled slowly across the courtyard with the big trapper, Will Reed. The two were engaged in a lively conversation, a fact which did not altogether please him. They walked like two people more interested in each other than in where they were going. Neither seemed to notice the flowers that bloomed on the trellis and lined the adobe-tiled path. Nor did they look up at the blue sky and admire the clear, cloudless weather. No. Each looked only at the other as they walked aimlessly.

Sunlight glinted on the raven black hair of Francesca as if to illuminate the vast difference between her and the copper-haired mountain man. They were a world apart: separate cultures, vastly different lives, different religions. So what was it about this Yankee that so animated the face of Don Pedro's daughter?

He frowned as he considered the question. Perhaps it was those differences that interested Francesca. Yes, that must be the explanation. The very things that drew Francesca to Will Reed now would certainly cause her great heartache if the friendship developed into anything more. She would be better with one of her own kind. Perhaps a man like Captain Zuniga?

At that moment the trapper said something amusing and Francesca burst into laughter. She was enjoying herself far too much.

Don Pedro rocked up on his toes in a gesture that signified his displeasure. Why did she not have a chaperon? Where was Doña Eulalia, who should have been walking within earshot of the couple?

"Doña Eulalia!" Don Pedro called his sister, but he did not leave his place at the window.

His eyes widened as Francesca stooped to pluck a bright orange poppy which she then tucked behind the ear of Will Reed. More laughter!

Once again, Don Pedro called the delinquent aunt. This time it was a bellow, raising the clatter of footsteps on the stair behind him. *She'd better be here in a hurry,* he thought irritably. As Francesca's chaperon, Doña Eulalia had failed today and he would find out why.

A timid knock sounded at his door. Don Pedro called his permission to enter, but instead of his sister it was her servant girl who appeared.

He turned from his watch to glower momentarily at the poor girl. "Where is your mistress?"

"She sent me to say she is ill. She begs your pardon." The girl's hands trembled as did her voice. It was rare for Don Pedro to raise his voice in the house.

"Then you will have to do," Don Pedro said grimly. "Go tell Francesca I wish to speak with her alone. Now!"

The servant nodded, then hesitated. "Francesca . . ."

"She is in the courtyard," Don Pedro gestured out the window as if to give the frightened woman every clue as to his displeasure. "Go! Tell her to come to my study!"

Francesca's eyes were bright with amusement as she considered the poppy in Will Reed's hair. "I have often been amazed when a horse has been left to run the back pastures for a season, how much time it takes to get it presentable for riding. You have curried and combed out nicely for one so long in the mountains."

"I take it that is a compliment of sorts?"

"Proper tack. A good bridle and saddle. A few hours pulling the burrs from the mane. These help the appearance of a horse, but do not always mean he adapts to civilization."

Will smiled and shrugged. "I have not always worn moccasins, you know. It's just that man and beast must adapt to their surroundings or perish."

"They say you are as much an Indian as the Indians." She turned from him as if she suddenly noticed the flowers and had to stop and consider them.

"In some ways they are as civilized as you or I."

She whirled around. "I differ with you in that opinion. They are ignorant and godless and—"

"Ignorant of the ways of the white man, but like the wild horses, they know the tracks and trails of their world better than you imagine. To them, you might be considered ignorant, Francesca."

She tossed her hair as a mare might toss its mane. She did not like his reply. "They have no knowledge of God . . . or of the church."

At this, he did not argue. He looked thoughtfully at the sky as a blackbird sailed across it. He smiled slightly as though he remembered something . . . *someone.* . . "You are right in some ways," he conceded. "Death is imponderable to them. They have no real idea of what will come after this life." He shrugged. "But they are just as much eternal souls as you and I. Just as valuable to God as a mission priest, ranchero or ranchero's daughter."

"What do you mean?" she shot back, genuinely offended at his thinly veiled accusation. "That is why there are missions here."

"Jesus Christ was never brutal, never physically cruel. I have heard enough reports about some mission Indians to know that . . ."

Their conversation was cut short by the servant of Doña Eulalia who cleared her throat nervously behind them.

Both Will and Francesca turned to stare at her a moment before she found the courage to speak.

"Your father wishes a word with you, señorita," she ventured, looking toward the study window that framed the figure of Don Pedro. Francesca spotted her father, flushed, and then looked away. He had been watching them.

"Perhaps we shall continue our conversation later, Will Reed," she said in a suddenly cool tone. And then she brushed past him, hurried across the courtyard and into the house.

Her father's silence was ominous as he paced the length of his study. His hands were clasped behind his back; a posture he assumed when he was constructing decrees that must be obeyed the moment he pronounced them. Francesca wondered what she might have done to stir his displeasure.

Finally, Don Pedro spoke. "This Americano is not one of us." His opening words were like the death knell rung out by the mission bell after someone died. There was no mistaking the somber meaning.

"No, Father." She said what was necessary and required. Understanding the deeper meaning of his statement, she pretended only to hear the truth that Will Reed was quite different than anyone in California.

"You were talking with him." A stinging accusation, intimating that whatever they were talking about could not be entirely proper.

"About the Indians, Father."

Don Pedro frowned. Everyone knew of the immoral and inhuman practices of the Indians. Was the trapper speaking of the unspeakable to his innocent daughter? "What of the Indios?" he snorted.

Francesca phrased the discussion lightly. "Señor Reed would have made a dedicated priest, Father."

Don Pedro's expression betrayed his surprise. "What is that?"

"He has simply said all the things Mother used to say about them: that they are also eternal souls."

"Who . . . ?"

Her father was wading through his confusion, and Francesca was intent on keeping him away from his reason for calling her.

"Yes," she continued. "Señor Reed is convinced of the great value of the savages, Father. You must talk with him on the matter sometime. Almost word for word the things Mother used to say." She did not mention that Will had spoken of the brutality of the missions against many of the native population. Now was a time to be careful as she related her conversation with Will. If she wished to speak again with him, then she must walk softly through the maze of her father's disapproval.

"I should enjoy hearing his opinion, Francesca, but—"

She interrupted what she knew he was about to say. "Yes. I thought you might enjoy hearing his viewpoint. It is good for the mind to at least look at the ways of those who are so very . . . different from us." She did not add that often one found that there were not as many differences as one thought. "Perhaps after dinner then. You and Ricardo will enjoy his company. I have other things to attend to this afternoon, so I cannot join you. My day to teach the children." She rose and kissed her father on the cheek.

Don Pedro inhaled and looked around the room as if he was trying to locate his lost objections. What was it he was going to forbid her to do? What had he been so angry about?

"You cannot join us for luncheon?" He looked confused.

"I will eat at the mission. You know how the children look forward to their lessons. I cannot be late."

"So much like your mother," he muttered and kissed her on the top of her head. He now was certain his worries were unfounded. Francesca was too bright to fall in love with an outsider; too ingrained with the qualities of her own culture to seek for any fulfillment outside it.

She slipped out of the study unscathed and without any fatherly decrees ringing in her ears. *There is still some hope,* she thought as she changed her clothes. Her father might see the Yankee was not so different as he thought!

21

WHAT IS THE urgency of this meeting and what secrecy requires my arrival at this ungodly hour?" complained Captain Zuniga to Don Dominguez.

"Quiet down," observed the ranchero. "My servants may be awakened by the noise you are making. They may gossip all they wish among themselves, but I do not want them carrying tales to others."

"What tales? What others?"

"Something new has come up. Something that makes it more important than ever for Figueroa to favor *us* and for our other—uh—business to be more productive than ever."

"What can be so new about raising cattle? Have you figured a way to grow a second hide on a steer? Now *that* would be news," sneered the little captain.

The burly ranchero pulled himself up haughtily. "I have a mind to dismiss you and keep this all to myself."

The soldier knew that Dominguez never joked where greed was concerned and he was suddenly all ears. "Your pardon, Don Dominguez," he said. "What is the nature of your news?"

Somewhat pacified by the change in Zuniga's tone, the ranchero explained, "Yesterday a vaquero of mine chased some steers up Canyon Perdido. Last winter's rains caused a mudslide there that uncovered a dark-red rock face. The vaquero did not recognize the ore, but he thought it unusual enough to bring me a sample." Dominguez handed over a lump of rock.

"So?" questioned Zuniga. "It obviously is not gold or silver. This may be the land of precious metals in old fables, Don Dominguez, but California will never produce wealth from the earth."

"Ah, but you are wrong, my good capitan," asserted the ranchero. "This sample is cinnabar, the source of quicksilver."

The captain was all attention now. "Quicksilver? You mean the liquid metal used to refine silver and gold?"

"The very same," asserted Dominguez with finality. "Quicksilver grasps hold of silver and gold as eagerly as you or I. It is used to free the precious metals from the baser elements. Then the quicksilver can be burned away, leaving the wealth behind."

"So it is almost as valuable as gold?" asked Zuniga with a barely controlled squeak in his voice.

"At the moment, even more so. The gold and silver mines of Mexico are dependent on quicksilver from the state of Jalisco—"

"Which is now in turmoil because of the revolutions sweeping Mexico," noted Zuniga.

"Exactly," agreed Don Dominguez. "If we can produce quicksilver in quantity, every would-be ruler of Mexico will want us for his allies. We need not be content with a rancho in Santa Barbara. Oh no! We may soon control California!

"Capitan, I am going to need your help more than ever before. Cinnabar mining will require many workers and the preparation of the quicksilver is hazardous as well. We will need more Indios than ever, only not for Sonora; we will need them here!"

"And the location of the mine?" Zuniga was sure there was more to this. "It is on your own property?"

"By no means! That is why the secrecy is more important than ever.

Canyon Perdido is divided between the holdings of the mission and those of Rancho Rivera!"

"And what of the vaquero? What if he should wonder aloud to someone who might know what the ore is?"

The ranchero laid his fleshy chin into his palm in thought. "It would be wise to avoid unnecessary complications. I will have Juan and Iago arrange for him to meet a most unfortunate accident."

"But of course, Don Dominguez." Zuniga's eyes hardened until he gave a good impression of a snake.

22

"**Y**OU LIKE THIS Señor Reed." Francesca's aunt began her remarks without any preamble. She had called her niece into the parlor of the hacienda without any explanation. Francesca only expected the usual discussion of some problem with the servants or a complaint about an inferior grade of lard.

"What? What did you say, Aunt?" Francesca feigned incomprehension to cover her confusion.

"It is all right, child. Did you think that to another woman, even one my age, the signs would not be plain?"

Francesca shook her head and swallowed hard. "But Father would never . . ." she began, trying her best to sound dutiful.

Her aunt patted the needlepoint-decorated stool drawn up near her knees. "Sit here, child. Your father is exactly the subject I wish to speak with you about."

Doña Eulalia inclined her gray-haired head a moment and listened to the sounds of the house. It was mid-morning and the servants' duties took them all outside for the time. She nodded to herself in satisfaction that she and Francesca would not be overheard.

"Your father loves you very much and wants your best. Never doubt that. But he cannot replace the advice your mother would have given you. Neither can I, but I must do my best.

"What I wish to say is this: I too loved a young man once, a common sailor. 'Not suitable,' my father said." The old woman's voice dropped.

Francesca waited patiently, then impulsively reached out to her aunt's nervously fidgeting fingers. Doña Eulalia and her niece clasped hands.

At last she found her voice again. "I made plans to run away with him.

My father—your grandfather—found out. He had my sailor abducted and sent away on a galleon. I never saw him again.

"So," said the aunt, drawing both her figure and her voice erect. "What lesson is here? Be obedient, child. Be extremely careful to obey your father's wishes. Do not encourage Señor Reed. Be distant, cool, reserved, and, if need be, rude to your young man."

Francesca looked puzzled. "But that is exactly what Father wishes for me . . . Rude? . . . Oh! Yes, I see," she brightened. "I must be very obedient!"

Doña Eulalia chuckled a deep, throaty chuckle in which Francesca caught a fleeting glimpse of a young, headstrong girl who had loved deeply. "Just beware of looking into Señor Reed's green eyes!" she instructed. "Even I find it difficult to be properly reserved!"

In five days time, Ricardo was out of bed despite Padre Sanchez's admonitions. "My friend," the young ranchero said warmly to Will, "I feel fine. Never better, in fact. If I am to properly celebrate at the fiesta in your honor, I must get back on my feet."

Dressed for riding, but with a sombrero two sizes larger than normal to fit his bandages, Ricardo led the way to the barn. Ricardo's bay horse and the gray Flotada were saddled and awaiting them. They met Francesca coming out of the barn. Will touched his hat brim and started to speak, but Francesca turned her face from him and walked away.

"My father tells me that you ride well," commented Ricardo as Will stared after her a moment, then adjusted the stirrups and tightened the cinch.

"What? Oh, I spent some time on Cumberland ponies back home," acknowledged Will, "and when I came west, I found some pretty fair mountain horses; traded for them with the Crow and the Pawnee."

Will led the gray around the enclosure three times, then stopped to tighten the cinch again.

"Ah," observed Ricardo, repeating Will's actions with his own horse, "I see you are a true vaquero, who knows the paso de la muerte."

"The step of death? Oh, I get your drift," responded Will, climbing aboard Flotada. "I once had a real cinch-binder of a trail horse almost come over with me because I forgot to circle him after tightening the girth. I won't forget that lesson."

The two caballeros rode out together. Ricardo wore a rust-colored suit of velvet and Will was dressed in his dark green.

"Mi amigo, it feels good to be on horseback again," admitted Ricardo as they moved at a slow canter along the road.

Over two hills the riders turned aside from the road and loped across fields of orange poppies and dark blue lupines. They had no particular destination in mind; it was the joy of riding in the late spring air that beckoned them on.

"What are your future plans, amigo?" inquired Ricardo.

Will had to ponder this question for a time. "I'm not sure," he said at last. "My campañeros of the trail are all gone, along with our gear and furs. Maybe I can find someone to stake me to go back and try again."

"Have you not had enough hardship for one lifetime?" asked Ricardo. "Why not stay here and become a ranchero, or if that does not suit you, a merchant like others of your countrymen?"

Will had heard of the easterners who had come to California by ship. Some had accumulated fabulous wealth and prestige like Henry Fitch, now a trader in Pueblo de Los Angeles. Fitch had married Josefia Carrillo, daughter of a prominent San Diego family.

In the settlement around the presidio and mission of Santa Barbara, there were other easterners. Daniel Call was making a living as a carpenter after having jumped ship from the leaky China trader *Atala* back in 1816.

It was even rumored that Don Jose Maria Alfredo Robinson, born plain Alfred Robinson of Boston, hoped to marry into the de la Guerra family. His Yankee business acumen, if united with the de la Guerra riches and respectability, would create a trading operation of considerable force.

Will wondered how others from the East had been accepted so completely while he was treated with suspicion. Ricardo explained that it was the mode of his arrival that made the difference.

With their coastal network of pueblos and presidios, the Mexican government felt able to control immigration from the sea. But overland was another matter. The ranges of mountains that guarded California on the east had long been considered impassable. Now they had been breached, by energetic and voracious trappers and scouts, Americans from the new United States.

In time trade routes might be established and travel regulated so that the Mexican authorities would relax. But for now there was too much internal turmoil in Mexico to allow foreigners to come and go freely.

"So why don't you Californians develop the trading possibilities yourselves?" asked Will.

"It is not suitable for hidalgos to become merchants," commented Ricardo. His reply was without pretense or snobbery; he was simply stating the facts.

"You see, my friend," the young ranchero continued, "there is an order to the universe. Some men are born to rule and others to be ruled; some to be merchants and others to be craftsmen. The Lord God has made it so."

"But," interrupted Will, "what about the Indians? What is their role?"

"I have given this much thought," replied Ricardo seriously. "The holy fathers believed that the Indios could become gente de razón, by study and observation. But I no longer think this possible. They are too childlike to ever govern their own affairs or reason for themselves. They will remain servants forever."

"Seems to me I've heard that point of view from everyone except the Indians themselves," observed Will, reining Flotada back to a walk.

"Enough of this talk of merchandising. I have a powerful thirst," concluded Ricardo, also slowing the bay. "Let us turn aside here for refreshment."

The cantina Corazón del Diablo was as unimposing as its name was sinister. The Devil's Heart was a low adobe structure from which most of the whitewash had peeled. The weathered bricks slumped as if a good rain would melt the building altogether. The hitching rail outside, to which three horses were already tied, looked more substantial. Will noted that one of the horses was a mare.

Inside the saloon were three customers and the proprietress. An older man was seated at a table by himself. His spurs and leather leggings proclaimed him to be a vaquero.

The other two men leaned on the slanted pine plank that served as a bar. They were dressed in badly stained blanket serapes through which their heads protruded. Their unshaven faces were close together and they were laughing loudly at some private joke.

Just as Will and Ricardo were entering, the taller of the two coarse men at the counter spoke. In a voice meant to carry, he said to his companion, "Ugh! Hey, Juan, don't you hate the smell of cow? And have you noticed how those who herd cattle have the manners of cattle as well?"

The lips of the vaquero in the corner may have tightened at this remark, but he gave no other sign of having heard. He took a sip of his drink and set the glass back down.

Seeing Ricardo and Will, the man called Juan whispered something to his loud friend. The first man downed his drink in one gulp and shook off a restraining hand.

"I hear that to keep the vaquero docile they treat them just like the young of the herds—they make steers of them." At this statement, the short, fat woman behind the counter excused herself, saying she needed to go to her casa for more glasses.

Still the vaquero said nothing, but the provocative play was far from over. Now the loud man sauntered over to stand in front of the vaquero, stopping back from the rickety table and folding his arms across his chest.

"Say, you are a vaquero, a cowherd, aren't you? Tell us if it is true. Are you a toro bravo, or only a poor steer?"

With the last taunt still ringing in his ears, the vaquero threw the remaining contents of his glass into the tormentor's face, jumped to his feet and kicked the table out of the way.

When the loud man uncrossed his arms to wipe his face with one hand, he held a long, thin-blade knife in the other. He dropped into a fighting crouch and began to stalk the cowhand. "You are already as lean as an old steer, but maybe I can still trim you some," he jeered.

The vaquero picked up the three-legged stool on which he had been sitting and held it in front like a shield. The knife-wielder lunged in, drew a sweep of the stool, then jumped to the side, slashing the vaquero's sleeve.

"Say amigo, can't a body drink in peace in these parts?" asked Will mildly.

The loud man did not even glance toward the voice. "Keep out of this," he growled. "It is not your fight."

"Maybe not," admitted Will, "but I think I can see it evened out some." As he moved closer to the fight, Juan moved from the bar to confront this imposing white man.

"I would not involve myself, señor," suggested the fat-lipped one. "This is between Iago and the vaquero." With a smile he also drew a dagger-like blade from under his serape.

Will stopped moving and lifted his palms in a gesture of agreement and smiled in return. The two combatants continued to circle warily, blood dripping from the vaquero's arm.

The trapper had fixed his gaze on the eyes of the man facing him. Will called over his shoulder to Ricardo, "You know what my uncle taught me about situations like this? He said if a man insists on fighting bare-knuckles, oblige him; if someone gets the drop on you with a rifle, give him what he wants. But," the tautly nerved scout added, "do you know what he said to do if someone pulls a knife?" Will pivoted his shoulders slightly to the left as though turning to see Ricardo's reply.

Halfway through the pivot, he spun sharply back toward the right, his right hand doubled into a fist the size of the head of a sledge hammer. With his arm at its fullest extension, he backhanded his fist solidly against the ear of the man guarding him.

"He said I should break his arms," Will concluded, following up the right by stepping through with his left, flush on the man's nose. The fat-lipped one, already staggered sideways, flew backwards against the bar.

His arms bounced straight up over his head from the force of the impact. The knife jumped out of his hand and landed on the floor behind the bar.

At the sudden commotion, the loud man looked around to see the cause. This was all the vaquero needed. He swung the stool hard toward Iago's face.

Iago recovered to bring the point of his knife up to ward off the blow, but the stool knocked the blade from his hand.

"Things are looking a whole lot more even now," commented Will.

Juan grabbed a bottle from the bar and took a clumsy swing at the scout's head. Will caught the bottle in mid-descent, turned his back into Juan's rush, and lifting under the man's armpit with his other hand, flipped the cutthroat onto the floor.

Will stepped across the prostrate body with his right leg, keeping Juan's arm on the scout's left side. Dropping to his knees, Will fell onto Juan's chest. At the same instant he bent the man's elbow backwards over his thigh. There was a loud pop and Juan screamed once, then passed out.

Iago had never intended this to be a fair fight, and it was apparent his accomplice had been dispatched. Seeing the grim look on the vaquero's face, the coward bolted out the door.

"Your pardon, señors," apologized the cowboy, dashing past Ricardo and Will in his pursuit of Iago.

The failed assassin had already reached the buckskin mare and untied the reins when the vaquero reached his zebra dun. In an unhurried manner, the cowboy took down his reata and shook out a medium sized loop.

As Iago clambered aboard the saddle and spun the mare to flee, a floating ring of braided cowhide settled over his shoulders. He had time to experience an instant's feeling of escape before the rope reached its end and Iago burst backwards out of the saddle.

"What was that about, anyway?" asked Will, who had followed the men out of the cantina.

The vaquero shrugged, "Quién sabe? Who knows, Señor? Perhaps this one . . ." he gestured toward Iago with the spool of reata now coiled in his hands, "had been drinking bad liquor and it made him crazy."

Will studied the scruffy villain now seated sullenly in the dust and trussed up like a chicken. "I don't know," he wondered aloud, "he seemed bent on picking a fight with you. You sure you don't know him?"

"No, señor," said the old vaquero emphatically. "These are not vaqueros, not even jinetes, riders, I have seen before. They are likely ladrones from the cantinas of Pueblo de Los Angeles, robbers fleeing the law."

The motionless form of Juan had been dragged from Corazón del

Diablo and deposited in the dirt next to his partner. He had awakened once since being dragged out, but another scream from the pain of the shattered arm and he promptly passed out again. There was no need to tie him up.

A troop of horsemen headed by Captain Zuniga clattered up to the cantina. Zuniga reined to a sudden stop and threw up his hand to halt his squad of soldiers.

"There was a murder reported here and I . . ." he stopped mid-sentence and looked with surprise from Will and the vaquero who were standing, to the dust-covered prostrate forms of Iago and Juan.

"No, no murder," corrected Will, "an attempted one though. Your arrival is very timely, Capitan. You can relieve us of these two snakes."

"I am in charge here," barked the little captain, fairly launching himself from his horse. "Once again, Americano, I find you involved in suspicious circumstances. How do I know that you are not robbing these caballeros!"

The gray-haired cowboy who was no taller than the captain and even thinner, jumped in front of Will and confronted Zuniga. "These caballeros," he bristled, pointing at the two men groaning in the dirt, "are rateros, criminals! I, Diego Olivera declare it to be so!"

"You watch your tongue, old man, or I will arrest you *and* this Americano. Now be quiet while—"

Once again the captain was interrupted. This time it was by the voice of Ricardo, speaking from the door of the cantina. "Capitan Zuniga, I can vouch for what took place here. These two malditos provoked a fight with Señor Olivera and *my good friend* Señor Reed only took part to see that it remained fair."

The captain looked angry at Ricardo's presence, and visibly fought to control his emotions. The result was a hideous half-smile, half-grimace that when added to the scar on his cheek made Zuniga look especially evil.

"Ah, Don Ricardo, I did not see you there," said the captain awkwardly.

"Apparently not," concluded Ricardo. "Now, are you willing to take *my* word for what has happened?"

"Si, of course," mumbled the thwarted officer. Ordering his men to take charge of Juan and Iago, Zuniga turned and announced to the old vaquero and Will that they were free to go.

The cowboy only snorted as a reply and Will shook his head in disgust. As he and Ricardo mounted their horses, Will could not resist calling out, "By the way, Capitan Zuniga, how did you know that a murder had taken place here?"

The soldier snapped rigidly upright as if suddenly ordered to attention, then said woodenly, "The proprietress ran to where we were resting our horses by the stream and said that she feared a murder was *going* to take place. That is what I meant."

A few hundred yards back toward Casa Rivera y Cruz, Will and Ricardo were overtaken by Diego Olivera. "Señors," he called, "wait a moment, please."

They had reined up just under an arch of cottonwood tree branches that laced together over the roadway. "In the confusion, I did not properly thank you," Diego began.

"Not important," responded Will. "They needed to be taught a lesson and I suspect they got it."

The older man drew himself up proudly in his saddle. "You are both gentlemen and I am but a poor vaquero, and yet I am indebted to you. Please accept from me this token of my debt."

Diego untied a small leather pouch that had been hanging behind his saddle. "I note that you are a fine horseman and your beast is a true caballo bravo. Will you accept from me these spurs, as I see you have none?"

Will glanced at Ricardo, who nodded, silently saying *Do not wound his pride.* Will then smiled amiably and the old vaquero passed over the pouch.

"Should you ever need my service," Diego pledged, "you have only to send. I am employed by Don Jose Dominguez. Vaya con Dios!" He clapped his own spurs to his horse and shot away from the young men, waving a final salute over his shoulder as he went.

The spur that fell from the pouch was made of finely worked silver. Will sat on the veranda of the Rivera hacienda examining the old vaquero's gift.

The engraving on the curving side piece was almost worn smooth from years of service, but the spur retained the soft gleam of high quality metal. The rowel was four inches across and carried twelve blunted points. The broad leather strap that fit over the instep of Will's boot and the twin chains that went underneath showed the care of frequent oiling and polishing.

"Ah, my friend," observed Ricardo as Will tried on the spur, "you look like a Spanish vaquero now—let us see you with the other spur in place."

As Will shook the other spur free of the bag, a lump of rock also fell out. It was a dark red fragment of stone no bigger than the scout's thumb.

He held it up and inquired, "What do you suppose this is?"

"I cannot say. A good luck piece, perhaps?"

"If that's true, then I should return it to Señor Olivera. He may have forgotten it was in there."

Ricardo agreed but added, "Why not wait until the fiesta? Señor Olivera will most certainly attend and you can return it then."

"That's a good idea," Will replied, "and since these spurs are too valuable to use every day, I'll keep them in the bag for now."

Ricardo took a moment to reexamine the rock fragment. "I have seen something like this, but I cannot remember where." Shrugging, he handed it back to Will, who placed it with the spurs in the pouch.

23

"YOU SEEM VERY quiet this evening, mi amigo," observed Ricardo as he and Will walked through the fig orchard at the rear of the hacienda.

Will stopped and leaned his hand on a slender tree trunk. He studied the silver piping on the seam of his dark blue velvet trousers. Still without answering, he raised the sleeve of the jacket and pulled at the cuff of the white silk shirt.

"Ricardo," he said at last, "do I look like I fit in your society?"

"Most certainly," agreed his friend. "You appear as a true caballero bravo, only bigger and red-haired, of course."

"And do I express myself clearly in your language? Have I butchered too many phrases? Have I done things that are offensive?"

"What is this about?" Ricardo asked slowly. "Has someone been rude to you or critical of your speech? He will have to answer to me!"

Will grimaced, making a face between a frown and a silly grin. "That is the problem. It is not a he, it's a she."

"What?" demanded Ricardo.

"Your sister. Don't misunderstand, she has never been anything but polite. But I fear I have offended her."

"What do you mean?" asked the bewildered ranchero, looking back through the trees to the lighted outline of Francesca's window.

"Ever since a conversation we had . . . I meant no disrespect . . . I can't even remember what I said . . . she has been cool, distant. All we talked about was Indians and—"

"Say no more," instructed Ricardo. "It is not fitting that a gentleman such as yourself has to explain. I am certain you said nothing improper. I will speak with her and if she does not behave better, I will have Father instruct her." The young man strode purposefully back toward the house.

"Wait, Ricardo," Will called after him. "I didn't mean for you . . ." but his friend had already reentered the hacienda.

"Father," began Ricardo, bursting into Don Pedro's study, "I wish you to speak with Francesca."

Don Pedro was studying a map of the rancho, planning the location of another watering pond for the cattle. "Eh? What's that?" he said, his thoughts interrupted.

"I have spoken with Francesca about the way she speaks to Señor Reed. She gave me a most disrespectful reply. In fact, in words better suited for a muleskinner, she told me to mind my own business."

The elder ranchero stood and clasped his hands behind his back. "Is your sister too forward with the Americano?" he questioned, concern flitting across his brow.

"On the contrary, she has been rude to him. Señor Reed is a fine gentleman, a brave one who saved my life. He must be made to feel welcome in our home. She fails to uphold the courtesy of the house of Rivera y Cruz."

Don Pedro looked confused. One hand remained clenched behind his back while the other passed over the dome of his head. "Certainly, our hospitality cannot be questioned. Señor Reed is our honored guest. I . . . ah . . . I will speak with her."

Francesca repressed a smile as she watched her father pace the length of his study again. His hands were clasped behind his back; his attitude once again was that of the great Ranchero considering how best to pose his decree.

"Father," Francesca ventured timidly, although she did not feel timid. "I wish you would not pace so. It makes me feel as though I have displeased you in some way."

Don Pedro frowned, continuing his walk down to the window overlooking the courtyard where he had first observed Francesca talking so pleasantly with Will Reed. Had he not paced that day as well?

He slowly turned around to face Francesca. "Daughter, I do not understand your behavior," he said at last. Indeed, the tone of disappointment was inherent in his words.

Francesca opened her eyes wider, pretending her innocence. "Whatever have I done, Father?"

"Ricardo has told me—"

"Ricardo!" she scoffed in mock anger. "What does he know about my affairs?"

Don Pedro held up his hands to silence her, a gesture she meekly obeyed. "Now, now! It is not only Ricardo who has noticed, but I, myself, have observed your behavior."

"My behavior?"

"Coolness. To our guest."

"Guest?"

"To Señor Reed you have been . . ." he frowned and rolled his hands as if to make the right words come forth. "You have been more than cool. . . . You have been rude."

"I? Rude?" She protested, and yet she felt a sense of exhilaration. The days of coyness had paid off! Now, instead of instructing her that she must not speak to the American, her father was about to reprimand her for aloofness and command her to pay more attention to their guest. "But Father, he is a stranger. You said it yourself . . . quite different than us. Whatever is Ricardo talking about?"

"I realize it is difficult at times to be polite to one so . . . unlike us. His manners are . . . American . . . his speech is clumsy, but he is the man who saved your brother's life . . ."

Now it was Francesca's turn. Imitating her father's gesture, she raised her hand slightly. "You need not say more, Father," she replied repentantly. "I was not *aware* . . . that I might be offending him. Or being rude. I will try and do better. Really, Father. I will try and make up for it. I was not thinking of Ricardo or the great debt we owe."

The change in Don Pedro's countenance was marvelous to behold. He beamed. Yes, he had raised Francesca to be a proper hostess no matter how difficult the task. "Your mother would be pleased," he smiled. After kissing him lightly on the cheek, Francesca ran upstairs to bathe and change for supper.

24

RICARDO ENTHUSIASTICALLY DESCRIBED the planned events of the fiesta, explaining in detail the succession of trials of skill and courage that would occupy much of the day.

"And will there be a shooting match at this fiesta?" inquired Will.

"There will be the exercise of the lazadores, the ropers, and games of raya and once and—"

"Do any of those involve shooting?" persisted Will.

Ricardo looked dubious. "I doubt that a contest of firearms is planned. Most of the sports are from horseback and—"

"That'll work," said Will. "I'm a fair hand with a horse, but not even close to your vaqueros with their reatas. If I can get a rifle or a brace of pistols, I may be able to show you people a few things."

"We have nothing suitable in the hacienda," observed Ricardo thoughtfully. "Nothing but an old fowling piece. But I know where we may obtain something for you."

The rowboat beached on the white sand below the little community of Santa Barbara belonged to the *Paratus*. It was left on shore for the use of customers whenever the trading ship was in port.

"Ahoy, Captain Easton," called Ricardo as he and Will rowed toward the ship.

"Who's that?" responded Easton, glancing over the deck rails. "Well, welcome aboard, Señor Ricardo. Come up and introduce me to your friend."

The pair climbed a rope ladder to the teakwood deck of the vessel. The fact that Ricardo was a frequent visitor aboard *Paratus* was evident by the ease of manner with which he and Billy greeted each other.

"And this is obviously the American we've been hearing about from the ladies," acknowledged Easton with a nod in Will's direction. "You're certainly a long ways from home," Easton said in English.

The scout took an immediate liking to the trader's hearty handshake and broad smile.

"En Español, por favor," requested Ricardo.

"But of course," agreed Billy switching back easily to Spanish. "And no pirate dialect today either."

At Will's puzzled look, Ricardo explained that Billy put on a swashbuckling act that appealed to the ladies of Santa Barbara. "He adopts an air of mystery and danger because it's good for business," laughed Ricardo.

"Don't give away all my secrets," requested the pirate-merchant with mock ferocity, "or I'll be forced to cut out your heart and feed it to my pet shark!"

"Actually," said Will, "we are here on business." The scout proceeded to explain his intention of demonstrating a mastery of sharpshooting on the day of the fiesta.

"I think I have just what you are after," responded Billy. "Wait here." He disappeared below-decks for a minute, returning with a walnut case inlaid with teak and mahogany. He presented it, unopened, for both men to see the quality of the workmanship, then raised the lid with an expert salesman's touch.

Inside were a matched pair of dueling pistols. Their half-stocks were made of polished walnut and the octagonal steel barrels gleamed.

"These are .50 caliber, and as you see were made as percussion models, not converted flintlocks."

"They are beauties," agreed Will, hefting one to feel the balance. He drew a bead on a masthead to check the sights. "But too expensive for me, I'm sure."

"Nonsense," said Easton. "Take them as a loan. I'll back you in a gentlemanly wager or two and win enough for you to keep them as a gift."

"You place a great deal of confidence in someone you've never seen shoot," observed the trapper.

"You came cross-country living off the land, didn't you? What better recommendation might I need? Come below and we'll get powder and shot."

Ricardo preferred to remain on deck to watch the white clouds pile up on the peaks behind Santa Barbara. The breeze out of the northwest was refreshing and the earlier ocean calm had been replaced by small, dancing waves.

Easton escorted Will down a companionway, then past stores of trade goods. "We can't take long," he noted. "The way the wind is rising, we may have to slip our cable and run out behind the islands till this blows over."

He stopped in front of a double-locked cupboard. "Heard you lived with the valley Indians for a time," he said in English. "Was anything bothering them?"

"The usual tribal feuds, but I think I know what you're asking about. They had a curious way of talking about their people being 'taken by the West,' but then shutting up tight as a clam. Never figured out what they meant."

Easton's pony-tailed hair bobbed as he nodded his agreement. "I thought as much. I've come across some late-night shipping going on at a little cove north of here . . . and the cargo wasn't hides or tallow."

The trader offered no explanation of his mysterious words. He took a key on a string from around his neck and commented, "Powder's here in the Santa Barbara."

"Santa Barbara? Same name as the mission? Why is it called that?"

Easton regarded Will with a questioning look. "Not up on your Catholic saints, eh? Saint Barbara is the lady in charge of sudden calamity—explosions for instance."

Opening the locker, the trader removed a keg of powder and a sack of lead balls. These he passed to Will, along with a small tin of percussion caps.

Reaching into the back of the locker, Easton moved some more kegs around and came out with a cloth-wrapped package. Will could see several more similar packages. "There's also this," he said.

When unwrapped, the object revealed was a brand-new Hawken rifle. Will whistled sharply between his teeth in admiration.

".50 caliber, same as the pistols," noted Easton. "Only this will carry 350 yards and still knock down a grizzly or a man."

"Maybe I'll win the prize at the fiesta and be able to buy this," said Will.

"Nobody else knows I have it," said Easton, wrapping the gun again. "Let's keep it that way, all right?"

"Whatever you say," agreed Will.

"If you find you need it sooner than that fiesta, you know where to come," the trader concluded, securing the locker.

"Why would I need it at all?" asked the scout, frowning.

"You just remember what I called the powder magazine and that'll do for now," concluded Easton. "You had best get to shore. I'm going to have to get this ship underway."

Sensing a need for more courage than it had taken to face grizzlies or hostile Indians, Will had finally worked up enough nerve to take direct action with Francesca. After supper, he caught her by the elbow and asked if she would care to "walk a piece."

To his surprise, she agreed with no hint of reluctance. Saying that she needed a moment to collect a shawl from her room, she left Will standing by the front door, still stunned. As he waited for her to descend the stairs, the scout didn't see the raised eyebrows of his friend Ricardo and the answering nod of approval from Don Pedro.

The fig orchard was all shades of silver from the light of a full moon, sailing up over the surrounding hills like a brilliantly lit ship cresting a dark wave. When Will politely offered Francesca his arm, he was surprised again by the eagerness with which she accepted it.

For a time they strolled in silence. Will knew what he wanted to say, but was so pleased by his initial success that he did not want to take a chance on ruining it.

"Francesca," he said at last, "I'm afraid I was rude to you and offended you. If so, I'm sorry. I'm a plain-speaker and I value that in others, but I had no right to be critical."

The slim, dark-haired girl noted his earnestness, and answered sincerely, "Say no more, Will Reed. There was no offense for you to apologize for."

A hint of lavender wafting from Francesca electrified Will's senses. "But . . . but I sounded abrupt when I spoke about the treatment of the Indians. I did not mean you personally, of course. I meant that their path . . . if we want to show them a path . . ."

Francesca had turned to stand in front of him. Will's great rough hands engulfed her diminutive smooth ones. Her chin jutted up toward his and there was amusement in the sparkle of moonlight reflected in her eyes.

"Hang it all, Francesca," the scout complained. "Here I claimed what a plain speaker I am, and now I can't get words to even come out of my mouth right!"

She smiled up at him then, a dazzling smile of genuine affection and promise. "I understand that mountain men are men of action and not of words," she said.

25

WILL AND RICARDO rode out together to take part in the preparations for the fiesta. In Will's honor, a bull-and-bear fight was to take place.

The bull, a huge cinnamon-red toro bravo, was already pawing up the ground in a corral adjacent to the fiesta grounds. The proud bull tossed his head and charged the fences at the slightest provocation of passers-by. When they jumped hurriedly back, he would clash his four-foot-wide dagger-tipped horns against the posts as if saying *I dare you to step in and fight me.*

Ranchero hands were busy reinforcing the stockade and sprucing up the grandstands from which the high ranking guests would watch the action. The purpose of today's journey into the canyons above Santa Barbara was to procure the other combatant for the contest. Will and Ricardo, accompanied by six vaqueros, were going to capture a grizzly bear *alive.*

Will wasn't sure he approved of this venture, especially when the ideas were coming from a man who had nearly lost the top of his head to the crunch of a bear's jaws. But the vaqueros had made their preparations for the capture as calmly as if securing a half-ton of ferocious fury were an everyday occurrence.

The line of riders began to sweep across a hillside from a little creek that circled its base up to its crest. Will and Ricardo rode behind to observe, although the young ranchero chaffed at not being in the action. His father had made him promise not to take part; not because of the bear but because he might reinjure his head if thrown from his mount.

The vaquero highest on the hill got the first view of the next arroyo over. He gave a shout of discovery, then a moment later a cry of "la osa" in disappointment.

As they rounded the ridge, Will could see down into the canyon. At the bottom, along a stony creed bed was a large mother bear, accompanied by two cubs. The riders began to whistle and shout and slap their reatas against their leather chapedero leggings.

The mother bear stood erect at the noise and gave a sharp "woof" in alarm. The cubs darted across the creek and into the brush, encouraged by a swat from the mother when one did not move fast enough to suit her. Once the cubs were safely across, she too dropped down and rushed after them.

The riders watched until the trio of grizzlies disappeared over the next ridge to the east. As the vaqueros advanced again, Ricardo explained that it would never do to take back a she-bear, although her ferocity in defense of her cubs might be legendary. To pit a female bear against a male bull— what if the bear should win? "Unthinkable," Ricardo remarked, shaking his head.

Several canyons farther on, a vaquero in the middle of the line called out a warning. He had seen the head and shoulders of a great silver-tip bear rising from a thicket of sugar sumac on the hill opposite them.

A low, marshy area in front of the thicket was an ideal capture ground. Shaking out their tallow-smeared reatas, three of the vaqueros trotted their horses in a wide circle to get behind the bear and drive him down into the open.

The other three, backed by Will and Ricardo, slowly advanced to the edge of the clearing.

When the riders on the slope were in position, they began making noises to move the bear downward. "Hey, oso," they called. "We have come to invite you to a fiesta!"

Will and the others did not have long to wait. A few minutes passed and then a huge, hump-backed oso pardo viejo crashed through the brush.

At the last clump of willows opposite the waiting riders, the grizzly threw up his head and sniffed the air. Clearly he did not like something. He shuffled his feet and swung his head from side to side.

The flapping, yelling sounds coming toward him down the slope were enough to finally convince the great bear to move into the open. Out into the marshy space he swayed, then halted again at the sight of the advancing riders.

Immediately the huge bear stood erect, roaring his defiance. He made an almost human gesture of looking over his shoulder as if plotting an escape, then reckoning himself surrounded, he prepared to do battle.

Six riders advanced cautiously toward him, their mounts betraying nervous excitement by stamping and snorting. The vaqueros tried to close the circle evenly, constricting the circle all around.

The bruin, gray-muzzled and slavering, turned slowly around, judging each rider's approach like a boxer looking for an opening. "El Viejo," one vaquero muttered. The title was repeated by the others: Not just *an* old grizzly but *the* old bear of the mountains. Never captured, never bested in a fight, he had disemboweled a half dozen horses and mauled four men—two of them to death.

At last one of the riders, anxious for the glory of being the first to secure a reata to El Viejo, allowed his palomino to get in advance of the others.

Instantly the great bear charged. The vaquero waited coolly, then cast a perfect loop around the grizzly's neck. Two turns of the braided cord were taken around the horn of the saddle as the palomino reared and spun.

The huge bear sat back on his haunches and resisted the pull of the line. This was expected and was the reason why the reatas were covered in tallow. An oso pardo could pull in a horse and rider like a man landing a fish, unless the cord were greased so the bear could not keep a firm grip.

Two other vaqueros quartered the bear, preparing to add their loops to the capture. But El Viejo had not reached his advanced age by doing the expected. When he found that he could not draw in the horse, he simply turned his massive head to one side and bit through the taut rawhide with a snap.

The grizzly immediately charged the nearer of the approaching riders and this time the panicked vaquero made no attempt to cast a loop. It was all he and his bay horse could do to avoid the bear's rush. Even a miraculous leap to the side did not spare them a rake of El Viejo's claws, lacerating the man's leg and the horse's flank.

But the circle of riders continued to close in. The lazadores, three men of great experience with the reata, timed their approach to arrive together. Two loops were flung to snare the bear's head. His parted jaws closed over one, but the other settled around his neck, choking him.

The third man flung his loop so as to capture El Viejo's front paws. Will rode out to take the place of the man who had been injured.

The scout and the remaining vaquero urged their mounts toward the struggling bear. It was attempting to free itself from the noose around its neck by upward thrusts of its bound paws.

Will and the vaquero watched for an opportunity, then each encircled one of the bear's hind legs with a rawhide loop. With little urging from their riders, the well-trained horses pulled stoutly back on the reatas until the grizzly was stretched out on the ground.

The coil around El Viejo's neck was kept tight enough to choke off his wind; no one dared dismount his horse until the massive beast was uncon-

scious. The mounted men were enough to keep the bear spread-eagled on
the marshy ground, but the injured vaquero was busy tending his own leg
and his limping horse. So although he had made a promise to his father,
Ricardo was called on to get off his horse and secure the bruin's muzzle
and paws with stout rawhide straps so that the reatas could be released
before the grizzly choked to death.

But just as Ricardo bent to secure a strap around the bear's jaws, the
mammoth grizzly lunged! He had been shamming and was not unconscious at all!

The bear brought his bound paws upward toward his muzzle, intending
to catch Ricardo's leg between his murderous claws and his ponderous
head. Whether it was only instinct or a flicker of motion that caught Will's
eye, he never could say. But the American's shout of warning came just in
time: The young rancher flung himself backward from the bear's clutches,
and landed sprawling in the mud.

All the vaqueros immediately tightened their reatas. This time no one
approached the grizzly until a few pokes from a long stick proved him
unconscious.

The bear was trussed in three times the normal number of rawhide
straps and loaded aboard a bull-hide sled to be dragged back to the hacienda. The wounded man rode double behind another vaquero so that his
injured bay could be led carefully homeward.

Everyone noticed and commented on how close Ricardo's escape from
this second oso pardo had been: from the sweep of the bear's claws, his
boot had been slit from top to heel, just missing shredding the leg within.

26

THE MORNING OF the fiesta, dawn was rosy-tinted over the slopes
east of Santa Barbara and the wind unusually serene.

Will was up early, laying out his changes of clothing for the day's events.
He had been told that tradition demanded at least three different outfits
be worn in the course of the day: Green for the paseo, the parade that
would start the festivities; dark red for the afternoon's contests of skill and
bravery; black with silver for the evening's grand ball.

Will had donned the forest-colored suit and was attaching the emerald
green sash when he remembered the spurs given him by Diego Olivera.
The scout had placed the pouch in the top drawer of a night stand.

He pulled apart the drawstring of the bag and upended the contents onto the bed. As the spurs tumbled out, so did the curious lump of red ore. Will wondered again about the rock, then shoved it into his pocket, intending to return the piece to Olivera during the fiesta.

The scout picked up the spurs. He was going to carry them out onto the veranda before putting them on, so that the rowels would not gouge the floors as he walked.

That was when he noticed the blurred spot on one of the shanks. While all the rest gleamed evenly, a jagged outline on one limb surrounded an area that looked smeared with a thumbprint of grease.

Will tried polishing the spot to see if it would come off, but all his rubbing and buffing produced no change in the appearance.

Must have been like that a long time, he thought. *Strange I didn't notice the other day.*

Inspecting the outline of the faded area, another thought struck him. Will reached into his pocket and fished out the chunk of stone.

By the early light coming through the bedroom window, Will studied the spur, turning the dark rock over and over in his hand. At last he found a surface of the stone that looked familiar.

Will fitted the edge of the rock against the blurred area of silver. The outline was a perfect match. *What do you suppose makes that happen?* he wondered.

The scout puzzled over this curiosity for a minute before returning the ore to his pocket and picking up his hat. As he headed downstairs he thought, *Another thing to ask Olivera about his lucky rock.*

"How will we know when to release the bear?" asked Iago.

He and Juan maintained a healthy distance between themselves and El Viejo's enclosure. Sometimes the bruin demonstrated his savagery, roaring and tearing at the ground and the bars. But now, as at other times, he was dangerously quiet, waiting to rear up and plunge a raking claw through the fence.

"I will maneuver the Americano right into the gate," answered Captain Zuniga. "One of you must watch from under the stands and signal the other to open the gate." He pointed to the darkest corner under the seats. "In the meantime you must hide there."

"This oso pardo is already very angry. He will crush the Yankee like an eggshell. But where will he stop?"

"That is not our concern. We can blame whatever happens on the Indios and be rid of the interfering Señor Reed at the same time."

Zuniga looked up at the pink streaks lighting up the eastern sky and at the dark mass of the hulking grizzly. He rubbed the scar on his cheek thoughtfully. "Yes, it will all work perfectly. Now go, and be certain you stay well hidden!" he ordered.

Will stood on the veranda of the Rivera hacienda, watching the bustling activity of the courtyard. Grooms paid particular attention to their equine charges, currying and brushing the manes and forelocks and tails till not a single tangle remained. An Indian child of age ten or twelve made the rounds of all the horses' feet with a bucket and a brush, polishing the hooves until they gleamed in the sun.

From the balcony of the hacienda, a vaquero dropped a weighted reata. He allowed it to twist slowly until all the kinks had been removed from the braided line, then coiled it carefully up again.

Francesca came out of a door at the far end of the house and stood, not noticing Will. She was, he thought, the most beautiful woman he had ever seen. Her lustrous dark hair was gathered up on her head and pinned in place with a high comb. A fine lace shawl draped her ivory shoulders, while about her neck a silver cross on a black velvet ribbon sparkled at her throat.

It seemed to Will that all the clattering noises of the courtyard were suddenly replaced by a rushing sound. It reminded him of the sound of a swiftly plunging river makes as it echoes out of a mountain gorge. He stood entranced, staring at Francesca as if seeing for the first time the goal for which he had been searching.

27

WILL AND RICARDO sat on their ringside seats, which meant staying aboard their horses while watching the roping.

A big Chihuahua steer was loosed into the arena, and a moment later an Indian vaquero, mounted on a lineback dun, raced after him. Four lengths into the corral a loop of reata floated over the animal's head.

The dun set his heels and dug in, even as the roper was completing the second dally of braided rawhide around the high, flat horn. The lazadore expertly flipped the slack out of the reata so that it would not get under his mount's hooves.

An instant later the dark red steer hit the end of the cord and was jerked completely off his feet. The roper, who had carried a length of rawhide pigging string in his teeth, vaulted off the dun. He hogtied the steer before the long-horned animal had even twitched, let alone gotten back to his feet.

Ricardo waved his sombrero and there was a round of "Bravo!" and "Well done!" from most of the other riders. A few sat silently, looking sour.

"What's wrong with those men?" asked Will.

"Pay them no mind," suggested Ricardo, straightening his hat. "There are some who still dislike it that my father has trained Indios as vaqueros, and they are perhaps jealous."

Almost as if overhearing this remark, one of the unimpressed men rode forward into the starting position. As Will watched, the lazadore shook out his reata and tied the end fast to the horn of his saddle.

"I thought you weren't supposed to tie the reata," observed Will.

Ricardo was shaking his head. "It is still done by some. Father won't permit it. He says the impact when the steer hits the end of the line is too hard on the horse unless the cord can slip a little around the dally."

The vaquero in the starting gate glanced over where the Indian lazadore who had just roped was coiling his reata. His scowl gave a clear message: *I'll show you how it's done.*

When the rider nodded, another rangy steer was prodded from the pen and the vaquero went flying after the beast. His sorrel colt was young and eager and fast, and the loop of reata left the roper's hand in only two strides.

But the vaquero's haste proved his undoing. He had made his cast before the steer had settled on a course. At the moment of his throw, the lean, grouchy steer veered in front of the sorrel, almost under the horse's nose.

It was the vaquero's misfortune that his throw was good: the loop settled over the steer's neck even as the startled sorrel spurted *ahead* of the steer. All the frantic yanking and sawing on the bridle by the vaquero had no effect and the horse plunged on until he, not the steer, hit the end of the reata.

There was the sound of bursting rawhide and an exclamation of shock. The hard-tied line and the hard-charging colt combined to snap the saddle and its occupant backwards off the horse.

The vaquero hit the ground with a sickening thud. Then as his mount kicked itself free of the girth, he came within inches of having his head reshaped. The horse raced off, still kicking, across the corral.

The roper picked himself up, slowly. Everything seemed to be working and no bones were broken. Dusting off his leggings, he turned around to retrieve his saddle and the audience burst into laughter: he had split the seat out of his trousers!

Will and Ricardo rode around the side of the corral toward the open field where other contests of riding and roping were being held.

"Do you suppose that last vaquero learned something today?" asked Will.

"Perhaps. But he will not like it that he was bested by an Indian *and* made the fool. He may have learned not to tie his reata, but it will not make him treat the Indians any better."

Will pulled Flotada to a stop and pivoted in his saddle. "Ricardo," he said, "explain something to me. Spain's soldiers were in the New World for three hundred years, and many raised families with Indian wives. If most Mexicans are part Indio themselves, why are they so hard on the California tribes?"

"It is not the amount of Indian blood that matters. A family name that goes back to Castille or Aragon is our source of pride."

Ricardo swung his arm in a sweeping circle around the fiesta grounds. "You see the Indios haul water, stack firewood, drive cattle and tend the fields. We, my father and I, treat them well, but they will never be gente de razón. They are like beasts of burden. Some are more clever than others and trainable, but not ever fully civilized."

"What you mean by 'civilized' might change how you view the Indios, but does that give anyone the right to kill them or make slaves of them?" asked Will.

"Oh no!" exclaimed Ricardo. "Only those who willingly join the mission family have requirements placed on them which they must keep. Slavery is illegal and murder is still murder!"

"I wish I were as certain of that as you," shrugged Will. "The Yokuts were terrified of something to their west, and I don't think it was sharks or whales."

A large, grassy field next to the enclosure for the bull-and-bear combat was the scene for the fiesta. It was bordered on two sides by oak trees that provided shady seating for the onlookers.

Francesca and Doña Eulalia were busy organizing the massive amount of food that would be a major part of the fiesta. The quarters from four entire dressed steers were hanging in cheesecloth over the limbs of an oak.

A barbecue fire presided over by three cooks was already blazing and the first of hundreds of pounds of meat was sizzling on the spits.

"Wasn't that a grand paseo?" observed one of Francesca's god-sisters.

"You can't fool me, Margarita," teased Francesca. "You did not see the parade! You only had eyes for the younger son of Don Alfredo."

The girl being teased blushed until her ears turned pink. She retaliated by blurting out, "You should not talk, Francesca! I know one who was watching you!"

"Well, what of it?" Francesca countered. "Didn't he look splendid?"

"Oh, yes," agreed the younger girl. "And so masterful with his horsemanship. Aren't you excited to see how well he does in the contests?"

"I wonder what he will choose to wear for the lazo. I don't think his customs require so many changes of clothing."

"Well of course he won't change," responded the girl. "He must wear his field uniform until changing into the dress one for the grand ball."

"Uniform?" puzzled Francesca. "What are you talking about, Margarita?"

"Ah," countered the god-sister. "The question is *who* are you talking about?"

"Girls! Girls!" interrupted Doña Eulalia, clapping her hands. "The guests will be coming around for their midday meal soon and we are not close to ready. Francesca, run and check the pasole to see if it is seasoned properly. Margarita, you come with me. We must speed up the making of the tortillas."

Across the field, the contests for lazadores, ropers, and jinetes, or riders, were continuing.

"Trust Flotada," Ricardo was laughing. "He knows what to do even if you do not."

"What is this game called again?" inquired Will.

"It is *once,* you know, eleven. If father would permit, I myself would show you how it is done. But I will be here, applauding!"

Will and the gray horse took up their position at the end of a line of riders waiting a turn to compete. Will held Flotada a little to one side so he could watch the proceedings.

When the course was clear, each rider set out at top speed toward a bare patch of ground about fifty yards away. After reaching the edge of the bare space, each jinete did his utmost to set his mount back on its haunches. The parallel skid marks produced by each animal's hind legs looked like the number eleven; *once.*

A pair of boys too young to take part ran out to measure the length of the skid. Each rider got three chances, the best mark counting for the final competition. The vaquero just ahead of Will moved up and prepared his horse at the starting line.

"Vámenos!" he shouted to his white-painted bay. Horse and rider flashed across the ground to the edge of the cleared area. A quick jerk on the reins and the horse seemed to sit down abruptly. A plume of dust obscured the action and then the boys called out "Viente-dos!"

"Twenty-two feet!" exclaimed the rider behind Will. "Aiyee, he will be the winner for certain; my eighteen is outclassed."

Will approached the line with Flotada. A wave of a handkerchief announced that the marks had been smoothed out and the scoring zone was clear. As Ricardo had taught him, Will moved his boots slightly so that the loose chains on each spur made a tiny jingle.

Flotada was immediately alert. He flicked his ears back toward the sound, then forward toward the goal, all attention on the business at hand.

The scout's barest tap of the great rowelled spurs was all Flotada needed to bound forward with a great leap, as if crossing a bottomless canyon. In three strides the gray was already at top speed and running as if his life depended on it.

Will could see the clear space coming up quickly. He knew that he would have to anticipate the edge or they would fly past. He raised himself in his stirrups, preparing to gather his weight on the reins and . . .

Flotada needed no more signal than the shift of weight. His great gray body gathered beneath him, till Will's spurs amost touched the ground on either side. The scout found his face next to the horse's head as they slid.

"Viento-cinco!" called the boys as Flotada trotted back to the end of the line.

Some of the competitors who had not passed twenty feet on their first attempt now withdrew, leaving Will and six others.

"Well done, señor," complimented the jinete in front of Will.

"Not since the great days of Diego Olivera has a rider reached twenty-five feet."

"Olivera," asked Will. "Do you know him?"

"Sí, señor," responded the rider. "We both worked for Don Dominguez."

"You mean you no longer work there now, or he does not?" asked Will. "In any case, will he be here today?"

The vaquero's face clouded to a deep frown. "No, señor, he will not be here today," he said sadly, "unless his caballero spirit insists on one last rodeo. He was found, dead, only these two days since."

"Dead!" exclaimed the scout. "How did he die?"

"His throat was slit as he rode night herd, señor, and—"

A flash of sunlight gleamed off the polished side piece of Will's spur. "Those spurs, señor," asked the vaquero, his eyes narrowing, "where did you get them?"

"From Olivera. He gave them to me. Listen, I can't explain right now. Where is Capitan Zuniga?"

Will rode out of the line of competitors and circled the field looking for the captain. He found him by the barbecue fire, talking with Francesca.

"Zuniga!" Will demanded, vaulting from Flotada on a sudden stop that would have won the contest for certain. "Zuniga, Olivera is dead. Have you interrogated those cutthroats to see if they had a third accomplice? What were they after? Why were they hounding the old man?"

The captain had not turned to face the scout for any of these questions. Francesca's eyes widened at the raving torrent from Will, and Zuniga at last slowly turned around.

"You are very rude, Americano," observed Zuniga. "If you wish to discuss police business, I suggest that you come to my office next week." He began to turn away.

"Just a minute," demanded Will, closing his powerful hand around Zuniga's elbow. "Pardon me, Francesca, but the capitan and I need to have a talk."

"Of course," Francesca agreed. "I need to attend to other guests as well."

The captain shook off the restraining hand and warned darkly, "Never touch me again, Americano. And never interrupt my conversation unless you no longer have a use for your own tongue."

Will was not impressed, and stood with his hands on his hips. "I want answers, and I want them now. Who killed Olivera? What are you doing to find out? Who hired those criminals and why were they after Olivera in the cantina?"

The officer smirked with his eyes and puckered his thin face as if he smelled something bad. "You have a lot of questions, Americano. Too many that are none of your business. Just so that you will leave me alone, I will tell you: I don't know who hired those men or why, but perhaps they succeeded after all. They escaped from the presidio three nights ago."

"Escaped!" ground out Will. "How convenient. Left no trail either, I suppose."

"I do not like your tone, Miserio. You will apologize at once."

"Apologize," snorted Will, "I'd sooner—"

Ricardo had followed Will's hasty departure from the contest and now stepped between the two men. "Will," he requested, "no unpleasantness. This day is in your honor, after all. Your pardon, Capitan. We will discuss this with you at a more appropriate time."

Will stood staring into Zuniga's face. The squinted green eyes of the trapper locked with the shark expression of the soldier. At last it was Zuniga who turned and walked away.

28

WILL WATCHED ZUNIGA saunter off toward the plank tables, which were groaning under the weight of the noon meal. Will noted to whom the officer spoke and his manner, following Zuniga with his eyes as if the captain were a wild animal the trapper was tracking.

"Zuniga is a strong man and bad to cross, my friend," cautioned Ricardo. "And he is not without support from some rancheros because they agree with his toughness toward the Indios."

"It is not strength when a man brutalizes those who cannot defend themselves. And it is not toughness to leave a murder unsolved while two likely killers escape."

"Just so," agreed the young ranchero, "but do not provoke the capitan if you can help it. He has a reputation for dueling to the death."

The trapper turned to his friend and said seriously, "Ricardo, sometimes the quality of a man is just as apparent by his enemies as by his friends. I won't be looking to start a fight today, but Zuniga will bear watching."

"Bueno," agreed Ricardo with seeming relief that the matter was temporarily at rest. "Let us address ourselves to the food. We almost had a victory of yours to celebrate in the once, and now we should fortify ourselves for the afternoon's events."

The pair joined a group of fiesta-goers who were picnicking. Francesca invited Will to sit down while she prepared a plate of food for him. Ricardo was attended to by all three Gonzalez sisters.

Captain Zuniga had the appearance of a man strolling in the enclosure of the corral, walking off the midday feast. He wandered around the stockade until he was satisfied that no other fiesta-goers were present.

The officer stopped directly in front of the stands with his back to the platform. He kicked idly at the dirt with the toe of his boot and remarked over his shoulder, "Iago, can you hear me?"

"Si, we hear you," came the whispered reply.

"Get ready!" Zuniga hissed in return. "It won't be long now!"

After consuming barbecued beef, beans and tortillas, there were ripe strawberries for dessert. The ladies retired to a nearby tent to rest and change while the men returned to a similar structure provided for them. Will swapped his green suit for one of burgundy trimmed in black leather. He was saving the black suit finished in silver for the grand ball in the evening. He also picked up the wooden case of dueling pistols.

Many of the guests took advantage of the break in the events for a midday siesta. In fact, this idea, combined with the warm sun and hearty fare, so appealed to Ricardo that Will had to remind him that it was time for the shooting exhibition.

"I won't need Flotada to do the shooting for me," he joked. "I handle this part myself."

When Francesca rejoined them, she linked her arm through Will's and together they led a procession toward the corral. Halfway there, Don Pedro was seen approaching on his flashy black horse and the group stopped to wait for his arrival.

At Don Pedro's side rode Don Jose Dominguez, as grouchy as ever in his tight boots. A deep scowl appeared on his face at the sight of Will and Francesca holding hands.

Francesca's father tossed his hat back on his head and mopped his forehead with a silk handkerchief. He was handsomely dressed, as befitted the host of the fiesta. The rust-colored jacket he wore was trimmed in gold, just the reverse of his gold brocade vest with its rust-red piping.

The flowing tail of the sash that wound around the waist of his trousers carried the tones of burnt orange and gold down into a matching saddle blanket. He and the horse seemed to be made of one piece of workmanship.

"Good day, children," he called cheerfully. "I'm sorry to be late. Don Jose wished to discuss some business with me. Is everything to your liking?"

A chorus of "Sí, bueno! Most excellent!" responded to his inquiry.

"And where is this procession going? Surely it is too early for the combat of the great beasts?"

Ricardo left his three doting companions—Consuelo, Juanita and Arcadia—and stepped forward to explain. "We are going to the corral for a contest of marksmanship, Father."

Don Dominguez managed to look even more sour than before. "I suppose this is a Yankee invention."

"Pleased to make your acquaintance too," said Will, his eyes twinkling.

"Bah! No real man cares for anything but horsemanship," argued Don Jose. "Why not let the Americano try his hand at correr al gallo if he wants to show off?"

"What's this about a rooster?" asked Will, turning to Ricardo.

The young ranchero explained that a live rooster was buried up to its neck in a pile of sand. The object was to gallop past at full speed, lean down from the saddle and pull the fowl out by the head.

"Of course, the Yankee may not have the stomach for our sport," needled Don Jose. "Seems he'd rather play with guns."

"Of course I have the stomach for it," retorted Will. "You can put the pot on to boil right now."

"Boil? Pot? What nonsense is this?"

"To cook the dumplings that go with the chicken, of course!"

Don Jose seethed inside as laughter broke out from the group.

"If this is to be a contest, then there must be a challenger," demanded Ricardo. Facing Don Jose Dominguez, he continued, "Since it is you who issued the challenge, Don Jose, will you ride or do you have a champion to propose?"

Don Jose's smile glittered brittlely. "Capitan Zuniga has already agreed to ride against the Americano," he said. The captain was approaching on his lanky bay.

"To make matters more intersting," continued Dominguez, "I wish to propose that the course be laid out right in front of the gate into the corral."

The strategy behind this suggestion was plain: after leaning out of the saddle to grab the rooster's neck, a rider would have only a split second to sit upright again or risk being smashed against the stockade fence. A timid rider would be distracted by the upcoming obstacle and unable to concentrate.

At this point Don Pedro intervened. "I cannot permit this," he said. "Señor Reed is my guest and has never engaged in this sport before. It is not fitting to put him at such a disadvantage."

"I completely understand," said Zuniga through thinly veiled sarcasm. "I would not wish to embarrass anyone, especially the day's heroic guest . . ."

The scout's response was to step off Flotada without speaking and set to work tightening the girth and checking the bridle. As everyone waited to see what would happen, Will completed his preparations and stepped back aboard the gray. At last he spoke: "The way I was raised, a man who's still talking when he should be getting ready usually loses."

The little officer visibly swayed in his saddle as if the raging anger seen on his face was surging through his body. If he responded at all verbally, he would fall into Will's cleverly worded trap, yet if he stepped down to tighten the bay's cinch, he would be seen as following the American's lead.

Zuniga took the only course which his pride would permit. He urged the bay forward without speaking, as if to say, "What are we waiting for?"

The black rooster protested loudly and violently when two Indians tried to place him in a shallow hole in front of the corral. Dominguez swore at them to hurry up and cursed them for being fools and cowards when the rooster flogged and pecked and clawed them.

At last the two men finished and climbed the fence with twenty other mission Indians to watch the contest. Behind them the captive grizzly snarled and growled, rearing to swat the air. He was answered by the deep bellow of the bull from the enclosure across the corral.

The rooster, now buried to his neck, was silent, but his eyes darted around wildly. He pecked furiously at the ground as if he could make it release him.

"The passes will continue until one rider is successful, or until the other is unwilling or unable to continue," declared Ricardo. "Now, who shall go first?"

"Capitan Zuniga," blurted out Don Jose, before anyone else could speak.

Zuniga then settled his hat back on his head. He urged his horse toward the rooster with a sudden jab of his spurs that made the bay spurt forward.

The captain leaned far to the left out of the saddle. Holding his body parallel to the ground, his shark eyes fixed on the rooster's head.

The bay horse ran true and Zuniga's small fingers were closing over the rooster's neck when the captain glanced ahead at the fast approaching stockade fence. He jerked upright in the saddle, pulling the horse up just inside the gate. In his left hand he clutched nothing but air. The rooster was still buried in the sand.

At Will's touch of the spurs, Flotada leapt forward. The scout leaned even farther from the saddle than Zuniga, his fingers almost brushing the ground as he and the horse flew over it. He hooked the rowell of a spur in the girth. The American trusted the horse to run straight and true without any correction from his rider.

Nearer to the rooster they swept and closer to the corral fence. Flotada corrected his path, moved nearer in line with the target, then straightened out again.

The wall loomed up. Will's hand was open and on course with the rooster. His fingers closed, grasped, pulled—the scout's body snapped upright just before Flotada thundered through the corral gate.

Will looked down at his hand to discover that he clutched feathers. The rooster, even more wild-eyed, was still buried in the sand. Will trotted Flotada back to the watching group. Some of the Indians hopped off the stockade and fanned out to watch the next attempt.

Zuniga spent longer preparing for this run. The little captain tightened the girth on the bay and checked the straps of his spurs. When he mounted again, he nervously shifted his weight, testing the cinch.

As the bay sprinted down the course again, Zuniga hooked the spur of his right foot onto the saddle horn. His body hung downward alongside the horse with his head almost touching the ground.

The horse raced across the space and the officer's hand closed over the rooster's neck. His grip and the surging power of the bay combined to pull the flapping chicken free of the sand.

Zuniga's free hand reached up to grasp the saddlehorn to pull himself back upright. He began a triumphant swing of the rooster so that all could see that he had not missed again; that he was, indeed, the winner.

With Zuniga halfway back into the saddle, the bay horse shrieked an alarm. It plunged to a sudden stop that jolted the officer's handhold loose. Next it reared, flipping Zuniga's spur off the horn and plunging him to the ground. The black rooster squawked and fluttered free.

The horse screamed again, terrified, as El Viejo, the massive, hump-backed grizzly, confronted him in the middle of the corral gate. The trumpet of fright was cut off mid-shriek as the lumbering grizzly smashed a blow to the bay's head, breaking the horse's neck.

"El Viejo! Oso pardo! The grizzly is loose!" Shouts erupted from the crowd, and the people scattered in confusion like a frightened nest of ants.

Will's first reaction was get Francesca to safety. At a tiny signal from the scout, Flotada whirled and raced toward her. As Will leaned from the saddle, the vagrant thought flashed through his mind that he had warmed up for this necessity only a few moments before.

Gesturing for the girl to lift her arms, Will leaned from the saddle and swept her up behind him without stopping. Flotada sped to the corner of the stockade where the high posts were occupied by Indians who had scrambled up to safety.

Will handed Francesca up. He shouted to them to keep her safe. One of them replied, "We will protect her!"

Spinning the gray around, Will took the reata from the horn and shook out a loop. Other vaqueros were racing in toward the great bear from all around the rodeo grounds.

The first of the lazadores was already flinging his loop at the grizzly. El Viejo stood erect, roaring his defiance and slashing the air with his great claws.

Will saw Zuniga scramble out of harm's way and leap up to scale the stockade. From the speed of his escape, the wiry officer appeared unharmed.

El Viejo took the coil of ungreased reata that had settled around his neck and pulled it toward him. The horse at the other end of the cord was jerked sideways and gave a panicked neigh. The vaquero was forced to draw a knife and slash downward, parting the line.

The grizzly dropped to all fours and charged. Two more vaqueros dashed in to try to distract the bear. He took no notice and pursued the first horse and rider, rising from his crouching lunge to slash at the horse's hindquarters.

Without the greased rawhide cords, the vaqueros were in great jeopardy from the enraged bear. With his terrific power and cunning, he could keep pulling in hapless riders. The ropers who had charged to recapture him only a moment earlier, now drew back a safe distance from the snarling El Viejo.

Sensing the reluctance of his human opponents, El Viejo rushed toward a knot of riders, scattering them. He was headed back toward the wild canyons where he lived, intent on escaping, and not willing for any interference.

In line with his escape was the feasting area of the fiesta, and a group of terrified women and children. The grizzly was aimed straight at them.

Will shouted to Ricardo, "Slow him down some, any way you can!" Urging Flotada to his greatest speed, the scout galloped back to where the case of dueling pistols sat abandoned in the dust.

The pistols had already been loaded in readiness for the marksmanship exhibition. Will knew that the demonstration he was about to give went way beyond what he had planned.

The American thrust one pistol in the sash around his waist and the other he held in readiness. Flotada reversed direction, running flat out down the track of the grizzly.

Ricardo and the other vaqueros were having no success distracting the bear. No matter how they charged at him or made futile casts with their reatas, El Viejo never swerved or slowed except to bite through a lasso and force a threatened lazadore to abandon one.

Will pushed Flotada to overcome the horse's natural instinct for safety and run in close along the bear's flank. The stout-hearted gray obliged and soon the pair had overtaken the grizzly from behind.

Will leveled the pistol at a spot toward the back of the bear's skull and cocked the hammer. Even though the explosion of the pistol followed the click of the hammer by only a second, it was enough warning for El Viejo to swerve toward the horse.

Flotada jerked to the side and spurted past the bear as Will's shot clipped the grizzly's ear and creased his head.

One shot left and only thirty yards before the bear reached women and children too petrified to run. The scout and the gray horse raced ahead of the bear, crossed in front of him, and stopped directly in his path.

Shooting downward at the bear was risky at best because the shot could glance off the bear's ponderous skull. The trapper jumped from the horse and slapped Flotada out of the way.

Will dropped the discharged pistol and drew the other from his sash. He cocked it and drew a bead on the bear. It only took a count of two for the range to close and Will fired.

The lead ball entered the grizzly's gaping mouth as he roared his charge. In what was the best shot the young trapper ever made, the bullet pierced the bear's throat and tore out the back of his skull.

El Viejo's rampage turned into a crashing roll like a giant furry cannonball bouncing along the ground. The bear's carcass smashed into Will, bowling him over. The scout ended up half under the dead grizzly. One great paw was flung across the man's chest in the appearance of amiable companionship.

Captain Zuniga was yelling something as he jumped down from his perch on the corral. Will was struggling to get out from the monster's weight and could not hear what was said, but he could see the officer waving his arms and gesturing for his squad of solders to join him.

At Will's whistle Flotada rejoined him and the scout remounted as Ricardo rode up. "What has got Zuniga all worked up?" asked Will.

"He says that the Indians let El Viejo out on purpose. He is mad! He is yelling that they were trying to kill him."

"Now what?" fumed Dominguez. "You looked like a fool who needed to be rescued, and the Americano is now a hero to everyone, not just the Riveras."

Zuniga's eyes went cold and his hand closed over the hilt of the dagger he carried in his sash. Not surprisingly, the complaints from the blustering ranchero stopped abruptly. "May I remind you," hissed the officer in tones that left no doubt about his willingness to enforce respect by a knife thrust, "that I was the one nearly killed today? What happened to those idiots in the corral? I will cut off their hands and feet after I gouge out their eyes!"

Dominguez, who believed the captain would do exactly what he said, tried to shunt the officer's wrath aside. "Yes, they *are* fools! They claimed the gate did not open when they pulled and then sprang open by itself! But don't destroy them now, not tonight! We still need to move cargo while everyone is preoccupied with the dancing."

Zuniga thrust the half-drawn dagger back into the red velvet sash. "All right," he said, "but after the cargo and the Americano are both disposed of, they are mine to deal with."

Don Jose Dominguez was happy to agree.

29

THE SCENT OF honeysuckle was on the light breeze that blew down from the hills and wafted into the great tent. Where only a grassy field had been for the daytime events, an enormous canvas pavilion had sprung up to house the fandango.

Will, now dressed in his grand ball outfit of midnight black and silver, was standing outside the tarp by one of the guy-ropes. He watched scores of Indians carry plank sections into the tent and assemble them into a dance floor.

Dear God, he prayed, *how I thank you for sparing my life today. And Francesca's.* At the remembrance of sweeping her into his arms and carrying her to safety, a shiver ran down his backbone. *What if I had not been close enough to save her?* he shuddered. It never occurred to him to marvel that he felt more dread at the prospect of her death than he did his own.

Will was so absorbed in his thoughts that he missed hearing a rustle in the grass behind him. Even when it sounded again, his distracted mind dismissed it as a stray puff of wind stirring the canvas doorflap. From inside the tent came sounds of guitars tuning up for the first dance, the jota.

Will was dazzled by another memory: After his fight with the grizzly, Francesca had run up to him and thrown her arms around him. Even when she at last pulled back, the girl still gripped his arms and held him locked within the embrace of her eyes. *Never leave me,* her eyes had said. *Never frighten me like this again!*

Another scurrying sound reached the scout's ears. This time there was no mistaking the soft press of furtive human footsteps.

Will whirled around, his hands involuntarily grasping for knife or pistol, neither of which were there. "Who is it?" he demanded. "Speak up!"

"Not so loud," requested an urgent whisper. "Señor Reed, it is me, Paco."

"Paco! Come into the light. What are you doing skulking out there?"

"Shh, Señor Reed! Capitan Zuniga will have me killed if I am discovered!"

The American started to argue, then decided that the fear he heard in the mission Indian's voice was real enough. The scout stepped away from the lighted tent, into the pool of shadow around one of the oak trees. He was soon joined by a flitting shape dimly recognizable as Paco.

Even in the faint light, Paco's clothes were obviously ragged. The Indian's face was gaunt and his eyes were hollow.

"Tell me what this is all about," Will ordered in a low, hoarse voice.

"The grizzly today, señor. It was no accident! I was there, under the stands, I saw it all. It was Zuniga and the ones called Juan and Iago."

The trapper started at the link formed by that trio of names. "Go on," he said.

"They were supposed to kill you, but I fixed the great beast's gate so it would not open when they pulled."

"But why me? I mean, what are those three mixed up in?"

"It is not just the three," corrected Paco. "The fat ranchero Dominguez, he is in this also."

"In what? What do two murderers, the capitan of the presidio and a ranchero have in common?"

"Slaves," murmured Paco. "They are selling captured Indians to Sonoran mines. At first it was mission Indians accused of crimes, but to prevent suspicion—"

"Can you prove this?" demanded Will. "I can't go flinging accusations like this to Don Pedro or someone without proof."

"Prove it yourself, señor. I heard them say that they have cargo to move tonight. If either Zuniga or Dominguez leaves the fandango, follow and see for yourself!"

Francesca tried for the third time to catch Will's eye as they swirled past each other on the dance floor in the motion of the jarabe. Each glance she gave him went unanswered, as the scout always seemed to be looking somewhere else.

Anxiety caused her face to flush and her heart to beat faster. The warmth of the air in the tent made it natural for countless fans to appear, and Francesca covered her dismay behind vigorous waving.

At the end of the music, Francesca moved deliberately to where a square of canvas had been rolled up to admit some of the cool evening breeze. Will turned around once before he discovered where she had gone, then spotted her and maneuvered through the crowd to rejoin her.

"You seem very preoccupied, Will," the girl asked with concern. "Were you perhaps injured by El Viejo after all?"

"No, Francesca, I am all right. It's just—"

At that moment, Don Jose Dominguez, who had been in deep conversation with Zuniga near the doorway of the tent, stepped outside and disappeared. "Excuse me," Will said hurriedly. "I'll explain later, Francesca."

"But Will . . ." the girl blurted out, too late. The scout had already ducked through the tent flap and into the night.

Outside, the air was much cooler and moist with the first tendrils of fog drifting in from the channel. Will circled the canvas, ducking his head and murmuring an apology as he bumped into a pair of lovers kissing in the shadows.

The tracker melted into the sheltering fringe of trees and approached the line where the horses of the guests were picketed. A reata was strung between two trees and secured to them by stout iron rings. This cord formed the temporary hitching rail to which the lead ropes were tied.

Flotada recognized Will's scent and nickered a soft welcome. At the sound, Will froze in the darkness and knelt down so that he would not present a man-shaped outline.

Hoping the horse would remain silent, the scout peered out from behind the sheltering tree trunk toward the line of horses. Midway down the row he saw Dominguez untie his mount and swing aboard to ride off.

Will noted the direction the ranchero had taken and as soon as Don Jose was out of sight, he followed on Flotada. Will rode bareback, with a hackamore improvised from the lead rope. He did not want the silver fittings on the tack to give him away by their jingle or by a flash in the moonlight.

With his hat pulled low over his face, Will plucked the silver buttons from his jacket and stuffed them into his pocket. The gray horse and the rider dressed all in black moved like a specter over the California countryside.

The ranchero was riding at an easy trot, not hurrying, and Will easily kept pace with him. The scout reined to a stop every so often to listen for a change of direction, but the hoofbeats continued up the coast, angling toward the ocean. Dominguez never gave any sign he suspected that he was being pursued.

It was an hour's ride before the smell of salt spray and the low rumble of the breakers announced that the trail had arrived at the Pacific. Following was suddenly much more difficult as the crunch of the waves on the sand covered the sounds Will had been tracking.

Ahead there was a light. It was above the beach on a promontory that stood higher than the strip of sand. The American knew that no habitation existed in such a place, and his instincts told him this was the destination toward which Dominguez was headed.

Trusting that the noise of the surf would drown out his approach, Will rode around the landward side of the hill. He dismounted in a brushy gully back of the knoll, and left Flotada ground-tied.

When the scout had crept across seventy-five of the hundred yards that separated him from the building, he heard voices. Loudest and very angry sounding was the ranchero's.

"You fools . . ." Will could make out, ". . . him! Zuniga ought . . ."

The scout had reached the windowless rear of an adobe structure. It looked like one of the hide warehouses in which the rancheros stored cured leather in readiness for shipping. Will removed his boots so that they would not crunch on the gravel, and slipped cautiously around the side of the building.

Now the words of the conversation were clear. "Don't make any mistakes," Dominguez was saying. "This will be the last shipment to Sonora. We'll blame the grizzly attack on the mission Indians and use that excuse to round them up. Once our own mine is operating, we'll be too powerful for anyone to care if we increase our work force with some wild Tulere-ños."

A mine? thought Will. *And what was that about the Tule people?*

A growly voice that reminded Will of the cutthroat known as Iago asked, "What about the Americano?"

Dominguez replied, "We'll kill him and blame that on the Indians too. In fact, we can take care of Don Pedro and his son the same way!"

So it was true! Indians were being taken as slaves. Whatever else the scheme involved, the certain threat of death now hung over Will, Don Pedro and Ricardo.

Will wondered what his next move should be. He knew that he still could not go back and accuse Dominguez without proof; not as long as Zuniga was the law. The scout strained his ears as the slavers entered the building.

"The schooner will send in the boat when we signal. How many are left in this lot?"

Iago replied to Dominguez's question. "A half dozen after the two that died on the way here. But one that is left is an old man nearly dead, and there is a muchacho who won't be good for much."

Will was very near the opening of the shed. The wooden plank door stood ajar. A heavy beam that had been used to bar the door from the outside lay on the ground. The scout stooped to pick up the near end of the beam. His first thought was to trap the conspirators inside and bar the door.

Silently, Will lifted the heavy timber. The light of the lantern inside the building flashed around as the slavers inspected their captives. Ready to slam the door shut and drop the timber in place, Will raised the bar to waist height.

The back of his neck prickled. He pivoted sharply with the heavy beam and swung it against the adobe of the shed like a housewife swinging a carpet beater.

What he had caught between the oak timber and the wall was not carpet but a man. It was Juan, the desperado whose arm Will had broken in the cantina.

Juan's shattered arm was tied across his chest in a dirty bandanna. From the other hand flew the knife which he had intended to use on Will. The scout thought he heard the man's other arm crack in trying to ward off the unexpected blow, but whatever the damage to his arm, Juan was crushed against the bricks of the warehouse. He collapsed with a moan to the ground.

The scout spun back around and tried to jam the beam against the door. Too late! It crashed outward and Iago and Don Jose tumbled through.

"The Americano," growled Iago, launching himself at Will. There was time to fend off one slash with the beam, then the trapper threw it from him because it was too clumsy and slow. The murderer slipped aside as the timber crashed down.

Will had no blade with him, but he stooped quickly and retrieved one of his boots. Reversing it on his hand, he presented the great rowelled spur toward Iago's face.

Will was grateful that Dominguez was a coward at heart. The fat ranchero hung back in the doorway, content to let his henchman do the fighting and take the risks.

And even without a knife, taking on Will Reed involved some risks. When Iago stepped in and thrust the knife forward, he expected the scout to back up. Instead, Will drove his booted fist up under the blade arm, knocking it aside. He followed this move by raking the spur across Iago's face. Three parallel gouges appeared as if by magic, welling full of blood that was black in the dim light.

"Get him," ordered Dominguez.

Iago circled in front of Will, trying to force the scout out of position and trap the spur hand against the wall. When the American saw what was intended, he snapped his arm up, letting the heavy boot fly, rowell points first, at the cutthroat's eyes.

As the man ducked, the scout stepped quickly toward his assailant and a perfectly timed left cross met Iago's chin. The murderer staggered back, his vision unfocused. The gleam from Iago's dagger showed that he had dropped his knife hand.

Will followed the blow to the chin by stepping through with a right into Iago's chest. Now the man's eyes bulged and he choked for breath.

The red-haired trapper grabbed Iago's arm and knocked the knife from his hand by smashing it against the adobe wall. Just then ten thousand stars fell out of the Santa Barbara sky and hit Will on the head. Or so it seemed to him as he slumped to the ground.

When he came to, his wrists and ankles were bound and his hands and feet were tied together behind his back. His first thought was that Dominguez had joined the fight after all, but he was wrong: it was Zuniga.

While Will was lying face down in the dirt at his feet, the captain explained how Will had followed Dominguez from the fiesta, and he in turn had followed the American.

"Why are we wasting time?" demanded Iago, wheezing. "He has killed poor Juan. Let me slit his throat and throw him into the sea!"

Dominguez disagreed. "No, not here. We can still make it look like the work of the Indios. We should load this cargo at once and get away from here." Then a new thought seemed to strike him. "Wait! I have heard that the Americano is a great lover of Indians. What could be more fitting than for us to send him with them. No questions are asked at the mines, and no one ever returns."

Zuniga and Iago gripped the scout's arms and roughly tossed him into the warehouse. The door was shut and barred. Iago was left on guard while the other two went to the beach to signal the boat.

The body Will had landed on grunted, but made no other sound. The scout apologized in Spanish, then switching to Yokuts repeated, "I'm sorry."

"Sequoyah!" piped a thin treble voice.

"Blackbird! No! Is that you?" gasped the American.

"Yes," Blackbird whispered, a sob catching in his throat. "Oh, Will Reed! Grandfather and I were captured while gathering herbs. These awful men forced us to march across the mountains with almost no food and only a little water. We were thrown into this prison two days ago."

"Where is Falcon?" Will asked, trying to peer through the darkness.

"Grandfather is very sick," the boy continued anxiously. "He can barely move or speak. Grandfather. Grandfather. Can you hear me?" There was no response.

30

WILL HEARD DOMINGUEZ and Zuniga returning from the beach. Dominguez was cursing loudly. "That no good . . . He calls himself a capitan! He is a coward, a coward! A little breeze springs up and he must hoist a signal that says 'cannot land.' "

Zuniga was more pragmatic. "He does not want to be caught on a lee shore and get beached here."

"Bah! Now we have to guard these wretches for another day. Iago," Dominguez said testily, "you must stay here. We'll be back tonight."

"And the Americano?" Iago asked, drawing his dagger by way of suggestion.

"No, not now," Dominguez stopped him with a look. Then to the officer he explained, "Zuniga, you and I will use this ride to speak of what is best to do with Señor Reed and with Don Pedro. If we plan this properly, since you are the law, you can name me as executor of Don Pedro's property."

"And guardian of his daughter?"

"Exactly so," the ranchero agreed, "and I in turn can start calling you son-in-law as well as son!"

Hearing this plan, Will struggled with his bonds, but without result. "Blackbird," he whispered, "do you think you can undo these knots with your teeth?"

Face down in the darkness, Will could not see the boy's enthusiastic nod of agreement. The boy went to work on the thong that pulled the American's hands down toward his ankles.

It was slow going. Even though Blackbird was not trussed up like Will, his hands were tied behind his back. After working on the knots for several hours in the inky blackness of the adobe building, the length of leather strap finally came undone.

Now Will could sit up and move a little in order to put the bindings on his wrists into a better position for Blackbird to work. "Hurry," he whispered. "If Iago comes in to check on us, we'll never get another chance."

It was nearly daybreak when the rawhide that secured Will's hands was loose enough for him to strip it off. He pulled his wrists free, shaking his hands to restore some feeling to them.

Will had begun to work on the cords holding his feet when he heard a noise outside the shed. There was no way to pretend to still be bound, and even tearing feverishly at the leather, the trapper could not get his ankles untied in time.

He jerked himself upright, falling hard against the adobe brick wall next to the door. Leaning alongside the opening, his muscles coiled like snakes preparing to strike. His hands were clenched for the single, two-handed blow he would have one chance to make.

The door opened, but only a small crack. Then it creaked wider apart, but still no one entered. At last it was pulled all the way open, admitting the dim illumination of predawn, but no one stepped across the threshold. Positioned against the wall, Will could not see where the guard stood. Drops of sweat clung to the scout's forehead as he struggled to keep his body tense.

"Reed," a voice called out in English. "Will Reed, are you in there?"

"Easton!" shouted Will, lurching out from the warehouse. "Thank God it's you. How did you find us?"

"Paco here," said Easton, indicating the mission Indian standing behind him. "He watched Zuniga trailing you and followed him. After you got locked up for the night, he came to fetch me."

"But that's ten miles each way and three trips. How could you do that on foot?"

Paco grinned slyly. "I told you it was forbidden for my people to ride. I did not say we did not know how." He went past Will into the warehouse and with a smirk added, "I will untie the rest."

"And what happened to the guard?" asked Will.

"Iago?" responded Easton. "He never sticks around for a fight unless the two-to-one odds are in his favor. Too bad though. I think he has gone to warn Dominguez. We may be heading into trouble if we go back."

"Not if," Will pointed out sharply. "Don Pedro and Ricardo and . . . Francesca are in danger."

"Thought you'd feel that way," said Easton, tossing Will a burlap-wrapped bundle.

"What's this?" asked Will. When he pulled the twine, a buckskin suit and a new Hawken rifle tumbled out.

"Never met a man who could fight his best in unfamiliar rigging," Easton pointed out.

Paco reemerged from the adobe. "Señor Reed, the Yokuts want to go home. But the old man is very bad. Even if they carry him, I don't think he will make it back to their valley."

"Please, Will Reed," begged Blackbird at Will's side, "you must help my grandfather."

"Try not to worry, Blackbird, I'll see that he gets tended to." To Easton Will said, "We'll take him to Father Sanchez at the mission."

"Mate, we'll be headed straight into their hands," cautioned Easton.

"No matter," said the grim-faced scout. "It's time to take down the evil in the West."

31

IT WAS AN odd looking procession that rode into Pueblo Santa Barbara. Will in his buckskins rode on Flotada with Blackbird behind him. Billy Easton was riding a mule. Falcon was carried on a travois pulled behind Paco's horse.

The mission Indian looked nervously around as he rode. At the first sign of observers he jumped off the horse and walked alongside.

They reached the mission grounds without incident, but several onlookers witnessed their arrival, including Father Quintana. Blackbird and his grandfather were entrusted to the safety and care of Father Sanchez. Will and Easton mounted again to ride out to Don Pedro's rancho.

As they were leaving the mission compound, they were met by a quick-marching file of twenty soldiers and Captain Zuniga. Zuniga's uniform buttons gleamed in the sun and the feathered plume of his hat waved in the wind. "Halt," he ordered. "Señor Reed, I again place you under arrest." Zuniga was so confident of his authority that he gave only a negligent wave of his gloved hand to order his soldiers to form a line blocking the exit from the square.

"What am I charged with this time, Zuniga?" asked Will. "Does what I know about you make me a spy?"

"Silence!" shrilled Zuniga. "You are charged with wantonly murdering the man named Juan and with stirring up rebellion among the Indios."

"And how do you explain your dealings in slaves and your intended plot to assassinate Don Pedro Rivera y Cruz?" asked Will pointedly.

"Lies. The ravings of a spy desperate to save himself," retorted Zuniga. "Guards, take him."

"Not so fast there, Capitan," suggested Billy Easton, a Hawken rifle across his saddle bow. "I have seen your warehouse and your human 'cargo' and I confirm what Reed here says is the truth."

"Easton, you are charged with smuggling and trafficking in slaves. Soldiers, seize them both."

"Wait!" shouted the voice of Don Jose Dominguez. He stood on the red-tiled roof of the priest's quarters. Beside him, pointing a rifle at Dominguez' quivering face, was the mission Indian Donato. "They killed Iago! Capitan! Tell your men to give up their weapons or they'll kill me too!"

Atop the roofs around three sides of the square stood fifty stony-featured Indians. Most were armed with bows, but others had firearms.

Zuniga gave an animal-like scream of rage. He raised the pistol he was holding and fired it at Will. The lead ball passed under Will's arm and flattened itself against the courtyard fountain as Will and Easton jumped from their mounts to take cover.

A rifle boomed from the rooftop, then another and another. The whiz of arrows being discharged filled the air with the sound of angry, death-dealing bees. Flotada clattered across the courtyard in confusion. Easton's mule bolted, then struck by a stray bullet, fell over on top of a soldier.

Two of the soldiers went down with arrow wounds. The others took cover behind the adobe watering tank as a rain of arrows and rifle balls pattered around them.

Behind the fountain, Will waited, reserving his fire until Zuniga rose up with a musket. Will's shot crashed into the bricks just below the captain's head, lacerating his face with flying scraps of adobe.

"Stop! You must stop!" shouted Dominguez from the rooftop. He was fearful that the mission Indian Donato would blow his head off at any moment. "Listen to me! It was Zuniga! Zuniga caused this to happen!"

Wildly, aiming through eyes blinded by adobe-dust and anger, Zuniga rose and fired at the roof. His shot pierced Dominguez's throat. The ranchero clutched at his neck even as he toppled from the roof to land with a sickening thud on the pavement below.

Will fired at the same instant, and his shot hit the captain square in the chest. As Zuniga fell, three arrows and two lead balls pierced him, including one fired by his own soldiers.

At that moment, Father Sanchez came out of the mission. His arms upraised, he walked boldly into the center of the square. "Donato," he cried. "Lazario. You others. In the name of Christ, stop this killing at once!" Miraculously, rifles and bows were lowered. No more shots were fired. The revolt of the Indians of Mission Santa Barbara ended almost as soon as it had begun.

The group gathered in the parlor of the hacienda of Don Pedro Rivera y Cruz included Will, Billy Easton, Father Sanchez and Ricardo. Together they were sorting things out.

Will drew a leather pouch from his pocket and out of it dropped the small lump of dark-red stone.

"Cinnabar," exclaimed Don Pedro. "Is that what all this is about?"

"And, Father," added Ricardo, "at last I remember where I have seen such ore before: it comes from the Canyon Perdido, on lands shared by us and the mission."

The little council took in the implications of that thought, then Will asked. "What is going to happen to the mission Indians?"

"They have run away into the hills, but they will return when they find out that they are not going to be punished. The two soldiers who were wounded are recovering, and the only two killed, Dominguez and Zuniga, were guilty of goading the neophytes into rebellion and enslaving both neophytes and valley Indians."

"And what about Father Quintana?" asked Don Pedro.

"He also has fled," reported Sanchez, "and it would be best for him if he never returned."

"What will happen if Governor Figueroa decides to step in?" asked Will.

"I do not think we need to worry about that," suggested Don Pedro. "You see, I have today received notice that I have been appointed the governor's representative."

"That's it then, I guess," said Will. "Tell me, Father, how is Falcon? Is he going to live?"

"Live?" chuckled the chubby priest. "That old man is as tough as bullhide. He has already been telling me what herbs are missing from my medical garden! By the way," Father Sanchez continued, "the child tells me that he and his grandfather want to return here after visiting with their people. It seems that someone has told them about a certain path, and they wish to learn more."

32

FRANCESCA WAS STANDING on the balcony of the hacienda, watching the sun set over the sweeping coast of California. A breath of clean summer breeze twirled her fine dark hair and rustled the pleats of her skirt.

Will and Billy Easton were in the courtyard below, and both looked up at Francesca standing there. "Reed," Easton said, "your place is up there with her, so let's keep this goodbye short."

"Thanks for your help, Billy," said the scout, "and for the use of the Hawken."

"You keep that," Easton said, refusing the weapon Will offered. "Call it a wedding present, since I won't be here for the ceremony."

"Oh? Will you be back this way soon?"

"Doubtful," replied the pirate figure. "Things would be a bit uncomfortable for me around here when people start asking where the Indians got those rifles. Anyway, my job is done."

"What job was that?"

"Looking into the situation here in California for President Andy Jackson. He sent me. I am the American spy."